FIELD BOOK OF
SEASHORE LIFE

CHRIS E. OLSEN

Field Book of
SEASHORE
LIFE

BY ROY WALDO MINER

Curator Emeritus of the Living Invertebrates
American Museum of Natural History

G. P. Putnam's Sons New York

TO MY WIFE

EUNICE THOMAS MINER

SBN 399-10293-0

Ninth Impression

CONTENTS

Introduction

THE purpose of this book is to serve as a compact manual of the more common invertebrate animals inhabiting the shallow oceanic waters of the Atlantic Coast of North America from Labrador to the Cape Hatteras region of North Carolina. In breadth, the territory covered extends from the upper tide limit to the edge of the Continental Shelf. It includes, first, the tidal zone, that coastal belt which is alternately covered and exposed by the sea twice a day; and second, the region of shallow water which begins at the lower tidal limit at a depth of zero inches and extends, gradually deepening, until it reaches a sounding of about 100 fathoms (600 feet), at the edge of the terrace known as the Continental Shelf, beyond which the Continental Slope descends at a steeper gradient to the floor of the ocean, at a depth of about 2½ miles. It deals therefore with the animal life of the shallow temperate waters of our eastern seaboard. South of Cape Hatteras the sea is much warmer and embraces the region of coral reefs and other tropical marine life not included in this volume.

The book is intended first of all for the layman who has become interested in the invertebrate sea animals he has chanced to pick up along the shore; second, for the student whose attention is more seriously drawn to the life of the seas; and third, for the research worker who, it is hoped, will find it of service as a handy reference book, because its convenient form permits rapid orientation of the species concerned in his work. It is by no means exhaustive, since it would be impossible to include all of the thousands of species known to science from this region without swelling the work to undue proportions and thus defeat the avowed aim of compactness.

Necessarily, the subject matter must embrace the researches of numerous investigators, whose reports are embodied in large volumes or scattered through a great variety of scientific journals, most of which are inaccessible to the average student of sea life or involve time-consuming search through volumes and files in specialized libraries in scientific institutions. The writer remembers well when, as a young man, beginning his studies of marine invertebrates, he was continually baffled in his endeavors to identify species commonly occurring in his catches by the time necessary, first, to run down the appropriate literature, and then to handle the many and often bulky volumes it embraced. In this volume, it has been the writer's endeavor to bring together in compact form the essential facts, descriptions, and illustrations into a single handbook of pocket size, which may be carried into the field and utilized for instant reference and preliminary study. A list of important references is added, especially of works that contain bibliographies of the special groups for those who wish to refer to the original literature, or pursue researches further along individual lines. Obviously, a book of this size, dealing with the enormous field covered by the fifteen animal phyla, cannot include an extensive bibliography, so that only salient works can be mentioned here.

The heritage of the modern zoologist is the accumulation of facts and observations of a multitude of scientists since the time of Linnaeus, two centuries and more ago. We refer with respect, however, to pioneer observations before his time, and note the keen eyes and philosophic conclusions of Aristotle, in spite of obstacles, four centuries before Christ. Linnaeus was mainly responsible for the binomial system of classification, by means of which two Latin names, one for the *genus* and one for each of the *species* into which it is subdivided, are designated for each distinct kind of animal known, together with a terse description. This system is in universal use today for all living forms, both plants and animals. Linnaeus also grouped the genera together into *orders* and the orders into *classes*. More recently the higher grouping into the *phylum* (plural *phyla*) and the *subphylum,* as well as the interpolated *subclass, suborder, family,* and *subfamily,* have been introduced. These divisions and subdivisions have been necessary for the exact placing of the multitudinous species known, as well as to express their relationships to each other. The so-called popular name may seem easier to remember, but it is loosely applied, and often includes different species under the same current appellation. It is also necessarily restricted to familiarly known forms, whereas there are hosts of species that are commonly known and must be accurately classified. Hence, the necessity for the scientific name and its classification. While, in this book, the scientific name is always used, the popular name is also given, if there is one in current use.

The term phylum is applied to each of the fifteen main divisions of the Animal Kingdom, as generally recognized at the present time. These phyla are based on radically different plans of structure. A chapter in this book is devoted to each phylum, with an introduction explaining its chief characteristics, together with one or more index diagrams illustrating the anatomical structures associated with it and the technical terms which must be used for the various parts. Each of these figures, therefore, acts as an illustrated glossary for the group. Similar diagrams are given for many of the subordinate groups.

The following scheme of the phyla of the Animal Kingdom is adopted here:

(1) Phylum *Protozoa* (Microscopic one-celled animals)
(2) Phylum *Porifera* (Sponges)
(3) Phylum *Coelentera* (Hydroids, jelly-fishes, sea-anemones, corals, gorgonians, sea-pens, etc.)
(4) Phylum *Ctenophora* (Comb-jellies)
(5) Phylum *Platyhelmia* (Flatworms)
(6) Phylum *Nemertea* (Ribbon-worms)
(7) Phylum *Nemathelmia* (Round-worms, thread-worms)
(8) Phylum *Trochelmia* (Rotifers, wheel-animalcules)
(9) Phylum *Annulata* (Bristle-worms, earth-worms, leeches, etc.)
(10) Phylum *Arthropoda* (Crustaceans, arachnids, myriapods, insects, etc.)
(11) Phylum *Mollusca* (Snails, bivalves, chitons, octopuses, squid, etc.)
(12) Phylum *Chaetognatha* (Arrow-worms)
(13) Phylum *Echinoderma* (Sea-stars, brittle-stars, sea-urchins, sea-cucumbers, sea-lilies)
(14) Phylum *Prosopygia* (Moss-animals, lamp-shells)
(15) Phylum *Chordata* (Protochordates, fishes, amphibians, reptiles, birds, mammals)

All the above phyla have representatives in the sea and all except (4), (12), and (13) include fresh-water species. Only (2), (3), (4), (8), (12), (13), and (14) have no species on land. Phylum (7), containing the Nemathelmia, is composed mainly of parasitic and terrestrial species, there being only a few marine forms. In phylum (15), the Chordata, only the Protochordates are dealt with, being generally considered transitional species between the invertebrates and vertebrates. The true vertebrates, or back-boned animals, of course, are not included in this volume.

Some of the above phyla embrace thousands of species while others have only a few, but each is based on a distinct plan of organization that is not closely related to any of the other phyla, though there are closer alliances between certain phyla than in the case of others.

Each phylum is divided into the subgroups, above mentioned, to indicate both the systematic position and relationship of the different species. For example, the common Rock Crab, *Cancer irroratus,* is classified as follows:

Phylum Arthropoda
  Class Crustacea
    Subclass Malacostraca
      Series Eumalacostraca
        Division Eucarida
          Order Decapoda
            Suborder Brachyura
              Tribe Cyclometopa
                Family Cancridae
                  Genus and Species *Cancer irroratu,*
                  (Rock Crab)

This classification seems very complicated and is necessary only when the species of a phylum, such as the Arthropoda, is very numerous and highly diversified. Usually such subdivisions as subclass, series, division, and tribe are omitted and the systematist passes directly from phylum to class, order, family, genus and species. For example, the Common Starfish may be classified as follows:

Phylum Echinodermia
  Class Asteroidea
    Order Forcipulata
      Family Asteriidae
        Genus and Species *Asterias forbesii*

It must be stated, however, that some specialists introduce intermediate subdivisions even in this case.

It is obvious to the student of sea life, as he examines the shore at different localities, that the character of the substratum varies greatly and that the assemblages of animal and plant life vary with the environment. Long stretches of the coast consist of exposed sandy beaches, while sheltered bays are often bordered and floored with mud, or with sand mixed with mud in every degree of transition from pure sand, through sandy mud, to pure mud. In other places, where there are more swiftly moving currents or more wave-action, the bottom is gravelly, in certain localities of fine texture, and in others of coarse composition. Headlands composed of glacial soil with glacial boulders embedded may be bordered by rock-strewn beaches where the earth has washed away at exposed points or in intersecting channels leaving only the stones, rounded through erosion, during their glacial history, or through wave-action after being exposed on the beach.

Other parts of the coast are characterized by rocks rising as precipitous cliffs or bounding the shore by long stretches of shelving rocks, sometimes fractured by the force of storm-waves or split by the frosts of winter. At times, they are intersected by igneous dikes or they may be upheaved by deep-seated geologic forces.

The force of the tides produces profound effects along such shores as northern Massachusetts and Maine, where, together with the outlying coasts of Nova Scotia, they taper into the confining waters of the Bay of Fundy. In the lower portion of the tidal zone in such regions are many crevices and basins in the rocks always filled with water so as to form tidal pools even at the lowest tides. Animal and plant associations show close adaptations to these varied inanimate situations.

Along the dry upper part of sandy beaches, animal life is relatively sparse; but in the moisture-soaked lower stretches near the surf-line, the mole-shrimps (*Hippa talpoida*), the sand-hoppers and beach-fleas (Amphipoda) abound and, here and there, the moundlike burrows of sand-collar snails (*Neverita duplicata*) dot the level sandy floor. In the more sheltered muddy coves multitudinous species of sea-worms of diversified aspect burrow in the mud especially in the neighborhood of and among the roots of the eelgrass. Many of these become the prey of digging mollusks and mud crabs. Among the boulders in the inlets and guts scoured by the rushing tides only clinging animal and plant organisms can adhere to the rocks. Rock barnacles are anchored by their shells. Limpets cling by the suction of their valves. Encrusting sponges closely invest rocks and shells alike, especially those covering the valves of mussels and scallops. The latter, in turn, throw out holdfasts of silken fibers (byssus) cemented to neighboring rocks and shells by minute pneumatic discs. Multitudinous colonies of moss animals (Bryozoa) grow over all exposed surfaces, including the fronds of the algae which resist the force of the currents with strongly developed holdfasts. Between and under the boulders on the rocky points various kinds of crabs and strange-looking shrimp are found, while the submerged rocks may be covered with colonies of our delicate and fairylike only northern coral (*Astrangia danae*).

Remarkable concentrations of sea-animals and plants form veritable submerged gardens in the tide-pools at the bases of the cliffs in the more northern waters, including starfishes of contrasting colors and form, scuttling and concealed crabs of various species, clustered colonies of sea-anemones and delicate flowerlike hydroids, as well as encrusting and fingerlike colonies of sponges of contrasting and occasionally brilliant colors. Ascidians, like sea peaches, and the long-stemmed *Boltenia* abound, while such algae as the iridescent Irish Moss (*Chondrus crispus*), and red digitated dulse (*Rhodymenia palmata*), together with overshadowing fronds of brown kelp lend a garden-like character to the pools. These are living forms that cannot stand much exposure to the air and must always be submerged or at least continually washed by the waves.

Higher up on the rocks, in these regions of high tides, the cliffs are festooned with rockweed, among and beneath which the hard substratum is covered with mussels and colonies of the gay-colored purple sea-snail (*Thais lapillus*), which is called "purple" because of the red or purple fluid that it secretes (used as a dye by Indians in early times), but which actually has shells banded with contrasting color combinations, including browns, yellows, white, and orange. Above these, along the highest range of the tidal zone, is the white frieze of rock-barnacles and hosts of the acorn-snail (*Littorina litorea*), which can stand exposure to the air much longer than the other invertebrates of the rock community because of their ability to enclose sea water tightly within their branchial chambers to aerate their blood. Wharf-piles also have special associations of animals encrusting them below the low-tide mark, located there because of the advantage of the freshly aerated sea currents that flow past them.

In the outer waters along the coast, hosts of swimming and floating sea-organisms, such as jelly-fishes, ctenophores, medusae, and swimming mollusks abound. Many of these are luminescent at night. Among them the waters are swarming with minute crustacea, belonging to the Entomostraca, and microscopic Protozoa, as well as myriads of those tiny single-celled plant-organisms known as diatoms. These latter, being plants, obtain their food from the energy of the sunlight, through the process of photosynthesis, by which they unite carbon, oxygen, and hydrogen to form starches and sugars. They are the basis of the food of all sea life, for all animals from the Protozoa and Entomostraca upward feed upon them or upon the animals that do so.

In order to collect and study the many important and diversified sea creatures with which our coasts and coastal waters abound, it is necessary to adapt methods of securing them to the peculiar conditions and circumstances characteristic of each of the different classes of associations and environments above outlined. The larger animals occurring between the tides can, of course, be secured by turning over stones and by digging into sand or mud with a shovel or clam-rake. They should then be placed in a pail of sea water, but the smaller and more delicate forms should be separated into wide-mouthed jars or bottles of sea water, if it is desired to examine them further, while alive. Otherwise, they can be collected at once into vials containing alcohol or a 4-per-cent solution of formaldehyde, taking care to keep the latter away from hands and eyes.

Flat-tipped forceps are important for handling the smaller animals individually. It is best to wet the forcep tips with the collecting fluid, which causes the specimens to cling to them. Shallow-water forms can be collected by hand, or by nets. A water glass facilitates this kind of collecting greatly. This is a box or bucket with a clear glass bottom, aquarium cement or some other type of waterproof cement being used to make the joint water-tight. By looking through such a glass the ripples in the sea surface are smoothed out and the sea-bottom and the undersea life are rendered clearly visible. It can be used from a boat with great facility. Water goggles are very useful if one wishes to submerge one's head while hand-collecting or in shallow-water diving. Hand nets are indicated for collecting crabs, and fine silk nets of various types may be used in collecting surface forms, especially when towing after a boat at night. An electric torch can be used to attract specimens to the surface. Hand-collecting around rocks and in tide-pools is very productive. For wharf-pile collecting a scrape-net is most useful. This is a long-handled net with a scraping edge on one side of the hoop outside the net fastenings. For bottom-collecting, a small dredge is used from a boat. The dredge net should be strong and protected by a canvas bag open at the end. The net opening is framed by a rectangle of heavy iron, the meshes being tied through perforations around the inner edge and with a scraping edge outside. The limits of space in this volume prevent the author from giving detailed directions for collecting and handling specimens, but references will be found in the bibliography to one or two works that will be of great assistance in this respect. If there is a marine laboratory in the neighborhood, useful hints may be obtained by consulting members of the staff.

In examining and studying the catch, much can be done quite simply if one is living near the sea, provided a table with good daylight is available in some suitable shed or workroom. Shallow trays of glass or white enamel should be supplied with fresh sea-water, which can be kept handy in pails and renewed from time to time. Magnifying glasses or low-power dissecting microscopes are important. Much can be done with simple lenses of varying power especially if they can be supported to free the hands for the use of forceps and needles. While animals like hermit crabs and sea-worms are large enough for study of activities, many of their anatomical characters can only be seen with the aid of lenses. These are of course indispensable for the study and identification of minute forms. High-powered microscopes are required for some advanced work, but for general use, lower powered equipment is far more important. If you are a student in a seaside laboratory, you are fortunate, for the instruction and equipment there will open new worlds to you daily. For advanced workers, the prospects are illimitable, for even with the best training obtainable and with complete access to the rapidly developing modern scientific equipment, oceanographers are still only on the threshold of the seas.

The writer desires here to record his great indebtedness to those scientists who have helped him in building up this field book. As a project, it was framed many years ago and was developed gradually. A number of those who were most helpful are no longer living. The late Professor Gary N. Calkins took a great deal of interest in the work and suggested use of much material based on his studies of the Protozoa of the Woods Hole region. The co-operation and advice of Professor Alfred Goldsborough Mayer were of the highest possible value, during his later years, in connection with the medusae and ctenophores. Professor Edmund B. Wilson greatly encouraged the writer in his work on sponges, and freely offered the results of his early researches on pycnogonids for the section dealing with that subject. A great debt is owed to Mr. Frank J. Myers, who contributed the larger part of the chapter on rotifers and gave much sympathetic advice and collaboration both in the laboratory and in the field. Professor Raymond C. Osburn generously offered the results of his work on the Bryozoa of New England, and my colleague, Doctor Willard G. Van Name, furnished most of the material in the section on isopods, and contributed the section on ascidians. He was also very helpful in developing the chapter on mollusks. The writer drew freely from the results of many eminent zoologists throughout the entire work. The chief books utilized are listed as selected references at the end of the volume. It is of special importance, with all other zoologists, to acknowledge with pleasure and great respect, the indebtedness of the entire field of systematic zoology to that ubiquitous and farseeing student of marine life, the great Addison E. Verrill, for the many works embracing his encyclopedic and accurate observations and descriptions based on many groups of invertebrates. His work in connection with the annulates in a noteworthy succession of articles cited in the list of selected references and the magnificent series of monographs on the same group by the eminent British zoologist, W. C. McIntosh, published by the Ray Society of London, form the most extensive basis of our knowledge of the Annulata of the North Atlantic up to the present time. Redrawn and adapted selections from their illustrations are included in this field book.

The writer also wishes to express his sincere thanks to the authorities of the American Museum of Natural History for their permission to utilize the extensive facilities, especially including the library, during the many years of the progress of this work. The black and white drawings were made by W. H. Southwick and G. H. Childs, under the author's direction, for the most part as redrawings and adaptations from the illustrations of the scores of scientists listed in the bibliography, while the color plates were done by Chris E. Olsen and G. H. Childs, mostly from original material, also under the author's direction.

Finally, the author wishes to make special and grateful acknowledgment to his wife, Eunice Thomas Miner, for her valuable assistance and co-operation during the writing of the text and the preparation of the book for the press. It is his hope that the book may fill a need and be useful to students of the marine life of the region that it embraces. In that case, he will feel that the labor and attention devoted to it are fully justified.

ROY WALDO MINER

1

Phylum Protozoa

(THE SIMPLEST ANIMALS)

PROTOZOA are single-celled animals. All other animals consist of many cells. A cell is a microscopic bit of living substance, known as protoplasm, containing a central body, the nucleus, surrounded by more or less of the cell protoplasm (the cytoplasm).

Life is not known to exist except in the form of protoplasm and, excluding Bacteria, protoplasm is always organized in cells consisting of a nucleus and cytoplasm. The nucleus contains a concentrated mass of granules known as chromatin. This substance is essential to the life of the cell since it enables the latter to assimilate food, grow, and reproduce new cells like itself. Chromatin granules are also carriers to the next generation of the hereditary peculiarities of the parent cell. While concentrated in the nucleus, they exist in the protoplasm, if at all, only in scattered form. In the Bacteria, there is no nucleus, but the chromatin granules are scattered through the protoplasm of the organism. While the Bacteria, therefore, are microscopic bits of protoplasm, they do not have true cellular structure and are regarded as more primitive or, at least, as simpler creatures than Protozoa. There are many reasons to regard the Protozoa as having evolved from a more or less bacterial origin, especially as some of the more primitive protozoans have, not only a nucleus, but also chromatin granules in the cytoplasm as well.

Protozoa, though they consist of but a single cell, nevertheless have all the essential properties of living creatures contained in the cell body.

They move independently and are sensitive to their surroundings. They prey upon other organisms for food, or, in some cases, manufacture it by the aid of the substance known as chlorophyll, as plants do, and are, therefore, under such circumstances, indistinguishable from one-celled plants and are often classified as such. They ingest the captured food material, assimilate it, and excrete the indigestible remainder. They are thus enabled to grow. After they reach a certain size, the nucleus divides to form two nuclei, and the cytoplasm follows suit. In the end, the entire cell splits to form two new cells, each half the size of the parent. This method of reproduction is called fission. An interesting peculiarity is that the parent generation disappears in producing the two offspring. Obviously, no distinction of sex is required in this method. Reproduction by fission is often supplemented by the production of large numbers of tiny spores, which swim about and pair off two and two. Each pair unites to form one individual which develops the original form and starts a new series of generations by fission. Sometimes, these spores are of two sizes, the smaller pairing with the larger. This is a very primitive division into two sexes. In some cases (e.g., *Paramecium*), two complete individuals unite instead of forming spores. Their nuclei, after splitting, exchange half their nuclear substance with each other. The two resulting individuals then separate and reassemble their nuclei, each of which now consists of the mingling of the chromatin from the two individuals. This kind of union is known as conjugation and is said to renew the vitality of the organism. After this process, reproduction by fission proceeds in the usual way. Protozoa are considered to be the most ancient type of animal life on earth, just as Protophyta are regarded as the most ancient type of plant life. Thus all other forms of plant and animal life have evolved from them. If this is the case, there was once a time when Bacteria, Protozoa, and Protophyta constituted the entire life of the globe. They are represented now by millions surviving relatively unchanged in company with the hosts of "higher animals" that have been derived from them by the process of evolution, as the result of greater or less changes. It has taken many millions of years to bring this about.

The Protozoa not only evolved the types that were transitional to higher animals, but they also exhausted the possibilities of change within their own group. Finally, as they exist today, they are found everywhere in the world, in moist places from the Arctic and Antarctic regions to the Equator, from the highest mountains to the depths of the sea, and probably outnumber all other forms of life on the globe. Certain species even live in the tissues and body fluids of higher animals and, in the blood of man himself, they are the cause of many fatal diseases.

In this handbook, we shall deal only with typical species of Protozoa found in the sea.

There are five main groups of the Phylum PROTOZOA, as follows:

Phylum PROTOZOA

    Subphylum SARCODINA, Protozoa without definite shape;

    Subphylum MASTIGOPHORA, Protozoa with definite shape and with whiplike structures known as *flagella;*

    Subphylum INFUSORIA, Protozoa with definite shape and with very fine hairlike projections, known as *cilia;*

    Subphylum NEOSPORIDIA, blood parasites resem-

bling the *Sarcodina* in shape, which reproduce themselves before they are mature;
Subphylum TELOSPORIDIA, also parasites resembling *Mastigophora* which reproduce only after they
have reached the adult stage.

Since this handbook is not primarily intended to deal
with parasitic forms, only the Subphyla *Sarcodina, Mastigophora,* and *Infusoria* will be treated here.

SUBPHYLUM SARCODINA

This subphylum includes the *rhizopods* or "root-footed"
Protozoa. These Protozoa move about by projecting portions of their jellylike body so as to form *pseudopods* (literally "false feet"). Sometimes, these are blunt, club-shaped
projections; in other cases, they are filamentary or threadlike, or they may assume many other peculiar forms, even
blending together to produce a network. By means of
these projecting *pseudopods,* the organism pulls itself from
place to place by contracting them and drawing up the
main body to their position. The pseudopods are also used
as snares for capturing other microscopic organisms for
food. These creatures are engulfed in the protoplasm and
drawn in to be swallowed and digested by the body of the
animal. Reproduction is usually asexual, by fission. For the
most part, the rhizopods are free-living.

CLASS LOBOSA

In this class, the pseudopods are relatively short and
clublike. They are not filamentary, nor raylike, nor anastomosing. There are two orders in this class, namely, the
Amoebaea and the *Testacea.*

Order AMOEBAEA

Nuda are naked Lobosa. The protoplasm of the body is
either naked or bounded by a thin membrane of the same
substance, known as the *pellicle.*

Typical species of this group, occurring in salt water, are
as follows:

Amoeba proteus (Pallas). This species is illustrated
in the index diagram (PLATE I). It occurs for the most part
in fresh water, but is also known to be found in brackish
water. It is a jellylike drop of protoplasm, continually
changing in shape and creeping from place to place over
water plants and other material by extending pseudopods
from its body. It has a nucleus containing chromatin, the
granules of which are grouped into small bodies known
as *chromosomes.* In the surrounding cytoplasm are to be
seen globular structures, some of which contract rapidly
to eject indigestible or undesirable particles from the body.

These are the *contractile vacuoles*. Other globules (food vacuoles) are digestive in function, containing particles of food-material in process of disintegration. Other species of this same group are *Trichamoeba gumia* and *Mayorella gemmifera*. These are illustrated in PLATE 2, page 9.

Order TESTACEA
(PLATE 2)

These are the shelled *Lobosa*. The animals themselves are amoeboid in structure, but secrete shells, either from horny or calcareous material, within which they live. The pseudopods are light, slender threads, not blunt lobes, as in the preceding order.

Gromia lagenoides Gruber. This more or less ovoid body is enclosed within a pear-shaped chitinous shell which is quite flexible. There is an opening at the larger end of the shell. The pseudopods are filamentary and granular, forming a network beyond the shell opening, which is turned inward to form an internal tubular sleeve through which the protoplasm may pour freely outside, forming a thin layer around the outside of the shell, from which branch fine pseudopodia. This species feeds upon smaller Protozoa, captured by the pseudopods. The network of protoplasm entraps smaller single-celled organisms, whether diatoms or protozoans.

Actinophrys sol Ehrenberg. The spherical body has a dense granular endoplasm and an ectoplasm of bubble-like vacuoles shading gradually into the internal layer. There is a central nucleus and one contractile vacuole. The pseudopods stand out stiffly in all directions, their shape being maintained by fine axial filaments. This species occurs abundantly in both fresh and salt water.

Heterophrys myriapoda Archer. This organism shows some differential character between ectoplasm and endoplasm. There is one nucleus in the endoplasm. There may be one or many contractile vacuoles. The pseudopods extending out from all sides are thin and stiffened by an internal granular core. They are much longer than the body diameter. The internal portion of the animal has many yellow cells similar to the commensal bodies (xanthoplasts) in radiolarians. It is common among algae.

SUBPHYLUM MASTIGOPHORA
(See INDEX PLATE I, *Anisonema grande*)

The Protozoa belonging to this group possess a definite shape, the body being covered by a firm pellicle. They are especially characterized by one or more long whiplike structures, at least one of which is locomotor in function in free-swimming forms, and is also useful in securing the

PLATE 1

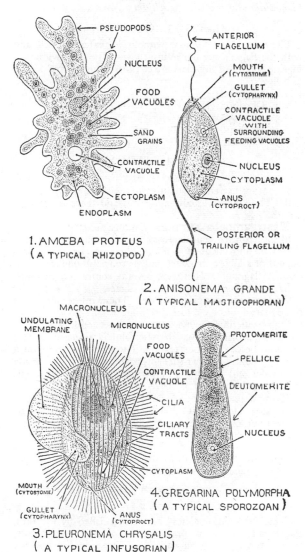

1. AMŒBA PROTEUS
(A TYPICAL RHIZOPOD)

Labels: PSEUDOPODS, NUCLEUS, FOOD VACUOLES, SAND GRAINS, CONTRACTILE VACUOLE, ECTOPLASM, ENDOPLASM

2. ANISONEMA GRANDE
(A TYPICAL MASTIGOPHORAN)

Labels: ANTERIOR FLAGELLUM, MOUTH (CYTOSTOME), GULLET (CYTOPHARYNX), CONTRACTILE VACUOLE WITH SURROUNDING FEEDING VACUOLES, NUCLEUS, CYTOPLASM, ANUS (CYTOPROCT), POSTERIOR OR TRAILING FLAGELLUM

3. PLEURONEMA CHRYSALIS
(A TYPICAL INFUSORIAN)

Labels: UNDULATING MEMBRANE, MACRONUCLEUS, MICRONUCLEUS, FOOD VACUOLES, CONTRACTILE VACUOLE, CILIA, CILIARY TRACTS, CYTOPLASM, MOUTH (CYTOSTOME), GULLET (CYTOPHARYNX), ANUS (CYTOPROCT)

4. GREGARINA POLYMORPHA
(A TYPICAL SPOROZOAN)

Labels: PROTOMERITE, PELLICLE, DEUTOMERITE, NUCLEUS

prey. This subphylum is divided into two classes, the *Flagellidia* and the *Dinoflagellidia*.

CLASS FLAGELLIDIA

These are *Mastigophora* without an external shell and with the flagella not borne in grooves. The free-swimming marine species of this class are comprised under five orders, as follows:

1. Monadida
2. Choanoflagellida
3. Heteromastigida
4. Euglenida
5. Silicoflagellida

Order MONADIDA
(PLATE 2)

These are extremely small forms with one or more flagella. The body is usually amoeboid and there is often no mouth.

Mastigamoeba simplex Calkins. This is an amoeboid species often considered to be transitional between the *Sarcodina* and the *Mastigophora*. The animal extends pseudopods of a lobose character, but there is also one large and distinct flagellum. There are several contractile vacuoles. It has been observed in decaying algae.

Codonoeca gracilis Calkins. These interesting small protozoans build a cuplike dwelling, usually goblet-shaped, though sometimes ovoid. At the upper end, there is a collarlike projection, which is absolutely transparent and seems to be of chitinous texture. The goblet is borne on a delicate stalk. The pear-shaped organism is situated inside the goblet and has one whiplike flagellum extending out into the water, which it beats continually.

Monas sp. Only one specimen of this genus was found at Woods Hole by Calkins, but they doubtless occur throughout our entire region. They have a very simple structure with a small ovoid body, either free-swimming or attached to algae by one of the two flagella. The main flagellum is about four times the length of the body. There is a posterior contractile vacuole.

Order CHOANOFLAGELLIDA
(PLATE 2)

These "choanoflagellates" are distinguished by the thin, transparent collar of protoplasmic material which surrounds the base of the flagellum. These species may be with or without a gelatinous test or envelope. They may occur singly as attached or free-swimming forms.

Monosiga ovata Saville Kent. This species has no stalk or, at most, a very short one. The form of the animal is ovate, tapering practically to a point, which bears a flagellum of considerable length. Around the pointed end of the body is developed a tumbler-shaped collar. Oil globules may be seen through the body. There is a contractile vacuole and nucleus in the upper portion of the organism.

Monosiga fusiformis Saville Kent. This species is flask-shaped, almost fusiform. There is a goblet-shaped collar at the upper end of the body and a short stalk or none at all. Two contractile vacuoles and one nucleus are known. It is found in fresh and salt water.

Codonosiga botrytis (Ehrenberg). The individuals of this species may occur either singly or in colonies. In either case, there is but a single elongate stalk with the individual or individuals borne at its upper end. The stalk is much longer than the body. The latter is naked but equipped with a collar around the base of the single flagellum. They have been found growing on red algae.

Order HETEROMASTIGIDA
(PLATE 2)

In this order, the individuals have two or more flagella, one of which trails behind the organism.

Bodo globosus Stein. The body is globe-shaped. The anterior flagellum is the shorter of the two and draws the body forward by its vibrations. The longer trailing flagellum curves under and extends out behind the animal. This species is quite common in sea water.

Bodo caudatus (Dujardin). In this case, the body is quite variable. At times it is oval, and at other times it is irregular in shape. The flagella are inserted in a small indentation below a forward-projecting prostomium. The contractile vacuole is in the forward part of the body near the base of the flagella. In this case, the anterior flagellum is usually longer than the posterior trailing flagellum. This species is also common along our coast.

Oxyrrhis marina Dujardin. The individuals of this species are considerably larger than those of the two preceding species. The body is ovoid expanding toward the rear, somewhat pointed anteriorly. Near the pointed end, there is a funnel-shaped cavity from which project two flagella, approximately equal in length. There is a central nucleus. Reproduction by fission occurs transversely throughout the body.

Order EUGLENIDA
(PLATE 2)

The species belonging to this order are comparatively large in size and all with quite definite shape. There may be one or two flagella and a mouth or no mouth at the anterior end. There is always a distinct pharynx. In some cases, the body is plastic and certain species have an eye-spot.

Astasia contorta Dujardin. This flagellate has a plastic, spindle-shaped body with a single flagellum. The cuticle is striped in spiral fashion; otherwise the body is colorless and transparent. A contractile vacuole is situated in the anterior projection near the base of the flagellum, which, in turn, rises from an oesophageal tube into which, also, the contractile vacuole empties. This species is common in decaying algae.

Anisonema vitrea (Dujardin). This flagellate has eight ridges separating eight concave facets, completely surrounding its definitely shaped, spindlelike body. There are two flagella; the shorter, forwardly directed one is locomotor in function while the other, arising near the base of the first, curves abruptly and extends backward behind the animal for a considerable distance. There is an anterior ventral groove from which the two flagella originate. A large number of food vacuoles are in the posterior portion. There is a central nucleus and a contractile vacuole in the forward part on the left-hand side. The animal is quite transparent and glassy in appearance. It is common in decaying algae.

Anisonema grande Ehrenberg. This species is shown in the index diagram as a typical flagellate with the various parts of the organism labeled for convenience.

Order SILICOFLAGELLIDA

This order contains but a single species, with a silicious skeleton as indicated below.

Distephanus speculum Stöhr. This is an odd and quite rare flagellate having a symmetrical silicious skeleton formed of two rings of different sizes parallel with each other and connected by bars of silicon. Six bars radiate outward from the wider ring and six short bars point inward from the shorter ring. The color of this flagellate is yellow. It has a single flagellum.

CLASS DINOFLAGELLIDA

This class consists of *Mastigophora* which may be naked or enclosed in a simple membrane or protected by means of a cellulose armor of two shells or of many plates welded together.

The uniform characteristic of the class is the possession of two flagella, arising close together, but one trailing behind and the other at right angles to the axis of the organism, vibrating in an arc of a circle. Both of these flagella typically occupy grooves.

The body of these dinoflagellates is of a definite form,

PLATE 2

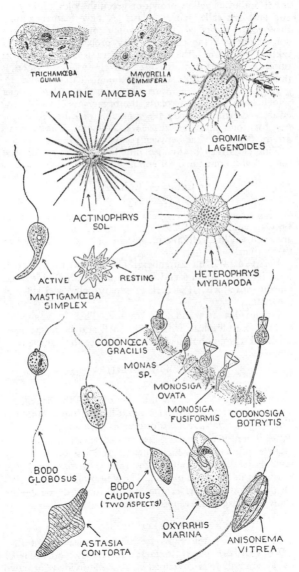

TRICHAMŒBA
GUMIA

MAYORELLA
GEMMIFERA

MARINE AMŒBAS

GROMIA
LAGENOIDES

ACTINOPHRYS
SOL

HETEROPHRYS
MYRIAPODA

ACTIVE   RESTING

MASTIGAMŒBA
SIMPLEX

CODONŒCA
GRACILIS

MONAS
SP.

MONOSIGA
OVATA

MONOSIGA
FUSIFORMIS

CODONOSIGA
BOTRYTIS

BODO
GLOBOSUS

BODO
CAUDATUS
(TWO ASPECTS)

OXYRRHIS
MARINA

ANISONEMA
VITREA

ASTASIA
CONTORTA

though often irregular in shape. A stigma and various small bodies of yellow-brown or greenish color usually occur and are called chromoplasts. A new feature among Protozoa is the *pusule* system, which consists of large sacs connected with the exterior. They probably function for taking fluid from the outside. There is a single, large nucleus. By means of the greenish chromoplasts, food is produced in plantlike manner, though capture and ingestation of small organisms also occur. In certain species which have lost chromoplasts, the organisms have become entirely dependent upon the ingestion of other forms of life for food and are, therefore, holozoic. These forms are on the borderline between plants and animals.

This class may be divided into two orders, as follows: the *Adinida* and the *Diniferida*.

Order ADINIDA
(PLATE 3)

This group includes a few chiefly marine forms with simple ovoid bodies, which may be naked or, if protected, are enclosed in a cellulose membrane or a cellulose shell of two valves.

Exuviella lima Ehrenberg. The shell is thick, ovoid, with its more pointed end forward and with an indented margin anteriorly. It is dark brown in color and slow of movement.

Exuviella marina Cienkowsky. This is a smaller form, more elliptical, with a thin shell and large granules scattered throughout its interior. The central nucleus is spherical.

Order DINIFERIDA
(PLATE 3)

This order includes all the rest of the dinoflagellates. There is always a ventral longitudinal groove (*sulcus*). The *longitudinal flagellum* originates here and trails backward. There is also a transverse or sometimes spiral groove (*girdle* or *annulus*) which may encircle the body spirally several times. This contains the *transverse flagellum* and is always in wavelike motion. The vibrations of the longitudinal flagellum drives the animal forward, while the transverse flagelium causes the animal to spin like a top.

Family Peridinidae

In this family, the transverse furrow is nearly central.

Peridinium digitale Pouchet. This is a globular or ovoid animal. It is contained in a shell divided into two similar halves by the transverse groove. The anterior shell is the larger. As the furrow runs around the shell in spiral

PLATE 3

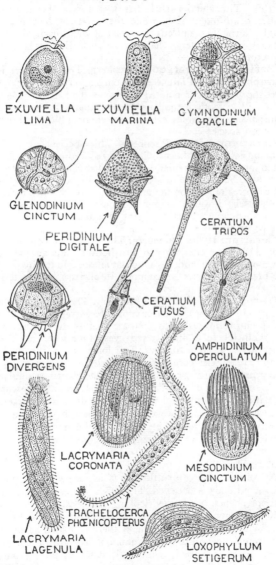

EXUVIELLA LIMA

EXUVIELLA MARINA

GYMNODINIUM GRACILE

GLENODINIUM CINCTUM

PERIDINIUM DIGITALE

CERATIUM TRIPOS

PERIDINIUM DIVERGENS

CERATIUM FUSUS

AMPHIDINIUM OPERCULATUM

LACRYMARIA CORONATA

MESODINIUM CINCTUM

LACRYMARIA LAGENULA

TRACHELOCERCA PHŒNICOPTERUS

LOXOPHYLLUM SETIGERUM

fashion, its two extremities are connected by a longitudinal furrow. The anterior shell has two forwardly directed spines of different size, while the posterior half has a single horn. The nucleus is spherical or ellipsoidal and located in the posterior half of the shell. This is a very common species.

Peridinium divergens Ehrenberg. The shell here is also spheroidal, the larger shell being anterior. There are two short divergent pointed horns on the anterior shell, each with a tooth at the base on the inner side. It is very transparent, sometimes colored brown or yellow. Also a common species.

Ceratium tripos Ehrenberg. This species has three long projections or horns. The body is more or less flattened and has a circular or somewhat spiral transverse furrow. The longitudinal furrow is quite wide and takes up the greater part of the anterior half of the shell. The shell, itself, is quite porous. Chromatophores, green or yellow-brown, are usually present. It is found in fresh and salt water.

Ceratium fusus Ehrenberg. There are two long horns terminating the elongate fusiform body of this animal. It is yellow in color and has chromatophores. Both this and the preceding species are common in algae, about floating timbers and old wharves.

Glenodinium cinctum Ehrenberg. The globular body is smooth with brown chromatophores arranged radially and pointing inward with the base against the interior of the shell. There is often a red eyespot present near the junction of the two furrows. The longitudinal furrow is small. The species occurs in both fresh and salt water.

Gymnodinium gracile Bergh. This species is similar to *Glenodinium* except that the shell is entirely absent. The animals are spherical with a practically circular transverse furrow which, however, in some cases, may be spiral. The flagella arise near the junction of the transverse and longitudinal furrows. The chromatophores are often not present so that ingestion of food is of animal character (holozoic).

Amphidinium operculatum Claparède & Lachmann. The ovoid body is flattened. There is a very small conical anterior portion of the shell looking like a cap. The longitudinal furrow extends throughout the entire length of the body with a contracting width. If there is a shell at all, it is extremely delicate. The chromatophores are brown or green, grouped radially with their bases extending outward and pointing inwardly toward a central granule. There is a posterior nucleus. It is common in fresh and salt water.

SUBPHYLUM INFUSORIA
(See INDEX PLATE 1, *Pleuronema chrysalis*)

The *Infusoria* are characterized by the possession of minute hairlike bodies known as *cilia* for locomotor and food-catching purposes or, instead of these, specialized tentacles for the same purpose.

CLASS CILIATA

These are *Infusoria* having cilia which are retained throughout their entire life history.

Like the *Mastigophora,* the *Ciliata* have a definite permanent shape, which is maintained by a firm pellicle. The anterior and the posterior ends can always be distinguished from each other. Symmetry is usually bilateral, though occasionally it may be radial.

Ciliata are the most highly developed class of Protozoa, as they have special organs for securing food; various external structures due to specializations of the pellicle; small contractile regions which are the prototypes of muscles in higher animals; and also, specialized nervous elements. Usually *Ciliata* are solitary, free-swimming creatures. Some, however, may be attached for the whole or part of their life history and a few may form branching colonies.

Ciliata are divided into four orders, as follows:
1. Holotrichida
2. Heterotrichida
3. Hypotrichida
4. Peritrichida

Order HOLOTRICHIDA

The species in this order have cilia covering the entire body, but without any distinction, except for length, between the cilia surrounding the mouth and those covering the rest of the body. The group is divided into suborders, the *Gymnostomina* and the *Trichostomina.* In the *Gymnostomina,* the circular mouth is closed except while food is being ingested and the structure known as the undulating membrane is not present. In the suborder *Trichostomina,* the mouth is always open and the undulating membrane is present.

Suborder GYMNOSTOMINA
Family Enchelinidae
(PLATE 3)

In this family, the mouth is either at the end of the body or near it. Food is swallowed, but without the aid of producing currents by ciliary action.

Lacrymaria lagenula Claparède & Lachmann. The body is more or less flask-shaped with a conical apex which may be protruded to a certain degree. The surface of the body is covered with longitudinal, slightly spiral stripes. The cilia cover the body uniformly, but a circle of longer ones surrounds the base of the conical proboscis. The macronucleus is slightly above the center of the body. There are two contractile vacuoles toward the posterior end. This species may vary from an elongate to a sub-globular form.

Lacrymaria coronata Claparède & Lachmann. This form is also flask-shaped and contractile. The contractile vacuole is at the posterior end. There is a short mound-shaped proboscis separated from the rest of the body by a deep groove. It is surrounded by a circle of long cilia inserted on the proboscis itself. The slightly spiral stripes are so deeply sunk into the cuticle that they give a fluted appearance to its surface. The endoplasm is blue-green in color. The body retains its shape quite permanently, due to the toughness of the membrane.

Trachelocerca phoenicopterus Cohn. This is a very long, slender protozoan (total length, 3 mm.). It may, however, contract to much smaller proportions. The anterior end is square or cylindrical, often with a four-sided mouth. The macronucleus may be a single, round body or it may be divided into two or several parts. The tail is pointed, with longer cilia than on the rest of the body except for the mouth region, where the longest cilia are situated.

Mesodinium cinctum Calkins. A deep indentation divides the body of this species into two parts, a short, oral region and a larger globular region for the rest of the body. The oesophagus is longitudinally striped. Rings of cirri take their rise in the groove. If there is more than one ring, an anterior set points forward around the mouth and the rest around the posterior part of the body. Four short tentaclelike prolongations may be extended from the corners of the mouth. The macronucleus is horseshoe-shaped.

Family Trachylinidae
(PLATES 3 & 4)

The species in this family often have the body drawn out into a long anterior process, the mouth often having a specialized framework.

Loxophyllum setigerum Quenn. The body is flat, with striped upper- and undersurfaces along which the cilia follow the stripes. It is very extensible and flexible. The anterior end often prolongs itself like a proboscis. The central portion of the body is domelike, containing

PLATE 4

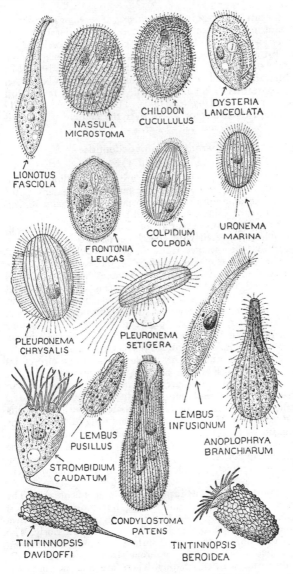

LIONOTUS
FASCIOLA

NASSULA
MICROSTOMA

CHILODON
CUCULLULUS

DYSTERIA
LANCEOLATA

FRONTONIA
LEUCAS

COLPIDIUM
COLPODA

URONEMA
MARINA

PLEURONEMA
CHRYSALIS

PLEURONEMA
SETIGERA

LEMBUS
INFUSIONUM

ANOPLOPHRYA
BRANCHIARUM

LEMBUS
PUSILLUS

STROMBIDIUM
CAUDATUM

CONDYLOSTOMA
PATENS

TINTINNOPSIS
DAVIDOFFI

TINTINNOPSIS
BEROIDEA

the nuclei and contractile vacuoles. Both mouth and anus are present.

Lionotus fasciola Ehrenberg. The elongate body is fusiform with a tapering or rounded posterior end. The anterior end usually forms an elongate proboscis which is flat and flexible. In this species, it is as long as the main part of the body. The contractile vacuole is double. Cilia are present only on the underside of the body. An elongate mouth extends beneath the proboscis for its full length, bordered by long cilia. The animal swims freely through the water or glides over the bottom. It is found in both fresh and salt water.

Family Chlamydodontidae
(PLATE 4)

The species in this family are mostly ellipsoid. The mouth usually is not terminal, but may be at any point from the anterior to the posterior end. It usually has an armature of spinose, rodlike stiffenings.

Nassula microstoma Cohn. The body is cylindrical, completely covered with cilia. The mouth is ventral from ¼ to ⅓ the distance from the apex. Well-defined spiral stripes mark the outer surface of the entire body. The circular mouth is at the bottom of a depression and is continued into the interior by means of a cylindrical oesophagus, which is supported by a skeleton of stiff rods. The body may be colorless or may be bright with red, blue, brown, or black pigment. There is a globular macronucleus in the center with a number of micronuclei attached to it. The contractile vacuole is posterior.

Chilodon cucullulus Müller. This common species is ovoid in outline. The anterior end is curved to the left with the mouth just over the angle. The posterior end has a broad, round outline. Only the ventral surface is ciliated and is also abundantly striated. The lines of cilia all converge at the mouth where they are longer. The mouth is in the middle of the body and about ¼ the distance from the anterior end. It is round in outline and is supported by from 10 to 16 rods. There are a number of contractile vacuoles. There are one macronucleus and one micronucleus.

Dysteria lanceolata Claparède & Lachmann. The body is also oval in this species, but more elongate. It consists of two valvelike portions, of which one is oval and the other is cut away obliquely and posteriorly. The cilia are only on the ventral surface. The mouth is between the two valves and has a throat armature similar to the other species in this family. There are one macronucleus and two contractile vacuoles. The animal moves in circles. It is practically transparent.

Family Chiliferidae
(PLATE 4)

The mouth is always situated in the anterior half of the body. Undulating membranes are present, either on the edge of the mouth or in the oesophagus.

Frontonia leucas Ehrenberg. The mouth is situated somewhat anteriorly and has an undulating membrane on its left edge only. The body is rather cylindrical in form with cilia of uniform length evenly distributed over the entire body. The mouth is always open and has a small longitudinally striped lip which continues into a long furrow toward the posterior end. The globular nucleus is on the right side of the furrow with a contractile vacuole opposite. The edge of the body is stiffened throughout with large trichocysts. It feeds on dinoflagellates and other forms of similar size. The color is dark brown to black.

Colpidium colpoda Ehrenberg. The oval body has the mouth situated about ⅓ of the distance from the anterior to the posterior end of the body at the bottom of a slight depression and continued to the interior by means of a tubular oesophagus within which there are two undulating membranes. The anus is terminal with a contractile vacuole situated near it. The spherical macronucleus is central with one micronucleus attached. The food is mainly bacteria. The body is striped externally from pole to pole with the cilia in longitudinal rows following the striations.

Uronema marina Dujardin. This is quite a small organism, oval in shape, slightly flattened ventrally. Widely placed striae mark the exterior from the anterior to the posterior end. There is a large mouth near the center of the body, surrounded by two rows of cilia. There is no oesophagus, but an undulating membrane extends down the mouth. This species is especially characterized by a single, long, stiff bristle extending from the posterior end. The central macronucleus is accompanied by one micronucleus attached to one side. The posterior contractile vacuole is situated near the anal opening. The animal moves swiftly and steadily forward in a straight line. It feeds mainly on bacteria obtained from decomposed vegetable substances.

Family Pleuronemidae
(PLATE 4)

A long groove (*peristome*) running along the ventral side terminates in the mouth. The body is somewhat flattened. An undulating membrane takes up the entire left edge of the peristome, and sometimes continues on around the end and toward the mouth. Sometimes, there is a smaller membrane on the right side.

Pleuronema chrysalis Ehrenberg. The ovoid body is narrower at the anterior end than at the posterior end. The peristome is ¾ of the body length, with its posterior end straight and curved along the left side. The body is covered with fine cilia arranged in longitudinal lines, except near the peristome. The small mouth is in the bottom of the peristome, just beneath the large undulating membrane which is highest toward the posterior portion. This membrane can be folded together inside the peristome. On the right side of the peristome are the largest cilia. The contractile vacuole with one attached micronucleus is in the anterior portion of the body. This species feeds upon Bacteria. It is found in both fresh and salt water.

Pleuronema setigera Calkins. The body is elongate and narrower than the previous species. It is described by Calkins as being somewhat "cucumbershaped." The peristome is shorter and deeper with a high, sail-like, undulating membrane entirely in the posterior part of the body, forming a pocket around the peristome. Another smaller undulating membrane runs down the inside of the peristome to the inside of the mouth. Long cilia cover the body. From three to ten especially long threadlike setae extend out posteriorly from the body. There are a central macronucleus and a contractile vacuole posterior to it.

Lembus infusionum Calkins. The body is long and almost fishlike in shape, tapering from a somewhat blunt posterior portion terminating in a long seta to a gradually narrowing anterior end, which is almost pointed. The mouth is situated near the center of the body. The cilia, anterior to the mouth, grade from short cilia to extremely long ones at the anterior end on the ventral side. On the dorsal side, they are much shorter and pass backward over the body and forward on the ventral side to the mouth, but all practically of the same size. The large macronucleus is centrally located with a small micronucleus near it. Posterior to the nuclei are six or eight contractile vacuoles in a row.

Lembus pusillus Quennerstedt. This is a much smaller species than the above. It is nearly cylindrical in form, with a somewhat narrower anterior end and a more rounded posterior end, bearing a long bristlelike seta pointed directly backward. The peristomial groove extends from the anterior end to the middle of the body with undulating membranes on the edges. There is only one contractile vacuole. The cuticle is distinctly striated lengthwise.

Family Opalinidae
(PLATE 4)

The species in this family have an oval form, but the body may, at times, be drawn out until it is wormlike in character. There is neither mouth nor pharynx.

Anoplophrya branchiarum Stein. The body may be cylindrical or pear-shaped. In the latter case, the broad end is anterior in position. The cuticle is striped lengthwise by indentations like those of a melon. Fine particles are seen throughout the body, probably the remainders of digested food fragments. The nucleus is cucumbershaped and granular, with a micronucleus on the concave side. The long cilia are sparsely inserted in the grooves. There is one contractile vacuole at the extreme posterior end. This species is occasionally free-swimming, but it is often parasitic upon the gills of the amphipod *Gammarus pulex*.

Order HETEROTRICHIDA

In this order, the cilia cover the entire body or they may be reduced to certain localized areas. A specialized adoral zone of membranelles is present. This order is divided into two suborders, the *Polytrichina* and the *Oligotrichina*.

Suborder POLYTRICHINA

This group includes *Heterotrichida* having a complete covering of cilia.

Family Bursariidae
(PLATE 4)

The triangular peristomial region ends in the mouth.

Condylostoma patens Müller. The body resembles an elongate sac, narrowing anteriorly and broad and rounded in the posterior region. It contains many brightly colored food granules. The triangular peristome terminates the smaller end and shows clearly the undulating membrane. The mouth is situated at the base of the triangle and opens into a short, narrow, and conical oesophagus. This species is very common.

Suborder OLIGOTRICHINA

In this suborder, the cilia occur only in certain localized areas.

Family Halteriidae
(PLATE 4)

In this family, there are no cilia in the region of the peristome. Otherwise, they occur only in connection with certain girdles around the body.

Strombidium caudatum Fromentel. These are small, transparent animals more or less pear-shaped with a prostomiumlike projection arising from the broad end. A ring of long cirri surrounds this end, just inside of which is an adoral zone leading down to the mouth at its posterior extremity. A strong caudal appendage tapering to a point terminates the narrow posterior end of the body. The large spherical nucleus is located centrally, while the contractile vacuole is posterior. The terminal appendage enables the creature to leap suddenly through the water, at intervals, after resting.

Family Tintinnidae
(PLATE 4)

The body of each individual is attached by means of a terminal stalk to the bottom of a cup-shaped house. The mouth-region at the flattened top of the animal is enclosed by two circlets of cilia, the outer of which is composed of thick, tentaclelike membranelles. The entire body is covered with cilia.

Tintinnopsis beroidea Stein. In this case, the shell or house is colorless, thimble-shaped, and with a rounded posterior end. The body of the animal is cylindrical. There are twenty-four membranelles.

Tintinnopsis davidoffi Daday. This species is similar to the preceding, except that the shell is much narrower in proportion to its length. It is provided with a spinelike stem of considerable length. The shell is chitinous and covered with a mosaic of silicious flakes.

Order HYPOTRICHIDA

In this order, the cilia are located only on the ventral side. There is a distinct adoral zone.

Family Oxytrichidae
(PLATE 5)

In this family, the cilia on the rather indefinite peristome are confined to the ventral surface and are uniform in size.

Epiclintes radiosa Quenn. The body of these creatures is elongate, quite narrow anteriorly and drawn out posteriorly into an elongate but retractile tail-like extension. The anterior end is characterized by five long cirri. The rest of the ventral side possesses cilia of practically uniform size. The tail-like appendage may be stretched out to twice the length of the body or contracted to body size. The peristome starts anteriorly on the right side and extends backward and to the left.

Amphisia kessleri Wrzesniowski. The body is elongate, slightly S-shaped, and expanded somewhat in the center. The peristome, down the right side, extends

PLATE 5

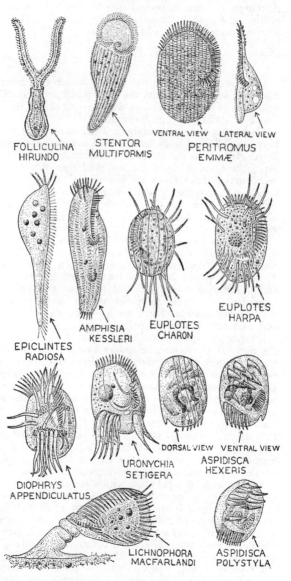

FOLLICULINA
HIRUNDO

STENTOR
MULTIFORMIS

PERITROMUS
EMMÆ

VENTRAL VIEW   LATERAL VIEW

EPICLINTES
RADIOSA

AMPHISIA
KESSLERI

EUPLOTES
CHARON

EUPLOTES
HARPA

DIOPHRYS
APPENDICULATUS

URONYCHIA
SETIGERA

ASPIDISCA
HEXERIS

DORSAL VIEW   VENTRAL VIEW

LICHNOPHORA
MACFARLANDI

ASPIDISCA
POLYSTYLA

for a considerable distance with a distinct adoral zone. A conspicuous line of preoral cilia borders the right side of the adoral zone. Three anteriorly located cirri form a triangular pattern.

Family Euplotidae
(PLATE 5)

Cilia are almost entirely absent, while the frontal, marginal, and ventral cirri are very much reduced. The anal cirri, however, are always characteristic of this family. There is a ribbonlike macronucleus.

Euplotes charon Ehrenberg. These remarkable forms have a small, oval body, usually with six or eight deeply fluted grooves on the carapace. The adoral zone extends ⅔ of the distance down the left-hand side of the body in a curving line. There are ten ventral cirri, seven of which are near the frontal border and three near the right edge. There are five posterior and four anal cirri. The macronucleus is horseshoe-shaped. The contractile vacuole is on the right side located posteriorly.

Euplotes harpa Stein. In this species, the body is more elongate than in the previous case. There are three teeth on the frontal margin. There are ten ventral cirri. The dorsal surface has eight longitudinal grooves. The adoral zone possesses a series of powerful membranelles extending in a curve from the mouth to the extreme right frontal margin. There are five long and rigid anal cirri and several smaller marginal cirri.

Diophrys appendiculatus Stein. At first glance, the form of this species resembles that of *Euplotes,* but at the posterior right, there is a large indentation or excavation in the body of the species. Anteriorly, there is a row of powerful membranelles which curve about and become gradually smaller as they reach the peristome and follow it down to the mouth, where they are of small size. There are seven large ventral cirri pointing generally forward and sidewise. There are five very large anal cirri which point posteriorly and extend beyond the posterior part of the body, uniformly curving to the left. From a region deep in the dorsal pit, and dorsal to the anal cirri, rise three large, pointed cirri, which are almost hooklike, as they curve at right angles to the right. Two small cirri are at the left end of the row of anal cirri. The macronucleus is divided into two parts which are elongate and almost cucumber-shaped, lying transversely and almost parallel to each other. There is a contractile vacuole lying above the bases of the five anal cirri.

Uronychia setigera Calkins. The most characteristic structures in this species are the enormous cirri which are situated posteriorly. There are two excavations in the posterior end of the body. The right excavation seats five great cirri, which are parallel to each other, one, at the extreme right of the row, being much larger than the other four. The left excavation has two conspicuous cirri, one larger than the other. There are three dorsal cirri located dorsally to those just mentioned, characterized by their sickle shape. The peristome is quite wide, converging to a hollow, at the bottom of which is the mouth. There are a spherical macronucleus and a micronucleus attached to its side. The contractile vacuole is situated posteriorly between the two sets of posterior cirri. This species is quite common.

Aspidisca hexeres Quennerstedt. The carapace of *Aspidisca heres* is elliptical with a spearlike projection at its left posterior border. There are eight very short, thick ventral cirri, which distinguish this species from all others. According to Calkins, they have very much the appearance of pointed paintbrushes and may separate into fine fibrils when the organism is moving slowly. In an excavation at the posterior end, six curved cirri, irregular in size, emerge parallel to each other. The peristome is situated posteriorly and has an undulating membrane. The nucleus is horseshoe-shaped.

Aspidisca polystyla Stein. This species is much smaller than the preceding and is closely related to it. It differs in the number of anal cirri, which are ten instead of six. There are eight ventral cirri in two rows with one of the second rows somewhat separated from the rest.

Order PERITRICHIDA

The cilia in this order are found only in the adoral zone and about the mouth.

Family Lichnophoridae
(PLATE 5)

The adoral zone is on the anterior part of the animal and is rounded or oval in shape, surrounded by a circlet of conspicuous cilia.

Lichnophora macfarlandi Stevens. The anterior end is that characteristic of the family, while the posterior end is developed like a stalk with a broad, sucking disc at its bottom with which it clings to the substratum. The adoral zone practically encloses the peristome. The macronucleus is long and beaded and may be broken up in several parts. The contractile vacuole is in the region of the mouth on the left side. The stalk is very contractile and can become attached or detached from the surface to which it clings. When detached, the organism moves about freely by means of its pedal disc. The nucleus is separated into five or six parts distributed throughout the organism.

Family Vorticellidae
(PLATE 6)

These may be attached or may swim about. They are peritrichous ciliates having the adoral zone in the form of a right-handed spiral.

Vorticella marina Greeff. These are protozoans of bell-like form. They may be colorless, or yellow, or green, through the presence of other small organisms. When not contracted, the cilia around the edge of the flowerlike body beat the water in successive rotation. The posterior end takes the form of a long threadlike stalk which attaches the animal to the substratum. This stalk, due to a highly contractile thread which extends throughout it from end to end, may be suddenly drawn down into a single-coiled structure, bringing the animal close to its base. The macronucleus is always long and sausage-shaped with a micronucleus attached. The bell of the organism is annulated horizontally. In this genus, though the animals occur singly and it is not a colonial form, nevertheless the individuals tend to remain in groups.

Vorticella patellina Müller. The body is flowerlike, widest at the anterior border from which it narrows directly to the top of the stem. The ciliary disc is only slightly elevated. The cuticle is not annulated. The whole creature is transparent.

Zoothamnium elegans D'Udekem. This species and its relatives grow in colonies which may be large or small. Otherwise, it is quite similar to *Vorticella*. The branching is quite frequent and always simply forked in pairs due to the fact that with each division of the animal, the stalk also divides. The border of the peristome is widespread, tapering posteriorly; otherwise, it is quite similar to *Vorticella*.

Cothurnia crystallina Ehrenberg. While these animals are similar to *Vorticella,* they are much more elongate and form a transparent vase-shaped "house" (*lorica*) to the bottom of which the aboral end of the animal is attached. These structures may be simply globe-shaped or may be vase-shaped. The basal part is maintained on a short stalk. The cups may be transparent or tinged with brown. The animal may extend the upper part of its body out of the cup or may contract until it is practically contained within it.

Cothurnia imberbis Ehrenberg. In this case, the lorica is expanded posteriorly, but is somewhat narrowed at the oral margin. It has an extremely short stalk. It is

PLATE 6

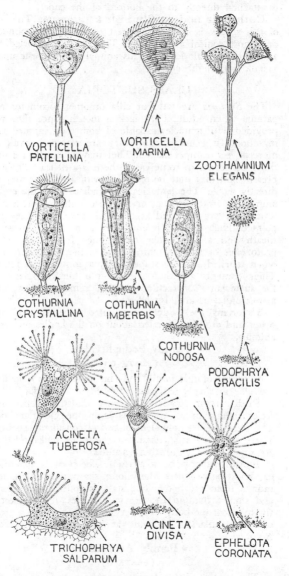

VORTICELLA
PATELLINA

VORTICELLA
MARINA

ZOOTHAMNIUM
ELEGANS

COTHURNIA
CRYSTALLINA

COTHURNIA
IMBERBIS

COTHURNIA
NODOSA

PODOPHRYA
GRACILIS

ACINETA
TUBEROSA

ACINETA
DIVISA

TRICHOPHRYA
SALPARUM

EPHELOTA
CORONATA

perfectly smooth and without annulations. The animal is attached directly to the bottom of the cup.

Cothurnia nodosa Claparède & Lachmann. The cup of this species is elongate, largest centrally, and rounded or almost conical at the base. The cup is supported by a stalk of variable length. This animal also is borne upon a stalk within the cup.

CLASS SUCTORIA

The *Suctoria* are without cilia or other locomotor apparatus when adult. They lack a mouth, since they are provided with tentacles capable of both food capture and ingestion. In general form, they are rounded, oval, or more or less trumpet-shaped. They may be single or sometimes branched. In some cases, there is a delicate "house" present and they may be provided with a stalk or may be directly sessile. The tentacles may radiate from the entire animal, or from the top, or may occur in groups. Sometimes they are knobbed at the end; sometimes they are pointed. Each tentacle is enclosed in an outer contractile sheath and a stiff inner tube. They feed upon other protozoans or rotifers which stick to the tentacular ends when touched and are stupefied by a poisonous secretion. Their contents are then sucked into the endoplasm of the suctorian. Contractile vacuoles, a micronucleus, and a macronucleus are also present.

Suctorians are widely distributed in fresh and salt water and are often carried about on the bodies of larger animals.

Family Podophryidae
(PLATE 6)

Members of this family may be stalked or not stalked, globular in shape, tentacles knobbed or pointed.

Podophrya gracilis Calkins. Short, knobbed tentacles radiate in all directions from the globular body. The stalk is extremely slender and of considerable length. There is a small nucleus situated near the stalk and there are one or two contractile vacuoles.

Ephelota coronata Wright. The body is spheroidal or almost pear-shaped. Many long, sharp, pointed tentacles radiate from the body. The stalk is considerably shorter and stouter than in the previous species. It is widest at the top near the body. It is very common and often grows on campanularian hydroids as well as on algae and *Bryozoa*.

Family Acinetidae
(PLATE 6)

The species of this family may be naked or may construct a *theca* or a "house." They may or may not be stalked. Their numerous knobbed tentacles are all similar to each other.

Acineta divisa Fraipont. This is a very delicate and beautiful species with a long, straight, slender stalk and a theca shaped like a wineglass, in which the animal is situated and rises, dome-shaped, above the delicate rim. The slender tentacles are all knobbed and stand out straight in all directions from the upper portion of the animal. They are said to move backward and forward slowly. The spherical or oval nucleus is located centrally with a contractile vacuole nearer to the surface.

Acineta tuberosa Ehrenberg. This is one of the larger *Suctoria,* situated in a cup so fragile that it can scarcely be seen, mounted on a straight stalk shorter than in the preceding species. The body is almost triangular in shape, having two upper, rounded angles, from each of which a group of tentacles stands out rigidly in all directions. The tentacles are knobbed. The endoplasm of this species shows many granules and is yellowish in color. The oval nucleus is quite large and the contractile vacuole is in the upper part of the body.

Family Dendrosomidae
(PLATE 6)

The species in this family are naked, having no theca or "house." The numerous knobbed tentacles are all alike and grow in various tufts. They may be simple or branched.

Trichophrya salparum Entz. These are small forms without stalks or cups. The more or less elongate body is irregularly lobed and variable in shape. The knobbed tentacles are borne upon the convex lobes. There is an oval or spherical macronucleus. It may even be bandlike or horseshoe-shaped. There are various contractile vacuoles. This species is often parasitic and is widely distributed in fresh and salt water.

2
Phylum Porifera

(SPONGES)

SPONGES are among the most abundant and most widely distributed of sea-animals. With the exception of one family, the fresh-water sponges, they are found in all seas of the globe ranging from shallow waters to beyond a depth of 1,300 feet. The bath sponges of commerce, with which the "sponge" is associated in the minds of most people, although from a commercial point of view the most important of the group, form but a single family, the *Spongidae*. The rest of the subkingdom with its great multiplicity of species is doubtless comparatively unknown to the average person. Even the commercial sponge, as it reaches us, gives but little idea of what a sponge really is, as it is only the supporting or skeletal part of the animal colony denuded of its fleshy coat of living tissue.

The living sponge is either a single animal or a colony of animals. It is always sessile, that is, attached to the sea bottom and incapable of locomotion. For this reason, it has often been regarded as a plant. But since, in more recent years, its life processes and larval history have become better known, especially since it has come under the eye of the compound microscope, its animal nature has become clearly established.

Sponges show all variations of form, size, and color. There are cakelike sponges, dome-shaped sponges, and fan-shaped sponges. Some are branched like trees; in others the branches reunite to form a complicated network. Some are shaped like huge cups or goblets; some gather in clusters of trumpet- and tubelike forms, and even the simplest and most primitive sponges are often shaped like graceful vases. All these forms are found in sizes varying from that of a pinhead to the height of a man.

Their color is as varied as their shape and size. They run through the whole chromatic scale from brilliant red, yellow, and green to the most delicate blue and deepest violet, in every gradation of shade and tint. Some are pure white, others are shining black, while still others reflect from their opal spicules all the colors of the rainbow.

As the form and color of sponges, however, may vary as much among members of the same species as among those of different species, these factors cannot be depended on for classification. The same sponge which, in deep water, shows the branching habit, in shallower waters appears as a flat encrusting colony; or a sponge which has a symmetrical vaselike form, many feet below the surface of the sea, where it is little disturbed by outer influences, may be of the same species as an irregular one-sided mass growing in shallow water or in the crevice of a rock. Again, a sponge, usually dome-shaped, may send out a fingerlike process from its upper surface which becomes branched and unites with the branches of other fingerlike processes. In other words, external form in sponges is not a constant or essential factor. It is purely a matter of environment, in which currents and gravity play an important part. This tendency to vary has made the arrangement of sponges, in an orderly and natural system, a difficult task, much complicated by the fact that, for many years, classification has been wrongly based upon these very factors. Since, however, the microscope has been developed to its present perfection, it has been found that the arrangement of the skeleton and the form of the spicules or skeletal units, together with the structure of the canal system, furnish more constant data for classification. This can be brought out more clearly in discussing the anatomy of the sponge.

ANATOMY

In considering the anatomy of sponges it is sufficient for our purpose to concern ourselves with:

1. General Structure,
2. The Canal Systems,
3. The Skeleton.

1. *General Structure*

This is best shown by the description of a simple sponge in which the general characteristics of the subkingdom predominate, unmodified by special conditions.

The simplest, most primitive, and, at the same time, most typical sponge is *Ascetta primordialis*, first described by Häckel (INDEX PLATE 7, FIGURE 1). This sponge is typically vaselike in external form. The circular opening at the top of the vase is known as the *osculum* (*osc*) in spite of the fact that it is excretory and has neither structurally nor functionally the characteristics of a mouth.

The walls of the vase are perforated with numerous openings or pores (*p*) which open directly into the hollow interior of the sponge, the *paragastric* or *atrial cavity* (*atr*). The walls are made up of three layers: 1st, the ectoderm, or outer layer; 2nd, the endoderm, or inner layer; 3rd, the mesoderm, or middle layer.

The *epithelium* or *ectoderm* (*ect*) is a thin layer of cells, generally arranged in mosaic form and known as "pavement cells." In the case of this species, however, the

walls of the cells have disappeared and left tne protoplasmic cell-contents continuous over the entire surface of
the animal. Such a layer is called a *syncytium*.

The *endoderm* (*end*) lines the paragastric cavity and
is made up of a layer of peculiar and characteristic cells
called "collared cells," or *choanocytes* (*cho*), found nowhere else among many-celled animals (see INDEX PLATE
8). They are so called from a collar-shaped rim around
the outer edge of the cell out of which extends a long
whiplike filament or *flagellum* (*fla*). The continuous
vibration of these flagella produces a current by means
of which the sea water, with its multitude of tiny animal
and plant forms, is sucked in through the pores. The
organisms are then seized upon by the choanocytes and
their digestible parts absorbed. What is left is discarded
and flows with the current out through the osculum at
the summit of the vase.

The *mesenchyme* (*mes*) is a thin jellylike layer between
the epithelium and endoderm. It contains scattered amoeboid cells and the reproductive elements, and originates
the skeleton.

2. *The Canal Systems*

In the form of sponge just described the mesenchyme is
extremely thin, but if, as in the majority of sponges,
there is a greater or less thickening of this layer, the
pores will no longer be perforations, but will become
transformed into tubes or canals which may branch and
be modified in various ways. This gives rise to three
general types of sponges which are therefore based mainly
on the arrangement and variations of the pore- and canal-
systems. These are known as:

(a) the Ascon Type, (b) the Sycon Type, and (c) the
Rhagon Type.

(a) *The Ascon Type* (INDEX PLATE 7, FIGURE 1). This
type is characterized by sponges having walls with a
thin layer of mesenchymal tissue (*mes*), and therefore,
with pores (*p*) opening directly from the outside into
the paragastric cavity (*atr*). The endoderm (*end*) is
always continuously lined with choanocytes or "collar
cells" (*cho*). *Ascetta primordialis*, therefore, is the representative of this group. Another example is *Leucosolenia*.
A complication of this type is shown by *Homoderma*,
which differs from *Ascetta* in having its surface broken
up by a multitude of radially arranged thimblelike prolongations or diverticula, each with a central cavity of
its own, opening into the main paragastric cavity of the
sponge and lined with a continuation of the endoderm
with its collared cells. In this case, the pores are found
only in the walls of the diverticula.

PLATE 7

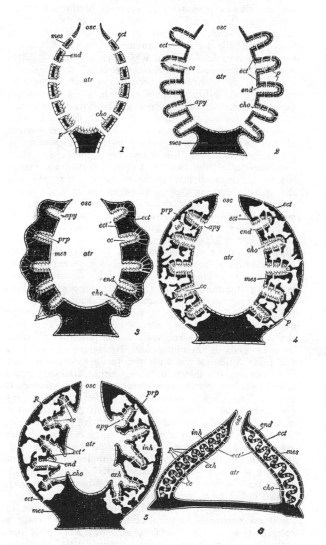

(b) *The Sycon Type*. In this type, as in the example just described (*Homoderma*), the walls of the paragastric cavity are prolonged into radially arranged branches called *radial tubes* (*cc*) but the choanocytes, instead of lining both the paragastric cavity and the radial tubes, are found only in the latter, while the former is invested with a layer of epithelial "pavement cells" (*ect*) like the outside of the sponge. The mouth of the radial tube by which it opens into the central cavity is called the *apopyle* (*apy*). In the simpler sponges of the Sycon type, such as *Sycon ciliatum*, the pores open directly into the radial tubes (INDEX PLATE 7, FIGURE 2) and the outer surface of the sponge is covered with papillae corresponding to the cavities within. In these forms, the mesenchyme (*mes*) continues to be thin. In other forms, however, the mesenchyme becomes greatly thickened and completely fills the spaces between the radial tubes, so that the outer surface appears comparatively smooth and free from the papillae (INDEX PLATE 7, FIGURE 3). Under these circumstances, since the pores cannot open directly from the outside into the radial tubes, they lengthen into *inhalent canals* traversing the mesenchyme. In still other forms (INDEX PLATE 7, FIGURE 4), the canals have expanded to wide cavities or *inhalent lacunae* (*inh*) opening to the outside by the pores and into the radial tubes by openings called *prosopyles* (*prp*). Another complication occurs in the *Leucons* (INDEX PLATE 7, FIGURE 5), where the walls of the paragastric cavity become folded in such a manner that the radial tubes lose their radial position and open into the folds or their branches. The openings by which the folds communicate with the paragastric cavity may then become narrowed and thus large irregular spaces called *exhalent lacunae* (*exh*) are formed, with the result that the radial tubes become mere tubular chambers (*cc*) communicating at the open end with the paragastric cavity (*atr*) only by the intervention of the exhalent lacunae (*exh*), and at their inner surfaces, through the apopyles (*apy*) with the inhalent lacunae (*inh*), and with the outside by the pores. As both the inhalent and exhalent lacunae are lined with "pavement cells" (*ect*) the choanocytes become restricted to the tubular *flagellate chambers*, as the radial tubes are now called.

(c) *The Rhagon Type*. The two preceding types of canal arrangement are peculiar to the sponges having a calcareous or carbonate-of-lime skeleton. The great majority of sponges, including those having "glass" skeletons, horny skeletons, or no skeletons at all, belong to the Rhagon type (INDEX PLATE 7, FIGURE 6). In this case, the flagellate chambers (*cc*) are very small and numerous and, instead of being tubular, are spherical. The mesenchyme varies greatly in thickness, and the canal system may become much complicated through the folding of the walls of the paragastric cavity and the development of wide mesenchymal cavities (*inh* and *exh*).

3. *The Skeleton*

One of the most remarkable features of sponge structure is the skeleton. It is, by far, the most reliable basis for classifying the sponges yet discovered, since it is comparatively unaffected by the external surroundings of the individual and therefore its peculiar features remain constant to the group of which it is characteristic. It may be composed of either fibers or spicules, and is secreted by the mesenchyme. Its function is to furnish a rigid supporting framework for the body and to act as a protection against the enemies of the sponge.

The fibrous sponges include, among others, those known to commerce. The skeleton is, in most cases, made up of interlacing and anastomosing fibers of a horny substance called *spongin,* closely akin to silk in chemical composition (INDEX PLATES 28 and 29). It is also secreted by the mesenchyme and is arranged so as to be a supporting basis to the layers of cellular tissue composing the soft parts of the animal. The fibers are of two kinds—first, a set of long stout *principal fibers* from ½ to 1 mm. in diameter, radiating from the base of the sponge to its surface; second, a complicated network of fine *connective fibers* interlacing among the principal fibers and supported by them. The connective fibers are extremely delicate, having a diameter of only .01 to .02 mm. and with meshes scarcely as large as their diameter. Grains of sand are often found embedded in the principal fibers, in some cases forming a considerable part of the skeleton, in others the entire substance. The spongin fiber is made up of a soft central core or *medullary axis,* surrounded with successive layers of the spongin substance. The classification of the horny sponges is based upon the minute characters of the network. A few sponges of small size have no skeleton at all, being supported by whatever rigidity their tissues may possess, but, with these exceptions, all except the horny sponges have skeletons made up of *spicules* instead of fibers. These are small needlelike bodies composed of either carbonate of lime or silicon. The latter is found combined with water in such proportions as to form a substance chemically resembling opal and of transparent, glassy appearance. Hence spicular sponges may be classified as calcareous or silicious according to the nature of their skeletons. Spicules may have one or two axes, or their axes may radiate in 3, 4, 5, 6, or even 8 different directions, and are found in a great variety of forms, some of which are shown in INDEX

PLATE 8. Those having one or two axes may be straight, curved, or bent at various angles. They may be pointed, rounded, or knobbed at one or both ends. They may be smooth or spined. Spicules having a greater number of axes may also have their arms pointed, rounded, or knobbed, or each arm may be branched, either once or twice, or to such a degree as to present a great variety of starlike figures (INDEX PLATES 11 and 12). Spicules occasionally assume extremely odd shapes. Some look like tiny cuff-buttons, others like anchors, horseshoes, and hooks of peculiar design, while still others are coiled like springs. As regards size, they may be divided into two classes: *megascleres,* or large spicules, and *microscleres,* or small spicules. The megascleres form the main supporting structure of the skeleton and are bound together in long fiber-like bundles which are either parallel, or cross each other so as to form triangular or square meshes. They are sometimes entangled and interlaced in all directions like felt, clinging together with their hooks and projections. In the Hexactinellid sponges, the megascleres are of three axes at right angles to each other and are arranged with points overlapping. During the life of the sponge, these grow together and finally form a perfectly rigid network (INDEX PLATE 11). The microscleres, on the other hand, are not supporting in function. In fact, in most cases, their use is unknown. They are found embedded in the fleshy parts of the sponge and are so minute as to be distinctly visible only under a high power of the microscope. They are extremely valuable for determining species.

REPRODUCTION AND DEVELOPMENT

Sponges may reproduce either by budding (*asexual reproduction*) or by means of eggs (*sexual reproduction*). Reproduction by budding is brought about by an outgrowth of cells from the side of the sponge involving all three layers. This finally develops into a miniature of the parent sponge, as far as structure is concerned, and becomes narrowed at the base until it is only attached by a stem, and finally drops off. It then becomes fixed to the sea bottom and grows to maturity. Sexual reproduction on the other hand is only effected by the union of sexual elements within the tissues of the parent sponge. The male and female reproductive cells originate in the mesoderm of the same individual and unite to form the fertilized unicellular egg. The larva is developed from the one-celled stage, by a process of egg division or cleavage. It passes through 2-, 4-, and 8-celled stages by vertical divisions, at the end of which time it appears as a circular disc divided into eight equal segments. These again divide into a 32-celled stage by means of a horizontal or *equatorial* cleav-

PLATE 8

CLASS CALCAREA

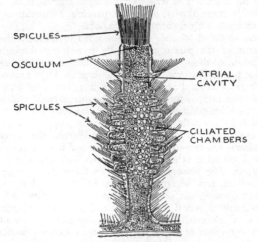

SPICULES

OSCULUM

ATRIAL CAVITY

SPICULES

CILIATED CHAMBERS

LONGITUDINAL SECTION OF A
TYPICAL CALCAREOUS SPONGE

CHOANOCYTES OR COLLARED CELLS
LINING CILIATED CHAMBERS

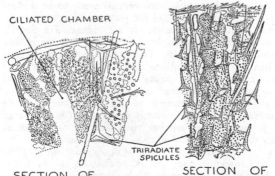

CILIATED CHAMBER

TRIRADIATE SPICULES

SECTION OF CILIATED CHAMBER

SECTION OF WALL OF <u>GRANTIA</u>

age, and then, by repeated divisions of the eight upper cells, a hollow sphere is formed composed of eight large granular cells and many small cells, each of the latter bearing a long flagellum or whiplike filament. The eight large cells divide more slowly, always remaining comparatively large, and are not provided with flagella.

At this so-called *blastula* stage, the larva issues from the endoderm of the parent and finally passes out through the osculum of the sponge. It swims rapidly about with its flagellate portion in front, and after a time the large granular cells grow around and enclose the flagellate cells. Soon a cup-shaped body is formed, known as the *gastrula,* which is covered with nonflagellate cells, and lined with a multitude of flagellate cells. The opening of the cup, or *blastopore,* now narrows and almost immediately the larva settles down and becomes fixed by the rim of the blastopore to a rock or some other object. The development is now very rapid. The blastopore closes; the flagellate cells develop collars and become choanocytes; the osculum or excretory opening perforates the free end; the side walls are pierced with pores; traces of the skeletal spicules begin to show in scattered mesenchyme cells as tiny needles of glass or carbonate of lime; and the body assumes a somewhat cylindrical shape. From now on, the animal possesses all the elements of a true sponge, and growth proceeds according to its nature and environment.

PHYSIOLOGY

This subject, in its application to sponges, is very imperfectly known. The following facts, however, can be definitely stated:

The adult sponge is attached and is incapable of locomotion. Its only outward movements seem to be a slow dilatation and contraction of the pores and osculum.

The choanocytes, however, are very active. The flagella are in constant vibration, and the collars are continually expanding and contracting. These cells are the chief organs of nutrition and respiration. The motion of the flagellum creates a whirlpool, by means of which the sea water and the organisms it contains are sucked down within the collar. The cell then seizes upon and absorbs the digestible organisms, while the constantly renewed sea water, being brought into closer relation with the absorbing tissues, causes the necessary oxygenation to take place.

Excretory products are, without doubt, cast out by these cells and, together with the indigestible organisms, borne out through the osculum by the main current of sea water.

It is also said that, during the winter, many choanocytes disappear, to be restored in the springtime. Thus a kind of hibernation seems to occur.

The growth of sponges is slow, five or six years being necessary to bring them to their full size. This, however, is very variable.

There is no muscular or nervous system. Instead, there is what has been called a "vague general sensibility" of the whole sponge. This shows itself particularly in the movements of the osculum and pores.

Sponges may grow together if placed in contact, or, on the other hand, fragments cut from a sponge can be made to live and grow separately. This peculiarity is utilized in connection with the artificial propagation of the commercial sponges. Sponges do not, however, regenerate parts which have been cut off, although the original sponge may go on growing as if nothing had happened.

POSITION OF SPONGES IN THE ANIMAL KINGDOM

The relation of sponges to other animal forms has always been very uncertain. The choanocytes of the endoderm seem to connect them with a group of colonial Protozoa known as Choanoflagellates (page 6). These are the only other animal forms which have "collared cells." In fact, certain colonies of Choanoflagellates (*Proterospongia*) very much resemble primitive sponges. On the other hand, sponges have often been grouped with the Coelentera, on account of the resemblance of the planula and gastrula larval stages to those of the jellyfishes; because of the fixed condition of the adult, the simple structure and the saclike internal cavity; as well as the supposed resemblance of the osculum to the coelenterate mouth. The latter resemblance is only apparent, however, as the osculum does not function as a mouth nor does it have the same embryological history. Sponges, moreover, differ widely from coelenterates in their lack of tentacles and "sting-cells" (*nematocysts*), and are peculiar in having pores, "collared cells," and spicular skeletons. These differences are so important that it has been necessary to recognize the sponges (Phylum Porifera) as a separate subkingdom (Parazoa), most probably having a common ancestry in some group immediately derived from the Protozoa.

CLASSIFICATION

On account of the difficulties besetting sponge classification, many very widely differing schemes have been proposed. The earliest were based largely on external forms and the chemical composition of the sponge skeleton. The latter basis is still used for the division into classes, but the former has been abandoned for the most part on account of the plastic nature of the framework of sponges and the consequent variability of their growth habits. Such internal features as the form and arrangement of the spicules, the extent of the choanocytic layers, and the general plan of the canal system seem to be more constant characters, and are utilized in all recent classifications. There is, however, much variability among internal characters also, and there are yet many perplexing problems to the spongologist, especially on account of the great number of intermediate forms and unexpected relationships. In fact a genealogical diagram of the sponges would not so much resemble a branching tree as a network with connecting fibers anastomosing in all directions, and most probably approximating in its appearance the bewildering skeletal labyrinth of the fibrous sponge itself.

PORIFERA

DISTINCTIVE CHARACTERS

1. Typically tube-shaped
2. Numerous incurrent pores for ingesting food and oxygen in water
3. Single osculum or excurrent opening for excretion
4. Branching system of incurrent canals and converging excurrent canals
5. Solitary or forming more or less complicated colonies, often intimately united, so that individuals are distinguished only by their oscula
6. Flagellated chambers with collared cells
7. Epithelium, endoderm, and mesenchyme
8. Spicules for support formed in mesogloea (lime, silicon, or acanthin)
9. Central cloaca, lined with collared cells in simplest type (*Ascon*)
10. Cloaca lined with epithelial cells, opening into thimble- or tube-shaped chambers lined with collared cells (*Sycon*)
11. Cloaca and canals lined with epithelium; collared cells confined to groups of spherical chambers situated between systems of incurrent and excurrent canals
12. Spongin fibers secreted in mesenchyme
13. Free-swimming, ciliated larva which reverses tissue layers in metamorphosis to sessile form

SIMILARITIES TO OTHER PHYLA

1. Early stages of sessile form resemble the colonial protozoan, *Proterospongia*
2. Collared cells similar to these of choanoflagellate Protozoa. Occur nowhere else in animal kingdom
3. Has two layers of cells with structureless mesogloea like coelenterates, but outer and inner cell layers are apparently reversed in the two groups

4. Certain cells have a degree of independence, reminding one of colonial Protozoa (amoeboid wandering cells)
5. Tube-shaped body and colonial habit reminds one of coelenterates, also fixed mode of life
6. Planula and gastrula stages common to both

DIFFERENCES FROM OTHER PHYLA

1. Differs from Protozoa in the dependence of most of its tissue cells upon each other, with increased complexity of structure
2. Its life history is that of a metazoan
3. Differs from coelenterates in having collared cells
4. Has no nematocysts
5. Outer and inner cell layers apparently reversed in arrangement
6. Osculum of sponge is at opposite extremity from blastopore, which is attached to bottom. Mouth of coelenterate corresponds to blastopore and is on free extremity of tubelike body
7. Possesses characteristic spicules very different from any skeletal structures of coelenterates

CONCLUSIONS

1. Sponges more closely related to Protozoa than to Coelentera
2. Sponges originated from flagellate protozoans, as their differences are merely complexities easily derivable from simpler protozoan structures
3. Derived from Protozoa on a line independent of that of Coelentera

DEFINITION OF PORIFERA

This phylum comprises many-celled animals of extremely low organization living attached to the sea bottom or on various shells and stones, each individual being typically of tubular shape. This is particularly seen in solitary species. Due to the colonial habit, however, through which each sponge buds off other individuals which remain attached, complex organizations are built up in which neighboring individuals become so closely associated that it is impossible to state where one sponge leaves off and another begins. Colonial masses thus formed may be irregular in shape or may be associated around a single axis to form tubelike colonies which, in turn, may themselves form complex clusters.

The body wall of each individual is pierced by countless pores through which water is sucked into the tissues of the sponge, finally reaching a cylindrical cavity, the gastral cavity or *cloaca,* which opens to the exterior by means of a large chimneylike vent, the osculum. The water pumped in through the pore collects in the gastral cavity and is ejected to the exterior through the osculum. The tissues of the sponge are composed of (1) an outer *epithelium;* (2) a middle layer, the *mesenchyme,* which secretes the supporting skeleton; and (3) the *gastral layer,* which is often broken up into several chambers lined with *collared cells* or *choanocytes.* These latter cells are found only in sponges and certain groups of Protozoa. Each choanocyte consists of a protoplasmic cell from the summit of which projects a transparent cylindrical membrane forming a collar. From within this membrane projects a single whiplike flagellum. The skeleton consists of needlelike spicules of lime or silicon which may have a single axis or may be branched in various ways. Or it may consist of a substance known as spongin, which is allied to chitin, and which may form a network entirely devoid of spicules; with spicules embedded in it; or simply as a cementing substance between neighboring spicules.

The phylum Porifera is divided into three main classes as follows: Class 1. *Calcarea* (*Calcispongiae*); having calcareous spicules. Class 2. *Hexactinellida* (*Hyalospongiae*); having silicious spicules. Class 3. *Demospongiae;* having a skeleton of silicious spicules and spongin, or of spongin without spicules of any kind.

CLASS CALCAREA (CALCISPONGIAE)
Limy Sponges
(INDEX PLATE 8)

This group contains the simplest and most primitive sponges of tubular or vaselike form. The skeletal spicules are formed of carbonate of lime ($CaCO_3$). These spicules may either have a single axis (Monaxonid); have three radiating parts (Triaxonid); or have four-rayed parts (Tetraxonid).

The individuals may be grouped in colonies or may be solitary and with a whitish color. They are divided into two orders; *Homocoela,* with individuals having a single central cavity lined with collared cells, and the order *Heterocoela,* having a central cavity from which branch cylindrical chambers radiating on all sides.

Order HOMOCOELA

This is the simplest type of sponge. The thin walls of each tube are composed of two cell layers, an outer layer at the epithelium, made up of flattened, close-set cells, and an inner gastral layer made up of collared cells lining the entire gastral cavity. Between the two layers is a thin structureless layer which secretes a supporting

PLATE 9

LEUCOSOLENIA BOTRYOIDES
ENTIRE COLONY

LEUCOSOLENIA BOTRYOIDES
TUBES ENLARGED SHOWING SPICULES

LEUCOSOLENIA
BOTRYOIDES
METHODS OF
BRANCHING

LEUCOSOLENIA
CORIACEA
GENERAL APPEARANCE

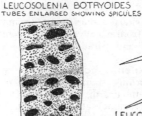

LEUCOSOLENIA CORIACEA
CANAL OPENINGS ENLARGED

LEUCOSOLENIA
BOTRYOIDES
SPICULES
(MAGNIFIED)

LEUCOSOLENIA CORIACEA
SPICULE (MAGNIFIED)

COLONY

GRANTIA
CILIATA

SPICULES (MAGNIFIED)

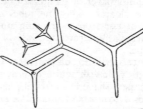

LEUCOSOLENIA CANCELLATA
SPICULES (MAGNIFIED)

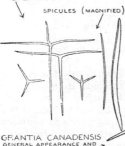

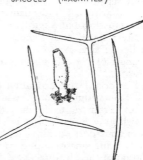

GRANTIA CANADENSIS
GENERAL APPEARANCE AND
SPICULES (MAGNIFIED)

skeleton of interlacing calcareous needles. These three layers are pierced at intervals by openings known as pores which open through special contractile cells known as *porocytes*. These may contract to close the pores or expand to open them. The *Homocoela* comprises about five families, only one of which is abundant in the shallow waters within our range. It is the Family *Leucosoleniidae*. This is the simplest of the sponge families with the characters of the order. Only one genus is known, *Leucosolenia* (PLATE 9), having the characters above mentioned.

Family Leucosoleniidae

The individual sponges are erect and finger-shaped, usually rising from a network of horizontal, stolonlike tubes. Monaxonid and triradiate spicules are the chief skeletal elements.

Leucosolenia botryoides (Fleming) PLATE 9. A small branching sponge made up of clusters of white cylindrical tubules of delicate close texture, each with an opening (osculum) at the summit. They are found between the tidal marks growing abundantly on the undersurface of stones, on rockweed and other algae. Each finger contains a central cavity (cloaca). A hand lens shows a thin single layer of triradiate calcareous spicules embedded in the cloacal wall. The tubes either branch from each other or rise from a creeping stolon.

Martha's Vineyard to Gulf of St. Lawrence; northern Europe.

Leucosolenia cancellata Verrill PLATE 9. A small sponge, yellowish white to brownish yellow, occurring in small pear-shaped, spherical, hemispherical, or irregular masses. It consists of quantities of intricately anastomosing tubes. The surface is irregularly pitted with deep depressions separated by thin, rounded ridges. The spicules are regular triradiate and quadriradiate, of unusual size, their rays tapering but slightly to terminate in somewhat obtusely pointed ends. The sponge varies from ¼ to 1¼ inches in size.

Coast of New England and Canada to Arctic regions; Europe.

Leucosolenia coriacea (Fleming) PLATE 9. A somewhat incrusting sponge which spreads irregularly over rocks. From ⅛ to ¼ inch thick, varying in color from bluish gray to dark brown. The walls are perforated with numerous oval openings set close together and continued as twisting anastomosing canals, penetrating the sponge substance in all directions. The spicules are triradiate, equiangular, and with thin, obtusely pointed rays.

New England coast northward; Europe.

Order HETEROCOELA

Sponges having cells of thimblelike ciliated chambers radiating from the central gastral cavity. Each of these chambers is lined with collared cells while the gastral cavity is devoid of them.

The *Heterocoela* is also divided into five families with three within our range.

Family Sycettidae
(INDEX PLATE 8; PLATE 10)

The flagellated chambers are elongate, thimble-shaped structures, radially arranged around the central gastral cavity, and projecting outward from the body of the sponge, not covered by a dermal cortex. Triaxon spicules support the walls of the chambers, forming a regular pattern. The collared cells (*choanocytes*) are typically segregated in the flagellated chambers.

Sycon protectum Lambe PLATE 10. A small, egg-shaped sponge with a large osculum surrounded by a fringe of slender spicules as long as the body itself. Total length, ⅛ inch. The sponge encloses a large central cavity with minute radial tubes. Between them are triradiate spicules, regularly placed. The openings of the radial tubes are arranged in even rows. Oxeote spicules project from the outer surface between the openings of the pores. The dermal skeleton is composed of triradiate spicules having the arrangement shown in PLATE 10 around and over the openings of the tubes. Quadriradiate spicules are found in the gastral skeleton.

Coast of Nova Scotia in 56 fathoms.

Grantia ciliata (Fabricius) PLATE 9; COLOR PLATE II, 1. This sponge grows in small groups of tiny, finger-shaped individuals, elongate and cylindrical, with a surface covered over with small projections that give it a hairy appearance. The individuals are about ¾ inch to 1 inch in height, diameter about ¼ inch. The terminal osculum is surrounded by long, slender, shining spicules, often ⅛ inch in length. It is often closed by a thin membrane in life. The spicules are slender, triradiate, and quadriradiate, with gently curved rays of needlelike sharpness. Those surrounding the osculum are oxeote in form. The sponge is found growing in small clusters on seaweed, shells, and stones. Color, cream white.

New England coast to Arctic Sea; Europe.

Grantia canadensis Lambe PLATE 9. This species is similar to the preceding in size, growing in solitary fashion. Of a brownish red color with firm, compact texture. Quadriradiate and oxeote spicules, not so slender as those of *Grantia ciliata*. The body is smoother and without the hairy appearance of that species.

Leuconia (Leucandra) pumila Bowerbank PLATE 10. A very small tapering cylindrical sponge not more than ⅜ inch in length and ⅛ inch in diameter. It is characterized by triradiate, equally angular spicules varying in size from small to large, but always the same shape. Pores inconspicuous. Cloaca cylindrical, extended through the entire sponge.

Northern New England and Canada; Europe.

Family Grantidae

A clearly defined dermal cortex, pierced by pores, continuously covers the layer of flagellate chambers, so that they appear to be buried in the sponge wall. These may be either radial and thimble-shaped, opening into the gastral cavity by wide apertures, or they may be small and spherical, with narrow openings, and scattered irregularly through the thickness of the sponge wall.

Family Heteropidae

Sponges with distinct and continuous dermal cortex, as in the previous family, supported by a series of three-branched (triradiate) spicules of which a long ray is directed inward, alternating with inner triradiates with a long branch projecting outward (see *Heteropia rodgeri* in PLATE 10). The flagellated chambers are similar to those in Family *Grantidae*.

Heteropia rodgeri Lambe PLATE 10. This is a small cylindrical sponge found growing on seaweeds, with the character of the family described above. It is found in northern waters, especially in the region of Nova Scotia.

Family Amphoriscidae

This family has dermal membrane and flagellated chambers as in the two preceding families. It is distinguished by the presence of quadriradiate spicules in its subdermal layer, along with triaxons and monaxons (see PLATE 10).

Amphoriscus thompsoni Lambe PLATE 10. A small calcareous sponge, cylindrical in shape but contracted at the base of the osculum. Spicules, triradiate and quadriradiate, also oxea of two sizes. Arrangement as in PLATE 10.

Gulf of St. Lawrence.

CLASS HEXACTINELLIDA
(The "Glass" Sponges)

In contrast to the Class *Calcarea,* the sponges of this class possess silicious spicules instead of a calcareous skeleton. These are formed on three axes, and are therefore known as *triaxon* spicules. Typically these three axes cross,

PLATE 10

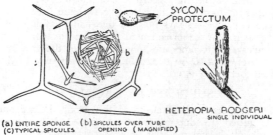

SYCON
PROTECTUM

(a) ENTIRE SPONGE (b) SPICULES OVER TUBE
(c) TYPICAL SPICULES   OPENING (MAGNIFIED)

HETEROPIA RODGERI
SINGLE INDIVIDUAL

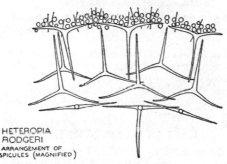

HETEROPIA
RODGERI
ARRANGEMENT OF
SPICULES (MAGNIFIED)

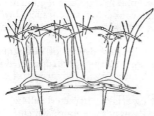

AMPHORISCUS THOMPSONI
ARRANGEMENT OF SPICULES (MAGNIFIED)

LEUCONIA
PUMILA
ENTIRE SPONGE

AMPHORISCUS THOMPSONI
ENTIRE SPONGE

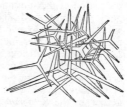

LEUCONIA PUMILA
TYPICAL SPICULES (MAGNIFIED)

forming six rays, hence the name of the Class *Hexactinellida*. These spicules may be separate or they may be welded together to form a rigid, latticelike skeleton (see INDEX PLATE II). The six rays may be unequally developed or some axes may be ornamented by spines or curved in various ways. In some cases, one or more of the axes may be entirely aborted, so that their typical plan may be disguised (see INDEX PLATE II).

SUBCLASS LYSSACINA

The spicules in the skeleton in this group are separate or, if united, it is due to adventitious causes, such as overgrowth of skeletal material occurring irregularly.

SUBCLASS DICTYONINA

The long main spicules (*hexactine dictyonalia*) are firmly united throughout life into a latticelike supporting network.

The Glass Sponges, in this region, are practically all found in deep water, and therefore are not included in this handbook, which is intended to cover the life of the shallow seas. They form, however, a large, diversified, and important group of sponges, including some of the most beautiful sponge species.

CLASS DEMOSPONGIAE

This is the most widely spread and dominant group of the Porifera. It includes all the well-known sponges and the vast majority of the species. They are cosmopolitan, extremely diversified in form, color, and appearance, being adapted to all conditions of sea life; one group even occurs in fresh water.

As they have reached the greatest degree of differentiation and complication possible to sponge structure, they are regarded as the most highly organized group of the phylum.

The *Demospongiae* are especially characterized by the possession of the substance known as spongin, which is organic in nature and allied to silk in its chemical composition. In one of its two forms it is a gluelike substance, in the other a fibrillar material secreted within cells. In the *Demospongiae*, silicious spicules may be cemented together in practically every proportion in various groups, there being none, or practically none, in the *Tetractinellida*; just enough to hold the needlelike monaxoid spicules together in the *Renierinae*; completely but closely covering the large but thickly set spicules of certain Chalinine sponges to form strong and stiff supporting fibers, while others of the same family have the supporting network of spongin fibers containing scattered, weak spicules em-

PLATE 11

CLASS HEXACTINELLIDA
("GLASS" SPONGES)

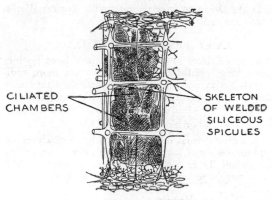

CILIATED
CHAMBERS

SKELETON
OF WELDED
SILICEOUS
SPICULES

SECTION THROUGH WALL OF
A TYPICAL HEXACTINELLID SPONGE

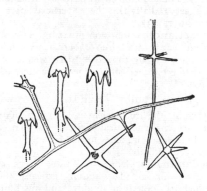

TYPICAL HEXACTINELLID
SPICULES

bedded in it. Finally, in the true commercial sponges, there are no spicules at all, the skeleton being entirely composed of elastic spongir

SUBCLASS TETRAXONIDA
(INDEX PLATE 12)

These are *Demospongiae* typically with four-rayed spicules, each ray representing an axis.

Order TETRACTINELLIDA

The megascleres in this order typically have spicules with one long, needlelike branch with three short, radiating branches at one end (*triaene* spicule), or they may be *desmas* (four-branched spicules with irregular sub-branches).

Suborder CHORISTIDA

There are no desmas in this group. The megascleres are all typically triaenes, while the microscleres are either *sigmas* (small T- or S-shaped spicules) or *asters* (small polyaxon star-shaped spicules).

Family Geodidae

This family is characterized by possessing a dense cortical layer made up of *sterrasters* (spherical star-surfaced microscleres). The tetraxon megascleres are triaenes, which are usually set radially in the superficial part of the sponge (see PLATE 13).

Geodia zetlandica Johnston PLATE 13. The incurrent and excurrent canals lead into *chones* (independent unbranched canals, usually capped by *sieve plates*). The cortex is well-defined and crustlike, due to the zone of closely set sterrasters.

Family Tetillidae

When present, the microsclere is always a sigma. The megascleres are characteristically *protriaenes* (i.e., triaenes with their three short branches turned forward). The skeleton is arranged radially.

Tetilla laminaris George & Wilson PLATE 13. This sponge forms a thin lamella, standing vertically, the lower part of which is rooted in muddy sand by bundles of fibers. The upper margin is rounded and thicker, while the surface of the sponge is thrown into vertical folds. The texture is dense and firm. The color of the living sponge is grayish brown. The horizontal length is always greater than the height. The size varies up to ⅔ inch. While the surface looks smooth, long slender spicules project from it everywhere and, though covered with minute pores, it has the general appearance of being solid. Sponges of thi

PLATE 12

ORDER TETRACTINELLIDA

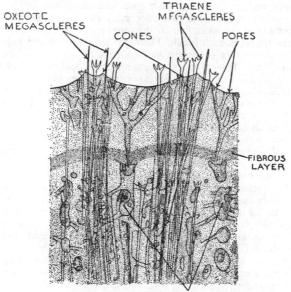

OXEOTE MEGASCLERES

TRIAENE MEGASCLERES

CONES

PORES

FIBROUS LAYER

INHALENT CANALS

VERTICAL SECTION OF A TYPICAL TETRACTINELLID SPONGE

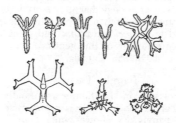

CHARACTERISTIC TETRACTINELLID SPICULES

genus are characterized by having no definite fibrous cortex. The pores and oscula are not located in the depressions.

Spicules are arranged in spiculo-fibers extended out radially in closely set brushes. The spicules composing these are needlelike oxea. They are of two sizes, the shorter tapering gradually at each end and abundant in the brushes and also in the root fascicles. The larger are thicker at the outer than at the inner end. Several of these are found in each brush. There are also very slender protriaenes which cover the whole surface of the sponge like fine hair. These are larger around each osculum. *Anatriaenes* characterize the fibers of the lower part of the sponge as well as the root fascicles. Sigmas are abundant in the outer layer of the sponge everywhere and in the walls of the canals and are extremely minute.

Abundant along the coast of North Carolina and probably to Buzzard's Bay.

Craniella cranium (Lamarck) PLATE 14. An egg-shaped sponge with evenly rounded surface thickly furnished with bristling spicules which project about ⅛ inch. The oscula and pores are quite inconspicuous. The dermal membrane is thin and of a clear, shining appearance. The color of the living sponge is pale green. The principal spicules are large and long double-pointed oxeas, collected into bundles, especially near the surface. Sigmoid and C-shaped microscleres are also abundantly placed. The interior of the sponge is made up of bundles radiating from a central axis toward the surface, either in star arrangements, or forming a curved pattern. The size of the spicule varies from about ¼ inch to ⅓ inch in length.

New England coast; Europe.

Craniella logani Dawson PLATE 14. A fossil species found in Pleistocene deposits (Leida clay) of Montreal and vicinity. The spicules resemble those of *Tetilla cranium* and are so well preserved that it is possible to infer their skeletal arrangement when alive. This fossil species is closely allied to *Craniella cranium* and gives a good idea of the geological range of this genus.

Pleistocene of Ontario, Canada.

Family Theneidae

The microscleres in this family are usually asters. The megascleres are triaenes. There is no characteristic cortex.

Thenea muricata (Bowerbank) PLATE 14. A small conical sponge with osculum near the center of the upper portion. Other specimens are found with the osculum located at one side.

East coast of Greenland, Davis Strait, Gulf of St. Lawrence, and New England coast. Also found from Norway to the coast of Portugal.

PLATE 13

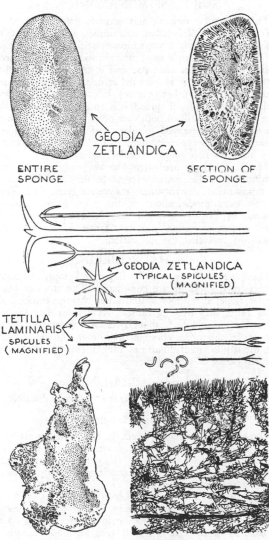

GEODIA
ZETLANDICA

ENTIRE
SPONGE

SECTION OF
SPONGE

GEODIA ZETLANDICA
TYPICAL SPICULES
(MAGNIFIED)

TETILLA
LAMINARIS
SPICULES
(MAGNIFIED)

ENTIRE SPONGE

SECTION OF SPONGE BODY

TETILLA LAMINARIS

SUBCLASS MONAXONIDA

This is a most difficult and variable group, embracing a large number of families, subfamilies, and species. The spicules are, however, always monaxonoid in type, i.e., they are built along a single axis, either in one or in both directions. In the former case, one end differs from the other (*style*). Typically, it is rounded at one end (*strongylote*) and pointed at the other (*oxeote*). If knobbed at the round end, it is a *tylostyle;* if spined, it is an *acanthostyle*. In the case of spicules built in both directions, they are known as *diactines,* i.e., two-rayed spicules. If diactines are pointed at each end, they are called *oxeas*. If both ends are knobbed, they are *tylotes;* if simply rounded, *strongyles*.

The microscleres are often like the macroscleres, and diminutives of their various forms. So they are referred to as micro-oxeas, microtylotes, microstrongyles, etc. Some groups have modifications of the aster form, straight, twisted, or double. Spongin may be absent, present in small quantities, or an important factor, in some groups practically replacing the spiculation.

Order HADROMERINA

These sponges are usually large and massive. Some species have stalks or are cup-shaped. The spicules often form a skeleton without spatial order or arrangement. At other times they may be radiate. As a rule, they do not form fibers or network, though certain species tend to be fibrous. In this order spongin may be absent, or, if present, usually in small quantities. Megascleres are usually of one kind only in a given species.

Suborder ACICULINA

In this suborder, the megascleres are always diactinal.

Family Stylocordylidae

These are pedunculate sponges. In the body, the skeleton forms strongly radiating, almost symmetrical fibers constructed of close-set bundles of spicules (see INDEX PLATE 15). In the stalk, these are placed longitudinally to form a strong supporting structure.

Stylocordyla borealis (Loren) PLATES 15 and 16. This peculiar sponge, with its long, slender stalk and more or less globular head terminating in an osculum, is quite variable in details but is readily recognizable. Though it has only been found by dredging in 200 fathoms or more, it is likely to be brought up by fishermen. The spicules are all double-pointed oxea, either straight or slightly curved, the larger ones having a swollen area at the middle.

Northeast coast of the United States, Gulf of St. Law-

PLATE 14

CRANIELLA CRANIUM
TYPICAL OXEOTE SPICULE

CRANIELLA CRANIUM
GROWING ON ISODICTYA
INFUNDIBULIFORMIS

CRANIELLA CRANIUM
TYPICAL SPECIMEN

CRANIELLA CRANIUM
CROSS SECTION

THENEA MURICATA
ENTIRE SPONGE

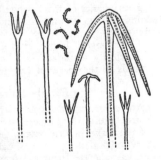

**CRANIELLA
CRANIUM**
TYPICAL SIGMOID
MICROSCLERES
(MAGNIFIED)

CRANIELLA LOGANI
TYPICAL SPICULES (MAGNIFIED)

rence to Nova Scotia; also northern European waters, and even the southern Atlantic Ocean.

Suborder CLAVULINA

The megascleres are monactinal, usually tylostyles, i.e., pin-shaped.

Family Clionidae

These are *Hadromerina* that bore into shells, often making extensive excavations.

Cliona celata Grant PLATE 16; COLOR PLATE II, 3. This sponge is common along the New England coast on gravelly and shelly bottoms from shallow water to considerable depths. It is very conspicuous, being of a bright sulphur yellow color, and grows into irregular massive forms, firm in texture. Low wartlike prominences, about ⅛ inch in diameter, are scattered over the surface in a well-developed specimen. This, like all members of its family, is a boring sponge, commencing its growth by penetrating dead shells and fragments of limestone in every possible direction, forming irregular and anastomosing galleries which increase in size until the substance bored is consumed. Then it protrudes from the surface and grows into thick irregular crusts, 8 inches or more in diameter, covering over and boring into other shells and stones in the process. As Verrill states, the boring habits of sponges are the principal agents in the disintegration of shells that accumulate over the sea bottom. This work, however, is aided to a certain degree by boring worms and mollusks.

The spicules of this sponge are tylostyles, that is, monaxons pointed at one end and with a rounded knob at the other.

The sponge is found from Cape Hatteras northward. It is especially abundant on the New England coast and extends to the coasts of Europe.

Family Spirastrellidae

An outer crust formed by *euasters* and *streptasters* (spiral asters). Megascleres, tylostyles, and styles.

Spirastrella andrewsi George & Wilson, PLATE 16. A cylindrical sponge with large cloacal cavity, often high and vase-shaped. Incurrent pores are found on the outside of the sponge while excurrent openings are within the cloacal cavity. The sponge is often excavated by canals which are inhabited by many shrimp. The external surface of the sponge, between incurrent openings, appears comparatively without pores, but is dotted with small, round subdermal cavities covered by a thin dermal membrane. These cavities are connected by small canals passing into the tissues of the sponge. The spicules are generally tylo-

PLATE 15

ORDER HADROMERINA

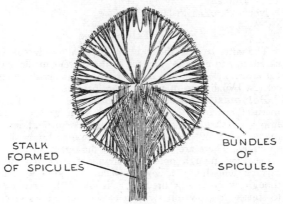

STALK
FORMED
OF SPICULES

BUNDLES
OF
SPICULES

SECTION OF *STYLOCORDYLA*

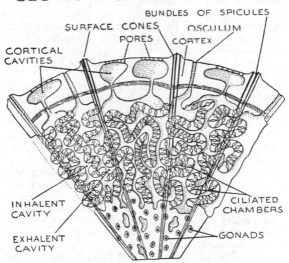

CORTICAL
CAVITIES

SURFACE CONES

PORES

BUNDLES OF SPICULES

OSCULUM

CORTEX

INHALENT
CAVITY

EXHALENT
CAVITY

CILIATED
CHAMBERS

GONADS

SECTION THROUGH WALL OF
TYPICAL SPECIMEN OF
HADROMERINA TO SHOW STRUCTURE

styles, knobbed at one end and either pointed or rounded at the other. The microscleres are mere spirasters which are twisted. Color in life, purplish black; dark brown when dried. The living specimen sometimes is covered with small actinians.

North Carolina to Jamaica.

Family Polymastiidae

The outer layer of the body has a specially differentiated skeleton, and a special skeleton is also present in the cortical layer. Tylostyles and styles are the characteristic megascleres. Usually, no microscleres are present.

Polymastia robusta (Bowerbank) PLATE 16. Forms incrustations over shells and stones. As it grows it rises into a number of long, slender, fingerlike projections, as many as 28 of these having been counted in a single specimen. There are no openings at the outer ends of the projections, though pores are abundant over the entire surface. The living sponge is yellow or gray in color, though, when freshly dredged, it is said to be orange-red to scarlet. It grows on rocks in patches sometimes several inches across. The spicules are tylostyles of which one variety is long and slender, sharply pointed at one end and with a conspicuous knob at the other. The diameter is largest in the middle. A shorter, curved tylostyle, thicker and stouter in appearance and with no conspicuous knob, is also abundant in the cortex.

Gulf of St. Lawrence; northeastern New England coast; England.

Polymastia mammillaris (Johnston) PLATE 16. This species is similar to the preceding, except that the body of the sponge is bristling with projecting spicules, while a number of projections are flattened or straplike, often with an unusually broad projection in the center and a stout oscular tube. The color in life is yellowish. Spicules are slender tylostyles, those in the main fibers being the slenderest and straightest and with almost no knob at the rounded end. The spicules form the dermal layer of the cortex and are slightly curved with a fairly well-developed knob. Those from the inner layer of the cortex are long and slightly curved with a conspicuous knob. The projecting tylostyles, which cause the bristling appearance, are thicker than the last named.

Gulf of St. Lawrence; coast of Nova Scotia and northeastern United States.

Trichostemma hemisphericum (M. Sars) PLATE 17. This species includes oval sponges related to *Polymastia*, but have more rounded, knoblike papillae, instead of elongate or straplike projections. They may be 2 to 3 inches in length, 1½ inches broad, and with a rimlike

PLATE 16

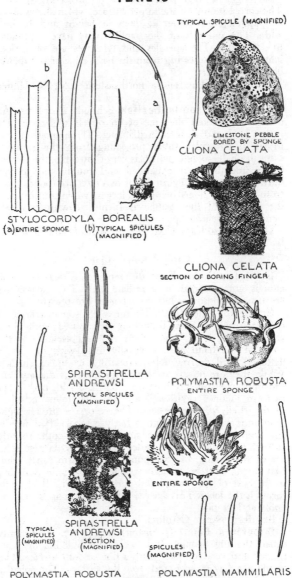

TYPICAL SPICULE (MAGNIFIED)

LIMESTONE PEBBLE
BORED BY SPONGE
CLIONA CELATA

STYLOCORDYLA BOREALIS
(a) ENTIRE SPONGE   (b) TYPICAL SPICULES
(MAGNIFIED)

CLIONA CELATA
SECTION OF BORING FINGER

SPIRASTRELLA
ANDREWSI
TYPICAL SPICULES
(MAGNIFIED)

POLYMASTIA ROBUSTA
ENTIRE SPONGE

ENTIRE SPONGE

TYPICAL
SPICULES
(MAGNIFIED)

SPIRASTRELLA
ANDREWSI
SECTION
(MAGNIFIED)

POLYMASTIA ROBUSTA

SPICULES
(MAGNIFIED)

POLYMASTIA MAMMILARIS

basal edge, ¼ inch wide, formed of projecting spicules. The cortex is only on the upper surface, which shows about 60 papillae, each about ⅛ inch in height and ¼ inch wide. The summits of the papillae may have a pinhole-like osculum. The spicules and tylostyles are of various lengths, those projecting from the basal edge of the sponge being the longest.

Gulf of St. Lawrence; northeastern coast of United States.

Tentorium semisuberites Schmidt PLATE 17. An oval sponge about the size of an olive. It is about 1⅛ inches long and ¾ inch in diameter. There are from one to six tiny oscular tubes projecting from the rounded summit of the sponge, which is very contractile, the surface being smooth when expanded and rough and uneven during contraction. Tylostyles of two sizes are found, those from the main fibers being the largest while the cortex at the summit of the sponge is furnished with relatively slender and delicate spicules.

Greenland to Cape Cod; also Shetland Islands and Arctic Seas.

Family Suberitidae

In this family, there is no differentiated cortex. The skeleton is not arranged on a radiate plan. The megascleres are usually tylostyles. No microscleres are present.

Suberites undulatus George & Wilson PLATE 17. A sponge, often massive, branching or covered with close-set projecting lobes. The colony is about as large as the palm of the hand and is usually oval, with the small, flattened, and narrow lobes crowding its upper surface. While they are mostly somewhat flattened at the top and lean in various directions, they often fuse with each other to form inclined cavities. They are often found attached to the shells of live oysters. The color, in life, is light gray and, while the sponge is fairly compact, it is fragile and somewhat elastic. The spicules are smooth, slightly curved tylostyles with rounded heads. The largest sizes are in the middle of the sponge. They form fairly compact fibers, entirely without spongin, apparently radiating in the base of the sponge and pursuing longitudinal tracts through the lobes. This species is fairly common in muddy pools at low tide.

Beaufort, North Carolina.

Suberites ficus (Johnston) PLATE 17. Commonly called the Fig Sponge. It is somewhat bulblike or pear-shaped and very compact, with a fine smooth surface. The oscula are few or scattered over the surface. The spicules are tylostyles. The sponge, often about 3 inches in height, is attached by its narrowed stalk to shells or other solid

PLATE 17

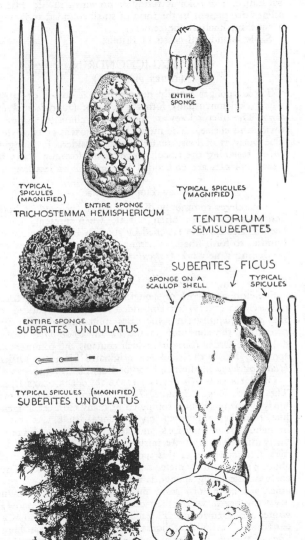

TYPICAL
SPICULES
(MAGNIFIED)

ENTIRE SPONGE
TRICHOSTEMMA HEMISPHERICUM

ENTIRE
SPONGE

TYPICAL SPICULES
(MAGNIFIED)

TENTORIUM
SEMISUBERITES

ENTIRE SPONGE
SUBERITES UNDULATUS

TYPICAL SPICULES (MAGNIFIED)
SUBERITES UNDULATUS

TRANSVERSE SECTION OF LOBE
SUBERITES UNDULATUS

SUBERITES FICUS

SPONGE ON A
SCALLOP SHELL

TYPICAL
SPICULES

substance. The color is ruddy or brownish in life. Microscleres are present in the form of small rounded rods with a swelling knob at the center.

Sable Island and coasts of Britain.

Order HALICHONDRINA
(INDEX PLATE 18)

These sponges usually do not have a cortex or crust. Their skeleton usually forms a network (*reticulate skeleton*). The microscleres are monaxon in character (sigmas, toxas, and chelae). The megascleres are oxeas or tylostyles. The body is of loose texture, with considerable spongin, either fastening the spicules together or forming fibers in which spicules are embedded to a greater or less degree.

Family Haploscleridae

Megascleres commonly diactine oxeas (pointed at both ends); microscleres often absent; when present, never chelae. The spicules fastened by spongin longitudinally in bundles to form fibers, or arranged as the sides of meshes, producing a network (*reticulum*).

Subfamily Chalininae

Skeleton a network of spongin fibers, in which diactinal megascleres (oxeas) are embedded often much reduced in size and quantity; in some cases quite insignificant, approaching the condition in the Family *Spongidae* (page 84) in the Order *Keratosa,* which contains the commercial sponges. This order doubtless originated from the Order *Halichondrina* in the neighborhood of this group.

Chalina oculata (Pallas) PLATE 19; COLOR PLATE II, 2. The Eyed Finger Sponge. This common sponge forms upright bushy colonies composed of many close-set, fingerlike branches supported on a slender stalk. As these branches grow, they fork and subdivide so as to become fairly numerous and are fairly large in height and thickness. Characteristic of this sponge are many round oscula about 1/10 inch in diameter scattered over the surface. The color of the living sponge is a soft orange-red. These colonies are often torn from their anchorages and thrown upon the beach, where their dead skeletons, almost snowy white, are often found. The substance of the skeleton is a network of cylindrical horny fibers, within which long lines of minute spicules are embedded, forming a more or less central core for each fiber. The spicules are oxea of various sizes.

This species is abundant from the Arctic Circle, along the Canadian and New England coasts, as well as along the coasts of England and Western Europe.

PLATE 18

ORDER HALICHONDRINA

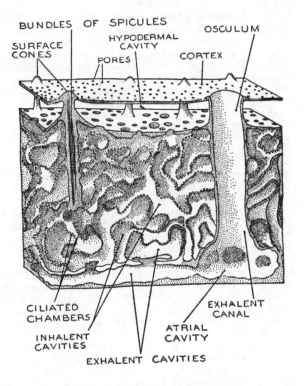

BUNDLES OF SPICULES

SURFACE CONES

HYPODERMAL CAVITY

OSCULUM

PORES

CORTEX

CILIATED CHAMBERS

INHALENT CAVITIES

EXHALENT CAVITIES

ATRIAL CAVITY

EXHALENT CANAL

PERPENDICULAR SECTION OF A MONAXONID SPONGE

Subfamily Renierinae

The spicules are either oxeas or strongyles (i.e., either pointed at both ends, or rounded at both ends), either forming an irregular skeleton or in just sufficient quantity to cement the spicules together, there seldom being enough developed to cover the spicules completely. Microscleres are absent.

Halichondria glabra Bowerbank PLATE 19. This sponge forms thin coats of incrustations ⅛ inch or less in thickness over stones and pebbles. The surface is smooth and shiny and pale yellow in color. The pores are so small as to be inconspicuous. The translucent dermal membrane is largely responsible for the shiny surface of the sponge. The spicules are extremely slender oxea varying in length.

North American and English coasts.

Halichondria caduca Bowerbank PLATE 19. A massive sponge of irregular shape with a rough and uneven surface. The scattered oscula give it a pitted appearance. The color, when dried, is light gray. The spicules form loose bundles of very irregular character and are only slightly cemented together with spongin. They are slender oxea of various sizes.

Northern coast of North America and England.

Halichondria panicea Johnston PLATE 19; COLOR PLATE II, 5. The Crumb of Bread Sponge. This sponge forms irregular masses, incrusting rocks and stones. It is of a yellowish color, shading into green. On the underside of stones and along their edges, the sponge is erected into close-set papillae or fingers, often adherent to each other and even forming tubular chimneys. These are grayish green on the outside, and the orifices of the oscula are lined with yellow. The sponge is soft and friable and crumbles easily in the hand. The spicules are oxeas with occasional strongyles.

Arctic Ocean to New England, North Pacific, Europe.

Reniera heterofibrosa Lundbeck PLATE 19. The sponge forms small irregular cushions from which arise series of low tubes with oscula, which give a lobelike effect. The surface is rough and woolly because of projecting spicules. Large, round oscula surmount the papillae. They vary from 1 to 2 mm. in diameter. The skeleton forms an irregular network of fibers thickly sown with spicules, which are curved oxea of fairly uniform length.

Iceland, Davis Strait; North American coast.

Reniera tubulosa Fristedt PLATE 19. Forms thick incrustations on stones and seaweeds with cone-shaped oscular tubes varying in height, surmounted by oscula. The skeleton is an irregular network thickly sown with spicules pointing toward the surface, as well as transverse spicules

PLATE 19

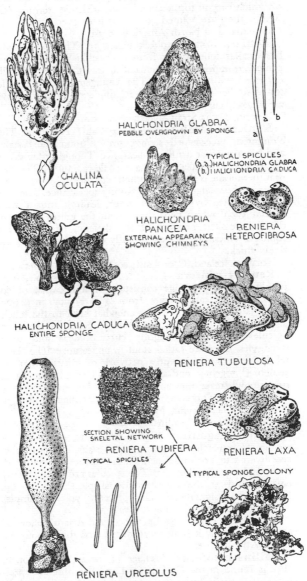

CHALINA
OCULATA

HALICHONDRIA GLABRA
PEBBLE OVERGROWN BY SPONGE

TYPICAL SPICULES
(a.a.) HALICHONDRIA GLABRA
(b.) HALICHONDRIA CADUCA

HALICHONDRIA
PANICEA
EXTERNAL APPEARANCE
SHOWING CHIMNEYS

RENIERA
HETEROFIBROSA

HALICHONDRIA CADUCA
ENTIRE SPONGE

RENIERA TUBULOSA

SECTION SHOWING
SKELETAL NETWORK

RENIERA TUBIFERA

TYPICAL SPICULES

RENIERA LAXA

TYPICAL SPONGE COLONY

RENIERA URCEOLUS

arranged singly. These are slightly curved oxea the ends of which vary in form, some having a slender termination, while others are pointed quite shortly or even rounded.

Greenland to North American coast.

Reniera laxa Lundbeck PLATE 19. This species also has oscular tubes rising from a crustlike base. They are conical, cylindrical, or somewhat flattened, and occasionally coalesced with each other. The arrangement of the skeleton is similar to that of the preceding species. The spicules are slightly curving oxea.

Iceland, Davis Strait, North American coast.

Reniera urceolus (Rathke & Vahl) PLATE 19. This elongated, tube-shaped sponge grows upon short stalks and has a peculiar urnlike appearance. Though often growing singly, some specimens have coalesced tubes. The dermal membrane is thin and without spicules. The projecting fibers of the sponge give a soft woolly appearance. The tube is surmounted by a large osculum leading into a wide oscular canal which runs throughout the entire length of the sponge. The network of the skeleton has somewhat square meshes. Spicules are slightly curved oxea comparatively thick.

Norway, Iceland, Greenland; coast of North America.

Reniera tubifera George & Wilson PLATE 19. An irregularly shaped sponge consisting of a network of coalesced, cylindrical branches, from ⅛ to ⅓ inch in diameter. It is quite fragile and is somewhat hard to the touch. The specimen illustrated is about 6 inches in diameter. Spicules are smooth, slightly curved oxeas and some strongyles. They are rather stout in appearance. The skeletal framework consists of a network of spicules that are cemented together end to end with a small amount of spongin wherever they meet or cross. The meshes are 3, 4, or 5 sided. The color of the living sponge is pink or reddish purple, varying to brown.

Beaufort, North Carolina.

Gellius flagellifer Ridley & Dendy PLATE 20. A sponge of somewhat irregular massive shape. It varies in size from 1 to 2 or more inches and is somewhat flattened. It crumbles easily when dry. The spicules are oxea, slightly curved, and of the characteristic shape shown in the figure. Small sigmata are also present, typical examples of which are shown in the illustration.

Davis Strait, Gulf of St. Lawrence, and Atlantic shore of Canada. Probably it is also well distributed throughout the entire Atlantic Ocean.

Gellius arcoferus Vosmaer PLATE 20. This sponge, also, is found in the Gulf of St. Lawrence and the specimens are usually quite flat, about 5 inches across and ¾ inch in thickness. The sponge is grayish yellow in color.

Greenland, Gulf of St. Lawrence, and the Atlantic Ocean generally. Usually in depths of from 78 to 80 fathoms.

Gellius laurentinus Lambe PLATE 20. Closely related to *Gellius flagellifer,* but differs in the small size of the microscleres which are sigmata, but not their characteristic shape. The sponge grows in small rounded masses with oxeote spicules forming a close network. It is fragile and crumbles easily. The oxea are slightly curved and more or less abruptly pointed at the ends.

Gulf of St. Lawrence, coast of northeast North America, and Atlantic Ocean.

Eumastia sitiens O. Schmidt. PLATE 20. A sponge consisting of a cluster of fingerlike projections coalesced at the base. The colonies are about 3 inches in length, 2 inches high, and 2 inches broad, although they vary considerably in these dimensions. The spicules are oxea of fairly large size.

Greenland, River and Gulf of St. Lawrence, and south coast of Nova Scotia.

Subfamily Spongillinae

These are typically fresh-water sponges found in streams and lakes, but as some species occur in brackish water as well, they may be briefly mentioned here. They grow in irregular masses on sticks, stones, and water plants to a size of from 4 to 6 inches in diameter.

They vary from brown to yellow in color, and may be green when growing in sunlight, due to the presence of multitudes of minute green, single-celled plants (zoochorellae) in their tissues.

Spongillidae have a thin, crustlike dermal membrane, like a roof over the subdermal spaces, supported by pillars made up of spicule bundles embedded in spongin. Reproduction is more frequently asexual by means of gemmules. These are spherical brood-sacs, containing reproductive cells and surrounded by two concentric dermal membranes separated by a close-set row of erect *amphidiscs* (dumbbell-like rods with a disc at each end). Typical genera are *Spongilla, Ephydatia,* and *Heteromeyenia.* As they are not primarily marine forms, they are not illustrated here.

Subfamily Gelliodinae

Conspicuously thick, elongate fibers form the chief skeleton containing many spicules, which, in certain species, are replaced by sand grains and fragments of other foreign bodies (*arenaceous fibers*) embedded in abundant spongin. The microscleres are sigmata.

Phoriospongia osburnensis George & Wilson PLATE 20. This sponge forms a thin incrustation over alcyonarian corals. It has a fairly smooth surface, about 1 mm. thick.

The pores of the sponge are abundantly scattered over the surface and are quite conspicuous. The spicules are strongyles which are rodlike in form with rounded ends. The microscleres and sigmata are abundant in the dermal membrane and isochelae are also present, scattered through the dermal membrane. The shapes of these spicules are shown in the figure.

Beaufort, North Carolina, 13 fathoms.

Subfamily Phloeodictyoninae

These are massive sponges with thin, fingerlike processes rising out of a thick cortex. The skeleton is a network of fibers formed of spicules supported by stronger elongate vertical fibers. The microscleres are either sigmas or lacking entirely.

Phloeodictyon nodosum George & Wilson PLATE 20. The basal portion of this sponge incrusts pieces of shells. From this arise several slender fingerlike processes to a height of 1¼ inches or more, terminating in rounded, closed ends. The sponge apparently absorbs portions of the shell upon which it is seated. Color, light brown. Pores on the projections fairly conspicuous. No oscula can be seen. Spicules are slightly curved slender oxeas tapering gradually to sharp points.

Beaufort, North Carolina.

Family Poeciloscleridae

In this family, the megascleres are almost always monactinal, being oxeas, styles, tylostyles, and the like. The microscleres are of various kinds, especially chelae.

Subfamily Esperellinae

The skeleton is made up of embedded fibers, none of which is echinating (i.e., made up partly of spicules projecting sidewise to form spines). Their texture, therefore, tends to be soft and pliant. The spicules of the outer layer are similar to those of the inner layers.

Mycale ovulum O. Schmidt PLATE 21. This sponge is almost always found on hydroids, algae, or branching bryozoa where they form cushionlike, rounded or ovoid growths, at first clinging to one side and gradually growing around the branching stems. According to conditions of growth, they vary from ¼ inch to more than 2 inches in diameter. The projecting bundles of spicules give the surface a soft, woolly appearance. Numerous, often close-set pores occur in the dermal membrane which is thin and is supported by the projecting spicules of the lower layers. In the smaller specimens, there is usually but one osculum while, in the larger growths, several may occur mounted on slight projections. Among the spicules and

PLATE 20

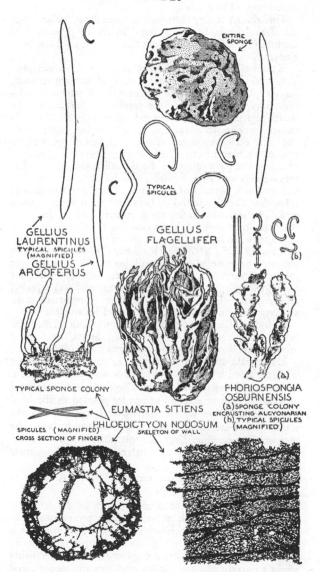

ENTIRE SPONGE

TYPICAL SPICULES

GELLIUS
LAURENTINUS
TYPICAL SPICULES
(MAGNIFIED)
GELLIUS
ARCOFERUS

GELLIUS
FLAGELLIFER

(b)

TYPICAL SPONGE COLONY

EUMASTIA SITIENS

PHLOEDICTYON NODOSUM

FHORIOSPONGIA
OSBURNENSIS
(a) SPONGE COLONY
ENCRUSTING ALCYONARIAN
(b) TYPICAL SPICULES
(MAGNIFIED)

SPICULES (MAGNIFIED)
CROSS SECTION OF FINGER

SKELETON OF WALL

the megascleres are more or less curved styli. The microscleres are all *anisochelae*.

This species is very abundant in Greenland, Iceland, and the Farö Islands. It is also found in the neighborhood of Denmark, the Baltic, and along the coast of northern New England.

Esperella fristedtii Lambe PLATE 21. A slender, flexible, and almost cylindrical sponge of upright growth, supported by a short, narrow stem with an expanded holdfast. Except for the stem, the sponge is characterized by sharp, thornlike, rather flattened projections set vertically on the sponge. Its pores and oscula are not easily made out. The skeleton consists of a central axis of spicules, arranged in fibers, from which smaller fibers are given off at a right angle to support the thornlike projections. The megascleres are long, straight, slender styles, rounded at one end and pointed at the other. There are also smaller tylostyles, slightly curved or bent and resembling crooked pins. The microscleres are small palmate anisochelae.

Davis Strait to the Atlantic Coast of the United States.

Esperella lingua Bowerbank PLATE 21. Large, massive forms fairly lobate in character, 6 inches or more in length, and covered with small pores. The spicules are tylostyles, varying from about ½ mm. to more than one mm. in length; straight, rounded at one end and tapering at the other. There are also palmate anisochelae, small sigmata, and fine, needlelike spicules of microsclere size.

Found off Greenland and Nova Scotia, Gulf of St. Lawrence, northeast coast of the United States, as well as around the British Isles and northern coast of Europe.

Esperella minuta Lambe PLATE 22. A small sponge with flattened oval head and slender stalk, about ¾ inch in length. No osculum known. The skeleton is composed of loose strands of spicules upwardly pointed in the head but forming fibers with a somewhat spiral twist in the stalk. Others are found projecting from the surface. The megascleres are either large, sharply pointed styli, or small tapering tylostyli. The microscleres are small palmate anisochelae.

Davis Strait to northern coast of North America at depths of about 200 fathoms.

Esperella lobata (Montague) PLATE 22. An irregular branching sponge with short, lobelike projections, scattered oscula, and inconspicuous pores. When dried, it is light brown in color and is usually found growing on hydroids, etc. The spicules are tylostyles, the larger being slightly curved, and the smaller ones straight, slender, and sharp. The microscleres are palmate anisochelae.

Shores of England, to North American coast.

PLATE 21

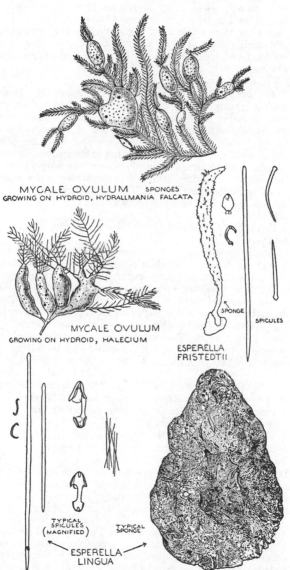

MYCALE OVULUM SPONGES
GROWING ON HYDROID, HYDRALLMANIA FALCATA

MYCALE OVULUM
GROWING ON HYDROID, HALECIUM

SPONGE

SPICULES

ESPERELLA
FRISTEDTII

TYPICAL
SPICULES
(MAGNIFIED)

TYPICAL
SPONGE

ESPERELLA
LINGUA

Esperella modesta Lambe PLATE 22. A small, lobe-like sponge growing on branching seaweed, somewhat brown in life, with a firm somewhat rigid texture. The oscula are large, made up of tylote spicules, slightly curved and rather stout. It has also slender curved styli; the microscleres are sigmata, and palmate anisochelae are present.

Coast of Nova Scotia.

Esperiopsis forcipula Lundbeck PLATE 22. These leaflike sponges, light yellow in color when preserved, have a rather firm consistency with folded surface, and thin dermal membrane, numerous pores on one side of the sponge, while the other has no pores and is thickly provided with spicules which lie parallel to the surface. Oscula simple, oval to irregular in shape, and of varying size. Skeleton with spicules arranged in branching fibers often running more or less parallel. The megascleres are slightly curved styli. The microscleres are variously formed isochelae.

Davis Strait, Coast of North America, depth 80 to 100 fathoms.

Esperiopsis obliqua George & Wilson PLATE 22. A branching sponge with more or less cylindrical branches, which are smooth or knotty on the surface on arising from a common base, but occasionally coalescing. It is bright red in color and varies in height from $2\frac{1}{2}$ to 8 inches. The dermal membrane is thin with numerous pores. The oscula are 1 mm. or less in diameter, scattered or arranged in longitudinal rows. The megascleres are styles, slightly curved and tapering toward the rounded base, as well as to the point. Small spines are found on some of the styles; others are strongyles, being rounded at both ends. Slender, pinlike tylostyles are also found. The microscleres are isochelae, sometimes with twisted stem or toxa. These form a skeletal framework of fibers with connecting branches.

Beaufort, North Carolina.

Stylotella heliophila Wilson PLATE 22. This very abundant sponge is common in shallow water where it is found on the bottom attached to shells or wharf piles. It is incrusting, or grows up in fingerlike lobes, either singly or fusing with neighboring lobes to produce a continuous mass. Small, cone-shaped projections are scattered over the surface. The color of the sponge, in life, is orange, often verging toward a greenish tint. The oscula are usually at the ends of the vertical lobes or at the ends of branches from their sides. The pores are very numerous ·in the dermal membrane, which is translucent. The spicules are styles, straight or slightly curved. They are irregularly scattered in the interior, where they occasionally give a network appearance, or may be arranged in fibers. The

PLATE 22

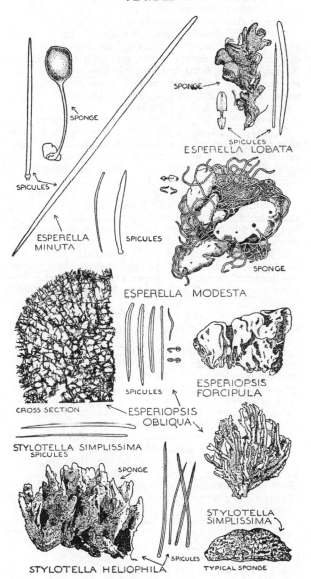

SPONGE

SPONGE

SPICULES

ESPERELLA LOBATA

SPICULES

ESPERELLA
MINUTA

SPICULES

SPICULES

ESPERELLA MODESTA

SPONGE

CROSS SECTION

SPICULES

ESPERIOPSIS
FORCIPULA

ESPERIOPSIS
OBLIQUA

STYLOTELLA SIMPLISSIMA
SPICULES

SPONGE

STYLOTELLA
SIMPLISSIMA

STYLOTELLA HELIOPHILA

SPICULES

TYPICAL SPONGE

spongin substance is meager, merely holding the spicules together where they come in contact.

New England coast, from Hatteras northward.

Stylotella simplissima (Bowerbank) PLATE 22. A thin, incrusting, lobelike sessile sponge with smooth or even surface and minute oscula, and with pores difficult to make out. It forms leaflike projections about ½ inch in height. The skeleton is arranged in bundles of spicules which are composed of long, slightly curved or straight styles. Color, when dry, light brown.

Shores of New England and northern North America.

Stylotella pannosa (Bowerbank) PLATE 23. A massive sponge, very rough and ragged in appearance, light yellow in color. The skeleton is constructed of an open network of compact fibers with spicules in the form of slightly curved styles.

British Isles to New England coast of North America.

Artemesina arcigera O. Schmidt PLATE 23. A round, somewhat flat, cushion-shaped sponge, about 2 inches in length, rather oval-shaped, and of firm consistency. Preserved specimens are yellowish white to gray, with an almost velvety surface, due to the projecting spicules. The oscula may be circular or of irregular shape with projecting thickened margina, and about 3 mm. in diameter. The pores are very small and circular. The spicules are tylostyles.

Dredged from 400 or more fathoms from Iceland, Greenland to Spitzbergen, and eastward to Nova Scotia on the North American coast.

Hamacantha implicans Lundbeck PLATE 23. A flat, cakelike sponge with an external crust characterized by close-set spicules, parallel to the surface, or projecting to give a shaggy feeling to the outside. Oscula found at the summit of the scattered rounded or conical papillae are characteristic of this species. These sponges grow as incrustations on shells of mollusks, on worm tubes, and on stones, so that, when sectioned, the lower portion is found to contain foreign bodies, such as pebbles, etc., embedded within the sponge tissue growing around these fragments. Large cavities are found within the interior, especially close to the surface. The sponge is 2 inches or less in diameter. The megascleres are styli, straight or slightly curved.

Coast of Europe to Newfoundland, in depths usually exceeding 170 fathoms.

Desmacidon palmata (Johnston) PLATE 23. An extremely common and characteristic species of the Atlantic coast, a foot or more in height, and of coarse and tough texture. The colonies consist of large, fingerlike lobes, which may be branching and extend like parallel fingers.

PLATE 23

STYLOTELLA PANNOSA
PORTION OF SPONGE SURFACE

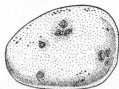

ARTEMISINA ARCIGERA

STYLOTELLA PANNOSA
TYPICAL SPICULE

ENTIRE SPONGE

VERTICAL SECTION SHOWING CAVITIES
HAMACANTHA IMPLICANS

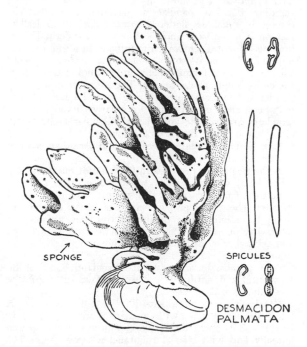

SPONGE

SPICULES

DESMACIDON PALMATA

In life, it is of a straw-yellow color. The fibers are smooth and of uneven thickness. The oscula are scattered.

Common in the British Isles, Nova Scotia, and along the northeast coast of United States. This is the "Mermaids' gloves" of the Shetlanders.

Desmacidon peachii Bowerbank PLATE 24. This is a more or less oval sponge, about one inch in diameter, having scattered oscula on its surface and large pointed styli evident at its basal end and usually turned in that direction. These styli are stout and slightly curved. The microscleres are sigmata of two or three sizes. There are also bundles of very slender rhapids which are extremely abundant in the dermal membrane among numerous small sigmata.

One hundred fathoms or more from Greenland to Nova Scotia and northern New England.

Asbestopluma cupressiformis Carter PLATE 24. A slender, erect form found growing on shells or similar material. A slender stem about ¼ the length of the entire colony supports the main sponge structure and is irregularly cylindrical and shows upon its sides small branches, standing out like papillae at irregular intervals. The sponge is sometimes flattened toward the top in leaflike fashion. The surface is smooth. A transparent dermal membrane is present. Each branch terminates in a minute osculum. The skeleton is composed of an axis of densely bound spicules arranged longitudinally and extending throughout the entire length of the sponge. The megascleres are long, slender styli or sometimes verging toward tylostyli. They may be straight or somewhat irregularly curved. The microscleres are palmate anisochelae. Globular embryos are often found in the tissues of the sponge.

Farö Islands, Iceland, Greenland, and Canadian coast of North America.

Asbestopluma pennatula O. Schmidt PLATE 24. Another long, slender sponge, supported upon a stalk, of which the base is coated with a sheath containing special spicules. The sponge proper consists of lateral branches issuing from either side of the central axis giving it a somewhat plumelike character. The megascleres are styli and tylostyli, the microscleres are palmate anisochelae and sigmata.

Farö Islands, Iceland, eastern Greenland, Gulf of St. Lawrence, and northeastern United States, at depths of 100 fathoms to deep water.

Cladorhiza nordenskioldii Fristedt PLATE 24. A long, slender sponge, with a stem about 11 inches in length and ¼ inch thick having minute branches placed laterally and with biserial subbranches upon them. The megascleres are smooth styli, thickest at the middle, about

PLATE 24

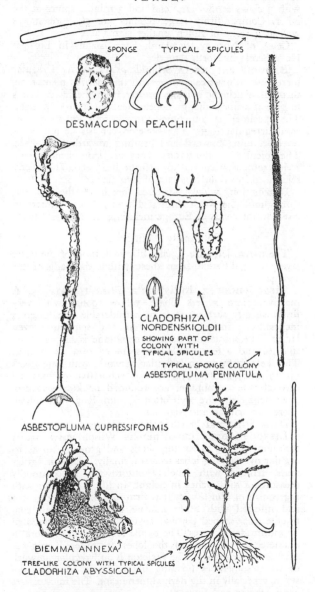

SPONGE TYPICAL SPICULES

DESMACIDON PEACHII

CLADORHIZA
NORDENSKIOLDII

SHOWING PART OF
COLONY WITH
TYPICAL SPICULES

TYPICAL SPONGE COLONY
ASBESTOPLUMA PENNATULA

ASBESTOPLUMA CUPRESSIFORMIS

BIEMMA ANNEXA

TREE-LIKE COLONY WITH TYPICAL SPICULES
CLADORHIZA ABYSSICOLA

⅔ mm. in length. The microscleres are small anisochelae with 3 claws at the large end and 3 minute spines at the other. Comparatively large sigmata are also present, as well as a series of much smaller sigmata.

Coast of Norway, Scotland, Farö Islands in Europe; Nova Scotia in North America.

Biemma annexa O. Schmidt PLATE 24. An irregular incrusting or massive sponge with thin dermal membrane, through which the spicules project from the lower layers to give it a finely shaggy appearance. No spongin present. The specimen is sometimes thrown into leaf-shaped or small irregular folds. The skeleton consists of numerous fibers running upward and bending toward the surface. The spicules are numerous. They are long, slender tylostyles, somewhat curved toward the head end. The microscleres are toxa and sigmata of two sizes.

Distribution, widely scattered north of the equator, throughout the West Indies, Florida, North American coast, to the coasts of Europe including the Mediterranean.

Subfamily Dendoricinae

The megascleres are usually diactinal, those of the outer layer being different from those within the body of the sponge.

Lissodendoryx indistincta Fristedt PLATE 25. A massive, more or less lobate, yellow sponge with very finely shaggy surface. It is of considerable size, often 4 inches by 3 inches in dimension, and sometimes even larger. The substantial dermal membrane is supported by spicules and a few oscula are scattered over its surface. The skeleton forms an irregular network, with long fibers toward the surface. The various subdermal cavities, all through the membrane, are rounded or kidney-shaped. The megascleres are styli often ½ mm. long. The microscleres are chelae and sigmata.

Davis Strait and North Atlantic Ocean.

Lissodendoryx carolinensis Wilson PLATE 25. A common sponge, incrusting shells and growing up as irregular overlapping lobes to form, finally, a large irregular mass, fringed with lobelike outgrowths. It commonly measures 4 to 8 inches in height. In life, it is white with a greenish or bluish cast. It is firm and brittle, overgrown and infested with other marine organisms. Small contractile, tube-shaped papillae cover the surface, penetrated by multitudes of pores. The oscula are ⅛₆ inch or more in diameter, at the ends of the lobes or scattered over the surface of the sponge. The skeleton is an irregular network of styles sometimes forming fibers. There are also tylostyles, especially in the dermal membrane. The microscleres are isochelae and sigmata.

PLATE 25

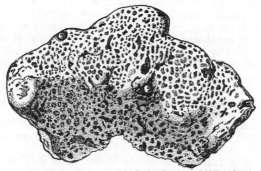

LISSODENDORYX INDISTINCTA

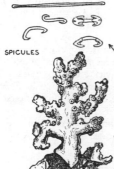

SPICULES

TYPICAL
SPONGE

LISSODENDORYX CAROLINENSIS

TEDANIA
SUCTORIA
ENCRUSTING
SPECIMEN ON
ALLOPORA

MELONANCHORA ELLIPTICA
SINGLE PAPILLA

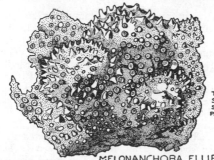

TYPICAL
SPONGE
SHOWING
PAPILLA

MELONANCHORA ELLIPTIC

Widely distributed along the eastern coast of the United States especially around Beaufort, North Carolina.

Tedania suctoria O. Schmidt PLATE 25. An incrusting sponge, becoming massive and sometimes branching. The dermal membrane is solid, supported by special dermal spicules. Oscula are scattered sparsely over the surface on special papillae. There are other papillae furnished with pores. The skeleton forms an irregular network. The megascleres are styli, and tylostyles are found in the dermal layer. The microscleres are on slender rhaphids. This sponge grows on other marine organisms.

Distribution is extremely wide throughout the North Atlantic from Europe to Davis Strait and the coasts of Newfoundland.

Melonanchora elliptica Carter PLATE 25. An incrusting or massive sponge, often with projecting lobes. The surface is closely set with wartlike papillae, cylindrical in shape or with rounded ends, often expanding terminally, supported by a network of spicular fibers. Pores are found in the meshes of this network. The oscula are spout-shaped and occur sparsely in the spaces between the papillae. The dermal skeleton contains very close horizontal spicules and fibers. The megascleres are styles, while the dermal membrane contains tylostyles and strongyles. The microscleres are very peculiar. They are known as *sphaerancorae,* which are typically two elliptical rings intersecting each other at right angles.

This species has a wide distribution from Scotland to Newfoundland and the eastern coast of North America to the Caribbean Sea.

Subfamily Ectyoninae

The skeletal fibers are equipped with laterally projecting (i.e., echinating) spicules, which are, themselves, usually spined.

Myxilla incrustans Johnston PLATE 26. Incrusting and irregular massive sponges somewhat resembling *Halichondria panicea* superficially. The surface is characterized by winding grooves and lobulate projections. The oscula are often on conical projections. The sponge usually grows attached to the sea bottom, so that the basal portions are filled with sand and gravel. It also grows on various species of bivalve shells and sometimes as crusts on barnacles, worm tubes, and other organisms. It is yellow to orange in color, rather fragile and moderately hard. The dermal membrane is thin and transparent, supported by fanlike bundles of spicules. The pores are numerous, being scattered thickly over the surface. The main skeleton is a network consisting of meshes which are triangular or four-sided, each side being formed by a spicule. Megascleres are

PLATE 26

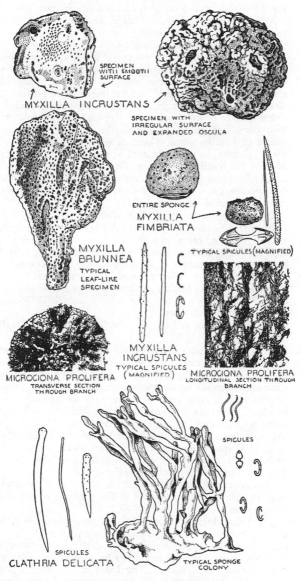

MYXILLA INCRUSTANS

SPECIMEN WITH SMOOTH SURFACE

SPECIMEN WITH IRREGULAR SURFACE AND EXPANDED OSCULA

MYXILLA BRUNNEA

TYPICAL LEAF-LIKE SPECIMEN

ENTIRE SPONGE

MYXILLA FIMBRIATA

TYPICAL SPICULES (MAGNIFIED)

MICROCIONA PROLIFERA

TRANSVERSE SECTION THROUGH BRANCH

MYXILLA INCRUSTANS

TYPICAL SPICULES (MAGNIFIED)

MICROCIONA PROLIFERA

LONGITUDINAL SECTION THROUGH BRANCH

SPICULES

SPICULES

CLATHRIA DELICATA

TYPICAL SPONGE COLONY

spined styli, straight or slightly curved. Microscleres are three-toothed *isoancorae spatuliferae* and sigmata.

Widely distributed from Europe and the British Isles to the Gulf of St. Lawrence.

Myxilla brunnea Hansen PLATE 26. This species of *Myxilla* is erect and often somewhat leaf-shaped or lobed, attached at the base to shells or stones. Sometimes, the base is narrowed to a short stalk. The living sponge is dark orange in color and lighter inside. The surface is characterized by many grooves spaced by sinuous ridges. Otherwise it is shaggy from projecting dermal spicules. The pores are numerous, set in the dermal membrane, round or oval in shape. The oscula are circular openings about ½ mm. in diameter with larger oscula around the edge of the leaflike expansions. The main skeleton consists of quadrangular meshes. The spicules are *acanthostyli* and *acanthostrongyles,* straight or slightly curved. Microscleres are isoancorae of two sizes.

Davis Strait and northern Canadian coasts.

Myxilla fimbriata (Bowerbank) PLATE 26. A cushion-shaped sponge, often almost spherical, with a smooth, slightly shaggy surface. The dermal membrane is supported by fan-shaped bundles of spicules. The main skeleton is formed by an irregular network of quadrangular and triangular meshes. The megascleres are straight or slightly curved icanthostyli. The microscleres are three-toothed isoanchorae of two sizes.

The distribution is from the Shetland Islands to Davis Strait.

Microciona prolifera Verrill PLATE 26; COLOR PLATE II, 4. This very common sponge forms incrustations on shells and wharf piles but develops into large clusters of close-set, fingerlike lobes, bright orange-red in color. These fingers branch and reunite. They may be 6 inches in height. Oscula are scattered over the surface, while the pores are extremely numerous between them. Canals, passing just beneath the dermal membrane, form irregular subdermal spaces. Megascleres are styles which are smooth and slightly curved. There are also small spinose styles. The microscleres are isochelae and toxas.

This species is abundantly distributed along the American coast from New England to Cape Hatteras and the West Indies.

Clathria delicata George & Wilson PLATE 26. An erect sponge with numerous long, slender, fingerlike processes somewhat separated from each other, rising from a common incrusting base and often branching into two or three forklike subbranches. The bases of the fingers are usually more slender than the upper portions. In life, they are dull reddish brown in color with a soft elastic texture.

PLATE 27

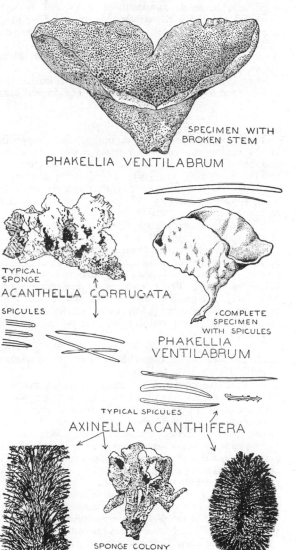

SPECIMEN WITH
BROKEN STEM

PHAKELLIA VENTILABRUM

TYPICAL
SPONGE
ACANTHELLA CORRUGATA

SPICULES

COMPLETE
SPECIMEN
WITH SPICULES

PHAKELLIA
VENTILABRUM

TYPICAL SPICULES

AXINELLA ACANTHIFERA

SPONGE COLONY

LONGITUDINAL SECTION

CROSS
SECTION

The skeleton is an irregular network of fibers turned upward and outward, composed of styles and tylostyles cemented together with considerable spongin. The megascleres are stout, sharply pointed tylostyles, with small spines on the head, or sharp but twisted styles. Some of the tylostyles are spined throughout their length. Microscleres, palmate isochelae or toxa.

From Prince Edward Island along the entire Atlantic Coast of the United States, often found growing on oyster shells.

Family Axinellidae

These sponges are usually of upright form expanding into a conical cup supported upon a stem. They may also be fan-shaped or branched. The megascleres are usually monactinal, i.e., styles or tylostyles, but are of relatively little importance, the spongin fibers being the chief supporting factors. The latter are usually soft, radiating, and often terminating in plumose tufts.

Phakellia ventilabrum (Johnston) PLATE 27. A cup-shaped sponge, often with a short, rather slender stalk. The cup is often 6 inches across the mouth, a total height of about 5 inches or more. The growth in the young sponges is often fan-shaped. The surface is smooth or somewhat ridged. The minute oscula are scattered, the pores inconspicuous. The color is pale yellow with a tint of green. Spicules are slightly curved styles tapering to one end. The slender styles, which are twisted in form, also occur.

From Great Britain to the Gulf of St. Lawrence, northeast coast of the United States and as far south as Brazil.

Acanthella corrugata George & Wilson PLATE 27. This is a sponge made up of folded, leaflike expansions with the folds growing together to form cuplike spaces. It narrows below to a short stem. Height about 2½ inches, width 4 inches. The leaflike edge is quite thin. The sponge surfaces are thrown into parallel wrinkles radiating toward the margin, with somewhat conelike projections. The color, in life, is bright orange-red. The texture is somewhat cartilaginous. There are a few scattered oscula, about 1 mm. in diameter. The pores are scattered over the surface. The megascleres are styles of two sizes: a stout slightly curved spicule and a very slender, smooth, and often wavy spicule.

This species is fairly well distributed along the Atlantic Coast, but especially in warmer waters.

Axinella acanthifera George & Wilson PLATE 27. The sponge body rises from a narrow stalk, expanding and dividing into flattened, leaflike lobes with irregular

PLATE 28

SUBCLASS KERATOSA
ORDER DICTYOCERATINA

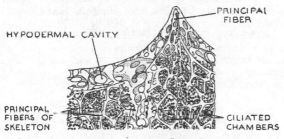

PRINCIPAL FIBER

HYPODERMAL CAVITY

PRINCIPAL FIBERS OF SKELETON

CILIATED CHAMBERS

SECTION OF WALL OF COMMERCIAL SPONGE (SPONGIA)

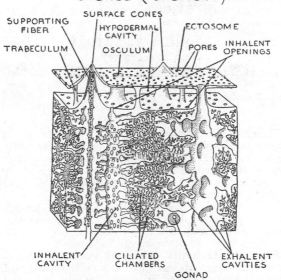

SUPPORTING FIBER

SURFACE CONES

HYPODERMAL CAVITY

ECTOSOME

TRABECULUM

OSCULUM

PORES

INHALENT OPENINGS

INHALENT CAVITY

CILIATED CHAMBERS

GONAD

EXHALENT CAVITIES

PERPENDICULAR SECTION OF COMMERCIAL SPONGE (SPONGIA)

margins, from a three-dimensional cluster. The surfaces are covered with numerous pores. The oscula are not conspicuous and are usually at the bottom of grooves. The skeletal form has a central axis composed of longitudinal fibers which are cemented by a considerable amount of spongin. Peripherally, the skeleton of radial fibers is prolonged from the axial fibers, curving outward toward the surface, branching as they do so. They enlarge to brushlike projections at their outer ends, giving a plumose appearance. The spicules are curved styli of various sizes, long and slender, short and slender, and short and stout. The smaller ones are spinose.

Atlantic Coast of the United States.

SUBCLASS KERATOSA

This subclass contains the sponges with skeletons composed of spongin fibers only, and without hard spicules of any kind, whether calcareous or silicious. They are often spoken of as the "Horny Sponges."

This subclass is divided into two orders; (1) *Dictyoceratina,* (2) *Dendroceratina.*

Order DICTYOCERATINA
(INDEX PLATE 28)

The skeleton of these sponges is a network or "feltwork" of anastomosing fibers. They include the commercial sponges and their relatives.

Family Spongidae

These are the commercial sponges. The skeleton is entirely composed of spongin fibers during their entire life history. However, inclusions of sand grains and other particles of foreign origin are often grown around by the sponge tissues and, if so, naturally become functional in aiding to support the skeleton.

In this family, the horny fibers are solid. The network has a very close mesh. There is a series of strong supporting fibers interconnected by a finer network of delicate fibers which anastomose with each other.

Spongia officinalis (Linnaeus) PLATE 30. This is the typical sponge of commerce. It is widely distributed through tropical seas in the eastern Mediterranean and the West Indies. The chief American sponge regions are found in the Bahamas and off the west coast of Florida. It is characterized by a skeleton composed entirely of horny fibers of spongin. Spicules are entirely absent. Thus the skeleton, when denuded of its animal tissues, becomes a resilient mass of silken fibers, giving the sponge its commercial value. The American varieties of this sponge are *Spongia officinalis* var. *obliqua* which is the

PLATE 29

SUBCLASS KERATOSA
ORDER DENDROCERATINA

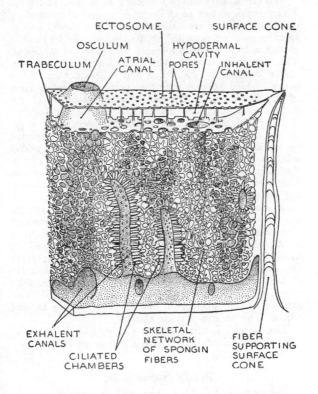

PERPENDICULAR SECTION
SHOWING GENERAL STRUCTURE

Common Reef Sponge; *Spongia* var. *dura,* the Hard Head Sponge; *Spongia* var. *barbara,* the Florida Yellow Sponge; and *Spongia* var. *graminea,* the Grass Sponge. *Coscinoderma lanuga* and *Hippospongia gossypina* are also commercial species found in West Indian waters.

Hircinia ectofibrosa George & Wilson PLATE 30. The general surface of this sponge is that of a standing plate more or less vertically produced into single, leaflike lobes, which are flattened or somewhat cylindrical. The colony is from 2 inches to more than 5 inches in height. The surface is covered with cone-shaped mounds connected together by the ridges and valleys between, thus being divided up into round or polygonal concave areas of small size. As in the case of other members of the Family *Spongidae,* there are no spicules, and the skeleton is composed of a network of horny fibers. The cone-shaped mounds are vertical or oblique and are supported by radiating fibers. These are comparatively strong and solid and extend to the summit of the cone. At times, the fiber is composed of a loose, ladderlike bundle of fibers. Smaller fibers form a network of support, converging on the main fiber. The latter is usually filled with sand grains, shells of Foraminifera, and broken sponge spicules, which have been derived from the environment. The interior of the sponge supported by the skeleton is filled with branching and anastomosing canals which finally terminate in the relatively few oscula. The pores are extremely numerous. Characteristic of the interior of the sponge are the filaments, very slender, threadlike canals with terminal enlargements, oval in shape. The exterior of the sponge, in life, is pale, varying to soft purple. This sponge is quite elastic.

This species is characteristic of the Florida and the West Indian islands but occurs as far north as the coast of North Carolina.

Family Spongeliidae

The fibers in this family are solid. A large proportion of inclusions of foreign bodies are present in the pithless spongin fibers. Fibers separately rising from the base of the sponge, simple or branched, or they may be reticulate. Flagellated chambers large and opening by large channels into the excurrent chambers.

Pleraplysilla latens George & Wilson PLATE 30. The living sponge consists of the colorless incrustations usually found on oyster shells. It is quite inconspicuous but common. The surface is furnished with small, sharp, cone-shaped projections, about 1 mm. in height. Skeletal fibers of spongin extend to the summits of the cones. The remainder of the sponge consists of a delicate net-

PLATE 30

TYPICAL
COMMERCIAL
SPONGE

SPONGIA OFFICINALIS
SECTION OF SPONGE TISSUE (MAGNIFIED)

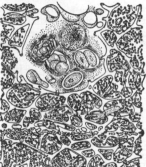

TYPICAL COLONY

**HIRCINIA
ECTOFIBROSA**

**APLYSILLA
LONGISPINA**
VERTICAL SECTIONS

PLERAPLYSILLA LATENS
VERTICAL SECTION

work. There is a dermal membrane covering a subdermal space from which numerous canals penetrate the interior, connecting with oval, flagellated chambers. Sand grains and other foreign particles are found in the main fibers.
Coast of North Carolina.

Order DENDROCERATINA
(INDEX PLATE 29)

The spongin fibers do not anastomose to form interconnecting meshes. Instead, they are *dendritic* (branching in tree-like fashion) and arise from a solid base of spongin.

Family Aplysillidae

The canal system has large, elongated chambers, so that the interior of the skeleton has widespread hollow spaces. Some members of the family (*Darwinella*) have spongin fibers that branch from a given center and are independent of other similar units, thus giving the impression of polyaxon spicules of spongin.

Aplysilla longispina George & Wilson PLATE 30. An incrusting sponge, sulphur yellow in color, turning indigo blue when plunged into alcohol. The body is soft but elastic, while the interior is full of extensive hollow spaces. The surface is covered with minute, acutely pointed cones supported by strong skeletal fibers, which may be simple or repeatedly branched. Fibers are generally without foreign particles though they may occur at times. There is a dermal membrane penetrated by short canals. The oscula are few and widely scattered, measuring up to ⅛ inch in diameter. The surface cones are supported by single strong fibers penetrating to its summit. Sometimes, they branch to support neighboring cones.

North Carolina and probably southward.

3

Phylum Coelentera

(THE POLYPS)

THIS group consists of a wide range of numerous and extremely diversified species. It is important, not only because of the abundance with which its manifold forms occur in the sea, but also because of its biological position in the animal kingdom.

While the coelenterates are extremely simple in their fundamental structure, the elementary plan has developed in protean variety through extremely striking phases of evolution to form the structural basis, histologically, of all higher types of animals.

The organization of a typical polyp is that of a tube, radially symmetrical in cross section, open at one end to form a mouth which is surrounded by a series of tentacles, each armed with batteries of "sting-cells" (*nematocysts*). The body wall is made up of two layers of cells, an *ectoderm,* or outer protective and sensitive layer, and the *endoderm,* which lines the cavity of the tube to form a digestive layer. These are separated by a membrane known as the *mesogloea,* which is thin and structureless, except that, in the higher coelenterates, cells migrate into it during the life history of the creature, thus forming a third but secondary cellular layer.

The food of the polyp consists of small, swimming organisms or, in the case of the larger species, even of fishes which may swim into contact with the "sting-cells" and be killed or stupefied by them, whereupon they are drawn into the central mouth by means of the adherent tentacles.

The "sting-cells" (nematocysts) are characteristic of all coelenterates. Each consists of a single specialized cell occurring in the ectoderm, containing a cavity filled with a turgid fluid surrounding a coiled hollow thread. The top of the nematocyst is prolonged into a trigger-shaped portion which extends to the outside and is pointed at the tip. It is known as the *cnidocil.* When this is brushed against by some swimming creature, the cell contracts violently, and shoots out the threadlike tube, turning it inside out as it does so. Barblike structures located within the hollow thread are thus brought to the exterior and penetrate the organism. At the same time a poisonous fluid is extruded, which will kill or stupefy the organism. Since the nematocysts are very numerous and are arranged in batterylike clusters, they form effective offensive and defensive weapons.

Reproduction is by budding (asexual method) or by free-swimming larvae hatched from fertilized eggs (sexual method). There is typically an alternation of generations. The asexual hydroid may bud off individuals like itself, which in some species separate completely from the parent, while in others, they may remain attached to form a colony of *hydroids* (*hydranths*). Certain of these, instead of being like the parent hydroid, form cup-shaped buds which eventually separate from the parent as free-swimming *medusae,* or jellyfish, each having an umbrella-shaped body fringed with stinging tentacles and possessing a centrally located pendant tube (*prostomium*) that hangs down from beneath the umbrella like the clapper of a bell and terminates in a mouth. These medusae, in turn, give rise to ova, or sperm cells. The fertilized egg settles down on some stationary object and develops a new hydroid stage which will repeat the process. Thus an asexual generation alternates with a sexual generation.

The Coelentera are divided into three classes: the *Hydromedusae,* the *Scyphomedusae,* and the *Anthozoa.*

The Hydromedusae are characterized by a typical alternation of generations in which there is a fully developed nonsexual hydroid stage as well as the sexual medusoid stage, as described above. The body structure is that of a simple two-layered tube, typical of the polyp, as already indicated. In the Scyphomedusae, the hydroid stage is minimized and often becomes insignificant, while the free-swimming medusoid stage is highly developed, as in the larger jellyfish. The true jellyfishes belong to this group. In the Anthozoa, including the sea anemones, corals, and gorgonians, on the other hand, the medusoid stage has entirely disappeared, while the hydroid stage is more fully developed, the lining of the polyp cavity being thrown into folds known as mesenterial ridges.

COELENTERA

DISTINCTIVE CHARACTERS

1. Typically tube-shaped and of fixed mode of life; secondarily free-swimming
2. Single mouth-opening at summit of tube for ingestion and excretion
3. Body-wall of two layers, ectoderm and endoderm, with thin structureless mesogloea between, derived from the ectoderm
4. Solitary or forming colonies by asexual budding; reproduce also sexually

5. Calcareous or corneous skeletal structures formed either as spicules secreted within the mesogloea, which may remain separate or afterward become united, or as external ectodermal secretions supporting the living polyps or containing them in calices
6. Presence of nematocysts
7. Polymorphism with division of labor
8. Alternation of sessile with free-swimming generations
9. Endoderm lining a digestive cavity and composed of gland cells, amoeboid cells, and occasionally muscle fibers
10. Ectoderm consisting of epithelial and interstitial cells, muscle fibers, and nerve cells
11. Free-swimming medusae, more highly organized than stationary polyps
12. Reproductive elements usually of ectodermal origin
13. Radial symmetry
14. Central cavity acts as stomach

SIMILARITIES TO OTHER PHYLA

A. *To Protozoa*
1. Early stages of *planulae* resemble *Volvox* and in-wandering takes place to form second layer similar to arrangement of cells in *Proterospongia* (Metchnikoff's Parenchymella theory)
2. Presence of nematocysts
3. Presence of wandering cells
4. Intracellular ingestion in forms like *Hydra*
B. *To Porifera*
1. Tube-shaped body of hydroids and fixed mode of life
2. Body-wall of two layers and mesogloea
3. Spicules of carbonate of lime in mesogloea
4. Colony formation by asexual budding
5. Early stages of development of planula larva

DIFFERENCES FROM OTHER PHYLA

1. Body-wall continuous and without pores; has free-swimming generations
2. Endoderm and ectoderm inverted as compared with Porifera
3. Spicules in mesogloea differ in structure and are intercellular instead of intracellular as in Porifera
4. No nematocysts in Porifera and no collared cells in Coelentera
5. Mouth corresponds with blastopore in Coelentera, contrary to case in Porifera, as regards osculum
6. Advance upon condition of colonies in Protozoa

CONCLUSIONS

1. Coelentera derived from Protozoa directly, but probably near base of Porifera stem, if not in common with it
2. Porifera and Coelentera represent two strongly divergent lines of evolution parting either shortly before or immediately after derivation from Protozoa.

CLASS HYDROMEDUSAE

The Hydromedusae, for the most part, are characterized by a typical alternation of generations. In the hydroid stage, the polyp is attached and is usually of colonial habit. It reproduces either by budding off other individuals like itself or by budding off a free-swimming sexual medusa and may be either male or female. Hydroids may be quite minute in size or, as in the case of certain solitary deep-sea hydroids (*Branchiocerianthus*), may be more than 6 feet in length. Sometimes, a colony will form a branching plantlike structure, each branch terminating in a polyp known as a hydranth. Every hydranth is connected through its stemlike base with the hydranths which terminate the other branches of the colony. Prolific colonies are often popularly termed "sea ferns." Practically all Hydromedusae are marine, although a few species are found in fresh water. The accompanying INDEX PLATE (31) gives the details of the principal structures of both the hydroid and medusoid stages. The terms indicated in this diagram will be utilized in describing the various species of Hydromedusae mentioned in this handbook.

The Class Hydromedusae is divided into five orders, within the geographical range covered by this book. In orders (1) and (2), the gonads, or reproductive organs, are of ectodermal origin. In orders (3) and (4), mentioned below, they are of endodermal origin.

(1) *Anthomedusae,* or true Hydromedusae, in which the polyps are naked
(2) *Leptomedusae,* in which the polyps are contained in a transparent cuplike *hydrotheca* (see INDEX PLATE 40)
(3) *Trachymedusae,* which have a conspicuous medusoid stage and minute hydroid stage when it is present
(4) *Narcomedusae,* with the hydroid stage lacking, and the medusae equipped with a scalloped or lobed umbrellar margin. These are animals of the open sea, only a few species being found along our coasts

PLATE 31

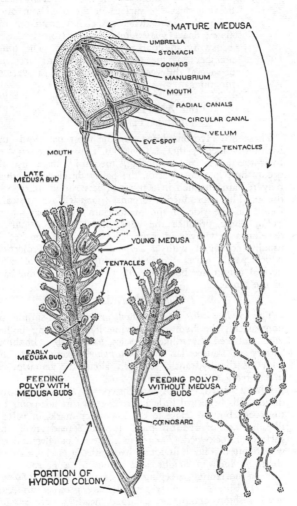

MATURE MEDUSA

UMBRELLA
STOMACH
GONADS
MANUBRIUM
MOUTH
RADIAL CANALS
CIRCULAR CANAL
VELUM
EYE-SPOT
TENTACLES

MOUTH

LATE
MEDUSA BUD

YOUNG MEDUSA

TENTACLES

EARLY
MEDUSA BUD

FEEDING
POLYP WITH
MEDUSA BUDS

FEEDING
POLYP WITHOUT
MEDUSA BUDS

PERISARC
COENOSARC

PORTION OF
HYDROID COLONY

HYDROID AND MEDUSA STAGES
OF A TYPICAL TUBULARIAN

(5) *Siphonophora,* mostly colonial Hydromedusae, floating near the surface in the open sea, often with the individuals suspended from an inflated float (*pneumatophore*) or from a cluster of swimming polyps (*nectophores*). The other members of the siphonophore colony are also of several different forms specialized for various functions

Order ANTHOMEDUSAE
(INDEX PLATE 31)

These are Hydromedusae, for the most part with the hydranths naked, that is, without a protective cup or hydrotheca. A free-swimming, medusoid stage usually occurs but, in some species, the partly developed medusa may remain attached in a more or less rudimentary condition. The reproductive organs (*gonads*) are typically found on the side of the manubrium (see INDEX PLATE 31*). These produce the eggs, which settle down to develop a new hydroid stage. The margin of the bell is usually equipped with a *velum,* a shelflike projection which partly closes the bell opening. Eyespots of ectodermal origin are borne on the bell margin at the base of the tentacles.

Family Clavidae

The *hydrocaulus* is branched or may be simple or nonexistent, the hydranths having long, tapering bodies with scattered threadlike tentacles, each with a knoblike battery of sting-cells. The *gonophores* grow from the body of the hydranth, scattered along the tentacles or in clusters.

Clava leptostyla Agassiz PLATE 32. The clublike hydroid. This beautiful little hydroid grows in tide-pools on the rocky bottom, close to the low-water mark, in velvetlike patches of reddish pink. It also spreads over the surface of rockweed (*Fucus*) in clustered patches and on wharf piles. The individual hydranths are club-shaped, about ¼ inch in height, and spring by a narrow base from a horizontal creeping network of stolons (*hydrorhizas*). Fifteen to thirty tentacles are grouped in scattered fashion about the enlarged head, which is surmounted by a porelike mouth. Just beneath the tentacles are berrylike clusters of reproductive buds (*sporosacs*). These are pink in the male hydranths and purple in the female. They correspond to the undeveloped medusae and never become free.

Common from Long Island to Labrador.

* *Sarsia eximia* (Allman).

PLATE 32

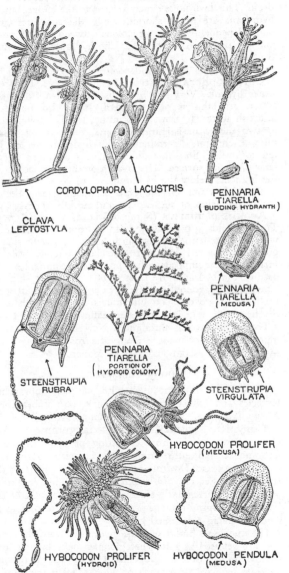

CORDYLOPHORA LACUSTRIS

CLAVA
LEPTOSTYLA

PENNARIA
TIARELLA
(BUDDING HYDRANTH)

PENNARIA
TIARELLA
(MEDUSA)

STEENSTRUPIA
RUBRA

PENNARIA
TIARELLA
PORTION OF
(HYDROID COLONY)

STEENSTRUPIA
VIRGULATA

HYBOCODON PROLIFER
(MEDUSA)

HYBOCODON PROLIFER
(HYDROID)

HYBOCODON PENDULA
(MEDUSA)

Rhizogeton fusiformis Agassiz. The fusiform hydroid. This hydroid is closely related to the above, but the hydranths are much shorter, while the sporosacs grow out independently from the stolons between the hydranths and are borne on short stalks. The hydranths have about twelve tentacles.

Massachusetts Bay, in tidepools.

Cordylophora lacustris Allman PLATE 32. The freshwater hydroid. Very few hydroids are known from fresh water, and this is one of them. It is also found in brackish water. It grows in a bushy, treelike colony, one to two inches in height, on stones, eelgrass, or wharf-piles. Each branch terminates in a hydranth which has ten to twenty fine, threadlike tentacles scattered irregularly over its surface. The oval sporosacs are borne on the branches below the hydranths.

Brackish water on the New England coast, also in the inland lakes of the eastern and middle states.

Acaulis primarius (Stimpson) COLOR PLATE III, 5, 5a. The hydroids grow singly from a rootlike attachment with a short stem. The hydranth has a long, club-shaped proboscis, covered by short tentacles scattered over its surface, each equipped with a bulblike extremity. At the base of the hydranth are clusters of a few long, filiform tentacles. The gonophores (reproductive organs) arise as a cluster of globe-shaped individuals around the base of the hydranth, with the tentacles scattered between them.

The distribution is throughout New England. It is of more frequent occurrence along the coast of Maine to Mount Desert Island and Grand Manan.

Family Codonidae

These are Anthomedusae with simple, unbranched tentacles and four to six radial canals, also unbranched. A ringlike gonad surrounds the manubrium.

Corynitis agassizii (Gemmaria gemmosa) McCrady PLATE 35. Hydroid consisting of cylindrical and unbranched hydranths, rising from creeping, horizontal, rootlike processes (hydrorhizas) growing on shells of the common mussel (*Mytilus edulis*) and on other mollusks. Tentacles are irregularly scattered around the stalk of the hydranth in spiral arrangement from crown to base, each tentacle having a terminal knob of nematocysts.

The medusae bud from the hydranth near the base and are released as somewhat globular bells having four narrow radial canals, a distinct velum, and two long opposite tentacles, from each of which rises a remarkable row of nematocyst batteries mounted on the tips of long, slender stalks. The basal bulbs extend up on the terminal portion of the radial canals and are covered with batteries of nematocysts, both at the bases of the long tentacles and of the intermediate rudimentary tentacles. The medusa was formerly known as *Gemmaria gemmosa,* until it was demonstrated to be the medusa stage of the hydroid, *Corynitis agassizii.*

Woods Hole, Massachusetts.

Slabberia (Dipurena) strangulata Haeckel PLATE 35. The hydroid is similar to that of the preceding genus. The medusa is quite small, only about 3/16 inch in diameter, and is beautifully tinted. It is oval in shape, varying to conical (var. *conica*) and hemispherical. It has four radial canals and four tentacles, slightly shorter than the height of the umbrella, with orange and green basal bulbs, brown ocelli, and is furnished with terminal orange knobs. The manubrium is green, shading into pink and red. It is narrowly constricted basally and in its middle portion.

Woods Hole, Massachusetts, to South Carolina.

Dipurella clavata (young of **Slabberia strangulata)** PLATE 35. High-shouldered bell about 3/16 inch vertically, with projection at summit. Outer surface dotted with nematocysts. Four radial canals with four tentacles unequally developed. Short club-shaped tentacles similar to those of *Dipurena,* but not so long, with longer terminal swellings and a median ring of nematocysts. Basal bulbs and ocelli also similar to those of that genus. Manubrium short and with gastric swelling. Color of tentacular knobs bright red with greenish tinge; basal bulbs orange to red or brown with black ocelli; manubrium shaded with green (Hargitt).

Woods Hole, Massachusetts; rare.

Corymorpha pendula Agassiz (Hydroid) = **Steenstrupia rubra** Forbes (Medusa) PLATE 32; COLOR PLATES III, 6, 6a; IV, 5. The beautiful and graceful hydroid of this species is solitary in habit and grows to nearly ½ inch in height. The hydranth at the summit has two rows of threadlike tentacles, one set encircling the mouth, the other composed of larger tentacles surrounding the base of the hydranth immediately beneath a ring of branching gonophores with medusae in various stages of development. The stalk (*pedicel*) is slender at the top, gradually becoming bulbous, or club-shaped, at the base. It terminates in a branched, rootlike hold-fast, which is ordinarily buried in the sand or mud.

The medusa, into which the gonophore buds develop, is free-swimming and has a rather irregular, dome-shaped bell with a conical prolongation at the top, which, in the male, may be of greater length than that of the medusa itself. It has a single trailing tentacle equipped with closely set rings of nematocysts. There are also three rudimentary tentacles.

The hydroid stage was originally described as *Corymorpha pendula* by Agassiz and as *Corymorpha nutans* by Stimpson. The medusa, which was not at first recognized as belonging to this hydroid, was named *Steenstrupia rubra* by Forbes.

This is one of the most beautiful of the solitary hydroids and, with its bent and nodding head, is often seen in Pamlico Sound, North Carolina, especially at Oregon Inlet and at Beaufort. It ranges southward to Tortugas, Florida. It is apparently identical with a similar species found in the Mediterranean Sea.

Pennaria tiarella McCrady PLATE 32. In the hydroid stage, *Pennaria tiarella* is found chiefly on eelgrass, seaweeds, stones, and wharves below the low-tide mark. The plumes of the feathery colony are about 4 to 6 inches in length, the main stems branching alternately. These stems are covered with a hard, chitinous *perisarc,* horny yellow to black in color. The polyp heads are flask-shaped, and the mouth is located at the end of a long, slender, conical throat tube. The mouth is surrounded by two or three irregular rows of tentacles, each crowned with a knob-shaped cluster of nematocysts. Medusa buds develop along the sides of the stem between the mouth and the base of the hydranth, which is also encircled with a row of long, flexible tentacles. The hydroid is white to rose color.

The bell of the medusa is ellipsoidal and rose-pink in color. It has thin, flexible walls, which in the female are often distorted by the presence in the manubrium of four or five large ova. There are four small, rudimentary tentacle bulbs at the base of each radial canal. Ocelli do not occur. The radial canal is frequently spotted with deep rose-pink, but the tentacle bulbs are pearly white.

Maine to the West Indies and Bermuda; shallow water.

Steenstrupia virgulata A. Agassiz PLATE 32. The bell of the medusa is pear-shaped, with a broad, flattened summit and no prolongation. There are four tentacles at the base of each of the four radial canals. One of the tentacles is large and conical, while the other three are merely rudiments. There is a wide velum. The manubrium is short and cylindrical, terminating in a circular mouth. The gonophores are located on the manubrium, which is light yellow in color, while the radial canals become intense pink as they reach the bases of the tentacles. The tentacles are milky white.

The species is recorded from Nahant, Massachusetts,

and also at Woods Hole, Massachusetts. The hydroid is not known.

Hybocodon prolifer L. Agassiz PLATE 32. The hydroid is abundant in tide-pools in Massachusetts Bay. It occurs singly or in small clusters, with no indication of a branching habit. The handsome orange hydranth terminates the stem, which is about two inches in height and which also displays orange bands of pigment. The body of the polyp is "flask-shaped with a broad base; the mouth is situated at the extremity of a narrow, cylindrical neck, which is capable of extension." There are two circlets of tentacles with clusters of gonophores between. Each circlet is composed of about sixteen tentacles. The range of this species is from New England to Iceland, Norway, and the British Isles. In other words, it is found along the entire North Atlantic coast on both sides.

The umbrella of the medusa is of a flattened cone shape, with a long, vaselike, tapering manubrium, terminating in a four-lobed mouth. Only one tentacle is developed, the other three being extremely small and rudimentary. Medusa buds grow from the base of the tentacle, these also developing but one tentacle each. An orange tinge is extensively developed in the manubrium and bases of the tentacles. Because of the presence of the single tentacle, the umbrella is asymmetrical in shape.

Hybocodon pendula Haeckel PLATE 32. Only the medusa is illustrated here. It is somewhat flatly tapering at the summit of the bell, with thickened, gelatinous substance in this region. A single well-developed tentacle is also present. The manubrium is well developed and is equipped with nematocysts. It is tinted pink and lilac and is dotted with pink granules.

The hydroid is not illustrated here because it is not found in shallow waters, occurring in from one hundred to ten fathoms along the New England coast. Like *Hybocodon prolifer,* it is of solitary habit, with a stem embedded in the sand, anchored by rootlike prolongations.

Hybocodon pendula ranges from Vineyard Sound to the mouth of the St. Lawrence River. The medusa is particularly abundant in April and May.

Syncoryne (Sarsia) mirabilis (Hydroid) (L. Agassiz) PLATE 33. Hydroid colony growing 1 inch or less in height, in small tufts of elongate slender stems, sparsely branching. Each stem is covered with a definite perisarc of transparent chitin without annulations, and terminates in a long bulbous hydranth which projects entirely beyond the end of the perisarc. The lining of the body cavity of the hydranth is rose-red, which gives the impression of that color to the entire colony. The medusa develops on the side of the hydranth body as an elongate bud with four rudimentary tentacles and four radial canals visible. The sexual products may be extruded from the sides of the large manubrium, before the medusa itself is set free. The full-grown, liberated medusa is a beautiful, hemispherical, and transparent bell, up to ½ inch in diameter. It has four long thread-like tentacles and a very long, slender, greenish manubrium hanging far below the margin of the bell. A black "eye" or ocellus is situated within a greenish bulb with a brown center at the base of each tentacle. Gonads are borne upon the manubrium, causing it to swell so as to fill the subumbrellar cavity as they mature.

Very common from February to May, from Narragansett Bay to Greenland and Scotland.

Sarsia (Syncoryne) mirabilis (Medusa) L. Agassiz PLATE 33.* This medusa is bell-shaped and very minute, being about 1/16 inch in height. The basal bulbs of the four tentacles are orange colored, with black ocelli. The manubrium extends beyond the velum and terminates in two successive bulbous expansions just above the mouth. These are blue above, shading into green below. The upper part of the manubrium is orange and bears its gonads closely set about its base. Medusae are also budded directly from the manubrium.

Woods Hole, Massachusetts.

Stauridia (Sarsia) producta Wright PLATE 33. The hydroid is characterized by a basal series of tentacles without knobs. The tentacles, with knoblike batteries of sting-cells, are confined to the upper portion of the hydroid and resemble those of *Syncoryne mirabilis,* which, however, has no knobless series of tentacles.

The medusa is egg-shaped and has thick, gelatinous walls and four tentacles, 1½ times the height of the bell. There are no medusa buds.

British seas.

Hydrichthys mirus Fewkes PLATE 34. The hydroid grows parasitically on a small fish, *Seriola zonata.* It develops a basal network of connecting tubes under the scales of the fish. The hydroids, bearing more or less degenerate hydranths, arise from the side of the main axis, becoming branched as they grow. The stomach cavities communicate freely with each other.

The medusa buds are found at the ends of the branches in various stages of development. In the free-swimming state, the medusa has at first two tentacles, but two more develop during the growth of the medusa. PLATE 34 shows

---

* See also INDEX PLATE 31 [*Sarsia eximia* (Allman)].

PLATE 33

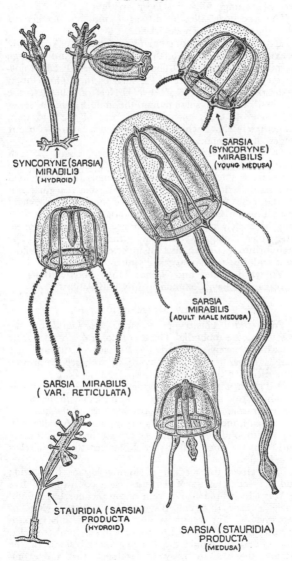

SYNCORYNE (SARSIA)
MIRABILIS
(HYDROID)

SARSIA
(SYNCORYNE)
MIRABILIS
(YOUNG MEDUSA)

SARSIA
MIRABILIS
(ADULT MALE MEDUSA)

SARSIA MIRABILIS
(VAR. RETICULATA)

STAURIDIA (SARSIA)
PRODUCTA
(HYDROID)

SARSIA (STAURIDIA)
PRODUCTA
(MEDUSA)

a colony attached to a fish, a detail enlarged, and a free-swimming, fully developed medusa.

The specimen illustrated was found by Fewkes in Narragansett Bay, Rhode Island.

Ectopleura dumortieri (Van Beneden) A. Agassiz PLATE 34. The hydroid of this species was found in large numbers at Newport, Rhode Island, by Alfred Goldsborough Mayer, clinging to the stem of the leptomedusan hydroid, *Obelia*. There are two circlets of tentacles, one of small tentacles surrounding the mouth, and a series of coarser tentacles encircling the base of the hydranth, immediately above which are the medusa buds in various stages of development.

The medusa is ovoid, or pear-shaped, about ⅛ inch high by 1/16 inch wide. The jelly (mesogloea) of the umbrella is thick, with four radial canals deeply situated and connected with a circular canal at the marginal rim of the bell. Eight vertical rows of nematocysts extend from the rim to the apex of the outer surface. The four long, delicately tapering tentacles are often tightly coiled. They have yellow basal bulbs with reddish ocelli. The manubrium is shaped like an inverted vase, with yellow base and tip; median portion pink.

Vineyard Sound and Woods Hole, Massachusetts, to Narragansett Bay. Common in July and August.

Family Margelopsidae

Four radial clusters of tentacles are found on the margin of the umbrella. There are no oral tentacles. The gonad completely surrounds the stomach. There are four simple radial canals. The hydroids are free-swimming, with medusae budding from their sides.

Margelopsis gibbesi Hartlaub PLATE 35. The genus to which this species belongs is remarkable in having a free-swimming hydroid with two whorls of tentacles. In this species, the tentacles are tapering, with a tip terminating in knob-shaped batteries of sting-cells. The medusae bud from the side of the hydroid between the two circlets of tentacles.

The bell of the medusa is slightly higher than wide and has four clusters of tentacles, each consisting of five or six, which branch out from a conspicuous basal bulb. Each tentacle is equipped with about fifteen rings of nematocysts. The velum is well developed. The mouth opening is round without prominent lips or oral tentacles. The gonad surrounds the stomach on all sides. In the female, the ova are so well developed that they completely crowd its surface and conspicuously nearly fill the bell cavity. The tentacle bulbs are yellow and have no ocelli. The manubrium varies from yellow to green.

PLATE 34

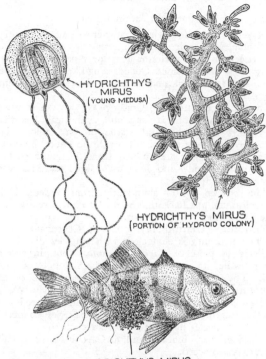

HYDRICHTHYS
MIRUS
(YOUNG MEDUSA)

HYDRICHTHYS MIRUS
(PORTION OF HYDROID COLONY)

HYDRICHTHYS MIRUS
(HYDROID COLONY ATTACHED TO FISH (SERIOLA ZONATA))

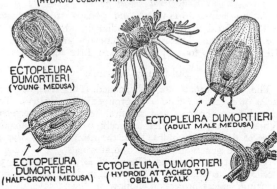

ECTOPLEURA
DUMORTIERI
(YOUNG MEDUSA)

ECTOPLEURA
DUMORTIERI
(HALF-GROWN MEDUSA)

ECTOPLEURA DUMORTIERI
(HYDROID ATTACHED TO)
OBELIA STALK

ECTOPLEURA DUMORTIERI
(ADULT MALE MEDUSA)

The species ranges from Pamlico Sound, North Carolina, to Charleston, South Carolina.

Family Cladonemidae

Mayer lists the following characteristics of this family:
"Tentacles branch dichotomously or complexly, or give rise to a linear series of nematocyst-bearing filaments along their abaxial sides. Gonads ring-like, or segregated upon the interradial and adradial sides of the manubrium."

Zanclea gemmosa McCrady PLATE 35; COLOR PLATE IV, 4. The hydranth is long and cylindrical, less than 1/25 inch in height, and sessile on the stolon. The tentacles are scattered spirally over the entire hydranth body. The medusae are budded from the lower part of the hydranth body and have two short tentacles with clusters of nematocysts.

The species occurs abundantly from Woods Hole, Massachusetts, to Charleston, South Carolina, usually associated with incrusting Bryozoa.

Zanclea (Gemmaria) costata Gegenbaur PLATE 35. The hydranth is elongated, with tentacles distributed similarly to those of *Zanclea gemmosa*, but, instead of being sessile, it is connected with the stolon by a short stalk. The medusae are budded from the base of the hydranth. The tentacles have batteries of nematocysts at their ends. The medusae have two tentacles, covered with papillae bearing rows of nematocyst batteries connected with the tentacles by a threadlike attachment.

It occurs from Block Island to Cape Hatteras, usually on sargassum weed.

Family Oceanidae

Anthomedusae, in which the gonads are segregated and developed upon the interradial or adradial sides of the manubrium. The marginal tentacles are unbranched. The mouth has four lips. There are three subfamilies.

Subfamily Tiarinae

The radial canals are unbranched. The marginal tentacles are separate and not grouped into clusters. The tentacles are hollow, and no oral tentacles are present. When present, the ectodermal ocelli are upon the abaxial sides of the tentacle bulbs. With the exception of *Calycopsis,* all the genera have four radial canals.

Stomotoca dinema (Peron & Lesueur) PLATE 36. According to Mayer, the 4-mm.-high bell has a large, tapering, apical projection, hollow in the female, usually solid in the male. There are two long, opposite tentacles with tapering, hollow, basal bulbs. There are no ocelli.

PLATE 35

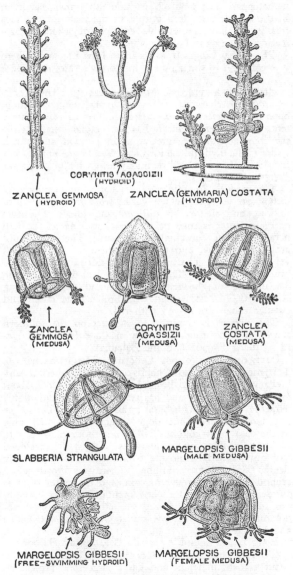

ZANCLEA GEMMOSA
(HYDROID)

CORYNITIS AGASSIZII
(HYDROID)

ZANCLEA (GEMMARIA) COSTATA
(HYDROID)

ZANCLEA
GEMMOSA
(MEDUSA)

CORYNITIS
AGASSIZII
(MEDUSA)

ZANCLEA
COSTATA
(MEDUSA)

SLABBERIA STRANGULATA

MARGELOPSIS GIBBESII
(MALE MEDUSA)

MARGELOPSIS GIBBESII
(FREE-SWIMMING HYDROID)

MARGELOPSIS GIBBESII
(FEMALE MEDUSA)

The tentacles are equipped with wartlike clusters of nematocysts. The stomach is yellowish brown to green in the female and deep purple in the male. Mayer says this is the most remarkable example of sexual dichromatism among the Hydromedusae.

The species ranges from southern New England, where it is common in the summer, to Tortugas, Florida, where it is rare.

Stomotoca rugosa Mayer PLATE 36. The genus *Stomotoca* is characterized by medusae having two long, opposite tentacles with a varied number of rudimentary tentacles between them. It has four radial canals, while the four gonads are interradial in position and much folded. The hydroid is identical with *Perigonimus,* but the medusae are not all definitely assignable to particular *Perigonimus* species.

The medusa *Stomotoca rugosa* has a conspicuous projection on its apex, which varies from short and blunt to long and slender in different individuals. The two opposite tentacles may be ten times as long as the bell height, but they are highly contractile. The basal bulbs are large, hollow, and tapering. There are no ocelli. A velum is present. The mouth is four-sided and the manubrium flask-shaped. The gelatinous bell is transparent, the interior of the tentacle bulbs and stomach being brick red, often variegated with brown. The radial and circular canals are tinged with red.

This species is common in summer off the southern shores of New England south of Cape Cod. It ranges to southern Florida and the Bahamas.

Perigonimus jonesi Osborn & Hargitt PLATE 36. This medusa of curious habits has a hemispherical umbrella with a rounded projection at the apex. It is about 1/16 inch in diameter and has two filamentous and highly retractile tentacles with basal bulbs and ocelli. The other two tentacles are undeveloped, being represented only by the basal bulbs and ocelli. There are four radial canals, the two leading to the tentacles being well developed and quite broad, while the two intermediate canals are slender and delicately outlined. There is a broad velum around the subumbrellar margin, and the manubrium is quite short with a four-lobed mouth. Strangely enough, this medusa has been found on only the legs and abdominal appendages of the spider crab, *Libinia* (Osborn and Hargitt).

Long Island Sound, especially Cold Spring Harbor.

Turris vesicaria A. Agassiz PLATE 36. The bell is about 1 inch in height and has a large solid projection, much more fully developed than in *Turris pileata.* There are sixteen long tentacles and forty-eight short ones. They

PLATE 36

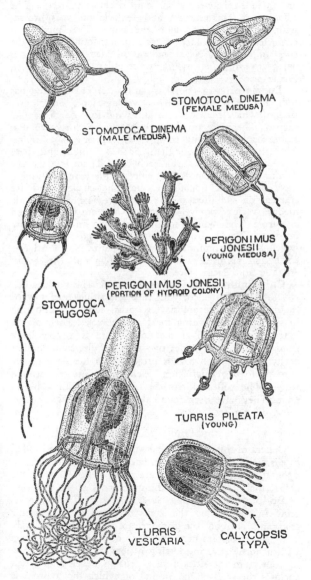

STOMOTOCA DINEMA
(FEMALE MEDUSA)

STOMOTOCA DINEMA
(MALE MEDUSA)

PERIGONIMUS
JONESII
(YOUNG MEDUSA)

PERIGONIMUS JONESII
(PORTION OF HYDROID COLONY)

STOMOTOCA
RUGOSA

TURRIS PILEATA
(YOUNG)

TURRIS
VESICARIA

CALYCOPSIS
TYPA

are arranged so that three of the rudimentary tentacles are included between each pair of long tentacles. The color of the manubrium and tentacle bulbs is brown, with dark red ocelli upon the latter. This medusa is characteristic of colder waters, being found along the coast of northern New England in May and June, and being recorded as especially abundant near Eastport, Maine.

Turris pileata (Forskal) PLATE 36. This medusa has thin side walls and usually a well-developed apical projection, which may be conical, cylindrical, or pineapple-shaped. There are usually twenty-four to thirty-two tentacles, having laterally compressed, tapering basal bulbs. The tentacles are longer than the bell is high, and there is an ocellus at the base of each bulb. There is a narrow velum. The stomach is four-sided, with four lips and a short neck. The gonads are horseshoe-shaped, and are situated on the sides of the stomach. The color of the medusa varies from yellow to red, or from brownish red to purple. The radial and circular canals may be yellow or green. The hydroid is probably *Perigonimus repens,* which is quite common around the entire North Atlantic coast and is even widespread throughout the South Atlantic and Pacific Oceans.

Calycopsis typa Fewkes PLATE 36. The medusa bell is somewhat elongated, with thin walls thickened toward the summit. There are sixteen radial canals, terminating in sixteen corresponding marginal tentacles. Each of the latter is club-shaped at the end. There is a very large stomach, filling the upper two thirds of the subumbrellar cavity. Four sets of gonads project from the sides of the four principal radial lines, each made up of fernlike ridges. The bell and tentacles are white, with a bluish tinge. They have been found floating in deep water near the Gulf Stream.

Subfamily Margelinae

Genera of this subfamily possess four unbranched radial canals. Oral tentacles, or nematocyst knobs, are present upon the lips. The tentacles are solid. When present, the ectodermal ocelli are upon the inner sides of the tentacles.

Podocoryne carnea Sars PLATE 37. The hydroids grow in colonies on the shells occupied by the hermit crab and also on the carapace of the horseshoe crab. They form colonies here, made up of a network of fibers with a horny covering having a network of spines growing out from the sides until a crust is developed, which encloses the shell of the animal on which the hydroid is growing. The polyps belonging to such a colony are of two forms: feeding polyps and reproductive polyps. This is transitional to the condition in *Hydractinia,* where there are several different forms of hydroids which are truly polymorphic. The individuals of such a colony are known as *polypites,* as contrasted to the single polyps in other species. Each polypite has twelve to sixteen stiff tentacles encircling the mouth region, and the medusa buds project from the sides of the polypite in this stage of development. After they are fully mature, they bud off the colony and swim away as independent medusae, which finally give rise to eggs. These in turn settle down to form a crust similar to that of the parent colony, new individuals arising by budding. This is a very widespread species, being found upon the Atlantic coast of America and Europe extending as far as the Arctic on the one hand and to Cape Colony and the tip of South America on the other. They are very abundant on the southern shore of New England.

The medusa is somewhat pear shaped and is about 3½ mm. in height. There are twenty-four to thirty-two marginal tentacles, which are usually about as long as the height of the bell. They are not very flexible and are often carried curled upward. There is a well-developed velum. Four radial canals are present around the flask-shaped manubrium. There are four oral tentacles around the mouth.

Podocoryne fulgurans (A. Agassiz) PLATE 37. The bell of this species is also pear-shaped and is not so large as the previous species, being about 1 mm. in height. There are eight to sixteen long, marginal tentacles, and, as in the case of the preceding species, they are quite stiff and curled upward. There are four slender, radial tubes. When first set free, each medusa has eight marginal tentacles. The manubrium is salmon red or colorless. This medusa is very abundant at Narragansett Bay, Rhode Island, in the summer. Generally speaking, it is the smaller size which distinguishes *Podocoryne fulgurans* from *Podocoryne carnea.*

Turritopsis nutricula McCrady PLATE 37. The hydroid forms a colony with slightly branched stems, each branch with a single terminal hydranth, which is club-shaped and with filiform tentacles scattered over its sides. The medusa buds are found mainly at the bases of the hydranths, each one having a short stalk. The stems of the hydroids and the medusa buds themselves are covered with perisarc, which on the stems is thick and incrusted with accumulations of foreign matter. It forms a thin capsule around the medusa buds. When first set free, the medusae have eight tentacles, and as they mature, these become quite numerous, ranging from forty to seventy.

The bell of the medusa is somewhat pear-shaped, and it is less than ¼ inch in height. The tentacles, when extended, are almost as long as the height of the bell but are very contractile. They have large basal bulbs, with an eyespot on the underside. There is a well-developed velum. The tentacles are abundantly equipped with nematocysts. The medusa has four radial canals and a circular canal around the margin. The manubrium is large and nearly fills the bell cavity. It bears four large gonads. The mouth is extended into four lobes. The stomach shows yellow to orange tips, which are also evident in the tentacle bulbs. The ocelli are deep orange or brown.

This species ranges from southern New England to the West Indies.

Stylactis hooperi Sigerfoos PLATE 37. This species grows in colonies on the shells of the common mud snail (*Ilyanassa obsoleta*), covering it densely. It forms a network (hydrorhiza), closely incrusting the snail shell with spines rising here and there. The hydranths are of two kinds: feeding hydranths and reproductive hydranths. The former are about 1 inch in length, with slender, unbranched stems terminating in a proboscis with a simple, circular mouth. The proboscis is surrounded by a circlet of long slender tentacles, varying in number from about fifteen to thirty or more. They are equipped with nematocysts. The reproductive hydranths are about ⅓ to ¾ as long as the feeding hydranths. They also have mouths but in addition bear four or five medusa buds below the bases of the tentacles. The hydranths are slightly pinkish white in color.

The medusa, when full-grown, is practically a swimming sporosac. It has an oval bell, with velum, and a circlet of very rudimentary tentacles. The bell is almost completely filled with gonads, which are liberated shortly after the medusae are set free from the hydroid. The medusa dies soon thereafter. The sexes are separate.

The species is distributed along the coast of New England but is especially abundant from Woods Hole, Massachusetts, to Cold Spring Harbor.

Bougainvillia superciliaris L. Agassiz COLOR PLATES III, 2, 2a; IV, 3. The hydroid colony grows in clusters about ½ inch in height, having irregularly branched primary and secondary subdivisions. It is usually attached to rocks. Each polypite has from fifteen to twenty slender tentacles in a single circlet. The medusa buds grow from the sides of the stem, encircled in a thin, chitinous capsule. The chitinous perisarc of the hydroid colony merges, gradually thinning out into the stem of each hydranth. The medusa is less than ½ inch in diameter, with a thick, gelatinous bell. In the subumbrellar cavity, there is a four-

PLATE 37

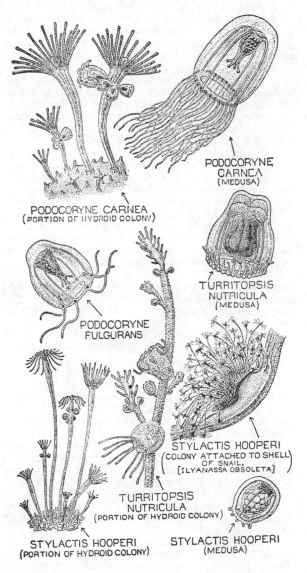

PODOCORYNE CARNEA
(PORTION OF HYDROID COLONY)

PODOCORYNE
CARNEA
(MEDUSA)

PODOCORYNE
FULGURANS

TURRITOPSIS
NUTRICULA
(MEDUSA)

STYLACTIS HOOPERI
(COLONY ATTACHED TO SHELL
OF SNAIL,
[ILYANASSA OBSOLETA])

TURRITOPSIS
NUTRICULA
(PORTION OF HYDROID COLONY)

STYLACTIS HOOPERI
(PORTION OF HYDROID COLONY)

STYLACTIS HOOPERI
(MEDUSA)

sided, flask-shaped manubrium, merging at the top into four radial canals which join at the angles. At the corners of the mouth are situated four treelike, branching tentacles. The four gonads are situated one on each side of the stomach. This and the tentacle bulbs are tinted reddish brown or yellow, the latter color also tingeing the substance of the bell itself.

This species is found on the North Atlantic shores from southern New England northward to Greenland, spreading also to the White Sea and Heligoland. The medusa appears early in April on the southern coast of New England. During the summer, however, it is found north of Cape Cod and along the coast of Maine.

Bougainvillia britannica Forbes PLATE 38. The hydroid, also known as *Bougainvillia ramosum,* has a stem which branches freely and a clublike hydrorhiza in which the branches do not anastomose. The perisarc forms annulations around the stem where it branches and extends over the base of each hydranth to form a cup into which the hydranth may withdraw. Each individual has about twelve filiform tentacles, making a regular circlet around the base of the conical proboscis (*hypostome*). They tend to be bent alternately forward and backward.

The medusa is oval in form. It has four radial tentacle bulbs which give rise to four clusters of tentacles. Eight conspicuous gonads are borne upon the manubrium. The stomach lining is orange-yellow to yellowish green or yellow-brown.

This medusa is widely distributed along the coasts of the North Atlantic Ocean on both the European and American sides.

Bougainvillia carolinensis (McCrady) PLATE 38. The hydroid grows in thick, feathery clusters, with stems forming loose networks often reaching a height of 12 inches. The adult medusa has an ovoid bell with a well-developed velum and trailing tentacles arranged in four clusters, each composed of about eight tentacles as long as the height of the bell. There are four radial canals. The four-sided manubrium is flask-shaped, with eight gonads surrounding its sides, which produce medusa buds directly. The gonophores of the hydroid colony are scattered over the stems and branches.

The species ranges from New Brunswick along the entire east coast, as well as to the east coast of the Gulf of Mexico.

Nemopsis bachei L. Agassiz PLATE 38. The hydroid grows in clusters on submerged wood and other floating objects. It produces colonies about 1 inch in height. The hydranths are characterized by a fold which separates them from the stem. The ectosarc of the stems is thin and

PLATE 38

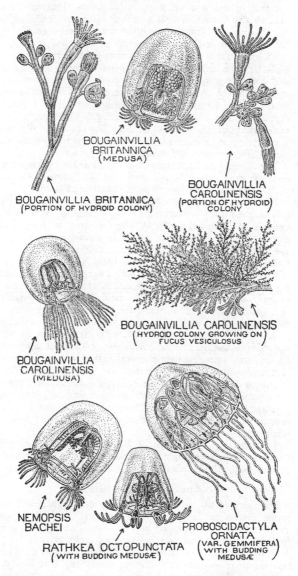

BOUGAINVILLIA
BRITANNICA
(MEDUSA)

BOUGAINVILLIA BRITANNICA
(PORTION OF HYDROID COLONY)

BOUGAINVILLIA
CAROLINENSIS
(PORTION OF HYDROID
COLONY)

BOUGAINVILLIA CAROLINENSIS
(HYDROID COLONY GROWING ON
FUCUS VESICULOSUS)

BOUGAINVILLIA
CAROLINENSIS
(MEDUSA)

NEMOPSIS
BACHEI

RATHKEA OCTOPUNCTATA
(WITH BUDDING MEDUSÆ)

PROBOSCIDACTYLA
ORNATA
(VAR. GEMMIFERA)
WITH BUDDING
MEDUSÆ

transparent. They are irregularly annulated at the bases of the side branches. Each polypite has twenty-four tentacles around the mouth, which is seated at the extremity of a funnel-shaped proboscis. Medusae may be seen encircling the hydranths just above the circle of tentacles.

The medusa is flattened when first set free but becomes globular as it develops. The tentacles increase in number and form four radial clusters of about fourteen tentacles each, of which the middle pair are contractile and longer than the rest, terminating in a knoblike cluster of nematocysts. There is a well-developed velum. The four radial canals bear the much-folded gonads. The short manubrium has a four-sided mouth and four radial clusters of oral tentacles. These organs are yellow to orange in color.

The species ranges from Woods Hole, Massachusetts, through Long Island Sound, and it is also found in Chesapeake Bay and as far south as Fernandina, Florida.

Rathkea octopunctata (Sars) Haeckel PLATE 38. The bell is practically a truncated cone in shape, with eight clusters of marginal tentacles. Each cluster, in turn, has eight tentacles, although in the fully grown medusa these are reduced to four or five in each cluster. The tentacle bulbs are large and pigmented brownish green to black. There is a well-developed velum. There are four radial canals. The length of the manubrium is about ⅓ the distance from the apex of the bell to the opening of the velum. It is quadratic in section, while the mouth has four prominent lips, each of which has a pair of oral tentacles ending in knob-shaped clusters of nematocysts. Medusae bud from the sides of the manubrium, with the oldest buds near the top and the youngest near the oral tentacles. As these mature and assume the form of medusae, another generation begins to develop buds on the stomach walls. At first these young medusae have only four radial tentacles. When set free, they possess sixteen. The hydroid stage appears to be absent, since medusae are formed directly from the parent medusae.

This species ranges from the British Isles, Norway, and Greenland to New England. It has been found in Narragansett Bay, Rhode Island.

Subfamily Dendrostaurinae

Members of this subfamily have no oral tentacles. The radial canals are branched. The marginal tentacles arise singly and are not grouped into clusters. The tentacles are hollow. There are no cirri or marginal clubs present.

Proboscidactyla ornata (McCrady) PLATE 38. The bell is about ⅕ inch in diameter, rather flat and flaring, with a slightly conical elevation at the summit. The young medusa has four main radial canals, which branch as it matures, so that the adult has from twelve to sixteen terminal canals distributed to the marginal canal. The tentacles also are four in the young but keep pace with the development of the radial canals so that in the adult there are twelve to sixteen. The manubrium is short, with four-sided lips. The gonads are formed at the base of the manubrium. The ocelli are reddish brown, while the gonads are from yellow to greenish yellow in color. The hydroid is unknown.

The medusa is especially common in Narragansett and Buzzards Bay but rare at Beaufort, North Carolina. In fact, it is found around the entire coast of North America, from New England to the Bahamas.

Family Eudendridae

Loose treelike colonies, arising from a branching, tangled hydrocaulus, characterize this family. The hydranth has a single whorl of threadlike tentacles surrounding a funnel-shaped projecting mouth (hypostome). There is no medusoid generation. Male sporosacs bud in a whorl underneath the tentacles, while the female sporosacs are located above them.

Genus **Eudendrium.** This is the only genus of the family *Eudendridae,* of which about twenty-two species are known to exist along the Atlantic coast of North America. Six of these are illustrated here.

Eudendrium ramosum (Linnaeus) Ehrenberg PLATE 39. The stems of this hydroid are more or less cemented together in bundles (fascicles) and are abundantly branched. The hydranths are usually on the upper side of the series of the alternate but pinnately arranged branches. There are annulations at the base of each branch. The hydranth has twenty-four tentacles. Gonophores are borne on the stems some distance below the hydranths. The species occurs abundantly from New Brunswick, in the Bay of Fundy, in Labrador, along the New England coast and the Atlantic coast generally to Charleston, South Carolina. They also occur at Bermuda and at Trinidad Island.

Eudendrium dispar L. Agassiz PLATE 39. The colony of this tubularian hydroid may be four inches in length, branching frequently but irregularly. The stems of the hydroids (pedicels) are almost completely annulated. The hydranth has twenty-eight tentacles. Gonophores are found in a whorl below the hydranths. The species occurs from New Brunswick to Stonington, Connecticut.

Eudendrium carneum Clarke PLATE 39. The colony may be a foot in length and abundantly branched, with the branchlets alternate. The stem tends to be fascicled, with annulations at the base of the branches and pedicels.

The hydranth has about twenty-four tentacles. Distribution is from southern New England to Beaufort, North Carolina. It is also said to be found in Puerto Rico.

Eudendrium tenue A. Agassiz PLATE 39. The stem is simple with irregularly placed branches, which are long and slender. The hydranth has about twenty tentacles. The male gonophores are in close-set whorls, while the female gonophores, according to Nutting, are globular and scattered over the hydranth body and pedicels. The species occurs from Nova Scotia to Massachusetts Bay and to Newport, Rhode Island.

Eudendrium album Nutting PLATE 39. This is a very small colony, usually not more than ⅓ inch in height, although the hydranths have long and slender pedicels. Each individual has twenty-six to thirty-two tentacles. The gonophores are small and few. The species is found on floating seaweed and on wharf piles at Woods Hole, Massachusetts, as far north as New Brunswick, and along the Atlantic coast to Florida.

Eudendrium capillare Alder PLATE 39. This is also a small colony about ⅜ inch tall, with irregular, short, and stout branches. The hydranths have about twenty to thirty tentacles. The female gonophores are quite conspicuous and are borne in whorls. The range of this species is from New Brunswick to Woods Hole, Massachusetts.

Family Hydractinidae

There is but one genus. Family characters as described below.

Hydractinia echinata Fleming COLOR PLATE III, 7, 7a. This remarkable species grows in colonies of polymorphic individuals occurring in patches on rocks and especially covering the mollusk shells inhabited by living hermit crabs, to the surface of which they give a velvety appearance when expanded. Under magnification, they are seen to be composed of several types of hydroid individuals, connected at the base by a network of stolons penetrating the limy crust covering the surface of the shell. The various individuals composing the colony include nutritive zooids, generative zooids, defensive zooids, and sensory zooids.

The nutritive zooids have simple, tube-shaped bodies, terminated by a mouth surrounded by a basal whorl of filiform tentacles. These do the feeding for the colony, passing along digested food through the basal stolons to the other types of zooids, which are not furnished with mouths. The generative zooids are generally shorter than the nutritive zooids. They have no mouth or tentacles, although they are furnished with nematocysts at the summit. They bear gonophores below the hydranth, which

PLATE 39

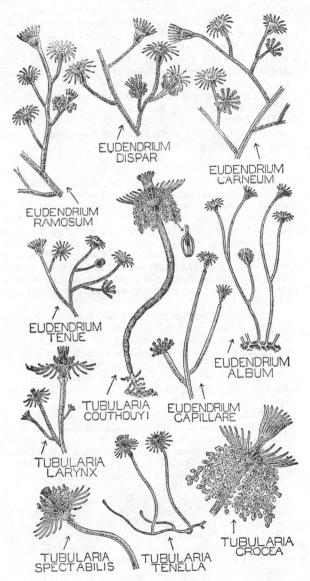

EUDENDRIUM
DISPAR

EUDENDRIUM
CARNEUM

EUDENDRIUM
RAMOSUM

EUDENDRIUM
TENUE

TUBULARIA
COUTHOUYI

EUDENDRIUM
CAPILLARE

EUDENDRIUM
ALBUM

TUBULARIA
LARYNX

TUBULARIA
SPECTABILIS

TUBULARIA
TENELLA

TUBULARIA
CROCEA

are seen to be in various stages of development. There is no medusa stage, the gonophores producing sporosacs. The defensive zooids are usually more abundant toward the margin of the colony. They are intermediate in size and slenderer than the other zooids. The summit is encircled with batteries of sting-cells. They are very flexible and usually coiling and uncoiling. The sensory zooids are quite like the defensive zooids, except that they have no batteries of sting-cells, but are instead well supplied with nerve cells of a sensory function.

This species is abundantly distributed from Labrador and New Brunswick along the entire New England coast and southward to North Carolina.

Family Tubularidae

The family comprises only the genus **Tubularia**, which consists of single, unbranched individuals, or the branching is from a horizontal creeping stolon which does not form a network. The hydranths are comparatively large with two whorls of tentacles, the basal circlet consisting of larger tentacles than in the case of the oral circlet, which forms a close cluster immediately around the mouth. The gonophores grow in grapelike clusters attached to the stem just above the lower circlet of tentacles and usually hang down below them. Five species are illustrated here.

Tubularia couthouyi L. Agassiz PLATE 39. The hydroid is solitary, growing up from a branched, rootlike stolon. The hydranths are sometimes ⅓ inch in diameter. There are about thirty to forty basal tentacles and as many as fifty shorter and smaller oral tentacles. The gonophores grow in long clusters, each with four radial canals. The range is from New Brunswick to the southern New England coast.

Tubularia larynx Ellis & Solander PLATE 39. The stems of this colonial form are much branched and form a tangled cluster at the base. They are much annulated. The tentacles are about twenty in number. The clustered gonophores have no radial canals. The distribution is from the Gulf of St. Lawrence to Vineyard Sound.

Tubularia spectabilis A. Agassiz PLATE 39. This hydroid is irregularly and sparsely branched. There are about twenty tentacles each in the oral and body whorls. It occurs from Nova Scotia to Vineyard Sound.

Tubularia tenella (L. Agassiz) PLATE 39. These are quite small colonies, not more than ¼ inch or so in diameter. There are about eighteen tentacles in each of the two series. The loosely clustered gonophores have no radial canals. The species occurs from Nova Scotia to southern New England.

PLATE 40

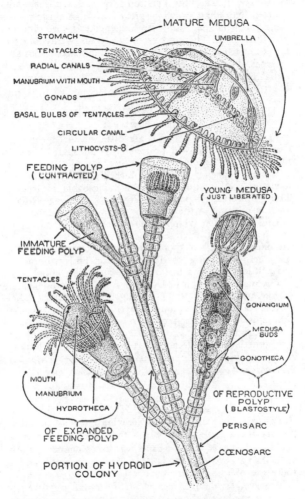

MATURE MEDUSA

STOMACH
TENTACLES
RADIAL CANALS
MANUBRIUM WITH MOUTH
GONADS
BASAL BULBS OF TENTACLES
CIRCULAR CANAL
LITHOCYSTS-8

UMBRELLA

FEEDING POLYP
(CONTRACTED)

YOUNG MEDUSA
(JUST LIBERATED)

IMMATURE
FEEDING POLYP

TENTACLES

GONANGIUM

MEDUSA
BUDS

GONOTHECA

MOUTH
MANUBRIUM
HYDROTHECA

OF REPRODUCTIVE
POLYP
(BLASTOSTYLE)

OF EXPANDED
FEEDING POLYP

PERISARC

CŒNOSARC

PORTION OF HYDROID
COLONY

HYDROID AND MEDUSA STAGES
OF A TYPICAL CAMPANULARIAN

Tubularia crocea (L. Agassiz) PLATE 39; COLOR PLATE III, 1, 1a. This handsome species, with its pink-hearted hydranths, grows in great flowerlike clusters, with bases much tangled but with long pedicels spreading out into fluffy tufts. There are from twenty to twenty-four tentacles in each of the two series. The gonophores are in long racemes. The radial canals are reduced to four compressed radial processes. The range is from the Bay of Fundy to Palm Beach, Florida.

Order LEPTOMEDUSAE
(INDEX PLATE 40)

In this order the hydroids are distinguished by the fact that the hydranths are protected by transparent, goblet-like enclosures known as hydrothecae, while gonophores terminate branches in the manner of the hydranths but have no mouth and therefore are incapable of feeding. The *gonotheca,* or protective envelope, is elongated to a narrow opening at the top. The hydranth is reduced to a central stalk upon which medusae are seen to be budding in various stages of development. When fully developed, the medusae detach themselves, work their way out of the narrow opening of the gonotheca, and swim off as independent medusae to form the sexual generation.

The medusae in this order differ from the Anthomedusae in having their gonads developing upon the radial canals instead of on the manubrium as in the case of the Anthomedusae. There are reasons to believe that the Leptomedusae originally evolved from primitive species of the Anthomedusae. Nine families are recognized, as follows: *Campanularidae, Campanulinidae, Hebellidae, Lafoeidae, Halecidae, Synthecidae, Sertularidae, Idiidae,* and *Plumularidae.*

Family Thaumantiidae

This family has characters showing its relationship to the Anthomedusae, from which the Leptomedusae originated, and may be considered as near to the connecting link with that group. Like the latter, there are no lithocysts, but there are marginal sensory clubs (*cordyli*).

The gonads, though located on the radial canals, as in all Leptomedusae, show continuity with the manubrium, on the walls of which they are to be found in Anthomedusae.

In the Thaumantiidae, the radial canals may be simple and unbranched, or they may have side branches ending blindly without connecting with the circular canals or, finally, they may have side branches which do connect with the circular canals.

Laodicea cruciata L. Agassiz PLATE 43. The bell of this medusa is 1 inch or less in diameter. The adult bell is somewhat flattened at the summit, but it is so flexible that it may assume a variety of shapes as it contracts on one side or the other. The relatively long tentacles, ranging from seventy to one hundred and fifty in number, are usually tightly coiled at the tips and stand stiffly out from the margin of the bell. There is a brown eye-spot at the base of each tentacle. Between the tentacle bases may be found short, spirally coiled cirri, more or less alternating with short club-shaped organs (cordyli). There is a narrow velum. The manubrium with its four-lobed mouth is continuous with the four gonads which extend along the radial canals, often for a considerable distance. Tints of light green characterize the manubrium, gonads, and basal bulbs of the tentacles. The hydroid grows from a creeping, rootlike stolon as a single unbranched polyp having a long, narrow hydrotheca with sharply pointed teeth at the margin. The polyp is retractile within the hydrotheca, which it can close by folding down the teeth. This species is common along the southern shores of New England, Cuba, and the West Indies in shallow waters, but has not been recorded from northern New England, though apparently it occurs on the European coast.

Melicertum campanula Agassiz COLOR PLATE IV, 1. This pear-shaped medusa is about 1 inch in height and strikingly beautiful in outline and proportions. The margin of the umbrella is characterized by about seventy radiating long and slender tentacles grading at their base into conical basal bulbs. They arise close together without space for ocelli or other sense organs. There is a distinct and wide velum. The manubrium is short and wide with fluted sides and flaring lips, eight in number. There are also eight sinuously developed gonads running the entire length of as many radial canals. The endoderm lining these and the central stomach are bright orange-yellow, shading to pale yellow in the thick gelatinous substance of the bell. The eggs, when extruded, give rise to free-swimming ciliated, planula larvae, which are pear-shaped. These attach themselves to the sea bottom by their larger end. The narrower free end lengthens into a tubular projection which becomes the stem of the elongate hydroid with a funnel-shaped hydrotheca and about twelve stumpy tentacles united to each other by a thin basal membrane.

This species is abundantly distributed along the New England coast, north of Cape Cod, which appears to be a barrier to its southern extension.

Family Campanularidae

The hydroids have a cup-shaped hydrotheca always at the end of a branch. The hydranth has a trumpet-shaped proboscis with a single wreath of threadlike tentacles. The gonophores may produce either free medusae or sporosacs. There are sense organs (lithocysts) on the margin of the umbrella, and the gonads are found on the radial canals.

Campanularia verticillata (Linnaeus) PLATES 41, 42. The colony forms a plantlike growth with main stem fascicled. The hydranths grow in successive whorls along this main stem as in the figure on PLATE 42. The hydrotheca are large and broad with annulated stems. The margin of the hydrotheca has from twelve to fourteen blunt teeth. The gonangium is prolonged to form a neck and is sessile directly on the stem.

Distribution, from Labrador along the entire New England coast.

Campanularia angulata (Hincks) PLATES 41, 42. The hydroid colony is about ⅜ inch in length, usually unbranched, or with few branches, the stems of the hydranths being annulated. There is a somewhat zigzag appearance to the main stem.

Casco Bay, along the southern New England coast, and Chesapeake Bay.

Campanularia flexuosa Hincks PLATES 41, 42. This is also an unbranched colony, though in some cases branches occur sparsely. The hydrothecae are given off evenly on each side of the main stem. The *gonangium* is large, about 2½ times as large as the hydrothecae. The medusae are formed on a central stalk and released to swim away independently.

From Gulf of St. Lawrence to Long Island Sound. Especially abundant on wharf piles at Eastport, Maine, and on floating seaweed in the Woods Hole, Massachusetts, region.

Campanularia hincksi Alder PLATE 42. This hydroid is unbranched and with a terminal hydranth. It rises from a horizontal stolon, from which also the gonosomes are budded forth.

Georges Bank, the New England coast, and the coast of Florida.

Campanularia volubilis (Linnaeus) PLATE 42. In this species, the hydranths arise unbranched from a stolon. The hydrotheca is long and slender with about ten blunt teeth. The gonangium has a short stem and is flask-shaped.

From Nova Scotia along the New England coast to Woods Hole.

Campanularia poterium (L. Agassiz) PLATE 42. This species also arises from a stolon with a tapering, unbranched, and fully annulated stem. The hydranths are

PLATE 41

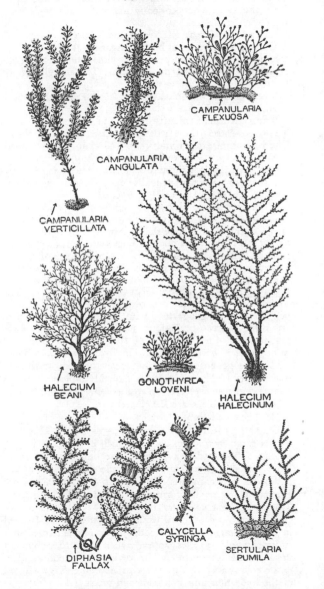

CAMPANULARIA
ANGULATA

CAMPANULARIA
FLEXUOSA

CAMPANULARIA
VERTICILLATA

HALECIUM
BEANI

GONOTHYREA
LOVENI

HALECIUM
HALECINUM

DIPHASIA
FALLAX

CALYCELLA
SYRINGA

SERTULARIA
PUMILA

about twice as long as wide. The gonangium also arises from the stolon independently and is usually well filled with sporosacs.

Labrador and coast of New England.

Campanularia amphora (Agassiz) PLATE 42. The colonies are small and branched with annulations at the beginning and end of the branches. The margin of the hydrotheca is without teeth.

From Grand Manan along the New England coast to Barnegat, New Jersey.

Campanularia minuta Nutting PLATE 42. This species has long, sparsely branched stems arising from the stolon. The hydrothecae are quite small and abundantly toothed.

Southern New England coast and Tortugas, Florida.

Campanularia edwardsi Nutting PLATE 42. The hydranths are slender, gradually expanding to a toothed margin. The stem is sparsely branched.

From New Brunswick along the New England coast.

Campanularia neglecta (Alder) PLATE 42. This colony is evenly and symmetrically branched. It may reach a height of slightly less than 1 inch with a rather zigzag contour to the main stem. The gonangia are flask-shaped and sessile directly on the stem.

Bay of Fundy and New England coast.

Campanularia calceolifera Hincks PLATE 42. The colonies of this species are considerably over 1 inch in height with a zigzag stem with forked branches. There are three to six annulations at the base of each main branch but with the stems of the hydranths annulated throughout. The margin of the hydrotheca is without teeth. The gonangia arise from near the base of the hydranth stems. The gonangium expands rapidly from its base and curves over the top to form a closed tube within which the sporosacs are developed.

New England coast.

Gonothyrea loveni Allman PLATES 41, 44. These hydroids grow in colonies about ½ inch or more in height, having a branched, wavy stem. The branches are annulated just above their junctions, while the pedicels of the hydranths are annulated throughout. The gonangia are elongated and sessile, forming a club-shaped termination. The hydrotheca is longer than wide with ten to twelve clearly cut and flat-topped teeth. The sporosacs are formed in the gonangium on a slender stalk and enlarge until rudiments of tentacles appear when their development stops, so that there are no free-swimming medusae. The entire colony is shown in PLATE 41, and an enlarged figure of the hydranths and gonosomes in PLATE 44.

From Hudson Bay and the St. Lawrence River, and the

PLATE 42

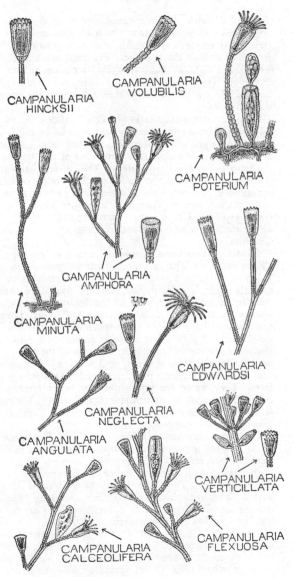

CAMPANULARIA
HINCKSII

CAMPANULARIA
VOLUBILIS

CAMPANULARIA
POTERIUM!

CAMPANULARIA
AMPHORA

CAMPANULARIA
MINUTA

CAMPANULARIA
EDWARDSI

CAMPANULARIA
NEGLECTA

CAMPANULARIA
ANGULATA

CAMPANULARIA
VERTICILLATA

CAMPANULARIA
CALCEOLIFERA

CAMPANULARIA
FLEXUOSA

New England coast generally, to Watch Hill, Rhode Island.

Genus **Obelia**. The numerous species belonging to this genus have a branched stem which may be simple or fascicled with flowerlike hydranths and with gonangia arising from the axils of the branches. The medusae are set free. They have eight or more marginal tentacles but no oral tentacles. The sense organs, or lithocysts, are situated around the margin of the umbrella between the bases of the tentacles.

Obelia commissuralis McCrady INDEX PLATE 40, PLATE 43. The colony is bushy and may be as much as 8 inches in length with a somewhat zigzag stem presenting a handsome appearance. It is annulated at the junction of the branches and hydranth stems. The medusa has sixteen tentacles and four narrow radial canals giving a cruciform appearance. The gonangia arise on short pedicels from the axils of the branches. They have a distinct collar. The medusae are free. This species ranges from the Maine coast along the entire New England shore to Charleston, South Carolina.

Obelia dichotoma (Linnaeus) COLOR PLATES III, 3, 3a; IV, 2; PLATE 43. This is a small hydroid growing in erect colonies, either as a single stem without branches or frequently irregularly branched, usually not more than 1 inch in height. The pedicels of the hydranths branch off alternately at regular distances from each other, immediately above the origin of the hydranth pedicels. The hydrothecae are goblet-shaped with smooth margins. The gonangia rise immediately from the axils of the stem. They are sessile, elongate, obovate, and with a collar around the terminal opening, through which the medusae are freed. They are of the type shown in INDEX DIAGRAM 40. A striking feature is the brilliant luminescence. The range is from Massachusetts to Charleston, South Carolina, on wharf piles and eelgrass.

Obelia gelatinosa (Pallas) PLATE 43. This species is often referred to the genus *Campanularia*. It has fascicled stems, which may grow in extensive clusters. The larger branches are thick and dark in color. The smaller branches are transparent. The pedicels of the hydranths vary in length. The hydrothecae are slender and long. The gonangia are club-shaped with a small opening at the top. The margin has about ten teeth.

This hydroid is found in shallow water growing abundantly on seaweeds from Cape Cod to South Carolina, being especially common on the southern New England coast on wharf piles. It has spread around the entire Atlantic coast, occurring also on the European and Mediterranean coasts.

Obelia plana (Haeckel) PLATE 43. This is a similar species with hydrothecae given off alternately from a slightly zigzag stem and annulated pedicels, about 1½ times the length of the hydrothecae. The colony may be as much as 8 inches in length. The hydrothecae are shallow and flare widely. The margins are untoothed. The gonothecae occur in the axils of the stems and are ovate in shape. The opening at the top has a tube-shaped collar. They occur at moderate depths in the Woods Hole, Massachusetts, region and in Long Island Sound. The medusa has twenty-four tentacles, and its gonads are on its radial canals.

Obelia geniculata (Linnaeus) PLATE 43. This hydroid grows about 1 inch in height with swelling joints from which the hydranths are given off alternately. The hydrothecae are as broad as they are high, with no teeth, and stand out sharply from the stem. The gonangium branches out from the axils. Its narrow collar is typically shaped like that of *Obelia*. The stems of the hydroid grow from a creeping stolon. They occur on seaweed near the low-water mark and have sparse branches. The medusae have sixteen to twenty-four tentacles and four gonads located on the radial canals near the center of the bell. They are quite transparent and often swim with the bell turned inside out. The tentacles are quite numerous.

The distribution is abundant on the Atlantic coast of America and occurring, in fact, throughout the world.

Obelia longissima (Pallas) PLATE 43. This species is quite appropriately named, as its long branches and abundant secondary branches give it a very fluffy appearance along a floating stem which may be a foot in length, tapering like a plume. The main stem is only slightly zigzag and black to brown in color. The delicate branches are light yellow and nearly transparent. The branches near the base are the longest and become gradually shorter near the tip of the colony. The hydrothecae are long and narrow with a fluffy circle of tentacles around the opening, which has very small, delicate teeth. The gonangia grow from an axillary position.

This hydroid ranges from New Brunswick to southern New England, occurring at Stonington and New Haven.

Obelia bidentata Clarke PLATE 43. This species is characterized by its long tubular hydrothecae, with teeth having two cusps on the summit of each, mounted on longitudinally grooved and deeply indented cups. The gonothecae and medusae are not known.

The distribution is along the coast of southern New England and Long Island Sound and, surprisingly, in the Malay Archipelago as well.

Tiaropsis diademata L. Agassiz PLATE 43. The bell of this medusa is somewhat flattened on the top with sloping, slightly concave sides and is about ½ inch in diameter. The tentacles are numerous, forming a close-set fringe around the umbrellar margin. There are eight sense organs situated adradially. There is a narrow velum. The radial tubes are slender, running straight from the base of the manubrium with its concave walls. The gonads develop on the radial canals and are cream colored. The stomach is of a deeper yellow, matching the bases of the fringelike tentacles. The hydroid is not known. This medusa is extremely abundant along the New England coast from March to May and disappears during the summer months. It is also known to occur as far north as the White Sea.

Clytia volubilis Lamouroux PLATE 45. The medusa is about ⅕ inch in diameter. It is broad and shallow with sixteen lithocysts. The velum is well developed. The four radial canals are narrow and connect with the threadlike circular vessel. The manubrium has four lips, and the gonads are at about the middle of the radial canals. The hydroid arises from a creeping stolon and has single hydranths mounted on slender pedicels, conspicuously toothed at the top and bottom. There are fifteen to twenty long, slender tentacles surrounding the dome-shaped proboscis, which has a round mouth opening at the summit. The gonothecae arise from the stolon separately with which they are connected by a short pedicel. The gonothecae are conspicuously ringed. Four or five medusae are developed from the central gonocoel and emerge from the opening when fully developed. The hydroid has also been known as *Clytia bicophora* L. Agassiz (PLATE 44), but, in that species, the gonothecae arise from the pedicels of the hydranths instead of from the stolon.

Both these species are very abundant upon the northern coast of Europe and upon the New England coast of North America.

Clytia noliformis (McCrady [Hydroid]) PLATE 44. The medusa stage, *Clytia folleata* (McCrady) (not illustrated), forms a hemispherical bell about ⅛ inch in diameter. It has sixteen contractile tentacles around the margin, equally distant from each other. Each has a sense organ in its basal bulb containing a spherical lithocyst. The four gonads are on the radial canals near the circular canal. A pale green color suffuses the various organs. The hydroid stage [*Clytia noliformis* (McCrady)] may be the same as *Clytia cylindrica* L. Agassiz (PLATE 44), though the hydrothecae are larger and more expanded than the slender, cylindrical ones characteristic of *Clytia cylindrica* (see below). In this stage, it is often found growing on

PLATE 43

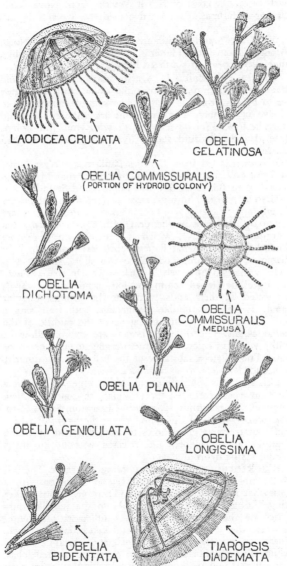

LAODICEA CRUCIATA

OBELIA GELATINOSA

OBELIA COMMISSURALIS
(PORTION OF HYDROID COLONY)

OBELIA DICHOTOMA

OBELIA COMMISSURALIS
(MEDUSA)

OBELIA PLANA

OBELIA GENICULATA

OBELIA LONGISSIMA

OBELIA BIDENTATA

TIAROPSIS DIADEMATA

sargassum weed in the Gulf Stream and off Bermuda as well as on the coast of North America from Nova Scotia to Cape Hatteras. Four or five medusae, when fully developed, emerge.

They are found abundantly along the coast of North America from Cape Hatteras to the West Indies, though they also appear off southern New England in summer.

Clytia cylindrica L. Agassiz PLATE 44. The hydroid stage arises unbranched from the stolon with elongated stems bearing concave teeth at the summit, about ten to twelve in number. The hydranths are quite minute and must be looked for on seaweed, growing from fine stolons (see also the hydroid stage, *Clytia noliformis,* described above).

It is distributed from Georges Bank to the West Indies and the Gulf, but is especially abundant from Massachusetts Bay to Buzzards Bay and Long Island Sound.

Clytia grayi Nutting PLATE 44 (cp. with *Phialidium languidum* PLATE 45). The medusae of this species are stated by Mayer to be identical with *Clytia volubilis* Lamouroux (PLATE 45), which is described on page 128. They have a somewhat flattened bell less than 1 inch in diameter. There are about thirty-two short, slender tentacles with two lithocysts in each successive space. There are a well-developed velum and four slender radial canals connected at their ends with the also slender circular canal. There is a tubular manubrium with four simple lips. The gonads are situated at about the middle of the radial canals. The different organs are cream yellow or milky white in color, sometimes verging toward green or pink. The jellylike substance of the bell is extraordinarily thin and flexible.

This species is common during the summer off the New England coast from Eastport, Maine, to southern New England and extending sparsely to Charleston, South Carolina. Some species of this genus retain the hydroid, which buds out from its gonophores to form a gonad in which medusae are developed and released without an intervening sessile hydroid stage.

Blackfordia manhattensis Mayer PLATE 45. The bell of the medusa is less than ½ inch in diameter with a somewhat strawberry-shaped bell. There are about eighty fringelike tentacles extending up into the jellylike substance of the bell. Two or three lithocysts are found between the tentacles with several concretions in each. There are four slender radial canals and a well-developed velum. The manubrium has four elongated, ruffled lobes. The sinuous gonads occupy a considerable portion of each radial canal. The manubrium is green, the color fading out along the radial canals. During the fall, this medusa

PLATE 44

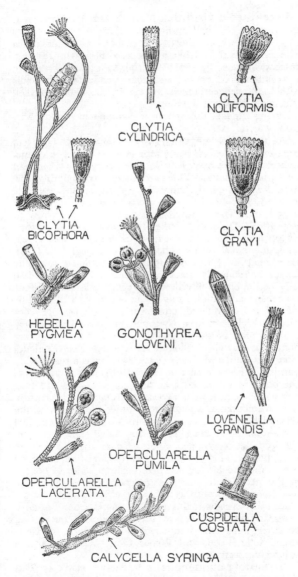

CLYTIA
CYLINDRICA

CLYTIA
NOLIFORMIS

CLYTIA
BICOPHORA

CLYTIA
GRAYI

HEBELLA
PYGMEA

GONOTHYREA
LOVENI

LOVENELLA
GRANDIS

OPERCULARELLA
PUMILA

OPERCULARELLA
LACERATA

CUSPIDELLA
COSTATA

CALYCELLA SYRINGA

is abundant off the New Jersey coast from Sandy Hook southward.

Blackfordia virginica Mayer PLATE 45. The bell is approximately ⅝ inch in diameter. There are about eighty long tentacles with short, conspicuous basal bulbs. The manubrium is shaped like a four-sided flask with curving, much convoluted lips, each tapering to a point. There are a well-developed velum and four slender radial canals with long, slender gonads. In the female, these are conspicuously lobulated with eggs.

During the fall, this species is common in shallow Virginia waters.

Staurophora mertensii Brandt PLATE 45. This is a large medusa, the bell being four to eight inches in diameter and of a substantial, jellylike consistency. It is a flattened hemisphere in outline. There are between two hundred and three hundred short, fringelike, spirally coiled tentacles crowded close together with a brown eyespot at the base of each one. The velum is well developed but narrow in proportion. The mouth takes the form of a four-lobed slit opening into a stomach, which extends well down along the radial canals almost to the circular vessel. On these canals, it is thrown into much convoluted sacs. The gonads continuously accompany these convolutions. The color of the organs is yellowish green, while the umbrella has a transparent bluish tinge. The white, crosslike appearance of the convoluted, cruciform stomach is quite conspicuous. The medusa is abundant around the New England coast, north of Cape Cod, but, in the early spring months, it may also be found off southern New England.

Eutima mira McCrady PLATE 45. This is a remarkably beautiful medusa occurring abundantly along our coast. The bell has a rounded apex and concave sides and four long tentacles, each with a conspicuous tapering basal bulb. The prostomium is about 3 to 4 times the length of the bell and has a long, slender peduncle extending from the trumpet-shaped stomach to the four-sided, ruffled mouth. The gonads are grouped along each of the radial tubes from the base of the peduncle nearly three-fourths of the way to the circular canal. There is also a series of gonads on the peduncle itself. The general color is light blue sometimes tinged with green.

Generally speaking, this medusa ranges from Beaufort, South Carolina, southwest to Tortugas, Florida, but during the latter part of the summer, it is often found off Newport, Rhode Island, and Woods Hole, Massachusetts, in varying numbers.

Eucheilota duodecimalis A. Agassiz PLATE 45. This is a very small but beautifully graceful medusa with a slightly more than hemispherical bell. It is about ⅒ inch

PLATE 45

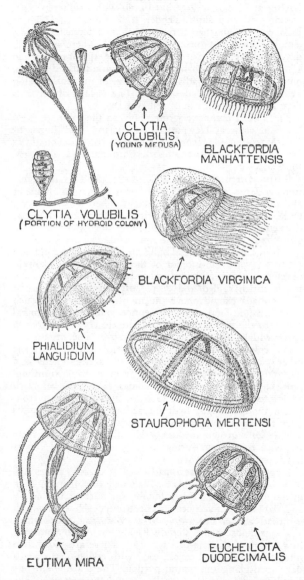

CLYTIA
VOLUBILIS
(YOUNG MEDUSA)

BLACKFORDIA
MANHATTENSIS

CLYTIA VOLUBILIS
(PORTION OF HYDROID COLONY)

BLACKFORDIA VIRGINICA

PHIALIDIUM
LANGUIDUM

STAUROPHORA MERTENSI

EUTIMA MIRA

EUCHEILOTA
DUODECIMALIS

in diameter. There are four slender tentacles, each one having at its base a large basal bulb with a spherical concretion and two short, slender, and conical cirri. Three lithocysts are attached between each two tentacles on the circular canal, thus being twelve in all. There is a well-developed velum. The manubrium is quadrangular in section and quite short. The gonads are situated on the outer portion of the radial canals, those of the female being extremely large and conspicuous. The organs of this medusa are tinged with light yellow-green.

The species occurs very commonly on the southern New England coast at Newport, Rhode Island, and Buzzards Bay, Massachusetts. It is also said to occur occasionally as far south as Charleston, South Carolina, and Tortugas, Florida.

Tima formosa L. Agassiz PLATE 46. This is an extremely large medusa. The bell is 4 inches in diameter and more than 2½ inches in height. There are thirty-two tentacles around the margin, eight of them equaling the diameter of the bell in length. Eight are intermediate in size. Sixteen of them in the intervening spaces are about 1 inch in length. The basal bulbs are long and tapering and recurve toward the interior of the bell. There are a well-developed velum and four radial tubes. The mouth opening is much ruffled and deeply divided into four parts. The gonads extend above the mouth region in a much convoluted fashion along the entire length of the radial canals to the bell margin. The peduncle above the mouth flares widely toward the stomach above. The organs are cream colored to pink and opaque, while the bell and the other parts of the medusae are transparent. There is a hydroid stage which developed from a free-swimming, pear-shaped planula which becomes elongated before it settles to the sea bottom, to form a slender stem from which the cup-shaped hydrothecae branch. The hydranths have twelve long tentacles.

The fully grown medusa is abundant along the New England coast from spring to early summer and occurs north of Cape Cod in winter.

Zygodactyla groenlandica L. Agassiz PLATE 46. This beautiful medusa has a flattened disc from 4 to 5 inches in diameter. The subumbrellar surface is shallow and flat or slightly concave. The trumpet-shaped stomach is broad above, narrowing to a cylindrical tube which again expands to the slightly flaring mouth, terminating in a fringe of delicate oral tentacles. There are more than ninety narrow radial canals, each with convoluted gonads developed along the central portion. There are about one hundred long, slender tentacles around the margin of the umbrella. These tentacles, as well as the circular canals

PLATE 46

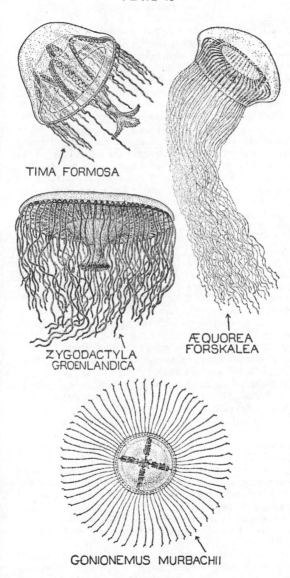

TIMA FORMOSA

ZYGODACTYLA
GROENLANDICA

ÆQUOREA
FORSKALEA

GONIONEMUS MURBACHII

and the gonads, are of a delicate purplish pink with a fainter tinge of this same color suffusing the rest of the medusa.

It is found from the southern coast of Long Island to Beaufort, North Carolina, during summer and autumn. Mature individuals are abundant off the New Jersey coast in October. It is strictly a creature of the open sea.

Aequorea forskalea Peron & Lesueur PLATE 46. This large and extremely beautiful medusa has a flattened, cap-shaped, slightly conical umbrella, which may be 8 to 16 inches in width and ½ inch in height. There are fifty to three hundred tentacles around the margin. These, in different species, have an extraordinary variation ranging from very short to more than three times as long as the diameter of the bell. The manubrium is quite short, flaring to a ruffled margin. The gonads are grouped along the numerous radial canals for nearly the entire length. The colors of these organs range through blue, brown, rose, red, violet, and milky white. It is one of the most variable of all the medusae.

The distribution is wide, extending from Tortugas, Florida, along the entire Atlantic coast of North America, Europe, and the Mediterranean coast.

Lovenella grandis Nutting PLATE 44. The stems of the hydroids are unbranched and rigid, growing from a common stolon. The hydrothecae branch off alternately from the main stem on short pedicels. Each is closed at the top by an operculum with ten to twelve wedge-shaped segments. The long and slender gonangium grows from the axils where the hydrothecae branch off from the main stem. It is more tubular than the hydrotheca. This hydroid produces bell-shaped medusae.

They are abundant on the New England coast, especially in the Woods Hole region and Narragansett Bay.

Opercularella lacerata (Johnston) PLATE 44. The hydroid colonies have a somewhat branched stem arising from a creeping stolon to a height of from ⅗ inch to 1 inch. The entire stem is annulated throughout its sinuous branches. The hydrotheca is spindle-shaped, the operculum continuing its outline so as to come to a point when its segments are closed. The enclosed hydranth possesses about fourteen or fifteen tentacles. The gonangia are bulb-shaped and sessile on the stem.

This species is distributed from Nova Scotia and New Brunswick along the entire New England coast to Long Island Sound.

Opercularella pumila Clark PLATE 44. The hydranths spring in varying lengths from a creeping, branching stolon. The hydrothecae are shaped like those of the preceding species but are much smaller and arise from the stolon independently. The gonangia are fusiform rather than oval and much larger than the hydrothecae.

They occur on wharf piles and similar structures from New Brunswick to Woods Hole and eastern Long Island Sound.

Cuspidella costata Hincks PLATE 44. The hydrothecae are cylindrical in shape and apparently made up of two or three segments. The uppermost terminal of the conical operculum is made up of many segments which converge to a point when closed. The gonosome is unknown.

It has been found sporadically in Fishers Island Sound and off the Gaspé Peninsula.

Calycella syringa (Linnaeus) PLATES 41, 44. The stems of this species are quite minute and simple. The hydrotheca is tube-shaped. An operculum, or cover, of eight to nine hinged angular segments surrounds the circular opening coming to a central peak when closed. The hydranths arise from a creeping stolon found on the surface of algae, as in the illustration on PLATE 41. The pedicel is always annulated.

This species ranges from Hudson Bay and the Gulf of St. Lawrence to Long Island Sound. It is especially abundant along the entire New England coast to Long Island Sound.

Family Lafoeidae

The hydroid is either sessile on a branching stolon or attached to a fascicled stem. The hydrotheca is tubular with no teeth or margin. It is open at the top with no operculum. There is usually no diaphragm. The gonangia are gathered in masses (*coppinia*).

Hebella (Lafoea) pygmaea Hincks PLATE 44. The stolon of this species is a creeping stem with a short annulated pedicel, but the surface of the hydrotheca is smooth and not corrugated. It has no diaphragm, and the gonangia grow in a mass to form a coppinia.

New England coast.

Lafoea dumosa (Fleming) PLATE 48. The stem of this species is fascicled, stiffly erect, and extensively branched. The hydrothecae are curved and tubular, abundantly growing from the main stem from which they are free except at the base. The gonangia form a coppinia, the individual capsules being hexagonal. The mass of gonangia is often pierced by elongated hydrothecae.

Occurs abundantly from Labrador along the entire New England coast.

Lafoea gracillima (Alder) PLATE 48. This species is quite similar to the above, the branches being also dense and bushy. The stems are fascicled. The hydrothecae are long, slender, tubular, and slightly curved. The coppinia is quite similar to that of the above species.

Found off the Nova Scotia and the New England coasts at depths varying from ten to four hundred fathoms.

Family Halecidae

The hydrothecae of the species of this family are extremely short, shell-like tubes in which the hydranths are seated. They are so shallow that the hydranth is exposed even when contracted. The margin is smooth and ornamented with bright dots. The gonophores give rise to attached sporosacs, more or less medusoid in shape, but never reaching a free-swimming condition.

Halecium beanii Johnston PLATES 41, 48. This is a densely branching hydroid forming a complex treelike growth with the hydranths arising alternately from both primary and secondary branches. The gonophores are elongated, arising from the main branches and showing conspicuously in the colony.

From the Bay of Fundy along the New England coast to Long Island Sound.

Halecium halecinum (Linnaeus) PLATES 41, 48. The colony is bushy, arising in clusters of several main stems with the branches going off in pinnate fashion and the hydranths arranged alternately upon these branches. The gonangia occur in rows on the secondary branches.

From the Bay of Fundy along the New England coast and Long Island Sound.

Halecium articulosum Clark PLATE 48. The round stem is fascicled and has an irregular, stunted appearance. The terminal branches are white. There are short internodes, each with one stunted hydrotheca on its shoulder. The female gonangia are large and mitten-shaped with the opening on one side near the distal end. The male gonangia are tubular. The species occurs generally along the New England coast from the Bay of Fundy to Long Island Sound at depths from five to about thirty fathoms.

Halecium gracile Verrill PLATE 48. This is a bushy, luxuriantly branched colony with a fascicled stem. The branches are long, slender, and more or less alternate. The hydrothecae are like expanded goblets, sometimes two or three of them appearing to be nested. The gonangia of the female arise from the axils between the main stem and the hydrothecae. They are asymmetrically developed, bulging out in front away from the main stem, the narrow neck having a projecting tubular collar.

The species occurs from New Brunswick to Martha's Vineyard and Long Island.

Halecium tenellum Hincks PLATE 48. This delicate colony is sparsely branched and about ⅜ inch in height.

The trumpet-shaped hydrothecae are given off alternately and at a considerable distance from the wavy subannulated stems. The bladderlike, irregularly oval gonangia arise from the axils of the branches of the main stem.

This species is found along the North American coast from New Brunswick to Florida in depths varying from eight to forty or fifty fathoms.

Diphasia fallax (Johnston) PLATES 41, 48. The main stem of this species is erect and branching to form graceful clusters terminating in tendril-like fashion. It may reach 4 inches in length. The hydrothecae are in two rows, the individuals being practically opposite to each other. They are short and stout. The gonangia are large and conspicuous. The male is fusiform in shape with four projecting lobes at the four-sided distal end. The female gonangium is still larger and terminates in four long projections.

This species occurs abundantly from the Bay of Fundy, along the New England coast, to the Woods Hole region and Narragansett Bay. It has also been recorded in deeper water off Charleston, South Carolina.

Diphasia rosacea (Linnaeus) PLATE 48. This is a delicate colony reaching about 4 inches in length with sparse, alternating branches and slender, obtusely bent hydrothecae, opposite to each other, having a single undivided operculum. The hydranths are quite slender. The male gonangium is pear-shaped with eight long ridgelike divisions. The female is larger and has two long, low lobes and six shorter ones.

The species occurs from Labrador to Vineyard Sound in depths from nine to fifty fathoms.

Family Sertularidae

Colonial hydroids having sessile hydrothecae, most of which bud from both sides of the stems and branches, the hydrothecae being in close contact with the stem structure. In some cases (*Hydrallmania*) the hydrothecae spring from only one side of the stem, with their apertures turned alternately to the right and left. In most of the genera, however, the hydrothecae are seated on the stem in two longitudinal rows, either opposite to each other or alternating. These colonies are often mosslike, or fernlike, sometimes producing beautiful, delicately branched plumes, which float out into the water.

Hydrallmania falcata (Linnaeus) PLATES 47, 49. This colony has a long, slender, undulating stem from which branches are given off more or less alternately, each having secondary side branches of fernlike aspect. The colony, as a whole, often grows about a foot in length. The hydrothecae occur only on the secondary branches and are tubular in shape. They are seated on only one side of the branch but bend alternately right and left. There is an egg-shaped gonangium, which may rise from either a primary or secondary branch. It is smooth and without spines.

This species is distributed from the Arctic Ocean and Labrador along the entire coast of New England to Long Island Sound.

Sertularella gayi Lamouroux PLATES 47, 49. This species forms a colony with relatively stiff primary, secondary, and tertiary branches, on the last two of which the hydrothecae bud off alternately. The colony, as a whole, may be 6 inches in length. The hydrothecae are broad with about one third of the base attached to the stem with four teeth on the margin. The gonangia are on the upper side of the branches and are long and slender.

This species is distributed from Georges Bank along the entire Atlantic Coast to Florida, the West Indies, and Leeward Islands. Along the Gulf Coast, it extends as far as Yucatan.

Sertularella rugosa (Linnaeus) PLATES 47, 49. This species has small, usually unbranched colonies growing abundantly from the stems of various seaweeds in all directions. The stem of the colony is more or less annulated and rough. The hydrothecae are alternate and have horizontal ridges or rings. The margin has four weak teeth. There is an operculum of four triangular sections. At intervals, a conspicuous gonangium branches off instead of a hydrotheca. It is also ridged, with four teeth on the margin.

This species ranges from Labrador and the Gulf of St. Lawrence along the New England coast.

Sertularella tricuspidata (Alder) PLATES 47, 48. This species grows in very delicate, loosely branching colonies from the stems of seaweeds with fairly numerous gonangia springing conspicuously from both stems and branches. The hydrothecae are alternate and somewhat separated from each other, with three teeth on the margin, and enclosed at the aperture by an operculum having three valves. The oval gonangia are conspicuously ornamented with about eight or nine horizontal, thin, shelflike ridges around the urn-shaped gonotheca.

This species occurs from Labrador, along the entire New England coast, to New Jersey.

Sertularella abietina Linnaeus PLATE 48. From the stout, main stem of this species, the large primary branches extend in pinnate fashion. The hydrothecae are crowded closely together, alternately tapering from a large base to a narrow opening. The gonangia are oval and nearly smooth.

PLATE 47

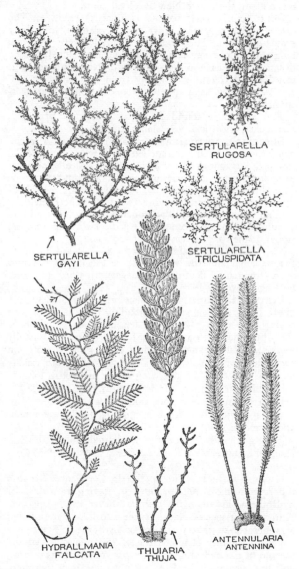

SERTULARELLA
RUGOSA

SERTULARELLA
GAYI

SERTULARELLA
TRICUSPIDATA

HYDRALLMANIA
FALCATA

THUIARIA
THUJA

ANTENNULARIA
ANTENNINA

The range is from Labrador and the Gulf of St. Lawrence along the entire New England coast.

Sertularella polyzonias (Linnaeus) PLATE 49. The colonies of this species grow from a slender, irregularly branching stem. The branches themselves are relatively long and undulating. The hydrothecae are situated at some distance from each other. They are relatively large and urn-shaped, extending obliquely from the somewhat zigzag stem. They have four teeth and a four-parted operculum.

This species is found from Labrador to Cape Cod, Nantucket, and the Long Island Sound.

Sertularia cornicina (McCrady) PLATE 48. The colony grows with an unbranched stem from a threadlike stolon to a height of about ½ inch. The hydrothecae grow in opposite pairs, one pair to each internode of the colony. They bend abruptly from the main stem, the margin of their terminal aperture having two teeth. The operculum consists of two sections. The gonangia are urn-shaped and annulated, growing from a short pedicel, directly from the stolon at the base of the stem of the colony.

This species occurs abundantly from Vineyard Sound to the Bahamas and the west coast of Florida. It is found most frequently floating on sargassum weed or other floating seaweeds.

Sertularia pumila Linnaeus PLATES 41, 48; COLOR PLATE III, 4, 4a. The stiffly upstanding main stems of each colony may reach 2 inches in length. They usually have their branches placed opposite to each other occasionally with secondary branchlets. They often grow in tufts on *Fucus* and other seaweeds. The hydrothecae are exactly opposite to each other and cling to the main stem for two thirds of their tubular, curving length. The gonangia are urn-shaped and have a wide opening with a shallow rim at the summit. They occur irregularly on the main stem and branches.

This species is abundantly distributed from Labrador, along the entire New England coast, to Stonington, Connecticut.

Genus **Thuiaria**. The species in the Genus *Thuiaria* differ from those in *Sertularia* in having two rows of hydrothecae in which the pairs are never strictly opposite. A number of species, however, seem to have a transitional arrangement in that the pairs of hydrothecae are nearly opposite. Another characteristic of this genus is that the margin of the hydrothecae never has more than two teeth, and the operculum is closed by not more than two flaps. In some species, the gonangia are smooth; in others, there are two spines on the shoulders.

PLATE 48

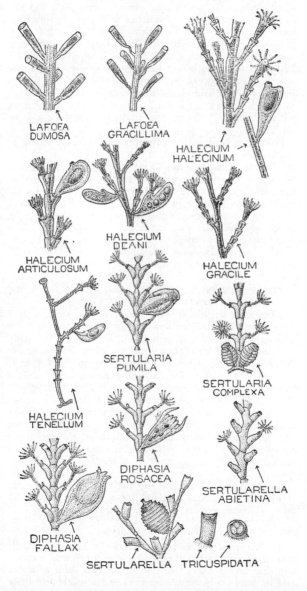

LAFOEA DUMOSA

LAFOEA GRACILLIMA

HALECIUM HALECINUM

HALECIUM ARTICULOSUM

HALECIUM DEANI

HALECIUM GRACILE

HALECIUM TENELLUM

SERTULARIA PUMILA

SERTULARIA COMPLEXA

DIPHASIA ROSACEA

SERTULARELLA ABIETINA

DIPHASIA FALLAX

SERTULARELLA TRICUSPIDATA

Thuiaria thuja (Linnaeus) PLATES 47, 49. The colony is about a foot in length, consisting of a rigid and zigzag main stem with the branches forming a symmetrical spiral of palmate growths making a stiff, dense tuft. It is popularly called "bottlebrush." The branchlets of the stem are somewhat flattened, and the small, alternate, tubular hydrothecae are adherent throughout nearly their entire length. They have no teeth, and there is but one flap to the operculum. The abundant gonangia often form rows at the base of the branches. They are oval, or urn-shaped, with a collared aperture and smooth exterior having no spines.

From the Gulf of St. Lawrence and Georges Bank to Nantucket.

Thuiaria cupressina (Linnaeus) PLATE 49. The colony has a somewhat wavy stem from which the plumelike tufts of branches take off alternately. It may grow to twelve inches or more in length. The pairs of hydrothecae alternate and are largely adherent to the stem. The margin of the aperture has two rather inconspicuous teeth. The operculum has two flaps. The gonangia are quite characteristic, being triangular in shape, with two conspicuous horns on the shoulders on either side of the circular aperture.

The distribution is abundant along the Canadian and New England coasts from Labrador to Long Island Sound.

Thuiaria argentea (Linnaeus) PLATE 49. This is a conspicuous species, its colonial tufts being a foot or more in length. The branches arise from all sides of the stem, and each branchlet divides into two parts. The name of the species comes from the rather silvery, shiny appearance of the colony. The hydrothecae are fairly distant from each other and regularly alternate. For the most part they are embedded in the stem. The margin has two teeth, one of which is usually longer than the other. The operculum has two flaps. The gonangia spring from near the base of the hydrothecae and have an elongated, triangular form with two well-developed shoulder spines and an aperture at the summit of a moderately projecting collar.

Common from Labrador and the Gulf of St. Lawrence along the entire New England coast, and the middle Atlantic shores generally, to Cape Hatteras.

Family Plumularidae

In this family the colonies have a characteristically plumelike effect since the hydrothecae are found on only one side of the branch instead of on two sides as is the case in the Family Sertularidae. They are sessile and more or less adherent to the stem. Nematophores are always

PLATE 49

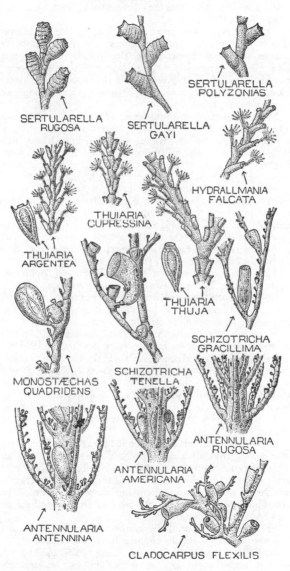

SERTULARELLA
RUGOSA

SERTULARELLA
GAYI

SERTULARELLA
POLYZONIAS

THUIARIA
CUPRESSINA

HYDRALLMANIA
FALCATA

THUIARIA
ARGENTEA

THUIARIA
THUJA

SCHIZOTRICHA
GRACILLIMA

MONOSTÆCHAS
QUADRIDENS

SCHIZOTRICHA
TENELLA

ANTENNULARIA
RUGOSA

ANTENNULARIA
ANTENNINA

ANTENNULARIA
AMERICANA

CLADOCARPUS FLEXILIS

present, usually between the hydranths on the main stem and branches. The branches bearing the hydranths are called *hydrocladia*.

The gonangia are large, often bladderlike structures which give rise to planulae instead of medusae. More species of hydroids belong to this family than to any other. They are mostly tropical, but a number of species, examples of which I give in this field book, are found along the Atlantic coast of North America throughout the temperate zone.

Monostaechas quadridens (McCrady) PLATE 49. This colony has a very striking appearance as it consists of a thin, elongated stem dividing into two branches, which in turn divide again to produce a series of long, slender hydrocladia rising vertically and parallel with each other from the upper side of the stem. Each of these consists of a series of short internodes, a cup-shaped hydrotheca, partly adherent, growing out diagonally, on nearly every other internode. The margins of these hydrothecae are entire. The oval·gonangia rise from a stemlike projection just beneath a hydrotheca. The nematophores are borne on very slender, elongated stems springing from the bases of the hydrothecae or even from the vacant internodes.

The distribution is from Martha's Vineyard along the coast to Cape Hatteras, Charleston, and Florida.

Schizotricha gracillima (Sars) PLATE 49. The colony grows to a height of 2½ inches with a fascicled, zigzag stem from which double branches are given off alternately. The hydrothecae are cup-shaped and partly adherent to the stem on about every other internode. They are about the same diameter as their depth. The nematophores are large and with two chambers. The gonangia occur in pairs on the lower part of the stem near the axil. They are cylindrical. The nematophores are scattered over the stem.

Along the New England coast at depths from ten to twenty fathoms.

Schizotricha tenella (Verrill) PLATE 49. This delicate colony is about 2 inches in height, its slender, zigzag stem bearing branching hydrocladia. The hydrothecae are small and attached on every other internode with two or three nematophores occurring between them. The gonangia grow from near the base of the hydrotheca as curved, clublike projections.

This species occurs off the southern New England coast and southward in depths from eight to ten fathoms.

Antennularia americana Nutting PLATE 49. The colony is about eight or ten inches in height, sparsely branched, if at all. There is a stout stem with branches (hydrocladia) in whorls giving a brushlike appearance.

PLATE 50

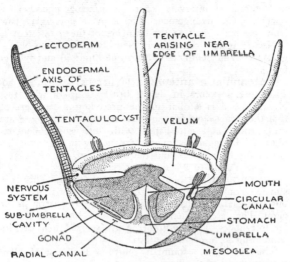

ECTODERM

ENDODERMAL AXIS OF TENTACLES

TENTACLE ARISING NEAR EDGE OF UMBRELLA

TENTACULOCYST

VELUM

NERVOUS SYSTEM

MOUTH

CIRCULAR CANAL

SUB-UMBRELLA CAVITY

STOMACH

GONAD

UMBRELLA

RADIAL CANAL

MESOGLEA

A TYPICAL TRACHYMEDUSAN
SHOWING ANATOMY

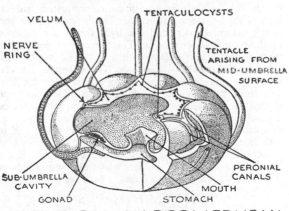

VELUM

TENTACULOCYSTS

NERVE RING

TENTACLE ARISING FROM MID-UMBRELLA SURFACE

SUB-UMBRELLA CAVITY

PERONIAL CANALS

GONAD

MOUTH

STOMACH

A TYPICAL NARCOMEDUSAN
SHOWING ANATOMY

For the most part, the hydrothecae occur on every other internode. They are small and cup-shaped. Between the hydrothecae at intervals occur small nematophores in a fairly regular arrangement. The obovate gonangia grow from the axils between the branches of the main stem.

New England coast from New Brunswick to Narragansett Bay in depths of fifty to one hundred and twenty fathoms.

Antennularia antennina (Linnaeus) PLATES 47, 49. This species occurs in dense, brushy clusters with few branches and is similar to the preceding species except that the stems have few internodes. The hydrothecae are quite small and cup-shaped with intervening nematophores. The gonangia appear frequently in the axils between the hydrocladia and the main stem.

Bay of Fundy to Narragansett Bay.

Antennularia rugosa Nutting PLATE 49. This is a sturdy colony reaching a height of 6 inches or more without branches. The hydrocladia occur in whorls of six or eight. They are swollen below and have long and irregular internodes. The hydrothecae are sparse, their cavities containing septa or thickenings.

This species was found by Nutting southeast of Nantucket in forty-six fathoms.

Cladocarpus flexilis Verrill PLATE 49. The colony may be 9 inches in height with a long central stem from which the hydrocladia are given off on either side to form a feather-shaped structure. The branches have very closely set internodes, and the hydrothecae are adherent by their entire inner margin. The aperture of each hydrotheca has a large median tooth and several small tooth-shaped projections on either side. The gonangia are very numerous and arise thickly from all sides of the stem and from the bases of the hydrocladia. They are club-shaped in appearance with a round, ovate, somewhat depressed opening at the top of the hydrotheca. There are two nematophores at the base of each hydrocladia and on each internode.

The distribution is Vineyard Sound and along the Atlantic Coast southward to Alabama in depths from thirty-five to about one hundred fathoms or more.

Order TRACHYMEDUSAE
(INDEX PLATE 50)

In this order, the hydroid stage appears to be completely lacking in most cases and, when present, is of minute size and more or less insignificant, while the medusae are of large size with four, six, or eight radial canals bearing gonads on the subumbrellar surface. The alternation of generations, therefore, usually appears to be absent. The medusae give rise directly to medusae instead of hydroids, although the hydroid stage may be present, but incipiently developed, in the gonads. Specialized sense organs in the form of lithocysts project on the margin of the umbrella, or they may be enclosed in pockets. A velum is present around the bell margin.

Family Olindiadae

This family includes medusae having a velum, in which the tentacles either arise from above the margin of the exumbrella or, in some cases, from the bell margin itself. Most of the tentacles have adhesive pads and various types of gonads upon the radial canals.

These are shallow-water, bottom-living medusae. The adhesive pads near the outer ends of the tentacles assist them in getting about over the sea bottom. A set of tentacles may also radiate from the margin of the velum. The former series are quite stiff, while the latter are flexible, hollow, and with or without adhesive pads. Batteries of nematocysts occur in ringlike groups. Gonads are developed on the walls of the radial canals, often as convoluted ruffles.

Gonionemus murbachii Mayer PLATE 46; COLOR PLATE IV, 6. This beautiful and delicate little medusa has an umbrella about ⅘ inch in diameter and about half that measurement in height. The tentacles are ¾ as long as the diameter of the bell and extend out stiffly on all sides. These are sixty to eighty in number and are equipped with successive series of ringlike batteries of sting-cells. Near the tip of each tentacle, there is an adhesive organ equipped with nematocysts, beyond which the tentacle sharply bends to a right angle. These pads enable the medusa to cling to seaweed and other objects on the sea bottom. The spindle-shaped manubrium is cruciform in cross section while the four lips are abruptly recurved. There is a series of marginal sense organs, each separated from its neighbor by two tentacles, and consisting of a small club. There are four straight radial canals extending from the manubrium to the bell margin, on each of which there is a much-ruffled gonad which, if straightened out, would be longer than the radial canals. The manubrium itself is dark brown tinged with pink, while the lips are whitish. A bright green pigment spot is at the base of each tentacle. This medusa is very abundant in Eel Pond, at Woods Hole, Massachusetts. Its range extends from the Woods Hole region to Noank, Connecticut.

Family Petasidae

This family is closely related to the Olindiadae on one hand and to the Geryonidae on the other. It differs from the Olindiadae in its simple tentacles, while in the latter family, the tentacles are equipped with adhesive pads. The gonads of the Petasidae are saclike and stand out in compact bunches from the radial canals, whereas in the Geryonidae, the gonads are leaflike expansions. Certain species are characteristic of fresh water.

Microhydra ryderi Potts PLATE 51. This remarkable medusa is budded off from a hydra of the same name occurring in a fresh-water stream near Philadelphia. The hydra is a simple tube attached at one end and with a mouth at the other devoid of tentacles. It reproduces asexually by budding off individuals like itself. The medusa is budded off from one side of the tube and is characterized by possessing eight tentacles, four radial canals, and four lips. It has neither lithocysts nor ocelli. It is quite minute, being about 1/40 inch in diameter. The adult medusa is not known. The hydroid devours the minute organisms known as rotifers, capturing them by means of its sting-cells.

Craspedacusta sowerbii Lankester PLATE 51. This peculiar medusa was probably native of South America or the West Indies and was doubtless brought to Europe and the United States with tropical water plants naturalized in the tanks of botanical gardens. It was first described by Lankester from a water-lily tank containing *Victoria regia* in Regent's Park, London, and has since been found in other water-lily tanks in European countries and the United States. It feeds upon *Daphnia*, a minute fresh-water crustacean. The adult medusa has a hemispherical bell about 1/2 inch in diameter. There are about 200 marginal tentacles which apparently were produced in fours, as they vary in length according to age and four of them are by far the longest. They are attached to the bell some distance above the margin and are very contractile. There are no ocelli. There are about 128 lithocysts suspended from the margin at irregular intervals between tentacles. There are four radial canals, each bearing a gonad. The manubrium with the mouth at its end extends considerably below the level of the bell margin.

The hydroid grows in colonies of two or three individuals from a common base. It is attached to the undersides of leaves floating on the water surface in the lily tanks. The polypites are about 1/4 inch long, cylindrical, and have no tentacles.

Aglaura hemistoma Peron & Lesueur PLATE 51. The bell of this curiously cap-shaped medusa is about 1/4 inch in height in the female, and about 3/8 inch in the male. The female has a circlet of from forty-eight to eighty-five rigid tentacles radiating from the bell margin with slightly club-shaped ends. The stomach is flask-shaped and bears a circlet of eight oval gonads around its stem. The mouth

PLATE 51

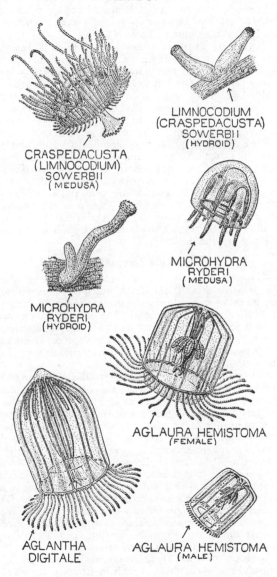

CRASPEDACUSTA
(LIMNOCODIUM)
SOWERBII
(MEDUSA)

LIMNOCODIUM
(CRASPEDACUSTA)
SOWERBII
(HYDROID)

MICROHYDRA
RYDERI
(MEDUSA)

MICROHYDRA
RYDERI
(HYDROID)

AGLAURA HEMISTOMA
(FEMALE)

AGLANTHA
DIGITALE

AGLAURA HEMISTOMA
(MALE)

has four lobes. The male has very short stublike tentacles. The species is common in warm and tropical waters and may be captured abundantly by the surface townet. It is distributed throughout all seas.

Aglantha digitale Haeckel PLATE 51. This beautiful and graceful medusa is nearly 1¼ inch in height with a series of eighty to one hundred long, almost S-shaped, brittle tentacles. The bell comes to a rounded point at the apex. One of the most important characteristics of this species, which it possesses in common with all the others of the genus, consists of the eight long, slender gonads attached to the eight radial canals on the subumbrellar surface. The long peduncle is spindle-shaped and extends from the apex of the subumbrellar surface until it terminates in a four-lobed mouth at the level of the bell margin. The medusa is very translucent and displays iridescent colors. The gonads are pale yellow while the stomach and tentacles are pink. There is no fixed hydroid stage for either *Aglaura* or *Aglantha* as the development is direct. There is an *actinula* larva which is transformed directly into the medusa.

Family Geryonidae

"Trachymedusae with 4 or 6 radial-canals upon which the leaf-like gonads are developed. The lithocysts-clubs are in enclosed sacs buried in the gelatinous substance of the bell above the ring-canal. The stomach is mounted upon a peduncle. There may be blindly-ending, centripetal canals between the radial canals. Development is through a free-swimming actinula, which becomes transformed into the medusa." (Mayer)

Genus **Liriope.** Four-rayed Geryonidae with four radial canals, four lips, four gonads, and one or more blind, centripetal canals in each interradial quadrant. With four primary solid, radial, four permanent, hollow, radial, and four solid, interradial tentacles, all twelve of which may or may not be found upon the medusa at one and the same time. Eight enclosed lithocysts, four radial and four interradial. Development direct.

In common with other Trachymedusae the species of *Liriope* are very widely distributed, being abundant in all warm seas although unknown from polar regions. The species are exceedingly difficult to separate, for the shape of the gonads, length of peduncle, and the number of centripetal canals are apt to be variable, and also change greatly in appearance as growth proceeds.

Liriope exigua Quoy & Gaimard PLATE 52. This beautiful medusa is about ½ inch in diameter. It possesses an almost perfectly hemispherical bell with a narrow velum. There are four hollow tentacles undulating from

the margin, the long, gracefully tapering peduncle terminating in a four-lobed trumpetlike mouth. Also, on the
margin, there are eight enclosed lithocysts. Four heart-
shaped gonads are situated on the four radial canals.
They are quite conspicuous as they are rosy red in color,
although in some specimens they may be green. The medusa develops directly from an actinulalike larva.

This species is found throughout the warm parts of the
Atlantic and Mediterranean Oceans.

Liriope conirostris Haeckel PLATE 52. This species
is somewhat over ½ inch in height and possesses a rather
elongate thimble-shaped bell and a long tapering manubrium. The gonads extend nearly the entire length of the
radial canals and are leaf-shaped, adorned with green
streaks. Green spots are seen on the stomach and upper
part of the manubrium. The four long trailing tentacles
are equipped with ringlike batteries of sting-cells.

This species has been found in our waters off the coast
of Virginia.

Liriope catharinensis F. Müller PLATE 52. The gelatinous substance of the bell of this species is very thick.
It is shaped like a flattened cone. The gonads of several
shapes found on the radial canals are green in color. The
bell may be ¾ inch in height.

The species is found abundantly from Brazil to Cape
Cod, Massachusetts.

Liriope scutigera McCrady PLATE 52. The bell has
slightly sinuous sides rounding into a flattened top. It is
about ¾ inch in diameter. The four tentacles are pink.
The yellow manubrium, with its open four-parted mouth,
hangs some distance outside the bell and is yellow-green
in color. The gonads on the four radial canals are flattened
oval and pale green in color.

This is a very abundant species found along the entire
Atlantic Coast of North America south of Cape Cod.

Order NARCOMEDUSAE
(INDEX PLATE 50)

In this order, the hydroid stage is apparently entirely
lacking, the young medusae reproducing directly from the
parent medusae. In the development, the egg hatches into
an actinula larva, and this is transformed directly into
a medusa by the outgrowth of the bell so that the tentacles of the actinula become those of the medusa and the
bell grows out between the tentacles. Gonads are found
along the radial canals or upon subumbrellar pouches.
There is a large, lens-shaped stomach cavity centrally located, often with radiating pouches or canals. The bell
margin is characterized by lappets with a delicate velum
bridging over them, which forms a continuous ring, par-

tially closing the opening of the umbrella cavity. The umbrella also has freely projecting sensory clubs arising from thickenings equipped with bristles. A cushionlike pad (*peronium*), acting as a support, is situated beneath the base of each tentacle, which are always solid and extend stiffly from the outside of the midumbrellar surface of the medusa, at the notches between the lappets.

The *Narcomedusae* are, therefore, a specialized group not related to the *Anthomedusae* and *Leptomedusae*.

Pegantha clara R. P. Bigelow PLATE 52. In this species, the twenty-eight tentacles are equal in number to the lappets and grow out from between their notches. Every other tentacle is longer than the intervening ones. The insertions of the long tentacles are farther above the margins than those of the short tentacles. They are all slender and taper to finely pointed tips. There is a simple ringshaped velum with powerful circular muscles. The bell is more than 2 inches in diameter and nearly an inch thick. It is milky in color.

This species was found by Professor R. P. Bigelow in the Gulf Stream.

Cunoctantha octonaria Haeckel PLATE 52. The somewhat flattened bell has eight tentacles projecting stiffly from its outer circumference, arising about midway between the margin and the apex. They have almost no motion, but each contains many sting cells. There are twenty-four sense organs in the adult, each upon a small elevation of the bell margin, which is known as the sensory cushion. There is a complex velum consisting of a ring-shaped membrane, but also extending upward as eight wedge-shaped webs between the eight loops of the nerve cord. The cone-shaped manubrium terminates in four angular lips. The medusa is completely transparent with slight tinges of green near the tentacles and lips. One curious fact in connection with its development is that the larva produces other larvae like itself by budding.

This medusa is found in all tropical seas and is common from Charleston to Beaufort, North Carolina.

Order SIPHONOPHORA

This order of the hydroids includes free-swimming colonies of individuals which are specialized for different functions, with their structures varying according to the function in each case. Such colonies are termed polymorphic. The colony as a whole, therefore, possesses individuals exemplifying a division of labor similar to that of the various types of organs in the body of higher animals. Thus, digestion is performed by digestive individuals; reproduction by reproductive individuals of two different sexes; swimming by special swimming individ-

PLATE 52

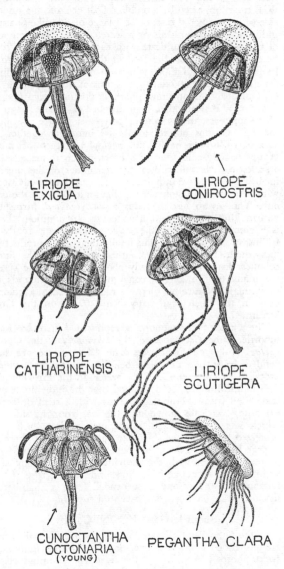

LIRIOPE
EXIGUA

LIRIOPE
CONIROSTRIS

LIRIOPE
CATHARINENSIS

LIRIOPE
SCUTIGERA

CUNOCTANTHA
OCTONARIA
(YOUNG)

PEGANTHA CLARA

uals, and so on. The various kinds bud from a common axial tube supported by a bulblike float or from the underside of a chambered disc, or of a large bladderlike floating individual filled with air or a secreted gas. The members of the colony communicate with each other through connecting tubes so that the food of the feeding polyps may be passed along to those which do not have the feeding function. When the axial tube is present, the upper end is kept afloat by the pneumatophore, or floating polyp (INDEX PLATE 53). Beneath this, in a number of species, a series of nectophores, or swimming polyps, is grouped around the axis. Groups of individuals are bunched together in successive clusters below the nectophore, each of these groups usually consisting of a *bract,* which is shaped like a scale, to cover and protect the remainder of the cluster, including a nutritive individual and a *gastrozooid* equipped with a mouth and stomach for digesting food for the colony. The group also contains a *dactylozooid* furnished with a long tentacle and nematocysts. In addition, there is a club-shaped polyp, the *palp,* which is apparently a feeling or tasting polyp; and finally there are reproductive individuals, the *gonozooids,* either male or female. Such colonies float or swim slowly about and, in some cases, are many feet in length, containing many thousands of individuals. Naturally, there is room for such a colony only in the open sea, many being found in the Gulf Stream.

The Order Siphonophora is represented here by four suborders: the *Calyconectae,* the *Physonectae,* the *Cystonectae,* and the *Disconectae.* The Calyconectae are suspended from one or more bell-like nectophores which propel the colonies through the water. In the Physonectae, the colonies may be so organized that the individuals are suspended from a bulb-shaped float with a stem or corm extending vertically down into the sea, from the sides of which sets of specialized polyps may project, each one protected by a bract or shield. In the Cystonectae, there is a large bladderlike float, the shape of which may undergo protean changes, with the individuals of the colony suspended from one edge of its lower side. In the case of the Disconectae, the colony is suspended from a chambered disclike float, having a large central mouth.

Suborder CALYCONECTAE

In the Suborder Calyconectae, the groups of individuals are suspended from one, two, or more swimming organs (nectophores). Apparently, this is a condition which is secondary to suspension by a float, for there is what appears to be a rudiment of a previous small float within the jellylike substance of the swimming-bell.

PLATE 53

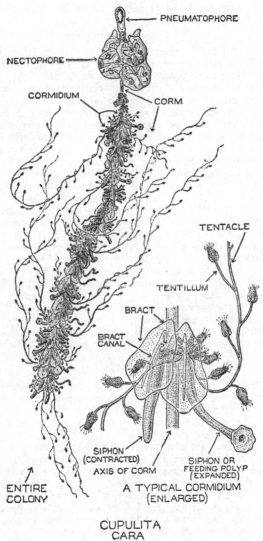

ENTIRE COLONY

A TYPICAL CORMIDIUM (ENLARGED)

CUPULITA CARA

There are two families in this Suborder, the *Monophyidae* and the *Diphyidae*. In the former family there is but one nectophore, while in the Diphyidae there are two nectophores.

Family Monophyidae

In this family, there is but one nectophore (swimmingbell), which may be miter-shaped or spherical. This may be primary and persistent throughout the life of the organism; or secondary, a temporary primary nectophore having been formed and then thrown off, after having budded off a secondary nectophore which is the persistent swimming-bell. The *cormidia* (groups of individuals) are suspended at intervals on a main stem. These are detached as free-swimming *Eudoxia* or *Ersaea* sexual generations (*Ersaea picta*, PLATE 55).

Sphaeronectes gracilis (Claus) PLATE 55. This species has a spherical primary swimming-bell (nectophore) which is retained throughout life. As in other members of this suborder (*Calyconectae*), the colony is kept afloat only by the swimming motion of the nectophore, though there is a rudiment of a float (pneumatophore) and oil globule, which may be seen through the thick gelatinous upper portion of the bell. A deep, ectodermic pit on one side gives rise to a stem (stolon) from which groups of polymorphic individuals (cormidia) are budded forth. Each group in this species consists of a feeding polyp; a fighting polyp, or tentacle, equipped with stinging-cells (nematocysts); a reproductive polyp (gonad), and a swimming-bell (nectophore). Each cormidium becomes detached as a reproductive generation (*Eudoxia*).

Family Diphyidae

In this family, the primary nectophore is discarded, leaving two pyramidal nectophores instead of *one* as in the Family Monophyidae.

This is a diverse family with many species, of which several are described here.

Diphyopsis campanulifera Eschscholtz (= *D. compressa* Haeckel) PLATE 54. This beautiful species has two angular and tapering nectophores or swimming polyps of similar size, placed one behind the other. The first one is a little larger than the other, with the contractile swimming organ on its ventral side. It is strongly compressed laterally and there are five prominent ridges meeting in the slender pointed top of the nectophore.

The second basal nectophore is of the same length as the first but narrower. It is the contraction of these two nectophores that drives the colony forward and keeps it at the surface. Between the nectophores, two wings have

PLATE 54

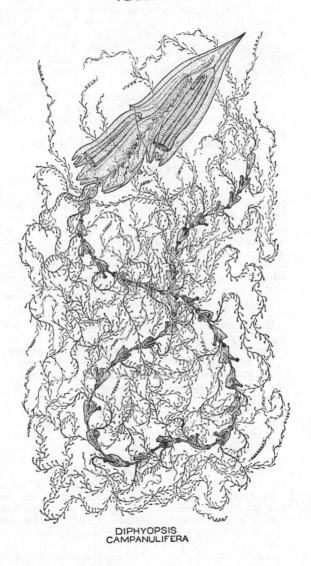

DIPHYOPSIS
CAMPANULIFERA

grown together to form a canal from which springs the
common stem of the colony, a slender tubule extending
for a considerable length into the water. Attached to this
stem, at regular intervals, are series of cormidia. In large
specimens there may be ninety or more, each one with a
protective bract which is something like a cape, enclosing
a feeding polyp, a tasting polyp, and a long, threadlike
tentacle with numerous branches bearing powerful sting-
cells. These extend far down into the water and sting to
death the small creatures which form the food of the
colony. They are digested by the feeding polyps in each
cormidium.

This species occurs in the open sea and especially in the
warm waters of the Gulf Stream.

Ersaea picta Chun PLATE 55. This is the free sexual
generation of *Diphyopsis picta* (Chun), the polygastric
generation closely related to *Diphyopsis compressa*
Haeckel, above described, the fertilized eggs of this generation developing into the adult form.

Diphyes bipartita Costa PLATE 55. This species differs from *Diphyopsis compressa* chiefly in the fact that the
second nectophore is attached to the first by a more
elongated neck so that it is less compact in its structure,
while the apex of the first nectophore is shorter and
blunter than in the case of *Diphyopsis*.

Subfamily Abylinae

Diphyidae with two angular, pyramidal, or prismatic
nectophores of different size and form. The basal nectophore is three-sided-pyramidal, asymmetrical, and much
larger than the symmetrical apical nectophore. Bracts six-
sided-prismatic, with a vertically descending phyllocyst, and
two lateral, horizontally diverging canals, arising from its
apex.

Abyla quincunx (Chun) PLATE 56. This species consists of a single nectophore or swimming polyp, having five
angular ridges surrounding the opening of the nectophore,
which give the name to the species. The axis of the colony
buds from a cavity at one side and is shown here in the
initial stages of its growth with several cormidia beginning to develop. Above the origin of the axis may be seen
a small vestige of an oil globule which does not become
functional in this genus.

Abyla pentagona Eschscholtz PLATE 56. This is a
similar species shown in the figure in approximately the
same stage of development.

Abyla trigona (Quoy & Gaimard); **Abyla perforata**
Gegenbaur PLATE 56. These two related species are shown
here with the axis in progressive stages of development.
In *Abyla trigona,* the tentacles bearing sting-cell batteries

PLATE 55

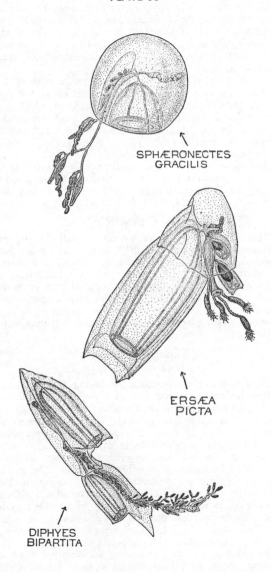

SPHÆRONECTES
GRACILIS

ERSÆA
PICTA

DIPHYES
BIPARTITA

are developed first and are shown in successive stages, with the most fully developed terminating the axis. In *Abyla perforata,* the cormidia show the various component individuals more fully developed. All the species of this genus are found in open seas and are brought up through the Atlantic Ocean by the Gulf Stream, spurs from which may bring them nearer to our coast.

As the cormidia fully mature, they become detached as a free-swimming stage generally spoken of as the free-sexual generation, the various individuals of which may produce male or female gonads. After fertilization takes place in the open sea, the larva grows into a new asexual polygastric generation.

Aglaisma gegenbauri Haeckel PLATE 56. The free sexual generation of *Abyla pentagona* is referred to as *Aglaisma gegenbauri* because it was formerly supposed to belong to a different genus until the life history was known.

Suborder PHYSONECTAE

These are siphonophores having a small float (pneumatophore) continuous with a long axial tube from which bud nectophores (swimming polyps) and successive groups with similar assortments of specialized individuals. Each group (*cormidium*) consists of a protective bract, a palp (feeling and tasting organ), a gastrozooid (feeding polyp), having a tentacle equipped with a series of stinging batteries, and a gonozooid (reproductive individual).

Family Agalmidae
(INDEX PLATE 53)

This family is characterized by having attached to its long axis two alternating rows of nectophores in addition to the successive groups of individuals.

Cupulita cara (A. Agassiz). There are four to six nectophores in each row. The cormidia vary in the number of specialized individuals in each group. The nectophores are locked together obliquely, their winglike projections fitting closely together in dovetail fashion. The float above them is comparatively small, forming an elliptical cavity containing a bubble of oily substance with no connection to the axis of the colony or to the outside. The coloration of this colony is well described by A. Agassiz. "The float is a brilliant garnet color; from it hangs the rosy-colored axis, with its pale swimming bells, and farther down, the scale, protecting the different kinds of feeding polyps, with their various kinds of tentacles projecting in all sorts of angles and curves from the main axis of the body, like the festoons of a chandelier; the

PLATE 56

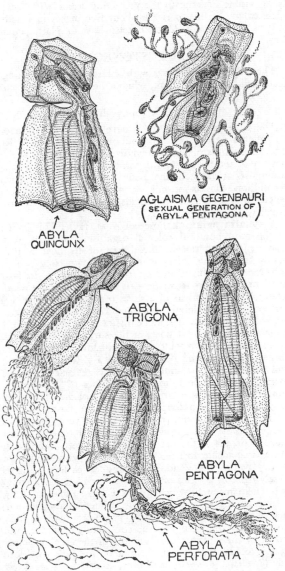

ABYLA
QUINCUNX

AGLAISMA GEGENBAURI
(SEXUAL GENERATION OF
ABYLA PENTAGONA)

ABYLA
TRIGONA

ABYLA
PENTAGONA

ABYLA
PERFORATA

darker colored polyps, tipped and mottled with scarlet, being visible underneath the protecting scales." The complete colony of this species is about five inches in length.

It is found from Massachusetts Bay to Narragansett Bay.

Suborder CYSTONECTAE

These are siphonophores with a large, hollow, floating, bladderlike pneumatophore, without nectophores or bracts.

Family Rhizophysaliidae

The large pneumatophore is developed in the form of an inflated pear-shaped sac with thin, translucent walls. The encircling structure known as the *coenosarc* is at the bottom of the float with the cormidia arranged in a successive series horizontally along its ventral side. Each cormidium consists of one or more gastrozooids, with tentacles, as well as dactylozooids, palps, and *gonodendra* (treelike branched gonads).

Physalia pelagica Bosc COLOR PLATE V. This is one of the most beautiful colonial organisms of warm seas. The delicate translucent membrane of its float is brilliantly tinted with colors which may range from a deep ruby-red to a brilliant blue or from red to green. Its float continually changes its shape as it trims itself to the wind. The upper part consists of a series of bubblelike chambers surmounted by a longitudinal red crest running lengthwise along the float. It may be 14 inches in length and is quite conspicuous as it floats at the surface of warm seas.

Numerous gastrozooids of a brilliant blue color are clustered beneath the float, each with a terminal mouth and bearing one or more ribbonlike tentacles from its base. There are also salmon-pink masses of gonodendra, bunches of fingerlike, green palps completing the series of delicately fluffy individuals beneath the float.

The tentacles, above mentioned, are very contractile and extensible and, on windy days, will stretch down into the depths of the sea from 40 to 50 feet, thus acting like a drag-anchor to keep the float from being blown too swiftly before the wind. The edge of each tentacle is closely beset by a series of blue, beadlike batteries of stingcells (nematocysts), which give the most powerful sting known among marine organisms. Fishes coming in contact with them are completely paralyzed and, as they struggle, are drawn up by the contracting tentacles until seized by the multitudinous mouths of the feeding polyps (gastrozooids) which suck them dry. One little species of fish (*Nomeus gronovii*), however, is said to swim freely beneath the *Physalia* float without being affected by the tentacles, giving a good example of the principle of symbi-

PLATE 57

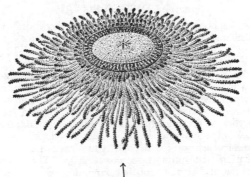

↑
PORPITA
LINNEANA

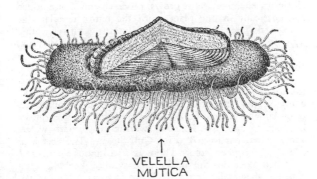

↑
VELELLA
MUTICA

osis or natural copartnership, which so often occurs in nature between unrelated organisms. The little fish acts as a lure, tempting other species within range of the tentacles and thus providing more food for the *Physalia* while, in turn, the Physalia protects the fish and enables it to dine off the "fragments from its master's table."

Suborder DISCONECTAE

Siphonophores in which the colony is suspended from a chambered float without nectophores or bracts.

Family Chondrophoridae

In this family, a single central gastrozooid is suspended from a many-chambered float, is surrounded by numerous blastostyles, which, in turn, are encircled by numerous dactylozooids. These grow out beneath a common coenosarc which is the pneumatophore, which also contains a network of tubes and is completely enveloped by the coenosarc which projects beyond it to form a float.

Porpita linneana Lesson PLATE 57. The disclike float is flat and circular and is surrounded on all sides by the radiating series of blastostyles and dactylozooids. It is about 1 inch in diameter and is colored a bright blue shading into a beautiful iridescent green in the center. *Porpitas* are often seen from vessels crossing the Gulf Stream and, as stated by Mayer, they are sometimes so numerous as to "fleck the ocean for miles with specks of brilliant blue." The pneumatophore, at first, is a single chitinous chamber. As it grows, other chambers are added concentrically in one plane until the entire circular disc is formed. The chambers all communicate with each other by pores in their walls and occasionally with the exterior. They are peculiar to warmer waters and are especially abundant from South Carolina to the West Indies.

Velella mutica Bosc PLATE 57. The general construction of the float in this species is similar to that of *Porpita*, being many-chambered. Its shape, however, is quite rectangular and it may be 4 inches in length. It is exquisite in coloring and, like *Porpita*, swarms in southern waters and is borne northward in the Gulf Stream. The float is of a deep, blue-green color. There is a chitinous-chambered, gas-filled float on the upper side with a keel-like crest running diagonally across it. There is a large central gastrozooid underneath and the under side of the disc is practically entirely covered with the numerous smaller gastrozooids and reproductive individuals which surround it. Projecting from beneath the outer edge of the disc is a series of numerous long, bright blue tentacles.

PLATE 58

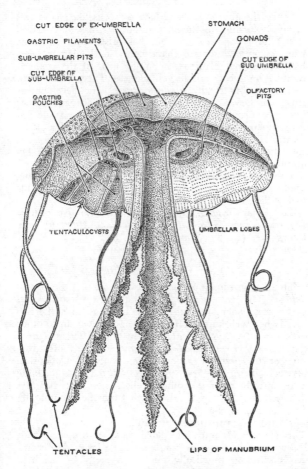

A TYPICAL SCYPHOZOAN
WITH PORTIONS REMOVED TO SHOW
INTERNAL STRUCTURE

CLASS SCYPHOMEDUSAE

While the *Scyphomedusae* have a medusalike shape, this group, according to the best authorities, has not derived from the *Hydromedusae,* but has arisen independently. The *Scyphomedusae* are characterized by having tentacle-like entodermal filaments upon the floor of the stomach cavity. The gonads are also entodermal. There is no velum such as occurs in the *Hydromedusae.* The development from the larvae is quite characteristic. The egg hatches into a hydroidlike form which is anchored on the sea floor, resembling a vase, with mouth and tentacles at the summit. Instead of reproducing by budding, however, it splits horizontally into successive saucerlike fragments, beginning at the top. These develop tentacles and a central mouth and, inverting themselves, swim off as medusae, gradually developing into the final adult form. This hydroidlike larva is known as the *scyphistoma.*

The Class *Scyphomedusae* is divided into five orders: (1) the *Cubomedusae,* (2) the *Stauromedusae,* (3) the *Coronatae,* (4) the *Semaeostomeae,* and (5) the *Rhizostomae.*

Order CUBOMEDUSAE

The Cubomedusae consist of a single family, the *Carybdeidae.* The *Carybdeidae* are confined to tropical and warm seas. They are highly specialized and their life history is not well known. In fact, their relationship to other orders of the *Scyphomedusae* is in doubt. The shape of the bell and a velumlike diaphragm resemble those structures of the *Hydromedusae,* but there is no real relationship between them, as these structures of the Cubomedusae arise entirely from the subumbrella, whereas in the *Hydromedusae,* the velum arises both from the subumbrella and the exumbrella.

Tamoya haplonema F. Müller COLOR PLATE VI, 3. This species has four interradial tentacles provided with leaflike spines known as *pedalia.* It has a large, deep stomach taking up practically the entire cavity of the bell. Between the tentacles, the sides of the umbrella are flattened so that it is given a quadrangular appearance. The umbrellar margin midway between the pedalia is notched to enclose, in each case, a sensory club, having a large median eye with two radial eyes on either side. The large eyes have prominent convex lenses. There is a velumlike organ known as the *velarium,* which is well developed and provided with branching canals. The genital organs are found in the angles of the umbrella extending down to the tentacle bases like frilled curtains. The bell is quite transparent. The tentacles are yellowish, tinted with purple. The genital organs are also yellow and there are large clusters of nematocysts (stinging organs) situated in the margin.

This active species is distributed abundantly from Brazil throughout the West Indies to Beaufort, North Carolina, Long Island Sound, and New York.

Chiropsalmus quadrumanus L. Agassiz PLATE 59. The most conspicuous organs of this species are the four branched handlike pedalia from which extend numerous tentacles. In the subumbrella, there are four radially situated pouches which give rise to finger-shaped extensions projecting into the subumbrellar cavity. The bell is about 4 inches high and 5½ inches wide. The tentacles are extremely flexible and equipped with numerous nematocysts. This jellyfish is erratically distributed, having been found both in Brazil and Beaufort, North Carolina, where it was obtained by H. V. Wilson about one mile offshore near the sea-bottom.

Order STAUROMEDUSAE

These remarkable medusae attach themselves to objects on the sea-bottom by means of an adhesive padlike organ at the end of a stalk, extending from the top of the bell, thus giving them a curious hydroidlike appearance. They are generally considered as being undeveloped or degenerate medusae which remain in their scyphistoma condition. It is thus an undeveloped medusoid creature attached upside down by an extension of its umbrella and with a mouth pointing upward. There are eight notches between as many marginal lobes, the latter of which terminate in clusters of hollow, knobby tentacles resembling pompons. At the bottom of each notch there is a padlike adhesive organ which may serve as an anchor.

Lucernaria quadricornis O. F. Müller PLATE 59; COLOR PLATE VI, 1. The disc of this species is 2 inches or more across and about 2½ inches in height. The bell is quadrangular in shape. Its margin has eight notches, four of which are about twice as deep as the alternate notches, thus bringing four series of two successive lobes close together. The summit of each lobe is crowned with pompons of more than a hundred tentacles. The stomach has four pouches lined by eight gonads. This species is extremely variable in color ranging through gray-green to various hues of brown.

It is very widely distributed on the coasts of Europe, Greenland, and North America, north of Cape Cod. It is comparatively rare on the American side.

Haliclystus auricula Clark PLATE 59. In this case, the disc is somewhat smaller than that of the previous species, but about 1 inch wide and 1 inch high. The bell margin is eight-sided with the notches and tentacles arranged as described for the order. There are the usual oval adhesive discs at the bottom of the notches. The color of this species is quite variable, the various individuals ranging through blue, green, yellow, olive, orange, red, pink, and violet. It is common in Massachusetts Bay and along the northern coasts of Europe.

Haliclystus salpinx Clark PLATE 59. The disc of this medusa is about 1 inch in width and not quite so high. The arms are comparatively short, separated by shallow notches. The border of the trumpet-shaped disc has a thickened margin, but the stalk is longer and more slender in proportion. It is four-sided in cross-section.

It is abundant off Mt. Desert Island, Maine, and along the rocky coast of New England generally.

Order CORONATAE

These are Scyphomedusae with solid marginal tentacles arising from the clefts between the marginal lappets and in the same line as the pedalia, which are of the same number as the lappets. The sense organs (*rhopalia*) also arise from between the lappets and alternate with the tentacles. Ocelli may or may not be present. The exumbrella is characterized by a circular, coronal furrow. The simple throat tube is short and has no curtainlike appendages as in the Semaeostomeae and Rhizostomae. The medusae are free-swimming and have no aboral stalk for attachment.

Family Periphyllidae

These are Coronatae with four interradial pedalia, bearing marginal sense-clubs and with four, or more, pedalia bearing tentacles.

Periphylla hyacinthina Steenstrup COLOR PLATE IV, 2. This species is remarkable for its high, narrowly pointed bell with gracefully curving sides surrounded at its base by sixteen marginal lappet pouches. The total height of the bell may exceed 6 inches and its width nearly 5 inches. A deep furrow indents the outline between the bell and the series of lappets. Twelve tentacles are inserted high up in the notches, grouped in series of three each between four lappets. Each two groups of three are separated by a notch having a marginal sense organ instead of the tentacle. There are, thus, four of these sense organs in the series of sixteen notches. The four clefts containing the sense organs are not as deeply cut as the other twelve. Within the umbrella cavity are four funnel-shaped interradial pits set against the central stomach, following its sides nearly to the apex of the umbrella. Eight U-shaped gonads embrace the sides of the four interradial septa. The central stomach

PLATE 59

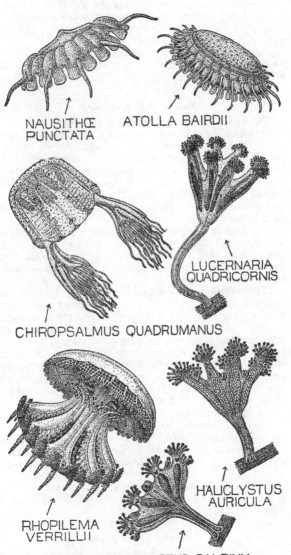

NAUSITHŒ PUNCTATA

ATOLLA BAIRDII

CHIROPSALMUS QUADRUMANUS

LUCERNARIA QUADRICORNIS

RHOPILEMA VERRILLII

HALICLYSTUS AURICULA

HALICLYSTUS SALPINX

is a four-sided prism divided horizontally into three parts.

A beautiful purple color lining the inside of the umbrella shows through the transparent jellylike substance. The sense organs are brown while the tentacles and lappets are of a translucent light blue.

This medusa occurs swimming on the surface of the North Atlantic from the Bay of Biscay to Cape Hatteras, at Martha's Vineyard, and even to Greenland and Spitzbergen.

Family Ephyropsidae

The *Ephyropsidae* are Coronatae with sixteen or more lappets, and eight or more tentacles alternating with eight or more rhopalia, arising from the slits between the lappets. Both tentacles and sense organs are in the same radii as sixteen radiating pouches rising from the subumbrella and separated from each other by sixteen septa, which may be complete or incomplete. The Ephyropsidae are very widely distributed in the open sea, being especially abundant in the tropics.

The Ephyra of this species is produced as a result of horizontal splitting (strobilization) of the hydroid. In the case of *Nausithoë punctata* Kolliker, the scyphistoma larva forms branches, thus reminding one of a hydroid colony, and it infests sponges.

Nausithoë punctata Kolliker PLATE 59. The flattened umbrella of this species has merely a slightly raised apex and is completely surrounded by large lappets having a diameter of somewhat over ½ inch. A deep furrow separates the disc of the umbrella from the encircling zone of lappets with their large convex pedalia. There are sixteen of these pedalia alternating with each other in possessing either a tentacle or a sense organ and overlapping the sixteen marginal lappets. The tentacles extend out abruptly from the margin of the bell. The simple mouth at the center of the subumbrella has four lips and is cruciform in appearance. Between the arms of the cross thus formed are four groups of cirri. The color of the medusa varies from green or light brown in the bell while the gonads are brown, red, or yellow. The umbrella has reddish spots, especially on the lappets.

This species floats on the surface in all tropical or warm seas and on the Atlantic Coast. It is only occasionally found north of Cape Hatteras.

Family Collaspidae

The *Collaspidae* are Coronatae with numerous marginal sense organs alternating with an equal number of tentacles. The marginal lappets are twice as numerous as the tentacles.

Atolla is the only known genus with three clearly distinguished species.

Atolla bairdii Fewkes PLATE 59. This is a flat disc-shaped medusa varying considerably in size from 1 inch to 6 inches or more. The central part of the bell is lens-shaped, surrounded by a convex rim from which project about twenty-two notches lying beneath the pedalia, from each of which springs a lateral tentacle. Outside the encircling angular ridge or rim, there are three overlapping zones of appendages. First, a circle of pedalia varying from eighteen to twenty-four, each one bearing a single tentacle. Second, a circlet of double-pointed sense organs situated outside the pedalia and alternating with them. The third or final zone is made up of elongated flaps or lappets, two for each of the sense organs.

A short and wide proboscis with four lips occupies the center of the subumbrella. The gonads, eight in number, surround the base of the proboscis. The jellylike disc of this species is a translucent milky blue, the surface sprinkled over with red patches, surrounded by the red-brown angular ring or furrow. Streaks of dark red extend inward like the spokes of a wheel on the subumbrella.

Atolla bairdii is very common and widespread in the North Atlantic, swimming at the surface and at considerable depths. It is especially abundant in the Gulf Stream off the coast of North Carolina.

Order SEMAEOSTOMEAE

"Scyphomedusae without a coronal furrow and without pedalia; with a simple, central mouth opening, the four perradial angles of which are developed into large curtain-like or gelatinous lips. With hollow tentacles and marginal rhopalia. The gonads are in saclike folds of the entodermal wall of the subumbrella with the interradial septal nodes in the stomach." (Mayer)

Family Pelagidae

The medusae in this family have eight or sixteen marginal sense organs with tentacles arising between the marginal lappets which, however, may exceed the number of the tentacles. In this family, for example, there will be eight or more tentacles and sixteen to sixty-four marginal lappets. The mouth is quadrangular with its corners perradial. The latter are greatly elongated into four rufflelike appendages known as mouth-arms. The central stomach is lens-shaped with simple radiating pouches extending under the umbrella. There are four symmetrical gonads forming pits in the floor of the subumbrella. The long ruffled mouth-arms, appearing like "double curtain-like fringes," are particularly characteristic of the Pelagidae.

Development in this family forms a free-swimming adult medusa directly from the planula, there being no hydroid-like scyphistoma stage.

Pelagia cyanella Peron & Lesueur COLOR PLATE VI, 4. The disc or bell is very active when the medusa is swimming, being almost globular when contracted, but flattened when expanded. It is about 2 inches or more in diameter. The outer surface of the umbrella is dotted with nemato-cyst batteries which radiate from the apex toward the margin of the umbrella. These are orange-red in color and quite numerous, giving the impression of dotted lines. There are sixteen marginal lappets, each shallowly indented in the middle. Eight tentacles spring from the notches between every other two lappets, sense organs occupying the notches between. The quadrangular throat tube projects below the margin of the umbrella. Its perradial lips are greatly elongated, hanging down in intricate folds to act as sensitive palps. The bell itself is purple-rose shading into blue. It is luminescent at night and is one of the most graceful and beautiful of all the medusae.

This species occurs abundantly in the Mediterranean where it is known as *Pelagia noctiluca*. It is apparently identical with *Pelagia cyanella,* which is the common form along our own coasts, occurring from the coast of Brazil and Florida to Cape Cod, being transported by the Gulf Stream.

Dactylometra quinquecirrha L. Agassiz COLOR PLATE VI, 5. This beautiful medusa has an umbrella which may reach nearly eight inches in diameter. As in the previous species, small wartlike clusters of nematocysts are scattered over the umbrella, being especially numerous at the apex. There are eight marginal sense organs, forty tentacles, and forty-eight marginal lappets with a ciliated pit close to each sense organ. The forty tentacles are golden yellow and stream down for a considerable distance through the water, partially veiling the four mouth lappets which prolong the corner of the quadrangular mouth with their flouncelike ruffles of rosy pink. This species is abundant in Narragansett Bay, Rhode Island, where the water is pure, but it ranges from the southern coast of New England to the tropics.

Family Cyaneidae

This family, like the preceding, possesses a four-sided central mouth surrounded by four perradial curtainlike lips. The tentacles, instead of being at the margin, are in clusters situated some distance back from it arising from the floor of the subumbrella. The four gonads are situated interradially in pockets in the wall of the subumbrella. Radiating from the stomach are numerous pouches giving rise to branching canals. While these medusae are related to the *Pelagidae,* the complex branching of the stomach pouches and the subumbrellar position of the tentacles separate them clearly from that family.

Cyanea capillata Eschscholtz var. **arctica** Peron & Lesueur COLOR PLATE VI, 6. The Pink Jellyfish. This is the giant jellyfish of the Atlantic Ocean. In England, it is spoken of as the "lion's mane." The great circular or lens-shaped disc may attain a diameter of 8 feet, while its numerous, long-trailing tentacles, 800 in number, when fully expanded, may be 200 feet in length. This is an extreme size, which is quite rare, for most individuals are not over 3 feet in diameter, with tentacles of 75 feet when fully extended. Specimens of about 1 foot in diameter are quite common along our coast and can be recognized by the rosy pink to brownish purple color of the stomach, shading out to the translucent yellowish margin. The central, quadrangular stomach has long foliated mouth-arms of rich brownish purple, while the gonads and tentacles are yellow to reddish brown. The powerful muscular system, which makes possible the rhythmical contractions of the disc, is brown to yellow in color. The umbrella margin is cleft into eight main lobes, each in turn partly divided by a median cleft with two shallow notches on either side of it. Thus there are thirty-two lappets divided by thirty-two indentations around the umbrellar margin. The jelly-like substance of which the disc is composed is very thick and resistant in the center of the umbrella, but the texture of the lobes is quite thin and delicate. There are eight marginal sense organs at the innermost point of the eight median notches. These are club-shaped and protected by a web joining the two lappets. As a whole, the structure of the sense organ is quite complicated.

The four gonads are situated on the subumbrellar floor on the four sides of the stomach. Radiating out from the stomach itself are sixteen stomach pouches which, at their outer edges, divide into numerous branching canals, extending out to the edges of the lappets.

It may readily be realized that this tremendous equipment of tentacles, with their thousands of powerful sting-cells, makes this jellyfish a formidable creature to contact in the open sea. The stinging power of the nematocysts, in some cases, is known to have been fatal to swimmers.

This remarkable jellyfish is abundant from the southern New England coast northward to the Arctic Ocean. It reaches its largest size in the colder waters while the individuals occurring south of Cape Cod are of comparatively small size. The medusae are found in southern New England until about the middle of June, when they disappear, but the mature specimens are abundant in the cold water off the coast of Maine, in August and September.

Family Ulmaridae

"Semaeostomeae with simple or branching radial-canals and ring-canals. Four interradial gonads. Four mouth-arms with folded curtain-like margins.

"The medusae of this family are closely related to the Cyaneidae, but different in that their radial-canals are placed in intercommunication by means of a marginal circular canal; moreover, the radial-canals are anastomosed in some of the genera, and this is never the case in the Cyaneidae." (Mayer)

Aurelia aurita Lamarck COLOR PLATE VI, 7. The White Sea Jelly. This is the common white jellyfish occurring all along our coasts and often thrown on the beach by storm winds or high tide. The disc of the adult medusa varies from 6 to 10 inches in diameter. In swimming, the umbrella varies from hemispherical to a more or less flattened disc. The gelatinous material of which it is composed is tough, thick at the center, but thin and delicate at the edge of the disc. There are eight marginal sense organs at the bottom of shallow indentations between the eight broad, flattened lappets. The extremely numerous, but short, fringelike tentacles completely surround the disc a little above the margin, alternating with the same number of numerous tiny lappets. The four-sided mouth-opening is extended perradially into four tapering sinuous mouth-arms, which are gelatinous in composition and are rather stiff-textured. The margins of the slot extending the full length of the mouth-arms are also equipped with numerous small tentacles. Four gonads are situated interradially between the mouth-arms and are horseshoe-shaped in appearance. Four radial, four interradial, and eight branching treelike adradial canals radiate through the transparent tissue of the jellyfish at the umbrella margin. The color of the jellyfish is a translucent milky white or a light yellow-brown. The gonads of the males are pale pink while those of the females are white.

This medusa occurs abundantly from Greenland to the West Indies. It is mature off the coast of Maine in September. In its development, the *Aurelia* egg hatches a larva which becomes a scyphistoma, and grows to a height of about ¼ inch, acquiring successively eight, sixteen, and finally twenty-four long tentacles. The scyphistoma divides horizontally into *Ephyrae* (larval jellyfish), which rapidly develop into the adult.

COLOR PLATES

II-IX

PLATE II

TYPICAL NORTHERN SPONGES

1. Tufted Sponge *Grantia ciliata* (Fabricius).
2. Eyed Sponge *Chalina oculata* (Pallas).
3. Sulphur Sponge *Cliona celata* Grant.
4. Redbeard Sponge *Microciona prolifera* Verrill. See also COLOR PLATE XXII, 7.
5. Crumb-of-Bread Sponge *Halichondria panicea* (Pallas).

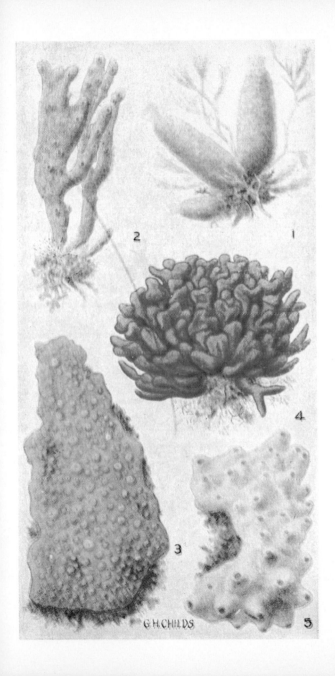

G.H.CHILDS

PLATE III

TYPICAL HYDROIDS

1. 1a. Pink Hearted Hydroid *Tubularia crocea* (Agassiz).

2. 2a. Long-tentacled Hydroid *Bougainvillea superciliaris* L. Agassiz.

3. 3a. Double-branching Hydroid *Obelia dichotoma* (Linnaeus).

4. 4a. Wreathed Hydroid *Sertularia pumila* Linnaeus.

5. 5a. Club-clustered Hydroid *Acaulis primarius* (Stimpson).

6. 6a. Nodding Nosegay Hydroid *Corymorpha pendula* Agassiz.

7. 7a. Spiny Polymorphic Hydroid *Hydractinia echinata* Fleming.

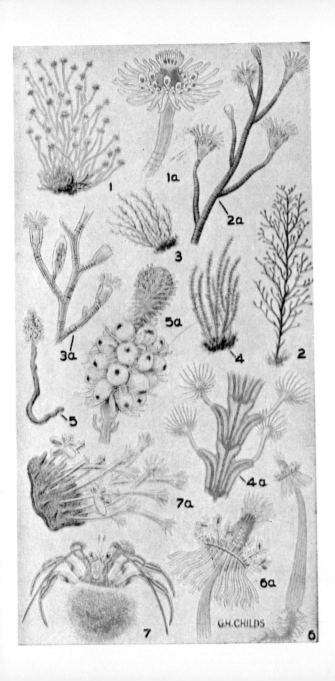

G.H.CHILDS

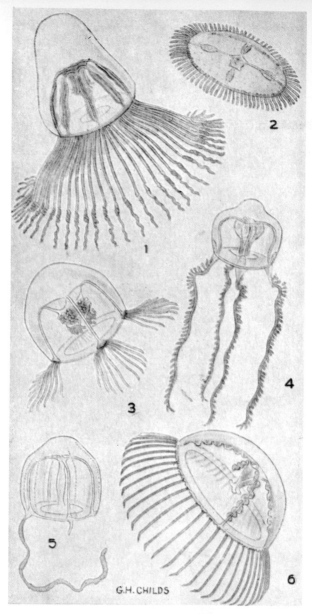

G.H. CHILDS

PLATE IV—HYDROMEDUSAE

1. *Melicertum campanula.*
2. *Obelia dichotoma.*
3. *Bougainvillea superciliaris.*
4. *Zanclea gemmosa.*
5. *Corymorpha pendula.*
6. *Gonionemus murbachii.*

PLATE V—PORTUGUESE MAN-OF-WAR
Physalia pelagica Bosc
Accompanied by the Man-of-War Fish *Nomeus gronovii*
Gmelin.

PLATE VI

TYPICAL SCYPHOZOAN JELLYFISHES
(SCYPHOMEDUSAE)

1. Stalked Scyphomedusan *Lucernaria quadricornis* Múller.
2. Lappet-bordered Jellyfish *Periphylla hyacinthina* Steen-strup.
3. Four-sided Jellyfish *Tamoya haplonema* F. Müller.
4. Luminous Furbelowed Jellyfish *Pelagia cyanella* Pèron & Lesueur.
5. Golden-fringed Furbelowed Jellyfish *Dactylometra quinquecirrha* (Desor).
6. Great Pink Jellyfish, Lion's Mane *Cyanea capillata* (Linnaeus).
7. White Sea Jelly *Aurelia aurita* (Linnaeus).
8. Many-mouthed Sea Jelly *Stomolophus meleagris* Agassiz.

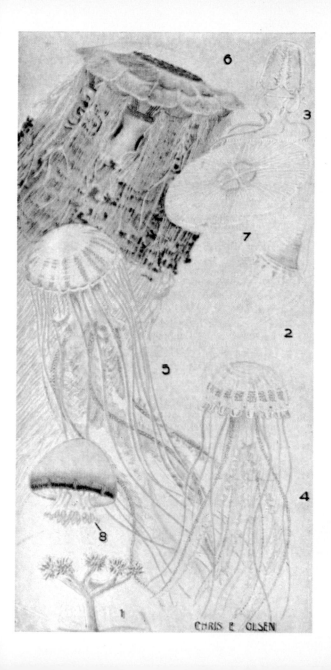

CHRIS E. OLSEN

PLATE VII

TYPICAL ANNULATE WORMS

1. Swift-footed Worm *Podarke obscura* Verrill. See also COLOR PLATE VIII, 2.

2. Clam Worm *Nereis virens* Sars. See also COLOR PLATE VIII, 3; PLATE 103.

3. Painted Worm *Nephthys picta* Ehlers. See also COLOR PLATE VIII, 4; PLATE 105.

4. Plumed Worm *Diopatra cupraea* Bosc. See also COLOR PLATES VII, 5; IX, 4.

5. Opal Worm *Arabella opalina* Verrill. See also COLOR PLATE VIII; PLATE 106.

6. Beak Thrower *Glycera dibranchiata* Ehlers. See also COLOR PLATE VIII, 7, 7a; PLATE 107.

7. Bi-tentacled Worm *Spio setosa* Verrill. See also COLOR PLATE VIII, 8; PLATE 108.

8. Fringed Worm *Cirratulus grandis* Verrill. See also PLATE 110.

9. Ornate Worm *Amphitrite ornata* Verrill. See also COLOR PLATE VIII, 9.

10. Trumpet Worm *Cistenides gouldii* Verrill. See also COLOR PLATE IX, 3.

11. Jointed Worm *Clymenella torquata* (Leidy). See also PLATE 115.

12. Sipunculid Worm, Mud Worm *Phascolosoma gouldii* (Pourtalès). See also COLOR PLATE IX, 15.

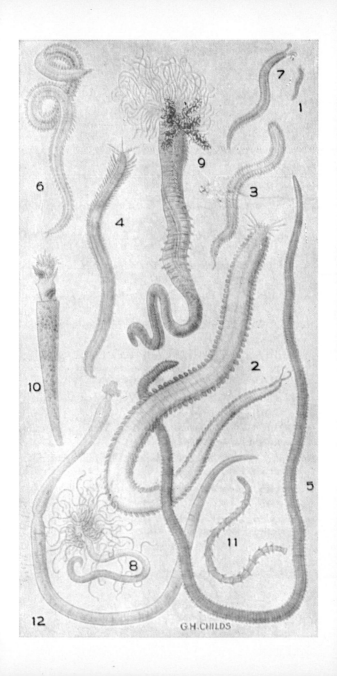

G.H.CHILDS

PLATE VIII

ANNULATE WORM HEADS

1. Scale Worm *Lepidonotus squamatus* (Linnaeus). Entire animal. See also PLATE 99.

2. Swift-footed Worm *Podarke obscura* Verrill. See also COLOR PLATE VII, 1.

3. Clam Worm *Nereis virens* Sars. See also COLOR PLATE VII, 2; PLATE 103.

4. Painted Worm *Nephthys picta* Ehlers. See also COLOR PLATE VII, 3; PLATE 105.

5. Plumed Worm *Diopatra cupraea* Bosc. See also COLOR PLATES VII, 4; IX, 4.

6. Opal Worm *Arabella opalina* (Verrill). See also COLOR PLATE VII, 5; PLATE 106.

7. Beak Thrower *Glycera dibranchiata* Ehlers. Showing proboscis everted; 7a, proboscis not everted. See also COLOR PLATE VII, 6; PLATE 107.

8. Bi-tentacled Worm *Spio setosa* Verrill. See also COLOR PLATE VII, 7; PLATE 108.

9. Ornate Worm *Amphitrite ornata* Verrill. See also COLOR PLATE VII, 9.

10. Coiled Worm *Spirorbis borealis* Daudin. See also PLATE 120.

11. Sabellaria *Sabellaria vulgaris* Verrill. See also PLATE 120.

12. Shielded Digger *Sternaspis fossor* Stimpson. Entire animal. See also PLATE 118.

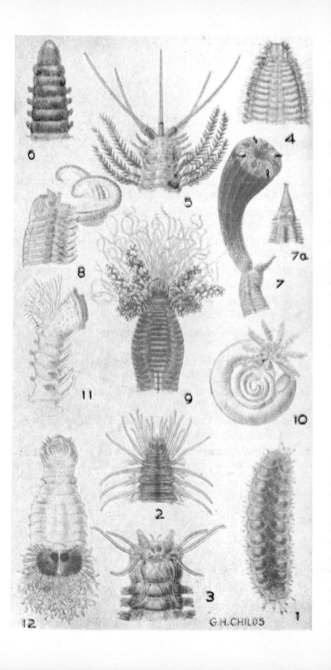

G.H. CHILDS

PLATE IX

SECTION OF SEA BOTTOM SHOWING PARCH-MENT WORM IN TUBE

1. 2. Parchment Worm *Chaetopterus pergamentaceus* Cuvier. In tube.

3. Trumpet Worm *Cistenides gouldii* Verrill. See also COLOR PLATE VII, 10.

4. Tube of Plumed Worm *Diopatra cupraea* Bosc. See also COLOR PLATES VII, 4; VIII, 5.

5. Mud Worm *Phascolosoma gouldii* (Pourtalès). See also COLOR PLATE VII, 12.

6. 7. Parchment Worm Crab *Pinnixa chaetopterana* Stimpson. Male and female.

8. Hermit Crab *Pagurus longicarpus* Say. See also COLOR PLATE X, 9.

9. Channeled Whelk *Busycon canaliculatum* (Linnaeus). See also COLOR PLATE XV, 16.

10. Common Scallop *Pecten irradians* Lamarck. See also COLOR PLATE IX, 10.

11. Mud Minnow. Common Killifish *Fundulus heteroclitus* (Linnaeus).

12. Eel Grass *Zostera marina* Linnaeus.

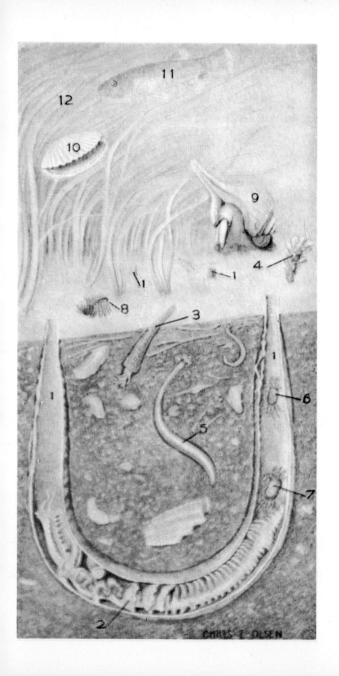

Order RHIZOSTOMAE

"Scyphomedusae without marginal tentacles, and with numerous mouths which are borne upon eight adradial, fleshy, branched arm-like appendages, which arise from the center of the subumbrella. The lips of the numerous mouths are bordered by minute, constantly moving tentacles." (Mayer)

This order comprises the most highly evolved Scyphomedusae. Due to the substantial gelatinous material of their discs and their large size, fossil impressions of them have often been found.

The umbrella of this species is dome-shaped, covered with nematocyst warts and with sense organs similar to those of the Semaeostomeae. It is, therefore, obvious that the Rhizostomae are descended from the Semaeostomeae.

Stomolophus meleagris L. Agassiz COLOR PLATE VI, 8. The bell of this magnificent species is more than 7 inches in diameter. It strangely resembles a large half-egg-shaped mushroom, an illusion attained by its thick, tough substance. There are eight marginal sense organs with sense-clubs deeply set within the niches between the lappets and protected by a partial web above them. The sense-clubs are hollow, slender-shaped with knoblike ends containing pigmented concretions. There are numerous marginal lappets, that is, 128 in all, with those bordering the sense organs longer than the rest. Eight adradial mouth-arms are joined together to form the convoluted stemlike mouth-tube. The lobes of the mouth-tube are double-forked at their ends. There is a large, ring-shaped stomach in the central part of the umbrella, prolonged into sixteen radial canals which give off an anastomosing network of branches throughout the tissue of the umbrella.

The muscular system of this medusa is highly developed and powerful, causing the umbrella to contract rhythmically with great strength and speed. The bell generally is of a milky bluish or yellow tint, showing brown reticulations over its entire surface. It is densely pigmented with brown around its margin with white or yellowish spots forming an indistinct pattern. This species is very common along the coast of North and South Carolina, Georgia, and Florida, but is not found north of Chesapeake Bay and never deeply within harbors.

Rhopilema verrillii Fewkes PLATE 59. The hemispherical bell of this remarkable jellyfish may be 12 inches in diameter. Its heavy gelatinous substance is quite rigid and, externally, is quite smooth except over the lappets, where the surface is sculptured in a complex manner and covered with so many minute projections that it resembles sandpaper. There are sixty-four of these lappets in all, six of which are of fairly large size with a small one at each end which makes a pair with its neighbor, so as to embrace a tiny mass of concretions of red pigment granules, thus making up eight marginal sense organs. The cross-shaped arm-disc is quite thick, being made up of four perradial columnar stems which are continued into eight tough, gelatinous mouth-arms about 7 inches in length, their terminal foliated projections being Y-shaped in cross-section. Multitudes of small mouths occur on their lower and inner sides, situated in undulating grooves, edged with clusters of nematocysts. These mouth-arms have a very complicated appearance and are connected with each other below the subumbrella. There are four heart-shaped genital openings at the top of the column, just beneath the umbrella. The cruciform stomach follows the general outline of the arm-disc with four open furrows extending down each column to the outer edge of the stomach, which gives rise, in turn, to sixteen main radial canals, which penetrate the substance of the umbrella to the marginal sense organs. They give rise to numerous side branches which anastomose to form a complicated network of small vessels. The umbrella itself is of a dull, light yellow color, while the mouths are deep yellow with brownish red irregular areas of pigment mottling their surface.

While rare, these jellyfish are occasionally found in considerable numbers in Long Island Sound, late in the summer, especially in August and September. During the rest of the year, they disappear in this region, but are found abundantly in Pamlico Sound off North Carolina.

CLASS ANTHOZOA (ACTINOZOA)
(INDEX PLATES 60 and 69)

The Anthozoa occur only as polyps, there being no free-swimming medusoid generation known in this group. While the Hydrozoa are characterized, for the most part, by a simple cylindrical enteron, the Actinozoa possess a more complex structure, the *stomodaeum*. Instead of the mouth leading immediately into the internal cavity (enteron), there is a short tube or gullet to which we apply the term, stomodaeum. It possesses two longitudinal grooves at the ends of its slitlike mouth, which continue through the internal gullet. These are known as the *siphonoglyphs*. The lower edge of the gullet terminates some distance below the mouth and is held in place by a series of partitions (*mesenteries*) connecting the gullet with the wall of the enteric cavity. These partitions are continued with free edges below the end of the gullet to the bottom of the interior, edged with a convoluted cord, the *mesenteric*

PLATE 60

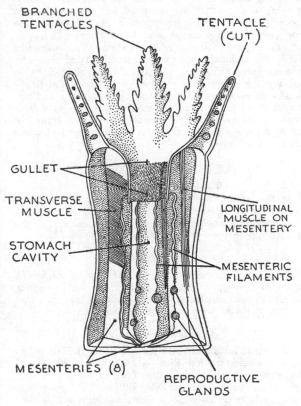

BRANCHED
TENTACLES

TENTACLE
(CUT)

GULLET

TRANSVERSE
MUSCLE

LONGITUDINAL
MUSCLE ON
MESENTERY

STOMACH
CAVITY

MESENTERIC
FILAMENTS

MESENTERIES (8)

REPRODUCTIVE
GLANDS

INTERNAL STRUCTURE
OF A
TYPICAL ALCYONARIAN POLYP

filament. On the walls of the mesenteries are muscular bands running lengthwise, known as the *longitudinal muscles,* which act as retractors. There is also a *parietal muscle* running obliquely across the lower end of the mesentery. The contraction of these muscles draws down the body of the anemone and, at the same time, retracts the tentacles so that they may be concealed within the body itself. The gonads are located in the mesenteries near the edge and are conspicuous when mature. Sexes are separate. The fertilized egg develops into a free-swimming larva, the planula, a minute egg-shaped ciliated body containing large endoderm cells and filled with yolk. After leaving the enteron, the embryo swims about and finally settles down to become attached by its broader end and transformed into a small polyp. There is also an asexual method of reproduction brought about by splitting the body of the anemone so that two polyps are formed where there was but one.

SUBCLASS ALCYONARIA
(INDEX PLATE 60)

In this group, the tentacles and mesenteries are always eight in number, the former being pinnate or branched. Only one siphonoglyph exists on the vertical end of the slitlike mouth.

Order ALCYONACEA

These are Alcyonaria with a skeleton of calcareous spicules of irregular shape embedded in the mesogloea, which, in some instances, are united into a branched axis, but for the most part are loosely embedded.

Family Cornularidae

Cornulariella modesta Verrill PLATE 61. The polyps of this species are less than ½ inch in length and are seated in more or less rigid cups (*calicles*) which, in turn, arise from creeping stolons. The soft body of a polyp may be entirely retracted into the hard calicle, which is then seen to be circular, with eight radiating grooves. The substance of the stolons and the calicle walls consists of strong spiny spicules, closely packed together. The tentacles are white and long, tapering gracefully from an expanded base.

Bay of Fundy, off the coast of New Brunswick and Nova Scotia, as well as the coast of Maine in depths of 35 to 100 fathoms.

Family Anthomastidae

The species of this family are red or purple in color and, when mature, are usually shaped like mushrooms

PLATE 61

GERSEMIA CARNEA (YOUNG COLONY)

GERSEMIA CARNEA (SINGLE CALICLE)

GERSEMIA MIRABILIS (PORTION OF COLONY)

GERSEMIA RUBIFORMIS (PORTION OF COLONY)

GERSEMIA RUBIFORMIS (SINGLE CALICLE)

GERSEMIA LONGIFLORA (SINGLE CALICLE)

DUVA MULTIFLORA (PORTION OF COLONY)

DUVA MULTIFLORA (SINGLE CALICLE)

GERSEMIA LONGIFLORA (PORTION OF COLONY)

DRIFA GLOMERATA (PORTION OF COLONY)

ANTHOMASTUS GRANDIFLORUS (YOUNG COLONY)

CORNULARIELLA MODESTA ('SINGLE CALICLE)

The polyps are comparatively large and retractile, possessing the usual eight pinnate tentacles. They are found in muddy bottoms attached by rootlike prolongations, usually in cool water. They have a very wide range and in all parts of the world, usually in deeper waters where the temperature is cool.

Anthomastus grandiflorus Verrill PLATE 61. This species grows in large, mushroomlike clusters with a thick expanding stalk surmounted by many large polyps. The colony may be from 3 to 5 inches in diameter with the individual polyp often 1 inch in diameter. They may be retracted into calicles. Vertical *siphonozooids* occur thickly between the polyps.

Off Nova Scotia and Newfoundland in 150 to 300 fathoms. It is often dredged up by fishermen.

Family Nephthyidae

Gersemia carnea Agassiz PLATE 61. This species grows to 5 inches in height and is prolifically branched. It is remarkably handsome because of its pale flesh or salmon color varying to light orange or pale red. When fully expanded, it is translucent with transparent polyps on the tips of its slender branches. The polyps expand to a considerable length, but are subject to extreme contraction. This species is common on stony or shelly bottoms from the southern part of the Gulf of St. Lawrence to moderately deep water near Block Island and Watch Hill, Rhode Island, and off Stonington, Connecticut. Most common in 10 to 30 fathoms but occurs down to 55 fathoms.

Gersemia mirabilis (Danielssen) PLATE 61. A very large species having a stout trunk with treelike branches given off in a bushy fashion with secondary and tertiary branchlets. The polyps are elongated. Clusters of these species often reach 8 inches in height.

Common on the Grand Banks of Newfoundland.

Gersemia rubiformis (Pallas) PLATE 61. This much-branching colony has stout pear-shaped clusters of lobes with a simple main stem characterized by a thick covering of red spicules, except near the base, giving the surface a finely granular appearance under the lines. The red color is especially characteristic. The stem is more or less bare with elongated branches often club-shaped, having clusters of numerous polyps.

Arctic regions to Bay of Fundy, Nova Scotia, and Newfoundland.

Gersemia longiflora Verrill PLATE 62. This is a loosely and openly branched species with elongated, nearly cylindrical stems. The stalk is somewhat bulbous at the base.

In deep water off New Jersey, Delaware, and on Georges Bank.

Genus **Duva**. The fully grown colony has a stout, considerably branched stalk. The tips of the branches are crowded with numerous small polyps, usually 3 to 5 in a cluster. The stalk and branches are usually naked, the latter often forming umbel-like groups at their tips. The polyps are only partially retractile.

Duva multiflora Verrill PLATE 61. The Sea-Cauliflower. When fully developed, this is a large treelike species about 4½ inches high and 3 inches broad. There is a large smooth stalk with very numerous branches, the polyps being crowded in clusters at their tips. When contracted they have a very cauliflowerlike appearance. The color is light red to pink. This is a larger species than *Gersemia carnea*, which it otherwise closely resembles. It is found off Nova Scotia and Newfoundland and is quite common in depths of 130 fathoms or more.

Drifa glomerata Verrill PLATE 61. This is an upright colony with a stout trunk which branches from all sides with short rather conical branches with crowded clusters of three to twelve polyps. Their surface is rough, covered with multitudes of thorny club-shaped spicules. The color is pale red, shaded toward brown on the stalk, and with translucent yellow or orange polyps when fully expanded. It is abundant on the Banks of Newfoundland.

Family Briareidae

Paragorgia arborea (Linnaeus) PLATE 62. This very interesting species occurs abundantly on the fishing banks off Nova Scotia and Newfoundland where it often grows to a great size, often 4 to 5 feet in height. The branches are quite irregular, separating and rejoining so as to form gnarled irregular projections often with swollen branching tips. Like all alcyonarias, the feeding polyps are surrounded by numerous siphonozooids.

Anthothela grandiflora (M. Sars) PLATE 62. This species has elongated polyps rising from raised calicles into which they may partially withdraw when disturbed. The branching structure rises from a spreading basal membrane. They are incrusted with eight groups of many converging spicules in the stalks of the tentacles, arranged in a V-shaped pattern with a circlet of numerous slender spicules below. It is buff or light yellow in color. It is found attached to shells, stones, etc., and is abundant off Nova Scotia and Newfoundland as far as the Banks.

Acanella normani Verrill PLATE 62. The Bush Coral. This is a very common species growing in closely branched, bushlike colonies a foot or less in height. The branches are usually sinuous in growth and often set at a wide angle to the stalk, the stouter branches at the bottom of the growth, the thinner ones more slender and roughly parallel to each other. The color of the colony is light chestnut brown, varying to orange and dark brown with polyps translucent when expanded. The main axis of the colony is white with orange-brown nodes. The elongated calicles are close-set in whorls around the branches, each with a cylinder of eight spines at the crown.

Abundantly distributed in deep water in the neighborhood of the banks off Nova Scotia and Newfoundland.

Family Chrysogorgidae

Radicipes gracilis Verrill PLATE 62. This colony grows in the form of tall, slender rodlike stems rising 3 feet or more from a branching rootlike base. The delicate crust covering the axis is made up of thin, oblong spicules resembling scales. The calicles of the polyps bud off obliquely from the side of the axis, well separated from each other. Their color is orange with often a pinkish cast. This species is often dredged off Georges Bank.

Family Keratoisidae

"Axis simple or variously branched, with long calcareous joints, which are often hollow, alternating with shorter horny joints. Branches, when present, sometimes arise from the calcareous joints, but more frequently from the more horny ones. Base calcareous usually divided into long, flat, irregular lobes serving as anchors in the mud of the sea-bottom." (Verrill.) The calicles are large and conspicuous, almost like series of elongated tumblers crowned with eight projecting spines. The sides of the calicle are also surrounded by circlets of spines.

Keratoisis ornata Verrill PLATE 62. The Gold-Banded Coral. This coral forms an irregular branching colony of a slender, gradually tapering form, occasionally over 4 feet in height. The calcareous joints are ivory white and are usually longitudinally grooved and very finely granular.

The chitinous joints are colored yellow or bronze, the smaller ones being of translucent amber color. It is distributed from 200 to 300 fathoms on the Banks off Nova Scotia.

Family Primnoidae

Primnoa reseda (Pallas) PLATE 63. This is a more or less massive growth up to 3 feet in height with the axis forming a trunk hard and calcified at the base. When living, it ranges from light red to a pale salmon pink. It is found on rocky bottoms from 50 to 150 fathoms, well anchored to large rocks.

PLATE 62

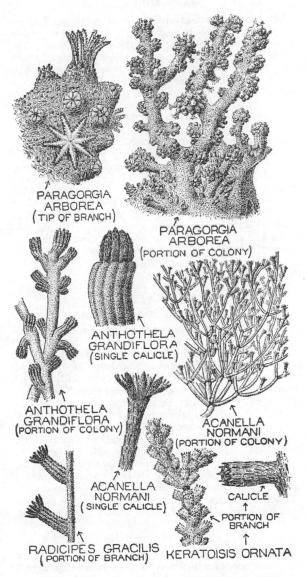

PARAGORGIA
ARBOREA
(TIP OF BRANCH)

PARAGORGIA
ARBOREA
(PORTION OF COLONY)

ANTHOTHELA
GRANDIFLORA
(SINGLE CALICLE)

ANTHOTHELA
GRANDIFLORA
(PORTION OF COLONY)

ACANELLA
NORMANI
(PORTION OF COLONY)

ACANELLA
NORMANI
(SINGLE CALICLE)

CALICLE

PORTION OF
BRANCH

RADICIPES GRACILIS
(PORTION OF BRANCH)

KERATOISIS ORNATA

Family Muriceidae

Lepidomuricea grandis Verrill PLATE 63. The peculiarity of this species is that the colony is more or less fanlike, its branches being practically in one plane. The calicles are cylindrical, or even more often conical, with margins protected by one or two rows of sharp-pointed spines. The outer crust is very thick and hard, but covered with a soft skin which obscures the spicules. The spines on the tentacles are arranged in a V-shaped pattern. This species appears abundantly off the Grand Banks and in Nova Scotian waters.

Acanthogorgia armata Verrill PLATE 63. This species forms a profusely branching colony with a horny and fibrous axis, giving it a rough appearance. The elongated, cylindrical, spiny calyces of the polyps are profusely and irregularly sessile on all the branches, often being crowded close together. The upper part of the polyp is slightly capable of retraction. The spindle-shaped spicules are so arranged that they form eight spiny ridges on the outside of the calyx, terminating in as many serrate extensions surrounding the cup-opening, like a delicate coronet.

This colony is found in fairly deep water along the Atlantic Coast of North America.

Order PENNATULACEA
(SEA-PENS AND SEA-FEATHERS)

The characteristic alcyonarian organisms, included in this order, consist of two parts: a *stalk,* which may be imbedded in the sand or mud of the sea-bottom, and an upper part termed the *rachis.* The latter has plumelike branchlets or *pinnae,* bearing the polyps, and may be shaped like a feather, a rod, or a broad plate. The central axis, when present, may be calcareous or of horny substance, its outer layers taking the form of a crust in which many spicules are imbedded. The polyps are dimorphic, comprising a series of larger individuals (*autozooids*), having the usual polyp structure, as well as a series of smaller polyps (*siphonozooids*), with no tentacles, gonads, or mesenteries. These regulate the incurrent and excurrent flow of water throughout the canals of the organism.

A few deep-water species are included here, with those from shallower water, to illustrate the range and evolution of the group.

Family Protoptilidae

Scleroptilum gracile Verrill PLATE 64. This is a deep-water species which was dredged by a "Challenger" expedition in 1467 to 2369 fathoms. It is bright orange in color. Specimens are often found with brittle stars clinging

PLATE 63

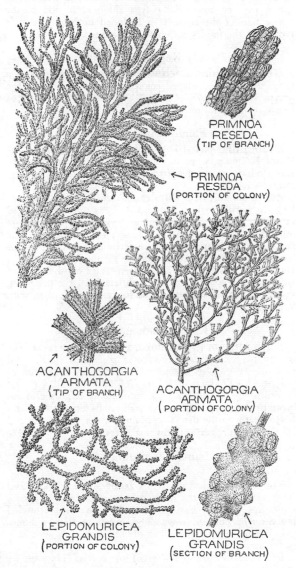

PRIMNOA
RESEDA
(TIP OF BRANCH)

← PRIMNOA
RESEDA
(PORTION OF COLONY)

ACANTHOGORGIA
ARMATA
(TIP OF BRANCH)

ACANTHOGORGIA
ARMATA
(PORTION OF COLONY)

LEPIDOMURICEA
GRANDIS
(PORTION OF COLONY)

LEPIDOMURICEA
GRANDIS
(SECTION OF BRANCH)

to them. It grows from 6 inches to a foot in height and has a row of flowerlike polyps along each side of the upper half of the stem. It is included here because it is typical of the family to which it belongs.

Family Kophobelemnonidae

Kophobelemnon tenue Verrill PLATE 64. This is a long, slender, club-shaped colony with a number of large polyps situated spirally around the stem. It was dredged in 499 to 2369 fathoms.

Family Umbellulidae

Umbellula bairdii Verrill and **Umbellula guntheri** Kolliker PLATE 64. These species belong to a rare and curious genus, hitherto dredged from 1731 to 2033 fathoms.

At the summit of a tall, slender stem, a close cluster of large flowerlike polyps is grouped. They may be deep red in color, shading toward orange red or purplish red in other polyps, each with eight long pinnate tentacles. The flexible stem of the colony is often 2 feet or more in length. It terminates at the base in a long, hollow, muscular bulb. It has been found in deep water off the coast of Greenland. *Umbellula guntheri* differs from the preceding species in having longer and perfectly smooth polyps with lanceolate clusters of zooids.

Family Anthoptilidae

Anthoptilum grandiflorum (Verrill) PLATE 64. The colony of this species grows over 2 feet in height and measures 1 inch in diameter. It has many hundreds of polyps. It is dredged in 302 to 1106 fathoms and was first described by Verrill, in 1879, from many large specimens brought in by the Gloucester halibut fishermen from off Nova Scotia on the deep water banks. Later, it was dredged by the "Challenger" off Buenos Aires.

Family Funiculinidae
(Sea-Pens)

The species included in this family have a short and stocky stem, while the more or less rectangular rachis is long and slender, having retractile autozooids crowded together in oblique rows. The much smaller siphonozooids run in a more or less double row along one side of the stem.

Funiculina armata Verrill PLATE 64. This species reaches a length of two feet or more. The autozooids are purple, with the rachis yellowish, on the underside, varying to brown above. This is a large and much-branched

PLATE 64

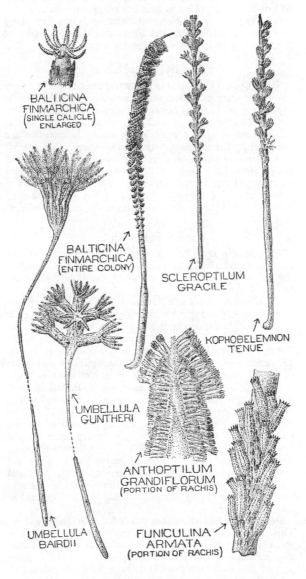

BALTICINA
FINMARCHICA
(SINGLE CALICLE)
ENLARGED

BALTICINA
FINMARCHICA
(ENTIRE COLONY)

SCLEROPTILUM
GRACILE

UMBELLULA
GUNTHERI

KOPHOBELEMNON
TENUE

ANTHOPTILUM
GRANDIFLORUM
(PORTION OF RACHIS)

UMBELLULA
BAIRDII

FUNICULINA
ARMATA
(PORTION OF RACHIS)

colony with a horny axis and long clavate, spinose calicles. When living, the color is pale orange or salmon.

The range is from Newfoundland to Nantucket, along the edge of the Continental Shelf and the upper part of the Oceanic Slope in 100 to 640 fathoms.

Family Virgularidae

Balticina (Pavonaria) finmarchica (Sars) PLATE 64. This colony has a tall wandlike stalk, frequently growing to a yard in height and to about 1 inch in diameter. Many have the axis stripped bare at the end and also at other places along the stem. These vacant spaces often are occupied by the actinian, *Stephanauge nexilis*. The base of this anemone becomes well developed at its sides and wraps around the stem of the pennatulid, while its edges coalesce to form a firm suture. The *Stephanauge* grows to rather large size. The weight of a cluster of five to nine polyps is considerable and bends over the axis of *Balticina* (see PLATE 73).

Family Pennatulidae

This family includes the typical sea-feathers with the pinnae symmetrically arranged in pairs on either side of the rachis. The siphonozooids are on the under side of the rachis.

Pennatula aculeata (Sars) PLATE 65. The Red Sea-Pen. This very beautiful and graceful species of sea-pen is widely distributed along the New England coast and has been found north as far as Nova Scotia, and south to the Carolinas. Individuals may be 4 inches or more in length. There are numerous spines among the siphonozooids in the rachis. On the Continental Shelf, it is very common from 60 to 300 fathoms and is even more abundant in deep water to more than a thousand fathoms. It is often brought in by fishermen and by dredging schooners off Gloucester and from the various fishing banks, as well as by the United States Fish Commission steamers, such as the "Fish Hawk" and "Albatross." The plumelike pinnae range in color from bright- to purplish-red, while the stalk is pale orange or yellow. There are, also, pink and rose-colored varieties, as well as albinos. Some varieties are found with longer pinnae. All are very luminescent in the dark.

Pennatula borealis Sars PLATE 65. The Great Sea-Pen. This is a much larger species, often attaining a length of 20 inches and breadth of 5 to 6 inches. It varies considerably in color. The edges of the pinnae and the bulbous part of the stalk are usually orange-red to purplish red, while the parts of the pinnae near the stalk and the lower part of the latter vary from yellowish to orange. The

PLATE 65

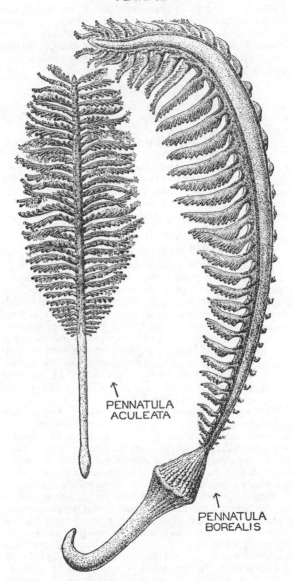

PENNATULA
ACULEATA

PENNATULA
BOREALIS

siphonozooids are usually numerous and red in color. There is a strong, bulbous, muscular enlargement near the top of the stalk. This organism is found along the northern New England coast from Newfoundland to the Woods Hole region, on the outer edge of the Continental Shelf, being dredged in 100 to 500 fathoms. It is frequently brought in by halibut fishermen.

Family Renillidae

In this family, the rachis is platelike and almost circular or kidney-shaped. The polyps are only on the front or upper surface. The stalk is soft.

Renilla reniformis (Pallas) PLATE 66. The Sea Pansy. This remarkable species has a generally flowerlike appearance, the rachis being rose pink or violet in color with an almost regular pattern of white polyps of two sizes, the autozooids, of typical form and almost transparent when expanded, surrounded by circles of siphonozooids, which are much smaller, without tentacles, and tubelike.

SUBCLASS ZOANTHARIA
(Sea-Anemones and Corals)

The polyps in the Zoantharia are cylindrical in shape with a very contractile body. The upper end is the oral disc, with a slitlike mouth in the center, and two siphonoglyphs, one at each end of the slit. Surrounding the mouth on the oral disc are radiating series of hollow tentacles arranged in either one circlet around the edge of the disc or in several or many circlets, completely covering the top. They may be in radiating rows or there may be two single circlets, one, the oral circlet, close around the mouth, usually on a raised prostomium; the other, the marginal circlet, around the outer edge of the disc. The mouth opens into the stomodaeum (pharynx).

The internal cavity (INDEX PLATE 69) is divided into radiating alcoves separated by thin partitions (*mesenteries*). The outer edges of these, in the upper part of the column, may be attached to the pharynx wall so as to close completely in the upper part of the compartments. Below the lower end of the pharynx, the compartments open freely like alcoves, as stated above. The mesenteries are arranged in pairs of different sizes, of which the longest are six in number and are the first to appear in the development of the polyp. There are muscle bands running from the top to the bottom of each mesentery, the two pairs corresponding to the siphonoglyphs, having their bands on the outer side of each pair. In the other four pairs, the muscle bands face each other. In the spaces between these six pairs of septa, there are six shorter pairs, which are the second series to develop in each polyp. In the third series to de-

PLATE 66

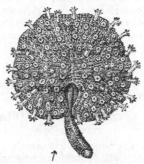

RENILLA RENIFORMIS
(DORSAL VIEW OF COLONY)

RENILLA
RENIFORMIS
(PORTION OF DORSAL)
SURFACE

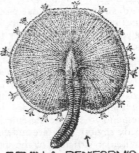

RENILLA RENIFORMIS
(VENTRAL VIEW OF COLONY)

ASTRANGIA DANAE
(PORTION OF COLONY)

velop, each pair occupies the twelve spaces between the first two pairs and so on. The free edges of the mesenteries are enlarged to form the mesenterial filaments, which are often much convoluted, and are equipped with sting-cells (nematocysts) and glandular cells secreting digestive fluids (enzymes). The detailed arrangement of these internal structures varies in different species of the sea-anemones.

The stony corals (e.g., *Astrangia danae* PLATES 66 and 75) are essentially similar in structure except that they secrete a stony skeleton.

Order CERIANTHIDEA
(PLATE 67)

These are anemonelike anthozoans, with smooth, muscular, often tapering, cylindrical bodies provided with a terminal pore. They are found buried in sandy bottoms with only the oral disc and two circlets of tentacles protruding. The latter are, respectively, an inner oral circlet and an outer marginal circlet. They are simple, slender, and tapering. The pharynx is slitlike and has one siphonoglyph, which, however, is not regarded as corresponding to the single siphonoglyph of the Alcyonaria. The body cavity is divided into as many alcoves or chambers as there are tentacles in each series, one tentacle of the oral series and one of the marginal series opening into each chamber. The mesenteries in this group are not paired, as in the true sea-anemones, but, in each case, simply correspond to similar mesenteries on the opposite side of the body cavity. They are indefinite in number. The retractile muscular structure of the species in this group is weak.

Family Cerianthidae

This is the only family and has the characteristics of the order.

Cerianthus americanus Verrill PLATE 67. There are 125 or more tentacles in each of the two circlets. When the body is fully extended, it may measure up to 6 inches in length. The general color is brown. The distribution is from Cape Cod to Florida, in shallow water.

Cerianthus borealis Verrill PLATE 67. This species is characterized by its large size, which is usually 7 to 9 inches in length and 2 inches in width of body, and measures from 5 to 6 inches across the expanded tentacles. Verrill records even larger specimens. One from off the Maine coast measured 18 inches long and 7 inches across the expanded disc.

A long, rough, and thick tube is constructed by this species, composed of mud and various other materials cemented together by hardened mucus. The tubes are

PLATE 67

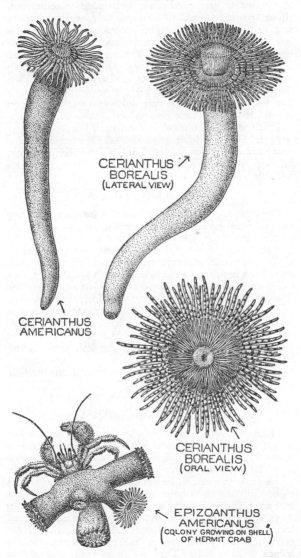

CERIANTHUS
BOREALIS
(LATERAL VIEW)

CERIANTHUS
AMERICANUS

CERIANTHUS
BOREALIS
(ORAL VIEW)

EPIZOANTHUS
AMERICANUS
(COLONY GROWING ON SHELL
OF HERMIT CRAB)

often 2 feet in length and fairly smooth inside. The body of *Cerianthus* varies according to its state of contraction, either tapering toward its terminus or sometimes swollen and urn-shaped. The marginal tentacles may be 150 to 200 in number, those in the inner rows being much longer than those in the outer rows. The oral tentacles are about ⅓ as long as the marginal ones. The color of the body in living specimens varies from dark chestnut-brown, tinged with bluish or purplish to an orange-brown or greenish gray. The disc is pale yellow-brown, being deeper around the mouth with fine radiating lines.

This species is abundant in the Bay of Fundy, off Casco Bay, the Gulf of Maine generally, off Georges Bank, and also off southern New England. It is a very common species in deep water. It is known to occur from 25 to 264 fathoms.

Order ZOANTHIDEA

These sea-anemones grow in colonies from an incrusting base or from stolons. The numerous tentacles are in one or two rows. Many species grow on shells of hermit crabs, sponges, and hydroids, and even stones on the sea-bottom.

Epizoanthus americanus Verrill PLATE 67. This anemone's body is more or less incrusted with sand grains. Colonies of several polyps grow out of a common expanded base of continuous fleshy substance. They are about an inch in height, with thirty-eight or more tentacles. In many cases, the flesh of the colony has completely absorbed the shell of a hermit crab, on which it is mounted, so that the crab is covered merely by the flesh of the colony base.

This species occurs in 20 to 400 fathoms from the Gulf of St. Lawrence to New Jersey.

Order EDWARDSIIDEA

These are small, slender, and solitary sea-anemones, which burrow in the sand with their tapering, almost pointed foot. When found, they usually are imbedded with only the oral disc protruding. The number of tentacles varies from fourteen to forty-eight. There are usually only eight fully formed mesenteries, while others are rudimentary. There are eight longitudinal ridges on the outer surface, corresponding in number with the eight mesenteries. They often are incrusted with sand and other foreign material. Some species adhere to stones, etc., by means of their sides. They are occasionally parasitic on jellyfish when young.

Edwardsia elegans Verrill PLATE 68. This beautiful and delicate species is from 3 to 6 inches in length and is

PLATE 68

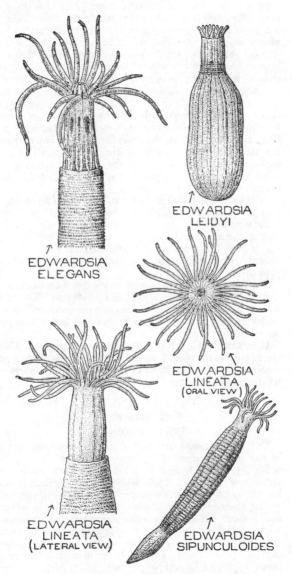

EDWARDSIA
ELEGANS

EDWARDSIA
LEIDYI

EDWARDSIA
LINEATA
(ORAL VIEW)

EDWARDSIA
LINEATA
(LATERAL VIEW)

EDWARDSIA
SIPUNCULOIDES

about an inch in diameter. There are sixteen slender and very mobile tentacles, varying from yellowish to pale flesh-color with a reddish or orange-red median stripe on the outer surface, extending to near the tip. Near the base of the tentacles there is a white or pale yellow spot, also an oval yellow spot with a V-shaped marking on the outer side of the base. The disc is somewhat cone-shaped and striped with eight lines of reddish or purplish brown, separating the eight labial lobes. These divide at each tentacle so as to pass along its sides. Square white spots often occur between the reddish lines. The upper part of the extensible body, more than an inch in length, has eight pale lines corresponding to the insertions of the mesenteries. Beneath the tentacle base is a series of lemon-yellow spots extending around this part of the body. There is also a band of eight oval, pale yellow spots, each divided by pale orange stripes.

This species is found at Eastport, Maine, under stones at very low tide, and is distributed southward to Cape Cod.

Edwardsia leidyi Verrill PLATE 68. Like the preceding species, there are sixteen tentacles. The length is 1¼ inches. It is peculiar in being parasitic on the ctenophore, *Mnemiopsis leidyi*. It is quite common from Vineyard Sound southward.

Edwardsia lineata Verrill PLATE 68. The number of tentacles in this species is eighteen to twenty. The color is generally brown. It is common among worm tubes and under or near stones, in 4 to 12 fathoms, from Vineyard Sound southward.

Edwardsia sipunculoides Simpson PLATE 68. There are twenty to thirty-six tentacles in this species. The length is more than 4 inches when extended. The color is brown. Its distribution is from Cape Cod northward.

Order ACTINIARIA
(Sea-Anemones)
(INDEX PLATE 69)

The sea-anemones are among the best-known animals of the ocean margin. They are most often seen at low water in tide-pools and in submerged areas among the crevices of the rocks. Their flowerlike appearance is well known to all persons wandering along the seashore.

The anemone's body consists of an *oral disc*, a *column*, and a *base*. The oral disc is flat, circular, and sometimes with a lobed margin. The tentacles may be few or many, and sometimes, in certain species, they cover the greater part of the oral disc. They may be arranged in two or many cycles or in radiating rows. When they are very numerous, they are apparently without arrangement. In the many species in which they occur, their numbers may

PLATE 69

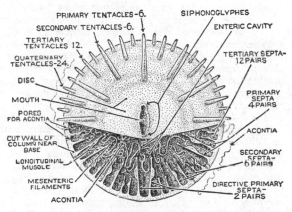

PRIMARY TENTACLES-6.
SECONDARY TENTACLES-6.
TERTIARY TENTACLES 12.
QUATERNARY TENTACLES-24.
DISC
MOUTH
PORES FOR ACONTIA
CUT WALL OF COLUMN NEAR BASE
LONGITUDINAL MUSCLE
MESENTERIC FILAMENTS
ACONTIA

SIPHONOGLYPHES
ENTERIC CAVITY
TERTIARY SEPTA-12 PAIRS
PRIMARY SEPTA 4 PAIRS
ACONTIA
SECONDARY SEPTA-6 PAIRS
DIRECTIVE PRIMARY SEPTA-2 PAIRS

APICAL VIEW WITH PORTION OF DISC AND COLUMN REMOVED TO SHOW INTERIOR

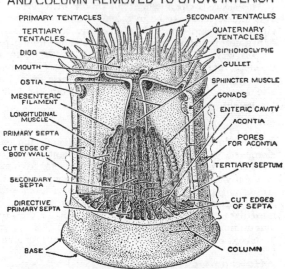

PRIMARY TENTACLES
TERTIARY TENTACLES
DISC
MOUTH
OSTIA
MESENTERIC FILAMENT
LONGITUDINAL MUSCLE
PRIMARY SEPTA
CUT EDGE OF BODY WALL
SECONDARY SEPTA
DIRECTIVE PRIMARY SEPTA
BASE

SECONDARY TENTACLES
QUATERNARY TENTACLES
SIPHONOGLYPHE
GULLET
SPHINCTER MUSCLE
GONADS
ENTERIC CAVITY
ACONTIA
PORES FOR ACONTIA
TERTIARY SEPTUM
CUT EDGES OF SEPTA
COLUMN

SIDE VIEW WITH PORTION OF DISC, GULLET AND COLUMN REMOVED TO SHOW INTERIOR

A TYPICAL ACTINIAN

vary from a few to hundreds and even to a thousand or more. The cylindrical body is known as the column.

Just above the base is a constriction which partly separates it from the column. The base itself is often expanded into a circular pedal disc, which can adhere to material on the sea-bottom, wrapping itself around shells, stones, or flattening out on the side of a rock. The anemone is able to travel from place to place slowly by extending portions of its pedal disc. The tentacles are simple, hollow, and taper to a point or to a ball-like enlargement equipped with batteries of sting-cells. The mouth is slitlike, although occasionally round, and usually in the center of a clear, smooth zone which separates it from the tentacles. Internally, the mesenteries are arranged in definite radiating patterns, usually in pairs with the muscle-bands facing each other, except in the case of the mesenteries on either side of the siphonoglyphs, which have their muscle-bands facing outward. In various species, certain of these septa are complete or incomplete depending upon the method of development. Gonads and mesenterial filaments are on the free edges of the mesenteries. There is no internal skeleton.

The sex-cells ripen while still in the mesogloea. Male and female cells may be in the same individual, but will ripen at different times so as to insure cross-fertilization. When fertilized, the egg produces a free-swimming pear-shaped larva, which settles down on the sea-bottom and develops into an adult polyp. Anemones may also reproduce asexually by splitting in half (transverse fission) and also by budding a smaller individual from the side of the parent.

Family Halcampidae

The column of this family is usually slender and much elongated, generally with a rounded or pointed end without a definite basal disc. The tentacles may vary from eight to twenty-four. There are but few mesenteries, and they are arranged on the principle of sixes (*hexamerous*). Sometimes there are more mesenteries than tentacles. The muscular system is feeble or lacking except for the strong longitudinal muscles of the mesenteries. The body may be naked or it may be covered with a coating of mucus, fine sand, etc.

Halcampa duodecimcirrata (Sars) PLATE 70. The tentacles here are short, usually twelve in number, in two cycles. The usually cylindrical column is very changeable in form, since it may be swollen in the middle or posteriorly, or it may contract to half its full length. It is usually covered with adherent grains of sand and small Foraminifera. There is a circle of small purplish brown spots near the lips and a concentric circle of the same color near the

PLATE 70

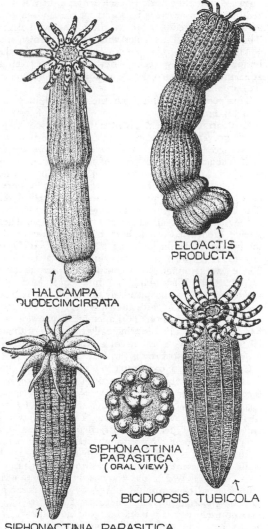

HALCAMPA
QUODECIMCIRRATA

ELOACTIS
PRODUCTA

SIPHONACTINIA
PARASITICA
(ORAL VIEW)

BICIDIOPSIS TUBICOLA

SIPHONACTINIA PARASITICA
(LATERAL VIEW)

base of the tentacles, the two connected by brown radial lines. The spots are oval, but with a pointed end extending outward. On either side of each tentacle there is a spot of reddish brown near the base and six crescent-shaped transverse spots of reddish brown alternating with flesh-color. The column is salmon-color with purplish brown spots.

The species of this genus occupy crevices in the sea-bottom and among rocks. They are able to creep about, adhering along their sides by means of very minute sucker-like organs.

This species is found from the Bay of Fundy to Eastport Harbor, Maine.

Siphonactinia (Bicidium) parasitica (Agassiz) PLATE 70. This and related species have one siphonoglyph prolonged into a three-lobed *conchula*. There are usually twelve tentacles and six pairs of mesenteries. The column is naked, soft, very changeable in form. There is no disc at the posterior end, but a central contractile pore. The circular muscles of the column are moderately developed. The body may be 3½ inches long when fully extended or it may contract to an elliptical or ovate shape. There are twelve grooves corresponding to the mesenteries, the latter being visible through the transparent wall. Tentacles are about ½ inch long, tapering from a swollen base. There is a terminal, often conspicuous pore at the tip of each tentacle. The mouth has nine equal lobes or folds and three others conspicuously rounded, forming a conchula in connection with the siphonoglyph. The conchula is capable of protrusion. This anemone is parasitic on jellyfish, to which it adheres principally by means of the mouth lobes. The body varies in color from flesh-color to light brown or greenish brown.

Common from Nova Scotia to Cape Cod in the summer.

Bicidiopsis tubicola Verrill PLATE 70. Like the other species in the family, *Bicidiopsis tubicola* is changeable in form and is capable of contracting and expanding its body cavity, especially when burrowing. The column-wall is soft and naked and nearly cylindrical, being three times as long as it is broad. It is obtusely rounded and perforated at the base. It is salmon-color, with somewhat translucent walls, the mesenteries showing through as pale whitish lines, between which the body is swollen and wrinkled transversely. It has minute suckers by which it can adhere to a neighboring surface. There are twelve strong, tapering, obtusely pointed tentacles, pale salmon-color, brown at the base and ringed with four bands of light brown. The mouth is salmon-colored inside and has a three-lobed conchula at one end connected with the siphonoglyph.

It is found at Eastport, Maine, burrowing in gravel and sand or under large stones.

Eloactis producta Andres PLATE 70. The body of this anemone is slender and very contractile. The tentacles are short, blunt, or with a knob at the ends. They surround the mouth in two rows, altogether twenty in number. The body has twenty longitudinal tuberculated ridges, one corresponding to each tentacle. The diameter is ¾ inch. It is whitish to salmon in color.

It occurs from South Carolina to Cape Cod, buried in the sand or on the underside of stones, in shallow water.

Family Bunodidae

The column is often of large size with a strong sphincter muscle and usually a tuberculated outer surface.

Bunodes (Tealiopsis) stella Verrill PLATE 71. These polyps are ½ inch or more in height. When well grown, they have about 120 long and large, smooth tentacles in about four or five cycles. The body-wall, except near the base, is covered with many longitudinal rows of adhesive suckers. The color of the column is translucent olive-green varying to flesh-color and to darker green. The disc shows a lighter shade of these colors and usually has six radial lines of opaque white running to the primary tentacles. Colonies of this anemone are found in large numbers in the crevices of ridges covered with algae at low tide and especially in sheltered tide pools. Sometimes it is buried in sand with only its tentacles exposed and, occasionally, it is found under stones.

It is distributed along the coast of Maine and at Eastport, Maine, and Grand Manan Island.

Epiactis prolifera Verrill PLATE 72. The most conspicuous characteristic of this species is the band of egg-pits which surrounds the outer surface of the body just below its middle. The height is ⅖ inch and the diameter, ½ inch. There are about ninety-six tentacles. The egg-pits may reach the number of thirty to forty.

Urticina (Tealia) crassicornis Müller PLATE 71. This is a very large, stout, and brightly colored species with many large, thick tentacles. The column has many longitudinal rows of very small suckers capable of becoming attached to foreign objects. The column is soft, flexible, and very changeable in form. The tentacles can be retracted and the column margin pulled in over the edge of the disc. The body-wall is streaked with bright red-crimson and dark red and blotched with lighter shades. The oral disc is marked by conspicuous double lines of bright red radiating from the mouth to enclose the bases of the tentacles. The tentacles are ringed with bands of red and white.

This species is especially abundant off Nantucket, Block Island, Watch Hill, and Fisher's Island Sound.

Family Boloceridae

These are large sea-anemones having numerous stout tentacles which are not retractile, but can be readily cast off. The usually smooth column secretes an abundant mucus. Usually there are no suckers or *verrucae*. The muscle structure is rather weak.

Bolocera tuediae Verrill PLATE 71. The large, cylindrical, orange or red body and the very large, nonretractile tentacles, which are easily cast off, distinguish this species. The column is smooth and stout, secreting mucus abundantly. The diameter across the tentacles often reaches 6 to 8 inches, while the longer tentacles are 2 to 3 inches in length. The body alone is 2 to 3 inches in diameter and somewhat tall, when expanded. The disc is deep orange-red in color with fine darker lines radiating from the mouth. The margin of the mouth is thrown into numerous thick folds of bright red. The two siphonoglyphs are bright red or rose-color varying to purple, and are formed by conspicuously thick folds with a deep groove between them. The tentacles are of the same orange-red color as the disc, more or less striped. The column is also orange-red and smooth. In some specimens, the body and the outer tentacles are white or salmon-color. The tentacles are equipped with powerful sting-cells and are capable of penetrating the skin of the human hands, especially when they are wet. This species ranges from the Bay of Fundy and the outer side of Nova Scotia, throughout the entire Gulf of Maine to Massachusetts Bay, Cape Cod, and Martha's Vineyard Island, in from 40 to 500 fathoms. A small crustacean (*Autheacheres dubenii* Sars) is often parasitic in the stomach of this sea-anemone and is usually the same color as its host.

Bolocera multicornis Verrill PLATE 72. This is also a large, bright red species with more than two hundred crowded tentacles, smaller than those of *Bolocera tuediae*. They are of the same color as the column and not banded. The disc is almost four inches in diameter, being about one-half the size of the previous species. The column is very short and thick so that the expanded anemone has the appearance of a red hemisphere covered with moving tentacles.

This species is found off Cape Cod in 33 to 90 fathoms and probably ranges to the northern fishing banks.

Epigonactis fecunda Verrill and **Epigonactis regularis** Verrill PLATE 72. These two species, illustrated at the top of the plate, have been dredged from the Banks off Nova Scotia and Newfoundland. They carry numerous

PLATE 71

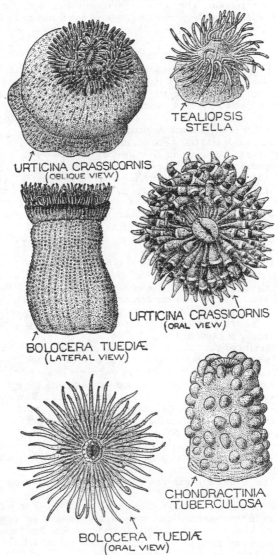

URTICINA CRASSICORNIS
(OBLIQUE VIEW)

TEALIOPSIS
STELLA

BOLOCERA TUEDIÆ
(LATERAL VIEW)

URTICINA CRASSICORNIS
(ORAL VIEW)

BOLOCERA TUEDIÆ
(ORAL VIEW)

CHONDRACTINIA
TUBERCULOSA

eggs and young imbedded in deep pits on the upper part of the column. The tentacles are stout and numerous. They have only been seen as preserved specimens so their color is not known (Verrill).

Family Paractidae

These actinians have no *acontia* or *cinclides*. There is a mesogloeal sphincter muscle which is either thick or diffuse. Usually, there are up to three or four and even more cycles of perfect mesenteries. The column is either smooth or wrinkled. The aboral disc is adherent and may be either large or much reduced.

Ammophilactis (Paractis) rapiformis (Lesson) PLATE 72. The body in this species is covered with fine longitudinal grooves. The mouth is surrounded by a circle of short, cylindrical tentacles, all of equal length. The column is about 3 inches in height and 1 inch in diameter. The surface is nearly smooth and pinkish in color. There is a small pedal disc. This animal is usually found buried in the sand near low-water marks.

Cape Cod to Cape Hatteras, extending to the coast of Europe.

Paractis perdix Verrill PLATE 72. This anemone is remarkable for its numerous tentacles, which may be nearly 400 in number, crowning the entire top of the column. This column extends upward for 3 or 4 inches with a broad oral disc, perhaps 5 inches in diameter. The tentacles are all practically of the same length. The column is usually not tuberculated.

Actinostola callosa Verrill PLATE 72. This anemone is massive, reaching a height of 6 to 7 inches, with the diameter across the oral disc 8 to 10 inches. The numerous tentacles are grouped in about four rows around the outer edge of the oral disc with a clear space between the inner row and the convoluted mouth. The inner tentacles are many times longer than the outer tentacles. The column is moderately tuberculated on the upper portion. The sphincter muscle is strong, as in the case of the other Paractidae. There are no acontia present. The pedal disc is quite distinct.

This species is distributed along the New England coast in 45 to 300 fathoms.

Stomphia carneola (Stimpson) PLATE 72. The column in this species is soft, smooth, and without verrucae or suckers. It is very changeable in form. The basal disc is thin and may be broadly expanded, but nevertheless can change its shape and contract to a small size. The oral disc is also very changeable, varying from flat to concave or convex. There are moderately stout and contractile tentacles, often as many as ninety-six, situated around the

PLATE 72

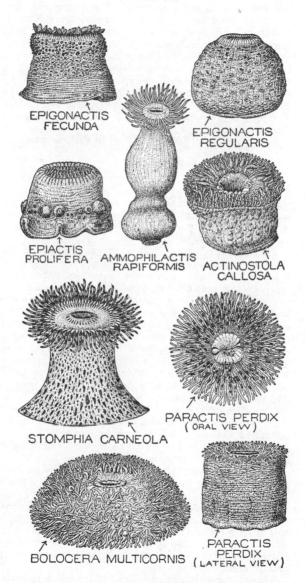

EPIGONACTIS
FECUNDA

EPIGONACTIS
REGULARIS

EPIACTIS
PROLIFERA

AMMOPHILACTIS
RAPIFORMIS

ACTINOSTOLA
CALLOSA

STOMPHIA CARNEOLA

PARACTIS PERDIX
(ORAL VIEW)

BOLOCERA MULTICORNIS

PARACTIS
PERDIX
(LATERAL VIEW)

margin of the disc. There are two siphonoglyphs. The labial lobes are numerous and small. The mesenteries, also, are quite numerous and thin. Normally, the column is cylindrical, higher than broad, and may become more elongated or extremely short. It may even be hour-glass shaped. The color of the column in this variable species is also changeable. It may be translucent pink, flesh-color, pale greenish, with the edges of the mesenteries showing through as paler stripes. Sometimes it is mottled and streaked irregularly with pale red, rose-red, or even scarlet. The tentacles are flesh-color, pink, ringed with two to three bands of carmine.

Bay of Fundy to Eastport, Maine, in shallow water.

Family Sagartiadae

These are actinians, as a rule, with numerous retractile tentacles, having acontia and usually also cinclides. The size and coloration of the column are extremely variable in the species included in this family. The sphincter muscle is mesogloeal and more or less diffuse. The mesenteries usually develop in multiples of six.

Sagartia modesta Verrill PLATE 73. The body of this anemone is cylindrical, and about five times as long as it is broad. It attaches itself to the sea-bottom, usually on a stone, by means of a strong pedal disc. There are sixty to one hundred tentacles situated about the margin of the oral disc. They are very delicate in texture and are slender and tapering. In color, they are gray, verging toward green, with dark spots near the base. The oral disc is somewhat yellowish with dark lines radiating upon it. The column is usually of a pale flesh-color. There is a tendency for sand-grains to adhere to the body because of the abundant mucus secreted here. Acontia are present, but apparently no cinclides. It is usually found at about the low-tide mark where it burrows among the sand and small pebbles. It is sometimes difficult to find because the coloration so closely mimics its environment.

Quite common in the Woods Hole region from Long Island Sound and Buzzards Bay to Vineyard Sound.

Sagartia luciae Verrill PLATE 73. This handsome species is between ½ to ¾ inch in height. The column is olive-green in color with more or less parallel, conspicuous, orange or yellow stripes. There are from twenty-five to fifty long and delicate tentacles. They are pale green, tinged with white. It reproduces both sexually and asexually; in the former case by means of ciliated larvae, in the latter by a simple division, which begins at the oral disc and proceeds down to the base.

Though formerly rare, this *Sagartia* is now quite abundant in the Woods Hole region and is spreading rapidly along the southern New England coast. It is not known north of Cape Cod.

Sagartia (Cylista) leucolena Verrill PLATE 73. This is a small and delicate species with an elongated, cylindrical body which may be covered with tiny papillae, usually in vertical rows. The body is quite translucent, so that the edges of the mesenteries show through its sides. There are forty to sixty tentacles, of which the inner series is the longest. They are very slender and taper to the tips. The color varies from a delicate flesh to white. Individuals may be 1½ inches in height. This species is quite common, adhering to the underside of rocks and in rock crevices. As it is quite sensitive to light, it tends to be found in dark corners among the rocks. Reproduction is largely sexual.

It is distributed from Cape Cod to North Carolina, and is quite abundant in the Woods Hole region and Long Island Sound.

Metridium dianthus (Ellis) PLATE 73; COLOR PLATE I. This species is one of the handsomest as well as one of the commonest to be found along our coast. It has a velvety-smooth column, up to 4 inches in height and 3 inches broad, crowned with a widely expanded oral disc, divided into waved lobes, covered with multitudes of small and slender tentacles. When very large, an individual may have as many as a thousand tentacles, while internally, there is a corresponding number of pairs of mesenteries. When the oral disc is in a more or less convex condition, it resembles a marine chrysanthemum. The column is dark chocolate-brown, sometimes blotched with white, and sometimes white, streaked and marked with brown. Cinclides are present. It may reproduce asexually by longitudinal fission, by budding from near the base, or by breaking off fragments from the edge of the expanded basal disc, each of which develops into a new individual. It also reproduces sexually in the usual way, by means of eggs fertilized by sperms which give rise to a free-swimming larva. It has a world-wide distribution around the Arctic region extending down through the North Atlantic to Long Island Sound and northern New Jersey, from low-water mark to a depth of 150 feet. It may often be found above low-water mark among stones, on wharf-piles, in tide-pools, and in rock crevices generally. It is most abundant and largest in size on the coast of Massachusetts and Maine and in the Bay of Fundy and Gulf of St. Lawrence.

Adamsia tricolor Lesson (**sociabilis** Verrill) PLATE 73. A strongly expanded pedal disc characterizes this anemone. It grows in colonies which have the curious habit of adhering to the shells of hermit crabs and to the larger crustaceans. It may be 3 inches in height and nearly 2 inches in diameter, with numerous tentacles, often as many as 500.

It is distributed from North Carolina to Florida.

Chondractinia tuberculosa (Verrill) PLATE 71. The body in this species is covered with remarkably large, prominent, often hemispherical tubercles, irregularly placed and not very numerous. The integument is very thick and firm except on the pink or red capitulum below the tentacles, where it is softer, slightly longitudinally ridged or nearly smooth, and probably capable of secreting a phosphorescent mucus. The lower tubercular part is usually covered with an adherent mud-colored epidermal secretion. The tentacles are numerous, dull red or reddish brown, rather long, usually not bulbous at the base or much tapered. The sphincter muscle is large and thick. The stomodaeum is also large and long. It has five deep lateral grooves, and four expanded intervening lobes on each side. The siphonoglyphs are well developed and deep. This species is known only in deep water.

From Georges Bank to the Grand Bank and in the Gulf of Maine.

Actinauge rugosa Verrill PLATE 73. The column of this species is peculiar in having a thick and almost rigid cortex. It is cylindrical with an expanded base, which stands out like a thin rim completely around the column. The upper part of the column has a transverse row of a dozen or more strongly compressed tubercles, which are scattered in position. They are somewhat irregularly placed appearing like small horizontal shelves. The whole column tends to be wrinkled. The upper edge is irregularly scalloped. There are usually ninety-six or more stout tentacles in about five cycles. They are fairly short and blunt when expanded.

This species ranges from Nova Scotia along the New England coast, in 50 to 100 fathoms.

Actinauge verrillii McMurrich PLATE 73. The cylindrical column is quite large and stout with tubercies or verrucae arranged in more or less vertical rows, occupying the upper ¾ of the column. The tentacles, while moderately stout, are not unusually large. The tips may vary from acute to obtuse. At the base of each marginal tentacle there is an elongate, swollen, basal lobe. In the larger specimens there may be 120 tentacles in several rows. The color is dull red, sometimes paling to pink. In many specimens, a dark brown epidermis obscures the red or pink color, while the tentacles vary from dull red to chocolate-brown. The basal disc often adheres firmly to pebbles and shells. This species may grow to 4 inches in diameter and 6 inches in height.

PLATE 73

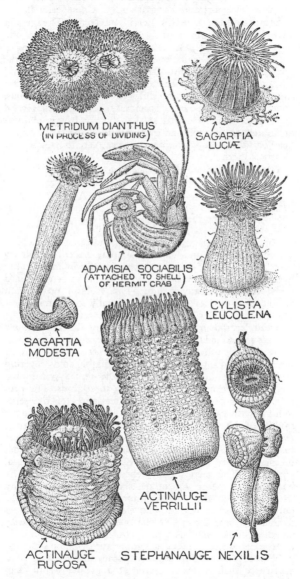

METRIDIUM DIANTHUS
(IN PROCESS OF DIVIDING)

SAGARTIA
LUCIÆ

ADAMSIA SOCIABILIS
(ATTACHED TO SHELL)
OF HERMIT CRAB

CYLISTA
LEUCOLENA

SAGARTIA
MODESTA

ACTINAUGE
VERRILLII

ACTINAUGE
RUGOSA

STEPHANAUGE NEXILIS

It is distributed along the Continental Shelf from Marthas Vineyard and Long Island to Chesapeake Bay.

Stephanauge nexilis Verrill PLATE 73. The greater part of the column wall is thin, flexible, and smooth. There are usually a few small obscure cinclides and many specimens have a transverse row of tubercles around the parapet of the oral disc. The capitulum is flexible and covered with folds, which can be retracted. The sphincter muscle is large and powerful. Tentacles are numerous, about 96 to 108 in larger specimens, arranged in several cycles and with somewhat swollen bases. Groups of these anemones are often found growing upon the stems of the Sea-Pen (*Balticina finmarchica* PLATE 64), to which they closely adhere.

They are common off Nova Scotia.

Order MADREPORARIA
(The Stony Corals)
(INDEX PLATE 74)

The coral polyps are arranged on the same principle as the sea-anemones and, like them, may be either solitary or colonial. They differ from them chiefly in their ability to secrete, from their basal ectoderm, an extremely hard skeleton of carbonate of lime. This is built up beneath and around the base of the body, usually in the form of a cup (*calyx*) into which the polyp can retract itself. The skeleton, as shown in the accompanying diagram (INDEX PLATE 74), is made up of radiating vertical plates or septa. These septa push the integument of the polyp into its interior so that it takes the form of radiating folds covering two sides and the inner edge of the septa. Within the body, the mesenteries alternate with these folds. The cup-like calyx is developed by the outer edges of the septa joining with each other to form a boundary wall. In the middle of the calyx, there often grows up a central column (*columella*). The polyps grow upward continuously, due to additions to their cylindrical base, which then becomes tubular and, at intervals, may be cut off by horizontal partitions. The polyps then reproduce by fission or by budding. As the growth of the skeleton continues during the division of the polyps, branches are formed as the polyps completely divide. The stony substance continues to increase in size until, in the open sea, coral reefs may be formed. For the most part, the latter are found only in tropical waters, having a temperature of not less than 70° Fahr. The reef-forming corals can only exist in comparatively shallow water, never at a greater depth than about 300 feet. A very few species occur as small growths in cold waters even up to the Arctic Ocean.

PLATE 74

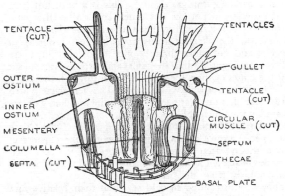

TENTACLE (CUT)

TENTACLES

OUTER OSTIUM

INNER OSTIUM

MESENTERY

COLUMELLA

SEPTA (CUT)

GULLET

TENTACLE (CUT)

CIRCULAR MUSCLE (CUT)

SEPTUM

THECAE

BASAL PLATE

INTERNAL ANATOMY OF A CORAL POLYP

LIVING TISSUES

CORAL SKELETON OR CORALLUM

CORAL POLYPS REPRODUCING BY
FISSION TO FORM A COLONY

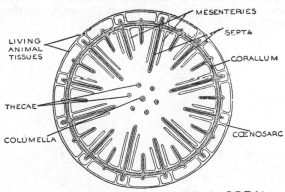

MESENTERIES

SEPTA

LIVING ANIMAL TISSUES

CORALLUM

THECAE

COLUMELLA

CŒNOSARC

TRANSVERSE SECTION OF A CORAL
POLYP TO SHOW RELATIONS OF
LIVING TISSUE TO CORAL SKELETON

Astrangia danae Agassiz PLATES 66 and 75. The principal coral found in this region, in shallow water, is the star coral (*Astrangia danae*). This is a beautiful little coral growing in patches not much larger than the palm of one's hand. Expanding from the top of the circular calyces are the delicate transparent polyps, grouped in clusters, and not more than ¼ inch in height. They are whitish or slightly pink· in color and are so translucent that the edges of their mesenteries show through the polyp wall as little vertical white lines. The tentacles which border the disc are comparatively few in number, but are covered with tiny papillalike batteries of sting-cells.

Oculina diffusa Lamarck PLATE 75. The Eyed Coral. This species grows in small branching treelike clusters in comparatively deep waters. The sides of its contorted branches bear the calyces of the coral polyps, which project conspicuously from the branches themselves.

They are distributed in cold seas, but their relatives are quite abundant in the coral reefs of the West Indies.

Flabellum goodei Verrill PLATE 75. These are solitary polyps, each forming a single calyx, the pointed base of which is imbedded in the sea-bottom. The sides are compressed and are fan-shaped, with projecting ridges. The mouth forms an elongate slit.

This and the following species are confined to the deep waters of the Atlantic Ocean. They are occasionally brought up by the dredge.

Flabellum angulare Moseley PLATE 75. This is similar to the preceding species except that the calyx is pentagonal in shape. It is beautifully symmetrical with the septa forming a radiating pattern in the interior of the shallow cup.

PLATE 75

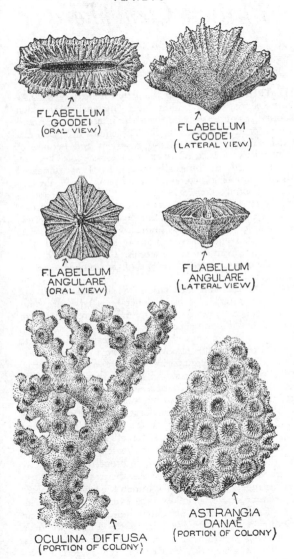

FLABELLUM
GOODEI
(ORAL VIEW)

FLABELLUM
GOODEI
(LATERAL VIEW)

FLABELLUM
ANGULARE
(ORAL VIEW)

FLABELLUM
ANGULARE
(LATERAL VIEW)

OCULINA DIFFUSA
(PORTION OF COLONY)

ASTRANGIA
DANAË
(PORTION OF COLONY)

4

Phylum Ctenophora

(THE COMB JELLIES)

(INDEX PLATE 76)

THE Ctenophora resemble the jellyfish because of their gelatinous transparent middle layer (mesenchyme) which fills out the entire space between the internal cavities and the ectoderm. They are like the Coelentera in the fundamental structure of the digestive system and because of the simplicity, or lack, of other organic systems. They are, however, distinctly biradially symmetrical as compared with the more or less complete radial symmetry of the coelenterates. Unlike the Coelentera, the Ctenophora have no nematocysts. They have a transparent muscular structure within the mesenchyme and the digestive system, which, while simple, is nevertheless branched according to a characteristic plan and forms a tubular system instead of a stomodaeum, as in the coelenterates. There is also a complex sense organ located at the end of the body opposite the mouth (aboral region).

Polymorphism and alternation of generations do not exist in this group. The more generalized types are spheroidal in shape, while the more specialized are flattened or equipped with bisymmetrical lobes and other features.

The most conspicuous characteristic feature peculiar to the Ctenophora is the possession of the so-called *"comb-plates."* There are eight rows of these on the external surface, passing from the aboral sense organ to the mouth region. Each comb-plate consists of a movable transparent plate, hinged at one side and with toothlike hairs projecting from its free edge. These plates beat the water successively and, due to the refringence of the rays of light broken up by the tiny teeth, cause a series of prismatic colors to pass rhythmically through the entire length of the row, while the effect of their motion is to propel the ctenophore through the water. In many species, there is a pair of tentacles arranged with biradial symmetry, each one situated in a *tentacle sheath,* a hollow tube extending into the interior of the organism on either side, usually with an elbowlike bend, and finally joining the alimentary tract. The nervous system resembles that in the coelenterates, consisting of a network underneath the epidermis with concentration into eight parts corresponding to the plate rows. There is no skeleton or excretory system. The reproductive organs (gonads) are located in the walls of the

PLATE 76

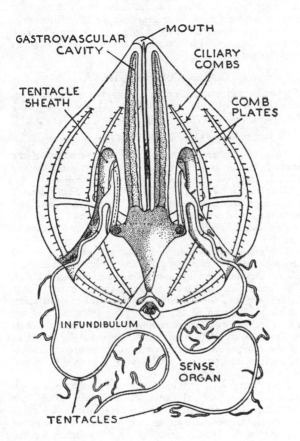

GASTROVASCULAR CAVITY

MOUTH

CILIARY COMBS

TENTACLE SHEATH

COMB PLATES

INFUNDIBULUM

SENSE ORGAN

TENTACLES

A TYPICAL CTENOPHORE

digestive system. There is no planula larva, development resulting in the so-called *cydippid* larva, which, when fully formed, resembles the more generalized adult ctenophores.

The ctenophores are divided into two classes: The *Tentaculata* (species with tentacles), and the *Nuda* (species without tentacles).

CLASS TENTACULATA

The Tentaculata, including the species with tentacles, may be divided into four orders: (1) *Cydippida;* (2) *Lobata;* (3) *Cestida;* (4) *Platyctenea.*

Order CYDIPPIDA

These are spheroidal forms with the branches of the stomach ending as blind sacs. They have two symmetrically placed, branched tentacles retractile into sheaths.

Mertensia ovum (Fabricius) PLATE 77. This animal is egg-shaped with the mouth at the more pointed end and with the apical sense organ at the broader end. The body is flattened sidewise and is somewhat over two inches in length.

The apical sense organ contains an irregular group of concretions. The two tentacles arise from symmetrically placed sheaths. They are long and branched on one side. The plate-rows, with their vibrating combs, extend about ⅘ the length of the animal. They are light pink in color, which is also true of the gonads, the tentacles, and the apical sense organ. The ctenophore ranges from the Arctic Ocean to the New Jersey coast. It is especially abundant off the coast of Maine, but seems to center around Labrador, where it apparently feeds upon sculpins. It is found swimming at the surface.

Pleurobrachia pileus Vanhoffen INDEX PLATE 76. The body is egg-shaped, but unlike *Martensia ovum,* it is not flattened, but nearly spherical, being about ⅘ inch in length and somewhat over ⅜ inch in breadth. The *apical sense-organ* is located centrally on the surface at the aboral pole. The eight rows of *comb-plates* are placed at equal distances around the body and extend nearly its entire length. The two *tentacles* arise from deep *sheaths* placed symmetrically on either side, into which the greater part of the tentacle may be withdrawn. The tentacles may extend as much as twenty times the length of the body and are branched on one side in the form of fine thread-like *filaments,* giving them the aspect of delicate plumes. The mouth is an extremely narrow slit at right angles to the long axis of the body. There is also the *stomodaeum,* which extends into the center of the ctenophore for not quite one half of its distance. From either side of the stomodaeum, a *perradial canal* extends out laterally to divide into two *paragastral canals*. These widely bifurcate and each, in turn, divides into two branches forming a Y-pattern. The bases of the *tentacular sheaths* are situated at the point of the first division of the paragastral canals. The final branches are known as the *adradial canals*. In this way, there is an adradial canal for each of the eight rows of comb-plates.

This beautifully transparent organism is tinged from milky-white to orange-yellow or brownish orange in the tentacles and stomodaeum. It is distributed from the Arctic Ocean, through all seas, to the Antarctic and Pacific. In America, it is found along the coast of New England to Cape Cod, though sometimes it is taken south of that point. During the summer, great swarms of this ctenophore occur off the coast of Nova Scotia and Maine.

Pleurobrachia brunnea Mayer PLATE 77. This species differs from the previous one by its longer egg-shaped body and by the opaque yellow-brown color of the stomodaeum. A row of brilliant purple spots extends halfway down each tentacle as well as along the side branches. The branches of the tentacles are fewer than in *Pleurobrachia pileus* and each ends in a large sensitive knob.

The range of this species is farther south than that of *Pleurobrachia pileus* and it has been known to occur in much greater abundance off the coast of New Jersey during the fall.

Hormiphora plumosa L. Agassiz PLATE 77. This is a warm-water form about the same size as the previous species. It is occasionally brought northward by the Gulf Stream.

Order LOBATA

The spheroidal body of these ctenophores is equipped with two large symmetrical, flaplike *oral lobes* and four *auricles*. The two tentacles are without sheaths.

Bolinopsis infundibulum (Muller) PLATE 77. The aboral end is narrowed to a blunt point and the large, paired, oral lobes are elongate lappets. They do not overlap each other. They are about ⅓ the length of the animal. The sense organ, at the aboral end, is situated at the bottom of a deep pit. It contains a mass of small white concretions. There are four auricles (fingerlike processes arising from the sides of the animal). They are flat and ribbonlike. The eight comb-plates arise from the aboral end and pass straight down to their destinations, four at the base of the auricles, while the other four extend down nearly to the end of the lobes.

This is an extremely common ctenophore of the northern New England coast. Cape Cod seems to act as a barrier as it has not been found south of that Cape. It is, however, very abundant off the coast of Newfoundland and northern Maine.

Mnemiopsis leidyi A. Agassiz PLATE 77. This is a large ctenophore, being about 4 inches in length. It is more or less pear-shaped in outline, including the oral lappets, each of which is about ⅔ as long as the animal and considerably wider. The four auricles are flat and ribbonlike; their edges lie in a deep groove that extends down the sides of the body. Both sides of the long, slitlike mouth are edged with a row of short tentacles. The central tentacle on each side is longer than the others. The creature is almost colorless, a slightly milky translucency making it visible to the eye. The ciliated combs are brilliantly fluorescent, especially at night. This species is common off southern New England in the summer, its range extending to the Carolinas. According to present knowledge, it does not occur as far north as Cape Cod.

Ocyropsis crystallina (Rang) PLATE 77. This animal is slightly less than 2 inches in length. The body is flattened laterally and is flanked by two large oral lobes which, by their flapping movements, drive the animal through the water. This activity naturally requires a powerful system of muscles. The auricles are about 1¼ inches in length forming ribbonlike flanges just across the lobes. This species is widely distributed over the tropical Atlantic, being occasionally brought northward by the Gulf Stream.

Leucothea ochracea Mayer PLATE 77. These are Lobatae with oral lobes of unusually large size, almost like butterfly wings. The auricles are long and thick and coiled, in spiral fashion, over the entire outer side of the body and the lobes. The outer surface of the body is covered with long conical papillae. The two middle tentacles are quite long. The distribution is from the Mediterranean to the warm eastern Atlantic, as well as Florida and the Gulf Stream.

Eurhamphaea vexilligera Gegenbaur PLATE 77. This is also a Florida species, but like all such forms, may be borne northward by the Gulf Stream. It is more than 1½ inches in length. The body is elongated and narrow and more or less flat. The aboral end looks like a transparent horn, while the posterior end is composed of the overlapping lappets of the lobes. When in motion, it resembles a transparent torpedo. Certain excretory pores between the combs of the cilia excrete, at times, a "brilliant rosin-red oily substance which is cast off if the animal be handled roughly or be suddenly disturbed, forming a fluorescent-looking, rosin-red cloud in the water surrounding the ctenophore." (Mayer)

This species is comparatively rare. It has been found

PLATE 77

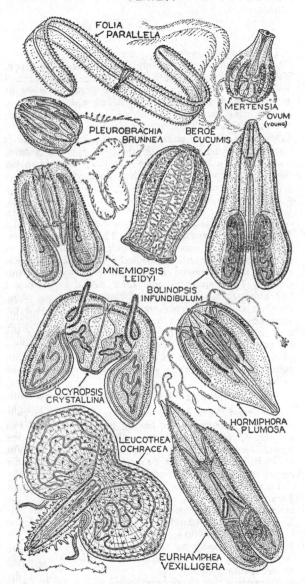

FOLIA PARALLELA

MERTENSIA

OVUM (YOUNG)

PLEUROBRACHIA BRUNNEA

BEROË CUCUMIS

MNEMIOPSIS LEIDYI

BOLINOPSIS INFUNDIBULUM

OCYROPSIS CRYSTALLINA

HORMIPHORA PLUMOSA

LEUCOTHEA OCHRACEA

EURHAMPHEA VEXILLIGERA

from the Mediterranean through the tropical Atlantic to Tortugas.

Order CESTIDA
(The Venus Girdles)

This order is noteworthy as containing, in two genera, *Cestum* and *Folia,* several species of a remarkable shape. They are long and ribbonlike, the body being compressed sidewise into a long band. The stomach and nerve organs are situated in the middle of the band, which extends in both directions as a flattened, ribbonlike structure. The two best-known species are *Cestum veneris* and *Folia parallela.* *Cestum veneris* is abundant in the Mediterranean and is also found in the tropical Atlantic. *Folia parallela* is much more abundant off the eastern American Coast than the other species and is therefore illustrated here.

Folia parallela (Fol) PLATE 77. This species is about 6 inches in length sidewise and about ⅜ inch in height. It appears to be a transparent ribbonlike creature which continuously rolls up and unrolls, swimming in undulating fashion near the surface of the sea. The stomach, the sense organ, and other fundamental structures are situated in the middle of the ribbonlike body, of which the aboral edge is nearly straight, not arched as is the case with *Cestum.* The four meridional tubes extend in a straight line along the middle of the ribbon to the outer edges, dividing it into an upper and lower half. They join the four subventral canals at the terminus. The tentacles form a double fringe along the upper and lower edges of the ribbon and, by their motion, send bands of rainbowlike hues along the border of the organism. The gelatinous substance of the creature seems to be tinged with faint yellow.

Order PLATYCTENEA

The ctenophores of this order are flattened vertically and are of creeping habit, having two tentacles and two sheaths. Comb-plate rows are only to be found in the larva. The species of this group have been said by some zoologists to be possible connecting links between the ctenophores and the flatworms.

There are four genera known in this order, *Coeloplana, Ctenoplana, Tjalfiella,* and *Gastrodes. Tjalfiella* was discovered off the west coast of Greenland. *Ctenoplana* was discovered off the Island of Sumatra and later was found by others off New Guinea and the coasts of Indo-China and Japan. *Coeloplana* was first found in the Red Sea and others in the Indo-China region. *Gastrodes* is a parasite in the tunicate *Salpa.*

As none of these have been found within the region to which this book is devoted, they are not illustrated or specifically dealt with here, except to say they may be degenerate forms of ctenophores with the significant habit of creeping on the sea-bottom, which gives them a generally flatwormlike appearance and accounts for the speculations regarding their being a connecting link as above-mentioned.

CLASS NUDA

This class includes the species of ctenophores without tentacles.

Order BERÖIDA

This order contains species with laterally compressed helmet-shaped bodies, showing a much-branched canal system with fine branches, sometimes anastomosing to form a network connecting various vessels in the anatomy of the organism. There are no tentacles, even in the larva. The stomodaeum is very wide, becoming a great sac with a short oral funnel. There are two genera with several species. The following species occurs in our range:

Beroë cucumis Fabricius PLATE 77. The body is helmet-shaped and compressed, the sense organ being at the aboral summit. The polar-plate surrounding the sense organ has a fringe of branched papillae. There are no tentacles or any tentacular vessels. The eight meridional vessels extend from the base of the sense organ to the broad mouth opening and are more or less parallel to each other. There are eight rows of comb-plates extending down the body immediately above the meridional vessels. Between the eight main vessels there is a complicated series of branched smaller vessels. In other species of this genus, these anastomose to form a connecting network between the meridional vessels. In the case of *Beroë cucumis,* however, the branches do not anastomose, so that the actual connection does not take place. *Beroë cucumis* has a pinkish cast, especially along the network of vessels, while the lines of comb-plates extend about ⅗ the length of the body, and by their successive movements, cause tracts of iridescent colors to travel down their flickering rows. The individuals of this species are about 1¼ inches long. They are found on the New England coast and especially off the coast of Maine. The range, however, extends southward to Chesapeake Bay.

5

Phylum Platyhelmia

(THE FLATWORMS)

THE phylum consists of flattened, soft-bodied worms, without segments, such as distinguish the annulate worms, without a distinctly separated head, and with no paired appendages. There is no body cavity, the space between the internal organs and the outer layer being filled with a networklike tissue, the *parenchyma,* containing various types of cells and subsidiary glands, as distinguished from the structureless jellylike mesogloea of coelenterates. It thus constitutes a primitive third layer. The two-layered Coelentera are, thus, often spoken of as the *Diploblastica;* while, beginning with the Platyhelmia, all higher groups in the animal kingdom are included under the term, *Triploblastica,* as possessing three fundamental cellular layers.

The outer body surface of the Platyhelmia is covered with moving cilia in the free-living forms or with an unciliated cuticle in parasitic groups. Likewise, there is a ventrally situated mouth in the former with a simple or branched internal digestive tube having no anus; while in certain of the latter (cestodes), both mouth and alimentary tract are absent, food being taken into the interior by absorption through the body wall.

The Phylum Platyhelmia is divided into three main groups, or Classes: (1) *Turbellaria* or free-living flatworms; (2) *Trematoda* or flukes; and (3) *Cestoda* or tapeworms.

Only the Turbellaria are free-living, both the Trematoda and the Cestoda being parasitic for the greater part of their life-history. Though they contain species, some of which affect marine life in an important way, they are not included here as being outside the limits set for this field book. The Turbellaria, however, comprise marine, fresh-water, and terrestrial species. Descriptions and illustrations of the important marine species occurring within our region will be found on the following pages.

CLASS TURBELLARIA
(INDEX PLATE 78)

The flatworms belonging to this class are free-living and have bodies covered with moving cilia. They creep over the bottom or on submerged plants and other material, or swim through the water by rapid undulations of their thin margins.

PLATE 78

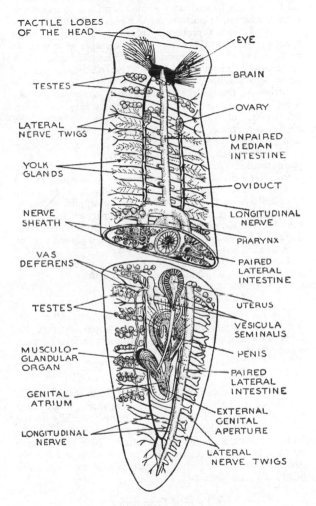

TACTILE LOBES OF THE HEAD

EYE

BRAIN

TESTES

OVARY

LATERAL NERVE TWIGS

UNPAIRED MEDIAN INTESTINE

YOLK GLANDS

OVIDUCT

NERVE SHEATH

LONGITUDINAL NERVE

PHARYNX

VAS DEFERENS

PAIRED LATERAL INTESTINE

TESTES

UTERUS

VESICULA SEMINALIS

MUSCULO-GLANDULAR ORGAN

PENIS

PAIRED LATERAL INTESTINE

GENITAL ATRIUM

EXTERNAL GENITAL APERTURE

LONGITUDINAL NERVE

LATERAL NERVE TWIGS

DIAGRAM ILLUSTRATING STRUCTURE OF A TRICLAD PLANARIAN

They are flat, often elongate, or cylindrical in shape. The mouth is located on the under-surface, either in the center, anterior, or posterior of this region. A pharynx may be extruded as a proboscis from the mouth. In some species it expands like a thin-walled trumpet to envelop its prey. In others, it is formed like a cylindrical tube which can be extended forward of the body. In some species, the intestine is a simple tube. In others, it has side-pockets or branches. In the Order Acoela, there is no intestine at all. Most Turbellaria are hermaphroditic, possessing both testes and ovary, but cross-fertilization between two individuals always takes place. Occasionally, there is asexual reproduction by transverse fission.

There is an excretory system consisting of one or two main trunks. These are divided into branches which, in turn, are subdivided into smaller capillarylike tubules, the smallest branchlets of which end blindly in a flame-cell, so-called from a flickering tuft of vibrating cilia within it. This is the first time this peculiar structure appears in the Animal Kingdom, to be repeated in certain higher groups. This system is not shown in the diagram, for the sake of simplicity.

The Class Turbellaria is divided into three subclasses: *Rhabdocoelida, Tricladida,* and *Polycladida.*

SUBCLASS RHABDOCOELIDA

The Rhabdocoelida are minute Turbellaria, either having no digestive tract, or having an unbranched digestive tube. The subclass is divided into three orders: *Acoela, Rhabdocoela,* and *Alloeocoela.*

Order ACOELA

These are minute turbellarians of delicate texture which are found in shallow waters along the shore, where there is plenty of seaweed. The mouth, located centrally on the under-side, leads directly into the parenchyma within the body, as there is no distinct intestine. These worms have no eyes, but a sense organ, the *statocyst,* is located directly over the brain. The color varies greatly but is usually bright and conspicuous.

Family Proporidae

One genital pore present. The mouth is variably located.

Childia spinosa von Graff PLATE 79. Like other members of this group, this species has no intestine. The mouth is situated on the under-side, just posterior to the middle of the animal. There is no pharynx, the food, consisting of minute sea-animals and microscopic plants, being taken directly into the parenchyma. Paired male penes are present, as well as paired oviducts usually filled with developing eggs. This species is about ½0 inch in length and light yellow in color. These tiny animals are usually found crawling over Sea Lettuce (*Ulva lactuca*), near the low-tide mark along the southern New England coast.

Anaperus gardineri von Graff PLATE 79. This is a similar species, red in color, shading into yellow anteriorly and posteriorly. The body is elongate, with no proboscis or intestine.

Family Aphanostomidae

The worms in this family have two genital pores, situated antero-posteriorly, first, the female, and then the male.

Polychoerus caudatus Mark PLATE 79. The body of the worm is about ⅛ inch in length, elongate, flattened, and leaflike. The approximately symmetrical sides convexly taper forward to a rounded anterior extremity. The posterior end is indented deeply between two rounded lobes, giving a smooth heart-shaped outline to the worm. In this posterior indentation there are usually three contractable caudal cirri, though in the adult worm, there may be as many as five. The margin is delicately thin, and undulates inward, while the worm is swimming. The transverse, oval mouth is located centrally on the under-side of the body. The light-colored, elongate digestive cavity, somewhat irregular in outline, may be clearly made out through the translucent body-wall. As usual among flatworms, the genital organs of both sexes are present in the same individual. The male genital opening is located posteriorly on the median line just forward of the base of the middle caudal cirrus, through which may protrude the oval or conical penis, marked by a *seminal vesicle* at its base into which empties the *vasa deferentia*. These may reach extensive proportions when filled with sperm.

The oviducts, on either side of the stomach, contain large grapelike clusters of ova, and unite on either side to open in common on the median line.

This worm is pale to deep red, or orange-red, the color fading away to a lighter tone over the digestive cavity. Underneath, it is whitish to yellowish in color. It occurs in large numbers in sheltered harbors, clinging to eelgrass, and feeding on minute crustaceans, along the New England coast.

Aphanostoma diversicolor Oërsted PLATE 79. This species is extremely variable in shape. When fully extended, the body is lanceolate, tapering sharply at both ends, especially posteriorly. The color also is variable. Usually, there are two sulphur-yellow spots situated on the back, one behind the other, bordered with a large area of blue or violet, which is forked posteriorly by a white V. The mouth is located beneath the center of the body. This is a tiny worm, not more than 1/12 inch in length.

It occurs along the southern New England coast, crawling over the algae at low-water mark. It is also found along the Mediterranean and western European shores.

Aphanostoma aurantiacum Verrill PLATE 79. This is a related species of the same genus. Its body, however, is broadest in front and evenly rounded. Like other flatworms, it is quite changeable in shape. The general color is light yellow, spotted generously with small specks of bright orange-red becoming paler toward the margins. A group of pigmented spots is situated anteriorly on the median line.

This flatworm is 1/17 inch in length. It usually may be seen crawling over algae, near the low-tide mark on the southern New England coast.

The worms in this group differ from these in the Order Acoela in possessing a complete, unbranched digestive canal only slightly connected with the body-wall by a few strands, otherwise being entirely separate and suspended in a fluid-filled cavity. An excretory canal also occurs. Testes, ovaries, and yolk-glands are enclosed by a membrane. The body is variable in shape, being elongate to thread-shaped, fusiform or leaflike. Sense organs, including two eyes, are often present.

Family Catenulidae

The mouth is at the extreme forward end of the intestine and therefore near the forward end of the body on the ventral side. The intestine is simple with a posterior excretory pore. Both testes and ovary are single, located posteriorly on the median line. Asexual reproduction also occurs.

Stenostomum grande Child PLATE 79. The body, in this species, is transparent and orange-yellow in color. The mouth is situated ventrally, near the forward end of the body. This animal is hermaphroditic, possessing both ovaries and testes. Reproduction is also asexual, budding off a chain of four to six individuals attached to each other in a line. A pair of eyes is situated directly over the brain on the anterior end, each with light-refracting organs.

Family Microstomidae

The mouth is near the forward end of the body. There is a simple pharynx and a pair of excretory tubes. Pigmented paired eyes and sense pits are present.

Microstomum davenporti von Graff PLATE 79. This species also forms an asexual chain of about four individuals, usually in a somewhat contracted resting stage. It is always swimming about with swift motions. There

PLATE 79

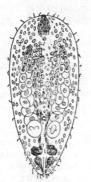

CHILDIA
SPINOSA

POLYCHOERUS
CAUDATUS

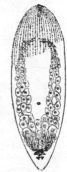

ANAPERUS
GARDINERI

APHANOSTOMA
DIVERSICOLOR

APHANOSTOMA
AURANTIACUM

STENOSTOMUM
GRANDE

MICROSTOMUM
DAVENPORTI

DALYELLIA
DODGEI

WOODSHOLIA
LILLEI

are usually numerous papillae on the posterior end. The body is whitish in color, without pigment, except that the intestine is lined with bright ocher-yellow cilia. There are no eyes. The species occurs on sea lettuce and rockweed in sheltered places along the southern New England coast and throughout Long Island Sound.

Family Dalyellidae

This family is characterized by possessing a large cylindrical pharynx opening into the forwardly located mouth. There is a single genital pore, paired testes, an ovary, as well as paired yolk-glands. Usually there are pigmented eyes.

Dalyellia dodgei von Graff PLATE 79. While this is preeminently a fresh-water species, it also occurs in brackish water along the New England coast. It is about 1 mm. in length and with its coloration mottled with sepia-brown. The anterior end is truncated so as to appear almost square in outline, with a slight concavity in the center. The body becomes expanded posteriorly, reaching its greatest width just back of the stomach, narrowing again to taper to a point behind. While it has no special color, it becomes so filled with green microscopic plant forms as to take their color. There are two distinct black eyes near the anterior end not far from the mouth.

Family Trigonostomidae

A small proboscis, enclosed in a proboscis sheath, opening by a proboscis pore, is located near the forward end of the body, on the ventral side.

Woodsholia lilliei von Graff PLATE 79. This flatworm is characterized by possessing a small conical proboscis in a proboscis sheath. The anterior end of the body is truncated and transparent and equipped with a pair of conspicuous black eyes. It has an elongated oval outline narrowing posteriorly to be terminated by a pointed lobe connected by a necklike constriction with the rest of the body. It is very abundant in the Woods Hole region of Massachusetts.

Order ALLOEOCOELA

Turbellarians with body-cavity greatly reduced, while the intestine is irregular and often sac-shaped. The gonads are without a definitive membrane, and filled with large numbers of follicles.

Family Plagiostomidae

A large pharynx is present in the anterior part of the body. The single genital pore is located posteriorly.

Plagiostomum wilsoni von Graff PLATE 80. The

PLATE 80

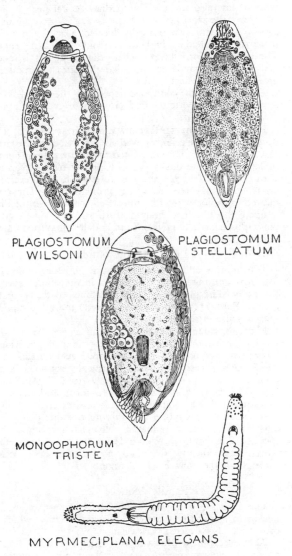

PLAGIOSTOMUM
WILSONI

PLAGIOSTOMUM
STELLATUM

MONOOPHORUM
TRISTE

MYRMECIPLANA ELEGANS

pharynx is sac-shaped and opens into a straight intestine without lateral branches. The median genital pore is situated near the tapering end of the body. Two conspicuous eyes are present symmetrically located near the anterior margin of the body. The body is about ⅛ inch in length. The general color is bright ocher-yellow, but this is modified by the multitude of imbedded rhabdites to produce a greenish yellow effect.

This is one of the commonest species in the Woods Hole region and most often found crawling over Sea Lettuce (*Ulva lactuca*).

Plagiostomum stellatum von Graff PLATE 80. The coloring of this species, as well as the shape of the eyes, readily distinguish it from related forms. It is about 1 mm. in length and the dusky greenish yellow of the pigment within its body is extremely characteristic. The eyes are branched into three diverging prolongations. They are located anteriorly in the midst of a network of fine tangled threads. The body is fusiform and tapers to a point posteriorly. It is very abundant in the Woods Hole region.

Family Pseudostomidae

The mouth and the genital pore, together with the pharynx, are united into one system in the hinder part of the body. The ovaries are also combined with the yolk-gland. Four eyes and dorsal ciliated groove form the special sense organs in this family.

Monoöphorum triste von Graff PLATE 80. In this species, both mouth and pharynx are situated posteriorly. There are two pairs of crescent-shaped eyes and a transverse groove passes around the evenly rounded head-region, separating the anterior eyes from the posterior pair. The body is symmetrically fusiform and tapers to a pointed tail. The translucent, colorless, ectodermal layer is sown with tiny, round and shining rhabditelike bodies, dark violet or black in hue, a color characteristic to this species. This is also a Woods Hole species and, together with those already described above, doubtless occurs throughout the New England region.

Family Monocelidae

The intestine is regularly lobulated throughout, terminating in a posteriorly directed pharynx, beyond which is the penis, also directed backward.

Myrmeciplana elegans von Graff PLATE 80. This is a narrow, elongate worm with a circle of cilia surrounding the anterior end, together with a series of tasting papillae. The brain is located anteriorly. The digestive tract is lobulated and extended through the greater length of the worm. The pharynx is at the posterior end of the intestine and is directed backward beyond which is the double, conical penis. A slight constriction separates the terminal portion of the body from the rest. The tail section is covered with small cylindrical papillae. The eyes are entirely lacking. This species occurs in brackish water in the Woods Hole region.

SUBCLASS TRICLADIDA
(INDEX PLATE 78)

The Subclass Tricladida are turbellarians having an intestine with three main branches prolonged into many side-branches, with a pharynx situated at the junction of the main trunks. One of the main branches extends anteriorly from the base of the pharynx, and the other two posteriorly from the same point, located symmetrically on either side. A well-developed proboscis may be extruded from the pharynx. In most species, paired eyes are present at the forward end of the body as well as a sensitive pair of tentacles. Mouth and genital pore are located at about the middle of the body or posterior to it. A ventral adhering organ or sucker is present in some species of this group.

The Subclass Tricladida is divided into three orders: *Paludicola,* or fresh-water Tricladida; *Maricola,* or Marine Tricladida; and *Terricola,* or Land Tricladida.

Only the Maricola, or Marine Tricladida, are described here, the others being outside our range.

Order MARICOLA

These are the turbellarian flatworms that live in the sea. For the most part they are found crawling over sea weed, stones, shells, and other material on the sea-bottom. They are usually carnivorous, devouring small sea-worms, crustacea, and mollusks. The mouth is located ventrally, at about the middle of the body or behind it. An eversible and highly extensible pharynx is protruded through the mouth to engulf the prey, which is swallowed and digested in the three branches of the intestine which meet at its base. The elaborately developed branchlets occurring along the course of the main trunks assist in this process. As seen in INDEX DIAGRAM 78, the nervous and reproductive systems of triclads are developed to a remarkable degree, the former including an anterior bilobed brain, eyes with lenses and optic nerve, with an abundant supply of tactile nerves to the sensitive anterior margin. These represent early stages in the evolution of cephalization, or specialization of the part of the body which first comes in contact with its environment to form a head.

Likewise, the hermaphroditic reproductive system is

highly developed, male and female elements both being present, with testes and yolk-glands repeated symmetrically on both sides of the body, a pair of ovaries placed well forward, and a uterus situated posteriorly on the median line. An atrium and single reproductive aperture, posterior to the mouth, is the common opening for both systems. An eversible and extensible penis insures cross-fertilization between two individuals.

Finally, while there is no actual external segmentation, this phenomenon is prophesied by the internal repetition of parts. Hence, it is obvious that the flatworm is significant as exhibiting initial stages of various anatomical systems characteristic of the higher animal phyla.

Family Procerodidae

The flattened body is characterized by an otocyst, but no sense-pits. The neck is variable but distinct.

Procerodes ulvae (Oersted) PLATE 81. This active and lively flatworm is about ¼ inch in length. The body is oval, almost tongue-shaped, in outline, but rounded and somewhat expanded posteriorly. It is arched dorsally and flat beneath. The neck is quite distinct, with head expanded to a rounded front and a pair of tapering, whitish tentacles which may be completely withdrawn. They are located just above the forward angle of the head. The eyes are large and black. The mouth is near the middle of the ventral side. There is a long, narrow, and cylindrical pharynx, nearly half the length of the body. This worm is dark brown, almost black, colored with a stripe of light gray or pale yellow extending along each side, occasionally blotched with lighter brown.

This species ranges along the entire New England coast from the Bay of Fundy to Long Island Sound, as well as along the northern European shores. It occurs near the low-water mark, sometimes in tide-pools among the algae and occasionally under stones.

Fovia affinis (Oersted) PLATE 81. Usually, the body of this species is almost parallel-sided, though it tends to be expanded posterior to the middle of the body. The head is a flattened oval in front, with slight indications of a neck. The corners of the head are prominently outlined and somewhat angular. The mouth, as usual, is nearly central. The stomach shows through the translucent body as a whitish area with bilobed, lateral branches. There are two eyespots situated centrally on either side of the median line near the forward end of the body. They are kidney-shaped and each has a transparent lens.

This species is light yellow in color, shading toward the grayish, as well as yellowish or brownish toward the margin of the body and on the underside. The pharynx

PLATE 81

PROCERODES
ULVAE

FOVIA
AFFINIS

PLANOCERA
NEBULOSA

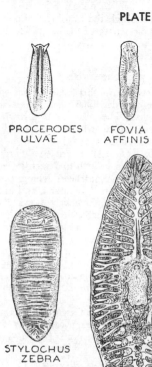

STYLOCHUS
ZEBRA

STYLOCHUS
ZEBRA

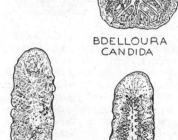

BDELLOURA
CANDIDA

EUSTYLOCHUS
=(STYLOCHUS)
ELLIPTICUS

IMOGINE
OCULIFERA

and stomach are visible through the translucent body-wall, extending nearly the whole length of the body. The length is from ¼ to ½ inch. The range is from Casco Bay, Maine, to southern New England.

Family Bdellouridae

There are two uteri present in this family, each with a separate opening to the outside. There are no rhabdites. There is a posterior sucker. The pharynx is thrown into narrow folds and is cylindrical when extended. Either ectoparasitic or commensal in habit.

Bdelloura candida (Girard) PLATE 81. This very active but small species is from ⅗ inch to 1 inch in length. It is shaped somewhat like a spearhead, being pointed anteriorly, widest two thirds of the way back, and broadly rounded behind, where a posterior sucker shows plainly. Its muscular undulating margin enables it to swim through the water rapidly. There are two eyes close together near the front, their dense color rendering them quite conspicuous. The cylindrical, white pharynx and much-branched intestine show clearly through the body-wall. This species is light in color, varying from grayish white to yellow, the brown foliate intestine contrasting sharply with it.

The range of this species is from Casco Bay, Maine, to Cape Hatteras, North Carolina, being commonly found on the gill-plates of the horseshoe crab (*Limulus polyphemus*).

SUBCLASS POLYCLADIDA

These are exclusively marine turbellarians, having the main gut dividing directly into multitudinous digestive branches, ramifying into all parts of the body. They are frequently of large size. Their thin, leaflike bodies enable them to swim actively by rhythmic undulating motions varying from flapping to tremulous, rippling vibrations. There are numerous eyes in the head-region, usually in two more or less symmetrical groups, with lenses, accumulations of pigmented granules, and refractive rods. Each eye is connected with the brain by means of an optic nerve. A pair of tentacles may or may not be present. There are usually also otocysts and sensory tactile cilia. Reproduction is always sexual. Two genital pores always exist. The mouth may be located anteriorly, in the middle of the body, or posteriorly.

The Subclass Polycladida is divided into two orders: *Acotylea*, Marine Turbellarians without suckers, and *Cotylea*, Marine Turbellarians having a ventral sucker.

Order ACOTYLEA

In this order, a sucker is not present. The mouth is situated in the middle of the under surface, or behind the middle, but never anteriorly. The pharynx is usually much folded when exserted. A pair of dorsal tentacles usually occurs. Development is normally direct, without passing through a typical "Müller's Larva" stage.

Family Planoceridae

This family includes the Acotylea with dorsal tentacles and with an approximately central mouth.

Planocera nebulosa Girard PLATE 81. The body is more than 1 inch long, oval in shape, thin and delicate at the edges, which undulate as it swims or creeps. A pair of long, slender, tapering tentacles is situated close together, not far from the anterior margin, flanked on either side by clusters of eyespots. The main cavity of the stomach shows through the translucent dorsal integument as a long median line. The color is quite variable, ranging through different shades of olive-green diversified by yellowish blotches. There may be a median pale dorsal stripe.

This species is found from southern New England to Charleston, South Carolina.

Stylochus zebra Verrill PLATE 81. This is a somewhat larger species than the preceding, being at least 1½ inches in length. The body is oblong in shape, with almost parallel sides slightly expanding toward the rounded front margin of the head and becoming gradually narrower posteriorly to taper convexly toward a bluntly pointed tip. While the worm is moderately thick along the middle of the back, the edges are often so thin as to be nearly translucent. A pair of rather close-set stubby tentacles is symmetrically disposed near the anterior end. Many eyespots are grouped in two clusters practically in contact on the median line. In some individuals, they are fairly well scattered over the head-region. There is also a series of marginal ocelli.

The color of the animal is yellowish brown, shading toward chocolate, with numerous, practically parallel, transverse bands of yellow or white, branching into narrower stripes at the margin, which suggested the specific name, *zebra*.

This species is quite abundant in southern New England, especially around Woods Hole, Massachusetts, where the worms are found in the dead shells of the whelk (*Fulgar*). This is the largest flatworm commonly found on our coast and is easily recognized by its conspicuous coloration.

Stylochus (Eustylochus) ellipticus (Girard) PLATE 81. In this species, the body is 1 inch in length and quite flat and thin, while its continually undulating margin is changeable in form. The paired tentacles taper to a point when fully expanded, but contract into nearly round balls when withdrawn. There are eight to twelve ocelli or eyespots. The mouth is situated about one third the body length from the anterior margin. The short, stumpy pharynx is eversible and may be extended quite a distance from the mouth-opening. The stomach has six or seven arborescent prolongations on either side, the smaller sub-branches forming a network. The color is a pale yellowish brown, varying to a mottled greenish or salmon color, graduating to a yellowish or whitish network.

This species is abundantly distributed from the Bay of Fundy and the coast of Maine to southern New England.

Imogene oculifera (Girard) PLATE 81. This curious flatworm has a large subcircular head-region, while the leaflike body tapers to an almost pointed posterior extremity. The extremely thin, almost translucent body is about ⅕ inch in length. The paired tentacles are conical, with spheroid tips, each containing a conspicuous eyespot. There are also two diverging lines of minute ocelli between the tentacles, forming an almost V-shaped group. The color is almost carmine-red, the stomach and its many branches showing through as lighter in color, those in front radiating fanlike from between the eyes to the circular margin of the head, while posteriorly along the axis of the body, they show a fern-shaped pattern.

This species ranges from southern New England southward as far as Charleston, South Carolina.

Family Leptoplanidae

The body of the species in this family is flat, thin, and leaflike. There are no tentacles. The mouth is nearly in the center of the body. The pharynx is large and lobed. There are usually four groups of eyes, two cerebral and two in the position occupied in the previous family by the tentacles, which are lacking here. The penis of the male genital apparatus is directed backward. The species in this family are very variable and difficult to distinguish when alive due to the density of the integument. The characters are best made out when the specimens are properly spread, killed, and prepared in the laboratory.

Leptoplana angusta Verrill PLATE 82. This species is comparatively narrow in proportion to its length. It much resembles a thin, elongated leaf with somewhat ruffled edges, undulating as it swims or creeps. The anterior margin of the head tends to be almost triangular in shape. The posterior end often has a slight notch at the

PLATE 82

LEPTOPLANA
ANGUSTA

LEPTOPLANA
ANGUSTA

LEPTOPLANA
ELLIPSOIDES

LEPTOPLANA
VIRILIS

LEPTOPLANA
VARIABILIS

LEPTOPLANA
VARIABILIS

LEPTOPLANA
VARIABILIS

DISCOCELIS
MUTABILIS

DISCOCELIS
MUTABILIS

TRIGONOPORUS
FOLIUM

TRIGONOPORUS
DENDRITICUS

EURYLEPTA
MACULOSA

median line. There are about six pairs of ocelli forming parallel lines located centrally at some distance from the head-region. The stomach branches, on either side, into numerous treelike lobes, variable in number in different individuals. The light brown color is also quite variable. The worm is about ½ inch in length and is found abundantly among hydroids and other small sea-animals from New England southward to the Carolinas. It has also been taken from the bottom of wooden vessels.

Leptoplana ellipsoides Girard PLATE 82. This flatworm has a broadly oval, but changeable body, quite flat, with very thin edges, which undulate rapidly when swimming. Groups of small black ocelli are present in paired clusters, the largest of which are the dorsal groups, each containing twenty to twenty-five ocelli.

The color varies through yellowish brown, reddish brown, and greenish brown, splotched with spots and specks of darker or lighter colors. There is a fairly uniform light-colored area running lengthwise from the groups of eyespots to the posterior region of the body. This worm varies from 1 inch to 1½ inches in length.

The range is from the Gulf of St. Lawrence to Casco Bay, Maine, where the species frequently occurs in tidepools and under stones from the low-water mark to 40 fathoms of depth.

Leptoplana virilis Verrill PLATE 82. The thin body of this worm has somewhat parallel sides and a broadly rounded head-region, the body narrowing posteriorly. Like the other members of this family, however, it is very changeable in shape. There are four clusters of black eyespots. The general color is light brown, diversified by darker and lighter specks and blotches. It is about ¾ inch in length.

This species occurs off Cape Cod and Nantucket Shoals from shallow water down to a depth of 31 fathoms.

Leptoplana variabilis (Girard) PLATE 82. As its name implies, this is an exceedingly variable species, three examples of which are figured in the plate. The body is oblong, varying from a narrow, elongate shape to a fairly broad elliptical outline. It has very black and conspicuous ocelli in four clusters, the two anterior groups being narrowly top-shaped. These are the so-called cerebral clusters. The posterior or dorsal clusters are practically circular.

The color varies from yellowish brown to light salmon, often variegated with orange-brown spots. There is a median narrow area of paler tint extending through the center of the body. This species ranges from Eastport, Maine, to Vineyard Sound, occurring in tide-pools under stones and on wharf-piles.

Discocelis mutabilis Verrill PLATE 82. The body of this worm is about ⅓ inch long and is quite thin. It tends to be broader in proportion than the previous species, having a rounded, hemispherical outline anteriorly and tapering somewhat posteriorly. Three pairs of cerebral and dorsal ocelli are irregularly located along the undulating margin. The general color grades from dark brown in the middle of the worm's body to a yellowish brown or pale yellow toward the edges. Sometimes the worm is practically translucent, with pale to golden-yellow spots.

It occurs from Woods Hole to Long Island Sound among the red algae.

Trigonoporus folium Verrill PLATE 82. This worm tends to be narrowed and somewhat pointed anteriorly, expanding centrally, and rounded posteriorly, so that it closely resembles a leaf. The thin edges usually undulate with a rapid motion. The inconspicuous eyes are grouped closely in paired triangular areas just forward of the anterior end of the stomach. The latter has quite convoluted lateral prolongations. The general color of the living worm is pale yellow to flesh-tint, the nervous system showing as a pink network through the translucent dorsal surface of the body. The stomach is distinctly brown. This species is from ¾ inch to 1 inch in length.

The distribution is from Eastport, Maine, to Long Island Sound, occurring from low-water mark to a depth of more than 50 fathoms.

Trigonoporus dendriticus Verrill PLATE 82. The body varies from an elongate, narrow form, with fairly squarish outline, to a broad form, tapering to a narrow rounded head-region, but becoming very broad posteriorly. The ocelli occur as four very narrow, elongate groups of very small but numerous eyespots, the cerebral clusters being very close together, their hinder ends somewhat overlapping the position of the anterior ends of the dorsal clusters, which are farther apart and more conspicuous. The color of the living worm varies from a pale yellow to a pinkish hue, with finely branched brown markings, the outline of the arborescent branched lobes of the stomach showing through the thin integument. The cerebral ganglia and complicated nervous system are reddish in color.

This species occurs off the coast of Cape Cod and southern New England generally.

Order COTYLEA

The Suborder Cotylea includes the Polycladida in which a sucker is present. It is located on the ventral surface posterior to the genital openings. The mouth is either in the middle of the body or located anterior to it. The pharynx is without folds in most cases, and is usually cylindrical or with a flaring opening. A pair of tentacles extending symmetrically from the anterior is often present. Development occurs through a free-swimming larval stage (Müller's larva).

Family Euryleptidae

The mouth is near the anterior end of the body. The pharynx is tubular and the stomach is long and narrow with branches which may be simple or, in some cases, forming a network. The ocelli are located on the anterior margin of the head-region and in the tentacles when they occur. There is also a pair of cerebral clusters.

Eurylepta maculosa Verrill PLATE 82. The body, though oval in outline, tends to be narrow and slender. It is about ½ inch in length. The front margin of the head-region is equipped with a pair of diverging fingerlike tentacles, as well as with groups of ocelli, which especially occur between the tentacles and on their front margins Many ocelli are also located in a patch on the mediar surface of the head, extending forward in a double fork with elongate streaks, representing the cerebral ocelli.

The color of this flatworm is pale pinkish, mottled with many small brown and purplish brown spots. The entire margin of the worm is punctuated with elongate spots radiating toward the edge like a border.

This species occurs in southern New England, especially around Woods Hole, Massachusetts, and the Elizabeth Islands near low-water mark and among the seaweed.

6

Phylum Nemertea

(RIBBON WORMS)

THIS is a very compact group of wormlike animals, showing so distinct an advance over the Platyhelmia in the features of their anatomy as to be considered worthy of being set apart as an independent phylum.

Generally speaking, they are soft-bodied, very contractile, cylindrical to flattened worms. They are usually quite elongated and frequently brightly colored. They vary greatly in size, certain species being less than 1 inch in length, while the largest forms may measure 30 yards or more. They are nonparasitic, though one group contains species of commensal habit. They are mostly marine, though a few forms live on land or in fresh water.

The body is unsegmented externally. The internal anatomy, however, tends to be repetitive in its parts, as if foreshadowing the segmental arrangement characteristic of higher invertebrates (INDEX PLATE 83).

The head is usually broad, truncated, and often flattened, while the posterior end is bluntly pointed. There are one or several pairs of eyes present in most species, usually paired or in symmetrical groups on either side of the head. The mouth, on the ventral side of the head, opens into a straight digestive tube (convoluted in a few species) terminating in an anus at the posterior end of the body, thus differing from the Platyhelmia, which have no anus. There are paired lateral pouches repeated throughout the greater part of the alimentary tract, the lining of which is completely ciliated.

The organ which is most peculiar to the Nemertea is the proboscis, which is entirely independent of the digestive system, and opens by a separate pore at the extreme anterior end of the body. It is above the digestive tube and is enclosed in a tubular sheath in a much-folded condition. The anterior end of the proboscis is attached to the inner wall of the sheath near its opening. When discharged, it is turned inside out, like a glove, for the anterior part is hollow. The posterior part, however, is thick-walled and muscular, and is thrust out without being everted. In many species, this portion bears a sharp spine at its summit, at its junction with the base of the hollow section of the tube. When the latter is everted, the spine is extruded and forms an excellent weapon of offense or defense.

The proboscis can be protruded for a considerable distance beyond the body and is used for the capture of its prey, coiling itself around it and drawing it down to the mouth.

Except for the Order Paleonemertea, which have no brain lobes, the nemerteans possess a brain composed of two ganglia located on either side at the anterior end, one on either side of the proboscis and connected with each other by a nerve-ring. Each ganglion usually consists of a dorsal and ventral lobe, the latter being continued backward on either side to form paired lateral nerve-cords. From the anterior lobes nerves are given off to the eyes and front of the head, while the proboscis is supplied by nerves from the nerve-ring. The lateral nerve-trunks, in certain groups of nemerteans (Order Paleonemertea), are connected with a nerve-plexus throughout the body, while in the more highly developed forms paired horizontal trunks are given off horizontally, in an almost segmental pattern.

The eyes vary from pigmented eyespots to more highly developed organs having a refracting lenslike portion, backed up with a pigmented layer as well as a layer of rods, forming a rudimentary retina. *Auditory capsules* are also present in some species; and other sense organs include a *frontal organ,* a disc-shaped area on the anterior end of the body, possibly having a taste function; sensitive *side organs* near the excretory pores, situated laterally toward the forward part of the body; and the characteristic paired *cephalic slits* or *cerebral organs* situated laterally on the head close to the brain-lobes. These are apparently quite important organs of sensation, varying from shallow, circular pits to longitudinal slitlike furrows, often complicated in structure.

There are three main blood vessels running longitudinally, one on the median dorsal line, the other two laterally, with transverse branches at regular intervals. An excretory system is also present, with flame-cells, similar to those of flatworms. Unlike the flatworms, the nemerteans are very seldom hermaphroditic, the sexes being separate. There is also an asexual tendency, for when nemerteans are handled or attacked they readily break up into fragments which will live independently and, under certain conditions, will regenerate the lost parts, thus showing a reminiscence of an asexual generation.

The PHYLUM NEMERTEA is divided into four orders, as follows: (1) *Paleonemertea;* (2) *Heteronemertea;* (3) *Metanemertea;* and (4) *Bdellonemertea.*

PLATE 83

INTERNAL ANATOMY OF A TYPICAL NEMERTEAN

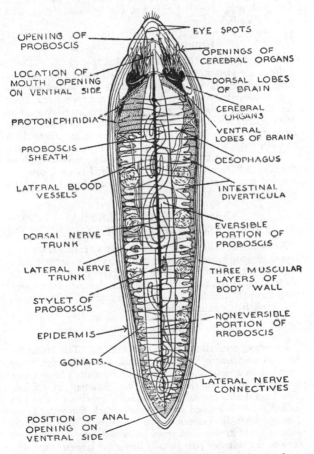

OPENING OF PROBOSCIS

EYE SPOTS

OPENINGS OF CEREBRAL ORGANS

LOCATION OF MOUTH OPENING ON VENTRAL SIDE

DORSAL LOBES OF BRAIN

CEREBRAL ORGANS

PROTONEPHRIDIA

VENTRAL LOBES OF BRAIN

PROBOSCIS SHEATH

OESOPHAGUS

LATERAL BLOOD VESSELS

INTESTINAL DIVERTICULA

DORSAL NERVE TRUNK

EVERSIBLE PORTION OF PROBOSCIS

LATERAL NERVE TRUNK

THREE MUSCULAR LAYERS OF BODY WALL

STYLET OF PROBOSCIS

EPIDERMIS

NONEVERSIBLE PORTION OF PROBOSCIS

GONADS

LATERAL NERVE CONNECTIVES

POSITION OF ANAL OPENING ON VENTRAL SIDE

(DORSAL VIEW)

Order PALEONEMERTEA
(PROTONEMERTEA and MESONEMERTEA)

Nemerteans with two muscle layers in the body-wall, having the brain and lateral nerve-cords lying either outside or imbedded in them. There is no spine, or stylet, in the proboscis. The brain is not divided into lobes. The mouth lies behind it.

Family Cephalothricidae

Cephalothrix linearis (Rathke) PLATE 84. This is quite a slender worm, about 2 to 3 inches long, with a long, pointed head. A small mouth is situated on the under-side of the body, quite some distance back from the tip, surrounded by more or less puckered lips. The color varies from light yellow or cream to flesh-color and even reddish or greenish white. Sometimes, there is a median red line extending lengthwise throughout the body.

This species occurs from Nova Scotia southward along the coast of New England to Long Island Sound, often in tangled masses of many individuals, including both adults and young.

Order HETERONEMERTEA
(SCHIZONEMERTEA)

Nemerteans with three muscle layers, comprising two layers of longitudinal muscle with a layer of circular muscles between them. The brain and lateral nerve-cords lie above the circular muscle layer and beneath the outer longitudinal muscle layer. The proboscis has no stylet. The mouth lies behind the brain.

Family Lineidae

Lineus socialis (Leidy) PLATE 84. The rounded body of this worm is very long and threadlike, gradually tapering to a slender bluntly pointed tail-end. The anterior border of the head is rounded but flattened in section. The lateral slits extend quite far back on either side. The mouth, also, is located some distance back from the head. The very small eyespots (often six pairs in mature individuals) are grouped in rows on either side of the head-region, the anterior pair usually being the largest. Dorsally, this worm is dark olive-green, though dark brownish, blackish, and red-brown individuals also exist. A pattern of lighter colored cross-lines is often found. The lower side of the body is always lighter than the upper side. This nemertean may be 10 inches in length, with a diameter varying from $\frac{1}{25}$ to $\frac{1}{3}$ inch. Like both the previous species, it may often be found in large masses of individ-

uals tangled together, though they easily disentangle
themselves to swim away.

The distribution is general throughout our region, from
the low-water mark under the entire tidal zone nearly to
the high-tide limit.

Lineus pallidus Verrill PLATE 84. The long and
slender body may reach 10 inches in length, with a distinctly wider head, equipped with quite long lateral slits,
cut deeply into the side of the head. The color is usually
pale yellow, blending anteriorly into reddish.

It occurs off the New England coast, buried in mud
from the tidal zone to a depth of 45 fathoms.

Lineus viridis (Fabricius) PLATE 84. As the name
implies, this is a green worm, occasionally varying from
olive to greenish black, somewhat paler beneath the head
region, with the lateral pits or slits reddish in some individuals. On each side there is a row of small light-colored
spots. Color varieties are also found verging toward brown
or reddish brown or even a uniform red.

The length of the body, also, is extremely variable, as
it is very soft and contractile. When extended, it reaches
a length of 8 inches. It is thickest anteriorly and tapers
gradually to a slender, pointed tail. A single row of ocelli,
varying from three or four to eight in number, is on
either side of the head. The lateral slits are quite long and
very deep. The mouth, situated slightly back of their posterior termination, can become considerably distended, as
well as the body itself, when swallowing a large worm
for prey.

This species is very common, being found throughout
the whole tidal zone and the shallow waters, from Greenland to the southern shores of New England.

Lineus arenicola Verrill PLATE 84. This is a somewhat smaller worm, being not more than about 4 inches
in length. It is long, slender, and slightly flattened. The
head is quite flat and capable of considerable distention.
The lateral slits are quite long, with a small, somewhat
triangular mouth on the median line, just posterior to
them. The color varies from flesh-color to purplish.

This may be a more or less southern species, as it is rare
as far north as New England. It has been taken in Long
Island Sound, however, near New Haven (Verrill).

Lineus dubius Verrill PLATE 84. This species is also
extremely slender. It is light green to dark olive-green in
color. The head is usually distinct, flattened and pointed,
being almost the shape of an arrowhead. About a dozen
ocelli extend backward on either side of the body. It is
usually 2 to 3 inches in length, and is found under stones
in the tidal area along the northern Massachusetts coast.

Lineus bicolor Verrill PLATE 84. This is a gayly colored species, easily recognized. Verrill's description follows: "Color, above, along each side of back a broad stripe of olive-green, yellowish-green, or brownish-green, separated by a median, dorsal, well-defined, broad stripe of yellow or yellowish-white, usually becoming clear white on the head, where it expands and blends with a white frontal area in advance of the eyes, the margins of head are also white. Lower surface pale greenish or yellowish-white."

It is a small worm, about 1½ to almost 2 inches in length. It is found on shallow bottoms among seaweed and hydroids along the coast of southern New England, in depths of from 2 to 24 fathoms.

Micrura inornata Verrill PLATE 84. This nemertean is easily recognizable because of its conspicuous coloration, which is bright cherry-red above, varying to a dark red, with a light-colored tail terminating in a white, threadlike prolongation. The head is blunt and flattened, without any ocelli.

This species is about 3 inches in length and ranges from the coast of Maine to Massachusetts Bay, on muddy bottoms, in 45 to 100 fathoms of depth.

Micrura dorsalis Verrill PLATE 84. In contrast to the preceding species, the color of this worm varies from pale yellow to orange on the forward part of the body, with a dark median stripe above and below, and irregular, pale blotches on the sides. The head is flattened and rather large and thick. There are no ocelli. The body is about 6 inches or more in length.

The species is well distributed off the coast of Maine, at the extreme low-water mark. It has not been recorded farther south.

Micrura affinis Verrill PLATE 84. This is a very common worm, occurring from Nova Scotia to Cape Cod on stony bottoms from 8 to 150 fathoms. It is especially abundant toward the northern part of its range. It is bright red in color, being darker and browner on some parts of its body. The head is characterized by being outlined conspicuously in white. The head is elongate, flattened, and somewhat spoon-shaped. The lateral slits are well developed and deep, also being marked by white margins. There are about four to six conspicuous black ocelli on each side of the forward part of the body, especially along the white border of the head-region. The tail terminates posteriorly in a long, slender, spikelike cirrus.

Micrura (Cerebratulus) leidyi (Verrill) PLATE 84. This worm has an elongate body, quite slender when fully extended, rounded anteriorly, becoming more flattened and somewhat wider posteriorly, so that Verrill places it

PLATE 84

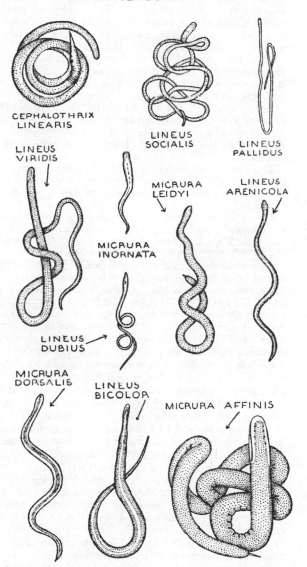

CEPHALOTHRIX
LINEARIS

LINEUS
SOCIALIS

LINEUS
PALLIDUS

LINEUS
VIRIDIS

MICRURA
LEIDYI

LINEUS
ARENICOLA

MICRURA
INORNATA

LINEUS
DUBIUS

MICRURA
DORSALIS

LINEUS
BICOLOR

MICRURA AFFINIS

in the Genus *Cerebratulus*. At least it must be transitional, for he admits that it is not so flattened as the typical species of that genus, nor "do the margins become so broad and thin." The caudal cirrus is relatively short, attenuated, and white in color. The head tends to be triangular and quite pointed, when extended. It has a large, long mouth with puckered lips, the anterior end of which is located medially between the posterior ends of the lateral slits, which are long, deep, and with extremely thin margins. The proboscis may be everted to a considerable distance, resembling a flesh-colored thread. The two ganglia of the brain are visible as dark areas through the thin flesh of the head-region. There are no ocelli in this species.

The entire body is rose to light purplish in color, but lighter ventrally. The internal organs, showing through the thin skin, modify the apparent color to darker or lighter mottlings.

This is a very common species. It occurs abundantly near the low-water mark, burrowing in the shallow, sandy bottom, from Cape Ann, Massachusetts, to Long Island Sound. It breaks into fragments very readily when captured.

Cerebratulus lacteus (Leidy) PLATE 85. This is the largest of all the American shallow-water nemerteans, the full-grown individuals often reaching a length of 20 feet and a width of 1 inch or more. The European nemertean, *Lineus marinus,* is, however, capable of attaining a much greater length, individuals of 90 feet or more having been observed. The body of *Cerebratulus* is comparatively thick anteriorly and somewhat narrower than the rest of the body, which rapidly becomes expanded and flattened for the greater part of its length, and has very thin edges. Though the posterior end is somewhat narrower, it is rounded and equipped with a long and delicate anal cirrus, which is often lost. The thin finlike margins of the worm are adapted for swimming, for the animals tend to burrow in the sand or mud of the shallow sea-bottom during the day, but emerge at night to swim actively about, thus having a tendency to nocturnal habits.

The greater part of the body is crowded with the internal organs, especially the lateral subdivisions of the stomach and the much-branched genital organs, which show through the body and modify its color. The general coloration varies from cream, through flesh-color, to salmon and pink. The internal organs modify this on either side so as to show a brownish band.

The head varies in shape from a bluntly tapering triangular outline, narrower than the portion posterior to it, to a broadly expanded spearhead, with a narrowed

PLATE 85

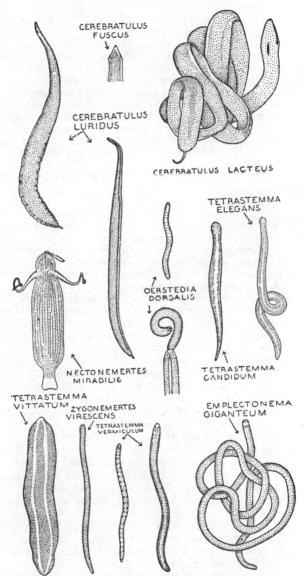

CEREBRATULUS
FUSCUS

CEREBRATULUS
LURIDUS

CEREBRATULUS LACTEUS

TETRASTEMMA
ELEGANS

OERSTEDIA
DORSALIS

NECTONEMERTES
MIRABILIS

TETRASTEMMA
CANDIDUM

TETRASTEMMA
VITTATUM

ZYGONEMERTES
VIRESCENS

TETRASTEMMA
VERMICULUM

EMPLECTONEMA
GIGANTEUM

"neck" connecting it with the rest of the body, or it may become semicircular.

There are no ocelli and the cephalic slits are long and deep, running the entire length of the head and nearly united by a shallow groove in front. The pits are lined with red, which is also the color of the lateral nerve-trunks showing through the margin of the entire body.

The mouth is a long narrow slit on the under side of the head. Through the large terminal proboscis-pore, the long, whitish, and slender proboscis may be everted more than 3 feet in length, in the large individuals.

This is a very common species, burrowing in sand and mud, near the low-water mark, in sheltered and quiet waters, from Maine to New Jersey, and southward to Florida.

Cerebratulus fuscus (Fabricius) PLATE 85. This species is similar to the preceding, but is smaller, the adults averaging about 2 feet in length. The color is not pink, but greenish gray to slate-color or olive, paler at the margins and underneath. The usual red line of the lateral nerve-trunks shows through to mark the border. The changeable head is often triangular in outline, though it may change without notice to a rounded form or may become bilobed in front. There are no ocelli. The mouth is large and vertically elongate.

This is a more northern species, being found in shallow water near the low-tide mark to a depth of 20 fathoms from Cape Cod, along the coast of Maine, to New Brunswick, Nova Scotia, and the Arctic. Its range also extends to Scotland and Northern Europe.

Cerebratulus luridus Verrill PLATE 85. This species, from 6 to 12 inches in length, is narrow and thick anteriorly, but broad, flat, and thin posteriorly. The broader part of the alimentary tract, with its lateral lobes and the branching genital organs are confined to this wide posterior region and do not extend forward into the narrow but thicker anterior region, except for the thin pharynx and proboscis apparatus.

The head is separated from the body by a narrow neck. It is very changeable in shape, as usual in this genus. The cephalic slits are large, long, and deep, and connected anteriorly by a shallow groove to the proboscis pore.

The color varies from chocolate-brown, through olive, to purplish brown, paler at the margin. Transverse bars of yellow or brown are caused by the lobes of the digestive tract showing through.

Its distribution is from Casco Bay to Buzzards Bay in sandy mud from 20 to 100 fathoms.

Order METANEMERTEA
(HOPLONEMERTEA)

In this group, the nemerteans have two muscle-layers, as in the case of the Paleonemertea, but the brain and lateral nerve-trunks are situated below them. The mouth is located in front of the brain. The proboscis has a sharp spine or stylet at the summit of the nonreversible portion, so that when the anterior part of the proboscis is everted this extends out as an offensive weapon. The intestine has a blind sac or caecum extending forward to the anterior part of the body.

Family Tetrastemmidae

The body is small and slender or, in some cases, short and stout. Two pairs of eyes are present. The lobes of the intestine alternate serially with the gonads. The lateral slits are anterior to the brain.

Tetrastemma candidum (Fabricius) PLATE 85. The body is very contractile, usually slender and proportionally elongated, and tapering to a point posteriorly. The head is typically wider than the body, narrowing to a neck. Two pairs of ocelli are present, one behind the other, forming a quadrangle. They are reddish brown in color.

The color of this species varies in alternating patterns of green and white or pale yellow. A grayish mottling betrays the location of the internal organs.

This is an active species, creeping rapidly over algae, hydroids, and various encrusting invertebrates in the tidal zone and in shallow water extending down to ten and twelve fathoms or more.

The range is from the Bay of Fundy to southern New England.

Tetrastemma elegans Verrill PLATE 85. This species tapers from the middle toward both head and tail. The head is oval and shapely, with a distinct neck, and small lateral pits. The four eyes are distinct and form a quadrangle. The color is a conspicuous pattern, consisting of two broad longitudinal stripes running the length of the body, separated by a broad median yellow stripe from the crown of the head, narrowing at the neck, and broadening to correspond with the shape of the body. A color of light yellow surrounds the neck. The brown stripes have slightly irregular borders and are sprinkled with light specks. The ventral surface of the body and head is light yellow.

This is a small worm, only about ⅘ inch long. It is common among seaweed and on wharf-piles along the southern New England coast from Woods Hole through Long Island Sound.

Tetrastemma vermiculus (Quatrefages) PLATE 85. In this case, the body is slender but changeable, usually rounded at both ends and of about the same diameter throughout. The four eyes form a quadrangular grouping, the antero-posterior distance being greater than the distance between the eyes of the same pair. All are connected by a dark line of pigment.

The dorsal coloration varies from light yellow to yellowish gray, or even salmon, speckled, especially laterally, with brown. It is paler on the ventral side.

This species is quite common, being found in tide-pools, on muddy bottoms, on rocks, and on wharfpiles, from the Bay of Fundy to Woods Hole, Massachusetts, and Long Island Sound, especially at Noank, Connecticut.

Tetrastemma vittatum Verrill PLATE 85. In this nemertean, the body is 2 to 3 inches in length and quite broad in proportion to its length, being about ¼ inch in breadth. As usual, there is considerable variation in form, tending to be at times cylindrical, at other times flattened somewhat. The head is smaller than the body and divided by a horizontal constriction about halfway between the two pairs of eyes, of which the anterior pair is closer together than the posterior pair. Forward of the constriction, that part of the head is rather conical or helmet-shaped.

The general color varies between dark or light olive-green, the olive also being yellowish in some specimens, and in others greenish brown to almost black. On the sides of the body there tends to be a mottled pattern, while ventrally, the body is generally paler. Anterior to the transverse groove, the head is striped with six green and six whitish or pale green stripes, converging at the tip, where the head is white in color.

This worm is commonly distributed from the Bay of Fundy, along the coast of Maine and southern New England, generally, to Vineyard Sound and Long Island Sound, on muddy bottoms, from the low-water mark to a depth of 25 fathoms.

Oerstedia dorsalis (Quatrefages) PLATE 85. The body, in this species, is about ⅖ inch in length, or less, rounded at both ends, and nearly cylindrical in section. The head is practically continuous with the body and has two transverse cerebral pits on each side. There are four ocelli, in two pairs, which are more distant from each other than the eyes in each pair. The proboscis pore is slightly ventral and not quite at the end of the anterior tip. The proboscis is quite long, its length, when everted, being about equal to three fourths of the body. Its surface is covered with multitudes of pointed papillae.

The body color is quite variable, mostly brown or reddish, either with a clear median stripe of lighter tint, *or* mottled and spotted with various shades of brown, with or without the dorsal stripe.

The distribution is general along the New England coast in shallow water and down to more than 20 fathoms. It also extends to the coast of Europe. It is quite common on stones and the piles of wharves.

Family Nectonemertidae

These are remarkable nemerteans, externally resembling a *Sagitta* (see page 692), but their internal organization shows that it is a true nemertean. The thin, flat body is rounded in front and tapers in fusiform manner to the posterior end. It is of definite shape as compared with the changeable outline of other nemerteans. It is highly muscular and equipped with lateral- and tail-fins, well adapted for swimming. The male has large tentacles symmetrically extending on either side.

Nectonemertes mirabilis Verrill PLATE 85. The flattened, symmetrical body is upwards of 2 inches in length. The thin margins, posteriorly, may be extended laterally as paired finlike expansions. The sides of the midregion are nearly parallel, abruptly narrowing back of the side-fins, and expanding again to a bilobed tail-fin, resembling the caudal fin of a fish. The entire body-surface is striated both longitudinally and horizontally as muscular layers. The head, bluntly rounded in front, is separated from the body by a constricted neck from the forward part of which a long, tapering cirrus extends on either side, tending to be coiled at the tip. The proboscis sheath is long, occupying the greater part of the body. The proboscis, when extended, is club-shaped. It is armed with a single spine. The large, straight intestine has symmetrically paired lobes somewhat alternately placed with reference to the repeated series of gonads. The general coloration is orange.

These nemerteans are open-sea dwellers, having been dredged from some hundreds of fathoms in the Atlantic Ocean, so that typically they do not belong in our region, but are included for comparison to show the swimming adaptations possible in this primitive group.

Family Emplectonematidae

In this family are included forms having the openings of the mouth and proboscis united. The body is long, very slender, and contractile. The head and body are confluent, without necklike constriction. The cerebral fossae are only slightly developed. The proboscis is quite small and thick.

Emplectonema giganteum Verrill PLATE 85. This is a large species, measuring, when fully extended, 7 to

12 feet, with a slender, rounded body about ⅓ inch in diameter. It is quite conspicuous, being bright orange-red to salmon in color, and of flesh-tint on the under side. There are many small, inconspicuous ocelli in four or more groups.

The range is from the coast of Maine to Marthas Vineyard and Block Island, from about 80 fathoms on the Continental Shelf to greater depths off the Banks. Often brought up by fishing trawls and dredges.

Family Amphiporidae

Comparatively stout-bodied and short nemertean worms. The lobes of the digestive tract are branched but not regularly alternating with the gonads. The anterior part of the proboscis thick-walled and eversible, exposing a lining of papillae, and a spine, or style, mounted at the end of the noneversible portion, surrounded by smaller rasplike stylets. The cerebral grooves are shallow and located transversely or diagonally on the side and ventral portion of the head. The eyes are very numerous, on the side and back of the head.

Zygonemertes virescens (Verrill) PLATE 85. The relatively flattened body, more than 1½ inches in length, is slender but broader in the anterior region, including a relatively large head, somewhat rounded on the front margin. The delicate and thin transverse cerebral grooves, on the sides of the head, continue transversely to the dorsal side, crossing the groups of ocelli, which are numerous and form large paired clusters laterally, arranged in rows. The color is light green, uniformly over the body, but in varying tones.

This species is common on wharfpiles and in shallow water among hydroids and other growths along the coast of southern New England.

The Genus **Amphiporus** includes numerous species, at least seventy being known, about eighteen of which are found on our coast. Twelve of these will be described briefly here:

Amphiporus angulatus (Fabricius) PLATE 86. The body is large and stout, round in section but flat ventrally. Head, wider than the neck, its sides spreading and oval in front, a conspicuous white spot on each side. The ocelli numerous in two dorsal groups. Proboscis comparatively large, its surface covered with papillae.

The coloration is deep purple dorsally, varying in some individuals to madder-brown or deep brown or plum-color. Others, occasionally, are reddish- or orange-brown. The head is whitish anteriorly, the spot, above mentioned, on each side, being triangular in shape. Proboscis reddish. Length, 1 to 1½ inches.

Very common at low-water mark from Massachusetts Bay north to Greenland.

Amphiporus multisorus Verrill PLATE 86. Similar to the above, but with a shorter, more compact head, abruptly separated from the body by a transverse groove. A pair of transverse slits occur laterally. Six clusters of ocelli, of three or four ocelli each, are paired on either side of the front margin of the head. Posterior to the above are two dorsal groups of six to eight ocelli each.

Salmon to flesh-color; lighter ventrally.

Coast of Maine.

Amphiporus tetrasorus Verrill PLATE 86. Differs from the preceding in having transverse cerebral grooves curving upward and forward on each side and, on the ventral side, laterally to the mouth. The ocelli form two converging clusters, nearly parallel to each other, on either side of the posterior part of the head.

General coloration, chocolate-brown dorsally, lighter beneath. The head is white anteriorly.

Coast of Massachusetts.

Amphiporus ochraceus Verrill PLATE 86. The long body is quite slender anteriorly, becoming broader toward the middle-region and tapering bluntly to the tail. The head is oval and serpentlike, tapering to a slender neck which gradually widens to join the body. The proboscis-pore and mouth are small. The numerous ocelli form a marginal row on each side of the frontal margin, while posterior to these are four more distinct eyes arranged in a quadrangular pattern. The brain ganglia show through as indefinite reddish spots.

The color of the body varies from light yellow to deep yellow or orange, especially anteriorly. There is usually a lighter median line. Through the translucent integument can be seen the internal organs, still lighter yellow in color, but giving a mottled appearance.

The length is 2 or 3 inches. The distribution is from northern Massachusetts along the southern New England coast, where it is common in the tidal area including tide-pools, under stones and among seaweed, hydroids and encrusting invertebrates generally; also on wharf-piles.

Amphiporus roseus Verrill PLATE 86. The body is short and stout, the sides nearly parallel, with an abruptly tapering tail. The head is transversely oval, wider than the body, with a distinct, groovelike neck, marked by a transverse slit on either side. The numerous ocelli are arranged in four groups in a crescent-shaped outline converging so that they nearly touch on the median line posteriorly.

The color is orange-red dorsally, lighter ventrally. The

length is somewhat less than an inch. The distribution extends from the Bay of Fundy to Massachusetts Bay.

Amphiporus mesosorus Verrill PLATE 86. This is also a bright red worm, with a flesh tint ventrally. The body is short, round, and rather stout, about ½ inch in length. The head is continuous with the neck. The numerous ocelli are grouped to form a triangular pattern on either side of the head.

This species is found along the Massachusetts coast.

Amphiporus frontalis Verrill PLATE 86. The body of this nemertean is large, elongate, and tapering only slightly to the bluntly rounded tail. It may reach a length of 5 inches with a breadth of ⅛ inch. The head is distinct, being broader than the body, and more or less triangular, though occasionally bilobed, in outline. The neck-region has a transverse ciliated slit on each side. The black ocelli are large and distinct, in a double row on each side of the head.

The color is white to pale gray or yellowish. A dark dorsal band runs along the median line. The internal organs show through, giving a mottled pale pink or yellow cast.

The distribution of this species is northern, being known to occur near the low-tide mark on the coast of Maine.

Amphiporus cruentatus Verrill PLATE 86. The body is quite translucent, so that the median and lateral blood vessels show through the light flesh-color of the integument in a conspicuous threadlike pattern of bright red. This species is quite variable in form, having a slender body, an inch in length when extended, tapering toward both head and tail. When contracted, it becomes quite short and stout. There is a row of eight to twelve ocelli on each side of the head, the largest being in front. The large proboscis is covered with a felt of long papillae.

This species occurs rarely off the southern New England coast in 4 to 10 fathoms.

Amphiporus agilis Verrill PLATE 86. This is a very active species, 1 inch to 1½ inches in length, almost snakelike in form and manner of movement. It has a slender tapering body with an oval, almost pointed head, wider than the body, and with a terminal proboscis-pore. The numerous ocelli are arranged on either side of the head in a long lateral line. Posterior to these a transverse groove completely crosses the dorsal surface of the head. The color is light orange-yellow, with a reddish median line running along the back. The light yellow internal organs show through the back in a networklike pattern.

This species is found from the Bay of Fundy to Massachusetts Bay, creeping rapidly over the sea-bottom or clinging to the underside of the surface-film.

PLATE 86

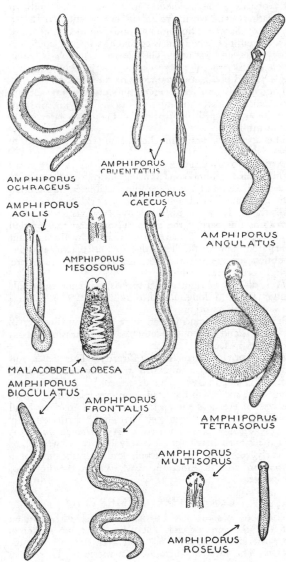

AMPHIPORUS
OCHRACEUS

AMPHIPORUS
CRUENTATUS

AMPHIPORUS
AGILIS

AMPHIPORUS
CAECUS

AMPHIPORUS
MESOSORUS

AMPHIPORUS
ANGULATUS

MALACOBDELLA OBESA

AMPHIPORUS
BIOCULATUS

AMPHIPORUS
FRONTALIS

AMPHIPORUS
TETRASORUS

AMPHIPORUS
MULTISORUS

AMPHIPORUS
ROSEUS

Amphiporus bioculatus McIntosh PLATE 86. The body of this species is about 1 to 1½ inches in length. It is a rather stout worm, round in cross-section, of about the same diameter throughout, and rounded bluntly at both extremities. The head is confluent with the body, not being separated by a neck. The transverse groove is barely visible. The name of the species is derived from the two single paired ocelli, near the front of the head.

The color is dark orange-red, sometimes orange or salmon, paler beneath, the internal organs showing through laterally as brownish mottled areas. There is a large, well-armed proboscis.

The species occurs throughout Long Island Sound to Block Island.

Amphiporus caecus Verrill PLATE 86. As the name implies, this is a blind species, being entirely without ocelli. The soft body is of about the same diameter throughout, with a rounded head, but without a necklike connection with the body. A whitish furrow, however, completely surrounds this part of the anatomy, marking the location of the cerebral slit. Two reddish areas show through the transparent skin of the head, due to the cephalic ganglia. Doubtless, this region may be sensitive to light, therefore, though ocelli are absent.

This, also, is a bright scarlet species, with the sides pale orange-yellow. A longitudinal, dark red stripe occupies a median dorsal position.

Specimens of this nemertean were first found by Verrill off Block Island in about 20 fathoms. They measured about 1½ inches in length.

Amphiporus superbus (Girard). This is a record by Girard of a specimen found by Stimpson off Grand Manan, in 1853, and described by the former as being "soft red" with the head "obtusely triangular," with one pair of eyes and the neck marked by a "narrow band of white." It has not been seen alive, but Verrill considers it likely to have been a variety of *Amphiporus angulare*. It is mentioned here, from a purely historic viewpoint, as an early record of the collection and identification of a nemertean on the American coast, within the limits of our range.

Order BDELLONEMERTEA

The body is short, flat, and flask-shaped with a median notch at the anterior end. There is a leechlike sucker at the posterior end, but in no other way does it resemble leeches. The internal anatomy is nemertean. There is a proboscis with a proboscis-sheath almost as long as the body, and, though it is without a style, there is a bulb and sac, which may be rudiments of such a structure. There are no ocelli or cerebral slits. There are two layers of muscles, an outer circular layer and an internal longitudinal layer.

Malacobdella obesa Verrill PLATE 86. This peculiar species is upwards of 1½ inches in length. The skin is covered with small star-shaped spots. The reproductive system fills most of the space between the intestine and the skin. Apparently, there are many reproductive openings on the back.

The color is yellowish white. This nemertean is parasitic or commensal in the gill cavity of the Soft Clam (*Mya arenaria*). It is closely related to, if not identical with, *Malacobdella grossa* (O. F. Müller). It occurs abundantly along the New England coast.

7

Phylum Nemathelmia

(ROUNDWORMS, THREADWORMS)

THE Nemathelmia are, for the most part, a parasitic group of organisms, with the features of their anatomy quite distinct from that of any other phylum in the animal kingdom. In fact, the relationships of the three main divisions, of classes assigned to the phylum, are problematic. Nevertheless, they seem to have more in common with each other than with any other phyla. They are all elongate unsegmented worms of simple organization. The great majority of them are internal parasites to other animals, either invertebrate, or vertebrate, or both. Some pass their entire existence as parasites; others are free-living during their larval period and parasitic as adults; still others reverse this condition, being parasitic during the larval period and free-living when adult. Some pass through the bodies of two or more hosts during their parasitic phases. A few live entirely free, in damp earth, fresh water, or salt water. They are unsegmented, with no serial repetition of parts either externally or internally. They have no appendages of any kind, except a few bristles, hooks, or, in a few instances, suckers. Their elongated bodies are tubular, often threadlike, and taper to both the anterior and posterior ends. They are covered with a thick, shining and smooth cuticle. In fact, they and the Kinorhyncha (page 283) are the only groups in the animal kingdom entirely without cilia of any kind, except possibly in the excretory organs of one group.

Internally, there is no closed vascular system or special arrangements for respiration, nor is there a true *coelom,* or body cavity, derived from out-pushing cells from the digestive tract and lined by a mesoderm, as in segmented worms and other higher animals. The digestive tract is reduced to extremely simple terms, being a straight tube from mouth to anus, or even lacking entirely.

The Phylum Nemathelmia is divided, for convenience, into three main classes: (1) *Nematoda,* or Threadworms; (2) *Nematomorpha,* or Hairworms; and (3) *Acanthocephala,* or Spineheads.

CLASS NEMATODA

This class contains, by far, the greatest number of the Nemathelmia. They are threadlike and pointed at both ends. They are usually shining white and may be found free-living in most soil or as parasites in plants, mammals, birds, reptiles, amphibia, fishes, insects, spiders, snails, and crayfishes. A number of them are dangerous to humans, horses, and dogs. Only a few are marine.

The species that are found free-living in the sea belong to the Family *Enoplidae*. They are very slender and hairlike. Their bodies are very smooth and transparent. They are distinguished by having eyes and by the development of fine hairs and bristles around the mouth. They move about actively, but never coil spirally. Among them is the species, *Enoplus brevis* Bastian, which lives among seaweeds and hydroids, swimming about in shallow water. It is greenish in color.

CLASS NEMATOMORPHA

This class contains the so-called Hairworms, or Gordian Worms. They resemble horsehairs, being very long, slender, and hairlike. They swim actively in fresh-water ponds and pools of stagnant water, in the case of the Family Gordiidae, to which the Genus *Gordius* belongs. The marine species is assigned to the Family Nectonematidae, of which it is the solitary representative, under the species name of *Nectonema agile* Verrill. This worm swims near the surface of the sea, rapidly undulating, and coiling and uncoiling. The males are from 2 to 8 inches long, and the females somewhat shorter. The body has two rows of fine bristles on each side throughout its entire length, which are easily broken off. It is often found off the New England coast.

8

Phylum Trochelmia

(WHEEL ANIMALCULES)

THESE are microscopic or submicroscopic animals, the largest of which are visible to the naked eye, being not more than ⅛ inch in length. There are about 1200 species known, mostly in fresh water. A few, however, about fifty species, live in salt or brackish water. It is with these that we deal in this chapter.

They are interesting historically, because they were among the earliest minute animals observed through the then newly invented microscope, more than two and a half centuries ago when first, the Rev. John Harris and later, Anton Leeuwenhoek saw myriads of minute living creatures, the existence of which had hitherto been unsuspected. Among the largest and most active of these were little top-shaped animals, spinning through the water, which had what appeared, to Leeuwenhoek, to be rapidly rotating wheels on their heads, so that he named them "Rotifera," or "wheel-bearers," and thought that, for the first time, he had discovered the principle of the rotating wheel in nature. He first published descriptions of them in 1703. Later, he discovered his mistake when, with improved lenses, he made out that the "wheels" were really wreaths of cilia beating the water in rapid succession, thus giving the illusion of rotation. Nevertheless, the name stuck, and they are still known as *Rotifera* or *Rotaria*. The name adopted for the phylum (Trochelmia) is derived from the Greek, *trochus,* wheel, and *helmins,* worm.

The ciliated anterior wreaths vary in details of position and extent; in fact, there may be one, two, or several of them. Typically, they surround a terminal bare, but sensory, region, and comprise an area known as the *corona* on the ventral side of which the mouth is located.

The posterior extremity is tapered and is usually provided with an organ adapted for clinging. The body is composed of ringlike joints, externally, reminding one of the segments of annulate worms. This is, however, a purely superficial character, affecting only the integuments; for, internally, the organs are entirely unsegmented.

Certain aberrant organisms, however, are ciliated ventrally, instead of on the anterior end, or, in some cases, lack cilia entirely.

The Phylum Trochelmia is divided into three classes, as follows:

(1) *Rotatoria,* with an anterior corona of cilia present.

as well as a complicated set of throat-jaws, situated in the pharynx, below the mouth-opening;

(2) *Gastrotricha,* having the ciliated area confined to the ventral side, and with no throat-jaws;

(3) *Kinorhyncha,* with cilia entirely lacking, and with the body armed with spines and bristles.

CLASS ROTATORIA

These are the true rotifers. Though the shape of the body is extremely variable, they are typically top-shaped, and there are always three body-divisions: head, trunk, and post-anal portion, called the foot. The corona of cilia is situated on the anterior end, toward the ventral side of which the mouth is located, as mentioned above. They are bilaterally symmetrical and provided with a proto-nephridial system. Circulatory and respiratory systems are, however, lacking. They may be oviparous or viviparous, and usually with separate sexes. They may be free-swimming or creeping, or they may be of fixed habits. Many species are solitary, and others form colonies. A few are parasitic.

A large number of species have a thin and flexible integument. Others develop a thickened portion in the middle of the body, known as the *lorica,* forming a stiff, protective armature, the surface of which may be smooth, granular, areolate, punctate, reticulate, keeled, branched, or spined, these being characters of value in differentiating the species.

The body-wall is composed of two layers, an inner layer of connected cells and the outer cuticle, showing the superficial segmented structure, already mentioned, and often patterned with longitudinal and transverse striations.

The well-developed internal musculature controlling the movement of the body-organs consists of longitudinal re-tractors crossing the internal cavity of the rotifer to con-trol the head and foot, as well as parietal muscles for extending these organs by hydrostatic pressure.

The cilia of the corona are in continual vibration, not only to aid locomotion through the water, but also to convey food to the mouth.

A *buccal canal* leads from the mouth to a thick-walled, muscular pharynx, called the *mastax* (INDEX PLATE 87), which encloses the throat-jaws (known as the *trophi*) and their musculature. Attached to the mastax, there are often salivary glands. The oesophagus arises from the dorsal part of the mastax and leads around it into the stomach, which is provided anteriorly with a pair of gastric glands. The intestine is straight and distinct. It empties into the cloaca and opens to the outside through the anal opening, situated dorsally at the junction of the trunk with the foot.

The excretory system is composed of a pulsating bladder emptying into the cloaca. In some species, the bladder is absent, the cloaca functioning instead. Emptying into the bladder are two long, sinuous, excretory tubes, called the *protonephridia,* a pair running through the body cavity on each side of the alimentary tract and anastomosing in the head. At intervals, along their course, are situated minute, club-shaped organs, called *flame-cells,* the free ends closed and each containing a bundle of long cilia in constant motion.

Below the intestine, on the ventral side of the body, lies the ovary. It is composed of two parts: the larger (*vitellarium*) contains a number of large nuclei, often exactly eight, and prepares the yolk for the developing egg. Confluent with the vitellarium is a smaller mass (*germarium*) containing many nuclei from which the eggs develop. An oviduct leads from the ovary backward to the cloaca.

The nervous system is composed of a *cerebral ganglion,* called the brain, situated dorsally in the head, above the mastax, from which radiate nerve-filaments to the various organs and sensory centers.

Most rotifers have rudimentary eyespots. There may be one, two, three, or none.

The antennae, typically four in number, are more often reduced to three by fusion of the two dorsals, which are situated on the head above the brain. The laterals are found on each side of the trunk in the posterior region, placed somewhat dorsally. The *retrocerebral sac,* an organ of unknown function, and *subcerebral glands,* when present, are dorsally placed; the sac is posterior to the brain with the glands, one on each side.

The foot encloses glands which secrete a mucilaginous substance, having the property of adhesion in water, which, in the majority of cases, passes through minute ducts to the openings at the tips of the toes, which vary in number from one to four, or may be absent entirely.

The primitive form of the corona may be considered, fundamentally, as a finely ciliated *buccal plate* forming a *circumapical band* surrounding a nude apical area. The latter sometimes carries sensory styles, setigerous papillae or membranelles, but never locomotor cilia. All the various modifications of the rotatorian corona may be derived from this primitive type.

The mastax encloses the trophi and is provided with muscles, glands, and sensory areas. The trophi (INDEX PLATE 88) are composed of a number of typical hard pieces and are very important in classification. The *fulcrum* is median and serves for attachment of two similar pieces, the *rami.* These three pieces, collectively, form the *incus.*

PLATE 87

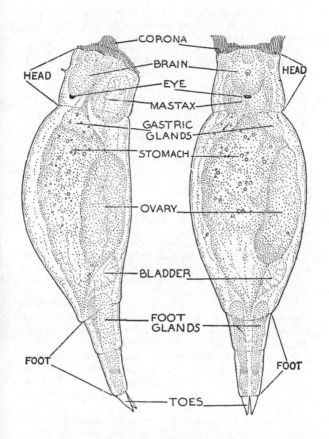

CORONA
BRAIN
EYE
MASTAX
GASTRIC GLANDS
STOMACH
OVARY
BLADDER
FOOT GLANDS
TOES
HEAD
FOOT

ANATOMY OF A
TYPICAL ROTIFER

The *manubria* are two lateral, similar pieces each of which articulates with a piece carrying one or more teeth, called the *uncus*. These four pieces, collectively, form the *mallei*.

The modifications of the various parts of the mastax give rise to a number of types connected by numerous intermediaries (INDEX PLATE 88), as follows:

Malleate mastax. The most primitive type, being the least specialized. All the pieces are about equally developed, permitting a feeble vertical movement of prehension and a horizontal movement of grinding.

Virgate mastax. Functions by suction. Derived from the malleate by elongation of all the parts in a direction perpendicular to the axis of the alimentary tract.

The fulcrum is long and expanded distally for attachment of a powerful muscle, the hypopharynx, which fills the domelike cavity formed by the rami and manubria. One end of this muscle is free and cuticular. On contracting, it tends to form a vacuum, sucking food particles into the mouth.

Cardate mastax. Functions by suction, but the manner and structure are entirely different from the preceding type. It oscillates as a unit on a transverse axis, while a complicated epipharynx supports the wall of the mouth.

Forcipate mastax. Functions by prehension. The entire organ is strongly compressed dorso-ventrally and is adapted to the capture and tearing apart of prey by protrusion through the mouth.

Incudate mastax. Functions by prehension. Differs from the preceding type by reduction of all the parts except the strong, pincerlike rami, which are protrusible through the mouth by revolving on a horizontal axis.

Ramate mastax. Functions by grinding. All the pieces are reduced except the unci, which are shaped like half moons and carry numerous, opposing linear teeth in the form of striations, several of which, near the middle, are stronger than the remainder.

Malleo-ramate mastax. Functions by grinding. Differs little from the preceding. The first few opposing, ventral teeth are detached and developed. The following teeth decrease rapidly in size, until reduced to simple striations.

Uncinate mastax. Functions by delaceration. The movement of the unci on the rami has been much increased by the development of an intermediate piece, the *subuncus.*

Among the oviparous rotifers, the most common type of individual, the nonsexual female reproduces exclusively by parthenogenesis. Its eggs develop invariably into females (*amictic females*), and multiplication by parthenogenesis may continue for many generations. However, the daugh-

PLATE 88

TYPICAL TROPHI, OR THROAT-JAWS OF ROTIFERS

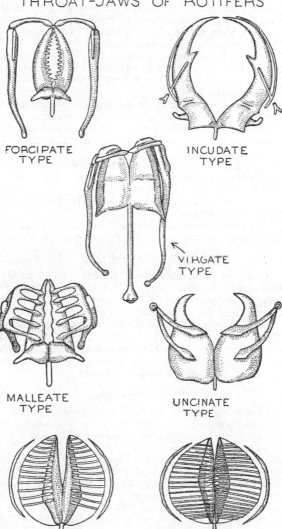

FORCIPATE TYPE

INCUDATE TYPE

VIRGATE TYPE

MALLEATE TYPE

UNCINATE TYPE

MALLEO-RAMATE TYPE

RAMATE TYPE

ters of the amictic female may be fertilizable (*mictic females*). Their eggs develop parthenogenetically into males, or, if fertilized, produce nonsexual amictic females with which the cycle begins anew.

While the majority of rotifers are potentially cosmopolitan, their distribution depends more on conditions of existence than on the means thereof. The following ecological groups have been suggested:

The Benthonic fauna. Free-swimming and gliding rotifers living on the substratum and among submerged aquatic vegetation in the littoral region of bodies of permanent water.

The Limnetic fauna. Free-swimming rotifers living in the open reaches of bodies of permanent water.

The Sapropelic fauna. Free-swimming rotifers living in temporary benthonic environments polluted by much decaying organic matter.

The Anabiotic fauna. Rotifers having the power of revival after desiccation, and living in moss where moisture may be permanent or temporary.

The Marine fauna. Rotifers living in brackish or saline waters of the ocean.

The Class Rotatoria is divided into three orders: (1) *Seisonidea;* (2) *Bdelloidea;* and (3) *Monogononta.*

Order SEISONIDEA

These are remarkably shaped rotifers with an elongate fusiform body, and a very slender, retractile neck, quite as long as the body itself, when fully extended. In the females, there are paired ovaries. The males are fully developed. The mastax is of the *virgate type* (INDEX PLATE 88), but in a specialized form known as *fulcrate.* There are no lateral antennae. The foot is without toes, but there is a terminal perforated disc instead. There is but one family, of which two species are known.

Family Seisonidae

This solitary family has the characters of the order.

Seison annulatus Claus PLATE 89. The head is terminated by a double corona, consisting of two little tufts of cilia, one on either side of the mouth. The head encloses a complicated glandular apparatus surrounding the terminal mastax of the modified virgate type, known as fulcrate, adapted for sucking. The long, slender oesophagus leads into a compact stomach with a wall consisting of large cells as in rotifers generally. The short intestine is quite reduced. The male genital organs open in the back of the neck in the male, while those of the female open posteriorly. This species is commensal on the small shrimp, *Nebalia* (PLATE 138).

Seison nebaliae Grube. This is a closely related species, also commensal on *Nebalia,* as its name indicates. Both species are cosmopolitan.

Order BDELLOIDEA

Apparently this order is composed entirely of females, with the ovaries paired, as in the preceding order, as males are entirely unknown. The mastax is ramate (INDEX PLATE 88). The lateral antennae are absent. The active, jointed body is telescopic at both ends. Toes, in this family, may or may not be present. When present, they are found at the tapering posterior end; two, three, or four in number. The corona is composed of two nearly complete separate wreaths of cilia. Four families are recognized, mostly in fresh water. A marine species is mentioned here.

Family Philodinidae

The two circular lobes of the corona are mounted on separate pedicels and are each bordered by a wreath of cilia. They are completely retractile.

Zelinkiella synaptae (Zelinka). This species is interesting because it is parasitic or, at least, commensal on certain species of *Synapta,* a genus of small, transparent sea-cucumbers (page 795), clinging either to the external surface or, sometimes, to the inner wall of the digestive cavity. It is eyeless, with a short but expanded corona, and ciliated cushions on either side of the mouth from which extend a beaklike projection. The last two joints of the foot are modified into a large sucker, by means of which it clings to the *Synapta.* It is less than 1/100 inch in length and, therefore, can be seen only with the aid of a microscope.

Order MONOGONONTA

This order contains, by far, the greater number of the Rotaria. Both females and males are present, the latter, however, of comparatively small size and insignificant. The mastax is of various types but never ramate or fulcrate. The lateral antennae are present, small tufts of cilia, especially innervated, placed symmetrically on either side of the outer surface of the lorica. The foot may have two toes or none.

Suborder PLOIMA

Only free-swimming rotifers are included in this suborder, none being fixed and stationary. Certain rare parasites attach themselves to their hosts by their throat-jaws, but never by means of the foot-region or a sucker. The foot is usually present, and is equipped with two toes. The corona is variable in type, often having several lobes fringed with coarse, compound cilia. The intestine is always equipped with an anal outlet.

Family Brachionidae

The corona has several lobes arranged transversely, each with tufts of strong, stiff cilia (*pseudotrochus*). The mouth is funnel-shaped. The mastax is malleate in type (INDEX PLATE 88). This is a large group, and is therefore divided into subfamilies.

Subfamily Brachioninae

Head and corona typical, without lateral lamellae or head-hood. Some species are without eyespots. When present, they are in the neck-region or frontal in location. Many species, at least seventy of which are marine.

Brachionus plicatilis Müller PLATE 89. This species has a rigid lorica, or armature, covering the central part of the body, with a characteristic saw-toothed anterior margin having three triangular pointed teeth on either side of a median notch. The long, wrinkled foot is sharply marked off from the body. There is a cervical eyespot. The four muscles that work the foot are clearly seen through the transparent lorica. Two huge gastric glands are attached to the stomach. Like all marine species of this genus, *Brachionus plicatilis* is very common.

Keratella cochlearis recurvispina (Jägerskoild) PLATE 89. In this species, the foot and toes are absent. A characteristically shaped lorica is present, which is well depicted in the figure, from which the species can be clearly identified. It is open anteriorly, is always tesselated, and terminates in a single spine. The eyespot is present in the neck-region and has a lens. This is a common marine species, found among seaweed near the shore.

Notholca striata (Müller) PLATE 89. The lorica is urn-shaped, with six spines on the frontal margin; two longer spines on each side flank a shorter spine. The posterior margin is rounded. The dorsal plate has twelve longitudinal striae. It occurs in both fresh and salt water. The membranous lorica changes its form as the body contracts. It is about 1/120 inch in diameter.

Subfamily Colurinae

There is a dorsal head-shield present in this subfamily, and the corona has lateral extensions or lamellae. There are paired lateral eyespots on the head.

Colurella adriatica (Ehrenberg) PLATE 89. The body is enclosed in a lorica which is laterally compressed and composed of two pieces placed laterally to each other, joined anteriorly but gaping posteriorly and ventrally. The dorsal head-shield anteriorly is hook-shaped and not

PLATE 89

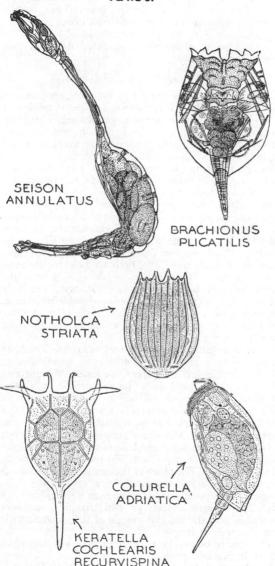

SEISON
ANNULATUS

BRACHIONUS
PLICATILIS

NOTHOLCA
STRIATA

COLURELLA
ADRIATICA

KERATELLA
COCHLEARIS
RECURVISPINA

retractile. The distinctly jointed foot is permanently extended, terminated by two slender, pointed toes, usually so closely appressed that they often look like a single toe. The species, in life, gives the impression of being a toe dancer, balancing on the tip of its closed toes, and then awkwardly tipping over.

Subfamily Lecaninae

The corona in this subfamily is, for the most part, unlobed; that is, without a *pseudotrochus* (see definition of the family). The mouth is not funnel-shaped. The lorica is composed of two plates, placed dorsally and ventrally, separated by a deep lateral groove. There are one or two toes, held in a diverging position.

Lecane grandis (Murray) PLATE 90. The lorica is subcircular, viewed horizontally, with the frontal border flattened. Viewed from the side, the lorica is seen to consist of two plates, one dorsal and one ventral, separated around the margin by a deep groove or sulcus but joined by a thin membrane. As the body expands and contracts vertically, the two plates move up and down like a pair of bellows. There are two slender toes with parallel edges and short, abruptly acute tips. Both are held widely separated as a rule. The members of this group have the curious habit of balancing on one toe, with the body bent at a right angle, held motionless; then, after a time, of swinging the body from one side to the other without letting go. Later, it will swim off to another location and repeat the process.

Proales reinhardti (Ehrenberg) PLATE 90. The body of this rotifer is elongated, slender, and spindle-shaped, with very flexible and transparent integument. A transverse fold separates the head from the rest of the body. The first third of the abdominal region rapidly increases in width, beyond which it gradually tapers to the tail. The two-jointed foot is quite long, with the toes slender and lanceolate in shape. The dorsal antenna is as usual, but the lateral antennae are at the base of the tail. The corona is somewhat oblique in position. The mastax is of a modified malleate type. The pharynx is fairly long. The stomach and pharynx are not separated by a constriction. The foot-glands are usually long, extending well up into the body. The eyespot consists of two triangular pigment cells and is near the anterior margin of the ganglion. It is about ¹⁄₁₀₀ inch in length.

This species occurs in both fresh and salt water, as well as in brackish pools.

Proales gonothyreae Remane PLATE 90. This is a related species, extremely interesting because of its habit of living commensally, if not parasitically, in the hydro-

theca of the leptomedusan hydroid, *Gonothyrea loveni*
Allman (PLATE 90; see also PLATES 41, 44). Apparently,
according to Remane, it fastens its mouth firmly to the
epidermis of the polyp, from which fact it is to be assumed
that it is a true ectoparasite rather than a commensal
organism. Other species of the same genus have similar
habits. For example, *Proales parasita* Ehrenberg and
Proales aureus Zawadovsky are parasitic in colonies of
the protozoan *Volvox*. Certain other rotifers are known
to be found habitually on the stems of hydroids, but apparently they feed on the diatoms and microscopic algae
which chance to be there. In the case of this species,
however, it seems to be intimately associated with its
host, laying its eggs either inside or on the outside
of the hydrotheca, and never leaving it of its own volition.
If removed, it crawls directly back to the colony, climbing
it with slow wormlike motions.

The head of *Proales gonothyreae* is moderately rounded
anteriorly. There is no constriction separating the head
from the rest of the body and there is the same gradual
transition in outline to the foot. There are two large and
well-developed conical toes on the foot. The corona consists of a ventrally situated, oval, ciliated area lying
entirely anterior to the mouth, with the cilia arranged
in seven transverse tracts across the ventral side of the
head. The internal organs have a normal arrangement,
except that the foot-glands are voluminous and extend far
up into the cavity of the abdomen. The mastax is considerably modified, correlated with the parasitic habits of
the animal, the malleo-virgate arrangement associated with
Proales being altered to accomplish the function of the
cardate type.

Family Lindiidae

In the Lindiidae, the corona is narrowed and oval in
shape, uniformly covered with almost feltlike cilia. Two
symmetrical antero-lateral extensions, known as *auricles,*
are equipped with long, powerful cilia providing efficient
propulsive power. The mastax is of the cardate type
(INDEX PLATE 88). The species of this family are oviparous.

Lindia tecusa Harring & Meyers PLATE 91. This
species is devoid of a lorica, the integument being leathery
and flexible, but the form is quite constant. The body is
elongate, spindle-shaped, and fairly slender. It is light
orange-brown in color.

The head is short, rounded anteriorly, with the neck
portion quite long and proportionately confluent with the
abdomen in outline, though the separation is clearly
marked by a transverse groove. The sides of the abdomen
are practically parallel for about two thirds of its length

and then taper somewhat to the toes. There is actually no foot, but the toes are indicated by short soft mounds that are retractile within the body.

The corona is situated on the ventral side, extending about a quarter of the body-length. No auricles are present. This species is viviparous, the embryo, before birth occupying about half of the interior of the parent, crowding and distorting the internal organs. The brain-ganglion is very large and pear-shaped. A very large eyespot is contained in a red, pigmented retrocerebral sac. This is a large rotifer, being 1/25 inch in length and visible to the naked eye. It is abundant in salt and brackish pools.

Family Notommatidae

The corona, in this family, consists of a marginal wreath surrounding a bare apical area and an evenly ciliated, usually somewhat ventrally situated buccal plate, the function of which is to propel food-particles into the mouth. The auricles are present in some species, absent in others. The mastax is virgate in type (INDEX PLATE 88).

Cephalodella mineri Harring & Myers PLATE 91. The body is rather short and almost cylindrical, a little convex dorsally. The head is moderately large and somewhat deflexed, with the neck not very distinctly marked. The lorica is thin and flexible, but with the plates well defined. The foot is rather short, conical, and well developed. The tail is very small, but with the toes strongly curved, broad at the base, and tapering to acute points. The corona is slightly oblique and convex, of regular outline. The virgate mastax is typical (INDEX PLATE 88). The brain ganglion is elongate. The eyespot is double and the two parts are located toward the front, fairly wide apart. The retrocerebral organ is lacking. The length is about 1/60 inch.

This species is very abundant among the water-weed, *Fontinalis novae-angliae,* in brackish running water on the New Jersey coast.

Family Trichocercidae

The corona is ventrally oblique, due to the forward curvature of the body. The mastax is a strongly asymmetric virgate (INDEX PLATE 88).

Trichocerca marina (Daday) PLATE 91. The corona consists of two small tufts of cilia mounted on elevations of the apical area. The anterior border of the lorica is cut up into sharp-pointed projections, with deep divisions between them. There is a transverse cervical groove, but the outline of the neck is otherwise continued into the abdomen. A well-developed stomach and a short in

PLATE 90

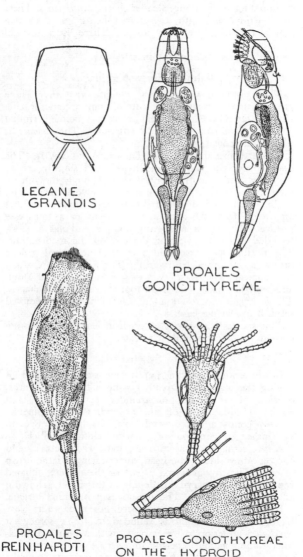

LECANE
GRANDIS

PROALES
GONOTHYREAE

PROALES
REINHARDTI

PROALES GONOTHYREAE
ON THE HYDROID
GONOTHYREA LOVENI

testine are present. The foot is very short and papilliform, terminating in two long, slender sharp-pointed toes. These are unequal in length, the shorter being less than two thirds the length of the longer. There is a cervical eyespot.

This species is abundant in salt water.

Family Dicranophoridae

The corona is narrow and oblique ventrally. There are two symmetrical apical tufts of long locomotor cilia situated laterally. A forwardly projecting, pointed, frontal rostrum terminates the lorica anteriorly. The mastax is of the forcipate type.

Encentrum marinum (Dujardin) PLATE 91. The body is elongate and spindle-shaped, and slightly arched from the dorsal to the ventral side. Though the integument is leathery, it is, nevertheless, somewhat transparent.

The head bends forward slightly and shows a distinct separation from the abdomen by means of a transverse groove. The corona is slightly oblique and has a short, rounded rostrum projecting dorsally on the median line. The flexible lorica is divided by a wide lateral groove into a dorsal and a ventral plate. The foot is short, stout, and conical. There are two toes, both short and stout, and set wide apart. The small foot-glands are pear-shaped. The forcipate mastax (INDEX PLATE 88) has double-pointed rami, broad at the base.

This species is nearly 1/125 inch in length. It is cosmopolitan in brackish and salt water.

Family Synchaetidae

In the rotifers of this family, the corona, instead of having the form of a wreath around a bare, apical area, consists of a number of rounded prominences, each equipped with a tuft of cilia or with a long, spinelike process consisting of several cilia closely appressed to each other, growing out of a narrow elongate follicle.

A projecting pair of auricles, like ear-lappets, extend one on either side of the head, each bearing a large brush of cilia. The hypopharynx, a part of the mastax, situated ventrally to the pharynx, is double in this family, showing as a V-shaped figure. The mastax is a modified virgate.

Synchaeta baltica Ehrenberg PLATE 92. The very large, bell-shaped body is rounded in front, somewhat narrowed posterior to the auricles, with a nearly parallel-sided abdomen, and tapering to a very short, stumpy foot with a pair of thick, blunt toes. There are four spinelike ciliary tufts on the corona. The auricles are large and broad, covered with vibrating cilia. There is a median dorsal antenna above the eye, while the lateral antennae

PLATE 91

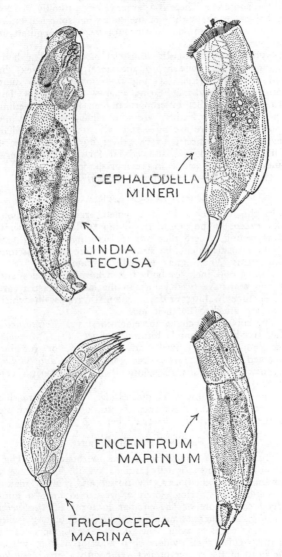

CEPHALODELLA
MINERI

LINDIA
TECUSA

ENCENTRUM
MARINUM

TRICHOCERCA
MARINA

are situated quite posteriorly, projecting on either side of the abdomen. There is a large, red eye, usually divided in halves, on the surface of the somewhat spherical brain.

This is a common marine species, cosmopolitan in range.

Synchaeta littoralis Rousselet PLATE 92. The body is more or less cone-shaped, the apical area convex, the abdomen cylindrical, tapering posteriorly to the stout, short, cone-shaped foot-bearing separate, pointed toes. The auricles are smaller in proportion than in the preceding species, but like it there are four ciliary spines on the apical area. There are three red eyes; one large, median cervical eye, connected by two diverging red nerve-tracts with two frontal eyes, situated far forward. The lateral antennae are situated as in previous species.

This species is common in brackish water.

Suborder FLOSCULARIACEA

In this suborder, the foot, when present, is without toes, except in the case of free-living adults or free-swimming young, where they are replaced by terminal foot ciliation inside a cuplike structure. There are numerous foot-glands. The mastax is malleo-ramate.

This group includes both free-swimming species and species that have fixed habits. In the latter case, they are either tube-dwelling or form colonial groups, in which they are attached by their toes.

The suborder includes three families: (1) *Testudinellidae*, free-living, nontube-forming species; (2) *Floscularidae*, adults either fixed and tube-living, or forming attached colonies, rarely free; and (3) *Conochilidae*, corona horseshoe-shaped, adults living in spherical colonies.

Since the Family Testudinellidae includes marine species as well as fresh-water forms, a typical example of the former will be described here.

Family Testudinellidae

These are free-swimming species without toes. They do not build tubes or jelly-cases to live in. They have a flattened, shell-like lorica, the dorsal and ventral plates, in some species, being closely appressed to form a thin-edged case, more or less circular in form (*Testudinella patina*); in others, somewhat thicker and oblong, with rounded edges uniting the dorso-ventral faces of a firmly welded shell, widely open anteriorly, from which the head of the rotifer projects, and with a small, slitlike opening posteriorly on the ventral side, to allow for the extrusion of the foot.

The corona is composed of a finely ciliated band sur-

PLATE 92

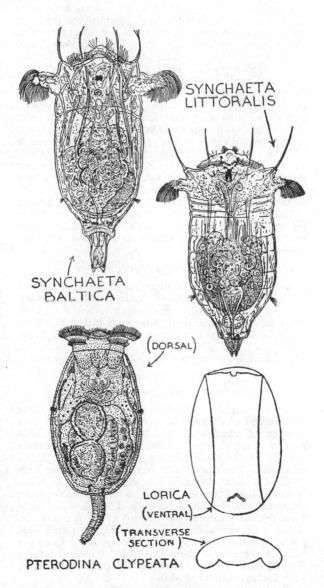

SYNCHAETA
LITTORALIS

SYNCHAETA
BALTICA

(DORSAL)

LORICA
(VENTRAL)

(TRANSVERSE
SECTION)

PTERODINA CLYPEATA

rounding the head and enclosing the mouth-opening on the ventral side, and of two strongly ciliated circles with long cilia: one borders the band anteriorly to form the ciliary wreath surrounding the apical area; the other forms the posterior border of the band. There are two frontal eyespots.

The species are both fresh water and marine.

Testudinella (Pterodina) clypeata (Müller) PLATE 92. The lorica is an elongate oval. It has considerable thickness, evenly convex dorsally, edges rounded and thick, curving in a semicircular roll to unite with the smaller convex, ventral side, as seen by the transverse section in the figure on the plate. The ventral side of the lorica is also depicted and shows the small, transverse slit for the projection of the foot. The lateral antennae show as small tufts on the sides of the abdomen above the middle, in the dorsal view. The internal anatomy is of the usual, normal, rotifer character and arrangement.

This is a very old species. It was first seen in 1786 in sea-water, in the Baltic Sea, by O. F. Müller, afterward described by Bory de St. Vincent in 1826 and by Ehrenberg in 1832.

Suborder COLLOTHECACEA

This is a group of rotifers with feet lacking toes, replaced by a ciliated cup in the free-swimming young. The corona consists of lobes, in some species elongate in shape, in others, quite short. A series of stiff setae extends out from the lobes. The mastax is uncinate (INDEX PLATE 88).

So far as is known, these are all fresh-water species.

CLASS GASTROTRICHA
(INDEX FIGURE, PLATE 93)

These remarkable little wormlike creatures are among the smallest of many-celled animals, those known being between .06 mm. and 1.5 mm. in length. They are elongate in shape, flattened ventrally, and somewhat convex dorsally. The back and sides are covered with spines, scales, or bristles. The ventral side is ciliated. It is principally by the motion of these cilia that the animals move about. A narrowing of the body in the neck-region distinguishes the head from the rest of the body. There is also a somewhat ventral mouth at the anterior tip of the body, together with the sense-organs consisting of paired eyes, paired sensory organs, and vibratory hairs having a locomotor function. There is a pair of *cement tubules*, the secretion of which helps the animal to cling to the surrounding medium at will.

The digestive canal is a straight tube, passing directly

from the mouth to the anus at the posterior end of the body. Protonephridia with flame-cells are also present. A large brain is at the anterior end of the head, connected by fine nerves with the sense organs and the longitudinal muscle fibers. Transverse fibers are lacking in the body.

The sexes, in Gastrotricha, may be separate, in which case the females are parthenogenetic. On the other hand, certain species are hermaphroditic, the male organs opening anterior to the female aperture on the ventral surface, in the posterior part of the body. The hermaphroditic species are practically all marine. As males have not yet been discovered in fresh-water species, it is assumed that the Gastrotricha here, possessing, as they do, only female organs, are entirely parthenogenetic.

Gastrotricha are very common in both fresh and salt water. They swim, jump, and creep actively about near the bottom or in the sand, wherever microscopic animals of other groups and microscopic algae and diatoms are found, and which also form the food on which they subsist.

The genera *Chaetonotus, Lepidoderma,* and *Ichthyidium* are particularly abundant, while *Dasydytes salticans* Stokes is one of the most active, as it possesses long, vibrating hairs as leaping organs.

Order MACRODASYOIDEA

Marine hermaphroditic species.

Order CHAETONOTOIDEA

Fresh-water and marine species. Only parthenogenetic females known, except the hermaphroditic species of a single family.

Family Chaetonotidae
Lepiderma, Chaetonotus, Ichthyidium.

Family Dasydytidae

Dasydytes.

CLASS KINORHYNCHA

(INDEX FIGURE, PLATE 93)

These are microscopic worms found in the sea, having an externally segmented body but internally unsegmented, and in this respect, resembling rotifers. The body-cavity has no peritoneal lining, therefore, in this respect also they show affinities to rotifers. The outer surface is entirely without cilia, this being a unique character among animals (except in the phylum Nemathelmia, page 262). Spines, bristles, and hooks, however, take their place and serve as locomotor and prehensile organs. The digestive tract is straight and terminates in the anus at the posterior end of the body, as in the Gastrotricha. The retractile head is specialized from the first ring of the body. It includes the mouth, surrounded by a series of hooks and long bristles, especially adapted for locomotion. The second ring forms the neck, also retractile in some cases, and often protected by an armature of plates. Two or four long bristles project from the posterior end of the body.

Order ECHINODERA

As this is the only order, the definition is the same as that of the class.

Suborder HOMOLORHAGE

Head and neck may both be retracted.

Family Pycnophyidae

Two bristles terminate the posterior end.

Pycnophyes frequens Blake PLATE 93. The specialized and retractile head and neck with their characteristic armature of spines are well illustrated in the figure, which shows the ventral side of this species. On the dorsal side, there is a characteristic arrangement of mid-dorsal spines, the first three and the last three being pointed and the rest rounded.

Suborder CYCLORHAGE

In this suborder, only the head is capable of being retracted. The neck is armed with a series of plates which act as an operculum, closing the opening after the withdrawal of the head.

Family Echinoderidae

The body is externally segmented into thirteen rings, the third and fourth rings being fused. Two bristles terminate the anal segment.

Echinodorella remanei Blake PLATE 93. Conspicuous lateral spines are present on the posterior border of the dorsal plates of segments eight to eleven. Mid-dorsal spines of considerable length occur on segments six to ten. A close-set fringe of small, even setae is present on the middle part of segment four, running around the ventral and lateral portions. A shorter row occurs ventrally and somewhat on segment five, and still smaller ones to a less degree on segment six. No eyes are present.

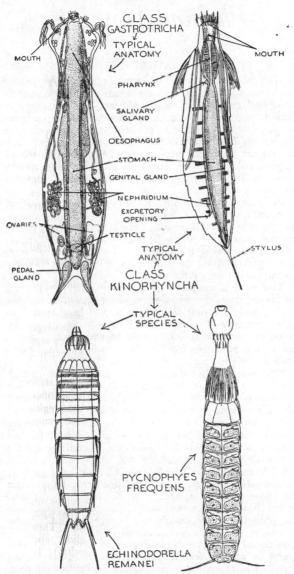

PLATE 93

CLASS
GASTROTRICHA

TYPICAL
ANATOMY

MOUTH

MOUTH

PHARYNX

SALIVARY
GLAND

OESOPHAGUS

STOMACH

GENITAL GLAND

NEPHRIDIUM

EXCRETORY
OPENING

OVARIES

TESTICLE

TYPICAL ANATOMY

STYLUS

PEDAL
GLAND

CLASS
KINORHYNCHA

TYPICAL
SPECIES

PYCNOPHYES
FREQUENS

ECHINODORELLA
REMANEI

9

Phylum Annulata

(SEGMENTED OR RINGED WORMS)

THIS phylum includes the true or segmented worms with elongated bodies, and the anterior segments specialized and modified to form a distinct head. A digestive tube surrounded by a true body-cavity (coelom) extends throughout the entire body, passing through the successive segments. The segments are more or less similar, but, in certain families, they may be fused, modified, or specialized for various functions. There is a tendency, however, for a repetition of parts throughout all segments (INDEX PLATE 95).

Each segment, typically, is equipped with a pair of unjointed appendages, known as *parapodia,* in contrast to the Phylum Arthropoda, which is characterized by jointed limbs. In certain families, these appendages are lacking in many of the segments. The successive segments are separated from each other by thin, muscular partitions, known as *septa*.

The head is composed of the most anterior segments. In some cases, the included segments are distinct, but bear organs showing adaptation to the head-region. In other cases, the head segments are more or less completely fused or compressed, so that their appendages are concentrated around and in front of the mouth, and are specialized for seizing, tasting, and tearing.

The parapodia, for the most part, are repeated on each segment throughout the greater part of the body. They are muscular projections of the body-wall, usually utilized for locomotion. In the Order Polychaeta, the parapodia are equipped with bunches of bristles (*setae*). These are usually lacking in the Order Archiannelida, and are entirely absent from the Hirudinea (Leeches). In the Order Oligochaeta, containing the earthworms and related forms, they are greatly reduced.

Internally, as above stated, the digestive tube traverses the entire series of segments from the mouth to the anus at the hinder end of the body. The mouth opens into the pharynx, which usually can be everted through the mouth to form a proboscis, to aid in securing food.

A dorsal vessel carries blood (red in some species, and green in others) forward toward the head-end of the body, dividing on either side to unite as a ventral tube, which returns the blood posteriorly on the ventral side.

A pair of coiled kidney-tubes (nephridia), in each

segment, constitutes the excretory system. Each nephridium is provided with an inner opening, often trumpet-shaped, and opening to the outside through a pore in the body-wall.

Breathing takes place through the whole integument of the worm. In the Polychaeta, special provisions are made for this function by means of branched gills or breathing organs. These are most fully developed in the segments immediately following the head-region.

The so-called brain is situated dorsally to the digestive tract in the anterior part of the head. A nerve-ring connects it with a paired ventral nerve-cord extending through the entire series of segments, with a pair of ganglia in each segment. The head is provided with paired sense-organs, including eyes, tactile organs and, in some cases, lithocysts, especially among the Polychaeta.

Reproductive organs become greatly developed during the seasonal breeding periods when they are filled with ova and sperm. They are localized in the lining of the body-cavity in each segment. The fertilized egg produces a top-shaped larva known as a *trochophore*. This is, at first, unsegmented, but becomes metamorphosed into the head-region of the worm, from which segments are budded off from the lower end to form finally the segments of the body of the adult.

The Phylum Annulata is divided into three classes: (1) *Chaetopoda,* or Bristleworms; (2) *Hirudinea,* or Leeches; and, (3) *Gephyrea,* or Mudworms.

CLASS CHAETOPODA

The Chaetopoda include those annulates which have paired appendages equipped with bundles of bristles (setae) for use in locomotion. These animals have a prostomium anterior to the mouth and a series of successive segments forming the rest of the body, more or less repetitive in their internal and external structures.

The class consists of the following four orders: (1) *Archiannelida;* (2) *Polychaeta;* (3) *Myzostomida;* and (4) *Oligochaeta.*

Order ARCHIANNELIDA

These simple, perhaps primitive, marine worms are of small size. They are considered by many as constituting a group close to the base of the ancestral line of the Annulata, having affinities with the larvae of the Order Polychaeta.

Family Dinophilidae

This family includes minute marine worms with a body of five or six segments, indicated externally by ciliated bands surrounding their short, cylindrical body (PLATE 94). The head, or prostomium, somewhat resembles a polychaete larva or trochophore, being top-shaped, and possessing two horizontal bands of cilia, a pair of eyes, and a number of anterior tactile bristles. There are no tentacles. The succeeding segments have at least one band of cilia each. The internal anatomy is not repetitive.

Dinophilus conklini Nelson PLATE 94. This is a tiny worm of from 1/50 to 1/25 inch in length. The body is transparent and has six segments. It is found along the New Jersey coast.

Dinophilus pygmaeus Verrill PLATE 94. About 1/35 inch in length with five trunk segments and whitish in color.

It has been found on wharf-piles in the Woods Hole region.

Dinophilus gardineri A. Moore PLATE 94. The color of this species is bright orange-red. There are six trunk-segments. The body is ciliated even between the ciliated bands.

It is found in brackish waters in the Woods Hole region.

Family Polygordiidae

These are threadlike archiannelids with numerous segments which are not always distinctly marked. There are no parapodia. The head not only has a prostomium with a pair of tentacles anterior to the mouth, but also a collar (*peristomium*) surrounding the mouth and without appendages. The general anatomy is annulate in character. The young are born as trochophore larvae.

Polygordius appendiculatus Fraipont PLATE 94. The worms of this species are about 1/5 inch in length. They have a salmon-colored body with a pair of long, terminal appendages, one on either side of the anus. They are distributed along the Atlantic Coast of North America as well as in the Mediterranean Sea. The larva is toplike anteriorly and segmented posteriorly.

PLATE 94

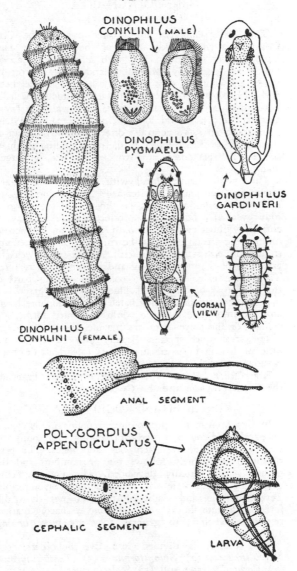

DINOPHILUS CONKLINI (MALE)

DINOPHILUS PYGMAEUS

DINOPHILUS GARDINERI

(DORSAL VIEW)

DINOPHILUS CONKLINI (FEMALE)

ANAL SEGMENT

POLYGORDIUS APPENDICULATUS

CEPHALIC SEGMENT

LARVA

Order POLYCHAETA
(INDEX PLATE 95)

This order embraces the greater part of the Class Chaetopoda and includes most of the seaworms. They have distinct segments, each with a pair of parapodia which are essentially swimming and breathing organs. The free-swimming species usually have many segments and all except the head-segments bear parapodia. Usually, a parapodium has two main parts, a dorsal lobe (*notopodium*) and a ventral lobe (*neuropodium*). Both have setae and a *cirrus* (a ventrally directed sensitive organ on the underside of each lobe). In the tube-building sedentary species, the parapodia are reduced in size or largely wanting.

There is a distinct head with special sense organs, including from one to ten tentacles, placed dorsally, and two *palps,* or tasting-organs, on the ventral side. Two to four eyes may be on the prostomium, or it may be entirely without eyes. The mouth, located on the peristomium (the second segment, bearing the mouth-opening) frequently possesses a proboscis. Among the polychaetes are some of the most colorful and beautiful sea-creatures. They often exhibit iridescent colors or various parts of the body may be bright red, blue, yellow, or green.

Like other annulates, they hatch out trochophore larvae and metamorphose into the adult segmented form.

Most of the polychaetes are marine, though there are a few fresh-water species. Usually they burrow in the sand or live in tubes constructed of calcareous or membranous material.

The Order Polychaeta is divided into two branches, the *Phanerocephala* and the *Cryptocephala*.

Branch PHANEROCEPHALA

In this branch, the prostomium remains in its typical ancestral condition as a lobe overhanging the mouth and usually has paired eyes, tentacles, and palps. The peristomium immediately follows the prostomium and the mouth is not usually developed. The body-segments, except in some species of the Suborders Spioniformia, Terebelliformia, and Capitelliformia, do not show differentiation into thorax and abdomen as sharply marked regions. Therefore, in general, they are more or less alike.

This branch is divided into five Suborders: (1) *Nereidiformia*; (2) *Spioniformia*; (3) *Terebelliformia*; (4) *Capitelliformia*; and (5) *Scoleciformia*.

PLATE 95

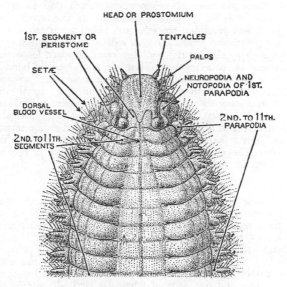

HEAD OR PROSTOMIUM

1ST. SEGMENT OR PERISTOME

TENTACLES

PALPS

SETÆ

NEUROPODIA AND NOTOPODIA OF 1ST. PARAPODIA

DORSAL BLOOD VESSEL

2ND. TO 11TH. PARAPODIA

2ND. TO 11TH. SEGMENTS

DORSAL VIEW OF ANTERIOR EXTREMITY

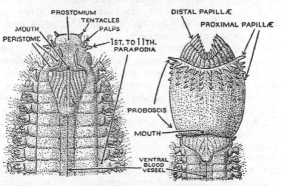

PROSTOMIUM

TENTACLES

MOUTH

PALPS

PERISTOME

1ST. TO 11TH. PARAPODIA

DISTAL PAPILLÆ

PROXIMAL PAPILLÆ

PROBOSCIS

MOUTH

VENTRAL BLOOD VESSEL

VENTRAL VIEW WITH PROBOSCIS INVERTED

VENTRAL VIEW WITH PROBOSCIS EVERTED

Suborder NEREIDIFORMIA

These are free-swimming worms which lead an active carnivorous life preying upon other sea creatures. They have well-developed tentacles and palps, as outgrowths of the prominent prostomium, as well as efficient paired eyes. The parapodia are also well-developed as paired locomotor organs on each segment. They are reinforced by bundles of setae as well as an *aciculum*, a stout, dark-colored, needlelike structure occurring in both the dorsal and central lobes of the parapodium. The bristles (setae) are usually jointed, though some unjointed ones are also present. The pharynx may be everted through the mouth to form a proboscis, often armed with chitinous hooklike jaws. The segments have septa and nephridia in regular repetition throughout the body.

Family Syllidae

These worms have a segmented, threadlike body with jointed and often very long tentacles and cirri. There are three tentacles on the rounded or somewhat rectangular head as well as four eyes. There are, usually, a pair of palps and two tentacular cirri. The mouth opens into a pharynx which may be completely everted with its chitinous wall.

Syllis gracilis Gruber PLATE 96. The head has three tentacles and two pairs of tentacular cirri, all *moniliform* (resembling strings of beads). The palps, elongate and flattened, are distinctly separate. The head is transversely oval in shape with four black eyes, the anterior pair wider apart. The body has eighty or more segments, brownish in color, paler anteriorly.

This species is common under stones in shallow waters, on sandy or muddy bottoms along the Atlantic seaboard.

Amblyosyllis lineata Gruber PLATE 96. This is a short worm with only sixteen segments. The body is ½ inch in length, tapering anteriorly and posteriorly. The head is small, shorter than broad, with one long slender median tentacle and two shorter ones. The palps are small and located on the ventral surface of the head. Each segment of the body is expanded laterally and dorsally to form a thin edge with constrictions where the segments are joined. The color is purplish brown, with yellow patches showing segmentally. The segments bear parapodia, each with a cone-shaped ventral lobe equipped with setae, while the dorsal lobe is represented by a long, coiling threadlike cirrus.

These worms live under stones, near the low-water mark, and are found throughout the northern Atlantic shores of both North America and Europe.

Sphaerosyllis brevifrons Webster & Benedict

PLATE 96. The head is short, very wide, almost fused with the palps, with sides rounded. There are six eyes, the posterior pair widely separated, and those on each side close together. The palps are short, coalesced, slightly emarginate in front. The antennae have a swollen, globular base and a short cylindrical outer part. The tentacular cirri are like the antennae, but a little longer. The buccal segment (*peristomium*) may be from one third to three fourths as long as the next segment. The body is colorless except for the eyes, which are red. The length is 1/25 inch. The number of segments is twenty-two. This species is found in sand at about the low-water mark.

Sphaerosyllis longicirrata Webster & Benedict PLATE 96. The head has the anterior and lateral margins regularly rounded, with the posterior margin very slightly convex and nearly straight. There are six eyes. The two posterior pairs are large, circular, and nearly on the same straight line. The anterior pair is very small just in front of the origin of the lateral antennae. The antennae are somewhat fusiform and irregularly constricted. The median antenna is one third longer than the head and palps. The tentacular, dorsal, and anal cirri have the same structure as the antennae. The anal cirri may be double the length of the dorsal. The buccal segment is as long as the second segment. The palps are large, convex externally, concave internally. The apex is blunt, rounded, with the anterior third free. They are connected by a thick membrane along their posterior two thirds. The pharynx occupies four segments, the stomach two. The body is colorless, the stomach is white, the intestines are brown or yellow. The worm is ⅕ inch long. It has thirty-three segments. It is especially common on shells at low water.

Sphaerosyllis fortuita Webster PLATE 96. This is a small worm about ⅛ inch in length, having a body of thirty-three segments. The head is oval and somewhat convex. There are four large eyes, also oval in shape, arranged in two pairs in the posterior part of the head so that the eyes of the second pair are nearer together than the first pair. The antennae are bottle-shaped, equal in size, with the unpaired antenna midway between the second pair of eyes, and the other two placed symmetrically in front of the first pair. The palps are large and conical in shape, their inner edges parallel and united on the midline for two thirds the length of the palps. The first segment is narrowed, but clearly distinct from the head. The tentacular cirri are shaped like the antennae. The dorsal cirri are also similar in shape to the antennae, but shorter, while the anal cirri are twice the length of the dorsal cirri. The delicate ventral cirri branch off from the basal joint of the parapodia, which are stout, cylindrical, and two-lobed.

This worm is found off the Virginia coast.

Autolytus (Proceraea) ornatus Verrill PLATE 96. This little but conspicuous species is white or cream-color, ringed with bands of bright red. It is about 3/5 inch in length.

The head is short, broad, and rather straight in front, but slightly bilobed behind. There are two pairs of moderately large eyes. The median antenna is white, very long, and slenderly tapering. The posterior tentacles are also slender, but not quite so long as the median tentacles. The inner antennae, the other two pairs of antennae and the tentacles are about one fourth as long as the median one. The tentacular cirri of the second segment are short, which is also the case for the dorsal cirri. This species has been found in Long Island Sound off New Haven and the Thimble Islands in 1 to 5 fathoms, living among hydroids and bryozoans.

Autolytus alexandri Malmgren PLATE 96. The head, rounded in front, has two pairs of red eyes, the anterior pair being farther apart than the posterior. There is a long tapering median cirrus. There are also two lateral cirri and two pairs of tentacular cirri, all slender and smooth. The body is about ½ inch long, tapering posteriorly and ending in two long and slender anal cirri. The general color is pale yellow, though the intestine, showing through the body, gives the impression of a dark band, with numerous small white specks. The dorsal cirrus of the parapodia is relatively short.

This species is abundant on the New England coast and is found in British waters.

Autolytus cornutus A. Agassiz PLATE 97. This is a small, flesh-colored species with conspicuous brown eyes. There is a green tinge toward the ends of the body and the dark greenish intestine shows through longitudinally. It constructs cylindrical tubes on seaweeds and branching hydroids. There is marked sexual dimorphism, the males and the females being very different in appearance. There is also a third form, different from either, which is asexual. These are the tube-builders, but are also seen swimming about. The sexual forms are found abundantly at the surface, especially toward evening, often creeping over the hydroids. The remarkable method of reproduction is noteworthy and has been thoroughly described by Alexander Agassiz. The eggs of the female are very numerous and are deposited in the body-cavity between the intestine and the outer wall along the entire body length. Soon, they accumulate in a pouch on the ventral side of the body from the twelfth to about the twenty-

PLATE 96

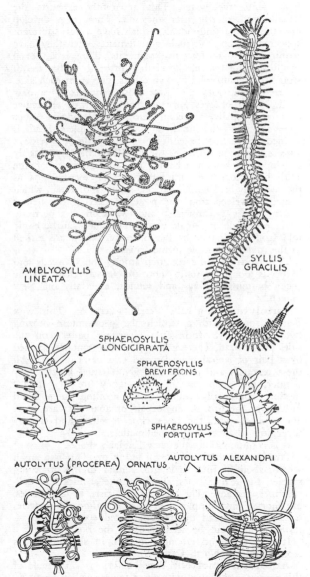

AMBLYOSYLLIS
LINEATA

SYLLIS
GRACILIS

SPHAEROSYLLIS
LONGICIRRATA

SPHAEROSYLLIS
BREVIFRONS

SPHAEROSYLLIS
FORTUITA→

AUTOLYTUS (PROCEREA) ORNATUS

AUTOLYTUS ALEXANDRI

sixth segment. Here, they hatch into young worms and escape into the water. This apparently exhausts the females and, shortly after, they die. These eggs develop into the asexual individuals, which have a very different appearance from the male and female. After they have acquired forty to forty-five segments, there is a dorsal swelling about the middle of the thirteenth or fourteenth segment, accompanied by two others, one from each side. These develop into the three front tentacles of a new head, a pair of eyes appears, then a pair of tentacular cirri, and, finally, a second pair of eyes and the other appendages of the head, so that a complete head is formed which may be either that of a male or a female. The segments posterior to the head become more highly developed and soon take on the characteristics of the adult body together with either ova or spermatozoa as the case may be. Finally, the new sexual individual, which actually develops from the posterior part of the neuter worm, breaks its connection and swims off as a perfectly developed male or female worm. The male can be easily told from the female by the antennae, which are forked in the male but simple in the female.

This worm is quite common among the seaweeds and hydroids along the south shore of New England on the rocky bottoms of bays and sounds, especially off New Haven.

Autolytus longilula Verrill PLATE 97. This is a slender species with a semicircular prostomium bearing two pairs of eyes forming a diverging pattern on the sides of the head. There is a long median tentacle, flanked by a pair of lateral tentacles and two pairs of cirri. All these tentacles and cirri are of about equal length, very slender, and with smooth sides. They are in constant motion, continually coiling and uncoiling in a spiral fashion at the tips. A single pair of anal cirri are short and conical, with the bases close together and usually diverging to form a V-shaped pattern.

It is common along the New England shores.

Autolytus varians Verrill PLATE 97. This is a small worm, about ⅜ inch in length, similar to the preceding species, the female being shorter, more slender and delicate in appearance. The tentacles and cirri, in this species, are shorter and stumpier than in *A. longilula*. This species is easily recognized by the bright red spots on the intestine which can be seen through the body-wall.

It is often found among hydroids, in shallow waters from Maine to North Carolina.

Autolytus emertoni Verrill PLATE 97. The male of this species is equipped with three much swollen tentacles. The median tentacle tapers to a coiling tip. The lateral

PLATE 97

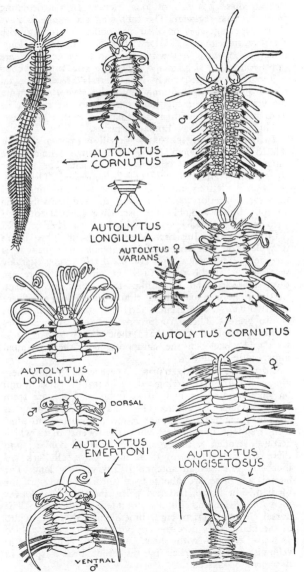

AUTOLYTUS
CORNUTUS

AUTOLYTUS
LONGILULA

AUTOLYTUS ♀
VARIANS

AUTOLYTUS CORNUTUS

AUTOLYTUS
LONGILULA

♂ DORSAL

AUTOLYTUS
EMERTONI

♀

AUTOLYTUS
LONGISETOSUS

VENTRAL ♂

tentacles are not only swollen but bifid at the tips. Behind these is a pair of long, slender cirri articulating from the first segment. The following six segments have short, tapering lobes on their parapodia. Beginning with the seventh segment, the dorsal lobe bears extremely long, brushlike bristles. In the female, the three tentacles are not swollen but slender and tapering. The anterior body segments have moderately long dorsal cirri. These increase in length, beginning with the seventh segment, the ventral lobes having long setae as in the male. The head is triangular with a large pair of eyes.

This is also a New England species.

Autolytus longisetosus Verrill PLATE 97. This is related to the previous species. The three tentacles are much longer, slenderly tapering, and flexible. The anterior six segments are short and closely appressed. The parapodia are relatively insignificant and without long cirri or setae. Posterior to this region, the segments become abruptly larger and, like the preceding species, equipped with larger parapodia, armed with long bunches of setae.

Odontosyllis lucifera Verrill PLATE 98. This species is typical of the worms in which it is included. The palps are comparatively short, largely separate, or at the most, fused at the base. There are three tentacles, and threadlike dorsal cirri are present. In the mature sexual phase, they become longer. There are two pairs of tentacular cirri and the ventral cirrus is also present. There is a proboscis, armed with a series of horny papillae which have their points turned backward. The setae on the parapodia have their terminal joint single or bifid.

Odontosyllis fulgurans Claparede PLATE 98. These are sexual forms occurring off the Virginia coast, found on shells and stones in 6 to 12 fathoms. They are from ⅕ to ½ inch in length. They may have as many as sixty-four segments. Setae are found on fourteen to nineteen segments, beginning with the twenty-first, which become swollen with eggs. The head is convex, and there are six eyes arranged in three pairs, all dark red in color. The median antenna is always very long. The lateral antennae are about two thirds as long as the median. The broad, flattened palps are somewhat longer than the head and bluntly rounded at the end. The dorsal cirri are four to eight times longer than the width of the body. They give the appearance of being wrinkled and are covered with short, stiff hairs. The color is yellowish white, marked by numerous brown spots in the form of crescents.

Streptosyllis arenae Webster & Benedict PLATE 98. The head in this species is convex, the sides, front, and posterior angles, regularly rounded. There are six eyes. The anterior pair are small and crescentic in shape. They are just behind and outside the origin of the lateral antennae. The antennae and tentacular cirri are wrinkled, but never annulated. The lateral antennae arise very close to the anterior margin of the head. The median antenna, longer than the lateral, arises from near the posterior margin of the head. The body is colorless anteriorly, but the oesophagus shows through as light brown in color. The stomach is white. Posterior to the stomach, the body is yellowish with numerous white specks. The length may reach ⅓ inch. There are fifty-five segments. This worm is found at the low-water mark in sand.

Paedophylax dispar Webster PLATE 98. This species has the usual rounded convex head and four large, circular eyes, laterally situated. The palps project for a distance nearly twice that of the head length. The median antenna articulates near the posterior margin of the head. The tentacular cirri are similar to the antenna. The dorsal and ventral cirri are similar, but a little larger. There are two anal cirri. The parapodia are fleshy and as long as one third of the width of the body. This worm is either colorless or white, tinged with red, marked with a white line between the segments. It may be dredged off the east coast of North America in 4 to 10 fathoms and is common on shells and stones.

Paedophylax hebes Webster & Benedict PLATE 98. The head in this species is very short, the width being more than double the length. The anterior angles are very broadly rounded. The anterior and posterior margins are but slightly curved. The eyes are six, the anterior pair being merely specks. The posterior pairs, on each side, are very close together; sometimes they are in contact. The palps are very large without any indication of division above. Their length is more than double the length of the head. The buccal segment is about one half as long as the second segment. Its cirri are very short. The body is widest in the middle and is gray or flesh-color. The length is about ¼ inch. There are forty-four segments. It is found on sand and shells from low water to 25 fathoms.

Paedophylax longiceps Verrill PLATE 98. This species is similar to the preceding, but with longer and narrower palps, extending forward. The head, itself, is very short and broad in proportion, with the two pairs of eyes crowded close together. The parapodia lack the elongate dorsal cirri, as is also the case with the other species of the genus. The stomach is short and thick-walled.

Occurs on the north shore of New England.

Eusyllis tubifex Gosse PLATE 98. This interesting species has a head with a ciliated collar. It possesses a proboscis armed with a single tooth, which is exposed when the organ is everted. The head is ovoid with two pairs of red eyes, the anterior being the larger. The median tentacle is longer than the two lateral tentacles. The body has more than fifty segments. It is light-colored anteriorly and translucent, showing the bluish white iridescent proboscis through its integument. The tail has two long, beaded (moniliform) cirri.

This species can be found in great numbers on the fronds of kelp (*Laminaria*) when tossed onshore by storm-winds on rocky coasts. It also occurs in deep water in such localities. These worms are tube-builders, secreting a translucent tube. When kept in an aquarium and irritated, they shine with a greenish light, given off from the ventral surface of each parapodium, flashing down the successive segments with brilliant flashes, to the affected part, and then fading away gradually.

Family Hesionidae

The species in this family have two pairs of eyes, two or three tentacles and, usually, a pair of two-jointed palps. The body is of moderate length. The proboscis may be protruded. In some species it is armed, in others, unarmed. The first four segments may be distinct, or more or less fused, and each has two pairs of tentacular cirri. The parapodia in the remaining segments have either one lobe or two lobes. The upper lobe is usually reduced to bundles of simple setae. The ventral lobe is equipped with compound setae. The dorsal and ventral cirri are threadlike.

Podarke caeca Webster & Benedict PLATE 99. The head is evenly rounded in front and at the sides, but nearly straight behind. There are no eyes. The antennae have cylindrical basal joints. An unpaired antenna, rising near the posterior margin of the head, is shorter and slenderer than the others. The most anterior pair are close to each other near the anterior margin of the head. Their length equals the length of the head. A lower pair rises from the undersurface of the head, just outside the upper pair. The first segment curves around the side of the head. There are six tentacular cirri on each side. A pair of these is based on each of the first three segments. The parapodia are quite large, pointed distally, and expanded at the base. The dorsal cirri do not extend beyond the parapodium. The ventral cirri arise from about the outer fourth of the foot and extend to about the end of it. The color of this species is yellowish white, crossed by many transverse bands variegated with yellowish brown spots and specks. It is found in sand at low water.

Podarke obscura Verrill COLOR PLATES VII, 1; VIII, 2. This curious little worm is found in great abundance at

PLATE 98

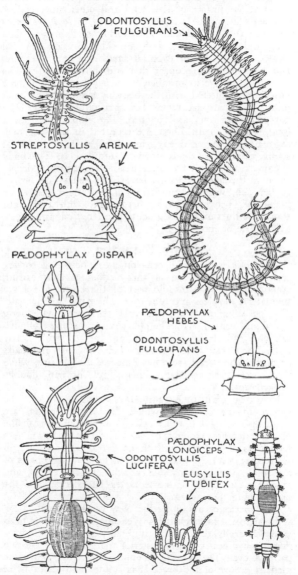

ODONTOSYLLIS
FULGURANS

STREPTOSYLLIS ARENÆ

PÆDOPHYLAX DISPAR

PÆDOPHYLAX
HEBES

ODONTOSYLLIS
FULGURANS

PÆDOPHYLAX
LONGICEPS

ODONTOSYLLIS
LUCIFERA

EUSYLLIS
TUBIFEX

Woods Hole, Massachusetts, among eel-grass and swimming at the surface of Eel Pond and other quiet waters, especially at night. It is closely related to *Podarke caeca* (PLATE 99), just described. The head is small, broader than long, indented in front, with the sides forming rounded angles. There are four eyes, all small and red. The anterior pair are farther apart than the posterior pair. The antennae are five in number, of nearly equal length, the outer one connected with the body by a short, thick basal joint. There are six tentacular cirri on each side. The parapodia are long and bilobed. The upper lobe has a long, slender cirrus. These are repeated in the successive segments, giving a deep, fringed effect, as the animal swims about with rapid sidewise undulations. The body is convex above and flat underneath, the segments deeply cut in at the sides. The color is variable, being dark brown to blackish, with a transverse band of light yellow or flesh-color, between the segments and with two light transverse lines on each segment. The length approximates 1½ inches, or more.

Family Polynoidae

The body is more or less elongate. There is a convex cephalic lobe, the base of the median tentacle arising anteriorly from the middle part of the body. There are two lateral tentacles and four eyes. The palps are elongate. The peristomium bears the first parapodia with long dorsal and ventral cirri. The pharynx is muscular, cylindrical, and capable of protrusion, and armed with horny jaws. The dorsal scales number twelve to thirty-five pairs or more. The dorsal setae have tapered simple tips, while the ventral setae are with either simple or with double-hooked tips.

Polynoë (Eunoa) acanellae Verrill PLATE 99. The species in the family to which this worm belongs are characterized by a double series of overlapping, scalelike plates, extending along the back. The figure shown here represents the anterior part of the dorsal region of a typical species, with the plates removed to show two pairs of the small, round pedicels of attachment cut across, and to give a clear view of the tentacles, lateral cirri, and the parapodia of these worms.

This species occurs along the New England coast.

Lepidonotus variabilis Webster PLATE 99. The head is oval laterally, divided longitudinally in the middle by a deep groove nearly to the posterior margin. There are two pairs of eyes. The middle antenna arises from above the median groove of the head. It is stouter and about twice the length of the lateral antennae. The upper part has a swollen area from which the tentacle tapers to a filamentary termination. The basal joint of the tentacular cirri is quite long in proportion and they are quite similar in appearance to the middle antenna. The palps are swollen at the base and taper rapidly to the pointed tips. They are a little shorter than the middle antenna. Twelve pairs of oval *elytra* (overlapping plates) cover the back. The posterior margins, fringed with tiny spinelike projections, are more rounded than the anterior margin, which is narrower and has a smooth border. The color of this species is quite variable. The head may be white, speckled with brown. The antennae and the cirri are white with a black or dark brown band encircling the enlarged portion. The palps are dark brown at the base, becoming lighter in color to white toward the tips. The general body-color is a variable brown, but the elytra are marked with white spots and minute brown spots. The anal segment is brown or black, while the segments preceding it have transverse stripes of brown. The length of this species is from ⅖ to ⅘ inch. It is found in shallow water along the eastern coast of Virginia.

Lepidonotus squamatus (Linnaeus) PLATE 99; COLOR PLATE VIII, 1. This worm is similar to the above, but with a larger and stouter head, the details of which may be seen readily in the figure. The body has twelve pairs of rough scales covered with small hemispherical tubercles, usually dark brown. Very common north of Cape Cod to Labrador and Iceland, extending along the New England coast and southward to Virginia. It is abundant in the Bay of Fundy from low-water mark to a depth of 80 fathoms.

Antinoë parasitica Webster PLATE 99. This is a minute parasitic form, about ¹⁄₁₂ inch in length, found under the elytra of *Lepidametria commensalis* (below). It has twenty-one setigerous segments. The head is divided in the middle into two lobes by a deep groove. The outline of each lobe is narrowly rounded with the margin on the sides at first slightly convex, then broadly concave, and slightly convex with a rather narrow posterior margin. The anterior eyes, about midway up the head, are crescent-shaped in form and widely separated. The posterior eyes are small and circular and located near the hinder margin of the head. The middle antenna has a basal joint, while the lateral antennae have none and are bottle-shaped with rounded, pointed tips. The palps are almost twice the length of the head and are cylindrical and smooth with an abrupt narrowing to fingerlike processes at the tip. The tentacular cirri are jointed from a cylindrical base. They are covered with papillae. There are twelve pairs of minute, transparent, and smooth elytra. They are very thin, without ground color, and with numerous light-brown specks and streaks. The dorsal cirri on the parapodia are long and project beyond the setae. The parapodia are practically cylindrical and bilobed. The setae of the dorsal lobe are very delicate, with finely toothed edges. The setae of the ventral lobe are of varied kinds. Common off the Virginia coast.

Antinoë sarsi (Kinberg) PLATE 99. The anterior margin of the head is double-pointed, as in *Lagisca floccosa,* described below. The posterior pair of eyes are close to each other and smaller than the anterior eyes, which are farther apart. Both pairs are on the posterior part of the head. The brownish median tentacle is fairly slender and tapers to a sharp point. The lateral tentacles are quite short and tapering. The palps are as long as the median tentacle, broad at the base, and taper to a pointed extremity. The tentacular cirri are also very long and slender.

This species occurs not only on the northern European coast but it has also been found from the St. Lawrence to Cape Cod on the Atlantic Coast, usually in fairly deep water.

Lepidametria commensalis Webster PLATE 99. The head is convex with rounded, though almost angular, sides. The eyes are circular and black, the anterior pair largest. There is no median groove. The lateral antennae have bases that are considerably stout and long, while the antennae themselves are straight-sided and taper to a filamentary brushlike point. The base of the middle antenna is very stout and cylindrical. This antenna is one third longer than the lateral antennae and of about the same shape. The tentacular cirri have a large joint like a truncated cone. They are slightly swollen near the tip. Both tentacles and cirri have two dark, ringlike bands. The elytra are transparent. The head is purple. The antennae are black at the base, verging into white, with a black ring on the larger portion. The terminal part is white. The setae and parapodia are golden-yellow, but there is a single, large pointed seta which is dark brown. This species found from southern New England to Virginia. The length is from 2 to nearly 4 inches. The number of segments varies from sixty to eighty. This is a commensal species, living in the tubes of the worm *Amphitrite ornata* (Verrill) (COLOR PLATES VII, 9; VIII, 9).

Lagisca floccosa Savigny PLATE 99. The median and lateral tentacles, in this species, are moderately short, as well as the tentacular cirri, and without an enlargement just below the pointed tip. The anterior border of the head is sharply indented on the median line to produce two acutely pointed areas extending forward on either side. The two pairs of eyes are at the lateral margins of the head, the posterior pair being close to the junction

PLATE 99

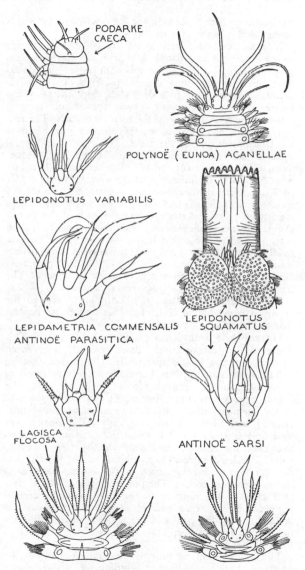

PODARKE CAECA

POLYNOË (EUNOA) ACANELLAE

LEPIDONOTUS VARIABILIS

LEPIDAMETRIA COMMENSALIS
ANTINOË PARASITICA

LEPIDONOTUS SQUAMATUS

LAGISCA FLOCOSA

ANTINOË SARSI

with the second segment. The body is covered with fifteen pairs of overlapping scales.

The species is found along the American and European shores of the North Atlantic.

Eunoa nodosa (Sars) PLATE 100. The body of this worm is broad and flattened. There are thirty-six segments having parapodia armed with setae, the dorsal setae being shorter than the ventral ones. The head is divided into two parts by a deep cleft, each division being narrowed to a blunt point. There is a distinct interval between them at the base of the median tentacle. The two pairs of eyes are conspicuous, the anterior pair being at the lateral margins of the head. The very small lateral tentacles arise close under the base of the long median tentacle. The powerful, broad, saberlike palps have six rows of short and minute cilia on each. The tentacular cirri are more slender than the median tentacle but of about the same length and apparently more flexible. There are fifteen pairs of scales covering the back of the worm, elongated, kidney-shaped, and with thick, densely ciliated margins and of somewhat leathery consistency. They are reddish brown or a mottled madder-brown in color, darker toward the anterior end of the worm. The first parapodia bear the tentacular cirri and have a few stout setae. The second parapodia have a long ventral cirrus.

This species ranges from northern Europe around the North Atlantic to the Gulf of St. Lawrence and beyond that to Cape Cod, Massachusetts.

Harmothoë imbricata (Linnaeus) PLATE 100. This species has a comparatively short body of thirty-seven segments bearing bristled parapodia. The median tentacle is long, with parallel sides, becoming slightly enlarged to a bulblike outline narrowing to a fine-pointed tip. The lateral tentacles are much shorter, attached below the base of the median tentacle, also with parallel sides and fine-pointed tips. The palps are longer than the median tentacle and saber-shaped. The tentacular cirri are more flexible than the tentacles and somewhat shorter than the palps. The head narrows to two blunt points, the indentation between them being much shorter and shallower than in the preceding species. The posterior pair of eyes is situated close to the junction of the head with the second segment. The anterior pair of eyes are slightly on the ventral side of the points of the anterior margin and are not visible from above. This worm is about 2 inches in length.

The distribution of this species ranges around the coasts of the North Atlantic, including the Mediterranean region, Scandinavia, the Arctic shores, and the American coastline south to Cape Cod, Massachusetts.

Evarne impar Verrill PLATE 100. This small worm is about 1 inch in length. The lateral tentacles are much smaller than the median tentacle and attached beneath it. The head is very deeply and widely divided, in front, into two lobes. There are four eyes, as usual, but the anterior pair are on the outer edges of the head, while the posterior pair is close to the second segment. The broad, bladelike palps are covered with minute papillae. There are fifteen pairs of scales, either with fine spines fringing the edges or, in some cases, smooth. They are greenish brown in color, distributed into somewhat regular bars and blotches. The ventral surface is pale or brownish in color. There are two long terminal styles. This species occurs between the tide marks, under stones, in crevices, and within mollusk shells. It is quite lively in its actions and, if touched, it is likely to break into pieces. It is brilliantly luminescent in the dark.

It occurs on both the European and American sides of the Atlantic.

Gattyana cirrosa (Pallas) PLATE 100. The comparatively minute lateral tentacles arise below the base of the long, stiff median tentacle. These and the tentacular cirri are covered with long cilia. The bladelike palps curve outward like scimitars. The head has two diverging, bluntly pointed lobes. The fifteen pairs of scales are kidney-shaped, except for the first pair. There are long cilia on the posterior and outer margins of the scales and a felting of minute spines on their surface. The color is pale olive to buff. Though not parasitic, this worm has often been found in the tubes of the larger worm *Amphritrite figulus* (Dalyell) (PLATE 111). It has also been found in the tubes of the Parchment Worm (*Chaetopterus pergamentaceus*, COLOR PLATE IX).

The range of this species is from northern Europe to Greenland and American shores as far as New England.

Family Aphroditidae

This family embraces annulates of ovate or oblong form, convex dorsally. There is a distinct prostomium with a pair of eyes, a median tentacle, and no lateral tentacles. There are two palps; the tentacular cirri are long. The buccal cirri are moderately long. There is a large and powerful proboscis. The first pair of parapodia has three dense tufts of setae. There are fifteen pairs of elytra on the second, fourth, and fifth segments, and thereafter on all alternate segments to the twenty-fifth, and then on every third segment.

Aphrodite aculeata Linnaeus PLATE 100. This animal is popularly known as the Sea Mouse. The dorsal side of the body is covered with a thick felt of matted hair, composed of the setae of the ventral division of the parapodia. In this case, they are long, silky, and iridescent. Their surface is perfectly smooth. The body is broad, with the head smoothly rounded in front. The median tentacle is quite small. It has a short basal joint and gently becomes club-shaped, finally ending in a narrow tip. There is an eye on either side of the median line. A pair of diverging palps, threadlike in shape, is present. The body is rounded, broadest in the middle, and tapers to a rounded point at each end. The back is convex, covered with dense, grayish felt in the middle and surrounded by the magnificent iridescent green and gold border of hairs and brown spines. This covering entirely conceals the fifteen pairs of scales and the indications of the forty-three setigerous segments, of which the body is composed. The underside is rough to the touch, so that the transverse ridges of the segments can be felt. When alive, it makes its way through sandy mud by means of its powerful ventral setae. Its back is kept clean by the currents of sea-water passing over it. The length of this species varies from 3 to 7 inches. It ranges from Massachusetts, northward to the Arctic, and around to European shores. Specimens have been found in the Adriatic Sea.

Laetmonice armata (Verrill) PLATE 100. This species, described by Verrill, and often found along this coast, is considered to be closely related to *Laetmonice filicornis* Kinberg, which is described below.

Laetmonice filicornis Kinberg PLATE 101. The eyes of this worm are borne on short peduncles, near the anterior border of the head. The back is covered with grayish felt, like that of *Aphrodite aculeata,* the Sea Mouse. The head-region is rounded and the body is covered with fifteen pairs of smooth, iridescent scales, ovoid in shape for the most part. The brownish iridescent spines, along the sides, are flat and flexible. Most of these have three teeth on each side. The tentacular cirri spring from the first pair of feet, which extend forward. These cirri, much longer than in *Aphrodite aculeata,* each have two tufts of tapering, fine-pointed setae. The first pair of setae spread out like fans and are directed anteriorly and medially. The second pair flanks it, with its spines much more compact. The two together seem to function as fenders to aid in protecting the mouth-region from sandy debris. The median tentacle is very slender and long, tapering to a fine point, though with a slightly bulbous expansion near the termination. It rises from the median line below and is ventral to the junction of the eye-peduncles. The still longer palps are robust and

PLATE 100

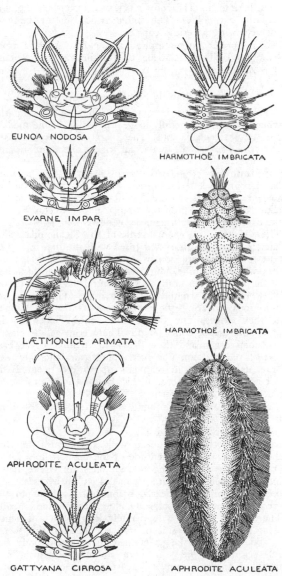

EUNOA NODOSA

HARMOTHOË IMBRICATA

EVARNE IMPAR

HARMOTHOË IMBRICATA

LÆTMONICE ARMATA

APHRODITE ACULEATA

GATTYANA CIRROSA

APHRODITE ACULEATA

armed with a series of long sharp papillae on either side, from base to tip. The body is flat, oval in outline, tapering at both extremities. The undersurface of the body is covered with spherical papillae.

This species ranges around the North Atlantic from New England and Canada to Scandinavia and Britain. It is sometimes found on oyster beds.

Family Sigalionidae

The cephalic lobe is rounded. The median tentacle, when present, is generally long, originating in the median part of the cephalic lobe. The lateral tentacles are fused with the base of the tentacular cirri. There are usually four eyes.

Sthenelais emertoni Verrill PLATE 101. The head has a rounded anterior border. A pair of *ctenidia* (sickle-shaped structures covered with toothlike cilia to an abundant degree, probably branchial in function) is at the base of the median tentacle, which is long and straight. These ctenidia are characteristic of the Sigalionidae. The later tentacles are short and fused with the first foot. The tentacular cirri are somewhat separate. The palps are proportionately quite long, slender, and smooth, attached to the base of the head on the ventral side, with a pair of scoop-shaped ctenidia at their base. The scales are numerous, covering the entire body. They are fringed at their edges. The dorsal and ventral lobes of the parapodia are of equal length. There is a well-developed branchial organ and three T-shaped ctenidia at the base of each parapodium. The overlapping scales alternate with branchial cirri on all segments up to the twenty-sixth. All the segments beyond this point have both scales and gills on each segment.

Sthenelais emertoni is found along the entire New England coast.

Sthenelais limicola Ehlers PLATE 101. This species has a transversely oval head with a brownish crescent-shaped marking on either side of the median line. There are two pairs of eyes, the anterior ones not visible, being hidden under the lateral tentacles at their base. The posterior pair show clearly, being just posterior to the median tentacle. The palps are long, slender, and smooth. The median tentacle is moderately long, with a flattened ctenidium on either side of its base. Though this worm is about 2 inches long, its delicate, elongate body has 128 segments. The scales are smooth, brownish, and translucent; they completely cover the back. The parapodia each have branchial processes and three ctenidia, in the form of ciliated pads.

This worm ranges along the Atlantic Coast of the northern United States to Canada, Norway, Britain, and the Adriatic Sea. It is found burrowing in the shallow sandy sea-bottom.

Sthenelais picta Verrill PLATE 101. The flattened body, though considerably elongated, is approximately the same breadth throughout. The back is convex, but the ventral surface is flat. The dorsal side is crowded with overlapping and imbricated scales, which exceed 150 pairs. These are almost crescent-shaped with a peculiar notch at the center of the anterior edge. The outer edge of each scale is fringed while the posterior edge is smooth. The scales of the anterior segments, for a considerable distance back, are covered with slightly elevated granules. The posterior scales are smooth. The anterior pair of scales immediately over the head are oval and finely toothed on the outer and anterior edges. The head is very small, rounded, and with the neck behind the eyes, of which there are four forming a quadrangle. The head is narrowed on its front border into an elliptical prolongation, which is the base of the median antenna. The first pair of parapodia are long and each has a pair of slender dorsal cirri nearly as long as the antennae and a large bundle of long, slender setae, which project beyond the scales and are golden in color. The general color may be gray with a brown median dorsal band varying so that the edges are also bordered with brown, with a black spot near the anterior margin. The head is dark brown with a red central spot and a light-colored spot on each side. The length may be 6 inches and the width about 4 mm. This curious species is often found burrowing in the sand around the low-water mark, extending down to 14 fathoms on shelly and muddy bottoms. It is quite common from Vineyard Sound to New Haven.

Sigalion arenicola Verrill PLATE 101. Superficially this species closely resembles Sthenelais picta and is found under the same circumstances and often in the same location on sandy bottoms around the low-water mark.

Pholoë minuta (O. Fabricius) PLATE 101. This is a very delicate and fragile species, hiding sluggishly under stones in the tidal area, especially in tide-pools. It is, at the most, not more than ¾ inch in length and like a delicate line in width; yet the body possesses forty-five to seventy segments. Its back is convex and the ventral side is flattened. The color varies from yellowish brown to pale pink, mottled with brown, throughout its double series of at least sixteen pairs of oval, overlapping scales. The round central attachment of each scale to the back shows through their translucent substance. The right and left series are separated from each other, showing a clear line along the middle of the back.

Like so many of the worms occurring along the coast of New England, this form extends its range circumboreally and down the European coast. Its body is so delicate, as mentioned above, that in order to collect it without damage it is best to place small stones in tide-pools over night, as suggested by McIntosh, and then put them into dishes of seawater for a few hours. If one then examines the waterline, these worms may be found.

Leanira hystricis Ehlers PLATE 102. This is a small, deep-water worm, not more than 2 or 3 inches in length, sometimes brought up by dredge. The scales are round, smooth, and translucent. The median tentacle is extremely small. The eyes, if present, are not visible from the dorsal side. The palps rise from the median line on the ventral side and are long, smooth, and taper to a point. The branchiae are absent from the anterior segments until the twenty-fourth, which has a very small one. Thereafter they occur on each segment, gradually becoming more and more elongate.

Family Phyllodocidae

These worms have a blunt, cone-shaped head, which may be heart-shaped or oval. There are two or three tentacles, the unpaired ones being posterior. There are two small eyes, rarely four. The body has numerous segments and two caudal cirri. The buccal segment has one to four pairs of tentacular cirri. There are no jaws. The dorsal and ventral cirri are leaf-shaped.

Phyllodoce groenlandica Oersted PLATE 102. The transverse region between the segments is densely ciliated. This worm is dark green with irregular brown markings. The gills, or branchiae, are brown with a light green margin. It is found at low tide in sand to depths of 25 fathoms, associated with sand and shells.

Phyllodoce fragilis Webster PLATE 102. This is a greenish worm, about 2 inches in length. The head is greenish white, wider than long, very convex, elongated, flattened. The body varies from light to dark green. It is widest in the middle, tapering in both directions, so that the first and last segments are very narrow. The cirri are generally yellowish green. The body and the dorsal cirri are marked with numerous dark brown spots. The eyes in the single pair are large, circular, and black, widely separated at the posterior part of the head. The two pairs of antennae are stout and cone-shaped, less than the head in length. The first segment has three pairs of tentacular cirri. The second segment carries the fourth

PLATE 101

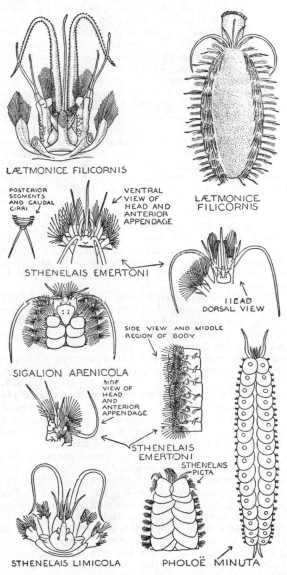

LÆTMONICE FILICORNIS

LÆTMONICE FILICORNIS

POSTERIOR SEGMENTS AND CAUDAL CIRRI

VENTRAL VIEW OF HEAD AND ANTERIOR APPENDAGE

STHENELAIS EMERTONI

HEAD DORSAL VIEW

SIGALION ARENICOLA

SIDE VIEW AND MIDDLE REGION OF BODY

SIDE VIEW OF HEAD AND ANTERIOR APPENDAGE

STHENELAIS EMERTONI

STHENELAIS PICTA

STHENELAIS LIMICOLA

PHOLOË MINUTA

pair of cirri, which are the longest of all. The basal joints are all cylindrical. The parapodia are cylindrical and bilobed with delicate setae. The dorsal cirri are in the form of broad heart-shaped expansions and function as branchiae or gills. They gradually become narrower toward the posterior part of the body. The anal cirri resemble the antennae. This is a common species along the New England coast, found on shells between tides.

Phyllodoce catenula Verrill PLATE 102. This species may be ¾ inch in length. The head is somewhat longer than broad, slightly heart-shaped on its posterior margin. The front is broadly rounded with a slight notch in the middle. The eyes are large and dark brown on the dorsal surface of the head, and the antennae and tentacular cirri are long and slender, the posterior two of the latter much longer than the others. The gills are larger and longer, ovate and leaflike with pointed tips. The proboscis has twelve rows of papillae on the basal portion. This worm is pale green in color on both the body and the gills with a median row of dark brown spots, one to each segment. The head is pale or greenish white. There are also two lateral rows, each having a spot. Common at Watch Hill, Rhode Island, at Woods Hole, and very common in the Bay of Fundy; from 4 to 50 fathoms.

Eulalia pistacia Verrill PLATE 102. This is a bright, yellowish green worm, often with darker markings posteriorly and toward the base of the appendages. It is about 1¾ inches in length. The body is fairly slender and somewhat flattened. The head is convex in outline and shorter than broad. The median antenna is slender and much shorter than the head. There is a pair of large brown eyes. The tentacular cirri are fairly long. The four posterior ones are much longer than the others. The narrow gills or branchiae taper anteriorly. They are ovate and leaflike on the middle segments, and are longer and taper posteriorly. The proboscis is long, club-shaped, and smooth, and somewhat striped longitudinally.

It is found in 6 to 12 fathoms in Vineyard Sound among ascidians. Another record is near New Haven in 4 to 5 fathoms, among hydroids.

Eulalia dubia Webster & Benedict PLATE 102. This worm has a dark green body and dark brown branchiae with green margins. There is a dark spot at the base of the parapodia, both dorsally and ventrally. The sides of the head are evenly rounded, with a transverse groove just back of the base of the antennae. The ventral antennae are concealed by the dorsal pair, but are otherwise similar to them. The median antenna is somewhat slenderer than the anterior pair. There are two large,

PLATE 102

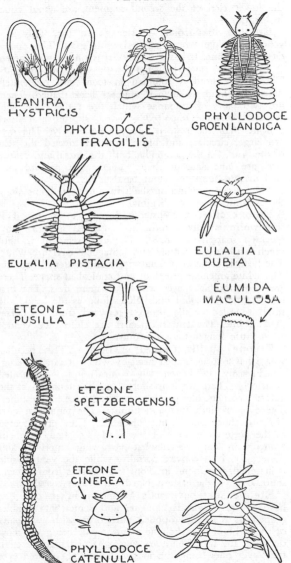

LEANIRA
HYSTRICIS

PHYLLODOCE
FRAGILIS

PHYLLODOCE
GROENLANDICA

EULALIA PISTACIA

EULALIA
DUBIA

EUMIDA
MACULOSA

ETEONE
PUSILLA

ETEONE
SPETZBERGENSIS

ETEONE
CINEREA

PHYLLODOCE
CATENULA

black eyes. The tentacular cirri on the first segment and the lower cirri of the second segment are about equal in length.

Eumida maculosa Webster PLATE 102. This is a yellowish white worm, spotted with gray. The appendages are white. It has a dorsal cirrus tinged with green. It may be ½ inch in length with sixty-five segments. The convex head is rounded in front and moderately notched behind, so that it appears heart-shaped. There are two pairs of antennae which are rather stout and similar. A single unpaired antenna, shorter and more delicate than the rest, is situated posteriorly. The eyes are large, circular, and black, situated toward the rear of the head. On the parapodia, both the dorsal and ventral cirri are lanceolate in shape. There is a pair of anal cirri arising from the stout basal joint.

This species is found on shells in 5 to 10 fathoms along the Atlantic Coast to Virginia.

Eteone cinerea Webster & Benedict PLATE 102. This tiny worm is only 2 mm. in length. It is light gray, speckled sparsely in brown. The anal segment is light green while the antennae and tentacular cirri are white. The head is dome-shaped anteriorly and flattened beneath. The white antennae are stout and conical in shape. There are two tiny, black eyes which are mere dots. The first body-segment is about one half as long as the head. The small rounded papilla projects forward from its dorsal median line. The tentacular cirri are short; the ventral are a little longer than the dorsal.

Eteone pusilla Oersted PLATE 102. This peculiar worm has a spade-shaped head by which it can be recognized easily. It is generally conical and is truncated anteriorly. There are four short, bladelike tentacles at the anterior corners, one pair clearly in advance of the other. The eyes are indistinct and minute. The tentacular cirri are also short and bluntly bladelike. They are situated at the posterior corners of the head. The body is about 2 inches in length, somewhat narrowing anteriorly and posteriorly. It is convex dorsally, while the ventral side is flattened. It is found in about 100 fathoms from Canada southward on the eastern North American coast.

Eteone spetzbergensis Malmgren PLATE 102. The head of this worm is elongate and somewhat thimble-shaped. It is evenly rounded anteriorly, with two pairs of short, blunt tentacles, the anterior pair being the most dorsal of the two. There are two pairs of tentacular cirri, the lower ones being the longer. Two light-colored eyes are situated posteriorly on the head. The body is more than 3 inches long, somewhat flattened, and slightly tapering anteriorly and posteriorly. The general coloration is pale yellow on the forward part of the body. Posteriorly, it tends to be flesh-colored.

Family Nereidae

The annulates in this family are conspicuous for their activity and muscular development. They are usually free-swimmers. The head is well formed and has eyes with prostomial tentacles. There are large, two-jointed palps. The buccal membrane is chitinous and is continuous with that covering the proboscis, which is armed with a pair of horny jaws, a series of horny teeth, and may be readily extruded. The body is elongate, sometimes rounded and sometimes flattened. The segments are quite similar. Usually the first have no parapodia, but have two tentacular cirri on each side. The parapodia almost always have two lobes and are nearly alike throughout the entire body. There are two cirri on the terminal segment.

Nereis virens Sars PLATE 193; COLOR PLATES VII, 2; VIII, 3. This is the Clam Worm, one of the largest and most common of our marine annulates. It occurs under stones or burrows in the sand or mud in sheltered bays and sounds, where it is common at the low-water mark and also between tides. It may attain a length of 18 inches, the larger forms being stout in proportion. It swims very actively with a sinuous method of locomotion and is very voracious, turning its proboscis inside out and thrusting it forward to seize worms and other marine animals with the two powerful jaws. When the proboscis is withdrawn, the jaws close at the same time. It can easily destroy worms and other creatures of its own size and much larger.

The worms of this species construct their tubes by exuding a viscid fluid from glands along the body which hardens into a translucent sheath. As the fluid is sticky, grains of sand adhere to it forming a flexible tube which fits the worms so closely that they can enter and leave it with considerable speed and move about within it, utilizing the bundles of setae with which their parapodia are equipped. They fall prey, in turn, to fishes such as the tautog and scup, which nose them out of the sand to devour them.

They leave their burrows, especially at night, and swim about in rhythmic undulations in large numbers. At this time they are readily destroyed by fishes. The free-swimming habit is probably connected with the season of reproduction when the males swim about in pools at low water to discharge their sperm. The number of segments varies with the size and age of the worm. In the larger individuals, there may be as many as two hundred. New segments are added at the posterior end just in front of the caudal segment, which always remains the same.

The head has two pairs of eyes and two pairs of antennae. There are four tentacular cirri, two dorsal and two ventral, of which the dorsal cirri are longer in the male than in the female, even measuring as long as the first nine segments. The male is easily distinguished from the female by its strong, steel-blue color, which blends into green at the base of the parapodia. These, in turn, are bright green in color and show the network of blood vessels within them with a contrasting effect. The female, on the other hand, is dull green, tinged with orange and red. Besides these colors in both sexes, the skin reflects prismatic hues from the light of the sun, often being brilliantly iridescent.

The parapodia or lateral appendages are remarkably complicated and very efficient not only as locomotor organs but also for respiratory purposes. They become more complicated and more highly developed toward the center of the body. The setae are also very characteristic and are remarkably delicate and specialized for various functions.

Nereis virens is widely distributed from southern New England, along the entire New England coast to Labrador, continuing around through the Arctic regions to the northern coasts of Europe and Great Britain.

Nereis pelagica Linnaeus PLATE 103. This species is smaller than *Nereis virens,* the large specimens being not more than 8 inches in length. The body is widest in the middle, tapering rapidly to the caudal region. The color is reddish brown. It is very common from Greenland to Virginia. In the northern part of its range it occurs under stones, but from southern New England to Cape Hatteras it occurs chiefly on shelly bottoms. It is found from the low-water mark to 100 fathoms. The general features of its anatomy are similar to *Nereis virens.*

Nereis fucata Savigny PLATE 103. This is a related species which is largely found off the New England coast. It has been dredged off Watch Hill, Rhode Island.

Nereis tenuis Webster & Benedict PLATE 104. This worm is without color, except for the red of the blood which shows through the transparent body. It is not quite 2 inches in length. The head is shaped like the bulb of a syringe, the small end being directed forward and divided by a median line to form two closely set bases for the slender conical antennae. The palps are slightly longer than the head, with terminal joints. There are four eyes, two on either side of the head, the posterior pair being slightly larger than the anterior. The proboscis is

PLATE 103

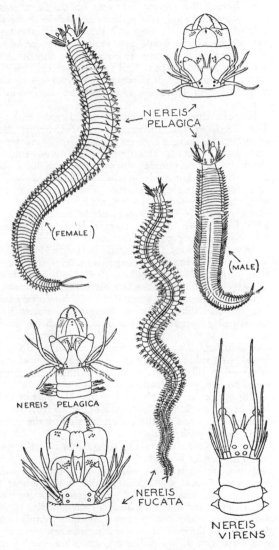

NEREIS
PELAGICA

(FEMALE)

(MALE)

NEREIS PELAGICA

NEREIS
FUCATA

NEREIS
VIRENS

made up of two ringlike segments with curved jaws, each having five rectangular teeth on the inner margin. The tentacular cirri, arising from a basal joint on either side of the head, are long and slender, each about twice the length of the head. The jointed setae are of three kinds, two with delicate terminal points, the other with a bluntly rounded apex. This is the most delicate *Nereis* known on our coast. It is extremely narrow in comparison with its length. It was found in 20 to 25 fathoms in mud and sand.

Nereis dumerilii Audouin & Edwards PLATE 104. The head, in this species, is characteristic of *Nereis,* generally speaking. The tentacular cirri, however, are very long, ranging, according to McIntosh, from one third, in small examples, to one fifth the total length in the larger. The body is usually 2½ inches long and of seventy to eighty segments. The general coloration varies around yellowish brown, except for the red dorsal blood vessel. The anterior part of the body is variegated with fine brown dots. It is more brilliantly iridescent than the posterior part of the body.

Epitokous Form. "The head in the epitokous male is short and rounded, the large, sometimes connate, eyes occupying the lateral regions. Body soft and delicate. Dorsal cirri of the first seven segments dilated and peculiarly modified. The ventral cirri of the corresponding feet are also dilated. At the compressed sixteenth foot the lamellae appear, and the pelagic condition is fully developed at the thirty-seventh foot, the great lobes being very thin, and finely and somewhat regularly veined. The dorsal cirrus has a series of prominent papillae on its lower edge. The long swimming bristles give a glassy sheen to the sides" (McIntosh).

This species is very plentiful in the Mediterranean Sea and its range is very wide extending to Norway and Sweden and across to the American side of the Atlantic as far south as Virginia.

Nereis (Nectonereis) megalops Verrill PLATE 104. The slender body in this species, as stated by Verrill, consists of an anterior portion containing fourteen setigerous segments and a posterior portion, much longer and slenderer, and consisting of very numerous short segments. The anterior portion is broadest in the middle, tapering both ways, while the posterior portion simply tapers gradually to the end. It is also characterized by complex parapodia with their lamellae and compound-bladed setae. The broad, oval head is somewhat convex and very smooth above. The four very large protruding eyes are a conspicuous feature, the anterior pair being the larger, covering the lateral side of the head and even a part of

PLATE 104

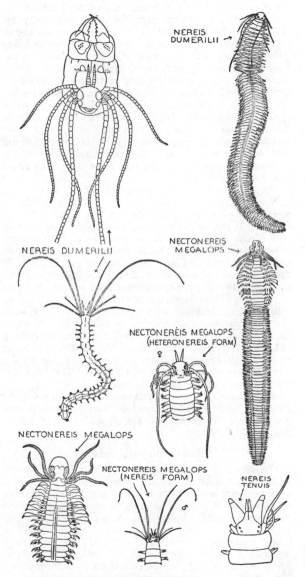

NEREIS
DUMERILII →

NEREIS DUMERILII

NECTONEREIS
MEGALOPS →

NECTONEREIS MEGALOPS
(HETERONEREIS FORM)

NECTONEREIS MEGALOPS

NECTONEREIS MEGALOPS
(NEREIS FORM)

NEREIS
TENUIS

the dorsal side. Two small antennae with swollen bases curve downward on the ventral side of the head. Of the eight slender, tentacular cirri, the upper pair is by far the longest. Two pairs are situated posteriorly and immediately in front of the larger eyes. Finally, a short lower pair is located near the mouth. Of the parapodia on the first seven segments, each has a large dorsal cirrus which increases in length from the first to the seventh segments. On the seven following segments, the dorsal cirri are smaller. All the ventral cirri are small. In the posterior region, there is a still further specialized series gradually decreasing in size toward the terminal segment. The worms of this species, about 1½ inches in length, are seen swimming actively at the surface not only in the evening, but also in the middle of the day, from about July 3 to August 11.

They are common in Vineyard Sound.

Nereis limbata Ehlers PLATE 105. This is also a common species, but grows only to the length of 5 or 6 inches. It can be easily distinguished from *Nereis virens* and *Nereis pelagica* by its slender, sharp, light amber-colored jaws, and by the parapodia, which are small toward the head and narrow or straplike caudally. It is brownish or bronze in color, in the anterior region, and marked with light-colored oblique lines toward the sides of the body. There is often a whitish border on each ring, thus marking the joints with pale bands. Posteriorly, both body and parapodia are reddish in color, while the main dorsal blood vessel shows through the integument as a red line. The male differs from the female by having more complicated appendages in the middle part of the body, which is also brighter red in color. The female is not characterized by this difference.

Nereis limbata is very common on sandy shores from New England to South Carolina. *Nereis virens, Nereis pelagica,* and *Nereis limbata* are all spoken of by fishermen as "Clam Worms."

Family Nephthydidae

The flattened head is usually quadrangular in shape, with a short tentacle at each anterior angle and one a little posterior to both on the first segment. There may be two eyes or none. The body is elongate and almost square in section, although convex dorsally and flattened ventrally. The segments are similar. There is usually a single cirrus on the terminal segment. The peristomial segment is usually fused with the following segment. The proboscis is large, with a pair of horny teeth, or none. The lobes of the parapodia are widely separated and bear a spine and a double row of setae of various types.

PLATE 105

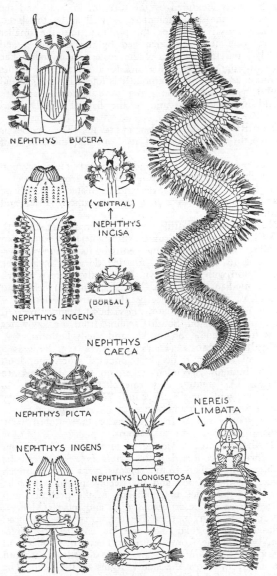

NEPHTHYS BUCERA

(VENTRAL)
NEPHTHYS INCISA
(DORSAL)

NEPHTHYS INGENS

NEPHTHYS CAECA

NEPHTHYS PICTA

NEREIS LIMBATA

NEPHTHYS INGENS

NEPHTHYS LONGISETOSA

Nephthys ingens Stimpson PLATE 105. This species can be easily identified by the form of its head and the position of the small antennae, as well as by the large, median, dorsal papilla on the proboscis and the smaller ventral one. It is also identified by the prominent and widely separated branches of the posterior parapodia. The setae are dark-colored. It grows to a length of 6 inches or more, and is quite common. It is found in Long Island Sound near New Haven in 3 to 8 fathoms, at Block Island in 29 fathoms, and in the Bay of Fundy from 10 to 60 fathoms.

Nephthys bucera Ehlers PLATE 105. This species is noteworthy for the form of its head and the length of its setae.

It burrows in mud and sand and is extremely common along the southern New England coast from Massachusetts Bay to Vineyard Haven and at Watch Hill, Rhode Island. It is found in 4 to 5 fathoms among rocks and sand.

Nephthys picta Ehlers PLATE 105; COLOR PLATES VII, 3; VIII, 4. This species can be distinguished readily from the other species of the same genus by its greater slenderness and its whitish body, mottled dorsally toward the head-region with dark brown. Frequently, there is a dark brown median dorsal line. The shape of the head and position of the tentacles are peculiar to this species.

It is found from Nahant, Massachusetts, and Vineyard Sound to Charleston, South Carolina, from the low-water mark to 8 fathoms, on muddy and shelly bottoms.

Nephthys caeca (Fabricius) PLATE 105. This is a species of small size, deeply pigmented when found on muddy bottoms. Specimens taken on sandy bottoms are colorless. Apparently, they can change their color to harmonize with their background. When swimming, they have a superficial resemblance to *Nereis limbata*.

The species ranges from Labrador to southern New England in from 7 to 50 fathoms.

Nephthys incisa Malmgren PLATE 105. This species was formerly confused with *Nereis ingens*. It can be readily distinguished from *Nepthys caeca* "by its much shorter prismatic body and the deeply incised parapodia as well as difference in papillation of the proboscis and characteristics of the setigerous rami and setae" (Moore).

Nephthys longisetosa Oersted PLATE 105. The head is nearly quadrangular. The anterior tentacles rise somewhat back of the frontal corners. They are slender and tapering. The second pair are blade-shaped and extend laterally from below the side margins of the head. The dorsal cirrus of the first parapodia is unusually long, curving forward, and similar in shape to the tentacles. The proboscis is quite characteristic. When fully extended, it is barrel-shaped, with about fifteen parallel rows of papillae extending lengthwise along its convex, cylindrical outer surface, marking it off like a pattern of barrel-staves. It possesses strong longitudinal muscle-bands, which contract to a rosette-shaped pattern when the proboscis is fully withdrawn. This species is found off the coast of New England and Canada and also around the British Isles.

Family Eunicidae

The head is triangular and semioval with lobelike palps more or less united. Only occasionally are there lateral tentacles. The eyes may be two or four or none. The body is long, typically wormlike, very often slender and rounded. It is iridescent, with numerous narrow segments ending in two or four anal cirri.

Arabella opalina Verrill PLATE 106; COLOR PLATES VII, 5; VIII, 6. Popularly known as the Opal Worm, this beautiful, iridescent creature is very long and slender, reaching a length of 18 inches or more, with a diameter of only 3 mm. The body is cylindrical in section, tapering gradually toward the small head. The segments are very closely marked. The general color is reddish to brownish, and the brilliant play of rainbow colors in each segment is especially noteworthy. The obtuse, cone-shaped head is bright orange. Its shape is variable and may change to become much longer than broad. There are four eyes in a transverse row, the two middle ones being the larger. The parapodia consist of a short, obtusely rounded papilla forming the base and bearing the setae, with an elongated curved and obtuse lobe arising ventrally. There are five to nine setae of various forms in each bundle.

This worm is quite common off the southern New England coast from Vineyard Sound to New Haven. It occurs from the low-water mark to a depth of 14 fathoms.

Diopatra cupraea Claparède PLATE 106; COLOR PLATES VII, 4; VIII, 5; IX, 4. One of the most beautiful annulates of the North Atlantic region is the Plumed Worm, *Diopatra cupraea*. It may be more than a foot in length, while its iridescent, armored body may be ½ an inch in width. It constructs a very interesting tube of tough, parchmentlike material, which tapers to a depth of 3 feet or more, while its upper end projects 2 to 3 inches from the surface of the sand or mud, forming a "chimney," which it builds, utilizing fragments of shells, bits of eel grass, seaweed, and other hard substances in the environment. These effectively camouflage the chimney, so that at first sight it looks as if these fragments were accidentally caught on a projecting stub. Internally, the chimney is very smooth, due to the parchment lining, which is continuous with the portion below the surface. The tube is large enough for the worm to turn around inside. The worm comes to the open top, extends its cirri and plumed head from the chimney, and even thrusts out most of its anterior portion in search of food animals that may stray within its reach, while, at the same time, it scouts around for additions to the tube. The anterior segments have paired, bright red, plumed gills, each of which is like a pulsating tree, with successive whorls of branches arising from the spiral, central stem. The scarlet color is due to the blood vessels, through which the blood penetrates the finest branches, to be purified by the oxygen in the sea-water.

This species is common in shallow water below the low-tide mark, from southern New England to Charleston, South Carolina.

Hyalinoecia tubicola (O. F. Müller) PLATE 106. This is a long, graceful worm, with about eighty-five segments, characterized by the brownish iridescence of its body, the double red line of the red dorsal blood vessels, showing through the thin integument, and the long series of red, smoothly tapering gills arising vertically from the dorsal lobe of the parapodia, beginning at about the twenty-third to the twenty-sixth parapodia and extending back to the last seven segments, which are without them. A pair of long anal cirri arise from the terminal segment. The head has a somewhat triangular frontal margin. Five long, slender, tapering cirri arise from annulated joints. There are no eyes. The palps are short and bulblike, situated close together on the median tip of the head.

This worm builds a translucent, horny tube, which it drags about after it. It is a remarkably widely distributed species, occurring along the North American coast from the West Indies northward. On the European side, it ranges from Scandinavia and the British Isles, along the shores of France and the Mediterranean Sea. It is even found in the East Indies, along the northern Australian coast and at New Zealand.

Drilonereis elizabethae McIntosh (= **Drilonereis longa** Webster) PLATE 106. This species is closely related to *Arabella opalina*. The head is more elongated, but it resembles it in being a simple cone with rounded summit; also there is a similarity in having four eyes in a straight line across the posterior border, and simplified parapodial limbs on all segments, except the first two, where they are completely lacking. Like *Arabella,* this species has a narrow, elongated body composed of many segments, all brilliantly iridescent, but peculiar in that

PLATE 106

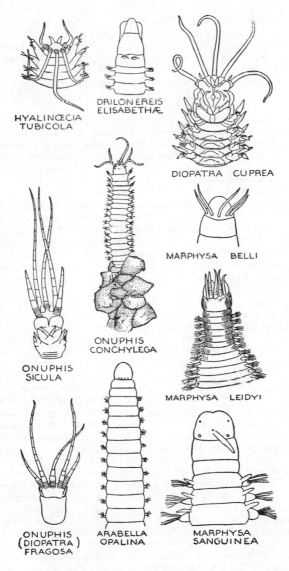

HYALINŒCIA
TUBICOLA

DRILONEREIS
ELISABETHÆ

DIOPATRA CUPREA

MARPHYSA BELLI

ONUPHIS
SICULA

ONUPHIS
CONCHYLEGA

MARPHYSA LEIDYI

ONUPHIS
(DIOPATRA)
FRAGOSA

ARABELLA
OPALINA

MARPHYSA
SANGUINEA

the color is concentrated in four longitudinal bands. The proboscis, also, is armed, as in *Arabella,* with a pair of powerful, black maxillae, each with about three teeth on the inner edge, a series of toothed dental plates of comparatively large size, and a pair of wedge-shaped brown mandibles, all most effective for attacking and devouring prey.

This species is abundant from New Jersey to Virginia, and also northward to Nova Scotia and in British waters in sandy and muddy bottoms.

Marphysa belli (Audouin & Edwards) PLATE 106. This is a beautiful species of which only the head is shown in the figure. The latter is very simple, showing affinities to the preceding species. It is rounded in front, conically dome-shaped. The median and two pairs of lateral tentacles are fairly long, tapering, and similar in shape, the median tentacles being the longest. There is a pair of eyes near the base of the inner lateral tentacles. The first two segments are without appendages.

The body of this worm is about 6 or 7 inches in length and is made up of many brilliantly iridescent segments, somewhat reddish in the anterior region. The posterior two thirds of the body is marked by a central, broad purple band, due to the dorsal blood vessel showing through.

Beginning with the third segment, the appendages have a simple, slender, tapering dorsal cirrus and a ventral, cone-shaped lobe bearing three spines and a bundle of various types of setae, all becoming longer as the body-width increases, and gradually diminishing in size as they approach the tapering tail. At about the fifteenth or sixteenth segment, a pair of beautiful red plumose gills, or branchiae, is added to each limb dorsally, continuing for about twenty segments, thus forming the branchial region of the body. Each gill has from ten to nineteen branchlets springing from one side of the main stem. These scarlet, feathery plumes wave from side to side in alternate unison, a beautiful rippling effect.

This species ranges along the eastern North American seaboard, as well as on the European side of the Atlantic.

Marphysa leidyi Quatrefages [= **Marphysa sanguinea** (Montagu)] PLATE 106. This worm is allied to *Diopatra cupraea* and has similar habits, but does not construct such perfect tubes. It occurs in shallow water below the low-tide mark, but is more frequently found in deeper water. It is a large and handsome worm, growing to a length of 6 or 7 inches in New England waters. Off the coast of Britain, it is recorded as being 18 inches to 2 feet in length. The body is largely flattened, but nearly cylindrical anteriorly. The general color is yellowish to brownish red and brilliantly iridescent. The branchiae are bright red, commencing about the sixteenth segment, as in the preceding species, which it closely resembles. The first pair of branchiae bear relatively few branchlets but farther along they have more numerous branchlets, all on one side, like flexible combs, also as in *Marphysa belli*. It possesses powerful jaws and is carnivorous.

The successive larval stages show a continuous series of developmental changes from the young to the adult. One of these is shown in PLATE 106, designated *Marphysa sanguinea,* the name given by Webster. In this young stage there is only one antenna, a slight median indentation on the frontal margin, and five eyes. In succeeding stages there are at first three, and then five antennae, and the organs generally multiply until they reach the adult condition shown in the figure marked *Marphysa leidyi*.

This species occurs from New Jersey to Vineyard Sound and around to European shores.

Onuphis sicula Quatrefages PLATE 106. The head of this species is similar to that of *Hyalinoecia tubicola*. The inner pair of lateral tentacles are as long as the median tentacle, if not longer. The outer ones are much shorter. They all have annulated basal joints (*cirrophores*). The maxillae are sharp-pointed. The gills begin on the fifth pair of appendages and continue, unbranched, to about the fiftieth segment. The tube built by this worm is constructed by strengthening a glandular secretion with gravel and shell fragments.

This species ranges from the Gulf of St. Lawrence, on the North American shores around to the European coast.

Onuphis conchylega Sars PLATE 106. The head is short and rounded. The five tentacles are shorter than in related species and have annulated basal joints (cirrophores). The first two segments have parapodia, as do all the rest. The branchiae begin on the eleventh or twelfth pair of limbs. The tube is built of pebbles and coarse gravel, and occasionally shells are utilized. It is lined with a glutinous secretion of great tenacity.

On the American Atlantic coast, this worm is found in great abundance near the edge of the Continental Shelf at 100 fathoms, and also in deeper waters, from the Arctic to Florida. On the European side, it extends from Novaya Zemlya and Scandinavia to the British Isles and the North Sea.

Onuphis fragosa (Ehlers) PLATE 106. The head is quite small and transverse in location, being wider than long. The tentacles are fairly short and delicately slender; the outer lateral pair less than half the length of the others. There is a yellowish proboscis.

This species ranges along the Atlantic Coast of North

America, southward to Florida, and on the European side from Norway to Britain.

Family Glyceridae

A pointed, ringed cone forms the head having four small tentacles at the tip. There is an elongate body, rounded, tapering anteriorly, and narrowing toward the tail, which has two short cirri. There are many narrow segments, each with two or more rings. The parapodia have a dorsal and ventral lobe. The proboscis is equipped with powerful muscles and can be thrown out rapidly in the form of a massive jaw with four hooked teeth at its club-shaped extremity.

Glycera dibranchiata Ehlers PLATE 107; COLOR PLATES VII, 6; VIII, 7, 7a; **Glycera americana** Leidy PLATE 107. These two species are quite similar. Each has an extremely small and acute head with four minute tentacles at the end, otherwise without appendages. The body is 6 to 8 inches in length, and tapers caudally. It is remarkably well adapted for quick burrowing. When free-swimming, these worms coil themselves in a loose spiral, rapidly rotating about its axis. They insert the pointed head into the sea-bottom and, as the body is rotated, it penetrates the sand or mud with such speed as to disappear instantly. They may be found, therefore, on sand or mud flats in shallow to moderately deep water. The color of the body is light purplish pink, with a pink line running dorsally through the entire length. The parapodia, also, are pink and quite minute. A significant difference between the two species is found in the gills. *Glycera dibranchiata* has simple gills on the upper and lower sides of its parapodia, while those of *Glycera americana* are branched in treelike fashion on the upper side, and are entirely absent on the lower side. Also, the parapodia themselves are differently shaped. These worms are popularly known as "Beak Throwers," because of their ability to evert the large saclike pharynx with great speed, turning it inside out to form a clublike proboscis, at the end of which there are four curved black hooks capable of seizing prey or of giving a sharp nip to an enemy. They have no true blood vessels, as in most other worms, but, instead, the cavity of the body between the alimentary tract and the skin is filled with red blood. Both of these species are found along the Atlantic Coast from southern New England to Charleston, South Carolina, from low-water mark to 8 or 10 fathoms.

Family Goniadidae

The cephalic lobe is elongate, tapering, with four equal terminal processes. It has horny teeth in two to five rows. The parapodia have two lobes in the middle and posterior part of the body.

Goniada gracilis Verrill PLATE 107. The body of this worm, which is less than 1 inch in length, is very slender and iridescent in color. The elongate, sharply conical head has eight rounded annulations, the basal one being furnished with a pair of tiny, red eyes. There are four slender antennae. The long, narrow parapodia are more than half the diameter of the body.

It has been found off Gay Head and along Cape Cod to Provincetown, Massachusetts, burrowing in clear sand or soft mud, from the low-water mark to 19 fathoms.

Goniada maculata Oersted PLATE 107. The head terminates anteriorly in a long, tapering process consisting of four segments and with four short tentacles at the tip. The tip is 4 or 6 inches in length, tapered anteriorly and posteriorly. It is rounded toward the head-region and flattened toward the tail, which terminates in two slender cirri. The proboscis has a row of about ten dark brown V-shaped denticles toward the base on each side. In extrusion, they diminish in size distally and to some extent proximally. There is also a circle of about twenty blunt conical papillae toward the end of the proboscis surrounding two lateral denticles. A series of X-shaped intermediate denticles, varying in size, forms a belt between the larger pair.

This species has a wide range along the North Atlantic Coast.

Family Sphaerodoridae

In this family, the head of the worms is conical in shape, with short papillae and four eyes. The proboscis is smooth. The rounded body is fusiform and with numerous segments. The parapodia are single-lobed and with a conspicuous globular papilla on each side.

Ephesia gracilis H. Rathke PLATE 107. The head is bluntly rounded, with papillae on the free border, the median and two lateral being the longest. There are four minute eye-specks, the anterior pair being nearer to each other than the posterior pair. The mouth-opening is immediately behind the tip of the snout. The length of the body may reach 2½ inches. It is elongate in shape, having about 120 segments. It tapers slightly anteriorly and more distinctly posteriorly, where it ends in a small, rounded tip with a large globular papilla on each side. Lateral papillae commence behind the snout, increase in size to the middle of the body, and again diminish posteriorly. Thinly distributed small papillae occur in rows on the general surface. The general coloration is straw yellow in front, the rest of the body being pale brown or dull reddish brown, the hues being darker over the intestine. Some specimens have a lilac or purplish tint along the ventral, setigerous lobes of the parapodia, which also have a spine and simple setae projecting, each with a tip shaped like a bill-hook.

This species is distributed from Greenland southward along the Atlantic Coast of North America.

Family Aricidae

"Head (prostomium) a pointed cone, with or without eyes, and devoid of processes. Peristomial segment without appendages. Body tapered anteriorly and posteriorly, flattened dorsally, rounded ventrally. Segments narrow. Proboscis a frilled rosette. Tail with two long cirri.

Aricidea fragilis Webster PLATE 107. As seen from above, the head is convex posteriorly, but anteriorly becomes somewhat concave to produce a shallowly S-shaped outline terminating in a narrowed prostomium slightly emarginate terminally. It may extend itself to about double its length, becoming acutely conical. There are two small, circular eyes situated laterally near the posterior angles. The delicate median antenna arises from practically the central point of the head. The parapodia of the first three segments are represented merely by cylindrical papillae without other parts except a bundle of setae. Beginning with the fourth segment, the cirrus is situated at the base of the branchia and is about one third the length of that organ which, in turn, is cylindrical. This is true of all the segments back of it except the non-branchiated posterior segments. There is a lobe on the external side of the cirrus except on the posterior segments above mentioned. The ventral ramus of each parapodium is also a tiny papilla, a little longer than the dorsal cirrus. On the fourth segment, it is about one half as long as the dorsal cirrus. On the segments posterior to the fourth segment, the ventral ramus becomes a fleshy, more flattened lobe to about the thirtieth segment. After the fortieth segment, the ventral rami are entirely without appendages.

This worm is about 1⅓ inches in length. Specimens have been collected with 170 segments. The head is white in color. The segments anterior to the fortieth are mostly bright red shading into white, which in turn shades into green. The anterior dorsal setae are golden yellow while those posterior to the segments bearing branchiae are white.

This species is only occasionally found burrowing in mud near the low-water mark.

PLATE 107

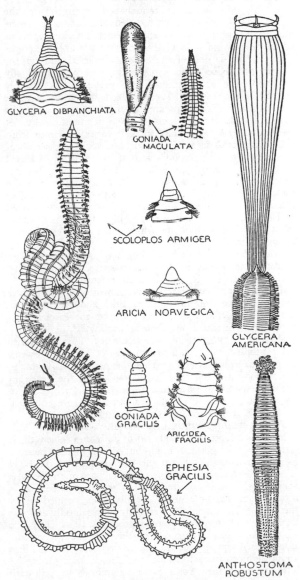

GLYCERA DIBRANCHIATA

GONIADA
MACULATA

SCOLOPLOS ARMIGER

ARICIA NORVEGICA

GLYCERA
AMERICANA

GONIADA
GRACILIS

ARICIDEA
FRAGILIS

EPHESIA
GRACILIS

ANTHOSTOMA
ROBUSTUM

Scoloplos armiger (O. F. Müller) PLATE 107. The head of this worm is cone-shaped, rising from the peristomial segment, which broadens the cone at the base, and is also seated on the still broader anterior segments of the body which converge to meet it, at an obtuse angle. The anterior region of the body is flattened and widens rapidly for about eight segments, then narrows gradually to about the sixteenth segment presenting a slightly convex outline. From that point on the body is more rounded, very gradually diminishing in diameter for its entire length of approximately 150 segments, when it terminates in a pair of anal cirri. It varies in length from 3 to 6 inches. The anterior region of about eighteen segments has lateral parapodia with short, stout, saw-toothed setae. From about that point on the parapodia become more dorsal in position, with the branchiae fairly near the middle line of the body. Outside of that is the bladelike dorsal cirrus, succeeded by the seta-bundle of the dorsal division of the parapodium. Finally, the double ventral lobes are situated laterally with a small cluster of setae between them.

The color of the body is deep red anteriorly shading gradually to orange in the more posterior segments. The back is suffused with a bluish green iridescence.

These worms live in sandy mud in which they find their food. They are found from the tidal zone to about 50 fathoms in northern seas. They occur on the eastern coast of North America from Canada northward.

Aricia norvegica M. Sars PLATE 107. This worm also has a pointed head, with no tentacles or eyes. A crescent-shaped groove separates it from the peristomial segment, which continues the cone-shaped outline of the head but rapidly expands at an obtuse angle. The branchiae begin on the fifth segment, of which about fifteen are equipped with setae. It lives in deep water on muddy bottoms.

Anthostoma robustum Verrill PLATE 107. This worm has a long, stout body up to 12 inches in length. It has an acutely pointed head, but the segments increase rapidly in diameter so that the thickest part of the body is in the anterior region. The posterior part of the body is very long, narrowing gradually to the caudal end. It is more or less flat or concave dorsally, and rounded below the parapodia. It is thicker vertically than laterally and has three rows of straplike, pointed processes along each side of the back and a pair of branched appendages on the side of each segment. It has a large proboscis, divided into about eighteen fingerlike lobes with much folded margins. The color of this worm is orange-yellow to yellowish brown. There are usually two rows of brown spots along the back and, posteriorly, there is a dorsal reddish line.

The branchiae are blood-red. When handled, this worm will break up with great ease, so that it is difficult to get an entire specimen (Verrill).

It occurs from Woods Hole to the New Jersey coast.

Suborder SPIONIFORMIA

The *Spioniformia* possess neither tentacles nor palps. The peristomium usually carries a pair of long tentacular cirri, and extends forward at the sides of the prostomium. The parapodia project only to a slight degree. The dorsal cirri may attain a considerable size, and act as gills throughout the greater part of the body. The chaetae are unjointed. Uncini are only present in the aberrant *Chaetopterus*. The body may present two regions more or less distinctly marked externally, but without corresponding internal differences. The buccal-region may be eversible, but there are no jaws. The worms are burrowers, or tube-builders.

Family Spionidae

The prostomial lobe is small, often with a bilobed margin. The eyes are often present and are frequently four in number. The proboscis is not conspicuous and seldom extruded. The anus is dorsal, usually surrounded by cirri, papillae, or with a sucker. The branchiae are of various forms, simple, strap-shaped, lanceolate, or like cirri. The parapodia are usually with two lobes with a lamella behind the double row of setae. The branchiae are simple.

Spio rathbuni Webster & Benedict PLATE 108. The head is oval, longer than wide, with slightly convex sides. The anterior end is emarginate. The posterior end is somewhat contracted. The anterior third forms an oval, flattened area in the middle of the head. The eyes are small and black and irregular in number, position, and form. They are situated on the oval space. They all differ from each other in certain respects. The tentacles are moderately stout, as long as the first eight segments, and taper to a slight degree. The large second segment envelopes the head on both sides as well as the anterior margin. An extensible proboscis is present. There are forty-nine segments altogether in this species within the body length, which is approximately ⅔ inch. This species lives in delicate sand tubes in the neighborhood of the low-water mark. It is found along the New England coast.

Spio setosa Verrill PLATE 108; COLOR PLATES VII, 7; VIII, 8. This species occurs abundantly near the low-water mark on sandy bottoms throughout Long Island Sound to Woods Hole and the Elizabeth Islands. It is usually more than 4 inches in length. The long and slender body is flattened over the dorsal region but more convex ventrally.

The head is rounded anteriorly, surmounted by a prominent cone-shaped median lobe which is flattened and turned up at the front. There are four eyes located at the summit of the head. On the first three or four segments, the upper lobe of the parapodia has a slender dorsal cirrus. The second segment, or peristomium, bears a pair of conspicuous tentacular cirri of considerable length, which tend to curl at the ends. The setae of the upper lobe are much longer and more slender than the others. The lower lobe is stouter and longest on the first three or four segments.

Scolecolepis cirrata Malmgren PLATE 108. This worm is 3 to 4 inches long and is chocolate brown in color, with bright red straplike dorsal breathing organs on the anterior third of the body. The front of the head is somewhat oval with rounded angles at the sides. Two large and conspicuous coiling tentacles (not shown in the figure) arise from the peristomium and are greenish in color. It is a northern species found in the Bay of Fundy, with its range extending to the Arctic and around to the northern European coasts. It is particularly abundant off Block Island and at Vineyard Sound in approximately 29 to 30 fathoms, as well as off Georges Bank from 110 to 150 fathoms.

Nerine heteropoda Webster PLATE 108. The top-shaped head is rounded and swollen at the base, coming to a conical point anteriorly. The second, or buccal, segment is fully as long as the head and cylindrical in shape. It bears a pair of long, slender, and tapering tentacular cirri near its posterior margin. Four small, black eyes are situated at the base of these tentacles, a group of two on either side. On the next segment, likewise on either side, there is a cluster of small setae with a rounded lobelike projection close to it. The following segment has a pair of small branchiae. These are repeated in each segment, increasing in size throughout the length of the body, until they practically touch each other on the back of the worm. On the anterior segments, the branchiae also bear a leaflike lobe with a short, rounded extremity. The ventral lobe of each parapodium, at first, is similar in structure to the dorsal lobes and divided into two parts. Toward the posterior portion of the worm, this division disappears while the end of the lobe becomes more slender and pointed. There is a fan of setae borne by each lobe of the parapodium. The worm has about forty segments within its total length of about ⅖ inch.

It is found in the Chesapeake Bay region.

Pygospio elegans Claparède PLATE 108. This is a small species, not much more than 1 inch in length, living in tiny sand-tubes. The head segment, shown in the plate, is more or less helmet-shaped and varies in proportionate

PLATE 108

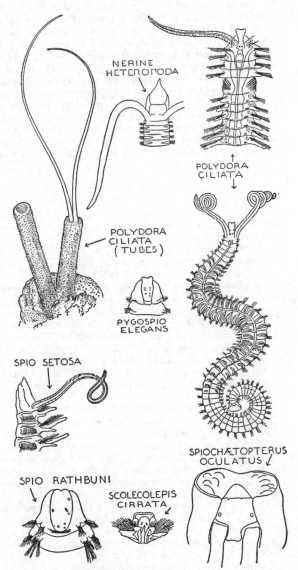

NERINE
HETEROPODA

POLYDORA
CILIATA

POLYDORA
CILIATA
(TUBES)

PYGOSPIO
ELEGANS

SPIO SETOSA

SPIO RATHBUNI

SCOLECOLEPIS
CIRRATA

SPIOCHÆTOPTERUS
OCULATUS

length. It is characterized by a distinct median, flat ridge which runs backward from the tip of the head to the end of the first segment. A variable number of paired eyespots are located on it. There may be two, four, or six of these. The figure shows a specimen with seven. There is a pair of long tentacles which springs from the mid-dorsal line of the peristomial segments. There are about forty segments, in all. The color is yellowish in the anterior segments, fading to white posteriorly. A red line shows the position of the dorsal blood vessel, while the digestive tract is marked by a brownish region about the middle of the body.

This worm is common on rocky coasts, between tides and in shallow water, in crevices among the rocks. On our coast, it is recorded as far south as Virginia. It occurs on both sides of the Atlantic.

Family Polydoridae

This species of this family are distinguished by having a considerably enlarged fifth segment with remarkably strong chaetae or spines. The anterior segments are without branchiae. There is a long pair of peristomial cirri, situated on either side of the prostomium. A flat, raised frontal ridge passes forward from the apex of the prostomium and around to the mouth on the ventral side.

Polydora ciliata Claparède PLATE 108. This very peculiar annulate occurs in large colonies building upright tubes in the sandy, muddy bottom at the low-tide mark. Shortly after the breeding season, the young are seen swimming freely at the surface of the water. The young worms are pale yellow in color with small, black spots between the parapodia. The antennae are white.

This species occurs abundantly along the coast of Massachusetts from the Woods Hole region to Nahant.

Family Chaetopteridae

The head-region is broad, flattened, and fused with various following segments. It has two long, grooved tentacles with an eye at the outer base of each. The mouth is large. The body has three regions: first, an anterior region, usually of nine bristled segments; second, a middle region of five segments, especially modified; and, third, a posterior region of a variable number of segments, each with a large dorsal lobe enclosing setae, and a ventral enlarged lobe with hooks. The fourth setigerous segment has setae which are especially powerful. These worms manufacture tubes, usually of a parchmentlike secretion and with two chimneys.

Chaetopterus pergamentaceus Cuvier COLOR PLATE IX. This worm, prominently pictured in COLOR PLATE IX, builds a U-shaped, parchmentlike tube buried in sandy mud. Hence the popular name, Parchment Worm. It is about 6 inches in length and is brightly luminescent in the dark. The tube is so built that its two chimneys extend above the sea-bottom. The anterior segments are coalesced to form a flattened shovel-shaped region, consisting of the prostomium, the peristomium, and several anterior segments. The broad mouth is at the anterior end of this section with a single pair of tentacular filaments, much reduced in size. The appendages of the middle segments of the body have united to form three circular "palettes," which fit closely to the interior of the tube and act like the pistons of a suction pump, drawing the sea water in through one chimney of the tube to flow out of the other. This incoming stream bears a multitude of minute organisms which form the food of the worm. They are abstracted by a special apparatus as the water current passes over its body and are taken up by a ciliated groove in the median line, which passes them forward in a continuous stream, to fall into the wide terminal mouth.

The rhythmic contractions of the circular palettes at the center of the body bring in sufficient current not only to supply the occupant of the tube, but to furnish food for two commensal crabs, male and female of the species *Pinnixa chaetopterana,* as well.

The sexes in this worm are separate and build separate tubes. Through the transparent integument of the body of the female worm may be seen the convolute yellow coils of the ovaries, which exude a continuous stream of matured pink-colored ova into the body-cavity of the abdomen, to be passed out, finally, through the anal opening. The testes of the male Parchment Worm also show through the abdomen wall, as whitish coils, which secrete the sperm, to be passed out of the body like the ova in the female. In each case, the ova and sperm are exuded into the tube, whence they are pumped out into the surrounding sea water to mingle and fertilize.

The chimneys of the Parchment Worm tubes can be seen in shallow water below the low-tide mark, especially in sheltered bays floored with sandy mud. They are especially abundant in the Woods Hole region. They range from Cape Cod to North Carolina on our shores and also in European waters.

Spiochaetopterus oculatus Webster PLATE 108. This species is closely related to the preceding, but is much smaller. The anterior region is composed of the buccal segment and nine setigerous segments. The middle region includes twenty to twenty-three segments, while the posterior region has numerous segments, variable in number.

As in the preceding species, the head is coalesced with the buccal segment and is prolonged backward between the bases of the other anterior tentacles. The tentacles project on either side of the mouth and are about an inch in length. There are two oval black eyes situated at the bases of the tentacles. The first pair of anterior parapodia are fleshy lobes, thick at the base, with a thin edge along the inner side, so that they are triangular in section. They bend over the body dorsally toward the mid-line and are directed forward, so that their flattened tips may be placed together.

In the posterior region, the cylindrical dorsal branches of the parapodia rise up vertically and terminate in a fleshy button. The ventral lobes are similar to those in the middle region, but are reduced in size. The anal segments have no appendages. They are conical in shape, close together, and divided below into lobes.

There is a densely ciliated groove running the entire length of the animal on the middle line. The edges of this groove may, at times, be brought together transforming it into a canal.

The anterior region is whitish above. The first six segments are white underneath with brownish specks blending into brownish purple. The middle and posterior regions are yellowish white above to light brown below.

The tube of the worm is clear white, gradually shading to yellowish white or brown. It has ringlike bands which may be black, white, or the color of the tube. It has a diameter of approximately 1 millimeter, while the length of the animal varies from 1 to 2 inches. It has been found in sand in low water off the coast of Virginia.

Family Magelonidae

This family was erected for the very remarkable and unique worm, *Magelona papillicornis,* which is the only species it contains. The outstanding characteristics are the flat, spoon-shaped prostomium; the two long tentacles (*peristomial cirri*); the ability to evert the entire anterior portion of the body, comprising the first eight segments, for respiratory purposes; and, the division of the body into three distinct regions, due to differences in its parapodial chaetae.

Magelona papillicornis F. Müller PLATE 109. The head, or prostomium, is large and spoon-shaped and acts as a dorsal roof for the peristome. The mouth is on the ventral side, through which the proboscis can be extruded. The anterior region of the body is composed of eight segments. It is quadrangular in cross-section, marked by dorsal and ventral longitudinal bands and similar parapodial armature. The second region consists of the single ninth segment, much narrower than the rest, and differing in structure from all the rest of the segments. The third region is

PLATE 109

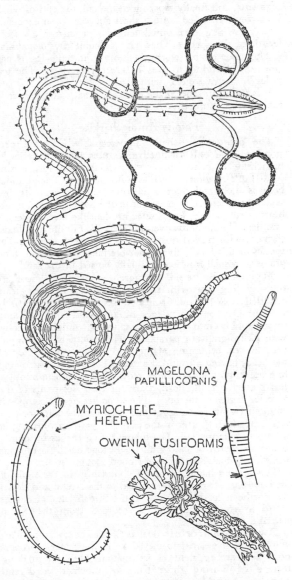

MAGELONA
PAPILLICORNIS

MYRIOCHELE
HEERI

OWENIA FUSIFORMIS

the longest, composed of the rest of the body, with many segments, and finally tapering to the tail, the end of which is convexly rounded, with a short anal cirrus on each side. The very long peristomial tentacles or cirri are characteristic of this species. They have a double row of papillae.

The color of this worm, including the tentacles, is pale rose-pink, blending to gray or green posteriorly. The tentacles are often banded with black.

It is found in sand at the low-water mark and deeper. It ranges from Europe to America.

Family Ammocharidae

The prostomium shades imperceptibly into the peristomium, the only distinctive features being a series of branching branchiae in certain species, probably arising from the peristome, which is without setae. The rounded body is short and slightly narrowed posteriorly, with few segments, decreasing in length in the posterior region and bearing setae. The dorsal setae are hairlike and in slender bundles. The numerous ventral setae are minute and hook-formed, with curved tips arranged in transverse rows. The species of this family live in flexible tubes coated with sand grains and shell fragments, usually buried in the sand.

Myriochele heeri Malmgren PLATE 109. These are tube-building worms of simple aspect, the reduced head, rounded dorsally and truncated ventrally, being entirely without eyes or appendages of any kind and blending imperceptibly into the short, tapering, simplified body, with its insignificant parapodia. The mouth is an oblique, vertical slot, beginning at the apex of the ventral side of the head, having a rounded anterior border and narrowing to a point, posteriorly. Three reduced pairs of seta bundles, just posterior to the head, mark the three segments of the anterior region of the body. The second region is composed of about twenty-seven segments, longer in the anterior portion and much shorter in the posterior part, terminating in a bluntly tapering tail. The tube is 2 to 4 inches in length. It is constructed of sand-grains held together by a mucous secretion, which also forms a smooth, tough lining.

This species has been found abundantly in the Gulf of St. Lawrence. It ranges northward to the Arctic and down the northern coast of Europe to the British Isles, at depths of 16 to 40 fathoms, and is recorded from the North Atlantic generally.

Owenia fusiformis Della Chiaje PLATE 109. This worm, though related to the above in the general proportions and arrangement of its anatomy, has the striking feature of bearing three pairs of much divided and branched branchiae from the peristome, the trunks of which are each divided into two stems, and then into four, and so on, except that the terminal branches are more numerous, short, truncated, and glandular. These extend from the tube-opening like a much-foliated nosegay of translucent, greenish blue, yellow and red-tinted fronds, surrounded by a collarlike fold of the body-wall inside the tube-opening. The animal is from 1 to 2 inches in length. The tube is constructed of closely set shell-fragments, held together by a tough mucous secretion.

This is a circumboreal species, extending from the shores of New England around the North Atlantic to northern Europe and British waters, in depths of 30–40 fathoms.

Suborder TEREBELLIFORMIA

The prostomium is a more or less prominent lobe (upper lip) with or without tentacles but without palps. The peristomium may carry cirri or "tentacular filaments." The parapodia are feebly developed. There are no ventral cirri. The dorsal cirri may exist and function as gills on some of the anterior segments. The chaetae are unjointed and uncini are usually present. The buccal region is not eversible and there are no jaws. These worms are burrowers or tube-builders and, for the most part, the tube-forming glands are grouped on the ventral surface of the anterior segments to form "gland-shields."

Family Cirratulidae

The head is distinct but small, with no appendages. The peristomial segment has the ventral mouth. The proboscis is always unarmed. Two segments without chaetae follow. The body is linear, filiform, elongated, with numerous narrow rings. Tentacles are present or absent, dorsal or ventral. The branchiae are long, filiform, contractile, and dorso-lateral in position, on many or a considerable number of segments. The corpuscles in the blood of *C. chrysoderma,* are flattened-fusiform in shape. In this and others, their color is identical with the liquid in which they float. The feet are biramous, with divisions separate; without setigerous processes or appendages; the superior division generally with capillary setae, or with setae and crotchets (hooks); and the inferior division with shorter setae or with these and crotchets or crotchets alone.

Cirratulus grandis Verrill PLATE 110; COLOR PLATE VII, 8. The Fringed Worm. This is a large, stout worm, 6 inches in length, with a diameter of ¼ inch or more. The head is very small and pointed, without distinct eye-spots. The body is more or less cylindrical anteriorly, but somewhat flattened posteriorly. The posterior end is obtuse, with the anus surrounded by a wrinkled border. The first seven segments following the mouth are without appendages. The eighth and ninth segments have two bundles of small setae on each side, together with two dorsal clusters of long, slender, branchial cirri. The bases of these clusters nearly meet on the mid-dorsal line. They consist of a large number of closely crowded cirri of various lengths. The parapodia, all along the body, are greatly reduced, consisting of very small bundles of setae connected by a slightly raised region. Along almost the entire length of the body, bundles of slender branchial cirri extend from the various segments, the annulations of which are very numerous and distinct. The color is yellow, shading into yellowish green, or orange to orange-brown and often with a play of iridescent colors beneath. The branchial cirri are translucent golden-yellow with a red central line, representing a blood vessel.

These cirri are continually extending and contracting, making a spectacular display. The Fringed Worm burrows in the mud and gravel beneath stones and constructs soft tubes which may entirely enclose it. It is very common, being found from the low-water mark to 6 fathoms of depth along the entire coast of New England.

Cirratulus cirratus (O. F. Müller) PLATE 110. This species is smaller than the preceding, but quite similar to it. The head is made up of the prostomium, with a row of eyes and a peristomium. It is about 3½ inches in length. It builds its tubes under stones. It replaces *Cirratulus grandis* north of Cape Cod, along the coasts of Maine and Europe.

Dodecaceria concharum Oersted PLATE 110. This little worm excavates its tubes in the shells of *Cyprina islandica,* found after storms on New England beaches, and of the scallop, *Pecten tenuicostatus,* in the Bay of Fundy. It is related to *Naraganseta coralii,* which burrows in the coral colonies of *Astrangia danae.* These were found by Verrill on the reef off Watch Hill, Rhode Island. They were dark greenish brown or black in color with brown-orange-colored branchiae.

Family Terebellidae

The upper lip of the prostomium is somewhat reduced and semicircular, usually forming an oval lobe above the mouth. The head is equipped with numerous grooved and ciliated tentacles, usually in two symmetrical bundles, springing from the peristomium. A thick roll behind the tentacles forms a tentacular membrane. The free border of the peristomium is the lower lip. The eyes are simple. The body is wormlike, tapering posteriorly, with smooth skin. The anterior region resembles a thorax, differing from the abdominal posterior region. The branchiae are in pairs on the second or following segments, branching, rarely thread-like. The anterior setae are in two rows from the eleventh

PLATE 110

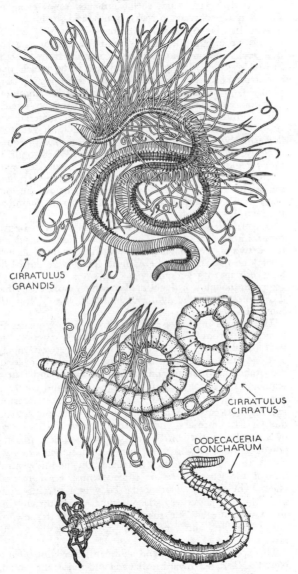

CIRRATULUS
GRANDIS

CIRRATULUS
CIRRATUS

DODECACERIA
CONCHARUM

segment, usually with wings. They build membranous tubes coated with mud, shell-fragments, sand, etc., and they may be adherent to rocks, stones, and shells.

Amphitrite ornata Verrill COLOR PLATE VII, 9; VIII, 9. This worm builds its tubes of mud and sand among and over rocks and on muddy shores. It may be from 12 to 15 inches in length. It has a flesh-colored body, which may vary from reddish to orange-brown, and three pairs of large plumelike, many-branched blood-red gills. It has numerous flesh-colored tentacles, which are always in motion, stretching out and contracting while gathering the materials for its tube construction. This is one of the most beautiful flowerlike worms along our coast. Its tubes have a round opening, ¼ inch or more in diameter. When built in sandy regions, it is surrounded by a low mound of sand, often widely different in color from that of the surrounding sea-bottom. It is common around and below the low-water mark, in sand and gravel, from Vineyard Sound to the New Jersey coast.

Amphitrite figulus Dalyell (= **Amphitrite brunnea** Stimpson) PLATE III. These were formerly considered to be two species, having been described simultaneously (1853) on both sides of the Atlantic. They were united by McIntosh in 1873 and this view has since been generally accepted, though it is doubtful as to which name really has the priority. Both the figures of McIntosh and Verrill are shown on PLATE III.

The worms in this species vary from 6 to 8 inches in length. The body is large in front but tapers posteriorly to the bluntly pointed anal segment. There are between ninety and one hundred segments. There are three pairs of blood-red branching branchiae on the second, third, and fourth segments respectively, continually expanding and contracting, similar to those in *Amphitrite ornata*. The seta-bearing segments (twenty-four in number) start with the fourth, though a rudimentary tendency to this feature is indicated by a papilla on the third segment. Each segment is composed of two body-rings, at first, but in subsequent segments, this number becomes increased. On the mid-ventral side of the worm there are fifteen scutes, or segmental plates. The general color of the body is a varying flesh tone, though, posteriorly, the intestine shows through as an orange streak. The tube, built of shelly fragments, minute pebbles, and sandy mud, crumbles easily in the fingers.

This species has a wide and abundant distribution from New England, northward to Canada and the Arctic Ocean, and around to Scandinavia, Britain, and European shores generally, including the Mediterranean Sea. It is found in

PLATE 111

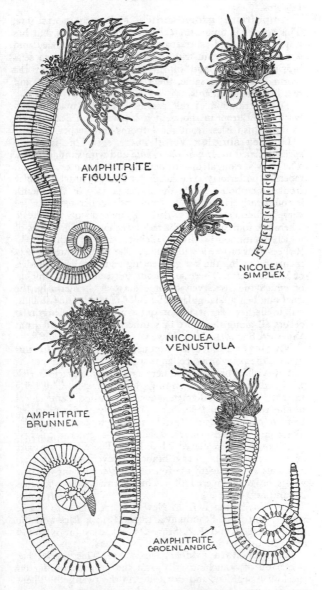

AMPHITRITE
FIGULUS

NICOLEA
SIMPLEX

NICOLEA
VENUSTULA

AMPHITRITE
BRUNNEA

AMPHITRITE
GROENLANDICA

shallow water, from the low-water mark to more than 100 fathoms.

Amphitrite groenlandica Malmgren PLATE 111. This species is quite similar to *Amphitrite ornata,* but has much shorter and more sparsely branched branchiae, with a much shorter main trunk. There are only nineteen seta-bearing segments and fifteen scutes. The length of the worm is about the same, there being between ninety and one hundred segments.

The distribution of this species is from Canada northward. On European shores, it is known from Scandinavia to the British Isles, from 100 fathoms and deeper.

Nicolea simplex Verrill PLATE 111. This is also a species related to *Amphitrite ornata* and with similar habits. The body is elongated, considerably swollen anteriorly, and tapering posteriorly. The head has a large, nearly circular frontal membrane, while the posterior fold of the mouth is comparatively small. The long and slender tentacles are very numerous and crowded together about the head. There are four small, bright red branchiae, the branches of which continuously divide dichotomously, with the V-shaped divisions at a wide angle. The fifteen anterior segments, following the last gill-bearing segment, have bundles of slender setae. There are about thirteen ventral shields, of which the last seven become narrower posteriorly, the final one being triangular. The color of the animal is light red to flesh color. It is not quite 2 inches in length. It occurs all along the shore of southern New England from Vineyard Sound to New Haven.

Nicolea venustula (Montagu) PLATE 111. In this species, the peristomial collar is small. A row of eyespots is clearly visible behind it. There are many tentacles, each with a distinct groove running along one side. The body increases slightly in diameter toward the middle and tapers to the rounded anal segment. The body is composed of forty to fifty segments (rarely seventy to one hundred). There are thirteen ventral shields. The general color is pale brown with scattered white spots. There are two pairs of branchiae with a few branches, seventeen setigerous segments starting with the fourth, the setae having narrow wings on their tapered tips. This worm builds soft tubes of sand and mud.

The distribution is from New England north to Arctic waters, and from Scandinavia to the British Isles and the Mediterranean and Red Seas. On our coast, it is found between tide-marks and in shallow waters.

Pista cristata (Müller) PLATE 112. This species has two pairs of branching gills with the setae beginning on the fourth segment and extending to the twentieth. There are no eyes. It is closely related to *Scionopsis palmata,* differing from it only "in the extent of the collar formed by the third segment and the structure of the branchiae," which, in the present species, have long stems, many and finely divided filaments, forming a dense and whorled, bushy structure. They spring from the anterior border of the fourth segment. The body is reddish orange in its general coloration, the scutes each having a bright orange stripe.

This species ranges from Virginia, northward to New England and the Atlantic Coast generally, and to the Arctic Ocean. On the European side of the Atlantic, it is found from Scandinavia to the British Isles and the Mediterranean Sea.

Scionopsis palmata Verrill PLATE 113. The elongated, slender body is composed of numerous segments of which seventeen, following the third segment, have fascicles of slender setae, and the remainder have only small hook-bearing lobes. The setigerous segments are all quite prominent, with rather long setae. The setae, beginning with the second setigerous segment, are also hook-bearing and these continue on smaller parapodia behind the last setigerous segment. There are about twenty rectangular ventral shields, of which the first are transversely situated. The following ones are approximately square, but become gradually quite narrow posteriorly, with the anal segment tapering to a sharp angle. The branchiae are quite large, with stout and quite long main stems, crowned with branching palmate tops, usually to the number of four or five, which spread out from the main stem to a feathery cluster. The branchial collar is formed from the margin of the third segment and is divided into two tapering prolongations pointing forward. From the margin of the second segment arises an expansion known as the tentacular collar, having a broad lobe on each side. The cephalic segment has a broad frontal membrane. The tentacles have very numerous, flesh-colored, slender processes extending out in close association with the branchiae.

The color, as a whole, shades from light red to dark reddish brown. The cross-annulations are often darker. The body is largely speckled with white and there is usually a row of bright red rectangular spots on each side connected around the lower part of the body by narrow transverse lines of red between the yellowish red ventral shields. The branchiae are usually green, also speckled with white. A network of blood vessels shows through the integument in all the segments. This worm is nearly 3 inches long. It is found from the low-water mark to a depth of one fathom from Vineyard Sound to New Haven.

Polycirrus eximius Verrill PLATE 112. This is a species with very numerous tentacles which characteristically extend in all directions. Irregular drops of blood forced into the tentacles distend them irregularly as the blood passes through their central canal. There are twenty-five setigerous segments, each with its bundle of slender setae. Posterior to these are seventy segments with hooklike processes (uncini). There are nine ventral shields, each one divided transversely by a median groove. The frontal lobe of the head is elliptical. The posterior lobe of the mouth is rounded. Both the body and the tentacles are bright red in color, though the former verges into yellow posteriorly. This species is found from Vineyard Sound to New Haven from the low-water mark to 10 fathoms.

Trichobranchus glacialis Malmgren PLATE 113. This is a small, brilliantly scarlet-colored worm about 1 inch in length, occurring on muddy bottoms at depths of 9 to 100 fathoms. The head is quite small and divided into two rounded lobes with numerous eyespots at their base. The peristomium forms a rolling lip. Three pairs of single, unbranched branchiae, threadlike in appearance, spring from the second, third, and fourth segments, and twist and turn in contorted and spiral movements. They are pale pink in color. The head proper, on the dorsal side, is separated from the first segment by a groove, and, on its double surface, gives rise to multitudinous tentacles of two kinds, *filiform* (threadlike) and *clavate* (club-shaped). The latter are grooved and streaked with red, while the former are pale pink. They are all in continuous movement. The body is largest anteriorly, with a rounded frontal margin. Posteriorly, it tapers through its seventy segments to the terminal anus, equipped with a pair of cirri.

This species ranges from New England, northward to the Arctic, and southward on the European coast to Britain, France, and the Mediterranean Sea.

Terebellides stroemi Sars PLATE 112. There is a pair of branching gills, each of which forms four tapering plumes of blood-red, branching out from a single stem. There are more than 100 delicate threadlike tentacles surmounting the anterior end of the body, which, in turn, has about sixty segments. This worm is about 3 inches long and occurs from 10 fathoms to the edge of the Continental Shelf from the Bay of Fundy to Vineyard Sound. Its range also extends around Greenland, Iceland, Spitzbergen, and the northern coasts of Europe. There are also records of its occurrence in the Adriatic Sea.

Thelepus cincinnatus (Fabricius) PLATE 112. This worm is about 6 inches in length. Its body-shape, in general, resembles that of typical terebellids, being enlarged anteriorly and tapering to the anal segment, which, in this

PLATE 112

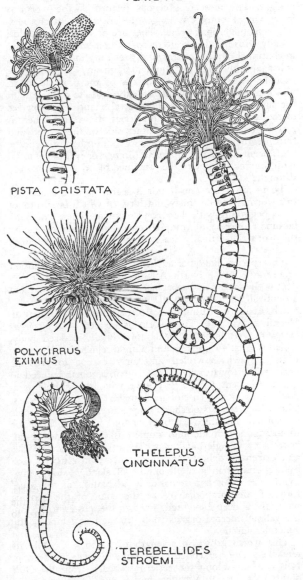

PISTA CRISTATA

POLYCIRRUS
EXIMIUS

THELEPUS
CINCINNATUS

TEREBELLIDES
STROEMI

case, is peculiar in having about twelve papillae at its margin. The most conspicuous feature of the worm is its crown of numerous long and powerful tentacles arising from the cephalic plate. They are orange to flesh-color, usually with red dots scattered over their surface. They are in continual motion, coiling and stretching in all directions, and enable the animal to pull itself in any direction. The cephalic plate is backed up dorsally by the cephalic collar, which passes down ventrally on either side to connect with the supra-oral arch above the ventral mouth. The surface of the collar is equipped with a series of eyespots. There is a pair of branchial tufts on either side of the second and third segments, each composed of a number of delicate, translucent, threadlike filaments, orange or yellow in color, with the fine red line of the contained blood vessel showing through.

There are about one hundred segments in the body of this worm, between thirty and forty of which bear tufts of setae, beginning with the second segment. These gradually become reduced and vestigial toward the posterior end of the worm, and finally cease altogether before the tail is reached.

This species, like other terebellids, has a wide distribution around the entire North Atlantic area at greater or less depths. In fact, it is probably cosmopolitan, being present around all the continents of the globe.

Chaetobranchus (Enoplobranchus) sanguineus Verrill PLATE 113. This worm is related to *Polycirrus eximius*, resembling it in its threadlike blood-red body, which is greatly elongated and without closed blood vessels. It is somewhat swollen anteriorly except toward the head, while toward the caudal end it becomes reduced to a mere filament. Unlike *Polycirrus*, which has simple parapodia, those of this species are branched except for the first pair, which consists of short, simple cirri. The second pair are forked. The third has three or four branches. Posterior to these, they divide into numerous branches which all arise from a single basal stem. These branches are slender and extremely delicate and are gathered in clusters, each branch ending in a small bundle of slender, sharp, sawtooth setae. This is a remarkable adaptation of the usual form of the parapodia. While the color of the body is naturally a deep blood-red, toward the posterior region, the yellow internal organs show through and modify the general coloration.

This worm grows to a length of 14 inches, while its tentacles may be extended to the same distance in addition. It is common along the eastern seaboard from the Gulf of St. Lawrence to Virginia, and is readily found at the low-water mark in mud and sand.

Family Ampharetidae

The cephalic lobe covers the mouth, the median part divided by oblique grooves; long, smooth, pinnate, or ciliated tentacles arise from the mouth. The peristomium surrounds the mouth forming the lower lip. The tentacular membrane is divided by two longitudinal grooves into three parts. There is a groove between the tentacles and the mouth. The body is wide in front, tapering posteriorly, with a variable number of segments, usually twenty to forty. There are four, rarely three, pairs of branchiae, which are thread-shaped and sometimes pinnate. The anal segment may be with or without two or more cirri. The posterior parapodia have dorsal cirri. These are tube-builders utilizing mud, fragments of algae, or shells for their houses.

Ampharete gracilis Malmgren PLATE 113. This worm grows to a length of from 1 to 1½ inches. It has a flesh-colored body which shades into green posteriorly, diversified by a conspicuous red median line caused by the dorsal blood vessel showing through the integument. The branchiae are light green. There is a bundle of setae on each side of the head in front of the gills, while the tentacular filaments are few in number. There are four pairs of filamentous, unbranched gills on the third and fourth segments. The body has from twelve to thirteen hook-bearing (*uncigerous*) segments posteriorly. The range of this species is from the Bay of Fundy to Marthas Vineyard and Block Island, in a depth of 10 to 90 fathoms. It is also found off the northern coasts of Europe.

Ampharete acutifrons (Grube) PLATE 113; **Ampharete setosa** Verrill (not illustrated). These are closely related to the above species. *Ampharete acutifrons* is somewhat shorter than *A. gracilis* and not so slender. *Ampharete setosa* has quite a thick body anteriorly, which tapers rapidly backward. The latter species has eight rather short branchiae. The fourteen segments have small bundles of long setae. The posterior portion of the body has about ten segments, without setae. The animals are small with two long, slender cirri. The general coloration is a translucent light yellow-green, except anteriorly, where it is tinged with bright blood-red. The branchiae are greenish. It is about ⅘ inch long and is found off New Haven around the low-water mark to about 6 fathoms. The tubes of both these species are about 1 inch long and covered with thick sand and mud (Verrill).

Melinna cristata (Sars) PLATE 113. In this species there are four pairs of long, evenly tapering branchiae arising from a double base on each side of the fourth segment. The dorsal collar has ten to twenty conical projections on its rim. Eighteen anterior segments are equipped with setigerous parapodia, beginning with the fifth segment. The body is about 2 inches in length tapering to the anus, which is provided with flaps at its aperture. The tube is of mucus, coated with mud. This species is found on both sides of the North Atlantic.

Amage auricula Malmgren PLATE 113. This is a comparatively short worm, about ½ inch in length. It is club-shaped, with a broad head-region, and tapers to the bluntly pointed tail-segment, with its terminal anus and two short caudal cirri. There are about twenty-eight segments, of which the third and fourth bear the long, smooth, tapering and unbranched branchiae, four on each side. The head is bent downward, with the lobes of the peristomium supporting it on either side and below. The threadlike tentacles are smooth. Fourteen anterior segments, including the gill-bearing third and fourth, have golden *chaetae*. *Uncini* (tooth-bearing hooks) occur, beginning with the fourth to the sixth segment. The tubes are covered with soft mud.

This species is distributed on both sides of the North Atlantic, ranging from New England to Norway and Britain.

Amphicteis gunneri Sars PLATE 113. The head-region of this worm is somewhat shield-shaped, with a ridge running forward on each side to the prominent lower lip, which is scalloped at the edge. The tentacles, about twenty in number, threadlike in shape, project from the mouth. There are four branchiae on each side, massive, long, and smooth, rising from the third, fourth, and part of the fifth segments. The chaetae begin on the parapodia of the third segment. On this segment, they are modified on either side to form the fanlike *paleae*, conspicuous golden, needlelike setae, arranged in an expanding curving cluster on either side, the concavity of the fan directed upward, and each containing fourteen to twenty setae. The seta segments number seventeen, occurring in tufts from cylindrical lobes of the parapodia. A club-shaped papilla is ventral to them on each segment. A flat scalelike lamella represents the ventral lobe of the parapodia and encloses the uncini, or hooks, which are continued to the end of the body beyond the termination of the seta-bearing segments.

The color of this species is pale yellow, blending to rose on the ventral side. The brown tone of the stomach and the green blood vessels show through the semitransparent integument. The branchiae are green, banded with brown, white, and yellow. The tube is constructed of mucus covered with mud in which fragments of algae tend to become imbedded.

The distribution is on both sides of the North Atlantic.

PLATE 113

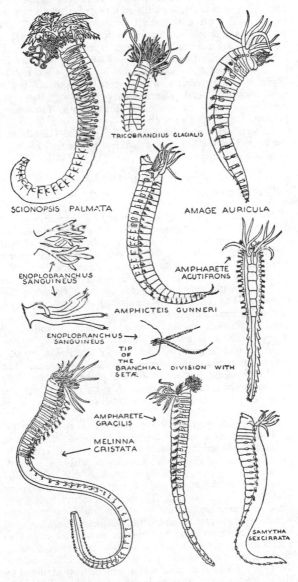

TRICOBRANCHUS GLACIALIS

SCIONOPSIS PALMATA

AMAGE AURICULA

ENOPLOBRANCHUS
SANGUINEUS

AMPHARETE
ACUTIFRONS

AMPHICTEIS GUNNERI

ENOPLOBRANCHUS →
SANGUINEUS
TIP
OF
THE
BRANCHIAL DIVISION WITH
SETÆ.

AMPHARETE →
GRACILIS

MELINNA
CRISTATA

SAMYTHA
SEXCIRRATA

Samytha sexcirrata (Sars) PLATE 113. This is a somewhat similar species with an elevated, smooth frontal-region and with a shortened peristomial segment. The tentacles are threadlike, smooth, and slightly enlarged at the tip. Three pairs of fairly long, tapering branchiae are borne on the third and fourth segments. The posterior lip is conspicuous and resembles the lip of a pitcher. The lateral line of parapodia on the successive segments, beginning with the fourth, comprises seventeen segments, converging ventrally at about the seventeenth. Hooks are present, each with five teeth.

This species ranges from New England to Canada and the Arctic; on the European coast, from Norway to Britain, in about 100 fathoms.

Family Amphictenidae

The head-region is obliquely truncate or semicircular, with two rows of powerful golden combs (*paleae*) made of hard, curved bristles, which exactly fit the opening of the tube. Above the combs is a firm area with smooth or fringed border. Beneath them is a membranous, fan-shaped veil margined with cirri. On the dorsal side of the mouth there is a group of contractile, grooved tentacles on either side. There are two tentacular cirri on either side, one arising from the side of the head, the other from the first segment. The body is of comparatively few segments, but of several differentiated regions: a peristomial region, a thoracic region without hooks, an abdominal region with a lamella for hooks, and finally, a posterior caudal region of five to six segments, usually bent at an angle, with a valvular flap above the anus. The bundle of setae has traces of wings on the tips. The parapodia are greatly reduced, as this is a tube-builder and manufactures a trumpet-shaped tube of carefully-welded sand-grains.

Cistenides gouldii Verrill COLOR PLATES VII, 10; IX, 3. This is a very remarkable and beautiful little worm, abundantly found burrowing in sandy mud. It constructs graceful, trumpet-shaped tubes which it builds of a single layer of sand-grains, carefully selected so that the smaller grains are at the small end of the tube and the larger grains at the large end. These are exactly and neatly cemented together by means of an adhering substance which resists water action. The obliquely truncated head of the worm emerges from the large end of the tube, into which it can retract when disturbed. Two pairs of long, tapering antennae extend forward, one on either side of the head. There is a semicircular veil in front, fringed by about twenty-eight long and slender papillae. Extending upward are two sets of long, golden setae (*paleae*), about fifteen in each set. These are slightly curved, closely set together, and have very sharp points. The worm utilizes these golden combs in digging its burrow, which it does, head downward. In front of the head is a crowded cluster of numerous, flattened, flesh-colored tentacles, each of which folds lengthwise, so as to form a groove underneath. There are two pairs of bright red branchial plumes on either side of the head region. The body of this worm is flesh-color, mottled with dark red and blue. It is stout, somewhat tapering, and quite smooth, the parapodia alone indicating its segmental repetition. These consist of fleshy lobes, each with a bundle of golden setae, diminishing toward the posterior end of the body, which is without setae and bent backward upon itself.

This species is abundant from Maine to North Carolina, at low-water mark, and to about 10 fathoms.

Suborder CAPITELLIFORMIA

The *Capitelliformia* have a pair of large, retractile, ciliated organs instead of prostomial processes, which they lack entirely. The parapodia do not project from the body. All chaetae are unjointed, being hairlike in the anterior part of the body and hooded crotchets posteriorly. There are no cirri. While there is no armed pharynx, the buccal region is eversible. There is no system of blood vessels, but red corpuscles are free in the coelom. All these worms are burrowers.

Family Capitellidae

At first sight, the members of this family resemble earthworms, since the head-region is pointed, and the body is round and seems to be practically devoid of appendages. These worms, however, have eyes in the form of pigment specks and two rounded tentacles on the head. There is an eversible burrowing proboscis, covered with papillae, which can be projected from the mouth. The long, reddish, distinctly segmented body is differentiated into two regions. The anterior region has nine to fourteen segments with rudimentary parapodia and fine setae. The posterior region has rows of retractile hooks and terminates in an anus having papillae. Also, in the posterior part of the body, there are branchiae at the ends of the rows of hooks, remaining permanently in view or being partially or wholly retractile. They contain a coelomic fluid with colored corpuscles and colorless plasma. In most of the segments, side-organs exist in a lateral groove anteriorly but, in the posterior regions of the worm, the side-organs project freely. There are cuplike organs on the proboscis, head, and body. There are no closed blood vessels, the circulatory system being represented by the coelomic haemolymph. Segmental organs exist in most segments, though in some species they are confined to a definite region.

Capitella capitata (O. Fabricius) PLATE 114. The entire body of this creature is conspicuously ringed, with many segments, and tapers at both ends. The color is blood-red. The head is sharp-pointed and conical but, unlike the earthworm, it has a pair of laterally situated eyes, with a papilla (*nuchal organ*) immediately behind each. The body is approximately 5 inches in length. An anterior region of about nine segments is differentiated because of their larger size, with the male copulatory opening between the eighth and ninth segments with two series of converging spines anterior and posterior to it. The sexes are separate. The female apparatus is situated between the seventh and eighth segments. Following the peristomial segment, which is without setae, seven segments are equipped with four rows of golden-colored bristles. Beginning with the ninth segment, there are hooks instead of bristles. All the segments posterior to the anterior region, are quite short and compressed. The red color of the body is in a continuous state of fluctuation, due to the motion of the red coelomic fluid through the waves of contraction passing through the body.

This worm is found near the low-tide mark in wet, gravelly places and under stones. It is cosmopolitan in distribution.

Notomastus latericius Sars PLATE 114. A similar species to the preceding. The head is conical and sharp-pointed, consisting of two rings. The first twelve segments are larger than those posterior to them. The latter have a central band on the ventral side marked by a double groove. The color is deep red, anteriorly, blending into brown, and then gray, posteriorly. The body is 6 to 10 inches in length.

This worm occurs abundantly in sandy bottoms from 80 to 100 fathoms in depth, and is often tossed ashore after storms. It is almost cosmopolitan in distribution.

Suborder SCOLECIFORMIA

The prostomium possessed by the species in this suborder rarely bears any sensory organs except in the Family Chlorhaemidae. The peristomium has no cirri, with the same exception. The parapodia are rudimentary or nonexistent. For the most part, dorsal cirri, acting as branchiae, are absent. This is also true of the ventral cirri. The chaetae are unjointed and uncini are not present. As in the Suborder Capitelliformia, here also, the buccal region is eversible, but there is no armed pharynx. The septa are irregularly existent. These worms are mostly burrowers.

PLATE 114

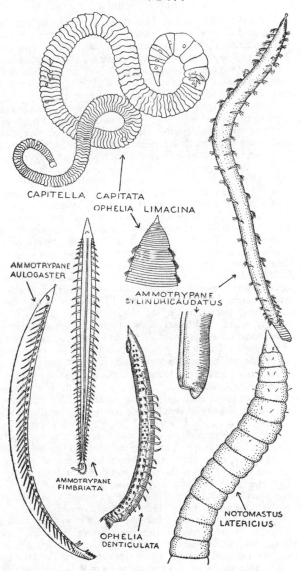

CAPITELLA CAPITATA

OPHELIA LIMACINA

AMMOTRYPANE
AULOGASTER

AMMOTRYPANE
CYLINDRICAUDATUS

AMMOTRYPANE
FIMBRIATA

OPHELIA
DENTICULATA

NOTOMASTUS
LATERICIUS

Family Opheliidae

The head is elongate and pointed, with slight differentiation, and ciliated organs may be extended from pits in the posterior portion. Eyes may or may not be present. The buccal segment is without tentacles, but usually has setae and a setigerous process. The short body is divided into two regions and, in some cases, slightly tapered toward each end. The anus often has valvelike processes.

Ammotrypane fimbriata Verrill PLATE 114. Among the worms found on muddy bottoms on exposed parts of the coast is this elongated, slender worm which tapers at both ends in streamlined fashion. It is thickest somewhat in advance of the middle of the body and has a generally convex outline on both sides. It is rounded above and somewhat less rounded underneath the body, with margins rising to a deep median groove on either side, which separates the upper and under surface. The head is quite pointed and has two small, black eyes. It has a small, almost spherical proboscis. The branchiae are quite long and slender. The posterior end of the body tapers to a small diameter and then enlarges to a spoon-shaped, deeply concave terminal structure. This peculiar appendage is fringed with a row of tiny, slender papillae. A pair of cirri arises from its base, ventrally, and a longer median cirrus extends from out its cavity. The color is purplish flesh-color, iridescent on the dorsal surface. There is a row of dark oval spots between the fascicles of dark gray setae on either side. The individuals of this species may reach a length of 3 inches. It is found from the Bay of Fundy to Buzzards Bay in 110 to 150 fathoms.

Ammotrypane aulogaster H. Rathke PLATE 114. Like the previous species, the body is fusiform. It tapers to a point at either end and consists of about fifty segments. The very sharply pointed head terminates in a curious stalked organ with a tiny knob at the summit (*mucro*). There are no tentacles or eyes, but there is a pair of posterior nuchal organs. The body is rounded dorsally and marked by faint cross-striae. Ventrally, there is a deep groove which extends the entire length of the body. Laterally, there are muscular ridges from which the parapodia are articulated. The latter consist of a long, straplike dorsal cirrus, ventral to which there is a small lobe bearing a cluster of fine hairlike bristles and a short ventral cirrus. The last pair of dorsal cirri, just above the anus, are larger, stout and muscular, and overhang the margin of a spoon-shaped organ, which terminates in a pointed cone. The hollow of this expansion faces ventrally and has a series of short cirri on its posterior border.

The coloration of this species is yellowish dorsally, with

brownish markings blending with flesh-color on the ventral side and ending in a red-tipped tail. The whole animal is suffused with a pearly iridescence.

This is a creature of very active habits, darting back and forth through the water with great speed, and plunging into the sandy mud of the bottom. It occurs below the low-tide mark and deeper.

This is a northern species, found on both sides of the North Atlantic.

Ammotrypane cylindricaudatus Hansen PLATE 114. This is related to the previous species, but has a longer and much slenderer body, which tapers to a pointed snout anteriorly, but is practically parallel-sided and tapers only very slightly posteriorly until quite close to the anus. The dorsal cirri on the limbs are much longer than in the preceding species, especially toward the tail-region. The mucro on the snout is club-shaped, rather than spherical, and the tail ends in an elongate cylindrical structure.

This species occurs in northern Atlantic waters, especially off the Gulf of St. Lawrence, generally in fairly deep water.

Ophelia limacina (Rathke) PLATE 114 (= **Ophelia denticulata** Verrill PLATE 114). The head is a pointed cone, which McIntosh suggests "may be useful in boring, as it is rendered tense by the waves of the perivisceral fluid, which also cause the proboscis to protrude as a pink frilled mass marked by fine grooves. The strong muscles of the region behind also probably aid in stiffening the pointed snout."

The mouth is opposite the first pair of parapodia. This worm is two inches or more in length and spindle-shaped. It is round dorsally, but deeply grooved ventrally. It is nearly parallel-sided, but converges rapidly toward the end of the body to the anus which is surrounded by a number of short cirri. In the forward part of the body, three rings are included in every segment. Posteriorly, these are reduced to a single ring each. The proboscis, when everted, is button-shaped.

The color is deep red, with a bluish iridescence, while the cirri have a golden hue. This seems to be a comparatively inactive and sluggish species.

This species ranges from Cape Cod northward to the Arctic and to European and British shores.

Ophelia denticulata Verrill PLATE 114. [= **O. limacina** (Rathke) PLATE 114]. This species, described by Verrill, is closely similar to *Ophelia limacina,* but is much slenderer according to his figure. However, it is considered by some to be a variation of the same species. It is recorded from the shore of New England.

Travisia carnea Verrill PLATE 115. This worm is about 3 inches in length, and is oblong or torpedo-shaped but very mobile and changeable. The head is acutely pointed, and the body also tapers to the tail, where it is terminated by a small, bluntly rounded papilla. The setae are small and slender and the branchiae begin on the third setigerous segment and continue to the twentieth. The segments of the middle part of the body have three annulations each. The color varies from light red to deep flesh-color, while the branchiae are bright red. It was first found by Verrill off Gay Head, Marthas Vineyard, in soft mud at a depth of 19 fathoms.

Travisia forbesi Johnston PLATE 115. This spindle-shaped worm is about 1 inch in length and is of a pale pinkish color blending to a pale yellow, laterally. It is mildly iridescent. The expanded anterior portion, of about fourteen segments, forms a distinct region in which the second segment consists of one ring and is without parapodia. The succeeding segments to the fourteenth have two to three narrow rings each; a parapodium comprising two clusters of bristles, of which the dorsal cluster is the larger; a filamentary branchia; and a circular pore. The mouth is situated on the ventral side between the second and third segments.

The second region begins with the narrowing of the anterior spindle-shaped part of the body, and consists of thirteen segments made up of rings that are broader antero-posteriorly, alternating with very narrow rings, there being one to a segment. Each segment here is equipped with a pair of parapodia with two lobes, with a short cirrus and a cluster of bristles just below the upper lobe.

This is also a sluggish creature and appears to be a scavenger, living among decaying algae and detritus.

It is found on both sides of the North Atlantic.

Family Maldanidae

The prostomium is usually united with the peristomium. There is a median keel with a nuchal organ on either side. The proboscis is well developed. The round, smooth body may be divided into anterior, middle, and posterior regions. There are but few segments (26 or 27). The long segments are few in number.

Maldane elongata Verrill PLATE 115. The body of this worm is extremely elongate and cylindrical. It is obliquely truncate at both ends. There are nineteen setigerous segments, much elongated in the middle of the body, with the head rounded obtusely in front. Most of the segments are biannulated. The body terminates in a caudal funnel with the anus dorsal to it. The color is dark to reddish brown and often iridescent. The apparently swollen parts of the rings are lighter in color, with blood vessels usually showing through. This species often attains a length of 12 inches, with a diameter of not more than ¼ inch. It is common along the New England coast, forming tubes of fine mud in the midst of sandy mud, at low-water mark.

Maldane sarsi Malmgren PLATE 115. The head-plate is longer than wide, and somewhat narrowed anteriorly, surrounded by a border. There is a distinct and high median keel, extending completely across the head-plate to the posterior margin. The fifth parapodial segment has an elongate gland the entire length of the segment.

The distribution is circumboreal. It is abundant in the North Atlantic at depths of 80 fathoms or more.

Clymenella torquata (Leidy) PLATE 115; COLOR PLATE VII, 11. This is another worm belonging to the same family as the above, but much slenderer. It constructs long, round tubes of sand and mucus for which it requires a nearly pure sand, in contrast to *Maldane*. Its tubes are long, nearly straight, and very neatly built. It is found in sheltered spots in coves or in the lee of rocks or ledges. It is very handsomely colored, being brick-red with bright red bands around the swollen parts of the rings. The peculiar color on the fifth ring always distinguishes this species, together with the funnel-shaped caudal appendage, which is surrounded by small papillae. The three rings immediately preceding the final segment are entirely without setae.

This species is found from the Bay of Fundy to the coast of New Jersey from low water to 60 fathoms.

Nichomache lumbricalis (Fabricius) var. **borealis** Arwidsson PLATE 115. The head-lobe of this species is fused with the buccal segment (peristomium), making a convex, oblique, and somewhat compressed head-region. The body is clyindrical, but slightly compressed. It is about 2 inches long and made up of twenty-six segments, of which twenty-two are equipped with setae. The two posterior segments are without setae. The anal funnel forms a deep cup with fifteen to twenty-two teeth on the margin and the anus is located centrally within. The color is light, mottled with madder-brown, pale yellow posteriorly. The anterior region is more or less colored crimson.

This species is likely to be found in rock-crevices, living in tubes of mud or sandy-mud, cemented together by mucus.

The range is North Atlantic on both American and European sides.

Leiochone borealis Arwidsson PLATE 115. In this species, the head-lobe is greatly reduced, with a more or less variable but well-developed margin. The eyes are located laterally. The seventh seta-bearing segment is long, with the parapodia near the anterior end. There are nineteen segments with parapodia, the five posterior segments being without them. There are long, threadlike anal cirri, the ventral being the longest. The body of this worm is between 2 and 3 inches long. The anterior segments are reddish brown in color. The seventh segment has a scarlet band posterior to the parapodia. The fragile tube is built of mucus, covered with sand-grains and shell-fragments.

This species is boreal in distribution, on both sides of the Atlantic.

Isocirrus planiceps (Sars) PLATE 115. The anterior border of the head-plate is not produced into a fingerlike projection, and the border is notched posteriorly, but not so deeply as in *Praxillella praetermissa,* and the margin is shallowly scalloped (*crenate*). The body has the typical shape for this family. There are twenty-five segments with setae and three with slightly curving spines. The anal funnel has twenty-seven short, conical teeth. The tube is not attached to the sea-bottom.

This species is recorded from the Gulf of St. Lawrence and off northern Europe in about 78 fathoms.

Axiothella catenata (Malmgren) PLATES 115; 116. In this species the anterior margin of the head-plate is broad. The border is not notched behind, forming an entirely complete rim. Eyes are lacking. The papillae of the proboscis have, for the most part, projecting summits. There are eighteen setigerous segments. The four posterior segments are without setae. Some of the anal cirri are long and slender and others are short and stout. The second and third parapodial segments are more or less completely glandular, near their posterior border.

This is practically an Arctic species, being most common around Spitzbergen, Greenland and the north coast of Siberia. There are records, however, along the coast of Norway, Denmark, Scotland, and the Shetland Islands, on the European side. It is also said to occur around Casco Bay, Georges Banks, and other parts of the northern Atlantic coast. These latter records, however, are considered by some to be doubtful (Arwidsson).

Rhodine loveni Malmgren PLATE 116. This worm has no head-plate. The buccal segment (peristomium) and the first parapodial segment are united and taper to a blade-like point. There is a keel between the nuchal organs. There are no eyes. The body is nearly cylindrical in sec-

PLATE 115

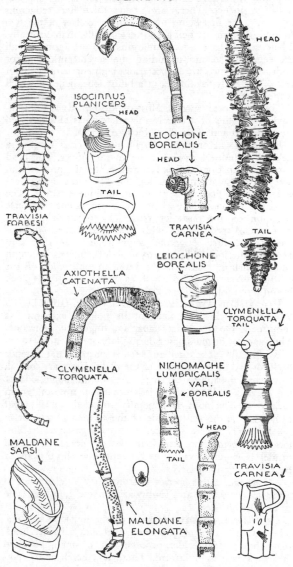

TRAVISIA
FORBESI

ISOCIRRUS
PLANICEPS
HEAD

TAIL

LEIOCHONE
BOREALIS

HEAD

HEAD

TRAVISIA
CARNEA

TAIL

AXIOTHELLA
CATENATA

LEIOCHONE
BOREALIS

CLYMENELLA
TORQUATA
TAIL

CLYMENELLA
TORQUATA

NICHOMACHE
LUMBRICALIS
VAR.
BOREALIS

HEAD

MALDANE
SARSI

TAIL

TRAVISIA
CARNEA

MALDANE
ELONGATA

tion and varies considerably in length, but usually approximates 2 inches. There are about thirty-five setigerous segments, the first being long, and the collars of the two following segments being shorter dorsally than ventrally. These collars have smooth margins and are found on all the segments to and including the seventeenth. One or both of the two most posterior segments are without setae. The body terminates in a blunt lobe, beneath which is the anus.

This is a boreal species. Most of the records are Scandinavian, but this or a closely related form is also reported from the Atlantic Coast of North America.

Rhodine attenuata Verrill PLATE 116. These are slender, cylindrical worms living in sand-tubes. The head is rounded in front and is represented by the prostomium and the peristomium fused together. In most cases, there is a cephalic plate present in an oblique position. The head has no appendages. There is a prominent transverse elevation on the posterior part. The posterior segment is funnel-shaped, often with scalloped edges. In this species, the first setigerous segment is very long and swollen anteriorly. This worm is about 2 inches in length and ⅟₂₅ inch in thickness. It is found in sandy mud off the southern New England coast as well as beyond Block Island from 6 to about 29 fathoms.

Praxillella gracilis (M. Sars) PLATE 116. The anterior tip of the head-plate, at its pointed extremity, is continued into a slender, tapering, fingerlike projection. The margins of the sloping head-plate are extended somewhat laterally. The median keel is narrow and extends back toward the lower edge of the plate. There are conical, flame-shaped papillae of large size on the outer side of the everted proboscis, crowded into rows, nine or ten in each row. The body is generally rounded dorsally, but rather flat on the ventral side of the segments posterior to the third. There are nineteen seta-bearing segments. Posterior to them there are four without setae. The anal funnel is rimmed with about twenty-five short teeth or cirri, and one long cirrus.

The range of this species is from New England northward to the Arctic and southward on the European side to the British Isles.

Praxillella praetermissa (Malmgren) PLATE 116. The anterior rim of the somewhat heart-shaped head-plate has no fingerlike process, but a small, rounded eminence is present instead. There is a notch at the posterior border. The proboscis is equipped with kidney-shaped papillae instead of conical ones. As in the above species, there are nineteen seta-bearing segments, followed

PLATE 116

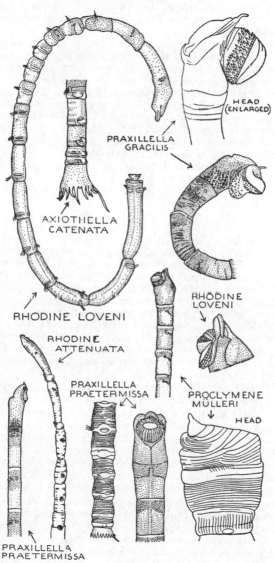

PRAXILLELLA GRACILIS

HEAD (ENLARGED)

AXIOTHELLA CATENATA

RHODINE LOVENI

RHODINE LOVENI

RHODINE ATTENUATA

PRAXILLELLA PRAETERMISSA

PROCLYMENE MÜLLERI

PRAXILLELLA PRAETERMISSA

HEAD

by four without setae. The anal funnel has about twenty-four small teeth around the rim and a somewhat longer anal cirrus on one side. The tube is like that of *Praxillella gracilis*.

Proclymene mülleri (M. Sars) PLATE 116. The head-plate is truncate obliquely forward. There is a conical projection centrally located on the front part of the plate, with a flaplike extension on each side. The keel is short and does not pass the middle of the plate. The plate-margin is slightly scalloped. There is a median groove on the somewhat flattened ventral side of the body. The dorsal side is rounded. There are nineteen segments with setae, the five posterior segments being without them. Small teeth, varying in number, encircle the rim of the anal funnel. There are two long cirri on the ventral side. The sides of the proboscis are wrinkled.

The distribution is circumboreal in the North Atlantic Ocean, in about 78 fathoms.

Family Scalibregmidae

This family is related to the Arenicolidae in various ways, but its species have characteristic peculiarities. There is a small prostomium, either with or without short, lateral processes. There are usually no eyes. The body is short and fusiform in outline, though this may take the character of an anterior enlargement. The branchiae also, when existent, are in the anterior region and four or five in number. The various segments are annulated. The lobes of the parapodia are equally developed and bear forked setae. A protrusible sense organ may be present between the lobes. There is a mouth, a pharynx, and a simple straight alimentary canal.

Scalibregma brevicauda Verrill PLATE 117. This is a burrowing species found on gravelly bottoms. Its comparatively short body tapers anteriorly to converge to a small truncated head with prominent angles. It expands toward the middle region, from which it tapers toward the tail. The ventral side is quite narrow and smooth along the middle line and is divided transversely into a series of small rounded prominences. Four anterior segments bear tuftlike branchiae with rather long bundles of setae, dorsally. There are dark spots and granules on the posterior margins of these parapodia, which have a generally granular surface. The parapodia of the middle region, covering about ten segments of the body, are indicated only by small bundles of slender setae. The caudal region includes about sixteen segments. The worm is dark brownish red in color tinged with yellow toward both the anterior and posterior extremities. It is about 1⅓ inch in length and is common off the southern New England coast.

Scalibregma inflatum H. Rathke PLATE 117. The almost square, truncate head has a lateral tentacle, standing out horizontally on each side, giving it a T-shaped outline. The body is about 3 inches in length, expanded anteriorly and suddenly tapering beyond to a much narrower breadth, which continues with almost parallel sides until it tapers moderately to the rounded tail region. It is convex, dorsally, and with numerous very narrow rings, which are combined into sixty-three or more segments, each of which has four rings, except the four anterior segments, with only one ring each. Beginning with the third segment, the parapodia have four or five treelike, blood-red branchiae, gradually increasing in size, on successive segments. There is also a dorsal papilla with a cluster of setae above each branchia. On the expanded part of the body the setae continue, but there are no branchiae. On the posterior, narrower part of the body, beginning about the fifteenth or sixteenth parapodia, the setae are accompanied by conspicuous dorsal and ventral cirri, leaflike in shape, gradually attenuating toward the tail, until they are entirely absent from the final three or four segments. The anus is surrounded by papillae, and the body is terminated by four or five long caudal cirri. The color of this species is brick-red, evenly covering the dorsal surface. The ventral surface is a grayer tone of the same color and somewhat iridescent.

This worm is abundant on both sides of the North Atlantic and in Arctic regions. It is found in sandy mud from the low-water line to about 80 fathoms.

Family Arenicolidae

In this family, the head is only moderately developed. It has no appendages and is bounded posteriorly by nuchal grooves. There are no palps nor tentacles. Only indistinct eyes are present. The elongate, rounded body is divided into three regions. The anal extremity is rounded and blunt. Four rings without setae occur between each two setigerous rings. The pharynx is globular and unarmed. The parapodia are rudimentary, the dorsal lobe having hairlike setae and the ventral, a vertical row of long hooks. There are no coelomic septa in the stomach region, but they are present at the beginning of the first, third, and fourth setigerous segments and also in the abdominal regions.

Arenicola marina (Linnaeus) PLATE 117. This is a large, stout worm which burrows rapidly and deeply into the sand just below the low-water mark. The head consists of the prostomium and peristomium fused together and it is without appendages. The proboscis, when everted, is covered with small filelike tentacles. The rudimentary parapodia are composed of bundles of setae anteriorly, while those in the middle region also have tufted branching gills dorsal to them. The annulated skin has indistinct segments, of which about twenty-one are setigerous, eight of them in the anterior region, and thirteen in the middle region. The color is green with brownish red-tufted gills. It may be 8 inches in length. It is found from Long Island Sound northward along the entire coast and also on the European side of the Atlantic.

Family Chloraemidae

There is a very small and short prostomium which can often be telescoped into the peristomium. It bears two short tentacles anteriorly. The peristomium is short and bears bundles of setae as well as short threadlike branchiae attached to it. The elongate setae of the anterior segments completely surround the head-region, which appears to be enclosed within a cagelike structure made up of these appendages. The worm-shaped body is more or less swollen anteriorly, or it may be fusiform and short. The surface is covered with mucus-secreting papillae which provide a layer of mucus to which grains of sand may adhere. The blood is green. The coelom has few septa. The parapodia are bilobed, surrounded by jointed setae of various types, often brilliantly iridescent, regularly arranged, and with characteristic joints.

Brada setosa Verrill PLATE 117. This is a rather small worm which burrows in the sandy mud and under stones. Its body slightly tapers at both ends, which appear to be obtuse or almost truncate. It is rounded above and flattened below and composed of seventeen setigerous segments. The skin is completely covered with small but prominent pointed papillae. In the parapodia, the upper bundles of setae are quite long, slender, and light colored. The lower fascicles are larger and composed of stouter, long, dark colored setae surrounded at the base by small cirriform appendages (Verrill). The worm is less than ½ inch in length with a diameter of ⅒ inch. It has been found off Gay Head at about 8 to 10 fathoms among mussels and other shells.

Flabelligera (Trophonia) affinis Sars PLATE 118. The body is quite slender and elongated. The skin is granular, anteriorly covered with small papillae. There are eight blunt, cylindrical branchiae or tentacular filaments on the head, which are thick and unequal in length. Two of the tentacles are stouter than the branchiae and

PLATE 117

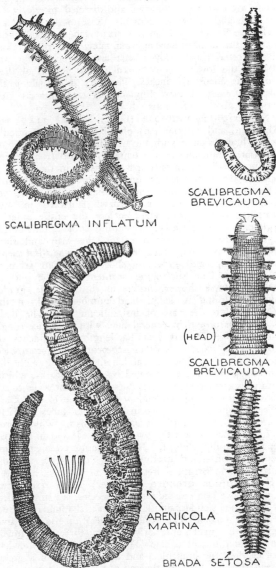

SCALIBREGMA INFLATUM

SCALIBREGMA
BREVICAUDA

(HEAD)

SCALIBREGMA
BREVICAUDA

ARENICOLA
MARINA

BRADA SETOSA

grooved ventrally. The fascicles on the four anterior segments are extremely elongated and directed anteriorly. On the fifth and following segments, those in the dorsal fascicles are hairlike and fan out, six to ten in each bundle. The ventral fascicles have approximately three stout, yellow setae. Posteriorly, the lower setae are longer, stouter, and curved, the lowest being hooklike. The length of these worms is about 2¼ inches. They are found along the southern coast of New England, as far south as New Jersey in about 20 fathoms.

Stylarioides plumosa (O. F. Müller) PLATE 118. The head and anterior part of this worm are retractile, acting like a siphon with the mouth contained within it. Two large and long brown tentacles extend from behind the mouth, diverging outward and rising in the midst of eight to ten green, slender, fingerlike branchiae. The first three segments give rise to many long, jointed, iridescent setae pointing forward and curving inward in such fashion that they completely enclose the entire anterior region, as if in a basket of shining spines. The fourth segment and, to a certain extent, the fifth and sixth segments have long tufts of similar setae, but separately arising, and gradually shortening from segment to segment. The succeeding segments, to the end of the body, have shorter clusters of similar setae, gradually diminishing in length and number, until on the anal segments they are of insignificant size. The body is a fuscous brown in general hue, with a surface rough with papillae. It may reach a length of 5 inches or more, with sixty to seventy segments, each composed of but one ring. The ventral lobes, beginning with the fourth segment, are represented by golden hooks, which, with the successive clusters of dorsal iridescent setae give a very handsome and resplendent appearance to this magnificent annulate. This worm builds its tubes in rich, black mud, replete with decaying organisms, which form its food. It occurs near the low-water mark and in shallow depths generally, along the North Atlantic Ocean margin, from New England northward to the Arctic, and on European and British shores.

Stylarioides arenosa (Webster) PLATE 118. Two palps, grooved on one side, in this species, are surrounded by numerous slender, simple branchiae, shading from red to green in color. The setae (bristles) of the first five segments are turned anteriorly, the first three being much longer than the branchiae. The tentacles are somewhat shorter than the branchiae, and are brown with a green thread running through the center of each filament, due to the green color of the blood. The body is about 2 inches in length, and round in section. It enlarges slightly in the

PLATE 118

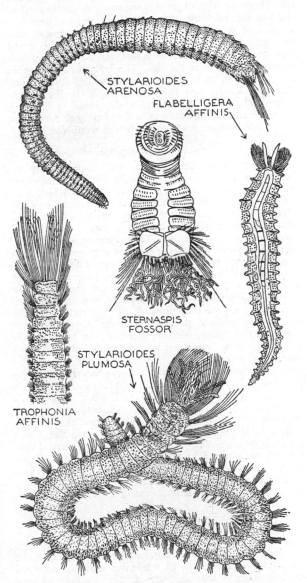

STYLARIOIDES
ARENOSA

FLABELLIGERA
AFFINIS

STERNASPIS
FOSSOR

STYLARIOIDES
PLUMOSA

TROPHONIA
AFFINIS

first few segments, then tapers gradually to the rounded tail. There are sixty to seventy segments, distinctly marked and bearing relatively short bundles of setae. There is a dorsal and ventral cluster of these in each segment with an elongated cirrus posterior to each cluster. The dorsal setae are amber-colored, while the ventral ones are dark brown but lighter at the tips. The body is covered with sand, which clings to each segment, making a dense coating. This species was first found by H. E. Webster in Virginia, between the tides. It is also found in England, though there is some doubt as to the identity of the species, as the branchiae are fewer in the British worm (McIntosh).

Family Sternaspidae

The features of this family, which contains only the Genus *Sternaspis,* are so well brought out in the following species, that no special definition will be needed here.

Sternaspis fossor Stimpson PLATE 118; COLOR PLATE VIII, 12. This curious worm is quite common off the entire New England coast from the Bay of Fundy and Georges Bank to Gay Head and the Woods Hole region, generally on muddy bottoms off the open coast. It is small and grublike, with about twelve segments and an oblique, flattened head bearing three rows of spikelike setae arranged in successive semicircles on either side of the papillalike mouth. Those in the outer semicircle include nine stout cirri, which are the longest of all. In the second series, the cirri are of medium size, while in the third series, that closest to the mouth, they are mere prickles. The cephalic end of the body is oblique and flattened with apparently three segments combined to form the head region. The seventh segment bears a pair of cylindrical, papillalike parapodia. Posterior to this, the segments increase rapidly in size, apparently overlapping each other and with a border of papillalike spines on the anterior edge of each segment. This part of the body is composed of seven segments. In the posterior region, there are two flat, horny plates, brown in color, facing forward on the ventral side, fringed with strong bundles of setae, which are longest toward the outer posterior corners beyond the setae. This entire region is fringed with a large series of flesh-colored tentacles which contract and expand in various directions.

Branch CRYPTOCEPHALA

The prostomium here is insignificant because the peristomium is greatly developed by growing forward so as to compress and even completely hide the prostomium. The tentacles are greatly reduced, while the palps have enlarged to such a degree that they are capable of taking on new functions with the result that their form is changed and adapted for such purposes. The body-segments of the worm are grouped into a sharply marked thorax and abdomen with both external and internal specialization.

This Branch is divided into two suborders: (1) *Sabelliformia;* (2) *Hermelliformia.*

Suborder SABELLIFORMIA

In this Suborder, the ancestral prostomium is very small and entirely hidden by the peristomium and the organs derived from it. The tentacles arising from the prostomium are very small and insignificant, while the palps, being organs of the peristomium, are greatly developed, branched, and act both as branchiae and sensory organs. The peristomium is without cirri or chaetae and usually has the form of a collar. The parapodia in this group are very feebly developed. There are no parapodial cirri (except certain derivatives in the Family Serpulidae). The chaetae are unjointed and hairlike in form. Uncini (hooks) are present as well as bristles. The body is divided into a thorax of nine segments and a clearly separated abdomen occupying the posterior part of the body with various external structures characteristic of each division. There is no eversible proboscis and no pharynx. On the thoracic segments there are secretory gland shields. These are all tube-building worms.

Family Sabellidae

The body, as a whole, is somewhat rounded or, at the most, slightly flattened. The thorax consists of from five to twelve segments with bristles of two different kinds; also, there are bristles of two kinds in a double row. The abdomen has numerous segments with bristles and hooks, each of one kind only. The first segment is partly enveloped by a collar more or less covering the branchiae. The latter form a funnel surrounding the mouth by bringing together the branching fan of branchiae on each side. In typical Sabellids, the fan has pinnae (branches) on the internal side of the stem, and on the external side in others. In certain species, there is a series of eyes on the external side of the rays. A pair of segmental organs, modified in the form of mucus-secreting glands, opens anteriorly by a single outlet. In this family, there is neither a thoracic membrane nor an operculum.

Sabellids build a cylindrical tube of mucine secreted by the glands, above-mentioned, of leathery or membranous consistency. Mud, sand, and other substances may adhere to the outside of this tube.

Sabella penicillus Linnaeus PLATE 119. This is a beautiful species, with a body 12 to 15 inches in length, above which two fans of delicate feathery branchiae spread in curving, slightly spiral fashion. The head-plate is divided into two pillars, one arising from either half of the plate, each trunk dividing again into thirty-five to forty or more delicate filaments, which send off on either side extremely fine short pinnae, in plumelike manner. In this species, these feathery structures are practically colorless, except for purple cross-bands occurring at regular intervals. The branchiae are without the eyespots that occur in certain other species of this genus. The body, convexly flattened, both on the dorsal and ventral sides, is divided into 150 to 200 segments.

The tube is parchmentlike and tough with mud adhering to it. This species is brought up by fishermen from time to time on the fishing banks from depths of 50 fathoms or more. It is also washed up after storms. It ranges along the North American coast from New England to Canada and the Arctic, as well as on northern European and British shores.

Potamilla (Pseudopotamilla) oculifera Verrill PLATE 119. This is another beautiful species, building tough but flexible tubes of fine sand and other material attached to the undersides of stones. It is about 2 to 3 inches in length and unfolds a wreath of gayly colored branchial plumes which are extremely variable in their patterns. They are often reddish brown, ringed with white, tipped with yellowish gray. There are ten or more branchiae on each half of the wreath, with one to three dark red eyes on the outer side. The worm's body is yellowish green in color, and has about sixty segments. It ranges from the Arctic Ocean to North Carolina. On European and British shores, it is represented by *Potamilla reniformis* (Linnaeus) and they may be the same species.

Potamilla torelli Malmgren PLATE 119. This is a small species, about 1 inch in length, the head plate and collar show close relationship with the preceding species, the latter structure having a narrow slit dorsally, as well as a deep cleft, ventrally. The branchial fans are of moderate size, with but comparatively few grayish plumes, not more than sixteen, and with pinnae diminishing in size toward the tips of the filaments, which end in a minute knoblike process. The collar is cream-color, the first seven or eight parapodial segments are reddish, and all are spotted with white dots. The distribution is cosmopolitan in moderate depths.

Euchone elegans Verrill PLATE 119. This beautiful species has a rounded, slender body which tapers posteriorly. The thorax takes up about one half the entire length and consists of eight setigerous segments. Each segment has two rings and a dorsal longitudinal groove. The circlet of branchial filaments, when expanded, is quite

PLATE 119

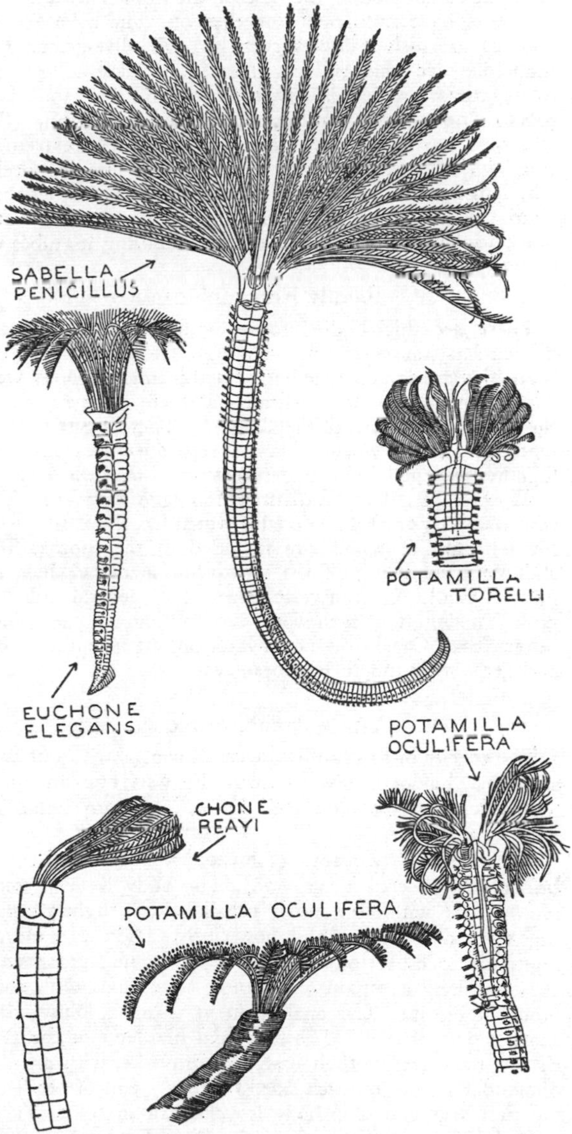

SABELLA
PENICILLUS

POTAMILLA
TORELLI

EUCHONE
ELEGANS

POTAMILLA
OCULIFERA

CHONE
REAYI

POTAMILLA OCULIFERA

conspicuous. The peristomium is bent backward and forms an open collar around the base of the branchiae. The gill filaments have numerous tiny eyespots. The color of the body is greenish yellow varying to dull olive-green. The branchiae are pale yellow, greenish, or flesh-color with many transverse bands varying between light and dark green. The collar is translucent, specked with white. The abdomen has about fifty narrow segments with extremely small bundles of setae. The anal segment has two ocelli. The length of this worm approximates 1⅛ inches. It occurs from Cape Cod to North Carolina, from the low-water mark to a depth of 5 fathoms, often building its tubes on oyster shells.

Family Eriographidae

These are thick-bodied forms with a thorax. The abdomen has transverse rows of hooks. The filaments of the branchiae are joined together by a thin membranous web. There are no eyes on the head, but there are eyespots on the terminal segment of the abdomen. There are two small tentacles. These worms live in separate tubes grouped together in a gelatinous material attached to shells, etc.

Myxicola infundibulum (Montagu) PLATE 120. The comparatively thick body of this worm has about sixty segments, eight of which are included in the thorax. The abdomen, consisting of the remaining segments, has numerous hooks in transverse rows. The general color is pink. The length of each worm is more than 2 inches. They range from Cape Cod northward on the Atlantic Coast and are also found in European seas.

Family Amphicorinidae

The species in this family are small worms with but four segments, having a few to about thirty-six branchial filaments with eyespots on their bases. They are found in fresh or salt water.

Amphicora fabricii (Johnston) [= **Fabricia sabella** (Ehrenberg) PLATE 120]. The body is very small and slender with very nearly parallel sides, slightly tapering toward the head and posteriorly. There are eleven segments, each bearing a fascicle of setae. The segments are about as long as broad and almost continuous with each other in outline. The anal segment is small, blunt, and bears a pair of ocelli. The branchial filaments of the two circlets have eyes at their base, all plumelike, with a series of slender pinnae on each side. There is a pair of ocelli on the first segment. The body is yellowish in color. These worms are found along the entire New England coast in the neighborhood of the low-water mark.

Family Serpulidae

Here the cephalic lobe is fused with the collar, which is usually equipped with fascicles of setae. It is open dorsally and fuses ventrally with the thoracic wall. Arising from the head-region is a pair of semicircular pinnate branchiae (a modification of the palps), resembling feathered plumes, with one or more of the dorsal branches modified to terminate in an operculum. The collar, above mentioned, is immediately beneath the crown of branchiae. This is actually an extension of the peristomium, having the function of smoothing the inside of the calcareous tube built by the species of this genus.

Filograna implexa Berkeley PLATE 120. Small worms forming intertwining masses of slender, whitish tubes, 2½ inches or so in height. There are eight branchial filaments. The color of the worm's body ranges from purple to pink. It is found along the New England coast to Vineyard Sound and in European seas.

Hydroides dianthus Verrill COLOR PLATE XXIII, 13. This is a common and very beautiful worm about 3 inches in length. The crown of branchiae is long and slender, radiating from the united base. There are about eighteen on each side, the ventral branchiae being longer than the dorsal ones. The pointed tips are without branches at the extreme end, but the pinnae are very numerous along the greater part of each branchia. These are plumelike and may be purple, banded with white and green. Often they are brown, banded with white and yellow. The greenish to greenish yellow collar is quite translucent. The branching veins show through as irregular, dark-green lines, due to the green blood of this worm. The body gradually tapers toward the posterior end. The collar is often one third as long as the body. It is attached, anteriorly, in the dorsal region, flared out above, and free dorsally below with undulating margins. Seven thoracic segments in the anterior region have bundles of long, pointed setae. There is a funnel-shaped operculum on one side with a long, slender stem, having a radiating rim composed of about thirty tooth-shaped spines. This closes the opening of the tube when the worm is withdrawn into it. Long, twisted tubes are built on mollusk shells. This species is very common from Cape Cod to Florida.

Hydroides norvegica Gunnerus PLATE 120. This is a similar species to *Hydroides dianthus* Verrill, and may be considered its northern and European form. Like that species, it builds calcareous tubes, often in coiled masses. The projecting heads have two fan-shaped series of branchiae with plumelike pinnae, fifteen to eighteen in number, with a color pattern variegated with pink. A dorsal filament on each fan has been modified into an operculum, one of which is fully developed, the other rudimentary. The functional one closes the tube-opening. When opened out, it is seen to be a double, handsomely patterned structure, composed of two superimposed starlike discs, the lower being the larger, and made up of twenty-five or more pieces, like a vase or flower cup surmounting a stem. The body of this species is of a reddish orange color. The shell has the appearance of smooth coils of limy material, showing lines of growth, thus differing from those of *Hydroides dianthus,* which have more irregular coils with a rough exterior. This is a cosmopolitan species, but especially abundant in northern waters at considerable depths.

Serpula vermicularis Linnaeus PLATE 120. This is another related species, having a collar separated by a considerable space dorsally, but otherwise continuous. The branchial filaments are bright red and have long, tapering tips. The body is reddish to orange. The limy shell flares somewhat at the opening and shows periods of growth by the remains of successive trumpetlike rims along its course. It is 3 or 4 inches in length and is usually coiled at its base, where it is attached to a mollusk shell, such as that of a scallop or even a mud-snail, like that in the figure on the plate. The main part of the shell is often freely erect, rough in texture, and occasionally adherent to the tubes of other serpulids. It is tinged with a pink or green color. This species is cosmopolitan in shallow water, below the lower tide mark, and to 60 fathoms or more of depth.

Spirorbis borealis Daudin PLATE 120; COLOR PLATE VIII, 10. The species of the genus *Spirorbis* build coiled snail-like tubes on such seaweeds as *Fucus* and *Chondrus crispus.* They are extremely common from southern New England to the Bay of Fundy and northward. *Spirorbis borealis* has nine branchiae besides the operculum, five on one side and four on the other. The branches are broad and the pinnae long. When they unfold from the opening of the tiny snail-like shell, the wreath of branchiae nearly equals the diameter of the shell itself. The operculum looks like a one-sided paddle and makes an efficient protective door when the animal is contracted within the shell. There is a broad collar with three paired bundles of setae. The branchiae are greenish white, verging into deeper green, which is the color of the blood. The tube is about ⅛ inch across its coil.

Spirorbis spirillum (Linnaeus) PLATE 120. It is doubtful whether this species can be separated from the above, with which, in fact, it may be identical. As described by Linnaeus from European specimens, it occurs in deeper

PLATE 120

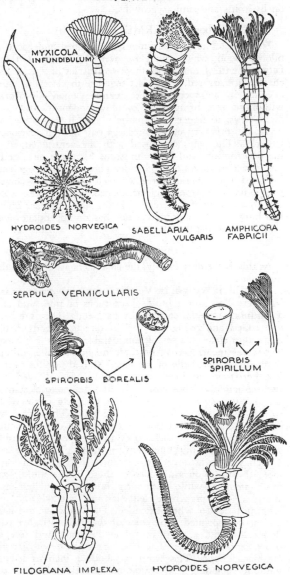

MYXICOLA
INFUNDIBULUM

HYDROIDES NORVEGICA

SABELLARIA
VULGARIS

AMPHICORA
FABRICII

SERPULA VERMICULARIS

SPIRORBIS BOREALIS

SPIRORBIS
SPIRILLUM

FILOGRANA IMPLEXA

HYDROIDES NORVEGICA

water than the *Spirorbis borealis* of our coast and is found on hydroids and similar growths.

Suborder HERMELLIFORMIA

The peristomium is enormously developed and forms a bilobed hood, which can close over the mouth. On the flattened end of each lobe, three semicircles of specialized chaetae are arrayed, which act together to close the tube-opening in an operculumlike manner when the worm withdraws into its tube. They move independently, like piano keys, to finger food particles into the mouth. The prostomium is very small, but has a pair of well-developed tentacles. The palps are fused with the ventral edges of the peristomium and bear numerous filaments on a complex series of ridges on each side. There are five segments included in the thorax, three of which have well-developed notopodia with strong chaetae. Dorsal cirri are present on the greater part of this region, acting as branchiae. There is a long tail-like abdomen which has no appendages and folds back on the thorax.

Family Hermellidae

As this is the only family, the characters are those of the Suborder.

Sabellaria vulgaris Verrill PLATE 120; COLOR PLATE VIII, 11. This worm builds hard tubes of fine sand and a glutinous material secreted by its glands. They are bent and coiled and twisted in various directions and usually form aggregated masses of considerable bulk, which may be several inches across, or there may be smaller groups of them on the shells of oysters. The body of the worm is rather stout and thick anteriorly, where it is divided into two semicircular lobes which can fit together to close over the mouth and form a practically complete circle when spread close to the opening of the tube. There are two slender, red, oral tentacles on either side of the mouth between the bases of these lobes and a tapering extension situated on the mid-line between them. The teeth are golden yellow, arranged in concentric halfcircles on each lobe; the inner ones are largest, those in the middle are more slender, while the outer ones are smallest and shortest. The prehensile tentacles are ciliated and are long and slender when extended. The branchiae are long and acutely pointed. The color of the body is rather pale flesh-color with a tinge of yellow or pink, and rose or brown spots ventrally. The lobes are whitish with irregular black marks. The worm is about 1 inch in length, without including the abdominal process which is described in the definition of the suborder above. It is very common from Vineyard Sound to New Jersey.

PLATE 121

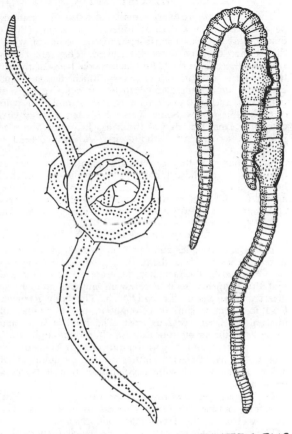

CLITELLIO
ARENARIUS

ENCHYTRAEUS
ALBIDUS

TYPICAL MARINE
OLIGOCHAETA

Order MYZOSTOMIDA

These worms are very small, disc-shaped creatures, parasitic on crinoids (Sea Lilies), ophiurans (Brittle Stars), and asteroids (Starfishes), to the bodies of which they either cling or become encysted. They are clearly worms belonging to the Class Chaetopoda, because, though the body is oval in outline, very much flattened and externally unsegmented, nevertheless it has five pairs of parapodia, each equipped with two setae and four pairs of suckerlike organs. Some species have ten pairs of cirri extending from the edge of the body. In others, the edge is simply serrate, but without cirri. A distinct head is not present.

Since, however, they are usually parasitic on deep-sea organisms or on those inhabiting the open seas, we shall here regard them as outside the limits of this volume, except for this brief mention, and to say that two genera and more than seventy species of this group are known.

Order OLIGOCHAETA

This Order includes the earthworms and certain fresh-water species allied to them. The group, as a whole, is characterized by the fact that there are no parapodia and that the segmental setae are few in number and project directly from pits in the body wall. The body segments tend to be quite similar throughout, but a number of internal specialized regions exist. The head is small and consists of the prostomium (a small projection in front of the mouth) and a peristomium, which contains the mouth but is otherwise similar to the prostomium. It differs from the following segments in that it possesses no setae.

The typical earthworms are mostly terrestrial and, therefore, outside the range covered by this book. The same is true of the fresh-water oligochaetes.

There are, however, a few species which occur within the upper limits of the tidal zone and may be observed by those studying the animals of the tidal area. Examples are given herewith.

Clitellio arenarius Verrill (= **Clitellio irroratus**) Verrill PLATE 121. The body is very slender and distinctly annulated. It grows to 2½ inches in length. The head is conical and a little elongated. The first segment bears setae. The following segments in the anterior region have fascicles of two or three setae, very short and small, with a slightly S-shaped curve. Some are slightly bent at the tip; others are strongly hooked. Farther back on the body, the setae are in groups of three or four and are somewhat longer. In some cases, the fascicles are forked. This species is light red in color. It has been found along the New England coast from Casco Bay to New Haven, under stones in the upper part of the *Fucus* zone, and very near the high-water mark.

Enchytraeus albidus Henle PLATE 121. This worm is white, slender, about 1 inch long, tapering toward both ends. There are three pairs of ventral seta-bundles on the first three setigerous segments. Beginning with the fourth pair of ventral fascicles, an additional series of dorsal fascicles commences, continuing throughout the entire body. This worm has no eyes. It is found near the high-water mark between the tides, in decaying or living plants.

CLASS HIRUDINEA

These are the leeches. They are typically segmented like the rest of the annulates but are usually flattened dorso-ventrally. Each segment consists of several rings, ranging from two to fourteen in number, depending upon the family concerned. This group is especially distinguished by the two suckers which are present; that at the hinder end being much larger, as a rule, than the small sucker at the anterior end. These suckers attach themselves to hard surfaces and are utilized for purposes of locomotion. There are no parapodia, no tentacles, and no setae. The head is continuous with the trunk. The mouth is located ventrally, but may be near the head end. Within the pharynx, there are three saw-toothed, chitinous plates in certain species while, in other species, a proboscis capable of piercing the skin of another animal may be thrust forward from the mouth. They may have several pairs of eyes. They possess both testes and ovaries and are, therefore, hermaphroditic, though the outlets for the sexual organs are so placed that copulation is required by two individuals.

While most leeches are found in fresh water, there are some marine species and a few terrestrial forms.

The Class is divided into two Orders: (1) *Rhynchobdellida;* and (2) *Gnathobdellida* (fresh water and terrestrial only).

Order RHYNCHOBDELLIDA

These leeches are without jaws, but have a proboscis which can be thrust out to pierce the body of another animal. They are found in fresh or salt water. The order is divided into two families: (1) *Ichthyobdellidae*; and (2) *Glossiphoniidae* (only in fresh water).

Family Ichthyobdellidae

This family contains both salt- and fresh-water species. parasitic on fishes and certain other animals. The body-segments are characterized by having more than three rings each.

Piscicola (Pontobdella) rapax (Verrill) PLATE 122. The body is long and slender when extended, but with the greatest diameter in the posterior half of the body. There are usually fourteen rings to a segment. The head is small and obliquely truncated. The general color is dark olive, with a row of rectangular, white spots along each side. The head and posterior sucker are light-colored, tinged with green. This species is parasitic on the summer flounder (*Chaenopsetta ocellaris*), which it actively attacks, attaching itself to the upper side.

Branchiobdella (Branchellion) ravenelii Diesing PLATE 122. This is one of the most remarkable of the parasitic leeches. It is characterized by having broad, leaf-shaped, lobed branchiae along the sides of the body. It has a large *acetabulum* (posterior sucker). The color of the worm is dark brown to dark violet, or purplish, speckled with white. It is a very active species, often found on a sting-ray (*Myliobatis freminvillei*), several of them being grouped together, according to Verrill, "on a large spot which had become sore and much inflamed by their repeated bites." It has also been observed off Charleston, South Carolina on a skate, and also out in the Atlantic Ocean on a Torpedo-Ray.

Trachelobdella (Cystobranchus) vividus (Verrill) PLATE 122. There are two clearly distinguished regions of the body. The anterior region includes the first eleven somites, of which the last three are narrowed to form the *clitellum*. The head includes five somites, made up of the first five primary rings (*annuli*). There are four eyes. The rest of the anterior region is composed of twenty primary annuli. The posterior region is considerably expanded and spindle-shaped, also constituting eleven somites among which are distributed numerous annuli. Finally, there are four preanal annuli. The body terminates in a large disc-shaped sucker. The color is brown to purplish, spotted irregularly with white on the back. The length of the body is 1 inch.

This species is found at Woods Hole, Massachusetts.

Trachelobdella rugosa Moore PLATE 122. This is a more or less flattened species, with a narrow anterior region of about eleven somites. The posterior region has a loose integument, much wrinkled and thrown into folds, narrowing posteriorly to the small transverse posterior sucker. The anterior sucker is also quite small and is

PLATE 122

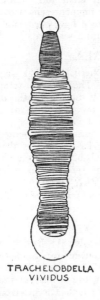

TRACHELOBDELLA
VIVIDUS

TRACHELOBDELLA
RUGOSA

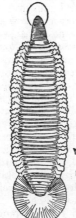

BRANCHIOBDELLA
RAVENELII

PONTOBDELLA
RAPAX

slitlike when contracted. The head is small and without eyes, though there are a few brown pigment cells across its anterior part. Specimens of this leech have been taken from the Red Snapper, off the Atlantic seaboard.

CLASS GEPHYREA

These marine worms show no external ringlike segmentation and have no parapodia. There is no serial repetition of internal parts. There is but one pair of nephridia. The sexes are separate and give rise to a free-swimming top-shaped larva (trochophore).

Though the Gephyrea do not resemble segmented worms, nevertheless, the trochophore larva indicates that they are related to the Annulata, probably in the neighborhood of the family containing the species, *Sternaspis fossor* (see PLATE 118; COLOR PLATE VIII, 12).

There are three Orders as follows: (1) *Echiurida*; (2) *Sipunculida;* and (3) *Priapulida*.

Order ECHIURIDA

These are Gephyrea which are peculiar in having a solid outgrowth of the dorsal portion of the head to form a long, spoon-shaped or troughlike extension like a proboscis. In some species this structure is very elastic and, occasionally, may be forked at the end. The grooved or hollow ventral side is ciliated, the motion of the cilia tending to sweep small organisms back toward the mouth, which is situated at the base of the proboscis. The sinuous digestive tube begins with an expanded pharynx and continues through the body to the posterior end, where the anus opens to the outside. There are no special sense organs except the proboscis, which is sensitive to touch and acts as an antenna or palp. There are no parapodia or other appendages, except two large setae on the ventral side not far from the mouth, and two circlets of setae around the anal region in *Echiurus*. The Echiurida live in the sand and mud or among stones in shallow water.

Echiurus pallasii Guerin PLATE 124. There are preanal bristles and two ventral hooklike setae on this worm. The body has a series of about twenty-two rings indicated by spines. The proboscis is spoon-shaped, but the ventral opening terminates somewhat above the base, thus making a cup-shaped structure around the mouth. The color is light yellow with orange-colored grooves inside the proboscis. The body, also, shades toward gray or orange. This burrowing worm may be 12 inches in length, with a proboscis about 4 inches long.

Its range is from Casco Bay, in the North Atlantic, along the entire eastern seaboard and also, through the

PLATE 123

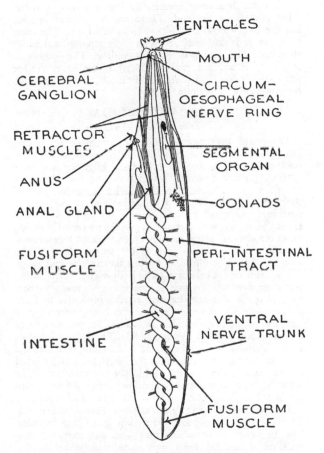

TENTACLES

MOUTH

CEREBRAL
GANGLION

CIRCUM-
OESOPHAGEAL
NERVE RING

RETRACTOR
MUSCLES

SEGMENTAL
ORGAN

ANUS

ANAL GLAND

GONADS

FUSIFORM
MUSCLE

PERI-INTESTINAL
TRACT

INTESTINE

VENTRAL
NERVE TRUNK

FUSIFORM
MUSCLE

INTERNAL ANATOMY
OF A TYPICAL GEPHYREAN

Arctic, to Europe. On the Pacific Coast, it occurs from California to Alaska.

Thalessema mellita Conn PLATE 124. This is a similar but much smaller species, having a proboscis somewhat pointed at the end. There are no preanal bristles, but the two ventral hooklike spines are present. The color of the body is dull brick-red with eight longitudinal bands showing. The proboscis is light yellow. The length of the body is about 1 inch, aside from the long, flexible proboscis. It has been found off Beaufort, North Carolina, commonly in sand-dollar shells.

Order SIPUNCULIDA
INDEX PLATE 123

These are long worms, 8 inches or more in length, burrowing in mud or crawling freely or in some cases, occupying snail shells. The cylindrical body has a slender anterior portion (introvert) which can be turned in like the finger of a glove into the thicker posterior part of the worm. The head, at the anterior end of the slender portion, is crowned by circlets of short and hollow tentacles. The body-wall has two layers of powerful muscles, an outer circular layer, and an inner layer of longitudinal muscles. In the thicker part of the worm, there is also a series of oblique muscles between the circular and longitudinal muscles. There is a large body-cavity, surrounding the digestive tube, which is narrow and extends from the mouth at the anterior end of the proboscis to form a loop near the posterior end of the body, only to turn forward to the anus, which is located on the middle of the extended body on the dorsal side. The looped intestine twines spirally as it does so. The sexes are separate, the products being discharged into the body-cavity and ejected to the outside through the single pair of nephridia. The larva is a trochophore, swimming about actively, and going through a metamorphosis into the adult worm.

Phascolosoma margaritaceum (Sars) PLATE 124. This species has a smooth, firm skin, pearl-gray in color. The proboscis is brownish gray and has four retractor muscles. There are no eyespots and no hooks on this structure. It has a continuous layer of circular muscles, which distinguishes it from *Phascolosoma gouldii,* as does the fact that the body is shorter and thicker.

It is a northern form, occurring off the coast of Newfoundland and Canada, in depths from 30 to 75 fathoms. Probably, it is also distributed continuously around the Arctic to European shores.

Phascolosoma gouldii Diesing COLOR PLATES VII, 12; IX, 15. This Sipunculoid Worm is the largest and most common of the group, often growing to the length of

PLATE 124

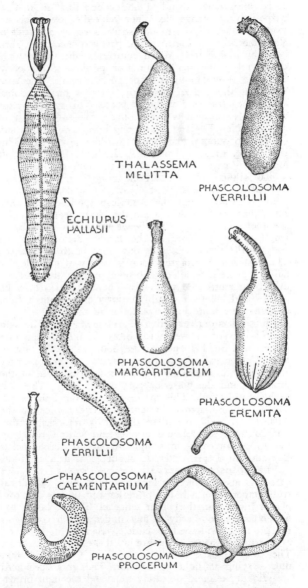

THALASSEMA
MELITTA

PHASCOLOSOMA
VERRILLII

ECHIURUS
PALLASII

PHASCOLOSOMA
MARGARITACEUM

PHASCOLOSOMA
EREMITA

PHASCOLOSOMA
VERRILLII

PHASCOLOSOMA
CAEMENTARIUM

PHASCOLOSOMA
PROCERUM

a foot or more and varying from ¼ to ½ inch in diameter. It is continually expanding and contracting, so that its shape is quite changeable. When relaxed, a long proboscis extends anteriorly, its mouth surrounded by a circlet of short tentacles in several series, partly connected at their bases by a thin web. When contracted, the worm withdraws the entire slender anterior portion of the body, enclosing it within the thicker posterior part. The anus is not at the end of the body, but lies on the dorsal surface near the base of the proboscis. This species occurs abundantly in shallow water along the entire coast of southern New England, burrowing in mud or sandy mud.

Phascolosoma procerum Moebius PLATE 124. This is a large, gray *Phascolosoma*, dredged abundantly off Marthas Vineyard Island, at depths ranging from 100 to 266 fathoms. It has also been found in the North Sea, especially off the west coast of Sweden at depths of from 9 to 35 fathoms, but the American specimens are five times the length of those from the North Sea, the largest specimen on record being between 7 and 8 inches in length, with 3 inches as the largest diameter of the body, while the proboscis is one third of that thickness. The posterior part of the body is narrowed to a slender tail-like process. Small dark brown papillae are scattered over both trunk and proboscis. The tentacles are in six groups and are twenty-eight to forty each, with a thin, smooth zone immediately posterior to them.

Phascolosoma eremita (Sars) PLATE 124. The skin is dark grayish or yellowish brown. Parallel transverse ridges and furrows encircle the body, especially posteriorly. Very small dark-colored papillae occur over the entire surface, being more numerous at the base of the proboscis and the posterior part of the body. The skin is thick and tough. This species ranges from Spitzbergen and Greenland across the entire Arctic border of the Atlantic. Gerould considers that it is remarkable that this Arctic species should also extend southward along the American coast, in shallow water, to Massachusetts Bay and, in deeper water, to about 40° North Latitude.

Phascolosoma verrillii Gerould PLATE 124. This species is about 1 inch in length with a thick, cylindrical trunk tapering to a blunt, posterior end. It has one row of not more than thirty-four tentacles. The proboscis has no hooks. A peculiarity is that under certain conditions the proboscis will shed its cuticle, retaining it, however, as a trumpet-shaped structure at the end of the body. The color is dark brown or steel-gray, with iridescent tints varying to light coffee-color. The gray specimens are said to be found on sandy mud and the light brown specimens on dark mud. Both the trunk and the proboscis are covered with conspicuous dark-brown papillae, more numerous at the base of the proboscis and the posterior end of the body. The largest are finger-shaped or conical, attached to the worm by a small neck. It ranges from Vineyard Sound to Cape Hatteras and is found in depths from 3 to 8 fathoms, near Woods Hole, and in 16 fathoms off Cape Hatteras.

Phascolosoma improvisum Théel PLATE 125. The surface of the skin is smooth except for conspicuous papillae at the posterior end of the trunk. From there, they grade to minute papillae which are scattered sparsely over the anterior part of the trunk and uniformly over the proboscis. This species measures about ½ inch in length. It is found in shallow water off Niantic, Connecticut, from a sandy bottom, 5 fathoms deep, to the New Jersey coast in green mud, 8to fathoms. It also occurs off the coast of Sweden.

Phascolion strombi (Montagu) [= **Phascolosoma caementarium** (Quatrefages)] PLATE 125. This is a very widespread species which occurs abundantly from Labrador to the West Indies. It is found off the Elizabeth Islands, Massachusetts, in shallow water, and is especially abundant from 20 to 150 fathoms. The trunk is about 1 inch in length, while the proboscis may be twice the length of the trunk. Some of the forms from shallow waters are much smaller. The species of this genus have holdfasts on the posterior part of the trunk with arrow-shaped or crescentic heads. Apparently, this is a genus that has evolved from *Phascolosoma*, having become considerably modified because of the habit of living within the shells of snails. As the body is too small for the shell, it fills in the extra room by cementing sand into a firm mass, leaving an opening to the outside through which the proboscis can be exserted to pull the shell around with it, from place to place. Sometimes a considerable chimney is built, surmounting the shell-opening, when the worm grows too large for its shell.

Dendrostoma alutaceum Grube PLATE 125. This species has a pear-shaped body swelling toward the posterior end, where there is a slightly raised papilla. The surface of the trunk, at first sight, seems to be smooth but, through a lens, it is seen that it is covered with very fine transverse furrows. The proboscis is cylindrical and comparatively stout. It terminates in six treelike clusters of numerous tentacles which are finger-shaped, slender, and each with a groove on its under-surface. They are light yellowish brown in color with specks of brown pigment on the underside. The anterior half of the proboscis is smooth, and yellowish brown in color, while the posterior half is covered with prominent backwardly pointed hooks. Below, at the base of the proboscis, the surface is covered by a design of rectangular blocks. The anus is at the junction of this zone with the trunk itself. The general body-hue is brownish flesh-color. This is a southern form ranging from Cape Hatteras to Key West.

Aspidosiphon parvulus Gerould PLATE 125. The species of this genus are so named because they have a shield in front of the anus and, also, one at the end of the body; the former covered with prominent spines, and the latter, by rounded or squarish plates. The proboscis is equipped with multitudes of tiny slender hooks, while the trunk is smooth, but overlaid with flat platelike structures of saucerlike shape, visible only through a lens, and largest posteriorly. The surface of the trunk, when contracted, is thrown into rectangular patterns by the contracting muscles beneath the surface. Most of the species of this genus are found in the Pacific and Indian Oceans. Several species, however, are in the Atlantic. Those here mentioned were taken off Cape Hatteras.

Order PRIAPULIDA

In this Order, the species have no tentacles, the anus is at the posterior end, and the proboscis is very thick and covered with spines. The trunk is thrown into horizontal wrinkles or stripes. The caudal part is covered with respiratory papillae. There are no organs for the special senses. The sexes are distinct.

Priapulus caudatus Lamarck PLATE 125. This animal, about 1 inch in length, is distinguished by a proboscis thicker than the trunk, with spines in longitudinal rows, and by the possession of caudal appendages covered by hollow papillae. The color is yellow or brown. It is found in Arctic seas.

Halicryptus spinulosus Von Siebold PLATE 125. This species is without appendages and has a comparatively short proboscis, being only one tenth to one twelfth the total body-length, with a surface armed with numerous spines in closely set circles. It has a flesh-colored body with a somewhat metallic luster and burrows in the sand, with the proboscis projecting from the surface, or so curved that both ends project into the water. It is said by some to make U-shaped tubes. This worm sheds its skin twice a year, in May and September. It is an Arctic species and occurs in from 2 to 50 fathoms.

PLATE 125

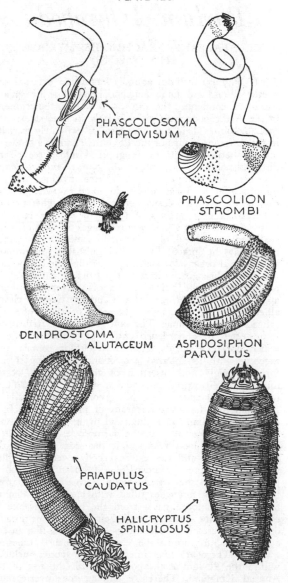

PHASCOLOSOMA
IMPROVISUM

PHASCOLION
STROMBI

DENDROSTOMA
ALUTACEUM

ASPIDOSIPHON
PARVULUS

PRIAPULUS
CAUDATUS

HALICRYPTUS
SPINULOSUS

10
Phylum Arthropoda

(CRUSTACEANS, ARACHNOIDS, MYRIAPODS, AND INSECTS)

THIS Phylum includes animals having an external segmentation and with jointed appendages. Unlike the Phylum Annulata, containing the segmented worms, the segments in the Arthropoda may differ greatly in size, shape, and specialization. Their number, also, is extremely variable in the different groups of the Phylum. There is a tendency for the body-segments to be grouped into three clearly distinguishable regions, the *head, thorax,* and *abdomen.* The segments comprising these three divisions may be quite similar as, for example, in some isopods; or they may be more or less easily detected in the higher groups, either by joints, by lines of fusion, or by the fact that each segment bears a pair of appendages, in spite of being coalesced, specialized, or reduced. In some cases, however, they may be practically indistinguishable. Arthropods have special organs for sight, either simple or compound; for touch, through sensitive tactile hairs or antennae; for taste, through the palps of the often complex mouth appendages; for hearing, through auditory hairs or closely allied balancing organs; for the sense of smell, often localized in the antennae. The outer surface of Arthropods is protected by a hardened cuticle of chitinous material which not only shields them from outside contact, but, together with its internal projections, gives opportunity for the origin and insertion of the internally located muscles. Their paired appendages are not only utilized for the special senses, these being concentrated mostly in the head, but for various means of propulsion, such as crawling, walking, swimming, and flying. The circulation of the blood takes place in the haemocoele. That is, there are no closed blood vessels, but the space between the internal organs and the external body-covering is filled with blood, aerated by means of gills (branchiae), which project out into the water usually as finely divided tree-like or plumose branches filled with blood and adapted to discharge impure gases from the body, and take in oxygen from the water through their thin wall-membranes or, in the case of air-breathing Arthropods, like insects and spiders, to receive the air into branched tubes or *tracheae.* There are five times as many species included within the Phylum Arthropoda as in all the rest of the Animal Kingdom. Therefore, among the invertebrates, they have been able to reach the highest levels of specialization and distribution. They have divided land and sea among them.

While a number of species are amphibious, the crustaceans are almost exclusively found in the salt and fresh waters of the globe, while the insects, spiders, and their allies, and the myriapods are almost exclusively terrestrial. The Phylum Arthropoda is divided into five Classes: (1) *Crustacea* (crabs, lobsters, shrimps, and water fleas); (2) *Arachnoidea* (spiders, mites, and King Crabs); (3) *Onychophora* (Peripatus); (4) *Myriapoda* (centipedes and millipedes); (5) *Hexapoda* (insects).

As the scope of this book includes only marine invertebrates, with few exceptions for convenience, only those Arthropoda that inhabit the sea or the intertidal zone will be considered here, for the most part. They are all included within the Class Crustacea, except a few Arachnoidea and one group of insects.

CLASS CRUSTACEA

This contains Arthropoda which breathe by means of gills or branchiae. They are segmented animals with two pairs of antennae and provided with segmental appendages, each of which is typically divided into an outer and an inner branch.

SUBCLASS ENTOMOSTRACA

The Entomostraca are small Crustacea in which the number of body-segments behind the head is quite variable. There is often an unpaired eye (the *nauplius* eye), occurring in some species, which seems to have persisted in the adult from a larval form, though a pair of lateral eyes, usually compound and not mounted on movable stalks, may also be present, except in rare cases.

Division BRANCHIOPODA

In this Division, the thoracic appendages are both respiratory and locomotor organs. In adaptation to these combined functions, they are flat and leaflike. The body may consist of numerous segments or it may be short, compact, and practically unsegmented. In most species, a carapace is present. There are two Orders: (1) *Phyllopoda*; and (2) *Cladocera*.

Order PHYLLOPODA

The species in this Order have an elongate body and distinct segments. They include the Fairy-Shrimps, the Tadpole-Shrimps, and the Claw-Shrimps. All are freshwater forms, and, therefore, are not included here.

Order CLADOCERA
(Water Fleas)

In this Order, segmentation is obscure or apparently nonexistent. There is a bivalved carapace, and four to six pairs of thoracic appendages. The first pair of antennae is vestigial, while the second pair is quite large, with two branches, and is used for swimming. The abdomen is small and usually doubled under the thorax. There is a single median compound eye. There are two Suborders: (1) *Calyptomera*; (2) *Gymnomera*.

Suborder CALYPTOMERA

The carapace encloses the entire body, which is very compact, with indistinct segments or none. The legs are leaflike and function as branchiae. The Calyptomera is composed entirely of fresh-water species.

Suborder GYMNOMERA

The carapace does not cover the head, limbs, and abdomen, and functions only as a brood-pouch in the females. The legs are prehensile. This Suborder is divided into two Tribes: (1) *Onychopoda;* and (2) *Haploda*.

Tribe ONYCHOPODA

In this group, the abdomen is merely a vestige. There are four pairs of compressed legs with clawlike spines. Both fresh- and salt-water species are included here.

Family Polyphemidae

As indicated by the definition of the tribe, the carapace does not enclose the legs and abdomen, but serves as a brood-sac. There are four pairs of legs, not specialized for respiration. The abdomen has two long, caudal spines, utilized for jumping. There is a large head with a single eye and large second antennae.

Evadne nordmanni Loven PLATE 126. This colorless species is very common in the shallow water along the Atlantic Coast. The head and thorax are continuous with each other. The brood-sac of the female is located quite high. The antennae are small. On the third pair of legs, there is a single spine on either side. It is about ½₀ inch in length.

Podon leuckarti (Sars) PLATE 126. This differs from the preceding species in having its head and thorax separated by a neck. The terminal part of the second antennae consists of two branches with six bristles on each branch. It is very common along the Atlantic Coast in company with *Evadne nordmanni*.

PLATE 126

CLADOCERA

EVADNE
NORDMANNI
(FEMALE)

PODON
LEUCKARTI
(FEMALE)

OSTRACODA

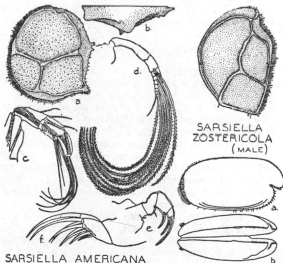

SARSIELLA
ZOSTERICOLA
(MALE)

SARSIELLA AMERICANA

(a) SHELL OF FEMALE, SIDE
(b) SHELL OF FEMALE, FRONT
(c) ANTENNULA OF FEMALE
(d) SWIMMING BRANCH OF ANTENNA, FEMALE
(e) JAW-FOOT OF MALE
(f) ABDOMINAL LAMINA OF FEMALE

CYLINDROLEBERIS
MARIÆ (MALE)
(a) FROM SIDE
(b) FROM BELOW

Tribe HAPLOPODA

The species in this tribe have six pairs of legs, the first pair being very long. The body is cylindrical. They are only found in fresh-water lakes in America and Europe and, therefore, do not come within our range.

SUBCLASS OSTRACODA

In this group, the body is not segmented. It is laterally compressed and always enclosed completely in a bivalved carapace, which can be shut by a retractor muscle. When the carapace is open, the locomotor antennae emerge and act as oars to propel the creature through the water. There are seven pairs of appendages, namely, two pairs of antennae, a pair of mandibles or jaws, two pairs of maxillae, the first pair of which is associated with the mandibles, and the second pair is leglike. Finally, there are two pairs of true legs. The abdomen is extremely short. In development, some pass through a larval stage, known as the *nauplius* stage. In others, this stage is passed through before birth.

The majority of the species in this Subclass are marine. The Subclass is divided into two Orders: (1) *Myodocopa*; and (2) *Podocopa*.

Order MYODOCOPA

The second antennae are divided into two branches, one being large, many-jointed, and adapted for locomotion, and the other vestigial. The valves of the shells have a deep notch in front for extruding the second antennae.

Sarsiella zostericola Cushman PLATE 126. The valves are irregularly ovate. Their surface is unsymmetrically divided into several areas by narrow ridges. The length is 1½ mm. This species is found among eelgrass and hydroids in the Woods Hole region of Massachusetts.

Sarsiella americana Cushman PLATE 126. This is closely related to the previous species and is found in the Woods Hole region.

Cylindroleberis mariae (Baird) PLATE 126. The valves are of elliptical outline, notched in front. This is a large species reaching 2 mm. in length. It is found with *Sarsiella zostericola*.

Order PODOCOPA

The second antennae are single-branched with sharp bristles used in walking or swimming. The shell is without an anterior notch. Most of the species are found in fresh water. The following are noteworthy examples of marine species.

Pseudocytheretta edwardsi Cushman PLATE 127.

PLATE 127

PSEUDOCYTHERETTA
EDWARDSI (MALE)

PONTOCYPRIS
EDWARDSI (FEMALE)
(a) FROM SIDE
(b) FROM BELOW

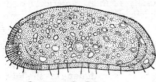

CYTHERIDEA
AMERICANA

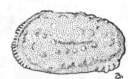

CYTHERE
DAWSONI
(a) FROM SIDE
(b) FROM ABOVE

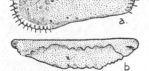

CYTHEREIS
VINEYARDENSIS (MALE)
(a) FROM SIDE (b) FROM ABOVE

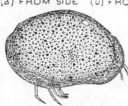

LOXOCONCHA
IMPRESSA
(FEMALE)

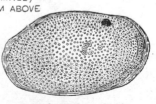

LOXOCONCHA
GUTTATA

This is a small, smooth species of elliptical outline, the surface bearing a few scattered hairs. The length is a little over 1 mm. It is found on sandy bottoms. It is the most abundant species in the Woods Hole region.

Pontocypris edwardsi Cushman PLATE 127. The shell is more or less triangular in outline with rounded ends and evenly covered with minute hairs. It measures .85 mm. by .47 mm. It is found in Eel Pond, Woods Hole, Massachusetts, during the late summer.

Cythereis vineyardensis Cushman PLATE 127. The shell is rough and largely composed of calcareous substance. It is rather hatchet-shaped in outline, with straight upper and lower edges, strongly rounded anteriorly and shallowly rounded posteriorly. Bristlelike hairs are evident around the anterior margin.

Loxoconcha impressa (Baird) PLATE 127. The shell is rather narrowed posteriorly with a notch at the upper posterior angle. The ventral margin has a flattened border. The shell is evenly punctate. It is common in shallow water among eelgrass in Vineyard Sound.

Cytheridea americana Cushman; **Cythere dawsoni** Brady PLATE 127. These are other related species, with shell characteristics as clearly shown in the accompanying illustrations.

PLATE 128

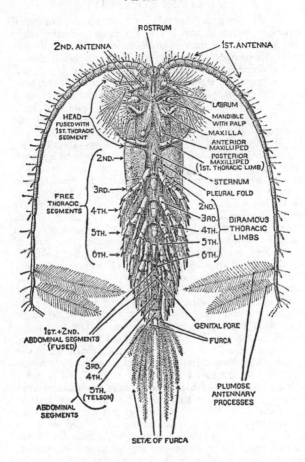

ROSTRUM

2ND. ANTENNA

1ST. ANTENNA

LABRUM

MANDIBLE
WITH PALP

MAXILLA

ANTERIOR
MAXILLIPED

HEAD
FUSED WITH
1ST. THORACIC
SEGMENT

POSTERIOR
MAXILLIPED
(1ST. THORACIC LIMB)

2ND. →

STERNUM

PLEURAL FOLD

3RD. →

2ND.

FREE
THORACIC
SEGMENTS

4TH. →

3RD.

4TH.

BIRAMOUS
THORACIC
LIMBS

5TH. →

5TH.

6TH. →

6TH.

GENITAL PORE

FURCA

1ST. + 2ND.
ABDOMINAL SEGMENTS
(FUSED)

3RD.

4TH.

5TH.
(TELSON)

PLUMOSE
ANTENNARY
PROCESSES

ABDOMINAL
SEGMENTS

SETÆ OF FURCA

A TYPICAL COPEPOD
(CALANUS HYPERBOREUS)
VENTRAL VIEW

SUBCLASS COPEPODA

In this group are included a vast number of small crustacea, many of which are of microscopic size, while the largest is less than ½ inch in length. Like all crustacea, their body is typically divided into head, thorax, and abdomen. In some cases, however, there is a fusion of the segments, especially of those included in the head and the thorax, thus producing a cephalothorax, which in many species is completely or partly protected by a shieldlike covering, the carapace. Each segment of the body, typically, has a pair of jointed appendages, utilized for locomotion and for breathing purposes. Usually, they have a single stemlike joint (*protopod*) from which branch two segmented terminal divisions. The outer branch is known as the *exopod* and the inner, the *endopod*. In various parts of the body, however, special functions must be performed so that these two branched appendages are often considerably modified. In the Copepods (INDEX PLATE 128), the head has six pairs of appendages, as a rule, as follows: two pairs of antennae, one pair of mandibles, one pair of maxillae, and two pairs of maxillipeds. The first pair of antennae (*antennules*) are not branched, but their ends may have two or three small branchlets (*plumose antennary flagella*). These may be sense organs, but often they serve for locomotion. The second antennae may either be two-branched or single and often are used as grasping organs. The mandibles, maxillae, and maxillipeds, as a rule, are well developed and functional. They may be reduced or absent in certain species. The thorax has six segments, each with a pair of legs. The first four are branched and utilized as swimming organs. The fifth pair are usually vestigial, but may be grasping organs in the male. The female usually lacks the sixth pair and this is also often true of the male. In identifying species, special attention should be given to the fifth pair. The sixth segment is provided with the genital organs. The abdominal segments, in some species, may be six in number, while there may be fewer, or even one in others. Copepods are of great importance in the economy of the seas, for they are directly or indirectly the basis of the food of all sea-animals.

The Subclass Copepoda is divided into eight Orders: (1) *Calanoida*; (2) *Cyclopoida*; (3) *Harpacticoida*; (4) *Monstrilloida*; (5) *Notodelphyoida*; (6) *Caligoida*; (7) *Lernaeopodoida*; and (8) *Arguloida*.

PLATE 129

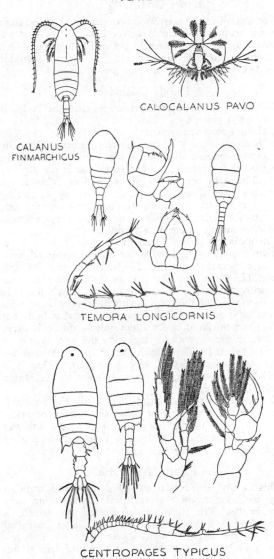

CALOCALANUS PAVO

CALANUS
FINMARCHICUS

TEMORA LONGICORNIS

CENTROPAGES TYPICUS

Order CALANOIDA

The movable joint is situated between the fifth and sixth thoracic segments. There is a very long pair of first antennae, having twenty-three to twenty-five segments. One of them is modified in the male. The second antennae have two branches and are not prehensile.

Family Calanidae

The first pair of antennae is longer than the body. A single sac is present.

Calanus finmarchichus (Gunnerus) PLATE 129. The head is separate from the first thoracic segment. The body is quite transparent while a red pigment is distributed in irregular blotches through it and sometimes in the appendages. The eggs are yellowish or reddish. This is an unusually large species, the female commonly measuring 4 mm. in length. It swims at the surface of the sea, sometimes in immense swarms, coloring the sea reddish. It is of economic importance as fish food.

Calocalanus pavo Dana PLATE 129. This is a remarkable species. The head of the male is separated from the first thoracic segments. The abdomen has five segments. The furca is smaller than in the female and much less richly plumose. The abdomen of the female has only two segments, but the furca is rich in broad plumes with a metallic iridescence while its very transparent body has orange and brick-red blotches, not only in the body itself, but also in the appendages, including the long bristles of the first antennae. The plumes can be spread, so that the name *pavo* (peacock) is very appropriate. This is a tropical pelagic species, sometimes brought to our region by the Gulf Stream.

Calocalanus plumulosus Claus. Only the female is known. It has a transparent body with orange or brick-red spots, both in the body and in the antennal and furcal plumes. One of the latter is developed to a great length forming a long trailing structure.

Family Temoridae

This family is characterized by a short and compact body with the straight symmetrical furca having very short bristles. The fifth pair of legs of the female is unbranched and symmetrical with an inner marginal prong on the terminal joint, shorter than the two terminal prongs. In the male, the fifth pair of legs is unsymmetrical. The left leg is quite irregular with a rod-shaped projection, while the distal portion of the right first antenna is unusually developed, as shown in the figure on PLATE 129.

PLATE 130

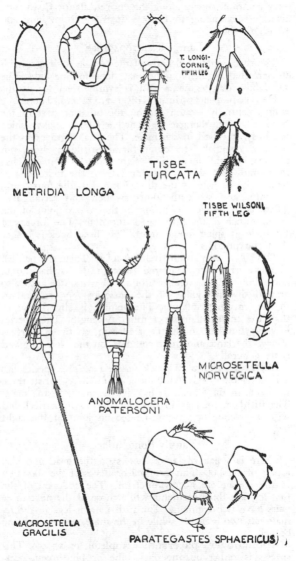

METRIDIA LONGA

TISBE FURCATA

T. LONGI-CORNIS, FIFTH LEG

TISBE WILSONI FIFTH LEG

MACROSETELLA GRACILIS

ANOMALOCERA PATERSONI

MICROSETELLA NORVEGICA

PARATEGASTES SPHAERICUS

Temora longicornis Müller PLATE 129. This is a very common species along the entire Atlantic Coast with its range extending to Europe. It is 1½ mm. long and bluish in color.

Family Centropagidae

The three-segmented body of the female is slender with its terminal segments somewhat bent to one side. The male has four segments and is symmetrical terminally.

Centropages typicus Kröyer PLATE 129. There is a single, centrally located eye on the anterior part of the head. The fifth thoracic segment has lateral hooks, which are unsymmetrical in the male. The anal segment in the male is vestigial. The outer furcal bristle is short, not plumose in the male. The right anterior antenna has its second joint sharply separated from the first. It is at least twice as long as the third joint with the fourteenth, fifteenth, and sixteenth joints swollen and rectangular. There is a conspicuous prong in the second joint of the outer branch in the fifth leg of the male. The forceps of the male grasping foot is stout. The distal hook is longer than the proximal.

This is a very transparent species. There is reddish pigment irregularly scattered through the cephalothorax and abdomen, especially around the mouth and also around the first joints of the posterior feet, as well as in the grasping antenna. The female is slightly larger than the male, attaining 2 mm. in length. This species is very abundant in the Gulf Stream, south of Marthas Vineyard Island, and quite common on the New England coast generally.

Metridia longa Lubbock PLATE 130. This species has a long, slender body with the abdominal region in three segments in the female. It has five segments in the male. The fifth pair of legs in the male is unsymmetrical and with a prolongation from the second joint of the right leg.

Family Pontellidae

There is a pair of lateral hooks on the head and also a pair of eyespots. The terminal branches of the abdomen in the female are not symmetrical. The endopod of the first leg has three segments while those of the next three pairs have two segments. The fifth pair of legs in the female has two branches while in the male, there is but one branch.

Anomalocera patersoni Templeton PLATE 130. This species is rather opaque dark blue or blue-green, occasionally iron-red. A series of dorsal black blotches occurs on the middle of the back and irregularly branching dark blue markings on the side of the thoracic segments. The digestive tube is bright green. The eggs are white or reddish. The female is 3½ to 4 mm. long; the male, about 3 mm. in length, has the right first antenna modified, some of the segments being unflattened. It also has an enormously developed ventral eye on the underside of the head. This species swarms at the surface and is important as fish food. It is quite common at Woods Hole after southwest winds and is especially abundant in the Gulf Stream.

Family Bomolochidae

The body is shaped like that of a *Cyclops*. Maxillae are present in both male and female. In the latter, they are located outside the other mouth-parts; but in the male, they are behind them. The second antennae are prehensile, but armed with claws.

Bomolochus albidus Wilson. This is a minute, entirely white species with a well-segmented body and sausage-shaped egg sacs. It is parasitic, being found in the gill-cavity of the Angler Fish (*Lophius piscatorius*), just above the pelvic fins.

Order CYCLOPOIDA

The movable joint is between the fourth and fifth thoracic segments. The thorax is much wider than the abdomen. The eggs are contained in two ovisacs, which are attached to the surface of the genital segment. The first antennae are long, with about seventeen segments. The second antennae have but one joint. The first four pairs of legs have two branches of about three segments each. The species live in fresh, brackish, and salt water, some burrowing in the sand and mud.

Oithona similis Claus PLATE 131. The cephalothorax and abdomen each have five segments with the first and second abdominal segments fused. The front of the female ends in a pointed beak, which is bent ventrally at right angles. The furca is shorter than the anal segment. The genital orifices are situated farther back than usual. The second basal joint of the mandibles has two hook-shaped bristles. The body is very transparent with reddish pigment distributed throughout the various segments.

Order HARPACTICOIDA

The movable joint is between the fourth and fifth thoracic segments. The body is quite cylindrical with the abdomen practically as wide as the thorax. The first antennae are short, having usually not more than eight segments.

Family Harpacticidae

The body is tapered posteriorly. The exopods of the first legs have two segments. The exopods of the third legs of the male are very stout and curve inward.

Clytemnestra rostrata Brady PLATE 131. The cephalothorax has four segments, consisting of the head and the first thoracic segment fused. The abdomen has five segments. The postero-lateral corners of the segments in the cephalothorax are prolonged into projections. The anterior antennae may be eight-jointed. The male has six segments in the abdomen, while the anterior antennae are specialized as grasping organs. The color is reddish, due to numerous rose-colored, brown, or light green oil-globules. The eyes are deep red and the ovaries dark gray, with a reddish tinge. The female is 1 mm. long, the male somewhat shorter. It is found in the Gulf Stream, about 60 miles south of Martha's Vineyard.

Oncaea venusta Philippi PLATE 131. In the female, the cephalothorax is pear-shaped with a granulated epidermis. The furca is four times as long as broad. There are two bristles on the second basal joint, long and slender, the outer branch of the feet with broad-edged, saw-toothed outer marginal bristles. In the male, there are short genital valves and a short, broad anal segment, practically oval. This species is carmine-red in color, densest in the cephalothorax and genital segment. The chitinous shield of the cephalothorax and the appendages are more or less violet. The eggs are blue. It is found in the Gulf Stream, south of Martha's Vineyard Island.

Sapphirina gemma Dana PLATE 131. This copepod has a flattened body. The thorax and abdomen of the female each have five segments with broad middle abdominal segments. The mandibles are hatchet-shaped. The maxillae are flat, oval discs. The male has leaf-shaped, broadened body-segments, iridescent in color. The furca of the female usually has a small point on the tip of the inner margin. The eggs are blue. The anterior antennae are five-jointed, with a long second joint. In the male, the length of the body is about 2½ times its greatest breadth. The eye lenses are on the ventral surface beneath the front. The furca, the fourth pair of feet, and the anterior antennae are like those of the female, but some of the following appendages are reduced. The female is transparent and the eggs are dull blue. The male has brilliantly blue coloration with reflections dazzling in the sunlight. It is iridescent with other colors as the animal changes its position (Dana).

It is found in the Gulf Stream, south of Marthas Vineyard.

Macrosetella gracilis (Dana) PLATE 130. The length

PLATE 131

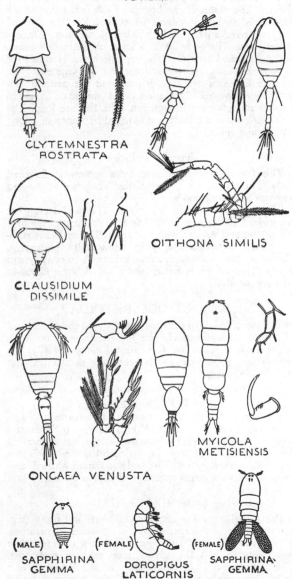

CLYTEMNESTRA
ROSTRATA

OITHONA SIMILIS

CLAUSIDIUM
DISSIMILE

ONCAEA VENUSTA

MYICOLA
METISIENSIS

(MALE)
SAPPHIRINA
GEMMA

(FEMALE)
DOROPIGUS
LATICORNIS

(FEMALE)
SAPPHIRINA
GEMMA

of the female is about 1½ mm.; that of the male somewhat shorter. The chitin of the body and the first joints of the limbs tend to be transparent violet in color. The internal organs are red, surrounded by yellowish oil drops The eye is deep red. The body itself is long, exceedingly slender, and compressed laterally. The cephalothorax is composed of four segments, and the abdomen of five segments. The anterior antennae are eight-jointed and the posterior antennae two-jointed. The antenna of the male is eight-jointed and grasping in function. The feet are long. The posterior part of the body is prolonged by means of a long and slender spine.

Family Tisbidae

This family is characterized by a somewhat flattened body. The thorax has lateral plates. The setae at the end segment are very slender.

Tisbe furcata Baird PLATE 130. The caudal branches are wider than they are long. The final segment of the fifth leg is long and slender with five setae. The male has rudiments of a sixth leg. The body is practically transparent. The ovary shows through as dark blue in color. The eye is red. This species is found along the Atlantic Coast to Chesapeake Bay.

Order NOTODELPHYOIDA

The movable joint in the male is between the fourth and fifth thoracic segments. In the female, there is no joint, but there is a pouch for incubation located dorsally; the articulation, in this case, is between the genital segment and the abdomen.

Family Doropygidae

This family has the characteristics of the order.

Doropygus laticornis Wilson PLATE 131. This and other related small species are parasitic or commensal in the gill-cavity of ascidians; in this case it is the Sea Grapes (*Molgula manhattensis*). The body is sausage-shaped, segmented, with the much narrower abdomen extending at a right angle.

Order CALIGOIDA

The movable joint is between the third and fourth segments, except in the species which are attached parasites, when there is no movable joint. The first antennae have two segments and the second antennae are prehensile. There are four pairs of swimming legs and rudiments of a fifth. There are two long ovisacs. Both sexes are parasitic and are found either in salt or fresh water.

PLATE 132

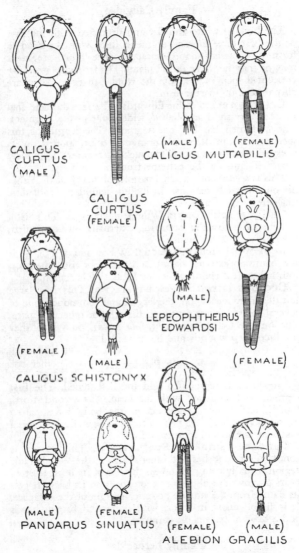

CALIGUS
CURTUS
(MALE)

CALIGUS
CURTUS
(FEMALE)

(MALE)   (FEMALE)
CALIGUS MUTABILIS

(MALE)
LEPEOPHTHEIRUS
EDWARDSI

(FEMALE)   (MALE)
CALIGUS SCHISTONYX

(FEMALE)

(MALE)   (FEMALE)
PANDARUS SINUATUS

(FEMALE)   (MALE)
ALEBION GRACILIS

Family Caligidae

The body is white and flat and depressed with the first or the first three thoracic segments fused with the head to form a horseshoe-shaped carapace. The fourth segment may or may not have dorsal plates. The frontal plates have crescent-shaped suckers on the frontal margin. They are all parasitic on marine fish.

Caligus rapax Milne-Edwards. The free-thoracic segment is very short and half as wide as the genital segment. The abdomen has but one segment. The length of this species is 6 mm. It is pale orange in color, spotted on its back with reddish brown. The suckers (*lunules*) are widely separated and on the extreme front of the body.

This is a common external parasite on many of the fishes of our coastal regions, including flounders, codfishes, mackerel, rays, sharks, etc.

Caligus schistonyx Wilson PLATE 132. This is a small species, usually occurring externally on Menhaden, sometimes on the Bluefish.

Lepeophtheirus edwardsi Wilson PLATE 132. This is a common external parasite on flounders and other bottom fishes. It is abundant in the Woods Hole region.

Cecrops latreillii Leach PLATE 133. This is a large but degenerate copepod, the largest and commonest one of several related forms found on the gills, or otherwise parasitic on the Ocean Sunfish (*Mola mola*), on which they produce deep wounds and lie imbedded.

Family Pandaridae

The body is segmented and much flattened. The first segment only is fused with the head. The second, third, fourth, and genital segments of the body have paired dorsal plates. The last pair is fused. The male has dorsal plates on the second segment only.

Pandarus sinuatus Say PLATE 132. This species is common on dogfishes and other sharks in the Woods Hole region, usually being found on the fins of its host. It often bears a growth of algae and protozoans on its back. It gets its name from the sinuate posterior margin of the carapace. It is light yellow in color, with horizontal brown bands and a brown spot on the carapace.

Family Lernaeidae

These are the largest of the parasitic copepods, often reaching a length of 8 to 10 inches, exclusive of the egg strings. The extremely elongate and unsegmented body is somewhat cylindrical and divided into three regions. First, a cephalothorax with horns or other processes; second, a thorax resembling a narrow cylindrical neck; and third, a trunk which takes up the rest of the body and is somewhat swollen and either straight or S-shaped. The paired egg strings are either club-shaped or long, threadlike structures. They may be straight or coiled or twisted at times into spirals. The antennae are dorsal with the second pair chelate. The mouth is like a sucking tube and may be protruded. The adult female buries or anchors firmly its head and part of its neck in the tissues of the host so as to bring to its mouth a source of abundant blood supply.

The male becomes sexually mature while still in a larval stage with a body something like that of *Cyclops*. It never attacks the tissue of its hosts nor is it anchored in any way, nor has anyone found it attached to or in company with the adult female (C. B. Wilson).

Lernaeenicus radiatus Lesueur PLATE 133. The body of the adult female is elongate and wormlike with a very long, slender neck and small, round head usually with five radiating processes. The egg sacs are long and stringlike. This is a parasite on the Menhaden and on other fishes. The head and neck are buried deeply in the body of the host, usually near the dorsal fin. The entire length, without counting the egg strings, is 40 mm.

Penella filosa Wilson PLATE 133. The cephalothorax in the female is somewhat spherical and slightly depressed. It is elongated at the head and covered with short prolongations that are often branched like a cauliflower. At the junction of the head with the neck, a pair of short, straight, and unbranched chitinous horns are given off. The neck is comparatively thick and of about the same diameter throughout. The first antennae are slender and three-jointed, close to the base of the second pair. The second antennae are two-jointed, both joints being of the same size, the terminal one having forceps like chelae with a strongly curved claw. This is a still larger species than the preceding, parasitic on the Swordfish and Ocean Sunfish. The rear part of the body is covered with a dense brush of minute plumose processes.

Family Dichelesthiidae

In this family, the general body-form is long and narrow. A carapace covers the head, which is fused with the first thoracic segment. The rest of the thorax is composed of free segments, which are sometimes equipped with rings or dorsal plates or both. The small abdomen is unsegmented. The long egg strings are thread-shaped. There are two pairs of antennae of which the first is slender and furnished with setae. The second pair is stouter and equipped with hooklike appendages. There are usually four pairs of swimming legs. The male is somewhat smaller than the female and is similar to it in having the head and the first segment fused and covered with the carapace. The rest of the thoracic segments, however, are fused and often covered with a dorsal plate, but never equipped with wings. The unsegmented abdomen is minute. This family is, for the most part, parasitic on marine fishes.

Lernanthropus pomatomi Rathbun PLATE 133. The first antennae are eight-jointed. The cephalothorax is much narrower than the thorax proper. The female is 7 mm. in length. The females are commonly parasitic on the gills of the Bluefish (*Pomatomus saltatrix*), which has been frequently taken from Vineyard Sound in Massachusetts and at Beaufort, North Carolina. The general color of this species is brown with the appendages light gray.

Nemesis pallida Wilson PLATE 133. This species has an oval carapace covering the head region. There are four-jointed thoracic segments followed by a much produced abdomen of several joints, longer in the male than in the female. In the latter, they are almost vestigial and bear a pair of egg strings.

Family Euryphoridae

In this group, the first three thoracic segments are fused with the head, while the fourth segment has two dorsal plates. The first three pairs of legs are branched, the fourth pair is unbranched and vestigial.

Alebion gracilis Wilson PLATE 132. This is an external parasite of sharks, especially of dogfishes, and the Pollack.

Alebion glaber Wilson. This is a similar species, also parasitic on dogfishes and sharks generally, and it is known around the Woods Hole region. The abdomen has two segments, with the fourth segment having rounded dorsal plates, which are lacking in the male. The color is grayish white and it is common along the Atlantic Coast.

Order LERNAEOPODOIDA

The copepods in this order have no movable articulation, their bodies being completely fused. The female usually is not segmented. The male is minute and remains attached to the body of the female, but he is free to move about. The female lacks swimming legs, though the male has one or two pairs. They are parasitic on both marine and fresh-water fishes.

PLATE 133

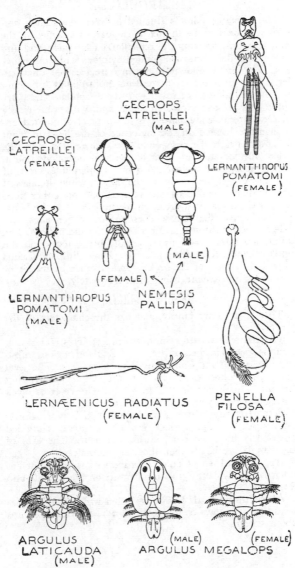

CECROPS
LATREILLEI
(FEMALE)

CECROPS
LATREILLEI
(MALE)

LERNANTHROPUS
POMATOMI
(FEMALE)

LERNANTHROPUS
POMATOMI
(MALE)

(FEMALE) — NEMESIS
PALLIDA

(MALE)

LERNÆENICUS RADIATUS
(FEMALE)

PENELLA
FILOSA
(FEMALE)

ARGULUS
LATICAUDA
(MALE)

(MALE)

(FEMALE)

ARGULUS MEGALOPS

Order ARGULOIDA

The movable joint is situated between the fourth and fifth segments of the thorax. A carapace is attached to the first segment, covering the cephalothoracic region and also protecting the branchiae located symmetrically on either side. The three following segments are free but unarticulated. The fifth and sixth segments, immediately following the movable joint, are fused with the abdomen. There are three eyes present, a median single, and two symmetrically placed, lateral, compound eyes. Two pairs of jointed antennae are located on the underside of the head in front of and beneath the compound eyes. There is a spinelike organ immediately in front of the siphon-shaped mouth, which secretes a poison. A pair of mandibles and of maxillae are at the bottom of the siphon, while the clawed and jointed maxillipeds are situated one on either side, modified into large suckers, on the underside of the body. In this order, the female does not carry her eggs, but fastens them to stones or other objects on the bottom. The adults are parasites of fishes, usually being found on the outer surface or in the gill-cavity. They cling to various objects by means of the suckers and advance by means of a walking movement, using them alternately.

Family Argulidae

This is the only family, and has the characters of the Order.

Argulus laticauda Smith PLATE 133. This is the commonest species in the southern New England region, infesting the eel, Tom Cod, flounders, skates, etc. The oval carapace is longer than wide with the abdomen extending behind. The length is 3⁵⁄₁₀ to 6 mm. The color is black variegated with yellow and brown markings.

Argulus megalops Smith PLATE 133. It is a parasite on flounders, sculpins, skate, etc. The carapace is divided posteriorly into two oval, leaflike segments. The eyes of the female are larger than those of the male.

Argulus alosae Gould. This species is similar but has a narrow body. It is found as a parasite on the Alewife and Smelt.

Argulus funduli Kröyer. A rather wide-bodied species found on minnows of the genus *Fundulus*. It often swims about freely.

PLATE 134

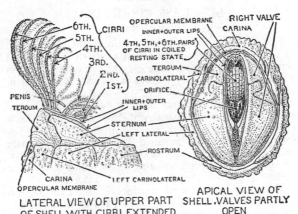

6TH. CIRRI
5TH.
4TH.
3RD.
2ND.
IST.

OPERCULAR MEMBRANE
INNER + OUTER LIPS

RIGHT VALVE
CARINA

4TH, 5TH, +6TH. PAIRS
OF CIRRI IN COILED
RESTING STATE

TERGUM
CARINOLATERAL
ORIFICE

PENIS
TERGUM

INNER + OUTER
LIPS

STERNUM
LEFT LATERAL
ROSTRUM

CARINA
OPERCULAR MEMBRANE

LEFT CARINOLATERAL

LATERAL VIEW OF UPPER PART
OF SHELL WITH CIRRI EXTENDED

APICAL VIEW OF
SHELL. VALVES PARTLY OPEN

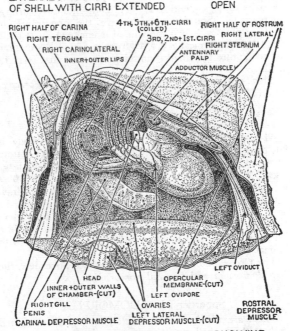

RIGHT HALF OF CARINA
RIGHT TERGUM
RIGHT CARINOLATERAL
INNER + OUTER LIPS

4TH, 5TH, +6TH. CIRRI
(COILED)

3RD, 2ND + IST. CIRRI
ANTENNARY
PALP
ADDUCTOR MUSCLE

RIGHT HALF OF ROSTRUM
RIGHT LATERAL
RIGHT STERNUM

LEFT OVIDUCT

HEAD
INNER + OUTER WALLS
OF CHAMBER - (CUT)
RIGHT GILL
PENIS
CARINAL DEPRESSOR MUSCLE

OPERCULAR
MEMBRANE - (CUT)
LEFT OVIPORE
OVARIES
LEFT LATERAL
DEPRESSOR MUSCLE - (CUT)

ROSTRAL
DEPRESSOR
MUSCLE

VERTICAL SECTION OF SHELL SHOWING
ENTIRE ANIMAL IN RESTING POSITION

SUBCLASS CIRRIPEDIA
(Barnacles)

The barnacles are shrimplike animals usually enclosed in a calcareous shell. They are of relatively large size as compared with the preceding group. The young are free-swimming, but as they become adult they attach themselves to other foreign objects, such as rocks, wharf-piles, drifting timbers, seaweed, often to the bottoms of ships, and even on whales, fastening themselves by means of a cementlike secretion from a gland in the next to the last joint of each anterior antenna. The body has a carapace that extends from the back of the head to cover the thorax, on either side of which it forms a fold which secretes the shells.

The appendages of the barnacles are quite characteristic. There is a pair of mandibles, two pairs of maxillae, and six pairs of legs, divided at their ends into two curling, many-jointed branches, which give the appearance of feathery plumes. When the animal is enclosed in its shell, these legs rhythmically project from it forming a casting-net to capture the small swimming creatures that form its food.

This Subclass is divided into two Orders: (1) *Thoracica;* and (2) *Abdominalia.*

Order THORACICA

This Order includes the true barnacles. The body is enclosed, upside down, in a calcareous shell to the bottom of which it is attached by the back of the head, while its legs are uppermost. As the valves of the shell open, these six pairs of feathery legs are thrust out to grasp and draw in the food of the animal.

Agassiz has said that the barnacle is nothing more than a little shrimplike creature, standing on its head inside a limestone house and kicking its food into its mouth with its feet (INDEX PLATE 134).

The Order *Thoracica* is divided into two Suborders, the *Lepadomorpha* and the *Balanomorpha.*

Suborder LEPADOMORPHA

These are the Stalked Barnacles, having an elongated body within a shell consisting of two valves, each composed of a number of large calcareous plates. The body forms a long or short stalk known as the *peduncle;* the part of the body enclosed by the shell being called the *capitulum.*

Of the three families composing this Suborder, only one, the family *Lepadidae,* is found within the range covered

PLATE 135

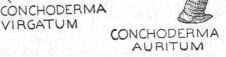

LEPAS
FASCICULARIS

LEPAS
ANATIFERA

LEPAS
HILLI

SECTION ACROSS
PLATES SHOWING
TOOTH ON
RIGHT SCUTUM

ANTERIOR
VIEW OF
BASAL PLATES
LEPAS HILLI

EDGEWISE
VIEW

LEPAS
PECTINATA

LEPAS
ANSERIFERA

CONCHODERMA
VIRGATUM

CONCHODERMA
AURITUM

by this book, the other two being confined to the West Coast of America or to deep water.

Family Lepadidae

The flattened body, enclosed in its shell, is mounted on a more or less slender, fleshy stalk. The shell consists of not more than five pieces: namely, two fan-shaped *scuta,* covering the lower part of the body; two *terga,* joined to the upper part of the *scuta* and covering the upper end of the body; and a median *carina,* or keel, at the hinge of the double shell. These are known as the Gooseneck Barnacles because of the shape of shell and stalk. They are hermaphroditic.

Lepas fascicularis Ellis and Solander PLATE 135. The plates of the shell, in this species, are very thin and paperlike. The carina has an angular bend. They often occur in bunches, in very abundant growths. The length of the shell is about 2 inches. The shell plates are joined closely together, fitting each other accurately. They are especially abundant in early summer, ranging along the Atlantic Coast from the Bay of Fundy southward to Florida; in fact, they are cosmopolitan, occurring attached to seaweed and other floating objects.

Lepas hillii Leach PLATE 135. The valves, in this species, are smooth and bluish white. The carina has a contracted neck and is well separated at the base from the scuta by soft skin. There is no *umbonal tooth* on the inside of either scutum. The shell is about 2 inches or less in length. There is no indication of radial striations on the shells. The range is along the coast of Canada and New England to Vineyard Sound.

Lepas anatifera Linnaeus PLATE 135. This species is similar to the preceding, but smaller. The carina is closely fitted to the other plates at its base. The right scutum has an internal umbonal tooth. This is absent on the left scutum. This species is very common, but ranges more southerly than *Lepas fascicularis.*

Lepas pectinata Spengler PLATE 135. The valves have more or less rough or even spinous ridges. The carina is conspicuously contracted above the base. This is found less commonly than the other species along the Atlantic coast.

Lepas anserifera Linnaeus PLATE 135. This is similar to *Lepas pectinata,* but is usually smoother, with the ridge on the scutum more distinct from the margin. The neck of the carina is not contracted as in *Lepas pectinata.*

Conchoderma auritum (Linnaeus) PLATE 135. In this genus the plates are vestigial, the body being covered with a leathery skin. The stalk is almost as broad as the body, but more contracted at the area of attachment. There are two earlike lobes at the upper end of the body. It is

PLATE 136

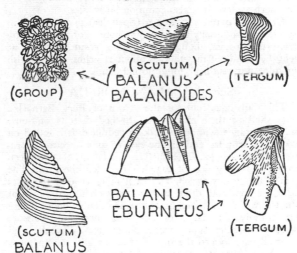

(GROUP)

(SCUTUM) BALANUS BALANOIDES (TERGUM)

BALANUS EBURNEUS (TERGUM)

(SCUTUM) BALANUS CRENATUS

(TERGUM) BALANUS CRENATUS

BALANUS IMPROVISUS

(TERGUM) (SCUTUM)

occasionally found on the bottom of ships coming from southern waters. It is also common on whales.

Conchoderma virgatum (Spengler) PLATE 135. This species is also usually found on the bottom of ships coming from the tropics, though its range is cosmopolitan. The length, including the stalk, is about 2 inches. It is grayish in color with six dark longitudinal bands.

Suborder BALANOMORPHA

This Suborder contains the Acorn or Rock Barnacles. The shell of these animals is attached directly on some solid substance, without a stalk or peduncle. It is found on rocks, wharf-piles, and, in the case of some species, on sea-turtles and whales. The shell is made up of thick, calcareous plates which fit together in a tentlike form. The plates are rigidly attached to each other around the sides of the animal, but there are two pairs of hinged valves at the top which may open and close like double doors. There are usually six plates forming the immovable portion, welded together with overlapping edges. Dorsally and ventrally are located the unpaired carina and the unpaired rostrum. There are two pairs of lateral plates on the side, all plates overlapping on both edges. The two pairs of side-plates have their ventral edges overlapping and their dorsal edges underlapping the neighboring plates. In every case, the edges that overlap are designated as *radii,* while those that underlap are called *alae*. The feather-feet are held uppermost. (See INDEX PLATE 134 for details showing shell, position, and anatomy of the animal.)

Family Balanidae

In this family, the carina is the only plate in which both the edges are alae. The bottom of each shell, in some species, is calcareous; in others, membranous. The plates of the wall are more or less porous, having tubes or cavities in their substance.

Balanus balanoides (Linnaeus) PLATE 136. This is the common Rock Barnacle. It has a membranous base to the cone instead of a calcareous one, as in other species. These are enormously abundant on the rocks along the Atlantic coast from the Arctic Ocean to Delaware Bay between the tide-marks. They become elongated when in crowded colonies. The diameter of the shell is less than ½ inch.

Balanus eburneus Gould PLATE 136. The Ivory Barnacle. This shell is low and broad. It is a fairly large, very smooth, white barnacle, usually growing at the low-tide mark in salt or brackish water. The base of the shell is calcareous in contrast to the previous species. It is common from Boston southward to the West Indies.

PLATE 137

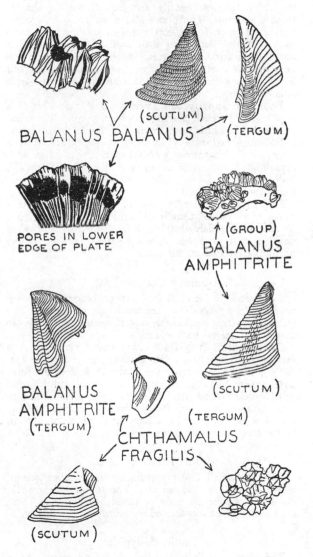

(SCUTUM)

BALANUS BALANUS

(TERGUM)

PORES IN LOWER
EDGE OF PLATE

↑ (GROUP)
BALANUS
AMPHITRITE

BALANUS
AMPHITRITE
(TERGUM)

(SCUTUM)

(TERGUM)

CHTHAMALUS
FRAGILIS

(SCUTUM)

Balanus crenatus Bruguiere PLATE 136. This is a very large species, usually very rough, with a sharply toothed aperture. The plates of the wall readily separate from each other. It is a northern species, being more common north of Cape Cod than south of it. The shell is about 1½ inches in diameter. The base is calcareous and very thin. It is exceedingly abundant on stones and shells below the low-tide mark, especially along the entire North Atlantic Coast.

Balanus improvisus Darwin PLATE 136. This is a very smooth barnacle, having very narrow radii. It is found in salt and brackish water from Nova Scotia to Patagonia.

Balanus balanus (Linnaeus) PLATE 137. This is a large, dirty-white, strongly-ribbed species, with plates well consolidated. It is quite common north of Cape Cod. The wall-plates have large, square, longitudinal tubes in their substance.

Balanus amphitrite Darwin PLATE 137. This is a rather small species, usually smooth and striated with pink or red. It is widely distributed in warm seas and often attaches itself to vessels. A white variety (*nivius*) ranges north to Cape Cod on our coast.

Family Chthamalidae

The plates of the shell wall are nonporous, not being penetrated by tubes. They are usually six in number. The rostrum overlaps the neighboring plates on either side, so that it has alae on both edges.

Chthamalus fragilis Darwin PLATE 137. This is a very small, fragile, somewhat flattened, grayish white barnacle growing on rocks in the tidal area. It does not form large clusters, but occurs singly, or in small groups, and occupies the highest part of the tide limit, even farther up than the more abundant *Balanus balanoides*. The shell has no calcareous base in this species. It ranges along the Atlantic coast from southern New England to the West Indies.

Order ABDOMINALIA

This is a small Order containing two families, one of which is found within our area. The animal has no shell, but has a segmented body protected by a mantle. There are three pairs of feet located posteriorly on the thorax.

Family Alcippidae

The slender stalk is attached to the substratum by a large chitinous disc. The mantle opens laterally. The legs are unbranched. The minute males are attached to the female.

Alcippe (Trypetesa) lampas Hancock. This species bores into the dead shells of the Moon-Shell (*Polynices*), when it has been deprived of its original inhabitant, and is being carried around by hermit crabs. It also attacks the shells of other barnacles and is about ¼ inch in length. It is reported from the Woods Hole region.

SUBCLASS MALACOSTRACA

All the larger crustacea are contained in this Subclass, including the shrimps, crayfish, lobsters, and crabs. The great majority of them have twenty segments, five of which belong to the head, eight to the thorax, and seven to the abdomen. Together, these are included in the Series *Eumalacostraca.* The only exception is a group of primitive *Malacostraca,* which belong to the Series *Leptostraca,* otherwise known as the *Phyllocarida.* They have an abdomen with eight segments. Throughout the entire Subclass, there are paired eyes, two pairs of antennae, a mandibular segment, and two maxillary segments. The eight thoracic segments carry the true limbs, the anterior of which are often turned forward so as to function to a certain degree in connection with the mouth. They are known as maxillipeds, while usually the last four (pereiopods) are turned backward and are used in locomotion. The abdomen, of six segments, bears a pair of double-branched swimming-feet (pleopods). Finally, the limbless, pointed, terminal segment is referred to as the *telson.* The openings of the excretory organs (green glands) are at the base of the second antennae. This is the uniform pattern on which all the Malacostraca are built with few exceptions. (See INDEX PLATE 156).

Series LEPTOSTRACA

In this group, the segments of the body are like those of the other Malacostraca, except that there are eight segments in the abdomen instead of six, as well as eight segments in the thorax, and the paired compound eyes are borne upon stalks. The eight thoracic limbs are biramous and each has a leaflike bract, thus causing them to resemble somewhat the leaflike limbs of the Phyllopods. The abdominal appendages also are biramous.

Nebalia bipes (Fabricius) PLATE 138. This is a small shrimplike form with slender body, more or less horizontally flattened, less than ½ inch in length. The eggs are carried by the female attached to the thoracic feet.

This primitive genus is also similar to the more primitive groups of the Malacostraca and therefore, is probably a connecting link between the two Series and also with the more minute crustacea already described under the previous groups. *Nebalia bipes* is found along the North Atlantic Coast among seaweed growing in shallow water.

Series EUMALOCOSTRACA

This Series includes all the rest of the Malacostraca and, as stated above, they differ from the Leptostraca in having seven segments and only six appendages on the abdomen,

PLATE 138

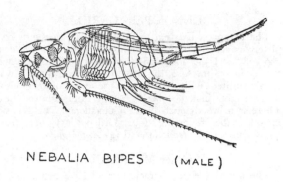

NEBALIA BIPES (MALE)

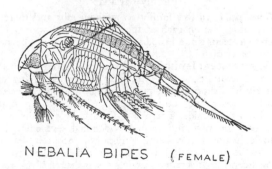

NEBALIA BIPES (FEMALE)

instead of eight. The Eumalacostraca fall naturally into three divisions: (1) *Peracarida;* (2) *Hoplocarida;* and (3) *Eucarida.*

Division PERACARIDA

The carapace, if it exists, in this group, does not completely cover the thorax, leaving at least four segments exposed, and the abdomen does not exceed the cephalothorax in width. Also, the first thoracic segment is always firmly united with the head. The eyes may be either mounted on footed stalks or seated firmly on the head. There is a brood-pouch beneath the thorax. The Division includes the following four Orders: (1) *Mysidacea;* (2) *Cumacea;* (3) *Isopoda;* and (4) *Amphipoda.*

Order MYSIDACEA

The anterior eight thoracic feet all have two branches. The two anterior feet, being nearest the mouth, are specialized to a slight degree as maxillipeds (foot-jaws). The eggs are carried in a pouch by plates beneath the thorax. In some species, the young hatch out as larval forms known as *Nauplii.*

Family Mysidae

The species in this family are without gills and there is an auditory sac on each of the six pairs of pleopods. The plates protecting the brood-sac are outgrowths of the posterior pairs of feet.

Mysis stenolepis (Smith) PLATE 139; COLOR PLATE X, 1. The more or less cylindrical thorax terminates anteriorly in a short, blunt, median projection, known as the rostrum, extending out between the eyes with a sharp tooth on either side. There is a distinct angle in the body between the first and second abdominal segments. The female is the larger, being almost 1¼ inches in length, while the male is slightly less than 1 inch. The body is translucent, each segment having a star-shaped black spot. There are also blackish markings scattered over other parts of the body. This species is important as the food of many fishes, being found in large numbers in the stomachs of the Shad and the Spotted Flounder (Verrill). It is very common in eelgrass from the New England coast southward.

Mysis mixta Lilljeborg PLATE 139. The telson has a quite broad and deep V-shaped notch with curved sides, at its posterior end. This species occurs in fairly deep water from Massachusetts Bay northward.

Erythrops erythrophthalma (Goës) PLATE 139. This species is readily distinguished by the very large ruby-red eyes. The legs are extremely slender, almost thread-

PLATE 139

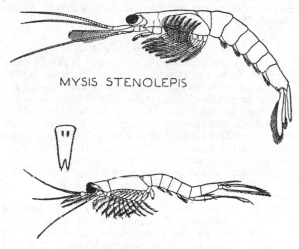

MYSIS STENOLEPIS

MYSIS MIXTA
MALE

ERYTHROPS ERYTHROPHTHALMA
FEMALE

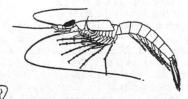

ERYTHROPS ERYTHROPHTHALMA
MALE

like. The telson is very short, not much larger than broad and truncate posteriorly. The distribution is from Massachusetts Bay northward.

Order CUMACEA

These are small, shrimplike crustaceans, generally ranging from about 5 to 15 mm. in length. The head and anterior part of the thorax are covered by a short carapace, leaving the posterior segments free. The abdomen is slender and more or less cylindrical. The eyes are not stalked, being sessile when present. The eggs are carried in a pouch under the thorax of the female. The male possesses a long slender second antenna as well as small limbs on certain of the abdominal segments. Most of the Cumacea live in the mud or sand and can be obtained by dredging or, at times, by means of tow-nets when they are swimming at the surface.

There are two pairs of maxillipeds and six pairs of *pereiopods* (walking legs), some of the latter having two branches. *Pleopods* (swimming legs) and *uropods* (tail appendages) are lacking in the female, while the male may have from two to five of the former.

Family Bodotriidae

In this family, the telson is not distinctly set off from the posterior part of the body. The male has five pairs of pleopods. The first three pairs of pereiopods are biramous.

Cyclaspis varians Calman PLATE 140. The cephalothorax is well rounded, as seen from the side. The carapace is slightly more than two sevenths of the total length and compressed, its vertical height being a little more than one half its length. The rostrum is short. The abdomen is very long and slender. The female is about ⅛ inch in length and the male, about ⅙ inch. It is found along the southern New England coast. There is no well-marked distinction between the thorax and the abdomen.

Leptocuma minor Calman PLATE 140. The carapace is slightly more than one fifth of the total length, moderately compressed. The rostrum is short and truncated. The eye is pigmented. The abdomen is stout and somewhat longer than the cephalothoracic region. The antennae consist of three segments. Only three pairs of pleopods are present in the male instead of the five pairs that are usually found in the Bodotriidae. This genus is doubtless transitional to the Leuconidae.

PLATE 140

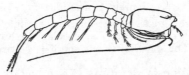

CYCLASPIS VARIANS
MALE

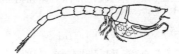

CYCLASPIS VARIANS
FEMALE

LEPTOCUMA MINOR
MALE

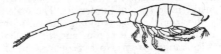

LEPTOCUMA MINOR
FEMALE

EUDORALLOPSIS DEFORMIS
MALE

Family Leuconidae

The thorax grades almost imperceptibly into the abdomen. The telson is absent. The male has only two pairs of pleopods. The mouth-parts are much less hairy than in other families.

Eudorallopsis deformis (Kröyer) PLATE 140. The body is short and stout. The median lobe of the carapace is not hollowed out. The first antennae are jointed between the first two segments. This species is distributed from Nova Scotia to Vineyard Sound.

Family Diastylidae

The anterior part of the thorax is clearly marked off from the posterior part. The male has two pairs of pleopods. The telson is present and distinct.

Diastylis quadrispinosa Sars PLATE 141. This species is very abundant on soft, muddy bottoms. It is distinguished by its pale flesh-color and the red-purple patch at the posterior part of the carapace. There are also two small spots of pink. It is found in depths of 18 to 35 fathoms from the Bay of Fundy to Long Island Sound and New Jersey.

Diastylis polita S. I. Smith PLATE 141. In the female, there are only three ridges on the carapace, as compared with four in the male. The first pair of legs is distinctly shorter in the male than in the female. The male also has a strong horizontal ridge running forward from the hinder margin. The male is 14 mm. and the female 12 mm. This species ranges from Nova Scotia to Block Island Sound.

Oxyurostylis smithi Calman PLATE 141. The genus, to which this species belongs, resembles *Diastylis* in general characters, except that the telson tapers to an acute point and has no apical spines. The carapace is not elongated. The antenna has a brush of hairs in the male and the next to the last segment of the antenna, in the female, is enlarged. The third and fourth pairs of legs, in the male, are biramous, as are two pairs of pleopods. The carapace is little less than one third the total length, considerably arched posteriorly and sloping anteriorly to the rostrum. It is, therefore, robustly fusiform in outline. All the leg-bearing segments are distinct. The abdomen is one sixth longer than the cephalothoracic region. The dorsal outline of the male is less arched than in the female. The telson is twice as long as the last segment, with about seven pairs of lateral spines. The first and second pairs of pleopods are branched, the exopod having two segments. This species ranges from Casco Bay to Louisiana.

PLATE 141

OXYUROSTYLIS SMITHI
MALE

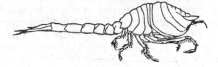

OXYUROSTYLIS SMITHI
FEMALE, NOT MATURE

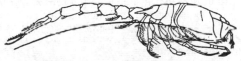

DIASTYLIS POLITA
MALE

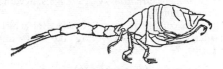

DIASTYLIS POLITA
FEMALE

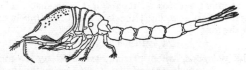

DIASTYLIS QUADRISPINOSA

Order ISOPODA
INDEX PLATE 142

The body of the *Isopoda* is more or less flattened above and below. They are all bilaterally symmetrical, except in the Family Bopyridae, which contains the parasitic species, with males and females differing in form and size, the males being permanently attached to the female near their genital organs.

The paired eyes are simple or compound. There are two pairs of antennae. The second antennae are much larger than the first with a five-jointed base (*peduncle*) and a many-jointed tapering *flagellum*. There is a pair of *mandibles* (hard jaws) and two pairs of *maxillae* (soft jaws) followed by a pair of *maxillipeds* (foot jaws). The thorax has, for the most part, seven free joints. There are seven pairs of jointed legs as in the Amphipoda, the first pair often differing from the succeeding ones. The abdomen is divided into six segments, each with a pair of appendages, though in various groups certain segments are fused together. The abdominal appendages are pleopods or swimming or breathing organs, as well as a pair of uropods on the terminal segment.

The isopods are mostly marine, except for a single, widely distributed fresh-water species and except for the Suborder *Oniscoidea,* which may have many terrestrial forms. The isopods are mostly scavengers, feeding upon dead marine animals.

The Isopoda consist of nine Suborders, of which seven will be dealt with here, covering the most important marine forms.

Suborder TANAIDACEA

This Suborder is often spoken of as the *Chelifera* because of its claw-bearing, first pair of legs. The head and first segment are fused, resembling a carapace. The abdomen has six segments, the last one being much longer than the rest.

Family Tanaidae

The pleopods, when present, are used for swimming. The two uropods extend backward from the terminal segment.

Tanais cavolinii Milne-Edwards PLATE 143. This species has three pairs of pleopods and a short pair of unbranched uropods. The segments are strongly constricted at their joints. The abdomen is composed of five segments, the first three of which are fringed with setae, long laterally, and short dorsally, by means of which this species is usually recognized. It is brown in color, pale

PLATE 142

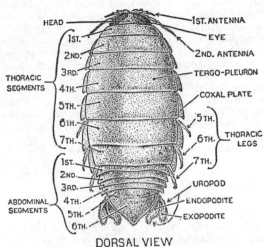

HEAD — 1ST. ANTENNA

EYE

2ND. ANTENNA

1ST.
2ND.
3RD. — TERGO-PLEURON
THORACIC
SEGMENTS
4TH. — COXAL PLATE
5TH.
6TH. — 5TH.
7TH. — 6TH. THORACIC
LEGS
7TH.

1ST.
2ND.
3RD. — UROPOD
ABDOMINAL
SEGMENTS
4TH. — ENDOPODITE
5TH. — EXOPODITE
6TH.

DORSAL VIEW

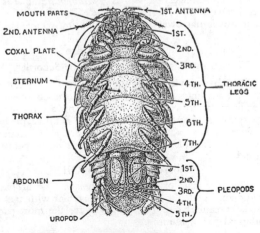

MOUTH PARTS — 1ST. ANTENNA

2ND. ANTENNA — 1ST.
2ND.
COXAL PLATE — 3RD.
4TH. THORACIC
STERNUM — LEGS
5TH.
THORAX — 6TH.
7TH.

1ST.
ABDOMEN — 2ND.
3RD. PLEOPODS
4TH.
UROPOD — 5TH.

VENTRAL VIEW

beneath. It is 5 mm. in length and is found on wharf-piles among the seaweed, from the water surface to a depth of 6 feet or more. It also occurs on sponges, barnacles, and oysters from Greenland to Long Island Sound, as well as on the European and Mediterranean shores.

Leptochelia savignyi (Kröyer) PLATE 143. The sides of the body are nearly parallel, without constriction between the thoracic joints. The head is long in proportion to its width. The abdomen has six segments, the first five being short in length and wider than the thoracic joints. The last segment is triangular in shape with two-branched uropods. The large compound eyes are seated on immovable peduncles. The first antennae and the first pair of legs in the male are longer than in the female. The male has large chelae while those of the female are small. The rest of the legs are locomotor in function. The color is white. It occurs abundantly in eelgrass and seaweed near the sea-surface. It is found from Cape Cod to New Jersey and its range also extends to Europe.

Suborder GNATHIIDEA

This Suborder contains a species with a large square head and powerful mandibles. The first thoracic segment is separated from the head by a suture and has two jointed broad appendages known as *gnathopods* and has three semitransparent calcareous plates. The seventh thoracic segment is narrower than the preceding segments.

Family Gnathiidae

This family has the characters of the Suborder.

Gnathia cerina (Stimpson) PLATE 143. In contrast to the broad plates forming the thorax, the abdomen is exceedingly narrow. Its first five segments are distinct, each carrying a pair of pleopods. The sixth segment is a pointed telson with a pair of two-branched uropods inserted at the sides of its base. It is said to be parasitic on fishes.

Suborder CYMOTHOIDEA

The first pair of legs is not chelate. The uropods are somewhat platelike in form and, together with the telson, make a caudal fan. The pleopods, for the most part, are adapted for swimming.

Family Anthuridae

The body is elongate, slender, and somewhat cylindrical. The head is small and inconspicuous. There are seven well-defined thoracic segments. The short abdomen has coalesced anterior plates.

Ptilanthura tenuis Harger PLATE 143. The head is no broader than the very long and narrow body. It terminates forward in a small, triangular projection. The eyes are small and round, situated on the margin of the head. The first antennae are short in the female, while, in the male, the flagellum of the second antennae is adorned with a conspicuous fringe of long, slender setae. The first six thoracic segments are longer than wide and equal to each other in length. The seventh segment is about one half the length of the preceding segments. The first five segments of the abdomen are fused on the median line, but the margins are distinct, the sixth joint narrower. The telson is long and trunk-shaped, being convexly pointed posteriorly. The uropods are narrow and pointed, but platelike. The color of this species is a mottled brownish. The males are 11 mm. in length, the females shorter. This isopod occurs from the surface to 19 fathoms in sand and mud. While it is rare along the coast of southern New England, it ranges from the Bay of Fundy to Long Island Sound.

Cyathura carinata (Kröyer) PLATE 143. This species apparently has eight thoracic segments. This is due to the fact that the first six abdominal segments are fused together so that, combined, they resemble an eighth thoracic segment. The two pairs of antennae are short and stout. The first thoracic segment is longer than the others, with a stout pair of legs turned forward. A fingerlike process with a slender curved spine suggests a chela. The remaining six pairs of legs are used for walking and are similar to each other. The telson together with the uropods forms a fanlike termination to the body. The length of this species is 20 mm. It is abundant between tides or around the low-water mark. The distribution is from Greenland along the entire eastern seaboard to Norfolk, Virginia.

Calathura branchiata (Stimpson) PLATE 143. This species somewhat resembles the preceding, but with narrower and longer thoracic segments. The abdomen is jointed and the telson is smaller and more pointed than in *Cyathura carinata*. The uropods are flattened and form a caudal fan.

Family Cirolanidae

The body is somewhat semicylindrical in form. The head is evenly rounded in front and not produced forward in the middle. The abdomen has six distinct segments. There is a pair of small lateral eyes. The first antennae are small. The peduncle of the second is five-jointed, the flagellum is long, slender, and many-jointed. The uropods are situated laterally to the telson, forming with it a caudal fan.

Cirolana concharum (Stimpson) PLATE 143. The head is almost rectangular; the anterior margin is rounded. Eyes are present. The first thoracic segment is produced around the sides of the head. The second and third thoracic segments are slightly shorter than the remaining four. All are similar in shape except that the sixth is somewhat contracted posteriorly. The narrower abdomen has six distinct segments, with the fourth forming an arc around the longer but narrower fifth. The triangular telson is truncated at its tip. It is fringed with setae around its sides and posterior border, as are also the uropods. This is a large species, averaging from 1 inch to 1½ inches in length. It is found abundantly from the sea-surface to depths of 18 fathoms, from Nova Scotia to South Carolina. It acts as a scavenger, devouring dead fish. It also feeds upon the Blue Crab and other animals.

Cirolana borealis Lilljeborg PLATE 143. This is a similar species, about ½ inch in length, very active and tenacious of life. It is a good swimmer and a savage devourer of fish. It may even bite the hand of a person holding it. Its limbs are spinous (Stebbing).

The second pair of antennae are long, extending beyond the posterior margin of the third thoracic segment. As in the preceding species, eyes are present.

Cirolana polita Harger PLATE 143. As in the other species of this genus, the peduncle of the second antennae is five-jointed. This pair of antennae is short as compared with the preceding species, reaching only to the middle of the first thoracic segment.

Family Aegidae

The broad, flattened body is continuously domed and smooth to the touch. The small head bears a pair of large compound eyes which nearly meet on the median line. The first pair of antennae arise almost in contact medially. They are shorter than the second pair. Both have a well-defined peduncle and many-jointed flagella. All the thoracic plates, except the first, show projecting coxal plates at the sides. The abdomen has six clearly defined segments, the posterior being large, almost triangular, and terminating in a point posteriorly. The edges of this segment as well as the uropods are abundantly fringed with setae. The pleopods are well adapted for both swimming and breathing.

Aega psora (Linnaeus) PLATE 143. The body of this species is oval, being broadest at the fourth and fifth thoracic segments. The dorsal surface is somewhat arched with very tiny scattered dots. The head is much wider laterally than long, and somewhat triangular, being produced to a point between the inner margins of the two

PLATE 143

TANAIS
CAVOLINI

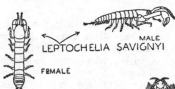

LEPTOCHELIA SAVIGNYI

MALE

FEMALE

GNATHIA
CERINA

CALATHURA
BRANCHIATA

CYATHURA
CARINATA

PTILANTHURA
TENUIS

CIROLANA
POLITA

AEGA
PSORA
(DORSAL)

CIROLANA
CONCHARUM

CIROLANA
BOREALIS

AEGA
PSORA
(VENTRAL)

NEROCILA
MUNDA

LIMNORIA
LIGNORUM

LIVONECA
OVALIS

eyes, which are very large and kidney-shaped, taking up most of the dorsal surface of the head. The first pair of antennae has a peduncle of three joints, the first two of which are flattened while the third is cylindrical. The flagellum has about twelve segments. The second antennae are much longer, extending beyond the first thoracic segment, when bent backward. It has a slender tapering flagellum composed of fifteen to twenty segments. The fourth, fifth, and sixth thoracic segments are much longer than the first three. All these segments, except the first, distinctly show leaflike coxal plates extending from beneath their outer edges. The terminal joints of the first three pairs of legs are strongly hooked. Those of the remaining legs are much weaker. The first five segments of the abdomen are extremely short. The last segment is large, triangular, and pointed at the tip, flanked on either side with the biramous uropods. The pleopods, the telson, and the uropods are strongly ciliated on their border.

This species is about 2 inches long and is distributed along the entire Atlantic Coast from Greenland and Hudson Bay to the mouth of the Mississippi. It is also found around the British Isles and on the coast of the North Sea. It is parasitic on skates, cod, and halibut, attaching itself to their skin.

Family Cymothoidae

The antennae, in this family, are small and fitted imperceptibly from peduncle to flagellum without a clear division. The head is triangular with large eyes. The coxal plates show clearly on both sides of all the segments, except the first. There are seven pairs of legs terminating in strongly curved hooks, which are, therefore, prehensile and adapted for parasitism on fishes.

Livoneca ovalis Say PLATE 143. The body is elliptical with strongly convex sides somewhat asymmetrical. It is nearly 1 inch in length and ½ inch in width. The first pair of antennae are widely separated. The head is set compactly into the first thoracic segment, which is broad and capelike. The six following thoracic segments are of about the same length. The width gradually narrows to the outline of the short and contracted first five abdominal segments. The last segment, or telson, is broadly and evenly rounded behind. The uropods are slightly longer than the telson, the outer ramus being longer. This species is widely distributed from Vineyard Sound, Massachusetts, along the entire eastern seaboard to the mouth of the Mississippi River. It is parasitic on the Bluefish, Sawfish, Scup, Sea Trout, Sunfish, and other fishes. As a rule, it attaches itself to the gills and the roof of the mouth.

Nerocila munda Harger PLATE 143. The head is quite distinct from the first thoracic segment. The body is symmetrical. The eyes are small, distinct, black in color, and widely separated. The posterior angles of the first thoracic segment are distinct or sometimes produced by acute angles, increasing gradually in length on the succeeding segments, the posterior ones often being comparatively long. The outline of the abdomen, as seen from above, is abruptly narrower than that of the thorax. The telson is regularly rounded and shield-shaped; the uropods, especially the outer ramus, being considerably longer.

Family Limnoriidae

The body is flattened and with parallel sides. The segments are well articulated and are capable of being rolled up into a ball. The head is short and very convex. The eyes are wide apart, being situated at the margins of the head. The legs are quite uniform in character and well adapted for walking.

Limnoria lignorum (Rathke) PLATE 143. In this species, the seven thoracic segments are clearly defined, the first being the longest, five of the remaining six with the coxal plates showing at the sides. The first antennae are larger and longer than the second. Both have bunches of setae on the terminal segment. The joints of the abdomen are practically as wide as those of the thorax, the first four being similar, and the fifth long and arching around the sixth joint, which is distinctly longer and crescent-shaped. The telson is broadly oval, rounded posteriorly, and fringed with setae. The tips of the uropods stand out from beneath its edge. This animal is gray in color and about ⅕ inch in length. It occurs abundantly in the neighborhood of the low-water mark, occasionally, however, extending to a depth of 10 fathoms. It is distributed from the Gulf of St. Lawrence, along the entire Atlantic and Pacific Coasts of North America, to the British Isles, the North Sea, and even to the Adriatic Sea. It is found burrowing in submerged timbers, penetrating them to ½ inch or more and causing great damage to docks.

Cassidisca lunifrons (Richardson) PLATE 144. This isopod has an oval body with quite a smooth surface-texture. The anterior border of the head is broader than the posterior border and is arched with the lateral angles acutely produced, while the posterior border is practically straight. The eyes are located at the posterior angles. The first pair of antennae is moderately developed and has a flagellum of six joints. The second antennae are longer, with the flagellum possessing eight joints. The first thoracic segment surrounds three sides of the head, the lateral borders being continuous with it in outline. The segments of the thorax are nearly equal and regular. The abdomen consists of two segments, the first, very short, and the second, large and with a bluntly pointed posterior termination, thus forming a triangular telson. The uropods fit closely against the oblique sides of the telson, the inner branch being large and with a pointed extremity. The outer branch is rudimentary and immovable, being distinguished merely by an indented notch partly separating it from the inner branch.

Family Sphaeromidae

The body is oval, convex, and capable of being rolled up into a ball. The seventh thoracic segment is regular and normal. The abdomen, however, consists of but two segments, the anterior segment being fused together, while the last segment is large and forms the telson, to which the double-branched uropods are attached laterally. The inner branch of the uropods is fixed. The outer branch is movable when present.

Sphaeroma quadridentatum Say PLATE 144. The body is ovate, its width being half its length. The head is short with the eyes at its outer margin. The frontal border curves around anterior to the eyes and is produced in a small median point. The first pair of antennae arises from the underside of the head and can be fitted into a groove. The peduncle consists of three joints, the first of which is the largest. The flagellum has about twelve very small segments. The second antennae are longer than the first, arising below them with five segments of varying length composing the peduncle, the first being the smallest. The flagellum consists of about fifteen segments. The posterior angles of the thoracic segments form a somewhat acute process, especially in the first four segments. The ambulatory legs are of normal character. The first segment of the coalesced abdomen is marked laterally by two depressions. The telson is long and rounded posteriorly and the uropods extend beyond it. This species is about ⅓ inch in length and extremely variable in color, diversified by whitish or pinkish marked patches with black edges. It is distributed from Vineyard Sound, Massachusetts, to Georgia and Florida, where it may be found under stones or among seaweed between the tides. The habit of rolling into a ball serves to distinguish this species from all other marine isopods.

Cilicaea caudata (Say) PLATE 144. This species may be distinguished readily because only the outer branch of uropods projects beyond the telson and is exposed. It is capable of folding under the inner branch. The outline of this species, seen from above, is practically straight, with

PLATE 144

CASSIDISCA
LUNIFRONS

SPHÆROMA
QUADRIDENTATUM

CILICAEA
CAUDATA

IDOTEA
BALTICA

IDOTEA
PHOSPHOREA

IDOTEA
METALLICA

CHIRIDOTEA
TUFTSI

CHIRIDOTEA
CAECA

EDOTEA
MONTOSA

ERICHSONELLA
FILIFORMIS

ERICHSONELLA
ATTENUATA

EDOTEA
TRILOBA

parallel sides, and truncated posteriorly, giving the impression of a rectangle. The first of the two abdominal segments is produced as a spine and generally has a medial lobe. The outer branch of the uropods is without spines. A horizontal sinus, transversely across the uropod, is armed with four teeth, two on either side forming a tubercle.

Suborder IDOTEOIDEA

This Suborder includes the species in which the uropods are situated laterally and ventrally, arching over the five pairs of pleopods, which act as branchiae. They open and close like valves to protect them and are attached to the outer margin of the telson.

Family Idoteidae

The broad oval body is flattened. The thoracic segments are normal and uniform in appearance. The first pair of antennae have a single-jointed flagellum. The second antennae may have single or many joints. The coxal plates may be distinct or fused with their segments. The first three pairs of legs have a hooklike *dactyl,* which bends back against the next segment to form a prehensile claw. The abdomen tends to have various segments fused to form a large telsonlike plate.

Idotea baltica (Pallas) PLATE 144. This species is nearly 1 inch in length, variable in color, but usually green. The abdomen is more than one third as long as the body. The large, round, conspicuous eyes are compound. They are situated at the extreme lateral margin of the head. The thoracic segments are of about equal length, the coxal plates being clearly shown. The legs are similar to each other, but longer posteriorly. The abdomen consists of two short segments, followed by a long, terminal segment, showing indications of fusion with those immediately preceding it. The telson has a convexly curving lateral margin ending in a triply toothed posterior margin, the central tooth of which is the longest. The males are often more than 1½ inches in length, while the females are ⅘ inch. The distribution is cosmopolitan. On our coast, it ranges from the Gulf of St. Lawrence to North Carolina. Locally, this isopod may be found on the southern Connecticut coast from New Haven to Stonington, at the sea-surface, on floating seaweed, or on the seaweed along rocky shores.

Idotea phosphorea Harger PLATE 144. The telson of this species ends in a sharp point and shows indications of fusion with a preceding segment. There are two abdominal segments immediately anterior to it. The head is broader than long. The round, compound eyes are at the extreme lateral margin. The first antennae are very short; the second are made up of a peduncle with one short joint and four long ones, bearing a flagellum with about twelve small segments. The coxal plates are clearly marked off, except for the first segment, and become gradually wider posteriorly. The ventral operculum, like the telson, tapers toward the posterior end. The color is usually dark green or brownish, with patches of yellow or white. The general color is darker than in the preceding species. It is about 1 inch in length and is distributed from the Gulf of St. Lawrence, along the entire coast of New England, at least to New Haven.

Idotea metallica Bosc PLATE 144. The body of this species has straight parallel sides and a long, squarely truncated abdominal plate. The head is wider than long, with a somewhat concave anterior margin. The large, round eyes are situated on the lateral margins. The first antennae are much shorter than the second antennae. The thoracic segments are nearly equal in size, the first curving around the head to some extent on either side. The coxal plates are very large and wide and increase gradually in width to the seventh, giving a saw-toothed appearance to the sides of the body. The legs are normal in character. The abdomen is composed of two short segments and a long telson, showing marks of coalescence with an adjoining short segment. The male is somewhat more than 1 inch in length, and the female is less than 1 inch. This species is cosmopolitan in distribution and on our coast it ranges from Nova Scotia to North Carolina. It is pelagic, swimming freely, in open water, and also among masses of floating seaweed.

Chiridotea caeca (Say) PLATE 144. This species has a broadly ovate, flattened thorax, with the abdomen nearly half as long as the whole body, tapering to an acute point posteriorly. The head has two concave notches at the median line to accommodate the basal joints of the antennae, with a triangular point between them. The head, also, has a deep notch, located laterally on either side. The small compound eyes are situated just back of these notches. The first antennae are four-jointed with the first joint very short. The second antennae also have a small first joint with four other approximately equal joints and a five-jointed flagellum. The thoracic segments are approximately equal in length. The first, however, surrounds the head on three sides. Except for the first segment, the coxal plates are clearly marked with the last four pairs showing dorsally as sharply pointed, posteriorly projecting processes. The abdomen has four segments, the first three of which are short, while the fourth forms the acutely pointed telson, as usual with indications of another fused segment. The opercular valves, underneath, are in two parts, protected by the telson. The color is variable, but usually a dark mottled gray. It is about ½ inch in length and is distributed from Nova Scotia to Florida. It is commonly found on sand-beaches along the New England and Long Island coasts, usually below high-tide mark, making little ridge-burrows visible at the surface, with a mound at the end. It is also found swimming about in shallow water.

Chiridotea tuftsi (Stimpson) PLATE 144. This is a similar species, but smaller in size and with a somewhat narrower head, twice as long as wide, fitting closely into an excavation of the first segment. The lateral margin has two lobes on either side, with the eyes just within the cleft between the lobes. The first antennae have three joints and a flagellum of one segment. The second antennae have a peduncle made up of five segments, the first of which is very short, and a flagellum of about twelve segments and longer than the peduncle. Except for the first segment, the coxal plates show clearly as posteriorly pointed projections, increasing in size toward the abdomen. The abdomen has four distinct segments, as well as a fifth partly coalesced with the long, pointed telson, bearing setae at its tip. This species is light reddish brown in color, speckled and marked with darker patches. It is over ⅓ inch in length, and distributed from Nova Scotia to Long Island Sound from shallow water to 25 fathoms. It is found on sandy shores, but more rarely than the preceding species. Its smaller size, much longer second antennae, and more conspicuous eyes readily distinguish it from *Chiridotea caeca*.

Edotea triloba (Say) PLATE 144. The ovate body is made up of conspicuously lobed thoracic segments rounded at their outer margins, giving the animal a scalloped appearance. The head is wider than long, with two conspicuous tubercles on either side of the median line, while the anterior margin has two broad hornlike projections, back of which the eyes are situated on lateral rounded lobes. The first antennae are much shorter than the second. The legs are similar to each other, all being prehensile with a slender dactyl folding back against the next joint of the leg. The abdomen is composed of a single segment, its notched outline indicating fusion with a previous segment. There is a large, rounded elevation in the middle of the telson, as well as another smaller one at the base, with a deep depression between, and a hollow toward the posterior narrowly pointed apex. It has a uniform muddy color which blends readily with the environment in which it is found. It is somewhat over ¼ inch in length and distributed from Maine to New Jersey on wharf-piles, in sheltered places and eelgrass, and among decaying vegetation from the surface to about 3 feet in depth.

Edotea montosa (Stimpson) PLATE 144. This is a species similar to the preceding, but somewhat larger with two low tubercles on the anterior margin of the head. The eyes are situated at the extreme lateral angles. The pairs of antennae are both short, the second being longer than the first, being made up of a few joints. The thoracic segments have similar rounded margins, the third and fourth plates being longer and wider than the others. The legs are all prehensile, like those of the preceding species, with the first pair much shorter than the others. The abdomen is a single segment with signs of coalescence with a preceding segment, the two converging with rounded lateral sides to a triangular apex. It is somewhat over ⅓ inch in length and is distributed from Nova Scotia to Long Island Sound, in mud and fine sand, on bottoms of from 8 to 25 fathoms. It is readily distinguished from the previous species by the more evenly rounded margins of the thorax and the convexly pointed form of the telson.

Erichsonella filiformis (Say) PLATE 144. The narrow body is made up of thoracic plates with notches and irregular outlines laterally. The coxal plates are all distinct, even on the first segment. The frontal margin of the head is deeply concave to accommodate the very large second antennae as compared with the much smaller first pair. The terminal joints in both pairs are ciliated. The legs are all approximately similar, each terminated by a weak dactyl which may have a grasping function to some extent. The abdomen is deeper and more arched than in other species. The color is dull. The length is a little less than ⅓ inch. The species is distributed from Long Island Sound and New Jersey to Florida and the Bahamas.

Erichsonella attenuata (Harger) PLATE 144. This is a much smaller species with a more regular outline to its body. It has short antennae. The terminal shield-shaped segment shows traces of a lateral tooth on either side near its base. The distribution is similar to the above.

Suborder ASELLOIDEA

The four or five pairs of abdominal appendages (pleopods) often used for swimming organs are here entirely branchial except in the case of the first pair, which are expanded and modified to form a thin opercular plate. The uropods (always two-branched) extend out posteriorly to the abdominal plate, which, in this Suborder, is composed of all the abdominal segments fused.

The second pair of antennae is always very long. The first thoracic legs are usually not chelate, though in some species they may be subchelate.

Family Janiridae

The sides of the head are expanded as lamellae. The eyes, when present, are usually on the dorsal border. The first pair of antennae are either well developed or rudimentary. The second antennae usually have a small scale, external to the third joint of the peduncle. The first pair of legs sometimes have a two- or three-clawed dactyl and are, therefore, prehensile. In some species, they do not differ from the other legs.

Jaera marina (Fabricius) PLATE 145. The uropods and the first pair of antennae are very small. This isopod has an oval body about ⅓ inch long, with three-jointed walking legs. The color is usually a marbled gray, though many variations are found. It is common in the tidal zone among seaweed and under stones. It ranges from Labrador to southern New England and is also European.

Janira alta (Stimpson) PLATE 145. The body of this species is slenderer than the previous one. Its legs are similar, but proportionately longer. There is a short, sharp rostrum projecting from the middle of the head. The antero-lateral angles of the head also project forward acutely. A pair of conspicuous eyes is situated dorso-laterally. The uropods are alike in both sexes and comparatively long, projecting posteriorly from the almost oval posterior plate, each from a separate notch with a tooth-like projection on the mid-line between them.

Suborder EPICARIDEA

These isopods are said by Künkel to be the most degenerate forms of isopods, all being parasitic on decapod crustaceans. The first thoracic legs are not chelae. Uropoda, when present, are terminal. The pleopods act entirely as branchiae and are not protected by an opercular plate. The full-grown female, in some species, is merely a simple sac filled with ova. The male is considerably smaller than the adult female and is usually parasitic upon her, clinging to her genital regions.

Family Bopyridae

In this family, the body of the female is segmented and asymmetrical; the male smaller, more slender, and symmetrical. The antennae are rudimentary. The legs, in some species, are rudimentary on one side.

Stegophryxus hyptias (Thompson) PLATE 145. This species is parasitic on the gills of the Hermit Crab (*Pagurus longicarpus*). It has been known in various localities from Woods Hole to Warwick, Rhode Island.

Phryxus abdominalis (Kröyer) PLATE 145. The head has two lobes. This species is very degenerate, the

thoracic branchial appendages being partly absent, with
the result that one side of the body of the female is greatly
swollen and much larger than the other. The abdomen
consists of five segments with the last three pairs of its
appendages wanting. It is parasitic in the shell occupied
by the Hermit Crab, where it sits on the left side of the
crab's back near the carapace and also near the attachment of the crab's eggs.

Ione thompsoni Richardson PLATE 145. This is another parasitic form. The female has side-plates present
on the head and on the thorax. On the abdomen, they are
branched in a treelike fashion, but the appendages of the
sixth thoracic segment are simple and cylindrical. In the
male, the second antennae are seven-jointed and the abdomen has six pairs of long, cylindrical appendages
(Stebbing). Isopods of this genus are parasitic upon various species of the Family Callianassidae (Page 504).

Leidyi distorta (Leidy) PLATE 145. The female,
which is illustrated in the plate, has a distorted asymmetrical body, with the thoracic feet ending in a blunt claw.
The seven pairs of the appendages have adhesive organs
nearly equal in size. The abdominal appendages have
plumelike, fringed branches. The first antennae of the
male are three-jointed; the second, seven-jointed. The abdomen has five rudimentary pairs of pleopods with two
long processes on the sixth abdominal segment. It is
parasitic on the Fiddler Crab (*Uca pugilator* PLATE 168).

Bopyroides hippolytes (Kröyer) PLATE 145. The
body of the female, though asymmetrical, has neither
side greatly swollen, as in the case of *Phryxus abdominalis*.
The segments of the thorax are distinct. The abdomen
has six segments. All the thoracic appendages are present,
though the pleopods on the abdomen are represented only
by fleshy ridges. The uropods are wanting. The male is
much smaller than the female. Its abdomen is fused into
a single plate without appendages. There are only vestiges
of the antennae. This species is parasitic on the gills of
various prawns, often showing externally as a swelling
under the carapace (see PLATE 145).

Probopyrus pandalicola (Packard) PLATE 145. The
female of this species is also asymmetrical. However, it
has all seven pairs of legs and though the segments of the
sixth abdominal segments are clear, no appendages are
attached to it. The abdomen of the male consists of a
single, fused plate without appendages. Only traces of the
antennae are present. It is widely distributed along the
northern border of North America on both the Atlantic
and Pacific sides and also around the North Atlantic to the
European coasts. It is parasitic on the gills of *Palaemonetes
vulgaris* (see PLATE 159) and other prawns.

Suborder ONISCOIDEA
(Sow Bugs, Pill Bugs)

This Suborder, for the most part, is terrestrial, containing many species of Sow Bugs and Pill Bugs, familiar to everyone as being found under stones, in damp, rotting wood, and especially under boards and logs. The only marine forms are one species in the Family *Oniscidae* and two species in the Family *Trichoniscidae*. This Suborder is divided into four families: (1) *Oniscidae* (terrestrial, except for one species); (2) *Armadillidiidae* (entirely terrestrial); (3) *Ligiidae* (entirely terrestrial); and (4) *Trichoniscidae* (terrestrial, except for two species).

Therefore, only the Families *Oniscidae* and *Trichoniscidae* will be defined here.

Family Oniscidae

This family contains the Sow Bugs. The flattened, oval body of these isopods consists of seven similar, thoracic segments of about equal length, except that the first is larger and embraces the rectangular, narrow head on three sides. The first antennae are inconspicuous. The second antennae are very long and consist of the usual peduncle with a short flagellum of only two segments. The uropods are two-branched, each branch consisting of a single joint. The abdomen has six segments of which the terminal one is triangular. The lateral plates end in posteriorly directed, pointed flanges; they are streamlined, however, on their outer edges. The species of this family are all terrestrial, except those of the following genus.

Philoscia vittata Say PLATE 145. The oval body of this species has a head which is longer laterally than from front to back. It has small compound eyes on the sides of the head. Except for the somewhat longer segment, the thoracic segments are approximately equal in length. The last three thoracic segments have their posterior angles produced backward, the seventh possessing the longest and most acute angles. The thoracic appendages are all walking legs, similar to each other except that they increase in length backward. The plates of the abdomen are much narrower and shorter than those of the thorax, the first two being partly overlapped by the last thoracic segment. The short telson is acutely triangular and flanked on either side by the two-branched narrow uropods. The color is brownish but variable, usually with a narrow, lighter stripe. It is about ⅓ inch in length and is found abundantly under stones, wood, and various forms of rubbish below the low-tide mark along the entire southern New England and New Jersey coasts.

PLATE 145

JAERA MARINA

PHRYXUS ABDOMINALIS

(DORSAL) (VENTRAL)
IONE THOMPSONI
FEMALE

IONE THOMPSONI MALE

JANIRA ALTA

LEIDYA DISTORTA

STEGOPHRYXUS HYPTIAS

BOPYROIDES HIPPOLYTES MALE

PROBOPYRUS PANDALICOLA

HEAD OF SHRIMP INFESTED WITH PARASITE

BOPYROIDES HIPPOLYTES FEMALE

PHILOSCIA VITTATA

ARMADILLONISCUS ELLIPTICUS

SCYPHACELLA ARENICOLA

Family Trichoniscidae

The head has distinct, but not large, lateral lobes, the frontal parts being rounded. The eyes are small or wanting. The first antennae have the last joint well developed and tipped with sensory hairs. The second antennae have three to five joints. The abdomen is not pointed posteriorly. The two branches of each uropod are conically tapered. The inner branch of the first and second pairs of pleopods, in the male, are modified for sexual purposes.

Armadilloniscus (Actinoniscus) ellipticus Harger PLATE 145. The flattened body is elliptical in shape. The head has a saucer-shaped outline with a triangular projection forward in the middle, the general shape being broader anteriorly than posteriorly. There is a pair of small, black, oval eyes on either side at the base of the triangular projection. The peduncle of the antennae is large and heavily jointed with a flagellum of four joints, the final one being very small, pointed, and tipped with setae. The head is set well back into the first thoracic segment. The six succeeding thoracic segments are produced laterally into posteriorly pointed lamellae. The seventh thoracic segment embraces and covers the ends of the first two abdominal segments. The three succeeding abdominal segments also have backward lamellae. The triangular telson is embraced by the large, flattened, and expanded peduncles of the uropods, the terminal joints of which are narrow, finger-shaped, and tipped with setae. The color is slate-gray. The length is about 4 mm. This species is common along the southern shore of Connecticut.

Scyphacella arenicola Smith PLATE 145. The abdomen in this isopod continues the outline of the thorax in being abruptly narrower. The head is round in front with no lateral lobes at the sides. Small tubercles are scattered over the dorsal surface, forming the bases of tiny spines. The eyes are prominent and round. The telson is narrow and triangular with a blunt, somewhat-rounded apex. This species is light in color with white spots and black dots irregularly scattered over the body. The length is not more than 4 mm. It is distributed from Nantucket along the southern New England and New Jersey shores to Maryland. It is found about high-water mark on sandy beaches.

Order AMPHIPODA *
(Sand Hoppers, Beach Fleas, etc.)

The Amphipoda, like the Isopoda, have no carapace, except that, at times, the head is fused with the first thoracic segment. The remaining six segments are always free-jointed with each other. The eyes are sessile; that is, they are not elevated on a movable stalk.

As distinguished from the isopods, the body of the amphipods is usually strongly compressed from side to side. In most species, the abdomen is made up of six segments, exclusive of the terminal segment which forms the telson (see INDEX PLATE 146). The gills or breathing organs are attached to the first joints of the thoracic legs on the underside. Therefore, the heart is also located anteriorly. This is in contrast to the isopods, where the gills are modified abdominal pleopods, with the heart located posteriorly. In the amphipods, immediately following the mouth, the first two appendages are the *mandibles* and *maxillae,* respectively. They are followed by the first and second gnathopods, appendages of the first two thoracic segments. Following them are five pairs of thoracic walking limbs, spoken of as *pereiopods.* These never consist of two branches. The first three pairs of abdominal appendages in the amphipods are termed *pleopods,* as they are adapted for swimming. The last three pairs of appendages are short, stiff, and used as leaping organs. They are known as the first, second, and third uropods. The color in amphipods varies greatly, but many species are adorned with bright colors such as crimson, red-brown, bright green, and deep blue-green, though usually those seen on the beach are various shades of gray, white, or simply translucent. Generally they are marine in habit. A few that live near the high-water mark among the seaweed are almost terrestrial. Some species also occur in fresh water. The Order Amphipoda is divided into three Suborders: (1) *Hyperiidea;* (2) *Gammaridea;* and (3) *Caprellidea.*

Suborder HYPERIIDEA

The amphipods in this Suborder have large heads, almost entirely occupied by a pair of huge compound eyes. The maxilliped has no palp. The gills are on three or four of

---

* It has not been practicable to illustrate sexual differences in the *Amphipoda,* except in a very few cases. In many *Amphipoda,* the gnathopods, more often the second pair, are conspicuously enlarged and modified in the males, but much smaller and simpler in the females. In the genus *Corophium,* for example, the second antennae are enormously enlarged in the males, but less so in the females.

the thoracic segments. The last two abdominal segments are fused to form the telson, which, together with the flat branches of the uropods, constitutes a tail-fan. There are seven pairs of thoracic legs. Three families of this Suborder are represented in our area.

Family Hyperiidae

The antennae of the female are quite small, while the second antennae of the male have long, whiplike flagella. There are five abdominal segments. The species in this family are parasitic on large jellyfish.

Hyperia galba (Montagu) PLATE 147. The head is wider than long, with great kidney-shaped compound eyes. The back is usually curved into a high arch. The pereiopods are similar in form and approximately equal in length, with almost no setae. The last two abdominal segments are fused together with the triangular telson and the leaf-like branches of the broad uropods, to form a terminal tail-fan. This species is about ⅜ inch in length. It is abundantly distributed from northern Europe to the Arctic Ocean through Greenland, Nova Scotia, and along the entire coast of New England. It is usually found in the White Jellyfish, *Aurelia aurita* (COLOR PLATE VI, 7).

Hyperia medusarum (O. F. Müller) PLATE 147. This species is characterized by the facts that the sides of its gnathopods are covered with setae and that it is usually found in the Pink Jellyfish, *Cyanea arctica* (COLOR PLATE VI, 6), as well as in other jellyfish. It is common along the coast of New England, north of Cape Cod.

Family Cystisomidae

The large eyes are not divided into two portions, as in the following family. The uropods are two-branched, the inner branch being fused with the peduncle. There is no mandibular palp.

Euthemisto compressa (Goës) PLATE 147. The third pereiopods are unusually long. The second and third pereiopods have a broad carapace. The body has a keel on the mid-line. The posterior two thoracic segments and the first two abdominal segments show a median spinelike tooth, projecting posteriorly.

Euthemisto bispinosa (Boeck) PLATE 147. This species also has a keel on the dorsal side. The last two thoracic segments are equipped with posterior teeth often curving upward. The *carpus* (hand) of the first pereiopods is conspicuously broad and dilated. The third pereiopods are extremely long, extending beyond the posterior end of the body, with an extremely narrow rodlike carpus furnished with spines, increasing in length toward the end

PLATE 146

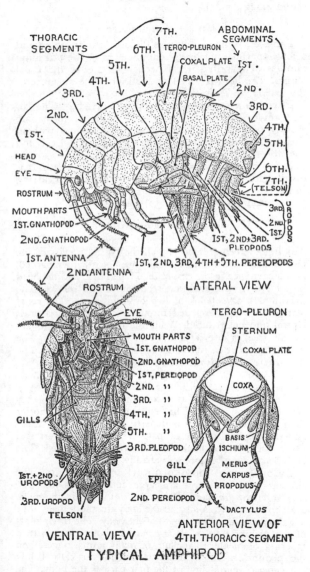

THORACIC SEGMENTS

ABDOMINAL SEGMENTS

7TH.
6TH.
5TH.
4TH.
3RD.
2ND.
1ST.

TERGO-PLEURON
COXAL PLATE
BASAL PLATE

1ST.
2ND.
3RD.
4TH.
5TH.
6TH.
7TH. (TELSON)

HEAD
EYE
ROSTRUM →
MOUTH PARTS
1ST. GNATHOPOD
2ND. GNATHOPOD
1ST. ANTENNA
2ND. ANTENNA

3RD.
2ND.
1ST.
UROPODS

1ST, 2ND + 3RD. PLEOPODS

1ST, 2ND, 3RD, 4TH + 5TH. PEREIOPODS

LATERAL VIEW

ROSTRUM
EYE
MOUTH PARTS
1ST. GNATHOPOD
2ND. GNATHOPOD
1ST. PEREIOPOD
2ND. ''
3RD. ''
4TH. ''
5TH. ''
3RD. PLEOPOD

GILLS

1ST. + 2ND. UROPODS
3RD. UROPOD
TELSON

VENTRAL VIEW

TERGO-PLEURON
STERNUM
COXAL PLATE
COXA
BASIS
ISCHIUM
MERUS
CARPUS
PROPODUS
DACTYLUS
GILL
EPIPODITE
2ND. PEREIOPOD

ANTERIOR VIEW OF
4TH. THORACIC SEGMENT

TYPICAL AMPHIPOD

This species is usually ⅗ mm. in length. It is generally found along the Atlantic Coast.

Family Phronimidae

The eyes, in this family, are divided into an upper and a lower portion, not being continuous as in the preceding families. The fifth pair of pereiopods are of the usual length. The head is very long vertically. The antennae of the female are vestigial.

Phronima sedentaria (Forskal) PLATE 147. The lateral angles of the first three abdominal segments are sharply pointed. The gnathopods are small and without chelae. The third pair of pereiopods are quite large and chelate or nearly so. The last thoracic segment is longer than the others. This species is over 1 inch in length. It is distributed throughout all the seas of the world, occurring inside the tests of the transparent colonial floating ascidians of the genera *Salpa* (PLATE 250) and *Pyrosoma*.

Suborder GAMMARIDEA

This Suborder includes the great majority of the Order Amphipoda, being practically all the typical species of the Order. The head and eyes usually are not greatly enlarged, as has been seen in the case of the Hyperiidea, and the head is not fused with the first segment of the thorax. The maxillipeds have palps of two or four joints. The coxal plates are well developed throughout. The abdomen is typical and not reduced. While the last two segments are usually free, in rare cases they may be fused together. The gills are present on five or six segments of the thorax. The first pair of uropods are always unbranched.

Family Orchestiidae

There are, typically, two compound eyes; rarely, they are vestigial or lacking. The first pair of antennae is shorter than the second. The mouth-parts are elongate vertically and the mandibles have no palp. The telson is short and thick with the terminal uropods not two-branched. The body is strongly compressed laterally.

Talorchestia longicornis (Say) PLATE 148. The circular compound eyes are large and conspicuous. The first antennae are short. The second antennae, in the male, are approximately as long as the body. In the female, they are about one third the length of the body. The three joints of the peduncle are well developed in both sexes, with a tapering filamentary flagellum of many joints longer than the peduncle. The mouth-parts extend vertically below the general ventral line of the first part of the body. The mandibles are without palps. The coxal plates are conspicuously developed along the sides of the body, grad-

PLATE 147

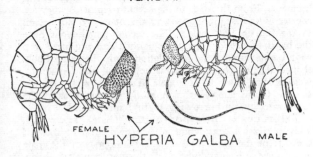

FEMALE   HYPERIA GALBA   MALE

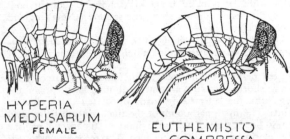

HYPERIA
MEDUSARUM
FEMALE

EUTHEMISTO
COMPRESSA
FEMALE

EUTHEMISTO
BISPINOSA
FEMALE

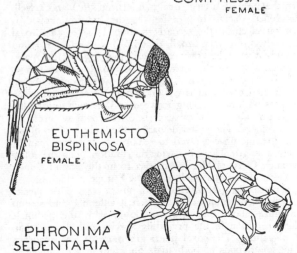

PHRONIMA
SEDENTARIA

ually increasing in size from the first to the fourth segments. From the fifth to the seventh segments, they are shorter. The first gnathopods, in the male, are subchelate; in the female, not chelate. The second gnathopods have the hand (*propodus*) greatly expanded and produced to a round lobe toward the articulation with the large hook-shaped dactyl. The second gnathopods of the female are weaker than those of the male. This is a very common species, found abundantly on sandy beaches around the high-water mark, burrowing to find moist sand.

Talorchestia megalopthalma (Bate) PLATE 148. This species has conspicuously large eyes covering most of the side of the head. The second gnathopods of the male are somewhat oval and about one third as long as the body. The antennae are shorter than in the preceding species, with which it is often found on sandy beaches. In both cases, the distribution is along the southern New England shore to New Jersey.

Orchestia agilis Smith PLATE 148. This species has large eyes and very short first antennae with a flagellum of not more than four joints and shorter than the three-jointed peduncle. The second antennae are also comparatively short, but with a stout peduncle, longer than the flagellum, the latter being made up of ten to 15 close-set joints. The first gnathopods of the male are subchelate and almost heart-shaped, with the joint of the dactyl on one lobe closing against the other lobe. The second gnathopods are chelate with a large oval palm (propodus) and a well-developed dactyl. In the female, the first gnathopod is without a chela; the second gnathopod has a small, oval propodus and very small dactyl. This species is found abundantly under seaweed near the high-water mark, especially where the seaweed is damp. It is the species which is disturbed when masses of seaweed on the beach are turned over, and is usually spoken of as the sand-flea. It feeds both on decaying seaweed and on such animal life as it can obtain. In color, it is olive-brown or green to light-colored. The posterior part of the body is often bluish and the antennae are red to red-brown. It is less than ½ inch in length. There is a wide distribution along the entire Atlantic Coast of North America from the Bay of Fundy to Cape Hatteras, as well as on the European side.

Orchestia palustris Smith PLATE 148. This species also has conspicuous eyes, short first antennae and second antennae about four times as long, with the peduncle slenderer than in the preceding species and shorter than its flagellum. The coxal plates are more or less quadrate. The gnathopods of both male and female are similar to the preceding species. The posterior angles of some of the abdominal segments are produced into acute points. The

PLATE 148

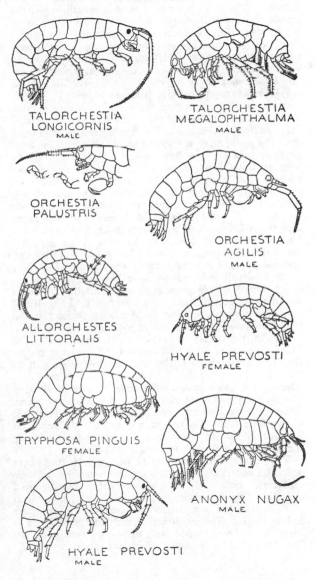

TALORCHESTIA
LONGICORNIS
MALE

TALORCHESTIA
MEGALOPHTHALMA
MALE

ORCHESTIA
PALUSTRIS

ORCHESTIA
AGILIS
MALE

ALLORCHESTES
LITTORALIS

HYALE PREVOSTI
FEMALE

TRYPHOSA PINGUIS
FEMALE

ANONYX NUGAX
MALE

HYALE PREVOSTI
MALE

color is olive-brown to olive-green with reddish-brown antennae. The male is nearly 1 inch in length, while the female is somewhat shorter. Generally speaking, it is of larger size, with slenderer second antennae and longer first antennae than the preceding species, and also with larger first coxal plates. It is usually found in salt-marshes some distance from the beach, among grass and weeds, and is, therefore, not associated with the preceding species.

Allorchestes littoralis Stimpson PLATE 148. This is a much smaller species than the preceding, being only ¼ inch in length. It has oval eyes, situated on either side of the mid-line of the head. The first antennae are longer than the peduncle of the second antennae, which, in turn, are comparatively short and peculiar for the comparatively long terminal joint of the peduncle, which is adorned beneath with a tuft of hairlike setae. The first gnathopods are squarish in shape and subchelate with their oblong propodus truncate at the end. The second gnathopods are stouter in the male than in the female, with the large, oval propodus forming an oblique palm over which the long, slender dactyl closes. The first uropods are the longest of the three pairs, the second being somewhat shorter, and the third, or internal uropods, the shortest of all. The telson is deeply indented on the mid-line, thus being bi-lobed. This species is green to olive-brown with red-brown antennae. It ranges from Grand Manan to Long Island Sound on rocky shores, near the high-water mark. It is also found on wharf-piles and in tide-pools.

Hyale prevostii (Milne-Edwards) PLATE 148. The first four pairs of coxal plates are much larger and deeper than the last three pairs. The first maxillae have a palp of but one joint. The palp of the maxillipeds is four-jointed. The second gnathopods in the male have a small wrist (*carpus*) somewhat overlapped by the preceding joint. There is a large, ovate propodus and a well-developed dactyl. The telson has two stumpy lobes. This amphipod is about ⅓ inch in diameter, and is distributed all along the New England coast to Long Island Sound.

Tryphosa (Orchomenella) pinguis Holmes PLATE 148. The anterior coxal plates are twice as deep as their segments, being quite conspicuous factors when viewed laterally. The first pair of gnathopods is slender with elongated carpus and narrow propodus. The eyes are kidney-shaped. The propodus of the first gnathopods is more or less cone-shaped with the dactyl closing on the narrow end. This is another abundant species.

Family Lysianassidae

The species in this family have a compact body with well-developed coxal plates. The first antennae have a short, stout base and always an additional and secondary flagellum. The cutting edge of the mandibles is not toothed. The second gnathopods are slender and flexible with the third joint long and narrow, and the hand (propodus) small, and covered densely with setae. The dactyl is only slightly developed and vestigial.

Anonyx nugax (Phipps) PLATE 148. The eyes in this species are large and well developed. They are elongated and wider below. The telson is nearly rectangular and divided on the median line by a deep cleft.

Lysianopsis alba Holmes PLATE 149. The antennae are short and alike in both sexes. The eyes are large and oval. The mandibles are without teeth and with a three-jointed palp. In the first antennae, the basal joint of the peduncle is stout and oval in shape, but longer than the next two, which taper almost imperceptibly into the flagellum, from the base of which, on the inner side, springs the small accessory flagellum. The second antennae are of about the same length as the first antennae and are also with a short flagellum. The first gnathopods are without chelae and normal in shape. The second gnathopods are quite long and slender, with a long carpus covered with hairs and a short, heart-shaped propodus, also densely hairy. The dactyl is extremely minute. The posterior two pairs of pereiopods are quite long, especially in the case of the last pair. The first pair of uropods are the longest with slender, pointed branches. The second pair is intermediate in length, while the inner pair is the shortest of the three. The telson is more or less rectangular, without clefts, and somewhat rounded posteriorly. The color of this species is white to yellowish white. It is ¼ inch in length. It is abundant in the mud at Woods Hole, and in mud and grass off the southern Connecticut shore.

Family Haustoriidae

Both pairs of antennae are unusually short, the first pair slightly shorter than the second. An accessory flagellum branches off from the base of the main flagellum. In the second antennae, the fourth joint of the peduncle is expanded to form a posterior, rounded lobe. Both pairs are densely equipped with hairs on the posterior side. The mandibles have a cutting edge without teeth. The gnathopods are weak. The pereiopods have broad expansions on their joints, adapted for burrowing. The uropods are double-branched, flanking a cleft telson.

Haustorius arenarius (Slabber) PLATE 149. The head is prolonged forward into a triangular rostrum. The eyes are small and round. The antennae are as indicated in the definition of the family. The body is rather flat and not arched, as is usually the case with amphipods. The first four coxal plates rapidly increase in size posteriorly. The last three are much shorter, the first two bilobed, the third with a spatulate lobe extending backward. The gnathopods are weak. Only the second pair is weakly chelate. The joints of the pereiopods have platelike spines, becoming successively larger until they are very wide in the last three pereiopods. No dactyls are present. The uropods are almost tubular in form with tufts of coarse spines. The telson is somewhat cleft in the middle. Among the most striking characters are the dense plumes of setae present on all the appendages. The color is pale yellow, closely resembling its sandy environment. This animal is about ⅔ inch in length and is distributed from Cape Cod to Georgia, on sandy shores, near the low-water mark. They are said to be the most rapid burrowers among the amphipods. They are usually recognized by the expansions on their joints and their extremely hairy appendages.

Family Ampeliscidae

The head is almost square in front, without a rostrum. There are usually two pairs of simple eyes. There is no accessory flagellum present on the first antennae. The second pair of antennae are longer and are situated at an interval behind the first pair. The gnathopods are weakly subchelate. The propodus and the next joint (carpus) are about equal in length. The first and second pereiopods are characterized by a very large and expanded fourth joint (*merus*). The telson has a deep cleft nearly to the base.

Ampelisca macrocephala Lilljeborg PLATE 149. The head is as long as the first three thoracic segments, with the front extending forward and squared off at the tip. The first antennae, in the female, are not so long as in the male, but with a very short peduncle and a comparatively long flagellum. The second antennae of the female have much longer joints on the peduncle and a flagellum of about the same length. The first four pairs of coxal plates extend forward diagonally and are about the same in size and quite deep. The first and second pereiopods are with long, needlelike dactyls. The fifth, sixth, and seventh pereiopods have their basal joints enlarged and produced distally, the posterior edges fringed with setae. The fifth and sixth coxal plates are shallow and bilobed. The third abdominal segment has a rounded and acute, saberlike projection at the postero-lateral angles. The deeply cleft and toothed telson is flanked with two pairs of uropods,

COLOR PLATES

X-XVI

PLATE X

TYPICAL SHRIMPLIKE CRUSTACEA

1. Opossum Shrimp *Mysis stenolepis* S. I. Smith. See also PLATE 139.

2. Mantis Shrimp *Squilla empusa* Say. See also PLATE 170.

3. Common Sand Shrimp *Crangon vulgaris* Fabricius = *Crago septemspinosus* (Say). See also PLATE 159.

4. Common Prawn *Palaemonetes vulgaris* (Say). See also PLATE 159.

5. Montagu's Shrimp *Pandalus montagui* Leach. See also PLATE 157.

6. Eel Grass Shrimp *Hippolyte* (*Virbius*) *zostericola* (S. I. Smith). See also PLATE 158.

7. Callianassa *Callianassa stimpsoni* S. I. Smith. See also PLATE 162.

8. Mole Shrimp. Sand Bug *Hippa talpoida* Say. Side view; 8a. Dorsal view.

9. Common Hermit Crab *Pagurus longicarpus* Say. Without mollusk shell. See also COLOR PLATE IX, 8.

10. Spinous Hermit Crab *Pagurus bernhardus* (Linnaeus). Withous shell. See also INDEX PLATE 163.

10a. Common Hermit Crab *Pagurus longicarpus* Say. With shell.

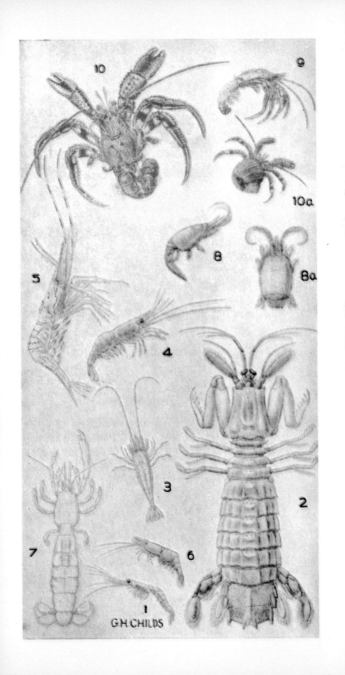

G.H. CHILDS

PLATE XI—LOBSTER AND LADY CRAB ON BAY BOTTOM. 1. Common Lobster *Homarus americanus* Milne-Edwards. 2. Lady Crab, Calico Crab *Ovalipes ocellatus* (Herbst). 3. Horshoe Crab, King Crab *Limulus polyphemus* Linnaeus. 4. **Sea Anemone** *Metridium dianthus* (Ellis). 5. Irish Moss *Chondrus crispus* (Linnaeus). 6. Pink Furbelowed Alga *Grinnellia americana* (Agardh). 7. Fingered Kelp *Laminaria digitata* (Linnaeus). 8. Ruffled Kelp *Laminaria agardhii* Kjellman. 9. Dulse *Rhodymenia palmata* (Linnaeus).

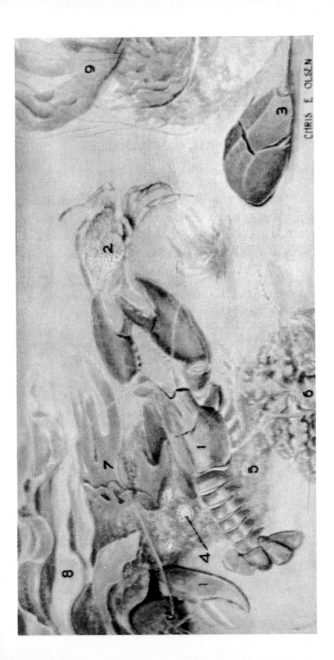

CHRIS E. OLSEN

PLATE XII

TYPICAL COASTAL CRABS

1. Common Spider Crab *Libinia emerginata* Leach. See also PLATE 169.

2. Toad Crab *Hyas coarctatus* Leach. See also PLATE 169.

3. Common Rock Crab *Cancer irroratus* Say.

4. Northern Crab, Jonah Crab *Cancer borealis* Stimpson.

5. Mud Crab *Panopeus herbstii* Milne-Edwards. See also PLATE 167.

6. Common Blue Crab, Soft-shell Crab *Callinectes sapidus* Rathbun. See also INDEX PLATE 165; PLATE 166.

7. Lady Crab, Calico Crab, *Ovalipes ocellatus* (Herbst). See also COLOR PLATE XI, 2.

8. Green Crab *Carcinides maenas* (Linnaeus).

9. Ghost Crab, Sand Crab *Ocypode albicans* Bosc = *Ocypode arenaria* Say.

10. Fiddler Crab *Uca pugnax* (S. I. Smith). See also PLATE 168.

G.H. CHILDS

PLATE XIII

MUSSELS, CLAMS, AND THEIR RELATIVES

1. Noah's Ark Shell *Arca occidentalis* Philippi = *Arca noae* Linnaeus. See also PLATE 179 (13).

2. Common Edible Mussel *Mytilus edulis* Linnaeus. See also PLATE 180 (6); COLOR PLATE XVI, 5.

3. Horse Mussel *Modiolus modiolus* Linnaeus. See also PLATE 180 (9).

4. Ribbed Mussel *Modiolus demissus plicatulus* (Lamarck). See also PLATE 180 (10).

5. Surf Clam, Hen Clam *Mactra (Spisula) solidissima* (Dillwyn). See also PLATE 185 (5).

6. Hard Shell Clam, Little Neck Clam *Venus mercenaria* Linnaeus. See also PLATE 183 (6); INDEX PLATE 178.

7. Disc Shell *Dosinia discus* Reeve.

8. Iceland Cockle *Cardium ciliatum* Fabricius = *Cardium islandicum* Lamarck. See also PLATE 182 (17).

9. Soft Clam, Long Neck Clam *Mya arenaria* Linnaeus. See also PLATE 186 (1).

10. Common Razor-shell Clam *Ensis directus* (Conrad). See also PLATE 185 (2).

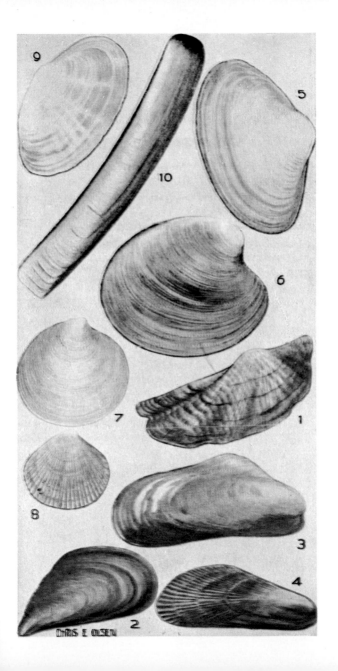

CHRIS E OLSEN

PLATE XIV

SCALLOPS AND OYSTERS

1. Smooth Jingle Shell *Anomia simplex* d'Orbigny. See also PLATE 181 (4, 5).

2. Prickly Pen Shell *Pinna muricata* Linnaeus = *Pinna rigida* Dillwyn.

3. Virginia Oyster *Ostrea virginica* Gmelin.

4. Iceland Scallop *Pecten islandicus* (Müller). See also PLATE 180 (1).

5. Common Scallop *Pecten irradians* Lamarck. See also COLOR PLATE IX (10).

6. Giant Scallop, Deep Sea Scallop *Pecten magellanicus* (Gmelin). See also PLATE 180 (4).

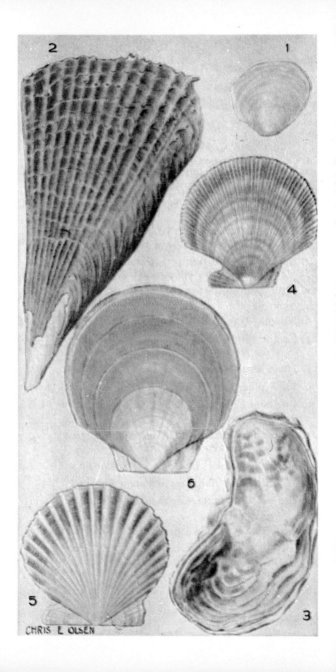

CHRIS E OLSEN

PLATE XV

MARINE GASTROPODS AND CHITONS

1. Hairy-girdled Chiton *Chaetopleura apiculata* (Say). See also PLATE 189 (5).

2. Red Chiton *Trachydermon ruber* (Linnaeus). See also PLATE 189 (7).

3. Common Tooth Shell, Tusk Shell *Dentalium entale* Linnaeus. See also PLATE 189 (4).

4, 4a. Tortoise-shell Limpet *Acmaea testudinalis* (Linnaeus). See also COLOR PLATE XVI, 6.

5. Little Sun Shell *Margarites (Solariella) obscura* Couthouy.

6. Smooth Top Shell *Margarites helicina* (Fabricius).

7. Fragile Purple Shell *Janthina fragilis* Lamarck = *Janthina janthina* Linnaeus.

8. Moon Shell *Polinices heros* (Say).

9. Sand-collar Snail *Polinices (Neverita) duplicata* (Say).

10. Common Periwinkle, Edible Periwinkle *Littorina litorea* Linnaeus.

11. Obtuse Periwinkle, Little Periwinkle *Littorina palliata* (Say). See also COLOR PLATE XVI, 5.

12. Duck's Foot Shell *Aporrhais occidentalis* Beck.

13. Waved Whelk *Buccinum undatum* Linnaeus.

14. Ten-ridged Neptune *Chrysodomus (Neptunea) decemcostata* (Say).

15. Knobbed Whelk, Giant Whelk *Busycon (Fulgur) caricum* (Gmelin).

16. Channeled Whelk *Busycon (Fulgur) canaliculatum* (Linnaeus). See also COLOR PLATE IX, 9.

17. Stimpson's Distaff Shell *Colus (Sipho) stimpsoni* (Mörch). See also PLATE 192 (7).

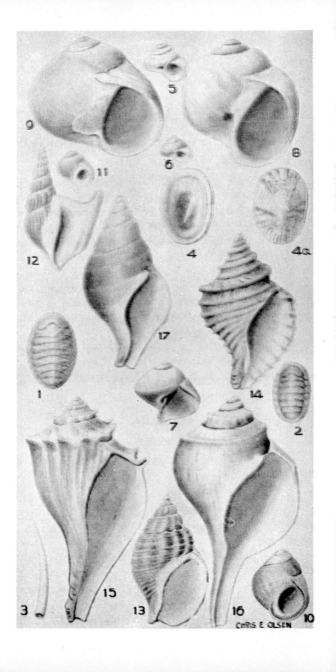

CHAS E OLSEN

PLATE XVI

INTERTIDAL MOLLUSK ASSOCIATION ON A ROCKY COAST

1. Purple Snail, Dog Whelk *Thais lapillus* Linnaeus. 1a. Egg cases.

2. Southern Periwinkle, Lined Periwinkle *Littorina irrorata* (Say). See also PLATE 190 (25).

3. Obtuse Periwinkle *Littorina palliata* (Say). See also COLOR PLATE XV (11).

4. Young *Littorina*.

5. Common Edible Mussel *Mytilus edulis* Linnaeus. See also PLATE 180 (6); COLOR PLATE XIII (2).

6. Tortoise Shell Limpet *Acmaea testudinalis* (Linnaeus). See also COLOR PLATE XV, 4, 4a.

7. Rock Barnacle *Balanus balanoides* (Linnaeus). See also INDEX PLATE 134; PLATE 136.

8. Knobbed Rock-weed *Ascophyllum nodosum* (Linnaeus).

each double-branched, with long, slender, and sharp terminal joints. The length is ⅜ inch. The color is whitish. This species is distributed from the Arctic regions to Long Island Sound. It is found, for the most part, among eelgrass on muddy bottoms.

Ampelisca spinipes Boeck PLATE 149. In this species, the postero-lateral angle of the third abdominal segment is not produced in an acute spine, but forms a right-angled corner. The coxal plates are similar to those in the preceding species. The back of the amphipod is not so strongly arched. The first and second antennae are much longer. The first three pereiopods are armed with sharp, posteriorly pointed dactyls. The third, fourth, and fifth basal joints are greatly expanded, the fifth with a margin fringed with setae. The telson is very narrow and nearly smooth. The color is almost white with a rose-colored or purple spot on the first coxal plate and other such spots sparsely scattered over the body. The length is ⅜ inch. Its distribution is both in the northern part of Europe and, on the American side, along the southern New England coast. It is very common on bottoms of sand, gravel, or mud, and among eelgrass, in shallow water, to 12 fathoms.

Byblis serrata Smith PLATE 149. There are two pairs of simple eyes toward the anterior part of the head at the base of the antennae. The antennae are very slender, the first pair much shorter than the extremely long second pair. In each case, the peduncle is slender and with the joints spiny on their lower margins. The coxal plate of the first gnathopod is broadly expanded and projects so far forward that it joins the entire length of the head laterally. It is fringed with setae on its outer side. The coxal plate of the second gnathopods also projects forward obliquely and, like the first, is fringed with setae. The third and fourth coxal plates cover the bases of the pereiopods, the fourth one having a curved indentation posteriorly, to fit the shallow bilobed anterior edge of the fifth joints of the fifth coxal plate. The sixth and seventh coxal plates are also shallow and bilobed. The basal joints of the fifth and sixth pereiopods are broad, oval expansions. That of the seventh extends posteriorly as an elongate, rounded plate, overlapping the lateral sides of the first and second abdominal joints. The third abdominal segment has rounded postero-lateral angles. The three pairs of uropods are biramous, extending beyond the narrow, rounded telson. This species is about ½ inch in length and is found abundantly on muddy and sandy bottoms along the southern New England shore.

Family Stegocephalidae

This family is characterized by its short head, deeply arched, compact body, and abruptly enlarged coxal plate.

Stegocephalus inflatus Kröyer PLATE 149. There is a prominent rostrum bent abruptly downward. There are no eyes. The first five coxal plates together form a compact semicircular lateral armor with the fourth plate equal in size to the three anterior ones. The terminal uropods have narrow, pointed branches exceeding the peduncle in length. The telson is pointed, but cleft on the middle line. This is a northern species found from Grand Manan to Block Island.

Family Phoxocephalidae

The rostrum, in this family, is expanded into a hood over the antennae. The fifth and sixth pereiopods are much longer than the seventh.

Phoxocephalus holbölli (Kröyer) PLATE 149. The palp of the first maxillae has but one joint. The second pair of gnathopods is larger than the first pair. The inconspicuous eyes are imperfectly developed. The coxal plates are all furnished with bunches of setae on the lower margin. The first three pairs of coxal plates are shallow and slightly bilobed; the last four pairs are elongate and almost quadrangular. The long, pointed telson is cleft medially to its base. Its sides are sinuously curved and hollowed out at the base of the biramous uropods. The color is yellow to orange. It is ⅕ inch in length and is distributed from the Arctic regions to Long Island Sound.

Paraphoxus spinosus Holmes PLATE 149. The anterior hood covering the bases of the antennae is without a keel, with a rounded triangular rostrum. The eyes are large in the male and somewhat smaller in the female. In the female, the first and second antennae are nearly equal in size, while in the male they are not much longer. The short flagella are very slender. The gnathopods are about equal in length and shape. The first and second pereiopods are about equal in size. The third is larger and with its basal joint expanded posteriorly into a rectangular plate. In the fourth pereiopods, the basal plate is more rounded and broader, while the fifth one is somewhat smaller. The first three coxal plates are about equal in size and somewhat rectangular, the fourth one being larger, rounded and hollowed on its posterior margin to articulate with the shallow fifth coxal plate, which has a posterior rounded lobe. The sixth and seventh are also shallow and rounded posteriorly. This is a slightly smaller species than the preceding. It is found off the southern New England coast.

PLATE 149

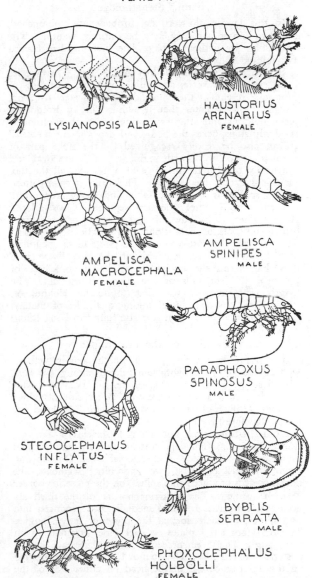

LYSIANOPSIS ALBA

HAUSTORIUS
ARENARIUS
FEMALE

AMPELISCA
MACROCEPHALA
FEMALE

AMPELISCA
SPINIPES
MALE

PARAPHOXUS
SPINOSUS
MALE

STEGOCEPHALUS
INFLATUS
FEMALE

BYBLIS
SERRATA
MALE

PHOXOCEPHALUS
HÖLBÖLLI
FEMALE

Family Stenothoidae

In this family, the terminal uropods are unbranched, but two-jointed, or they may be entirely wanting. The mandibles are without a palp. The first maxillae have a two-jointed palp.

Stenothoë cypris Holmes PLATE 150. This species is so called because its swimming motions, according to Holmes, resemble those of the fresh-water ostracod, *Cypris*. Holmes states that it swims "in an irregularly jerky manner and after swimming but a short distance, suddenly stops, flexes the body, and drops to the bottom." It can also be readily recognized by the huge pair of coxal plates on the fourth segment, which are oval and practically overlap the other coxal plates and all the thoracic legs except the last pair. The striking color-pattern of the species is also remarkable and easily recognized. According to Holmes, the first segment is rose-colored above. There is a row of rose-colored, or sometimes brownish, spots or bars along the middle of the back. The eyes are also rose-colored. The joints of the peduncle of the antennae are yellowish at the tip. There is a dark bar across the tip of the abdomen and base of the uropods. The gills have a tinge of rose-color. The length is 2 mm. It was first found by Holmes on wharf-piles at Woods Hole, among quantities of the hydroid *Pennaria* (PLATE 32). It is also found in Long Island Sound.

Family Acanthonotosomidae

In this family, the first pair of gnathopods is well developed, as compared with the related family *Bateidae*. The first three pairs of coxal plates are pointed below. There is a median dorsal crest on either side of which prominent tubercles are present or absent. The head has a well-developed rostrum.

Acanthonotosoma serratum (Fabricius) PLATE 150; INDEX PLATE 146. The segments are smooth and without tubercles on either side of the dorsal crest. On the posterior thoracic and first two abdominal segments, the dorsal crest is produced into spines, on the posterior border of each segment. The posterior border of the third abdominal segment is rounded medially and produced into two spines, on each side, at the posterior lateral angles. The first four coxal plates on each side terminate in an acute angle. The three succeeding coxal plates each have a posterior curved lobe. The round, black eyes are located on the anterior border of the head on either side of the rostrum.

Family Lafystiidae

The first antennae have no accessory flagellum. The maxillipeds have a small two-jointed palp. There is a broad thorax. These amphipods are parasitic on several species of fish.

Lafystius sturionis Kröyer PLATE 150. The head has a broad rostrum, flat in front. The fourth coxal plates are pointed below. The pereiopods are approximately equal in length and have strongly curved dactyls adapted for clinging. The eyes are small and rounded. The first antennae are somewhat longer and stouter than the second. Both pairs of gnathopods are comparatively small. The pereiopods are well developed and of fairly equal length. This species is about ¼ inch in length. It is parasitic on various fishes, having been found in the mouth of a Goose-fish, the back of a skate, and on the Angler (*Lophius*).

Family Calliopiidae

In this family, the amphipods have fairly regularly developed coxal plates, but not large. The first antennae have a short peduncle and a vestigial accessory flagellum, if it is present at all.

Calliopius laeviusculus (Kröyer) PLATE 150. The antennae are stout, the first being a little shorter than the second. There is no accessory flagellum. The mandibles have a large palp. The gnathopods are fairly strong with a large propodus and long, hooklike dactyl. The first four coxal plates are approximately oval, but increase in depth from in front backward. The last three coxal plates are shallow and somewhat bilobed. The last three pairs of pereiopods have a well-expanded basal joint, while the fourth joint (merus) has a posteriorly projecting terminal lobe. A low median keel is present on the first three abdominal segments. This species is about ½ inch in length and is distributed from Greenland and the Arctic, generally along the coast to Long Island Sound, and also on the northern coasts of Europe.

Family Pontogeneiidae

In this family, the body is compressed and not characterized by a prominent rostrum. The accessory flagellum is usually lacking in the first antennae. The body is otherwise moderately developed, no segments having a dorsal spine. The gnathopods are not unusually developed.

Pontogeneia inermis (Kröyer) PLATE 150. The body of this species is quite slender, with no unusual external characters and without a keel or projecting segmental spines. The eyes are kidney-shaped. The first and second antennae have short peduncles and quite long flagella, the second antennae being slightly longer. In the male, the antennae are more completely developed than in the female. The pereiopods are fairly slender and edged with bundles of sharp spines. This is a nearly colorless, practically transparent species with purple spots and purple bands on the antennae. It is not quite ½ inch in length. It is abundantly distributed from the Arctic Ocean to Fishers Island Sound.

Family Bateidae

In this family, the head has a stoutly projecting rostrum, tapering forward to a point. The eyes are large, placed laterally. The first coxal plate is vestigial, if not practically almost rudimentary, having no propodus or dactyl.

Batea secunda Holmes PLATE 150. The large eyes are situated posterior to the notch, on either side of the prominent rostrum. The second, third, and fourth coxal plates take up about one half the depth of the body. This species is nearly ¼ inch in length. The body is marked with blue to purplish or reddish brown spots. Its distribution is along the coast of southern New England in from 6 to 25 fathoms.

Family Gammaridae

In this family, the body is comparatively slender and with slender antennae, with accessory flagellum, when present, usually well developed. The gnathopods are usually powerful. The pereiopods are quite slender. The terminal uropods are often leaflike and project farther than the other two.

Carinogammarus mucronatus (Say) PLATE 150. This species has a strongly arched body and is very hairy, its appendages being all strongly ciliated. The eyes are kidney-shaped. The first antennae are a little longer than the second pair, the first joint of the peduncle being the longest. There is an accessory flagellum of three or four joints. The peduncle of the second pair of antennae is longer, but the flagellum is shorter in proportion. The first three coxal plates are deeper than wide; the fourth is almost quadrangular, but with rounded corners. The edges of all are ciliated. Both pairs of gnathopods are strong and with well-developed propodus and dactyl, forming efficient grasping organs. The two sides of the propodus are approximately parallel; the outer margin on which the dactyl closes is oblique. The first three abdominal segments have a conspicuous medial spine projecting backward to form a sharply acute tooth. This species is very abundant in brackish and salt water, especially among algae. It is olive-green with red spots on the first four abdominal segments, resembling *Gammarus locusta* in this respect. It is about ¼ inch in length, but specimens are

PLATE 150

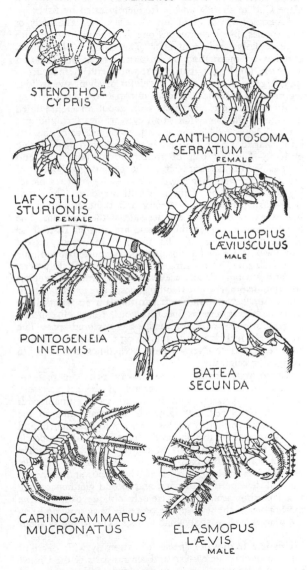

STENOTHOË
CYPRIS

ACANTHONOTOSOMA
SERRATUM
FEMALE

LAFYSTIUS
STURIONIS
FEMALE

CALLIOPIUS
LÆVIUSCULUS
MALE

PONTOGENEIA
INERMIS

BATEA
SECUNDA

CARINOGAMMARUS
MUCRONATUS

ELASMOPUS
LÆVIS
MALE

often taken much larger. It is abundantly distributed from Cape Cod to Florida and is frequently eaten by fishes.

Elasmopus laevis (Smith) PLATE 150. The body of this species, like the previous one, is strongly arched, with a moderately sized coxal plate. The fourth is the largest, and has an indentation on its posterior border. The first antennae are longer than the second, with a small accessory flagellum and a main flagellum of about twenty-four segments. The slender second antennae are about as long as the peduncle of the first, with about an eight-jointed flagellum. The somewhat small eyes are nearly round and black. The mandibles have a three-jointed palp, the last joint shaped like a knife-blade and adorned with a row of setae. The first pair of gnathopods of both male and female are of moderate size. The second gnathopods of the male are very large with a short, thick carpus blending into the outline of the powerful propodus. The dactyl is hook-shaped and very strong and stout, fitting into a hollow excavation on the inner side of the propodus. The second gnathopods of the female are smaller than those of the male, though similar to them in outline, except that the slender dactyl closes simply against their oblique outer margin. The last three pairs of pereiopods are powerful and strongly flexed backward. The terminal uropods are double-branched, extending posterior to the others. The telson is broad and cleft two thirds of its length. The color of this species is inconspicuous, being olive-brown or gray, mottled with rounded, lighter-colored spots. The length is ⅖ inch. It is found all along the coast of southern New England to New Jersey, sometimes occurring in sponges or eelgrass.

Gammarus fasciatus Say PLATE 151. The first antennae are longer than the second. A distinct accessory flagellum is present. The first and second gnathopods are well developed, but larger in the male than in the female. One peculiarity of this species is that the fourth and fifth segments of the abdomen have a rounded tubercle on the median dorsal part of the segment, bearing three tufts of spines. The sixth segment is without the tubercle, but with the three spine-clusters. The carpus and propodus are well developed in the first and second gnathopods, the dactyl closing against an extremely oblique palm. In the gnathopods of the female, the propodus is narrow and rectangular as well as somewhat smaller. The length is about ½ inch.

This is a fresh-water species of extremely wide distribution throughout the eastern and central parts of the United States in fresh-water ponds, under stones, and among pond weeds. Properly, it should not be included in this volume, but because of its typical structure and abundant distribution as well as its close relationship to marine species, it is useful to include it.

Gammarus locusta (Linnaeus) PLATE 151. This is the commonest species along the New England coast. It has a slender and compressed body with long and narrow, kidney-shaped eyes. The first antennae are longer and more delicately slender than the second antennae. There is a well-developed, eight-jointed accessory flagellum. The second antennae have a stout and long peduncle, with a much shorter flagellum. The first gnathopod of the male is equipped with a long, somewhat narrow propodus. The second gnathopods are much longer than the first, with a much more powerful propodus and dactyl. In the female, the gnathopods are smaller. The dorsal plates of the second and third abdominal segments have their lower margins produced into a sharp and acute spine. The three posterior abdominal segments have a median projection, with tufts of spines situated both on the projection and on either side of it. The general color of this species is olive-brown to reddish, with bright-colored spots of red, orange, or pink, due to globules occurring underneath the bases of the pleopods and first uropods. This species is about 1 inch in length, though some individuals may be practically 2 inches long, especially in the Arctic. It is abundantly distributed from the Arctic Ocean along the coast of Europe, on the one hand, to the Mediterranean, and along the entire New England coast in the United States to Long Island Sound, on the other. It is also distributed in the Pacific Ocean in both the United States and Asian seas, from Bering Sea southward. It is found at low-water mark, lurking under stones, and also occurring down as far as 50 fathoms.

Gammarus annulatus Smith PLATE 151. The first antennae, in this species, are shorter and slenderer than the second. The first four coxal plates are almost quadrangular in shape, but with rounded corners and much deeper than the last three plates, which are notched on their lower border. The body, itself, is long and slender. The first pair of gnathopods is smaller than the second pair, but exactly similar in shape. The length is ⅜ inch. This is a surface swimmer, but is also found among rockweed and under stones, between the tides, and occurs as well to 13 fathoms in depth. It is abundant along the New England coast from Eastport, Maine, to New Haven, Connecticut.

Gammarus marinus Leach PLATE 151. The eyes, in this species, are very narrow and kidney-shaped. The first antennae are much longer than the second, being nearly half as long as the body, with a very long first joint of the otherwise short peduncle. There is an accessory flagellum of seven joints, and a long main flagellum of about thirty or more segments. The length of this species is about ⅜ inch and.it is found in the upper part of the tidal zone below high-water mark, under stones. It is distributed on both the European and American sides of the Atlantic from the Mediterranean northward and down along the New England coast to New Haven, Connecticut.

Melita nitida Smith PLATE 151. This species has a quite slender body. The small oval eyes are situated laterally on a small projection near the base of the second pair of antennae. The first antennae are considerably longer than the second and with a small accessory flagellum. The four anterior coxal plates are almost rectangular and quite long. The fifth and sixth are short, with a double scallop at their lower edge. The seventh is a shallowly rounded flap. The first gnathopod is quite weak. The second is stronger, with a narrowly oval propodus and a hook-shaped dactyl, and is larger than that of the female, though the first gnathopods are about the same size in both sexes. The posterior three pairs of pereiopods have large, elongate basal joints and, as a whole, are quite powerful as adaptations for jumping. The terminal uropods are quite long, exceeding the other two clearly in length. The color is dark green. It is about ⅔ inch in length and distributed along the southern New England coast as far south as New Jersey, associated with seaweed or under stones, near the low-water mark.

Melita dentata (Kröyer) PLATE 151. The long, slender body is strongly compressed and arched. The oval eyes are situated at the base of the long, first pair of antennae with its multi-articulate flagellum and small accessory flagellum. The second antennae have unusually long joints and a short flagellum, but their total length is only about two thirds of that of the first antennae. The first four coxal plates are longer than the height of the first four segments in profile, the posterior margin of the fourth plate being somewhat excavated to fit the anterior margin of the fifth. The fifth and sixth are shallowly bilobed. The seventh is also shallow, but with a simple rounded outline. This species is yellowish in color, banded with dark red-brown. It is ⅜ inch in length and abundantly distributed from the Arctic to Buzzards Bay and Long Island Sound.

Family Amphithoidae

The body is slender and compressed. The fourth coxal plate is straight behind, overlapped by the fifth, which has a small lobe on its upper posterior margin. The accessory flagellum, if present, is very small. The second gnathopod is usually larger than the first and differently shaped

PLATE 151

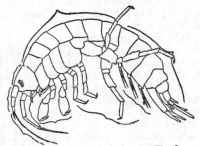

GAMMARUS FASCIATUS

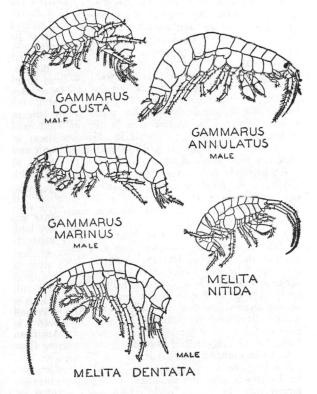

GAMMARUS
LOCUSTA
MALE

GAMMARUS
ANNULATUS
MALE

GAMMARUS
MARINUS
MALE

MELITA
NITIDA

MELITA DENTATA
MALE

from the smaller gnathopod of the female. The third pereiopod is directed backward almost parallel with the body. The fifth pair of pereiopods is the longest of all. The third uropods are short.

Amphithoë longimana Smith PLATE 152. The round eyes, in this species, are red in color. The first antennae are slender with an exceedingly long flagellum, equalling the length of the body. The second antennae are stouter and with a peduncle taking up three fourths of its length, terminating in a short flagellum, the total length being shorter than that of the first antennae. The first five coxal plates exceed in length the height of the body-joints. The first one is prolonged ventrally in front to cover the ventral side of the head. The second, third, and fourth coxal plates are similar in size and in their rounded, oblong shape. The fifth has a small lobe on the upper part of its posterior border. The first pair of gnathopods, in the male, is long and narrow. The second pair is much broader and stronger, with a triangular carpus blending into the outline of the expanded propodus. Both are bordered abundantly with setae. The first two pairs of pereiopods are weak. The third pair extends backward parallel to the body. The fourth and fifth pairs are by far the longest. The color shades from bright to pale green and to a bluish tint, or the body may be nearly transparent or reddish brown. This amphipod is ⅖ inch in length and is found mostly among seaweed in sheltered places, at the surface, near shore. It is distributed along the entire southern New England coast and to New Jersey.

Amphithoë rubricata (Montagu) PLATE 152. This is similar to the previous species, proportionately more slender, but reaching a large size. The first antennae are slender, with a somewhat short peduncle, and a very long flagellum. The second antennae have a longer peduncle and a short flagellum, the total length being not so great as that of the first antennae. The first coxal plate is narrow and produced forward along the lower side of the head. The color varies from green to red, often with light-colored spots along the median line of the back. It is nearly 1 inch in length and is found under rocks and among algae at low tide, especially on muddy shores. It is widely distributed on both the European and American sides of the North Atlantic, in this region occurring from Labrador to Long Island Sound.

Grubia compta (Smith) PLATE 152. This species, also, has a long, slender body strongly arched at the junction of the thorax with the abdomen. The first antennae are longer than the second, with a long multi-articulate flagellum and a minute single-jointed accessory flagellum. The mandibles have a three-jointed palp, while in the

PLATE 152

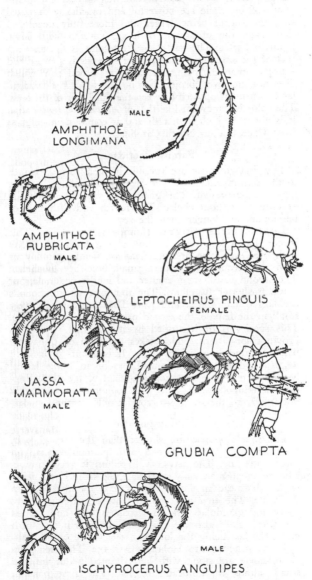

AMPHITHOË
LONGIMANA
MALE

AMPHITHOE
RUBRICATA
MALE

LEPTOCHEIRUS PINGUIS
FEMALE

JASSA
MARMORATA
MALE

GRUBIA COMPTA

ISCHYROCERUS ANGUIPES
MALE

maxillipeds it is four-jointed. The first and second gnathopods of the male are powerful and practically of equal size, the carpus being larger and more fully developed than even the propodus. Both are covered with long, plumelike setae. The dactyl, in the second, is shorter than that of the first. The third pair of uropods is shorter and stumpier than the elongate, narrower second pair which does not, however, project beyond the first. The triangular telson turns upward between the third pair of uropods. The color is somewhat like that of *Amphithoe longimana*. It is about ½ inch in length and is common in eelgrass from Cape Cod to North Carolina.

Family Photidae

The first antennae are variable in their relative length to the second antennae. The accessory flagellum may or may not be present. The gnathopods may be subchelate or entirely without chelae. The fourth and fifth pair of pereiopods are longer than the rest.

Leptocheirus pinguis (Stimpson) PLATE 152. This species has a long, slender, and almost horizontal body with oval eyes. The first antennae are slender but longer than the second pair with a small, accessory flagellum. The second pair have a stouter and longer peduncle, but a much shorter flagellum. The first pair of gnathopods are larger than the second pair. They are comparatively small in the female, the second pair being without chelae. This species is distinguished by its granular, chocolate-brown color-pattern, which takes the form of transverse bands surrounding lighter areas. It is about ½ inch in length, and distributed from Labrador to Long Island Sound. It is one of the most abundant of the New England amphipods, but especially common upon muddy bottoms from the surface to considerable depths.

Family Jassidae

The first antennae are shorter than the second pair. Both are abundantly adorned with plumelike setae on their underside. The accessory flagellum is very minute. The gnathopods are only subchelate, the second pair being larger than the first and with special modifications in the male. The first and second pairs of pereiopods are weak and glandular. The third pair is long and turned backward, as is also the case with the fourth and fifth pairs, the last being the longest.

Jassa marmorata Holmes PLATE 152. The two pairs of antennae are stout, with long, jointed peduncles and small, almost insignificant, flagella. The first pair of gnathopods is of moderate size with an oval propodus and hooklike dactyl, which functions by closing against projecting spines. The second pair of gnathopods, in the male, has an enormously enlarged propodus, with a projecting thumb-shaped process. The dactyl is also tremendously developed and, in both cases, a subchela is formed. The second gnathopods in the female are much smaller. The first and second pereiopods are not unusually long, but the third, fourth, and fifth are long, bent backward, and adapted for jumping. The ground-color of this species is reddish, but mottled with lighter spots. It is about ⅖ inch in length and is distributed along the Massachusetts and Connecticut coasts as far as New Haven. It is especially abundant among seaweed and hydroids on wharf-piles.

Ischyrocerus anguipes Kröyer PLATE 152. This is another remarkably developed species, similar to *Jassa marmorata* In the male, the first pair of gnathopods is comparatively small and subchelate. The second pair, however, has a long, curved basal joint, a comparatively small carpus, and an enormously curved propodus with a saberlike dactyl, which closes against a fringe of stout plumose setae, making a large and effective subchelate prehensile organ. In the female, the first gnathopods are like those of the male, but the second pair are very much smaller and of quite different form, the propodus being somewhat pear-shaped. The third, fourth, and fifth pairs of pereiopods project from beneath the body quite posteriorly, the body curving around behind them. The color of this species varies from greenish olive to pale crimson. Smith records specimens with transverse bands of orange-red, one to each segment, dotted with brown spots, while the legs were ringed with white, orange, or reddish bands. The length is ⅖ inch. This species is distributed around the northern Atlantic border, from the Arctic along the New England coast to Long Island Sound.

Family Aoridae

In this family, the body is very slender. The first pair of antennae is longer than the second pair and there is an accessory flagellum present. The first pair of gnathopods is larger and more conspicuously developed than the second pair. There are, however, sexual differences in these structures. The first and second pairs of pereiopods are typical and not unusually developed. The seventh pair of pereiopods is always longest. The uropods and telson are comparatively short.

Microdeutopus gryllotalpa Costa PLATE 153. The conspicuous distinguishing characteristics of this species are the extremely large first pair of gnathopods with their chelate claws. Instead of the propodus being large and swollen as in the various families of amphipods already described, it is the succeeding joint or carpus which has practically taken its place as a hand, while the propodus is reduced to a fingerlike process, extending forward and articulating with a dactyl or pointed terminal joint, a very efficient, pincerlike organ. The carpus has, in addition, three small, anterior, spinelike projections and a series of setae, against which the dactyl comes in contact, when bent downward. Two toothlike projections on the inside of the propodus also come into play to perfect this very efficient organ. The general aspect of this gnathopod is to give a cricketlike appearance to the amphipod itself, hence the species is named *gryllotalpa,* which is, incidentally, the scientific generic name of our common cricket. The second gnathopods are not at all of conspicuous size. The first antennae are quite long, the peduncle consisting of three joints, the first being of moderate size, the second joint the largest, and the third quite short. There is a long flagellum of about twenty segments with an accessory flagellum consisting of a single joint. The peduncle of the second antennae is longer than in the case of the first, but the seven-jointed flagellum is so short that the whole structure is only about ¾ inch. The distribution is circumpolar; on the European coast, it ranges from Norway to the Mediterranean Sea. On the North American coast, it seems to be known only from southern New England, and is found among seaweed and hydroids, especially on wharf-piles.

Microdeutopus damnonensis (Bate) PLATE 153. This species is somewhat similar to the preceding, but the first pair of gnathopods has a slenderer and proportionately longer carpus with a longer and acute toothlike anterior process. The grasping apparatus is similarly developed. The first antennae are also longer than the second but, unlike the preceding species, the accessory flagellum has two joints instead of one. This is a smaller species, being only ¼ inch in length. It has been found in the Woods Hole region and also around the British Isles.

Lembos smithi (Holmes) PLATE 153. In the first pair of gnathopods of the male, the propodus is larger and more expanded than the moderate-sized carpus which, however, is jointed closely with the former and appears like a single, expanded, club-shaped organ, with the dactyl articulating directly with the sinus of the propodus, the posterior angle of which has a stout spine. The second pair of gnathopods has a smaller subchelate propodus. The slender, last pair of pereiopods is much longer than any that precede. The telson is shield-shaped and rounded anteriorly. The body is mottled with reddish brown and black, though the dorsal side is gay with purple-orange or rose-colored bars, while both the first and second pairs

PLATE 153

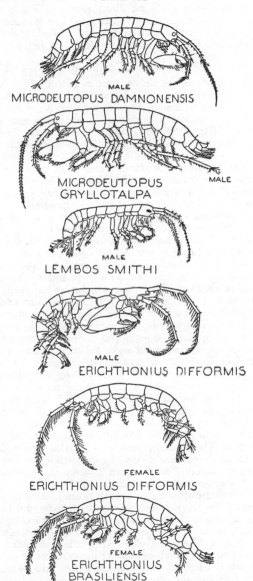

MALE
MICRODEUTOPUS DAMNONENSIS

MICRODEUTOPUS
GRYLLOTALPA
MALE

MALE
LEMBOS SMITHI

MALE
ERICHTHONIUS DIFFORMIS

FEMALE
ERICHTHONIUS DIFFORMIS

FEMALE
ERICHTHONIUS
BRASILIENSIS

of antennae are adorned with spots of orange to red and pink, two spots to a joint. This species is ¼ inch in length, and is distributed from Cape Cod to Cape Hatteras, forming tubes in the ascidian known as "Sea Pork" (*Amouroucium constellatum* COLOR PLATE XXIV, 9, 9a).

Family Corophiidae

The body of the slender species of this family is compressed vertically while the small abdomen is flattened from above to below. The antennae are variable. An accessory flagellum is present in some species and not in others. The gnathopods, also, differ in size. The fifth pair of pereiopods is the longest. The species in this family are tube-dwelling.

Ericthonius difformis Smith PLATE 153 (= **Erichthonius rubricornis** (Stimpson)). The antennae are slender and nearly equal, with long peduncles and short flagellum. The accessory flagellum, however, is absent. The two pairs of antennae are widely separated at the base, the anterior border of the head forming a lobe, on each side, between their bases and beneath the small, round eye. The first pair of gnathopods has a large carpus, broad at its junction with the smaller propodus. The strong dactyl is equipped with short spines. The second pair of gnathopods, in the male, has an extremely large carpus. Its lower distal angle is projected into an unusually strong, curved, acutely pointed spine, which forms a chela with the small, curving and narrow, but oblong propodus. The strong dactyl is equipped with a number of short spines curving backward under the spine of the carpus. In the female, the second gnathopods are small. The carpus is narrowly elongate and extends along one side of the oval propodus, so that it contracts the tip of the closing dactyl. The palm is well equipped with setae and large spines. The first and second pereiopods, in this species, are quite short, slender, and delicate. They are equipped with spinning glands. The last pair of pereiopods is the longest. The medially indented telson is equipped with hooklike spines and flanked by the narrow, two-branched serrate uropods. The first pair, however, is single-branched and does not extend beyond the other two.

Erichthonius brasiliensis (Dana) PLATE 153. This species has large, round eyes. Beneath these and between the antennae, the margin of the head is produced to a small, acute point. The antennae are approximately equal in length. The coxal plates are shallow, rounded lobes. The first gnathopods are shorter than the second pair. The carpus is narrow at its basal articulation and broad at its junction with the propodus, where it is also equipped with a rounded tooth. The propodus is triangular in shape, broad at the base and narrowed at its junction with the curved, spinelike dactyl. The second pair of gnathopods, in the male, has a triangular carpus prolonged into a curving process on its underside. This articulates with an almost quadrangular propodus, narrowed at its tip and with a strong, well-developed dactyl. The carpus and propodus of both pairs of gnathopods are furnished with long, hairlike setae. The first pair of two-branched uropods project somewhat beyond the other two pairs posteriorly. The telson is furnished with short, hooklike spines. It is shallowly bilobed along its posterior body, both lobes having circular groups of very short, hooklike spines. The length of this species is about ¼ inch. It is distributed on both sides of the Atlantic; on the American coast, extending from Woods Hole, Massachusetts, to Rio de Janeiro, Brazil.

Unciola irrorata Say PLATE 154. The body is narrow, but flattened. The cylindrical head is longer than broad, bearing antennae of similar shape, the first of which is somewhat longer than the second, and has a jointed, accessory flagellum. The peduncle of the second antennae is very stout in the male. The first pair of gnathopods, in both sexes, is much larger than the second pair. There is a strong cylindrical basal joint, a short carpus, a very large elliptical propodus with serrated spines on the palm, and a much longer, acute spine at its posterior end; the long, sharp, curved, and acute dactyl closes the full length of the palm and projects behind. The second pair of gnathopods is quite slender and more delicate, but well provided with spines and setae. The segments of the body are approximately equal in shape and blend imperceptibly from the thorax to the abdomen. The coxal plates are very shallow with indented border. The two posterior pairs of legs have oval basal joints, equipped with long setae. These pereiopods are longer than the rest. This is a brightly colored species showing variegated crimson blotches with a lengthwise median band of crimson spots on either side. Even the flagella and the propodus of the first gnathopods are gaily decorated with crimson. The length is about ⅗ inch. It is distributed from Greenland, along the North Atlantic Coast to New London, Connecticut, and Fishers Island Sound. This is a very common species found on muddy or sandy bottoms from the low-water mark to a depth of 500 fathoms. These amphipods are often found in the tubes of annulate worms.

Corophium cylindricum (Say) PLATE 154. The body of this amphipod is more or less flattened vertically and is comparatively straight, with even thoracic segments of about the same size, slightly increasing in length posteriorly, and blending imperceptibly into the abdominal segments. The fourth, fifth, and sixth abdominal segments, however, are fused together to form a long segment. In the female, the antennae are stout but comparatively short, the second pair of antennae being the more bulky of the two. In the first pair of antennae, the first joint is somewhat swollen and longer than the others; the second joint is about two thirds the length of the peduncle and consists of six segments. There is no accessory flagellum. The second pair of antennae is very stout, especially in the male. The third joint is the longest and of about the same diameter as the first two. The fourth and fifth joints are slender, gradually diminishing in size, while the sixth is quite small, but covered with setae. The next to the last joint in the second pair of antennae of the male is prolonged at its end into a curving, fingerlike process. The flagellum has only two segments, tufted with setae. The first pair of gnathopods is slenderer than the second pair. The body is purplish brown with a dark crossband at the posterior margin of each segment. The length is about ⅛ inch. It is found along the entire coast of southern New England, as well as on the New Jersey shore. It lives in soft tubes which are common around the base of eelgrass.

Corophium volutator (Pallas) PLATE 154. In this species, the second pair of antennae is very large and stouter than the first, the latter having only a short peduncle and a delicately tapering flagellum. There is no accessory flagellum. The segments back of the head are regular and gradually increase in size to the seventh. The thoracic plates are continued almost imperceptibly but the abdominal plates of the third and fourth are welded together. The pereiopods are quite weak except for the seventh pair, which are unusually long and utilized for jumping. The female is similar to the male but smaller in size.

Dulichia porrecta (Bate) PLATE 154. This is essentially a very slender amphipod. The coxal plates are extremely small, showing only their rounded ends, except that the second coxal plate, at the base of the second gnathopods, is acutely pointed at its lower anterior angle. The antennae are both conspicuous, the first pair being a little longer than the second and, if bent back, a little longer than the body. There is a very small three-jointed secondary flagellum. The first pair of gnathopods is quite small. The second pair is considerably enlarged by having a long, narrow basal joint with a greatly enlarged carpus. The latter has a long thumblike process about the middle of the lower border and a spine at its upper anterior corner. The propodus is quite small, toothed on its lower border, with a long, very acute dactyl. This, together with

PLATE 154

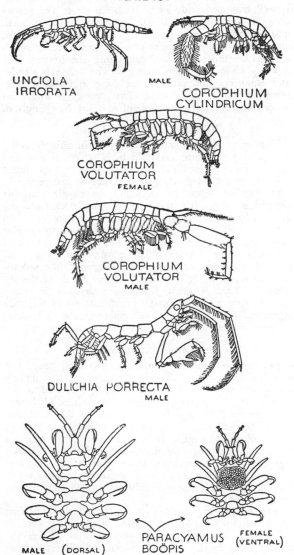

UNCIOLA
IRRORATA

MALE

COROPHIUM
CYLINDRICUM

COROPHIUM
VOLUTATOR
FEMALE

COROPHIUM
VOLUTATOR
MALE

DULICHIA PORRECTA
MALE

MALE (DORSAL)

PARACYAMUS
BOÖPIS

FEMALE
(VENTRAL)

the carpus, forms a very efficient grasping organ. The palm is well equipped with long, brushlike setae. The pereiopods of the third and fourth segments are quite weak and similar to each other. The gills are elongate, narrow, and conspicuous. The three posterior pairs of pereiopods are quite slender, the last pair being the longest. The tapering abdomen is also narrow. The telson is slender and elongate. The uropods are long and slender, terminating in brushlike setae. This species is found on muddy bottoms along the shore of northern New England.

Suborder CAPRELLIDEA

The very peculiar species included in this Suborder have a very elongated and thin body which, as has been stated, closely resembles that of a walking-stick insect when they are clambering around among the seaweeds. The peculiar forms of caprellids so closely resemble branching twigs that they are practically camouflaged, and are hard to distinguish from their surroundings. The head is fused with the first segment of the thorax. The remaining six segments take up the entire remainder of the body except for a miniature lobe forming a small knob at the posterior end, articulating with the seventh thoracic segment. This knob is all that is left of the abdomen. There is great individual variation in many species in the appendages and ornamentation of the body segments. They may be smooth, spinose, tubercle-bearing, or combinations of these characteristics.

Family Caprellidae

The body is a succession of long, cylindrical joints. The only indication of the first thoracic segment is a slightly dorsal groove. The first antennae are longer than the second. The second pair of gnathopods are much longer than the first. Pereiopods are lacking on the third and fourth thoracic segments, on each of which a pair of small, bladderlike gills is present. The three pairs of pereiopods situated on the fifth, sixth, and seventh thoracic segments are well developed and each ends in a propodus forming a subchelate clinging organ with the jointed, hooklike dactyl. These are utilized for clinging to seaweed and hydroids.

Aeginella longicornis (Kröyer) PLATE 155. The first pair of antennae are long. The three joints of the peduncle are slender and cylindrical, with the second joint the longest. The flagellum is only about one half as long as the peduncle. The second antennae are much slenderer and are about one half the length of the first. The flagellum is much shorter than the last joint of the peduncle and is, itself, only two-jointed. The first pair of gnathopods

PLATE 155

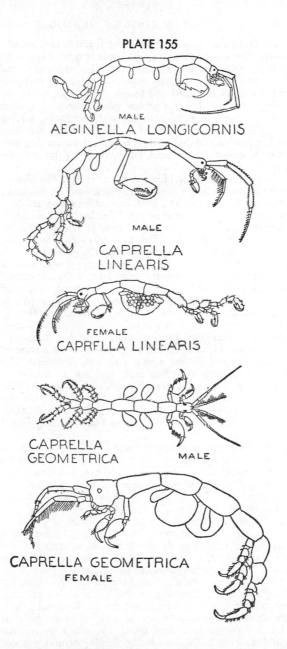

MALE
AEGINELLA LONGICORNIS

MALE
CAPRELLA
LINEARIS

FEMALE
CAPRFLLA LINEARIS

CAPRELLA
GEOMETRICA   MALE

CAPRELLA GEOMETRICA
FEMALE

arises from the fused head and first segment and is quite small. The second pair of gnathopods is quite large, with a huge propodus armed with tubercles and teeth, and terminating in a long, hooklike dactyl. The pereiopods are absent on the third and fourth thoracic segments, the only appendages being a pair of gills on each. The three posterior pairs of pereiopods are well developed, having long, slender claws, each comprising a large propodus and a hooklike dactyl. The vestigial abdomen has two pairs of minute appendages, one with two joints and the other with only one joint.

Caprella linearis (Linnaeus) PLATE 155. The slender body is much longer and more attenuated in the male than in the female. The first pair of antennae is about twice the length of the second. The latter has a single-jointed flagellum, but the peduncle is fringed beneath with long, hairlike setae. The first gnathopods are of the type usually found in amphipods. The second pair is powerfully developed. In the male, the second pair of gnathopods has an elongated basal joint, a slightly curved oval propodus, and an irregularly toothed and indented palm, with a strongly recurved hook. There is a pair of large saclike gills on the third and fourth thoracic segments of the male. In the female, the gills are slenderer, these segments also bearing thin, expanded, marsupial plates intended for breeding purposes. The three pairs of terminal pereiopods are strong and well developed. The female is smaller than the male and not so slender in proportion. The males are about ⅜ inch in length. This species is found on both sides of the Atlantic. On the American side, it is abundant from Greenland and Labrador along the entire New England coast to Long Island Sound.

Caprella geometrica Say PLATE 155. This is a stouter species than the preceding. There are no spines or tubercles on the body. The first pair of antennae is elongate and tapering. The second pair is nearly as long, the peduncle being fringed below by long hairlike setae and a flagellum consisting of two joints. The first gnathopods are small and nonchelate. The second pair are much longer and with a powerful, toothed and spined claw. There is a more or less quadrangular tooth at the distal end of the propodus and a sharp, forwardly projecting tooth at its inner posterior angle. The dactyl is strongly recurved and is excavated on its inner side to form a rounded indentation. As usual, the third and fourth thoracic segments in the male have only one pair of gills each for appendages. In the female, there are thoracic marsupial plates in addition. The dactyl is long and curved to a sharp point. The coloration is quite variable, some individuals being translucent and without color, and others reddish or mottled in various ways. The adult male is about ⅜ inch in length. This is the common caprellid of the southern New England coast. It is only rarely found north of Cape Cod, but extends southward to Virginia, however, especially among eelgrass, in sponges, and on wharf-piles.

Family Cyamidae

These amphipods are closely related to the Caprellidae so far as the forms of the limbs and the reduction of the abdomen are concerned. They are whitish, flat creatures with strongly indented segments, each one prolonged laterally and joined to the neighboring segments by contracted articulations. There is a single pair of antennae at the end of a proboscislike head. There are two pairs of gnathopods, the second of which is the largest, forming a claw of the usual type. The two succeeding segments have no pereiopods, but each one is equipped with a pair of long, fingerlike, breathing organs or gills. The last three pairs of pereiopods are enlarged and strongly clawed as in the Caprellidae. The abdomen is reduced to a rudimentary knob. The Cyamidae are parasitic on whales, living externally on their skin, and are commonly known as "Whale Lice."

Paracyamus boopis Lütken PLATE 154. This species is quite typical of the family with the characters described above. Illustrations of both the male and female of this species are shown in the plate. Note that the marsupial sacs of the female are filled with eggs.

Division EUCARIDA

In this Division, the carapace is enlarged, covering all the thoracic segments and fusing with most of them. The eyes are mounted on eyestalks (*peduncles*). The heart, as well as the gills, is located in the thorax. The eggs are carried by the inner branch of the pleopods beneath the abdomen. There is a complicated larval metamorphosis. This Division is divided into the following two Orders: (1) *Euphausiacea;* and (2) *Decapoda.*

Order EUPHAUSIACEA

These are shrimplike crustaceans with two-branched (*biramous*) appendages, including both pereiopods and pleopods. There are no special maxillipeds, these appendages remaining in their original primitive condition as the first pair of pereiopods, all of which are walking legs. The outer branches (*exopodites*) are utilized for this purpose while the inner branches (*endopodites*) form plumelike breathing organs. The pleopods are utilized for swimming purposes. The shrimp of this order are remarkable creatures in several ways and of undoubted economic importance. Their transparent bodies are highly luminescent at night, especially in certain localized parts of the body. Anyone who has been on long ocean voyages may remember how, at night, the steamship will pass through waves that are brilliantly luminescent, often for long distances. This is due to the euphausian shrimps which have small spherical organs of considerable luminous power, their light being directed and controlled by a complicated apparatus.

The body is colored brilliant red and, therefore, can be readily seen through the surface-water at some distance. When a vessel crosses through a vast swarm of these creatures, the captain of the vessel often refers to the reddened waves as "tomato soup." Millions of these shrimp, in such schools, are an abundant source of food for whales and other swimming creatures. Whalers in the South Pacific and other oceans of the world immediately look out for whales when the so-called tomato soup appears.

Family Euphausiidae

This is the only family in the Order *Euphausiacea* and, therefore, is to be described as having the characters of that Order. The carapace is connected with all the thoracic segments except the last. The egg-pouch is under the rear of the thorax and is membranous; i.e., it is not formed of stiffened plates. The pleopods are well developed in both sexes. These animals are highly luminescent, especially on the outer side of the eyestalk, on the base of the second and seventh pereiopods, and on the underside of the first four abdominal segments.

Nyctiphanes (Meganyctiphanes) norvegica (M. Sars) PLATE 157. This species is translucent, and has black eyes. The body and limbs are tinged and marked extensively with red. The telson is slender and acute, but a pair of long, flat spines, articulated on each side, extend beyond its tip. The basal joints of the first antennae bear a peculiar reflexed leaflet at their apex. The last pair of pereiopods is more or less rudimentary. The next to the last pair is also imperfect, lacking the three terminal joints. In the male, the exopod is present in both pairs of legs, but it is wanting in the female. The name, *Nyctiphanes,* is derived from two Greek words which mean "the night shining one," referring to the brilliant luminescence. This species occurs from Massachusetts Bay and off the Maine coast to the Bay of Fundy, the swarms coloring the surface reddish over large areas.

Rhoda (Boreophausia) inermis (Kröyer). This is a similar species of paler coloration and greater transparency. The basal joint of the first pair of antennae is without the apical leaflet characteristic of the preceding species. It is a northern form, occurring on both sides of the Atlantic and ranging south to the Vineyard Sound region, at least in winter.

Order DECAPODA
(Shrimps, Crayfish, Lobsters, and Crabs)

As the name indicates, this order contains the crustaceans that have ten thoracic legs; that is, five pairs of pereiopods. The carapace covers the entire thorax, often overarching the head as well, so that it is known as the *cephalothorax*. It is more or less cylindrical or compressed sidewise in some species, and, in others, somewhat flattened. The gills are on the thorax underneath the carapace, branching either from the bases of the legs or from the body-wall. Besides the five pairs of pereiopods, there are three pairs of leglike maxillipeds associated with the mouth-region. The first pair of pereiopods usually bear pinching claws (*chelae*) and are usually much larger than the remaining four pairs, the latter being ambulatory. The eggs are usually fastened to the pleopods, under the abdomen. The Order *Decapoda* is divided into three Suborders: (1) *Macrura* (lobsters, crayfish, shrimps, and prawns); (2) *Anomura* (hermit crabs and their relatives); and (3) *Brachyura* (true crabs).

Suborder MACRURA
(Lobsters, Crayfish, Shrimps, and Prawns)

This group is characterized by the large, well-developed abdomen, five segments of which bear double-branched pleopods (INDEX PLATE 156). The final segment, together with the flattened uropods, forms a tail-fan, the uropods representing the sixth pair of pleopods. The abdomen may be bent forward under the body. The pleopods are used for swimming. The *rostrum,* an anteriorly projecting structure above the eyes, is long and usually pointed. The first pair of antennae possess two or more flagella. The peduncle of the second pair is usually equipped with a large flattened scale, known as the *antennal scale.*

Section NATANTIA
(Free-swimming Shrimps)

These are the shrimps and prawns. They have a compressed body with a fully developed abdomen. The pleopods are adapted for swimming and used for that purpose.

Tribe PENEIDEA

These are shrimp that have the first three pairs of legs armed with claws. The first maxillipeds have no lobe on the base of the exopodite. The second maxillipeds have normal end-joints. The third maxillipeds are seven-jointed.

The plates terminating laterally at each joint are known as *pleura*. In this tribe, the pleura of the first abdominal segment overlap those of the second. The abdomen extends out posteriorly without a sharp joint. The gills are comparatively simple.

Family Peneidae

These are swimming shrimps with the first three pairs of legs having small chelae; the third pair is the largest. The last two pairs of legs are well developed, and there is practically a full set of gills. The rostrum and the second antennae are long, the latter having a large basal scale. This family contains the more southern shrimps and prawns.

Peneus setiferus (Linnaeus) PLATE 157. The rostrum is continued backward as a low keel, about two thirds of the length of the carapace. There is a furrow along each side of the anterior part of this keel. It is commonly found along the coast in shallow water from Virginia to the Gulf of Mexico. This is the most important market species of shrimp. Commercially, the larger individuals are known throughout their territory as prawns, the smaller as shrimp.

Peneus braziliensis Latreille PLATE 157. The dorsal keel on the carapace and the furrows on either side are continued practically the whole length of the carapace. It is less important commercially than the preceding species, but is found in the market and used for food in the northern part of its range. It lives under the same conditions and with the preceding species. It is distributed from Cape Cod to Florida.

Family Sergestidae

Either or both of the posterior two pairs of legs are rudimentary or wanting. The gill series is incomplete or wanting. The members of this family are pelagic.

Lucifer faxoni Borradaile PLATE 157. This is a small, transparent shrimp with the body extended forward into a long neck on which the antennae and long eyestalks are borne. This species has no gills. Like the other members of the family, it is pelagic, but occurs in Beaufort Harbor, North Carolina, in summer.

Tribe CARIDEA

The third pair of legs is without chelae. The first maxillipeds have a lobe on the base of the exopodites. The second maxilliped is peculiar in that its terminal joint extends as a narrow strip along the end of the joint before it. The third maxillipeds have from four to six joints. The pleura (i.e., the lower lateral extensions of the dorsal plates) of the second abdominal segment overlap those of the first segment, in addition to the usual overlapping of the next

PLATE 156

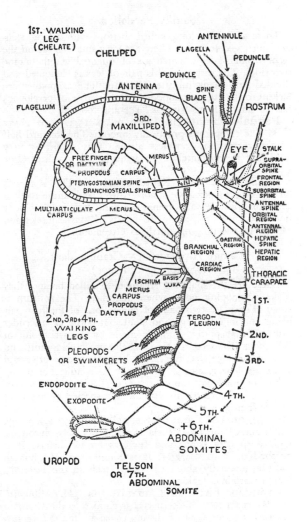

posterior segment. There is a sharp, dorsal bend to the abdomen. The gills are leaflike.

Family Pandalidae

These are rather long-bodied shrimps with a long, slender, upcurved rostrum. There are very small chelae on the second pair of legs, which are of unequal length on the two sides. The carpus of this pair of legs is elongated and divided into many minute segments. The exopodites are lacking on all the pereiopods. The first pair of pereiopods has no claw. The rostrum is large and toothed.

Pandalus montagui Leach PLATE 157; COLOR PLATE X, 5. The carapace is practically smooth. The forward half of the rostrum is toothless above. This species is very abundant in moderately deep water, chiefly north of Cape Cod.

Pandalus borealis Kröyer PLATE 157. This is a similar but larger species with more rostral teeth and a median spine on the third abdominal segment. It is found chiefly north of Cape Cod, along the coasts of Massachusetts and Maine, thence ranging north to Greenland.

Family Alpheidae (= Crangonidae)
(Snapping Shrimps)

These are the snapping shrimps, so called because they make a snapping noise when disturbed. The rostrum is small. There are two pairs of chelae, one of the first pair being enormously large and stout, but borne on a slender limb. The snapping sound is made by the wrist-joint of this chela. The second pair of chelae are both minute and both of the same size, the carpus being composed of several segments. The species of this family have either burrowing habits or may be commensal (i.e., having the habit of entering into partnership with another species). The species of this family are mostly tropical.

Crangon (Alpheus) heterochelis (Say) PLATE 157. The hand of the large chela is proportionately enormous, with deep depressions and furrows on its surface. It is notched on both margins. It is found from Virginia to Florida, especially about the oyster reefs in the Beaufort, North Carolina, region.

Crangon (Alpheus) armillatus (H. Milne-Edwards) PLATE 157. This species is similar to the *Crangon heterochelis,* but may be distinguished by the deeper furrows, enlarged posteriorly, on each side of the rostrum.

Crangon (Alpheus) normanni Kingsley [= **Alpheus packardii** (Kingsley)] PLATE 157. This species is peculiar in having the hand of the large chela smooth except for a transverse notch on the upper side near the

PLATE 157

NYCTIPHANES NORVEGICA

PENEUS SETIFERUS

LUCIFER FAXONI

CARAPACE AND ROSTRUM
OF PENEUS SETIFERUS (UPPER)
AND PENEUS BRAZILIENSIS (LOWER)

PANDALUS BOREALIS

CRANGON
HETEROCHELIS

PANDALUS
MONTAGUI

CRANGON
NORMANNI

ROSTRUM OF
CRANGON ARMILLATUS (LEFT) AND
CRANGON HETEROCHELIS (RIGHT)

SYNALPHEUS
LONGICARPUS

SYNALPHEUS
MINUS

end, and the hand is constricted above and below. The basal joint of the antennae has a small terminal spine, while the rostrum, itself, is practically reduced to a spine. This is the commonest snapping shrimp in the Beaufort, North Carolina, region. It is usually found among oyster shells.

Synalpheus longicarpus (Herrick) PLATE 157. The hand of the large chela is ovate in shape and smoothly inflated. The rostrum projects from the anterior border of the cephalothorax with concave sloping sides. The three anterior teeth are about equal. The eyes are set farther back than in *Synalpheus minus* (see figure). This species lives in cavities in sponges. It ranges from North Carolina southward.

Synalpheus minus (Say) PLATE 157. The rostrum, as seen in the figure, is short, broad, its anterior border having three acutely pointed teeth. It projects at an angle from the anterior border of the cephalothorax, the two round eyes being located upon it. The large cheliped has nearly parallel sides, shaped and articulated as in the figure. It is found along the Atlantic Coast from New Jersey to Florida.

Family Hippolytidae

These are shrimps with a well-developed rostrum, with two pairs of legs chelate, the second of which has the wrist divided into several small segments.

Genus **Spirontocaris** (= **Hippolyte**). The many species of this genus inhabit the northern seas, several ranging south to Cape Cod, on our coast, or a little beyond, though chiefly in deeper water.

Spirontocaris groenlandica (Fabricius) PLATE 158. The rostrum is small, with four large teeth on the back of the carapace. This species is best distinguished by the pointed side plates of the abdominal segments. The color is brownish red to dull brownish green. It ranges south to Marthas Vineyard Island in deeper water.

The remaining species, here dwelt with, have the side plates of the abdominal segments rounded below and not pointed.

Spirontocaris liljeborgii (Danielssen) PLATE 158. The rostrum is short with a deep triangular point and a midrib which projects conspicuously beyond the tip. There are several large teeth on the back of the carapace. The color is crimson, spotted with yellow. It inhabits northern waters and ranges south, though not commonly, to the Vineyard Sound region.

Spirontocaris spina (Sowerby) PLATE 158. This species is similar to the above, but the rostrum is unevenly truncated, the midrib projecting but little. The body is

PLATE 158

SPIRONTOCARIS
PHIPPSI

SPIRONTOCARIS
LILJEBORGI

COMPARISON OF ROSTRA
AND CARAPACES :—

SPIRONTOCARIS
PHIPPSI

S LILJEBORGI

S GROENLANDICA

SPIRONTOCARIS
GROENLANDICA

CARIDION GORDONI

SPIRONTOCARIS
SPINA

SPIRONTOCARIS
PUSIOLA

S PUSIOLA

S FABRICII

SPIRONTOCARIS
ZEBRA

S GAIMARDI

S POLARIS

SPIRONTOCARIS
POLARIS

S MACILENTA

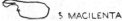

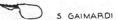

SPIRONTOCARIS
FABRICII

HIPPOLYTE
ZOSTERICOLA

LATREUTES
FUCORUM

TOZEUMA
CAROLINENSIS

translucent, mottled, and spotted with red, brownish red, and white. It ranges from Massachusetts Bay northward.

Spirontocaris pusiola (Kröyer) PLATE 158. This is a small species with a very short, straight rostrum, having very few teeth above and none below. The color is white with a few red or orange spots. It is found around Vineyard Sound, Massachusetts, sometimes in shallow water, and northward.

Spirontocaris macilenta (Kröyer) PLATE 158. The rostrum is very short, deep, arched, and with fine serrations above. The carapace is elongate and almost toothless. The range is along the coast of Maine and northward, chiefly in deeper water.

Spirontocaris zebra Leim PLATE 158. This is a species similar to *Spirontocaris polaris* (see below). The rostrum is still shorter and abruptly inclined downward. The body is banded with brownish red or orange, suggesting a zebra. It is found along the coast of Maine and northward.

The following species of *Spirontocaris* occur from Massachusetts Bay northward, chiefly at moderate depths.

Spirontocaris polaris (Sabine) PLATE 158. The rostrum is rather short, narrowly knifelike, with usually five to eight teeth above, including two on the carapace, and two to four below. A supraorbital spine is present on each side at the base of the rostrum.

Spirontocaris phippsii (Kröyer) PLATE 158. The rostrum has more teeth, and several below (eight to ten above, including three or four on the carapace). There are usually two supraorbital spines, one of which is very small, on each side. The body is semitranslucent, speckled, and mottled with brownish red.

Spirontocaris fabricii (Kröyer) PLATE 158. The rostrum is moderately long, usually without teeth above, except one or two at the base. There are several teeth below, two or three being on the carapace. There is no supraorbital spine. The color is white with small red spots.

Spirontocaris gaimardii (Milne-Edwards) PLATE 158. The rostrum is fairly long, with a few teeth above and below. There are two or three teeth on the carapace, which is narrower in the male. There is no supraorbital spine. The body is translucent, tinged with greenish brown.

Caridion gordoni Bate PLATE 158. This is a small shrimp occurring in rather deep water off northern New England and northward. The rostrum is curved downward, then up at the tip. There are seven or eight teeth above and only one below, near the end. The color is reddish.

PLATE 159

PALAEMON TENUICORNIS

PALAEMONETES
VULGARIS

PALAEMON
TENUICORNIS

CRAGO
SEPTEMSPINOSUS

SABINEA
SARSI

SABINEA
SARSI

SABINEA
SEPTEMCARINATA

SABINEA SARSI

SABINEA
SEPTEMCARINATA

SCLEROCRANGON
BOREAS

Hippolyte (Virbius) zostericola (Smith) PLATE 158; COLOR PLATE X, 6. This is a small shrimp, mottled greenish and brown, sometimes spotted with red, found among eelgrass from Vineyard Sound to New Jersey. The rostrum is straight and of the same length as the carapace, which has three spines located anteriorly. The abdomen is sharply bent at the third segment.

Hippolyte (Virbius) pleuracantha (Stimpson). This is a related species of similar habits, with a considerably shorter rostrum, occurring from New Jersey southward.

Latreutes fucorum (Fabricius) (= **Latreutes ensiferus**) PLATE 158. A very small shrimp with an upturned rostrum nearly as long as the carapace. The rostrum is truncated at the end. It is found in floating Gulf Weed.

Tozeuma carolinensis Kingsley PLATE 158. This is a very slender, transparent shrimp with a very long tapering rostrum with numerous teeth, situated below only. It is common in eelgrass in the Beaufort, North Carolina, region.

Family Palaemonidae

Included in this family are shrimp with somewhat small chelae on the first two pairs of legs, the second pair being usually the larger. The rostrum is compressed and armed with teeth.

Palaemon (Leander) tenuicornis Say PLATE 159. This is a stout-bodied shrimp found in floating Gulf Weed, though rarely as far north as Massachusetts.

Palaemonetes vulgaris (Say) PLATE 159; COLOR PLATE X, 4. This is the Common Prawn. The body is translucent with brownish spots. The rostrum has eight or nine teeth above and two or three below. It is abundant in eelgrass, in ditches, and salt marshes and similar places ranging from New Hampshire, south.

Family Cragonidae *

The shrimps in this family usually have a short, somewhat dorsally flattened rostrum. The first pair of legs are chelate, having a transversely closing finger. The second pair of legs are small, chelate in the usual way, with the carpus unsegmented.

Crago septemspinosus (Say) (= **Crangon vulgaris** Fabricius) PLATE 159; COLOR PLATE X, 3. The carapace has a dorsal spine posterior to the rostrum. The color is translucent, pale gray, with minute stellate dark spots. It is abundant throughout this entire region ranging from Labrador to North Carolina and less common in the

* Sometimes included in Crangonidae by various authors

south. This is the common Sand Shrimp. It always occurs in great numbers on sandy flats and in the tide-pools as well as in sandy bottoms in deeper water offshore. Its irregular gray color imitates that of the sand so closely that it is practically camouflaged when resting motionless on the bottom or when partially buried in the sand. Between tides it burrows into the moist sand to a considerable depth. Its enemies are such fishes as the Weak-fish, King-fish, Blue-fish, flounders, Striped Bass, etc., of which it forms the principal food. It reproduces, however, abundantly and therefore keeps ahead of its enemies.

Sabinea septemcarinata (Sabine) PLATE 159. This is a somewhat rough-surfaced shrimp of deeper water, north of Cape Cod.

Sabinea sarsii Smith PLATE 159. A similar species in appearance and distribution. It has more dorsal spines and a sharper rostrum.

Sclerocrangon boreas (Phipps) PLATE 159. A stout, rough species of very different appearance from *Crago septemspinosus*. It has three median dorsal spines on the cephalothorax. It is found north of Cape Cod, but usually in deeper water.

Section REPTANTIA
(INDEX PLATE 160)

This includes the lobsters and crayfish. The body is somewhat cylindrical. The abdomen is well developed and carried horizontally. The rostrum in the marine forms is small or absent. Chelipeds may be present or wanting.

Tribe PALINURA
(Spiny Lobsters)

The fully-developed abdomen is always held in an extended position except when it is used to propel the animal vigorously backward. It is symmetrical in shape and covered with spiny armature. Its lateral plates are well developed. The telson and the last pair of uropods with their broad, platelike outer and inner branches together form a well-expanded tail-fan. All pairs of legs are without chelae and are similar to each other. No large claws are present.

Family Palinuridae

The body is of large size. There is no scale at the base of the antennae. All legs are of the same length. The first abdominal segment has no appendages. The rostrum is small, if present. The eyes are not in separate orbits.

Panulirus argus (Latreille) PLATE 161. This is the West Indian Spiny Lobster or Sea Crawfish. It is a large animal of 8 to 16 inches in length. There are no pinching claws and the animal is entirely defenseless except for its spiny armature. The carapace has strong spines, two of which are hooklike, projecting anteriorly. The first antennae have strongly developed and spinous peduncles of large size, with long, many-jointed flagella capable of reaching some distance posterior to the body. The colors are variegated, with their patterns ranging through dark brown, red, and yellow, with certain bluish areas. This species ranges from North Carolina to Florida and the West Indies. It is quite common on coral reefs and under rocks in coral lagoons. Small individuals often occur in Beaufort Harbor, North Carolina. It is an exceedingly important food animal, the tail meat being highly prized.

Tribe ASTACURA
(Lobsters and Crayfishes)

These animals range from large to small size with a well-developed symmetrical body and an extended abdomen. As is the case with the Palinura, they are well armed, but without the spines characteristic of that tribe. The tail-fan is also broad. There is a well-developed rostrum. The outer plate of the terminal uropods is jointed by means of a transverse, suturelike joint. The second antennae have flagella.

Family Homaridae (Nephropsidae)
(American and European Lobsters)

These are the true lobsters. The rostrum has teeth along the sides. The first pair of pereiopods is very large, developed as pinching and crushing claws. The next two pairs are small with chelae.

Homarus americanus Milne-Edwards. PLATE 161; COLOR PLATE XI, 1. This is the American Lobster. The length may range up to 24 inches. Very large specimens are occasionally found, the largest one recorded having a length of 34 inches. The average length of the adult lobster captured for the market is 10 inches and the weight from 1½ to 2 pounds. The color varies through dark green shades, yellow to orange beneath, and sometimes with bright blue on the limbs, reddish markings being found also. Lobsters form one of our most important food resources, being caught off the coasts of the New England States and Canada most abundantly, the annual catches being well up into the millions.

Family Astacidae

This family includes the fresh-water crayfish and therefore is outside the range of this book, except to say that the body-form resembles a miniature lobster and that they

PLATE 160

ANATOMY OF THE COMMON LOBSTER (MALE)
HOMARUS AMERICANUS

PLATE 160

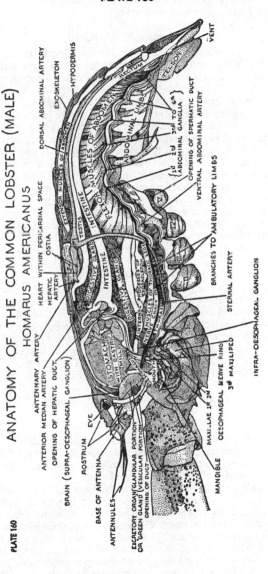

VENT

DORSAL ABDOMINAL ARTERY

EXOSKELETON

HYPODERMIS

TELSON

RECTUM

ANTENNARY ARTERY

ANTERIOR MEDIAN ARTERY

OPENING OF HEPATIC DUCT

BRAIN (SUPRA-OESOPHAGEAL GANGLION)

HEART WITHIN PERICARDIAL SPACE

OSTIA

HEPATIC ARTERY

EXTENSOR MUSCLES OF ABDOMEN

ABDOMINAL LIMBS

3rd TO 6th

1st 2nd (ABDOMINAL GANGLIA)

OPENING OF SPERMATIC DUCT

VENTRAL ABDOMINAL ARTERY

TESTIS

INTESTINE

FLEXOR MUSCLES OF ABDOMEN

DIGESTIVE GLAND

INTESTINE

DIGESTIVE GLAND

INTERNAL PROCESSES OR EXTENSOR MUSCLES OF THE LEG

FLEXOR MUSCLES OF THE LEG

STOMACH WITH GASTRIC MILL

MOUTH

ROSTRUM

EYE

BASE OF ANTENNA

ANTENNULES

EXCRETORY ORGAN GLANDULAR PORTION

OR GREEN GLAND (VESICULAR PORTION)

OPENING OF DUCT

MANDIBLE

MAXILLAE 1st 2nd

OESOPHAGEAL NERVE RING

3rd MAXILIPED

BRANCHES TO AMBULATORY LIMBS

STERNAL ARTERY

INFRA-OESOPHAGEAL GANGLION

are widely distributed in the streams, lakes, and swamps of the North American continent.

Suborder ANOMURA

This Suborder includes the Hermit Crabs and certain other groups intermediate between the *Macrura,* or shrimp-like crustaceans, on the one hand, and the *Brachyura,* or crabs, on the other. In the *Anomura,* the abdomen is more or less reduced, usually not symmetrical, and curved forward beneath the thorax. It is horizontally extended only in rare forms. The abdomen is usually imperfectly armored, the lateral plates being small or sometimes lacking entirely. The third pair of legs is always unlike the first and always without chelae or claws. The antennal scale, if present, is reduced to a small spine, instead of the large, leaflike scale of the *Macrura.* The last pair of legs is extremely different from the third pair and is turned upward on the dorsal surface of the animal or carried inside the gill chamber. The carapace does not cover the last thoracic plate. The Suborder *Anomura* is divided into four Tribes, as follows: (1) *Thalassinidea;* (2) *Galatheidea;* (3) *Hippidea;* and (4) *Paguridea.*

Tribe THALASSINIDEA

This tribe still has strong Macruran characters showing its relationship to the shrimps. It has a cephalothorax, compressed sidewise. The body is symmetrical, but the first pair of chelae is always highly unsymmetrical. The abdomen is unreduced and is carried straight out and unbent like the shrimps. The last pair of pereiopods is small, but not greatly reduced. The appendages of the sixth abdominal segment are efficient swimming organs. The animals of this group may be 2 to 3 inches in length. Usually, they burrow in sand or mud or hide beneath stones.

Family Callianassidae

The lateral plates of the abdomen are small. There are no vestiges of joints on the sixth abdominal appendages, but those of the third to the sixth abdominal segments are broad and well adapted for swimming.

Callianassa stimpsoni Smith PLATE 162; COLOR PLATE X, 7. The almost membranous armor is smooth and of shining texture. The cephalothorax is about one third the length of the abdomen. The anterior mid-dorsal region of the carapace shows a thickened oval patch or plate. The first pair of legs of the male are very unlike each other; the larger one has a long, narrow carpus articulating with the previous joint (*merus*) at its extreme upper angle. The last thoracic segment is free and bears a reduced pair of pereiopods. The fingers of the cheliped are hairy and with

PLATE 161

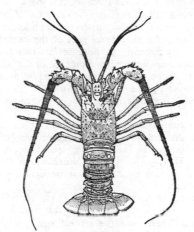

PANULIRUS ARGUS

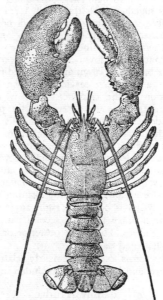

HOMARUS AMERICANUS

incurved tips. The uropods have broad blades. This species is common from Woods Hole southward.

Upogebia affinis (Say) PLATE 162. This is also a shrimplike species tending to carry its abdomen somewhat curved. Except for the dorsal part of the carapace and the legs, the body covering is more or less membranous. The carapace is somewhat longer than that of *Callianassa* and is nearly flat above, where it is covered with short, rigid hairs. Anteriorly, the carapace terminates in three points, the median of which is the longest, forming a rostrum. The eyestalks are hidden beneath the front of the carapace. The stout chelipeds are nearly equal to each other on the two sides, the chelae having a fringe of long hairs beneath. The distribution is from Long Island Sound to South Carolina. This species lives in burrows in the mud, between the tide-marks, and for some distance beyond the low-tide mark.

Calocaris macandreae Bell PLATE 162. The first pair of legs is unequal, though not so much as in the case of *Callianassa*. These and the second pair are chelate. The three posterior pairs are without chelae, very slender, and with the final pair turned backward along the abdomen. The uropods together with the telson form a conspicuous tail-fan deeply fringed along the posterior border.

Naushonia crangonoides Kingsley PLATE 162. This species has a somewhat cylindrical carapace with the rostral region in front being down-curved. The rostrum is flattened with a broadly triangular tip extending beyond the eyes. There is a transverse cervical carapace. Just above the pleural position of the carapace, there is a well-marked groove extending from the anterior to the posterior edges on either side. Otherwise, the carapace is smooth. It is about two-thirds as long as the abdomen, which also is smooth and without spines. The telson is longer than broad with a rounded posterior end. The eyes are on short peduncles, not visible from above. The antennae have a small basal scale. There is a triangular carpus on the propodus, twice as long as broad, forming an acute edge outside. The dactyl is bent at a right angle, curved at the end and with a sharp tip. The second pair of legs is the shortest and chelate. The three posterior pairs of legs are simple with flattened dactyls.

This species seems to be most nearly related to *Calocaris* and *Callianassa* and is, therefore, included in this family.

Family Axiidae

The streamlined carapace terminates anteriorly in a horizontal, flattened point (rostrum). One of the first pair of pereiopods is slightly larger than the other. The second pair are small, chelate, and equal to each other. The last three pairs are without chelae. The first segment of the abdomen is very short. The two branches of the uropods are flattened and leaflike, and practically of equal size. The uropod is split in the middle, forming two narrow, leaflike parts.

Axius serratus Stimpson PLATE 162. A small, lobster-like form without a rostrum. The other characters are those of the family. It is of very rare occurrence north of Cape Cod, but is somewhat more common to the South.

Tribe GALATHEIDEA

These crabs have a symmetrical body. The carapace is long, with a more or less rectangular outline, viewed from above, and with a surface more or less rough and spiny. The abdomen is as broad as the carapace and is always bent under the thorax. The first pair of pereiopods is much elongated, comparatively heavy, and chelate. The long dactyl closes tightly against a fingerlike process of the propodus. The next three pairs of pereiopods are without chelae, much elongated, more slender and covered with spines along each joint. The last pair of pereiopods is very much reduced and either turned up onto the posterior dorsal surface of the carapace or carried in the branchial chamber. Some of the species are said to carry shells temporarily on their backs, which may be held in place by this last pair of thoracic limbs. It is also suggested that when this pair is carried in the branchial chamber, they are utilized for cleaning it out.

Family Galatheidae

The abdomen, though usually turned under the body, is not folded closely against the thorax. Some of the species in this family are found along the shore, while others descend to deep water.

Munidopsis curvirostra Whiteaves PLATE 162. This species has eyes without pigment. Frequently, the eyestalk is elongated, extending through and beyond the cornea as spines. The eyes, therefore, are imperfect as the antennal flagella are often extraordinary long. The sense of touch takes the place of the rudimentary vision. The species ranges from 100 fathoms of depth, that is, at about the edge of the Continental Shelf, to about 2000 fathoms. Doubtless, the greater sensitiveness of touch is an important advantage on the dark sea-bottom. In this species, the quadrangular carapace is crossed by grooves dividing it into rhomboidal sections. The uropods and the telson together form a foliate tail-fan with the fringes of spines ornamenting the posterior ends of the leaflike lobes. In the illustration, the abdomen is extended to show its characters.

Family Porcellanidae

The abdomen is folded close against the thorax in the species included in this family, giving them a crablike form. They have small rather flattened bodies with a very hard shell. The last pair of legs is much reduced and directed forward alongside the carapace. The chelae are large and massive with flattened tapering fingers. While, generally speaking, this is a tropical family, several species are found in our region. In many cases, they are of commensal habits, that is, of entering into partnership with other species of animals.

Porcellana sayana Leach PLATE 162. The body is flattened, minutely granulate, and of rounded outline. The rostrum is obtusely rectangular with its tip bent down. The chelae are very strong and heavy. This species is found among oyster shells or living in partnership within the shells occupied by large hermit crabs. It occurs in the region of Beaufort, North Carolina. The "color in life, reddish or rusty brown with irregular longitudinal white lines, of which the median one is broadest and expanded anteriorly; hands and carpi with white spots on a red ground; smaller legs with transverse reddish bars. In alcohol, the red color disappears and the animal becomes perfectly white." (Hay and Shore.)

Porcellana soriata Say. The carapace is somewhat hexangular, much rougher than in the preceding species. The chelae also are rough, being covered with close-set tubercles. It is often found in the canals of sponges washed on shore near Beaufort, North Carolina.

Polyonyx macrocheles (Gibbes) PLATE 162. The carapace is transversely oval, one fourth wider than long. The slender antennae are somewhat longer than the body, with the basal segment enlarged. The chelipeds are unequal in size and quite long and twisted in shape. The carpus of the larger one is almost twice as long as the carapace of the animal. There is a fringe of long hairs on the inner margin. The fingers are very short and hook-shaped. They have teeth on the cutting edges. The abdomen is small, flat, and fitting close against the underside of the thorax. It is often found commensal in tubes of the annulate *Chaetopterus* (See COLOR PLATE IX, 1), along with the crabs, *Pinnixa chaetotopterana* (PLATE 168). The color is grayish white, mottled with brown. It ranges from North Carolina to Rhode Island and southern Massachusetts, where it is rare.

PLATE 162

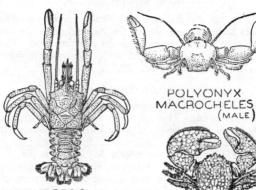

POLYONYX
MACROCHELES
(MALE)

MUNIDOPSIS
CURVIROSTRA

PORCELLANA
SAYANA

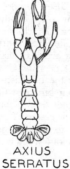

NAUSHONIA
CRANGONOIDES

AXIUS
SERRATUS

CALOCARIS
MACANDREÆ

CALLIANASSA
STIMPSONI
(LARGE CLAW)

NAUSHONIA
CRANGONOIDES

UPOGEBIA
AFFINIS

Tribe HIPPIDEA

These peculiar crabs have their limbs especially modified so as to form digging organs for burrowing in the sand. The shape of the organs and even of the body itself, strongly suggest the terrestrial moles. They are, however, closely related to the Galatheidea.

Family Hippidae

The first pair of legs may be subchelate. The rostrum is small or wanting. The carapace is cylindrical and sets closely around the body with lateral extensions curving round to cover the legs.

Hippa (Emerita) talpoida Say COLOR PLATE X, 8, 8a. Sand Bug. The first antennae are small. The second antennae are long and plumelike, due to the close-set, long hairs branching inward from the antennae. The tiny eyes are set on long, slender stalks. The first pair of legs is directed forward. The second, third, and fourth pairs of legs are strong, with leaflike extensions at their tips, fringed with cilia. The fifth pair of legs is reduced almost to threads. They are completely covered by the abdomen, which is bent so that the elongated, pointed telson, together with the sixth abdominal segment, lies closely fitted against the underside of the body. These are very active animals, burrowing in clean fine sand, especially at the edge of the water, to which they keep as the tide rises or falls. As the waves come in and cover their burrows, they leave them and actively scramble to a higher level to bury themselves anew. Almost immediately they emerge again, as the larger waves come in, and move to another new home so that, where they occur in large colonies, the edges of the waves seem alive with them.

Family Albuneidae

The first pair of legs is subchelate. There is a flattened carapace, the legs being exposed, as there are no expansions to cover them.

Albunea gibbesii Stimpson PLATE 164. The carapace has shallow S-shaped, lateral outlines, somewhat narrowed posteriorly, and broadened at the anterior margin. It is quite symmetrical. The front of the carapace has a very small rostrum situated at the bottom of a hollow, at the median line, formed by the sides of two triangular spines. There are about nine slender, curving spines on either side of these. There is also a strong salient spine on either side, slightly posterior to the anterolateral angle. The dorsal surface is somewhat corrugated with series of irregular lines indented transversely across the shell. The minute eyes surmount quite narrow, triangular eyestalks. Two

PLATE 163

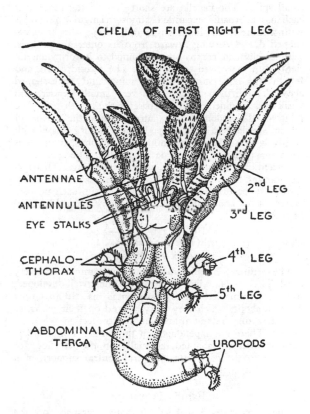

CHELA OF FIRST RIGHT LEG

ANTENNAE

ANTENNULES

EYE STALKS

CEPHALO-
THORAX

ABDOMINAL
TERGA

2nd LEG

3rd LEG

4th LEG

5th LEG

UROPODS

A TYPICAL ANOMURAN
(*PAGURUS BERNHARDUS*)
WITHDRAWN FROM SHELL

slender antennae extend forward for a considerable distance. The basal segment of the stouter antennae has a small spine. The flagella are short. The first pair of legs each has a broadly expanded, almost triangular propodus with a spine at the inner angle and a long, almost sickle-shaped dactyl curving inward from its outer angle. This, with an elongate carpus broadly joined to it, forms an efficient palm, narrowed to the wrist. The second, third, and fourth legs have stout irregular joints and sickle-shaped claws. The fifth pair of legs is very small, slender, and weak and is joined above the base of the fourth pair. The joints of the abdomen have lateral spines, the second of which are largest. The uropods have a large base with relatively small, branching joints. The telson of the male is triangular; that of the female is rounded. The color is an iridescent, light purple, with whitish markings. This species ranges from Beaufort, North Carolina, to the West Indies. It occurs on sand-flats exposed in extreme low water. It is abundant on the fishing banks (Hay and Shore).

Tribe PAGURIDEA
(Hermit Crabs)
INDEX PLATE 163

The ordinary hermit crabs are very common on every coast. They are familiar to everyone. Their well-developed, soft, and somewhat coiled abdomen is inserted in empty mollusk shells, which they carry around on their backs, so that they may retreat into them for protection when attacked. There are appendages on the sixth abdominal segment, which are adapted, especially on the left side, for clinging to the *columella,* or spiral central support, of a marine snail-shell.

Family Paguridae

These crabs have a hard, flattened carapace on the cephalothorax. The abdomen is usually not symmetrical, but elongate, tapering, and soft. The second antennae and the eyestalk are long. The first pair of thoracic limbs is large and both appendages have effective chelae or pincers, which are expanded and powerful. The last pair of limbs is reduced to very small size, curved backward, and then bending upward. The abdominal appendages are rudimentary or lacking, with the sixth, or last, pair, being adapted to hold the animal in the snail-shell which it occupies.

Pagurus (Eupagurus) pollicaris (Say) PLATE 164. This is the large hermit crab. The first pair of antennae is short. The second pair is much longer. The right claw is usually the larger of the two large claws on the first pair of limbs. The eyestalks have a dilated cornea. The palms

PLATE 164

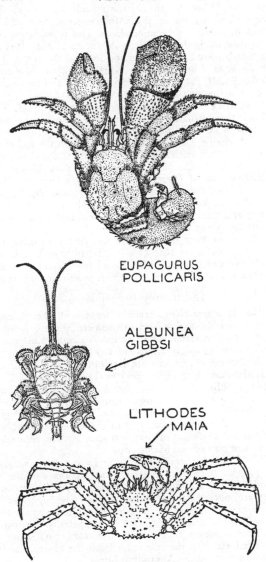

EUPAGURUS
POLLICARIS

ALBUNEA
GIBBSI

LITHODES
MAIA

of the hands are broad, quite flat, and covered by granular tubercles. When the animal has withdrawn into its shell, these claws remain at the entrance, so as to completely block it, acting as protecting doors. This is the larger crab, abundant along the coast from Maine to Florida. It is reddish or brownish when alive and inhabits the empty shells of *Busycon* (the Common Whelk), *Natica* (the Sand-Collar Snail), *Polinices* (the Moon Shell), and the shells of the large marine snails.

Pagurus longicarpus Say COLOR PLATE IX, 8; X, 9. This is the small crab found everywhere along the coast in shallow water with elongate, somewhat cylindrical, nearly smooth chelae. The eyes form a dilation on the end of the eyestalks. This species is abundant from Cape Cod southward to South Carolina. The adult inhabits the shells of *Littorina littorea* (Periwinkle), *Alectrion obsoleta* (Mud Snail), *Alectrion trivittata* (Embossed Mud Snail). It is found in rock-pools and behind sand-bars, as well as on sandy and muddy bottoms, where the water is shallow and sheltered, along the coast.

Pagurus bernhardus (Linnaeus) INDEX PLATE 163; COLOR PLATE X, 10, 10a. This is a fairly large hermit crab with rounded spinous chelae, found from Vineyard Sound northward, often in deeper water. It is also circumboreal.

Family Lithodidae

This is a free-living, crablike form with the abdomen bent under the thorax and unsymmetrically composed of heavy calcified plates. The rostrum is slender and pointed with thornlike spines on its sides. The appendages of the sixth abdominal segment are lacking.

Lithodes maia (Linnaeus) PLATE 164. This is a large, spiny, crablike Anomuran, almost transitory to the true crabs, having a small, elongate rostrum, with a few lateral, spinelike teeth, as mentioned above. The last pair of legs is greatly reduced and is carried in the branchial chambers. This is an inhabitant of northern seas, but has been taken in lobster pots off the Maine coast.

While the members of this family have a deceptive, crablike aspect because of the shortened thorax and the reduced, tightly adhering abdomen of heavy calcified plates, they are, nevertheless, members of the Tribe *Paguridea* because of the number of anatomical points in which they correspond to that family, including especially the unsymmetrical abdomen. This family, therefore, typifies one of the final stages in the transition from the Macrura to the Brachyura along the Anomuran line.

PLATE 165

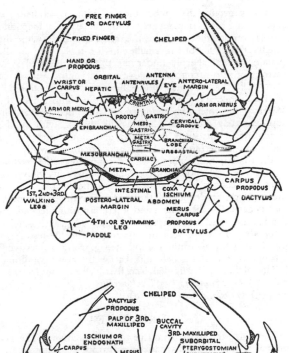

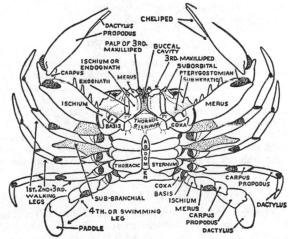

Suborder BRACHYURA
(The True Crabs)

In this group, the cephalothorax, with its carapace, is short and broad as compared with the usually long and narrow cephalothorax of the *Macrura* (shrimps); while the much-reduced abdomen, smaller in the male than in the female, is bent sharply under the thorax and fitted symmetrically into a concave groove on its ventral surface so completely that its dorsal side is flush with the ventral side of the thorax. This is in contrast to the condition in the *Macrura,* in which the abdomen extends out backward in approximately the same plane as the thorax, with all the abdominal joints well developed and not reduced. The abdomen of the female is broad and expanded, while that of the male is much narrower and confined to the median part of the underside of the carapace. There are only two pairs of pleopods in the male, enclosed between the abdomen and the underside of the thorax, modified as copulatory organs. On the other hand, there are four pleopods in the female, used for carrying the eggs. The sixth pair of pleopods is never present in either sex. The life-history of the Brachyura is quite complicated passing successively through several stages before it reaches the adult condition.

This Suborder is divided into five Tribes: (1) *Dromiacea;* (2) *Oxystomata;* (3) *Cyclometopa;* (4) *Catometopa;* and (5) *Oxyrhyncha (Maioidia).*

Tribe DROMIACEA

These are the most primitive of the Brachyura. The abdomen is not so much reduced as in other groups of the Suborder. The carapace is longer than wide, as in the Macrura and Anomura. Some authorities consider that this group is descended from the Anomura through the *Galatheidae,* and others say that it came directly from the Macrura through the group containing the lobster. However, the fact that the last two pairs of thoracic limbs have been reduced in the same way as in the Anomura seems to show its relation to that group.

Family Dromiidae

The eyes and antennules can be drawn into orbits. The last two pairs of thoracic legs are reduced in size and held dorsally. The sixth pair of pleopods is lacking or vestigial.

Hypoconcha arcuata Stimpson. The body is short, broad, and flattened. It is covered above by a parchmentlike skin. It utilizes its two reduced thoracic limbs to carry a large clam or other similar shell on its back for protection. Two oblique ridges meet in front on the anterior part of the lower surface of the body. This crab is occasionally dredged in the Beaufort, North Carolina, region.

Hypoconcha sabulosa (Herbst). This species is similar to the above and usually found with it. It differs from it principally in the fact that the lower surface is without the oblique ridges.

Dromia erythropus (G. Edwards). Sponge Crab. This species is typically a West Indian crab but has been rarely recorded from the Beaufort, North Carolina, region, its range probably having been extended by the Gulf Stream. It is interesting because of its habit of cutting out a piece of living sponge and holding it over its own head for concealment. To make this more effective, it usually settles down in the cavity made by cutting out the sponge fragment, the edges of the latter fitting back into the margin of the cavity from which the fragment was taken so that it seems continuous with the rest of the sponge body, thus concealing the crab.

Tribe OXYSTOMATA

The crabs in this group have a somewhat circular carapace. The mouth is triangular, instead of being square, as in the other Brachyura, with the apex pointing forward. The third maxillipeds do not have flattened coverings, as in the other crabs. The posterior thoracic limbs are often reduced and placed dorsally on the level above the other pairs. They usually burrow in sandy or gravelly bottoms.

Family Calappidae

The cephalothorax is rounded and covered with tubercles and granulations. The abdomen is completely hidden under the thorax. The antennae are quite small and the legs are normally developed.

Calappa flammea (Herbst) PLATE 166. Box Crab. This species has large, chelate claws with a toothed crest on the upper border. They are adapted to fit compactly against the front of the body so as to protect it completely. The color is buff or purplish, with a network pattern of purplish lines. This is actually a large tropical species which, nevertheless, occasionally ranges north to Long Island or southern Massachusetts. The size and position of the claws and the front pair of legs are such that it filters most effectively the gritty particles from the water which it sucks down to the branchial chambers.

Family Matutidae

This is a similar family, but with smaller claws, and with a carapace narrower posteriorly than in that family.

Hepatus epheliticus (Linnaeus) PLATE 166. The Calico Crab, or "Dolly Varden." This is a large and strikingly colored species with conspicuous rounded or irregular dark-bordered red spots on the back. It is also a tropical species, ranging north to Beaufort, North Carolina.

Family Leucosiidae

This family is characterized by its granular carapace, long claws, and comparatively small walking feet.

Persephone punctata (Linnaeus) PLATE 166. The evenly globular carapace has a granulate surface. There are three small, posteriorly directed, sharp and recurved spines on or near the rear margin. The color is grayish brown, marbled with darker irregular spots. The granules covering the carapace are white or often pinkish in color. It is a tropical species which ranges to the Beaufort, North Carolina, region, where it is comparatively sparse and widely distributed in shallow water. The greatly enlarged fifth segment of the abdomen in the female is usually distended by eggs during the summer.

Lithadia cariosa Stimpson PLATE 166. This is a small, stony-looking crab which is roughly pentagonal. It is found in the channels around Beaufort, North Carolina, and when caught, plays possum, pretending to be dead, then resembling a rough pebble. The chelipeds are stout, with angular joints, and with crested outer margins of the claws. They are light gray or yellowish in color. The female is said to have a few tiny red spots on the abdomen.

Tribe CYCLOMETOPA

In these crabs, the carapace is ovoid to circular. The frontal and lateral border are armed with conspicuous spines. There is no pointed rostrum. The mouth frame is square. The third maxillipeds are greatly flattened and, when brought together, form a double lid over the mouthparts.

Family Cancridae

The carapace is broadly oval and longest laterally. The last pair of legs are walking legs and not adapted for swimming. The first antennae are jointed, so as to fold lengthwise. The second antennae have short flagella. These are the typical crabs.

Cancer irroratus Say COLOR PLATE XII, 3. Common Rock Crab. The carapace is convex and covered with fine granulations. The anterior border, on either side of the middle line, has nine successive, broadly pointed teeth with finely granulated edges. Between each two teeth, the notch is continued onto the carapace as a short and conspicuous groove. The last tooth on each side, at the lateral extremity of the carapace, is mounted on a granulated ridge,

PLATE 166

CALAPPA FLAMMEA

HEPATUS
EPHELITICUS

PERSEPHONE
PUNCTATA

LITHADIA CARIOSA

PORTUNUS SAYI

PORTUNUS
SPINIMANUS

CALLINECTES
ORNATUS

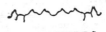

CALLINECTES
SAPIDUS

CALLINECTES
ORNATUS

ARENAEUS
CRIBRARIUS

but smaller than the rest. The front of the carapace, in the median line, has three teeth, with the middle one longer than the other two. The abdomen of the male is broad, with transverse granular ridges on each of the first three segments. The chelipeds are well developed, but of moderate size. The ground-color is yellowish with granulated purplish brown dots set so close together as to give it a brick-red appearance.

Cancer borealis Stimpson COLOR PLATE XII, 4. Northern Crab; Jonah Crab. The carapace is transversely oval, of greater proportionate width than in the preceding species. The surface in this species also is finely granulated. Its anterior margin on either side of the middle line is divided into nine quadrangular lobes, of which the margins are bordered with minute denticles. There are three median teeth, with the central one longer, as in the case of the previous species. The carapace, generally, is more deeply sculptured than that of *Cancer irroratus*, while the chelipeds are also heavier and more massive. The ground-color is brick-red above and yellowish on the ventral side. The same coloration is on the legs, but purplish mottlings give it a deeper color. This is found all along the New England coast, especially north of Cape Cod. It seems to prefer rocky situations exposed to ocean surf.

Family Portunidae

These are the Swimming Crabs. They have a transversely oval body, with the last pair of legs more or less adapted for swimming, except in *Carcinides maenas*. The terminal joints of these are approximately oval, and thus form effective paddles. The first pair of antennae fold back transversely.

Portunus sayi (Gibbes) PLATE 166. The anterior border of the carapace is arched and equipped with small teeth, six of which occur medially between the eye-sockets. The posterior and postero-lateral border together form a three-sided outline. A prominent sharp spine extends out horizontally at the extreme lateral angle. The terminal joint of the last pair of legs is flat and oval in shape, forming a pair of swimming oars. It is usually found in drifting Gulf Weed.

Portunus gibbesi (Stimpson). This is a similar species found in tropic and shallow seas, ranging north to Beaufort, North Carolina, where it occurs in deep channels. It is distinguished from *Portunus sayi* by having eight teeth instead of six on the mid-frontal border between the eye-sockets.

Portunus spinimanus Latreille PLATE 166. In this species, the carapace is similar to that of *Portunus sayi*, but the pair of teeth on the extreme lateral border are shorter. It is found at Beaufort, North Carolina, in deep channels, associated with *Portunus gibbesi*.

Callinectes sapidus Rathbun PLATE 166; COLOR PLATE XII, 6. Common Blue Crab, Hard-shell or Soft-shell Crab. This is the common crab of commerce, highly valued for its edible qualities. It is our most important seafood product, next to the lobster. The color is a variation of dark green shades, while the legs are suffused with bright blue, and sometimes with scarlet, longitudinal markings. This species occurs from Cape Cod southward to Florida and around the Gulf of Mexico to the Mississippi. The lateral angle of the carapace is armed with an unusually strong and sharp spine. The last joint of the last pair of legs is paddle-shaped. Between the eye-sockets there are six frontal teeth.

Callinectes ornatus Ordway PLATE 166. This is a similar species, but has eight, instead of six, frontal teeth between the eye-sockets.

Ovalipes ocellatus (Herbst) COLOR PLATE XII, 2; XII, 7. Lady Crab. Calico Crab. This is also a swimming crab, with the terminal joint of the last pair of legs broad and modified into oval swimming paddles. The carapace is about as broad as long. The general shape is circular. The anterolateral margins have five conspicuous teeth on either side, all of them quite similar to each other. The chelipeds are long in proportion to their width and with quite long, sharp, and serrated pincers. The color of the carapace is light lavender, with purple or purplish red spots making an even pattern over its light-colored back. It ranges from Cape Cod to the Gulf of Mexico, on sandy beaches, and is utilized for food in the southern states.

Carcinides maenas (Linnaeus) COLOR PLATE XII, 8. Green Crab. This differs from the other swimming crabs in not having the last pair of legs expanded as oval paddles. They are flattened but with pointed tips. The chelipeds are shorter in proportion than in the case of the Lady Crab.

Arenaeus cribrarius Lamarck PLATE 166. This species resembles *Callinectes* in having two very large lateral spines. It is distinguishable from it by being thickly dotted with small yellowish spots. It is chiefly found from Virginia southward, but also occurs in Vineyard Sound and off the coast of New Jersey.

Family Pilumnidae (Xanthidae)
(Mud Crabs)

The first antennae fold transversely. The carapace is usually transversely oval. The legs are not adapted for swimming. The color is a dull muddy hue harmonizing with the muddy bottom on which they are usually found.

Panopeus (Eupanopeus) herbstii Milne-Edwards PLATE 167; COLOR PLATE XII, 5. This and the other species of this genus and the related genera are commonly known as Mud Crabs. They are stoutly built crabs usually rather slow-moving, many being common on oyster-beds and other muddy bottoms covered with shells or stones. The chelae are stout and often have the fingers abruptly black or brown. This is the largest and stoutest of the native Mud Crabs. The black color extends slightly to the end of the chelae. The front of the carapace is of moderate width, the postero-lateral margins not strongly converging. The carapace is somewhat quadrate. The carpus of the cheliped is without a groove. The color of the immovable finger extends over beyond the line of color on the movable finger. This species occurs along the coast of Massachusetts, probably brought there with oysters. It is much more common southward.

Eurypanopeus depressus (Smith) PLATE 167. In this species, the back is only partly convex. The dark color of the fingers extends well onto the hand of the chelae. It is reported from Vineyard Sound, commonly in Long Island Sound and southward.

Neopanopeus texana sayi (Smith) PLATE 167. The body is less wide and the back more convex and uneven than in the preceding species. The dark color of the finger extends well onto the hand of the chelae. It is very common along the whole coast.

Hexapanopeus angustifrons (Benedict and Rathbun) PLATE 167. In this species, the dark color of the fingers does not extend at all onto the hand. It occurs from the Vineyard Sound region southward.

Rhithropanopeus harrisii (Gould) PLATE 167. This species is recognizable from the other Mud Crabs by the whitish finger of the large chelae. It is found chiefly in brackish estuaries along our whole coast.

Menippe mercenaria (Say) PLATE 167. Stone Crab. This is a very large, stoutly built crab with a very hard shell, purplish to brownish red in color above. It makes deep burrows in sandy shoals and is much esteemed as food. Though powerful, it is slow but not pugnacious. The carapace reaches almost 5 inches in width. It is found from North Carolina southward.

Eriphia gonagra (Fabricius) PLATE 167. It is easily recognizable by the many rows of flattened, rounded tubercles, like heads of nails studding the front or external surface of the chelae. It is occasionally found at Beaufort, North Carolina, but more abundantly southward.

Pilumnus sayi Rathbun PLATE 167. The frontal border of the carapace between the eye orbits is much more than

PLATE 167

PANOPEUS
HERBSTII

CLAW OF MALE

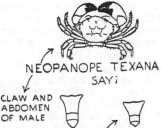

NEOPANOPE TEXANA
SAYi

CLAW AND
ABDOMEN
OF MALE

EURYPANOPEUS
DEPRESSUS
ABDOMEN OF MALE

HEXAPANOPEUS
ANGUSTIFRONS

EURYPANOPEUS
DEPRESSUS

RHITHROPANOPEUS
HARRISI

MENIPPE
MERCENARIA

ERIPHIA
GONAGRA

PILUMNUS
LACTEUS

PILUMNUS SAYI

half the greatest breadth of the carapace. It is often granulate or spinous and usually hairy. The lateral surface of the carapace is armed with small spines or spinules, which enables it to be easily recognizable among our native species. These are often quite scattered, and very long and stiff on both the body and limbs. The chelae and margin of the body have short, but sharply erect spines. This species ranges from North Carolina southward.

Pilumnus lacteus Stimpson PLATE 167. This is a similar species. The sides of the carapace have four anteriorly directed teeth. The body is covered with a whitish pubescence, easily rubbed off. It is often found on wharfpiles among ascidians from Beaufort, North Carolina, southward.

Tribe CATOMETOPA
(The Grapsoid Crabs)

In this tribe, the front margin of the carapace is quite broad. The carapace, generally, is very square in outline. Otherwise, these crabs resemble those of the Tribe *Cyclometopa* in general appearance, but the margin of the carapace is never provided with spines to the extent that they appear in that Tribe. The carapace never has a rostrum, but the front is usually bent downward on the middle line. The Catometopa include both fully marine, shallow-water forms, or entirely terrestrial species.

Family Ocypodidae

The carapace is square with narrow, raised, lateral margins, without teeth. The eyestalks usually are very long. They are jointed so that they may each lie horizontally in a groove along the front of the carapace.

Ocypode albicans Bosc (= **Ocypode arenaria** Say) COLOR PLATE XII, 9. Sand Crab. Ghost Crab. This species is colored like sand and runs swiftly sidewise on the tips of its toes. It makes burrows high up on sandy ocean beaches. Its movements are very rapid and it so nearly imitates its environment that, when it suddenly stands still on a white sandy beach, it seems to disappear; hence, the popular name Ghost Crab. It occurs along the sandy beaches of the eastern seaboard, north to New Jersey. Occasionally it has been found on Rhode Island beaches.

Genus Uca. Fiddler Crabs. The crabs in this genus have a very white and short body. The front of the carapace is considerably expanded and is at a right angle to the sides. These narrow somewhat and also meet the straight posterior border at a right angle. The eyestalks are very long and slender. In the male, one of the two chelae is enormous and held horizontally across the front of the body.

PLATE 168

PINNOTHERES
OSTREUM
MALE

PINNIXA
CHAETOPTERANA
FEMALE

PINNIXA
CYLINDRICA
MALE

PLANES
MINUTUS

SESARMA
RETICULATUM

SESARMA
CINEREUM

UCA PUGNAX
CLAW (MALE)

UCA PUGILATOR
INSIDE ASPECT OF CLAW
MALE

UCA MINAX

HETEROCRYPTA
GRANULATA

This gives it the name of Fiddler Crab. Both chelae are small in the female.

Uca pugnax (S. I. Smith) PLATE 168; COLOR PLATE XII, 10. The front of the male is practically 1 inch in width. There is a rough, oblique ridge on the inside of the large chela of the male. It is found along our coast northward to Cape Cod. It is very abundant and burrows in the mud and sand of salt marshes, digging a round hole with a fairly long tube and a horizontal chamber at the bottom.

Uca pugilator (Bosc) PLATE 168. This species is similar to *Uca pugnax,* without the rough ridge on the inside of the hand of the male. It occurs very abundantly, burrowing in sandy or muddy beaches northward to Boston, Massachusetts.

Uca minax (La Conte) PLATE 168. This is a much larger species, the carapace of the male often measuring 1½ inches in width. There is a rough, oblique ridge present on the inside of the hand of the male. Red spots occur at the joints of the large claw. It is found along our coast northward to Buzzards Bay, Massachusetts, and lives far up in salt marshes, in brackish or nearly fresh water.

Family Grapsidae

The carapace is square and the lateral margins are almost exactly parallel or slightly arched. The orbits and eyes are moderately large and are wide apart, being situated practically at the anterior corners of the carapace. The eyestalks are not much lengthened. These crabs may be found along the shore in fresh water or on land.

Planes minutus (Linnaeus) PLATE 168. This is a small crab with a somewhat four-sided carapace, found in floating Gulf Weed. The color is variable, being mottled from yellow to brown. Its range is cosmopolitan, for it is found both in floating masses of Sargassum Weed as well as in other seaweeds in the open seas. Its coloration often mimics the masses of weed in which it lives, rendering it practically invisible.

Sesarma reticulatum Say PLATE 168. The carapace is rectangular, as is the case with other Grapsidae, and has a convex surface. The eyestalks are short and stout. The lateral margin is toothed behind the angle of the eye-orbit. It burrows in salt marshes associated with *Uca pugnax* and occurs along our eastern seaboard northward to Cape Cod.

Sesarma cinereum Say PLATE 168. Wharf Crab. Wood Crab. The carapace is more flattened and more nearly square than in *Sesarma reticulatum*. This species is found on wharf-piles and under logs and driftwood along the shore. Its range is from Chesapeake Bay, southward.

Family Pinnotheridae

The carapace is round, convex, and with a frontal margin not clearly outlined. The eyes are quite small, often rudimentary. These crabs usually live as commensals in the mantle cavity of living bivalve mollusks or in worm-tubes of living marine worms.

Pinnotheres ostreum Say PLATE 168. Oyster Crab. The color is whitish or pink. The female is often commensal (i.e., living in partnership) in oysters, and is often found in oysters used for food. The male is free-swimming, smaller, and rounder.

Pinnotheres maculatum Say. Mussel Crab. The female of this species is similar to the above, but lives as a commensal in mussels, scallops, and other bivalve mollusks. It is found from Cape Cod southward.

Pinnixa chaetopterana Stimpson PLATE 168; COLOR PLATE IX, 6, 7. Parchment Worm Crab. The carapace of this species is very downy. Its body is elongated laterally and is cylindrical horizontally. It is commensal in the tube of the annulates *Chaetopterus* and *Amphitrite*. It is found from the Vineyard Sound and Woods Hole region southward in shallow, sandy, mud bottoms, especially in sheltered situations.

The male and female of this little crab are often found in the U-shaped tube of the Parchment Worm, *Chaetopterus pergamentaceus,* as stated above. These tubes are found imbedded in sandy mud with the two chimneys extending 1 inch or more above the sea-bottom. These two crabs are very seldom found outside of these tubes and, doubtless, as they grow up they would find it impossible to escape from them. In fact, the chimney openings of the tube are probably too small for the adult crab to escape. They feed on particles of the small and microscopic forms which are pumped through the tube by the rhythmical contractions of the worm.

Pinnixa sayana Stimpson. A much less hairy species than the above with slenderer limbs. It is usually found free in mud or sand, and is distributed from the Vineyard Sound region southward.

Pinnixa cylindrica (Say) PLATE 168. This species is said to be a commensal in the tubes of the Lugworm (*Arenicola marina* PLATE 117), or it may be swimming freely. It is distributed mostly from Chesapeake Bay southward.

Tribe OXYRHYNCHA (MAIOIDEA)

The crabs in this Tribe have a more or less triangular carapace, narrowing in front, and with a pointed rostrum. It is broad and rounded behind. The frame of the mouth-opening is square, with its front margins straight. There are nine pairs of gills, opening at the sides of the mouth-region. The first antennae are longitudinally folded.

Family Parthenopidae

The basal joint of the antennae is very small. The claw-bearing feet are a great deal longer and heavier than the other legs. The carapace is more or less expanded laterally to form a cavity containing the walking legs. It is almost flat, posteriorly.

Heterocrypta granulata (Gibbes) PLATE 168. This species holds its claw-bearing pair of arms stiffly before its triangular body as it walks over the bottom among the shell fragments, which its peculiar shape and sculptured surface mimic so closely that it is almost completely camouflaged. It is found along the coast of Massachusetts and southward.

Family Maiidae (Inachidae)
(Spider Crabs)

The basal joint of the antennae is well developed. The chelipeds are not much longer than the other legs. This is a very large family, including all the true spider crabs. They are commonly found in the Atlantic Ocean, along both the American and European coasts. It is noteworthy that the legs are much longer in old than in young individuals, a matter to be considered in identifying specimens of this species.

Podochela riisei Stimpson PLATE 169. The rostrum in this species is short. The dactyl in the walking legs is shorter than the propodus. The carapace is elongate, narrowed in front. The outer maxillipeds are somewhat foot-like with a large palp. The rostrum is somewhat rounded instead of being acute. The basal joint of the antennae has flat and thin lateral crests. The legs are very long in proportion to the body. It has been found among hydroids at Beaufort, North Carolina.

Metoporhaphis calcaratus (Say) PLATE 169. This species has even longer legs in proportion to its body than the preceding species. The carapace has an irregular surface. The antennae are long, showing a flagellum. This crab is not uncommon among hydroids and among dredgings in the Beaufort region.

Pelia mutica (Gibbes) PLATE 169. The carapace is rounded and somewhat saclike, narrowing in front. The walking legs are fairly short, but stout. Their joints are flattened. The orbits behind the eye form a cuplike structure into which the eye may be retracted without completely concealing it. The eyestalks are short. The basal joint of the antennae is broad with a terminal spine. It is

PLATE 169

PODOCHELA
RIISEI

METOPORHAPHIS
CALCARATUS

PELIA MUTICA

LIBINIA
EMARGINATA
YOUNG MALE

HYAS COARCTATUS

HYAS ARANEUS

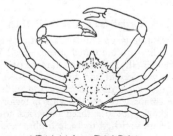

LIBINIA DUBIA

found among hydroids and similar growths on wharf-piles from Vineyard Sound southward. Its back may be overgrown with a sponge, often larger than the crab itself. The carapace is mottled with red.

Libinia emarginata Leach PLATE 169; COLOR PLATE XII, 1. Common Spider Crab. There is a median row of nine spines on the body. Its long legs and sac-shaped body cause it to resemble a huge spider. The carapace has a margin evenly rounded behind the rostrum. It is abundant, especially on muddy bottoms, in shallow water from Cape Cod southward.

Libinia dubia Milne-Edwards PLATE 169. Spider Crab. It is similar to the preceding species in habits, distribution, and form. It is distinguishable, however, by the smoother carapace having only six spines in a median row.

Hyas coarctatus Leach PLATE 169; COLOR PLATE XII, 2. Toad Crab. The body of this crab is so constructed with a wide shallow notch on each side, as to make it somewhat violin-shaped. The rostrum is divided into two parts, separated by a narrow slit. It is found on muddy or stony bottoms from Maine to Cape Cod. It also occurs farther south to Florida, but rarely, except in deeper water.

Hyas araneus (Linnaeus) PLATE 169. Toad Crab. This is closely allied to *Hyas coarctatus* and similar in distribution. The body, however, is not constricted to the same extent.

Division HOPLOCARIDA

The species in this Division are of large size. At least four of the thoracic segments are exposed and distinct, posterior to the small carapace. The eyes are mounted on a stalk. The eggs are carried in an enclosure formed by the maxillipeds. The heart extends through both the thorax and abdomen.

Order STOMATOPODA

These are quite large animals, sometimes reaching 1 foot in length. They are a unified group as all members of it have, fundamentally, the same characteristic structure. The abdomen is very broad and fully developed. The terminal telson is quite expanded, forming the widest part of the body. The carapace covers the four anterior segments but, as stated above, not the three posterior to it. There are five pairs of unbranched thoracic limbs, modified as maxillipeds, turning forward in the neighborhood of the mouth and ending in claws. The second pair is much larger and heavier than the others, and is specialized to form great, aggressive-looking, raptorial arms (reminding one of the insect known as the Praying Mantis), by means of which the members of this group seize their prey. The last three

PLATE 170

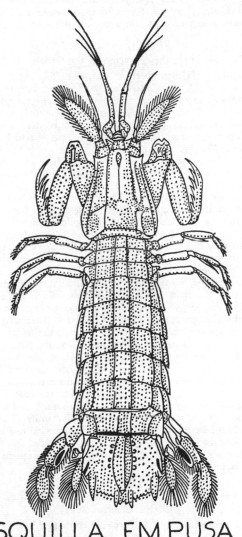

SQUILLA EM PUSA

pairs of thoracic limbs are slender, similar to each other and biramous. The pleopods are powerful swimming organs, also biramous. Series of small hooks on their endopodites link each pair together on the middle line.

Family Squillidae

This family has the characters of the Order.

Squilla (Chloridella) empusa Say PLATE 170; COLOR PLATE X, 2. Mantis Shrimp. The carapace of membranous texture has a longitudinal median ridge, with deep grooves, and two other ridges on either side. It is narrower anteriorly, flaring out to its posterior border, which is scalloped into three lobes, the middle one of which is the widest. The eyes are mounted on narrow stalks which diverge from each other to form a V. There are also four pairs of dorsal keels on the anterior five abdominal segments. The terminal joint of the second maxillipeds, which forms the raptorial claws, has six long teeth which become gradually longer distally. These fit into corresponding pits on the outside of the propodus which, in turn, closes against the back of the forward-directed basal joint. Smith describes this species vividly and regarding the second maxilliped, he says, "by means of this singular organ they can hold their prey securely, and can give a severe wound to the human hand, if handled unconsciously. It also uses the stout caudal appendages, which are armed with spines, very effectively. The body is usually pale green or yellowish green, each segment bordered posteriorly with dark green and edged with bright yellow; the tail is tinged with rose and mottled into rose and black; the outer caudal lamellae have the base and spines white, the last joint yellow, margined with black; the inner ones are black, pale at base; the eyes are bright emerald green; the inner antennae are dark, with a yellow band at the base of each joint; and the flagellum is annulated with black and white."

About 200 species are known in this family. The one described here is quite common from Cape Cod to Florida. It makes shallow burrows in mud between tides and below the low-water mark. There are usually several openings to each burrow.

CLASS ARACHNOIDEA
(Horseshoe Crabs, Scorpions, Spiders, Mites, and Bear Animalcules)

The great majority of the species contained in this Class live on land. Certain aberrant groups, however, are marine and, therefore, come within the limits of this book. They are, as follows: *Subclass Xiphosura,* including the Horseshoe Crabs, and *Subclass Arachnida,* represented here by two genera of Mites and a Water Bear.

SUBCLASS XIPHOSURA

This Subclass includes the Horseshoe Crabs, which are generally referred to the Class *Arachnoidea,* containing the spiders, scorpions, and their relatives. The Horseshoe Crabs, together with a few marine mites, are the only marine arachnoids. Apparently they were descended from the eurypterids, a great group which was very abundant in Palaeozoic times and is now entirely extinct.

Limulus polyphemus Linnaeus INDEX PLATE 171; COLOR PLATE XI, 3. The Horseshoe Crab or King Crab. The body consists of a cephalothorax, an abdomen, and a long, unjointed, spikelike tail. The cephalothorax, or carapace, takes up the larger portion of the body and is horseshoe-shaped. It is of leathery, chitinous texture and encloses, within its shell, the digestive, respiratory, and circulatory organs. The ventral surface of the carapace is somewhat excavated to make room for the five pairs of limbs with long, pincerlike chelae. A sixth pair has no chelae, but the terminal joints end with a number of elongate, narrow plates arranged in jointed circular cones and are used by the King Crab in pushing its way through the sand and mud of the sea-bottom. The first pair of appendages is quite small, but shaped essentially like the rest. They are known as the *chelicerae.* The basal joints of the other five pairs of legs are armed with a series of close-set spines which, through the motion of the legs, act as mills to help grind up the food. These joints (*chilaria*) immediately surround the centrally located mouth. The abdomen is connected with the cephalothorax by means of a transverse joint. Certain sutures and markings, on the dorsal side, together with six pairs of lateral spines, are vestiges of the former abdominal joints, which have now become completely welded into one abdominal plate. On the ventral side of the abdomen, there are six pairs of broad, platelike appendages, the first of which overlaps the rest and acts as a cover or operculum. The posterior five pairs are thin and bear breathing organs on the side against the body. Because of their overlapping, leaflike character, they are known as the gill-books. Underneath the base of the operculum are the two genital openings. The males are smaller than the females and have larger and heavier claws on the second pair of appendages for grasping the female. The King Crab possesses two large, conspicuous, compound eyes, situated at some distance apart on the upper side of the carapace, and two small simple eyes, situated close together on the middle line near the front border of the carapace. There is a fold of the carapace running antero-posteriorly, just above each eye, while a spine overhangs the eye itself. Its relationship to the arachnids, in general, is shown by the internal anatomy, which is more or less typical of that group. The King Crab increases in size from year to year, finally measuring up to 20 inches in length. The color varies from olive-brown to dark red-brown. It lives in the shallow margin of the ocean where it is found burrowing in the sand and mud, plowing it down with the front margin of the cephalothorax to obtain the small animals on which it feeds. It is very common along the eastern coast of North America, from Nova Scotia to Florida.

SUBCLASS ARACHNIDA

This is a large Subclass containing the air-breathing, land-living spiders, scorpions, and their relatives. A few rare exceptions are marine. In this Subclass there are only two orders containing marine forms, as follows: (1) *Acarina,* the water mites, including a single marine family (*Halacaridae*); and (2) *Tardigrada,* mostly a fresh-water group with a few marine species.

Order ACARINA
(Mites and Their Relatives)

The Acarina or mites are arachnids of small size, with unsegmented cephalothorax and abdomen separated by a transverse suture, but so arranged that the entire body is continuously spheroidal or ovoid in shape. There are four pairs of legs in the adult, as well as a pair of *chelicerae* and a pair of *pedipalps,* situated anteriorly. The chelicerae may have pincerlike chelae or they may be formed to act as piercing and sucking organs. The pedipalps, though five-jointed and leglike, are not used for walking, but are adapted in various ways, in different species, to act with the mouth-parts. The legs are also five-jointed, usually with more or less perfectly developed claws. Some species have eyes and others not. The anus is at the posterior end of the body.

Most mites are terrestrial and many species are parasitic. Only two of the families are aquatic, the *Hydrachnidae* and *Halacaridae.* The former contains fresh-water forms, while the *Halacaridae* alone have a marine habitat.

Family Halacaridae

This is the only marine family of this order. There are two genera mentioned here as examples.

Halacarus sp. PLATE 172. These little mites are less than 2 mm. in length and are often found in shallow water, crawling on the seaweeds on which they feed. They are also found on hydroids. There are usually three eyes.

PLATE 171

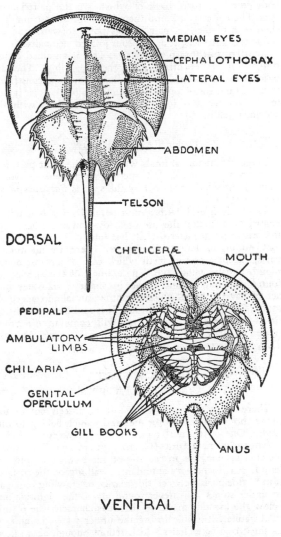

DORSAL

MEDIAN EYES

CEPHALOTHORAX

LATERAL EYES

ABDOMEN

TELSON

CHELICERÆ

MOUTH

PEDIPALP

AMBULATORY LIMBS

CHILARIA

GENITAL OPERCULUM

GILL BOOKS

ANUS

VENTRAL

LIMULUS POLYPHEMUS

In this species, there is a transverse joint dividing the oval body into two parts, back of which are the paired black eyes. The color is dark and there is a pointed rostrum. The chelicerae of the first pair of legs point forward, and are about the same length as the four-jointed pedipalps.

Scaptognathus sp. PLATE 172. This is an allied genus, similar in its essentials to the preceding. The anterior part of the body is vase-shaped with a constricted neck. The general appearance and coloration is shown in the figure. It is found in similar locations with the previous genus.

Order TARDIGRADA

These are minute animals which, for the most part, live in fresh water, but a few species are marine, a typical example of which is shown by the species *Batillipes mirus* PLATE 172.

The body is oval, with almost parallel sides. It is microscopic, necessitating the use of a low-powered microscope to observe its characteristics. It has four pairs of short legs, each ending in four to five claws. There are no mouthparts, except a pair of teeth which can extend out of the mouth and be withdrawn. The animals of this species are found crawling around algae in shallow sea-water and act as scavengers living upon minute animal and vegetable matter. They are retentive of life. It is said that, after being dried up for some years, they will come to life when placed in water. The digestive system is a straight tube. They are hermaphroditic.

CLASS INSECTA
Order COLLEMBOLA

There are a few species of seashore insects out of the many thousands inhabiting the land, which belong to this Order. One of the most typical is the following:

Anurida maritima (Guerin) PLATE 172. This small blue-black, wingless insect is not more than 3 mm. in length. It is found very abundantly walking on the surface-film of tide-pools, between tide-marks, or crawling on algae or under stones. It is never found above the high-tide nor below the low-tide mark, so that it is characteristic of this tidal habitat. It is able to breathe under water, because of its thick coating of hairs which retains enough air to keep it supplied for several days submerged.

In addition to the above, there are a few species that frequent the tidal zone including certain Hemiptera, one of which, belonging to the genus *Halobates,* has become adapted even to a sea life, for it has been found hundreds

PLATE 172

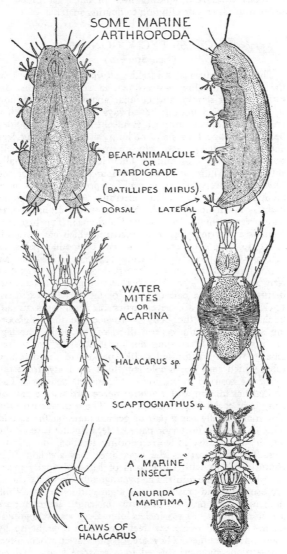

SOME MARINE
ARTHROPODA

BEAR-ANIMALCULE
OR
TARDIGRADE

(BATILLIPES MIRUS).

DORSAL   LATERAL

WATER
MITES
OR
ACARINA

HALACARUS sp.

SCAPTOGNATHUS sp.

A "MARINE"
INSECT

(ANURIDA
MARITIMA)

CLAWS OF
HALACARUS

of miles from land, gliding like an outrigger canoe on quiet tropical seas or clinging to floating material.

CLASS PYCNOGONIDA
(Sea Spiders)

These very curious, spiderlike animals are abundant in the sea from shallow water down to extreme depths. Because of their strange and peculiar anatomy, their position in the Animal Kingdom has always been in doubt. They are placed by most authorities in the group Arachnoidea because of their four pairs of long, slender, walking legs and a fifth smaller pair which remind one of the chelicerae characteristic of spiders. Their jointed legs, externally stiffened by chitin, proclaim them to be members of the Phylum Arthropoda, but in every respect, except for those mentioned, they are quite aberrant. Almost the entire body is taken up by its sharply segmented cephalothorax and a very minute unsegmented abdomen. The first segment is a tapering, fingerlike rostrum which has a mouth at its tip. The chelicerae and a pair of footlike palps, as well as short appendages bearing eggs, are located on this segment together with the first pair of walking legs and four simple eyes. The three posterior cephalothoracic segments each carry a pair of long, jointed legs (INDEX PLATE 173); thus there are seven pairs of appendages in all. Each segment of the body is attached to the neighboring segments for the central third of its width. The leg-bearing portion, extending out on either side, has a free lobe in which are located saclike pockets of the digestive tube, which runs the whole length of the body, from the tip of the rostrum to the end of the minute abdomen. The animal has a brain and a ventral nerve-cord with a pair of ganglia in each of the five segments. The sexes are separate. The male usually has a pair of genital pores on the second joint of the two posterior pairs of legs. In the case of the female, these exist in corresponding locations on all the legs. The male carries the eggs after they are laid. The young are born with three pairs of legs and finally metamorphose into the adult. The pycnogonids, along the shore, are usually found crawling over algae and hydroids. While the smallest are only about 1 mm. in length, larger species are often from ½ to 1½ inches long. Deep-sea pycnogonids having a spread of several feet have been brought up by trawls and dredges. They are bright scarlet when alive. The Pycnogonida are placed in a separate Class, divided into about ten families, in which more than 400 species are grouped. The four families known from this region are: (1) *Pycnogonidae;* (2) *Achelidae;* (3) *Pallenidae;* and (4) *Nymphonidae.*

PLATE 173

CLASS PYCNOGONIDA

MALE PYCNOGONID CARRYING EGG-MASSES ON
HIS OVIGEROUS LEGS

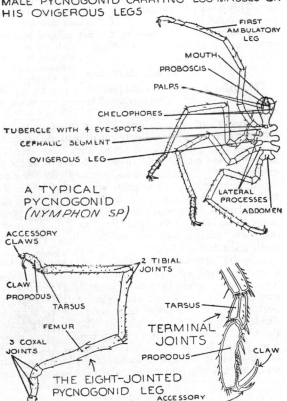

FIRST AMBULATORY LEG

MOUTH
PROBOSCIS
PALPS
CHELOPHORES
TUBERCLE WITH 4 EYE-SPOTS
CEPHALIC SEGMENT
OVIGEROUS LEG

LATERAL PROCESSES
ABDOMEN

A TYPICAL
PYCNOGONID
(NYMPHON SP)

ACCESSORY CLAWS

CLAW
PROPODUS
TARSUS
FEMUR
3 COXAL JOINTS

2 TIBIAL JOINTS

TARSUS

TERMINAL JOINTS

PROPODUS

CLAW

ACCESSORY CLAWS

THE EIGHT-JOINTED
PYCNOGONID LEG

Family Pycnogonidae

The body is very broad and stout. Chelicerae and palps are wanting. Accessory legs, ten-jointed, exist in the male but are lacking in the female. The legs are stout and the dactyls are without auxiliary claws.

Pycnogonum littorale (Gröm) PLATE 174. The body, in this species, is very broad and flat. The lateral processes are crowded, with almost no interval between them. Each segment has a conical tubercle on the median line. The very small eyes are black and widely separated. The abdomen is very slender. The walking legs are stout, the basal joints being quite thick. The color is light yellowish brown to dark brown. The legs are blackish toward their tips. This species is about ⅔ inch in length and it ranges, on our coast, from the Gulf of St. Lawrence to Long Island Sound. It is common in the Bay of Fundy, under stones, and is generally cosmopolitan.

Family Achelidae

The palps are six- to eight-jointed; accessory legs are present, ten-jointed in both sexes. The legs are stout, the dactyls with accessory claws.

Tanystylum orbiculare Wilson PLATE 174. The cephalothorax is circular, deeply cut in between the lateral processes. The prostomium is broad, with black eyes. The tapering abdomen is fairly large, slightly divided at the extremity. The chelicerae are rudimentary, consisting of a single, knoblike joint. The palps are a little longer than the rostrum. The accessory legs are larger in the male than in the female. The body-length is 1½ mm. This species ranges from Marthas Vineyard Island to Virginia, associating with hydroids and ascidians on wharf-piles. It may reach a depth of 14 fathoms.

Achelia spinosa (Stimpson) PLATE 174. The body is oval in shape, cut deeply between the lateral processes, which are separated by a clear interval. The eye-bearing tubercle is large, pointed, and prominent. The eyes are oval and black. The abdomen is comparatively long and slender, slightly divided at the tip. The accessory legs in the male are rather large. This species is very common from Grand Manan to Block Island Sound. Off the coast of Maine it is commonly found on hydroids, ascidians, and other animals, beneath stones near the low-water mark.

Family Pallenidae

The body is robust. The chelicerae are three-jointed and chelate. There are no pedipalps. The accessory legs are present, nine- to eleven-jointed in both sexes. The walking

PLATE 174

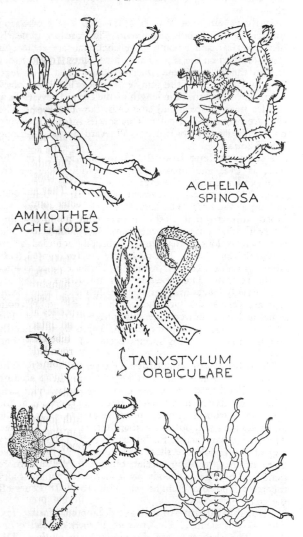

AMMOTHEA
ACHELIODES

ACHELIA
SPINOSA

TANYSTYLUM
ORBICULARE

PYCNOGONUM
LITTORALE

legs are very long. The dactyl is with or without accessory claws.

Pallene empusa Wilson PLATE 175. The eye-bearing tubercle is small, but prominent. The rostrum is nearly hemispherical and smooth. The chelicerae are short and stout, toothed on the second and third joints. The accessory legs in the male are one third as long as the other legs. They are smaller in the female. The legs are enormously long, over four times the length of the body. They are very slender near the base and stouter in the outer joints. The eyes are bright red in color. This species is found growing on tubularian hydroids from Vineyard Sound to Long Island Sound.

Pseudopallene hispida (Stimpson) PLATE 175. The body is oval and broad. The eye-bearing tubercles are small and rounded. The eyes are oval and light-brown in color. The eye-bearing segment is very large, being half as long as the body. The lateral thoracic processes are very broad and crowded close together with no intervening interval. The outer margins have hairy tubercles. The abdomen is longer than broad, abruptly rounded at its extremity, and hairy. The chelicerae are two-jointed, very stout, and amber-colored at the tip. They are twice as long as the rostrum. The accessory legs are slender. They are considerably longer and slenderer in the male. The walking legs are very stout, with the fourth and fifth joints about equal in length, but considerably longer than the rest. The fifth are slenderer than the fourth. The body is generally rough and hairy. This species occurs off Grand Manan Island.

Pseudopallene discoidea (Kröyer) PLATE 175. The oval body is somewhat narrower than in the preceding species. The lateral processes are in close contact with each other. The abdomen is pointed, but slightly double at the tip. The rostrum is obtuse, but convex in its outlines. The antennae are stout, but less so than in the preceding species. The chelae have acute, finely serrate claws. The accessory legs of the female are short and stout. The legs resemble those of the preceding species, but are longer and more slender. The legs and body are rough with conical hairy tubercles. The color is light yellowish brown. It occurs off the coast of Maine.

Phoxichilidium maxillare Stimpson PLATE 175. The body is slender. The rostrum is rounded and cylindrical. The chelicerae are three-jointed and chelate. The pedipalps are lacking. The accessory legs in the male are five-jointed. They are absent in the female. The legs are slender and the dactyls are stout and have auxiliary claws. This species ranges from Halifax, Nova Scotia, to Gloucester, Massachusetts.

PLATE 175

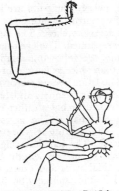

PALLENE EMPUSA

PSEUDOPALLENE
HISPIDA

PHOXICHILIDIUM
MAXILLARE

ANOPLODACTYLUS
LENTUS

PSEUDOPALLENE
DISCOIDEA

ANOPLODACTYLUS
LENTUS

Anoplodactylus lentus Wilson PLATE 175. The body is slender. The rostrum is cylindrical and rounded. The chelicerae are three-jointed and chelate. The palpi are lacking. The accessory legs are six-jointed, wanting in the female. The dactyls are without accessory claws. The lateral processes of the body are widely separated. The eye-bearing segment is broad, as long as the two following segments together. The abdomen is more than twice as long as broad, slightly split at the extremity. The ovate eyes are brown to black in color. The chelicerae are long, slender, and hairy. They are somewhat diverging with their bases rather close together. The chelae are stout and hairy. The accessory legs are covered with tubercles. The walking legs are very long and slender with stout dactyls. The female is slightly larger than the male, being over ¼ inch in length. This species is quite common in the tidal areas and down to 6 fathoms in Vineyard Sound. It is found especially on shelly bottoms clinging to hydroids and ascidians and climbing over them. It is usually deep purple in color. It has been taken as far north as the Bay of Fundy.

Family Nymphonidae

The body is usually slender, but may be broad. It has a large, tapering rostrum. The chelicerae, in most species, are chelate; in others, not chelate. The accessory claws are present or not. The pedipalps are present.

Ammothea achelioides Wilson PLATE 174. The body is very broadly oval and closely amalgamated so that the segments are not visible. The lateral are only slightly separated. The eye-bearing tubercles are prominent and acute. The chelicerae are chelate. The palps are very slender, longer than the rostrum. The accessory legs are very short and swollen. The walking legs are comparatively short and slender. The dactyl is prominent, nearly two thirds the length of the propodus and somewhat stout. Auxiliary claws are present and about two thirds the length of the dactyl. This species has been taken in the Bay of Fundy.

Nymphon stromii Kröyer PLATE 176. The body is quite slender, cylindrical, and rounded. The chelicerae are three-jointed and chelate. The pedipalps are five-jointed. The accessory legs are present in both sexes. They are stout, slightly hairy, and eleven-jointed. The walking legs are slender and the dactyl has auxiliary claws. The abdomen is small, tapering toward the extremity. The palps are much longer than the rostrum. It is found on muddy bottoms. The color, when living, is a light salmon-yellow, with legs often with broad reddish rings. The body of this species is about ⅜ inch in length; nevertheless, due to the length of its legs, it has a spread of 6 inches, and is the

PLATE 176

NYMPHON
STROMII

NYMPHON
STROMII

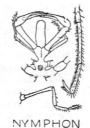

NYMPHON
MACRUM

NYMPHON
GROSSIPES

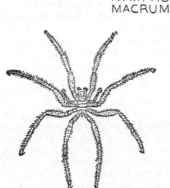

NYMPHON HIRTUM

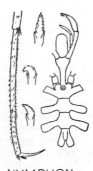

NYMPHON
LONGITARSE

largest species known from our coast. It is found from Halifax, Nova Scotia, to Massachusetts Bay.

Nymphon macrum Wilson PLATE 176. The slender body has extremely long and slender chelicerae with the claws of the chelae long, much curved, and when closed, crossing each other at a considerable distance from their tips. The accessory legs are separated from the first lateral processes by a clear interval. The terminal joint of the palp is very slender. The auxiliary claws are nearly two thirds the length of the dactyl. On the body itself, the lateral processes are separated by a space about equal to their width. The rostrum is about as long as the eye-bearing segment and nearly cylindrical. The chela is much elongated. The accessory legs are much longer in the male than in the female. This species is very distinct, much like the preceding species, but clearly distinguished by the large auxiliary claws. It has been found off Nova Scotia and the Gulf of Maine in deep water from 5 to 115 fathoms on muddy bottoms.

Nymphon longitarse Kröyer PLATE 176. This is another common species, extremely slender, with a smooth body and a very long neck, while the attenuated legs give it quite a spiderlike appearance. The chelicerae are slender and slightly hairy. The claws of the chelae are very long and slender, their tips crossing when closed. The accessory legs are remarkably slender. The color, when living, is light salmon or nearly white, sometimes irregularly striped across the body and legs with purple. It is somewhat over ¼ inch in length. It ranges from the Bay of Fundy and Georges Bank, along the coast of Maine and Massachusetts. It occurs on a variety of bottoms, but is more frequently found where there is much mud.

Nymphon hirtum Fabricius PLATE 176. This species a common species, similar to *Nymphon stromii,* but smaller and with a longer neck. The body is slender and quite smooth. The eye-bearing tubercle is very prominent and conical. The eyes are black and nearly round. The small tapering abdomen is often bent upward. There is a large rostrum. The chelicerae are slender, with a basal joint about as long as the rostrum. The palps are slender and so are the accessory legs. The walking legs are long, very slender, and sparsely hairy. The color, when living, is a light salmon-yellow, the legs often banded with reddish to light purple. It is an extremely common species, taken often from Labrador to Long Island Sound, in from 12 to 110 fathoms, on rocky, gravelly, and occasionally on muddy bottoms.

Nymphon hirtus Fabricius PLATE 176. This species is clearly distinguishable by its short, compact body and stout, very hairy limbs giving it an extremely spiderlike appearance. The spread of the limbs may be up to 3 inches. The later processes are scarcely separated. The eye-bearing segment is broad and stout. The tubercle is very elevated and rounded. The eyes are oval and black. The abdomen is slender and tapering. The chelicerae are very hairy and rather stout. The claws of the chelae are slender, acute, and very strongly curved, crossing each other at a considerable distance from the tips. The palps are stout. The accessory legs are much longer, larger, and stouter than in the female. The walking legs are quite stout and thickly covered with coarse hairs. The color of the species is a dull yellow. Adult specimens are often covered with living Bryozoa, sponges, and other material, which become attached to them. It is taken abundantly off Nova Scotia, and rarely off the New England coast.

11

Phylum Mollusca

(SNAILS, BIVALVES, CHITONS, SQUID, AND OCTOPUSES)

THE mollusks are one of the most important groups in the Animal Kingdom. Next to the insects, they include more species than any other animal subdivision, approximately 80,000 being known. The Phylum containing them is quite distinct from any other modern group, though the most primitive forms and the free-swimming larvae seem to point to an origin close to that of flatworms (Platyhelmia) (see page 224).

Paleontologically, they are one of the oldest groups of which we have definite knowledge, representatives being abundant among the fossils of the Lower Cambrian strata laid down at least 600,000,000 years ago. Because of their soft bodies, their shells alone are preserved in a fossil state, but their abundance and the relatively high organization of all mollusks seem to indicate that they must have existed for millions of years previously, perhaps as naked soft-bodied forms, incapable of leaving traces of hard parts in the rocks. It is conceivable that the comparatively acid seas of early pre-Cambrian times, when the oceans were more or less free from the salts that accumulated in later ages by erosion from the continents, made the formation of shells of carbonate of lime impossible. Later, when the seas accumulated much calcium in solution, shells were formed, perhaps at first, as one of the by-products of excretion, and later utilized and perfected as a means of protection.

The shell is the secretion of the mantle, a thin, fleshy fold of tissue that surrounds the upper part of a mollusk's body. As indicated above, it is largely of carbonate of lime, and is laid down as a deposit on a base of delicate horny substance produced by the animal, and spoken of as *conchyolin*. Usually, the shell is composed of three layers: an outer layer of horny integument, rough in character, or raised in hairlike projections in some shells; in others, a rough or smooth porcelainlike layer of vertical calcite crystals; beneath this, a second calcite or aragonite layer with the crystals laid in another direction; and, finally, a porcellanous layer like the first. Shells that have an iridescent or pearly lining are usually the more primitive species. In such cases, the two outer layers are very thin, while the inner pearly layer takes up the greater thickness of the shell. This is composed of thin minute plates of calcite arranged horizontally with their edges overlapping like tiny shingles. The light diffracted from the close-set lines produced by these edges causes the iridescent effect. The substance of this layer is generally spoken of as *nacre*.

From the economic standpoint, mollusks have always been of great importance to the human race. The bivalves, or two-shelled mollusks, furnish an enormous food-resource, while the gastropods, or single-shelled, snail-like forms, as well as the squids and octopuses, have contributed their part, though to a lesser degree.

The oyster, clam, and scallop fisheries are by far the most important. Millions of dollars are invested in their development, and thousands of men and great numbers of vessels are employed. Mussels, cockles, and razor-shells are also eaten, especially in foreign countries. Among the gastropods used for food in various parts of the world are periwinkles, whelks, conchs, and the luscious abalone.

For other economic products than food, the pearl-oyster is of outstanding importance, not only for the precious pearl occasionally produced, but also for the mother-of-pearl, which is used extensively for the manufacture of buttons, knife handles, inlays, and all kinds of fancy ornaments. All nacreous shells of other species have varying value in this respect, the most important being the fresh-water clams, abalones, top-shells, and the turban shells. Certain cowries have been used for money in the Far East and the Pacific Islands, while the American Indians used shells of the hard clam for making wampum. The tusk-shell also was utilized for this purpose by the Indians of the northwestern states. Shells have been used for various utensils, such as spoons, knives, dishes, and basins. Tritons and conchs have been widely used as trumpets. The Purple Snails were crushed by the ancients and by many native Indian tribes to obtain purple dye. Shells are ground for road-making and burned to obtain lime. Many of the beautiful species are used for ornaments, such as necklaces, shield decorations, earrings, and the like. The great Orange Cowrie is highly prized as a mark of rank by Fiji chieftains. The larger and more beautiful shells are used as household ornaments and curios, while shell-collecting, in itself, has a widespread general interest.

Externally, the body of a mollusk is typically divided into three regions: the *head;* the *foot;* and the dorsal region, or *pallium*.

The *head* occupies the anterior region of the body. It is equipped with the mouth-appendages, when they exist, and most of the special sense organs. The *foot* is on the ventral side and is a prominent feature, being the chief organ of locomotion. It is variable in size and shape, but always takes the form of a projection of fleshy consistency and is highly muscular and contractile. The *pallium,* or *mantle,* is a very characteristic molluscan structure. It takes up the entire dorsal part of the animal, and consists of a fold of skin enveloping the rest of the body to a greater or less degree, enclosing beneath it the breathing organs (*ctenidia*), and secreting, on its exterior surface, a protective shell of calcified material, which assumes great diversity in form, color, and ornamentation. It is the most familiar and conspicuous of molluscan features, as described above. Being a hard structure, covering a soft, but growing body, it must continually increase in size to keep pace with that of the body. Its area is increased around the margin by secretions from the edge of the mantle, which is thick and vascular, while the thickness is added to by secretions from the entire outer surface of the mantle itself. The horny epidermis, present on the exterior of the majority of shells, is also laid down by the mantle edge.

Special muscles fasten the shell to the body. These are paired and symmetrical in the various groups of mollusks, except the Gastropoda, where a single asymmetrical muscle attaches the body to the internal twisted spire of the shell, known as the *columella.* The soft body of the mollusk is unsegmented internally. The digestive system consists of a tube passing from mouth to anus. It is enlarged anteriorly to form the *buccal cavity,* or "throat," and includes the oesophagus. A sceond enlargement forms the stomach, which is followed by the tubular intestine. The latter is more or less straight in the primitive forms, like Amphineura, but is thrown into loops and folds in bivalves and snails. In the coiled or twisted body of the latter, the intestine may be twisted forward so that the anus opens anteriorly near the head.

In the buccal cavity may be found the *mandibles,* or jaws, and that characteristic structure peculiar to the mollusks, known as the *radula.* This is a ribbonlike organ, covered with transverse rows of tiny, rasplike teeth arranged according to different patterns in different genera and species, thus aiding classification. There is typically a central tooth, though this may be absent, with the others forming a symmetrical series on either side; the numbers, form, and size varying with the species. The radula usually moves backward and forward over the end of a cartilage, like a pulley, thus aiding the mandibles in grinding up the food.

A digestive gland, or liver, pours its secretion into the stomach, efficiently digesting the food and then absorbing it into the system. It also aids in excretion.

The important cavity, known as the *coelom,* found in varying extent and location in most animal groups above the Coelentera, like that forming the serous-lined peritoneal cavity of vertebrates, occurs among the mollusks, represented by the genital, pericardial, and renal cavities. These are entirely separate from the connective tissue-lined circulatory cavity, partly specialized as heart and blood vessels and partly composed of irregularly expanded blood sinuses. The blood may be colorless, or may be bluish or red; the latter color is due to the presence of hemoglobin in solution or in the form of corpuscles. Breathing may be taken care of by featherlike gills (ctenidia or branchiae). In Nudibranchs, it is performed by branched extensions of the mantle, and in air-breathing landsnails (Pulmonates), by means of a *vascular sac,* or lung. Excretion is largely the function of special *renal sacs,* or kidneys, which are usually associated with the genital cavities and the pericardium, in varying combinations in the different molluscan groups, in utilizing coelomic ducts to connect with the outside.

The specialized nervous system is composed of a series of paired ganglia connected by commissures, which send out fine nerves to the various organs of the body. This system is found, in varying degrees of complexity, throughout the different molluscan groups. The simplest and most typical system occurs in Amphineura. The most fundamental features are (1) the *cerebral ganglia,* paired ganglia, above or lateral to the mouth, with nerves supplying the eyes and tentacles; (2) the *pedal ganglia,* situated in the foot and below the oesophagus, supplying the foot; and (3) the *pleural ganglia,* above the pedal ganglia, and also below the oesophagus, innervating the mantle, branchiae, heart, and other visceral organs; the latter through the *visceral ganglia* (to which they send a nerve-trunk), as intermediary.

The Mollusca are also characterized by passing through a free-swimming larval stage in their life history, known as the *trochophore* or *veliger* stage. The trochophore is a top-shaped larva which, in its general characteristics, reminds one of similar larvae in the Phylum Annulata and the Phylum Prosopygia, as well as the top-shaped adult of Rotifera.

The Phylum Mollusca is divided into five main Classes, as follows: (1) *Amphineura,* or chitons and their relatives; (2) *Pelecypoda,* or bivalves; (3) *Scaphopoda,* or tusk-shells; (4) *Gastropoda,* or snails; (5) *Cephalopoda,* including squids, cuttlefishes, and octopuses.

CLASS AMPHINEURA

This Class includes the Chitons and related forms. They are the most primitive of living mollusks. Most of them have an oval, creeping body, either with calcareous spicules imbedded in the tough cuticle or with a jointed armor of eight transverse plates (INDEX PLATE 177). Externally, they have a certain serial repetition of body-parts, and breathe by means of a double row of repetitive plumelike gills (ctenidia). Internally, segmentation is also suggested by a ladderlike series of transverse nerves connecting the longitudinal, paired, pallial, and pedal nerve cords. Otherwise, however, there is no trace of segmented or repetitive parts in the internal organization.

The narrow mantle cavity is enclosed by an overarching fold of the integument around the lateral and posterior margins of the body. The primitive nervous system has just been described. There is usually a radula.

Order APLACOPHORA

The species of this Order have somewhat cylindrical, wormlike bodies, but no shell, which is represented only by calcareous spicules projecting from the mantle which covers the body completely, leaving only a median longitudinal groove on the ventral side. A ridge inside this groove is the vestigial foot. Two branchiae, the anus, and a pair of renal openings are located in the cloacal cavity at the posterior end of the groove, which is the remnant of a mantle cavity.

Neomenia carinata Tullberg. The body of this peculiar form is short, stumpy, and slightly curved. The two ends are symmetrical with the mouth and anal openings similarly placed and directed ventrally. There is a keel on the dorsal surface. The body is covered with spicules. There is no radula. This species occurs in the North Atlantic Ocean.

Chaetoderma nitidulum Loven. The body is wormlike, cylindrical, and about 1 inch in length. The head is distinctly marked by a transverse groove, separating it from the body. There is no ventral groove. The sexes are separate. This species occurs on muddy bottoms along the North Atlantic Coast at a depth of about 100 fathoms.

Order POLYPLACOPHORA
(Chitons)

This group is distinguished by the dorsal armature of eight transverse calcareous plates. In the various species, these plates differ in details of form, sculpture, and color patterns. The posterior margin of each plate overlaps the anterior edge of that behind it (INDEX PLATE 177). Each plate is composed of two layers, of which the lower (*articulamentum*) extends forward beneath the overlapping portion (*tegmentum*) of the plate in front. The surrounding fold of the mantle (*girdle*) secures the ends of the plates. In the surrounding mantle cavity, six to eighty pairs of branchiae are located. There is an insignificant head with no tentacles. Peculiar, special sense organs

PLATE 177

CLASS AMPHINEURA

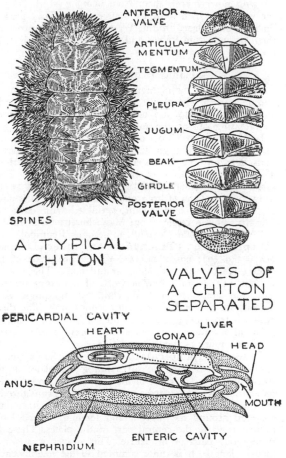

ANTERIOR VALVE

ARTICULA-MENTUM

TEGMENTUM

PLEURA

JUGUM

BEAK

GIRDLE

POSTERIOR VALVE

SPINES

A TYPICAL CHITON

VALVES OF A CHITON SEPARATED

PERICARDIAL CAVITY

HEART

GONAD

LIVER

HEAD

ANUS

MOUTH

NEPHRIDIUM

ENTERIC CAVITY

LONGITUDINAL SECTION OF A CHITON

(*aesthetes*) are in definite clusters on the shell surface. In some species, these are actually eyes. The foot occupies the entire ventral surface. It is used both for locomotion and as a sucker to hold firmly to the rocks.

Chitons are universal in their distribution, usually in shallow water, especially at the water's edge, where their clinging powers keep them from being washed away by the waves or pried loose by their enemies. They feed on diatoms and algae. In the West Indies, the natives pry them up with thin knives and cook them for food, under the name of "sea beef."

Family Ischnochitonidae

In this family, the plates are of comparatively large size and uncovered. The pleura are quite smooth. The anterior and posterior plates are articulated similarly. There are no radiating ribs on the anterior plates.

Lepidochiton (Tonicella) marmorea (Fabricius) PLATE 189 (6). The girdle is smooth, with no scales or hairs. The *umbo* of the posterior plate is situated anteriorly. The combined outline of the shell-plates is oval. Their surface is very finely granulated. There are from twenty to twenty-five pairs of branchiae. The total length is about 1½ inches. The color is buff, sprinkled with dark red. The distribution ranges from Massachusetts northward to the Arctic Ocean, and extends to become circumpolar.

Lepidochiton (Trachydermon) ruber (Linnaeus) PLATE 189 (7); COLOR PLATE XV, 2. The girdle of this species is covered with fine granulations. The shell is smooth, but shows a fine network of markings under a lens. The color is yellowish with red mottlings, while the interior of the shell is a conspicuous pink. The distribution is from Long Island Sound northward and circumpolar, also common on European shores. It occurs from low-water mark to about 80 fathoms.

Chaetopleura apiculata (Say) PLATE 189 (5); COLOR PLATE XV, 1. The girdle surrounding the plates in this species is hairy. The color of the shell is gray or yellowish, sometimes varying toward a red tinge. A keel runs through the center. The plates are sown with tubercles, irregularly scattered around the margin and tending toward longitudinal rows in the central part of the plates. There are twenty-four pairs of branchiae. This species is about ¾ inch in length. It is quite common in the neighborhood of the low-tide mark or below, along the entire east coast from Cape Cod to Florida.

Family Cryptochitonidae

The shell-plates, in this family, are reduced and largely covered by the smooth or, in the adults, somewhat hairy girdle.

Amicula vestita (Broderip & Sowerby) PLATE 189 (8). The shell-plates are nearly covered by the girdle, leaving exposed a series of central heart-shaped areas. The posterior plate has a slit on either side and a sinus located centrally. The shell-plates are light grayish, while the thin girdle covering them is brown, showing the outline of the plates beneath. These Chitons are about 2 inches in length. They occur commonly along the New England coast, north of Cape Cod in about 5 to 30 fathoms.

CLASS PELECYPODA
(Clams, Oysters, and Their Relatives)

These are the bivalves, or two-shelled mollusks. The mantle is divided into two lobes which completely enclose the soft-bodied animal, folding over the back and extending over the visceral mass, including the foot, on both sides. Each lobe of the mantle secretes a shell, which, at first, is very small, but as the animal with its mantle grows, the shell is enlarged to correspond, new successive layers being laid down underneath by the outer surface of the mantle, thus increasing the shell's thickness, and new material being added to the margin by the secretions of the mantle's edge, thus increasing the area. The successive stages are marked by the growth lines which can be readily seen on the exterior of the shell. The original shell is elevated above the hinge of the two valves forming a protuberance (*umbo;* plural, *umbones*) (INDEX PLATE 178). A ligament, or elastic band, holds the two shells together. Beneath this is the *hinge,* composed of interlocking teeth (*laterals*) which radiate forward and backward from the central teeth (*cardinals*) immediately below the umbones. The action of the elastic ligament is to keep the two valves open, but this is counteracted by two powerful muscles inside the shell, the anterior and posterior *adductor muscles,* the scars of which may be seen on the interior of the empty shell. In certain bivalves, such as the oysters and scallops, there is but one of these muscles, the posterior adductor, the other being not present. Two smaller scars mark the insertion of the *siphonal* and *pedal retractor muscles,* which pull in the siphons and foot respectively. A widely curving line connecting these (the *pallial line*) indicates the insertion of the many small muscles acting as retractors of the mantle margin. A wide indentation in this line (the *pallial sinus*), just below the posterior muscle scar, marks the position of the powerful siphonal retractor in species that possess large protrusible siphons. These latter structures are present in the majority of the bivalves and are modifications of the posterior mantle edges, which in these species are fused together at their edges, except posteriorly, where there are two openings, the lower or ventral one being the *incurrent opening* and the upper or dorsal the *excurrent opening*. Through the former, a current of sea water is brought into the mantle-cavity to aerate the gills and to furnish quantities of microscopic animals and plants for the mollusk's food. Through the latter, waste matter, the products of respiration, and ova and sperm from the gonads are expelled into the outside world.

In certain species, like the clams, these openings are prolonged in the form of tubes and are known as siphons. In more primitive species, such as the oyster, the mantle edges are open and the gills or branchiae merely establish a current flowing in over the anterior part of the branchiae, and flowing out near the anal portion.

The branchiae also show evolutionary modifications; primitive genera (*Nucula*) having elongate, narrow, and almost bipinnate ctenidia; while in forms like the common mussel, these have become broadened pairs of thin flaps on either side of the foot, each flap being reflected at its outer margins and turned backward. In the oyster and scallop, these reflected lobes are fused with the mantle at its inner origin and connected together by transverse processes in networklike fashion. This is the typical plan of the pelecypod gill.

The foot, among the bivalve mollusks, is merely a hatchet-shaped ventral prolongation of the visceral mass, extending downward on the median line between the two pairs of gill-flaps in such a position that it can be protruded between the two shells for locomotor or digging purposes. The hatchet shape of this structure is the origin of the name applied to the Class, namely, *Pelecypoda,* being derived from the Greek words, *pelekos,* hatchet, and *pous, podos,* foot.

The Pelecypoda are aquatic mollusks, most species being marine. They are of cosmopolitan distribution, mainly in shallow water on the Continental Shelf.

The Class is divided into three Orders: (1) *Prionodesmacea;* (2) *Anomalodesmacea;* and (3) *Teleodesmacea.*

Order PRIONODESMACEA

These are the more primitive Pelecypoda. The two lobes of the mantle are largely separate and open ventrally and posteriorly. No siphons are present, or are imperfectly developed. The gills are filiform and not reticulated. The shell is iridescent. nacre being present.

PLATE 178

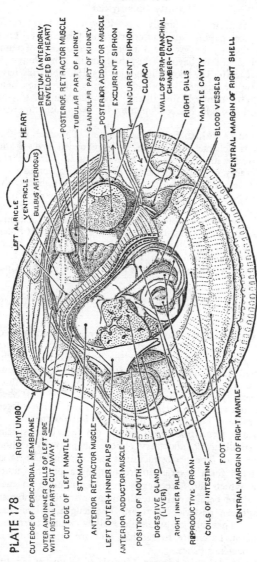

A TYPICAL BIVALVE, THE COMMON CLAM, SHOWN WITH LEFT SHELL AND MANTLE REMOVED

PLATE 178   RIGHT UMBO

CUT EDGE OF PERICARDIAL MEMBRANE

OUTER AND INNER GILLS OF LEFT SIDE
WITH DISTAL PARTS CUT AWAY

CUT EDGE OF LEFT MANTLE

STOMACH

ANTERIOR RETRACTOR MUSCLE

LEFT OUTER + INNER PALPS

ANTERIOR ADDUCTOR MUSCLE

POSITION OF MOUTH

DIGESTIVE GLAND
(LIVER)

RIGHT INNER PALP

REPRODUCTIVE ORGAN

COILS OF INTESTINE

FOOT

VENTRAL MARGIN OF RIGHT MANTLE

LEFT AURICLE
VENTRICLE
BULBUS ARTERIOSUS

HEART

RECTUM (ANTERIORLY
ENVELOPED BY HEART)

POSTERIOR RETRACTOR MUSCLE

TUBULAR PART OF KIDNEY

GLANDULAR PART OF KIDNEY

POSTERIOR ADDUCTOR MUSCLE

EXCURRENT SIPHON

INCURRENT SIPHON

CLOACA

WALL OF SUPRA-BRANCHIAL
CHAMBER (CUT)

RIGHT GILLS

MANTLE CAVITY

BLOOD VESSELS

VENTRAL MARGIN OF RIGHT SHELL

Family Solemyidae

The shell in this family has elongate, oval valves of equal size, gaping both anteriorly and posteriorly. They are covered by a thick, membranous *periostracum,* extending considerably beyond the shell itself. The hinge is without teeth. The foot is long and slender. The gills have one row of filaments pointing dorsally, the other ventrally. The mantle is fused below with an opening for the foot and a single, bilobed opening for use as an imperfect siphon.

Solemya velum Say PLATE 179 (1). The shell of this species is delicate and fragile. It is yellowish brown and is covered with a brown epidermis extending in scallops considerably beyond the fifteen radiating, impressed lines of the shell, often hanging down like a veil, hence the name. The latter is gray-blue within. It is usually buried in sand or actively swims about. It is about 1 inch in length. This species ranges from Nova Scotia to Florida.

Solemya borealis Totten. This is a similar, but much larger species, somewhat tan in color. It is about 2 inches in length and restricted to a more northern habitat than the preceding, ranging from Nova Scotia to the Connecticut coast.

Family Nuculidae
(Nut Shells)

In this family, the nutlike shell has valves of equal size, iridescent within. A large series of small even teeth forms the hinge, interrupted by a pit for the attachment of the ligament. The mantle is open ventrally and there are no siphons, nor is there a *byssus* (bundle of silken anchoring fibers) present. The gills are filiform. The oval shell has a one-sided, pointed umbo, with an olive-colored periostracum. The foot is adapted for burrowing.

Nucula proxima (Say) PLATE 179 (2). This species has a small, thick, and very oblique shape with a short anterior end. The periostracum is dark green. The large hinge-teeth form a series interrupted by a pit, on either side of which they are nearly at a right angle to each other, there being twelve teeth anterior to the umbones, and eighteen posterior to them. The length is less than ½ inch. They are common in shallow water from the Gulf of St. Lawrence to Florida, and are often found in the stomachs of fishes.

Nucula delphinodonta Mighels & Adams PLATE 179 (3). The shell is strongly ovate. There are three hinge-teeth posterior to the umbo and seven teeth anterior to it. This is a circumboreal species, ranging on this coast from

New Jersey to the Arctic. It occurs in from 6 to 100 fathoms.

Nucula tenuis Montagu PLATE 179 (4). This little shell is only ⅓ inch long and has quite a prominent umbo. There are approximately six teeth anterior to the umbo and nine posterior to it. It ranges from Labrador to Florida, in 4 to 100 fathoms, and deeper off Florida.

Family Nuculanidae (Ledidae)

The shell in this family has much the same character as in the Nuculidae, except that the valves are much drawn out posteriorly and are quite pointed at that end. Like the Nuculidae there is a line of teeth interrupted by a pit for the ligament, but, in this case, most of the teeth are posterior to it.

Nuculana (Leda) tenuisulcata (Couthouy) PLATE 179 (5). The shell is greatly elongated posteriorly. The mantle is open below, but there are small siphons adherent to each other. The shell is light green in color. The hinge has twelve anterior and sixteen posterior teeth. The measurements are about 1 inch long and ½ inch wide. It is quite common from southern New England northward, in shallow water, below the low-water mark.

Yoldia limatula (Say) PLATE 179 (6). This is a very attractive shell, with a smooth, polished surface, olive-green in color. It is quite compressed, with the straight, sloping, posterior end pointed, and gaping at both ends. There are two small, united siphons. The umbo is near the center, with twenty-two teeth anterior to it and eighteen on the posterior side. The shell is slightly less than 2 inches in length. This is a very active species. The long, extensible, and powerful foot enables it to leap for long distances. This species ranges from the Gulf of St. Lawrence to North Carolina and is quite abundant in moderate depths.

Yoldia sapotilla Gould PLATE 179 (7). This shell is not so large as that of the preceding species, being slightly more than 1 inch in length, but it is of similar coloration, being a pale yellowish green. It is so thin that it is translucent. The umbo is in the center, there being sixteen teeth on each side. It ranges from North Carolina to the Arctic Ocean, but is particularly abundant off Cape Cod, where it is much sought after by fish for food. It is found in depths of from 4 to 100 fathoms.

Yoldia myalis (Couthouy) PLATE 179 (8). This is a similar species to the preceding, but with a somewhat shorter slope to the shell posteriorly, and longer in proportion anteriorly. It occurs from Labrador to Massachusetts, in from 7 to 100 fathoms.

Yoldia thraciaeformis (Storer) PLATE 179 (9). This shell is somewhat kidney-shaped, rounded anteriorly, and considerably broadened posteriorly. It is open both anteriorly and posteriorly. It is about 2 inches long and more than 1½ inches wide, giving it a comparatively bulky appearance. The umbo is a little anterior of center, with twelve teeth on each side. The species ranges from Long Island Sound to the Arctic, in fairly deep water.

Yoldia obesa (Stimpson) PLATE 179 (10). The shell of this species is fragile and very small, being only ¼ inch in length and ⅛ inch wide. It is oval in shape, longer and somewhat tapering posteriorly. The umbones are nearer to the rounded anterior end than to the posterior. The hinge-teeth are small, ten being anterior and twelve posterior to the umbones. It is yellowish green in color. It is found off the New England coast in relatively deep water.

Family Arcidae
(Ark Shells, Box Shells)

This is a large family with many species found in all warm seas. The shell is heavy and boxlike, with a dense periostracum. The umbones are near the posterior end of the shell and are separated by a dorsal, diamond-shaped area for the externally situated ligament. The hinge consists of a long, even row of small comblike teeth, similar in size and shape. The mantle is open below. The large foot is pointed and with a heel-like lobe. Posteriorly, there is an opening shaped like the figure 8 to serve instead of siphons, which are lacking. There are two hearts and the blood, in some species at least, is red in color.

Arca occidentalis Philippi (= Arca noae Linnaeus) PLATE 179 (13); COLOR PLATE XIII, 1. The Noah's Ark Shell. This shell is heavy, oblong, and almost quadrangular. The prominent umbones are situated anteriorly, and quite far apart, due to the wide dorsal depression where the external ligament is attached. Both the anterior and posterior margins of the shell are truncated. Ventrally there is a wide gap in the mantle to permit the

---

Key to PLATE 179

1. *Solemya velum;* 2. *Nucula proxima;* 3. *Nucula delphinodonta;* 4. *Nucula tenuis;* 5. *Nuculana (Leda) tenuisulcata;* 6. *Yoldia limatula;* 7. *Yoldia sapotilla;* 8. *Yoldia myalis;* 9. *Yoldia thraciaeformis;* 10. *Yoldia obesa;* 11. *Arca incongrua;* 12. *Arca ponderosa;* 13. *Arca occidentalis (Arca noae);* 14. *Arca campechiensis pexata;* 15. *Arca secticostata (Arca lienosa);* 16. *Arca transversa;* 17. *Arca campechiensis americana;* 18. *Arca holmesi;* 19. *Pectunculus (Glycymeris) pennaceus.*

PLATE 179

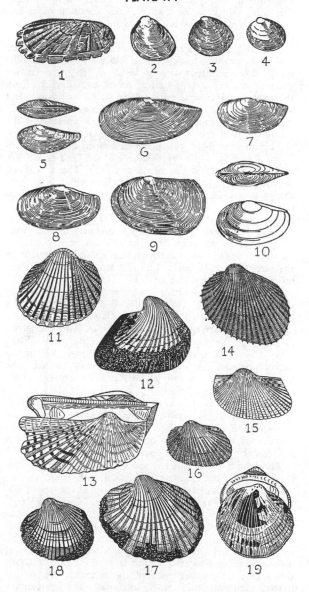

extension of the byssus; in this case there is a silken rope-like cord, which forms a strong attachment to rocks and hardens into plates of horny substance that may be shed and renewed.

The hinge, in this species, consists of a straight, even, and uninterrupted line of about fifty comblike teeth. The shell is ornamented with a series of about thirty-five grooved and expanding, fanlike ridges, radiating out from the umbo and crossed by tigerlike stripes of brown and yellow. A remarkable feature is the series of compound eyes, or ocelli, which Patten has shown occurs along the middle fold of the thickened mantle-edge of this species.

This shell is about 3½ inches in length. It ranges from North Carolina to the West Indies and the Gulf of Mexico.

Arca incongrua Say PLATE 179 (11). This is a short, rounded, and somewhat arched shell, with a wide ligamentary area and, therefore, well-separated rounded umbones. There are numerous small teeth forming the hinge, gradually becoming smaller from the two ends toward the center. The valves are unequal in size, with about twenty radiating flattened ribs on each side, and about ten additional ones around on the posterior side of the strongly arched shell. The ribs tend to have repeated cross-ridges on their surface.

This mollusk is white in color and about 2 inches in diameter, measuring the same in all directions across the shell. It is distributed from North Carolina to Texas.

Arca ponderosa Say PLATE 179 (12). The Ponderous Ark Shell. This is a heavy and greatly arched shell. When viewed sidewise, it is almost perfectly heart-shaped, as the valves are equal in size and symmetrically curved. The umbones are situated somewhat forward, strongly bent posteriorly, and are widely separated by the dark brown ligamentary area. There are about thirty-two radiating ribs, crossed by successive ridges, especially toward the ventral portion of the shell. The general color is cream-white, but the lower part of the valves is covered by a heavy, furry, dark brown epidermis.

The length of the shell is about 2 inches. The mollusk ranges from Massachusetts to Florida and Texas.

Arca campechiensis pexata Say PLATE 179 (14). The Combed Ark Shell. Bloody Clam. This is a large species, about 2½ to 3 inches in length. It is very abundant throughout its range and is noted for the fact that it has red blood, which is unusual among mollusks. The shell is obliquely oval, with round, almost hemispherical umbones, slanted anteriorly, and from these radiate about thirty ribs. The upper ends of the umbones are arched toward each other until nearly in contact. The ligamentary area is very narrow. The ribs are broad and flat, separated by narrow grooves which are often terminally fringed by tufts from the dark brown epidermis, or periostracum, which covers the lower part of the shell with shaggy fibers.

This species ranges from Massachusetts to North Carolina.

Arca secticostata Reeve (= **Arca lienosa** Say) PLATE 179 (15). This is a large Arca, about 3½ inches in length. It is elongated horizontally with the conspicuous umbones well elevated, and situated somewhat anteriorly, slanting moderately in the same direction. There are about thirty-five ribs. The hinge is quite long, and with numerous small teeth. It is white in color with a shaggy, brown periostracum.

The distribution is from North Carolina to Florida and Texas.

Arca transversa Say PLATE 179 (16). The Transverse Ark Shell. This species has a rhomboidal shell with the umbo directed moderately forward. There are about thirty-five ribs. The ligamentary area is long and narrow. The color is brown. The shell is about 1½ inches long and 1 inch wide. Its ribs are sculptured deeply and marked by cross-striae. The range is from New England to the Florida Keys.

Arca campechiensis americana Wood PLATE 179 (17). The American Ark Shell. This is a large species with the central umbo slanting anteriorly. There are about thirty-five ribs, each grooved longitudinally, and with deeply cut interspaces. The posterior end of the shell is expanded, while the anterior end is contracted. The ligamentary area is narrow, with umbones curving toward each other and nearly meeting on the median line.

This species is abundant from North Carolina to Florida and Texas.

Arca hølmesi Kurtz PLATE 179 (18). This is a closely related species but smaller. It is likely that the range is similar to the preceding.

Pectunculus (Glycymeris) pennaceus Lamarck PLATE 179 (19). The Feathered Bitter Sweet Shell. The shell is orb-shaped, with equal valves and with the hinge-teeth in a semicircle, all equal in size, but strongest at the ends. The animal has a crescent-shaped foot. The mantle is open and bordered with small ocelli. The umbones are high and nearly meet on the median line. The surface of the shell is marked with wide low ribs, marked, as well as the interspaces, with fine longitudinal lines. These are crossed by transverse lines giving a latticed effect. The shell is about 1¼ inches in diameter.

The Bitter Sweets are southern shells, ranging from North Carolina to Florida and the West Indies.

Family Pectinidae
(The Scallops)

This family includes the scallops of commerce and their relatives. The shell is orb-shaped, and with more or less unequal valves, the right valve being the smaller, and usually the one which is underneath. The mollusks may be either free or attached. In the latter case, either the under-shell may be fixed like an oyster, as in the genus *Hinnites,* or, in the case of young Pectens, a silken byssus may be secreted, the adults, however, becoming free in most species. The notch, through which the byssus was ma-nipulated, still remains in the shell and the byssus can be secreted at will. The adult scallops jump in rapid zigzag flights, by opening and closing their valves with such force that the expelled jet of water drives the animal a yard or more in a straight line through the water, after which it will shoot off in another direction, thus avoiding capture, if pursued. The mantle is open below. Its double edge is bordered with a curtainlike sensitive fringe, above which is a continuous row of steely blue eyes, each with a lens, retina, and optic nerve connected with the pallial nerve that runs around the edge of the mantle. The powerful single adductor muscle closes the shell and is opposed by the elastic ligament, the contraction of which, acting over the wide hinge as a fulcrum, snaps the shell open.

Each valve has radiating ribs, the ends of which closely interlock with the edge of the opposite valve. The umbo is a central, pointed beak. There are no teeth, but the liga-ment is quite long and narrow, holding the valves close together. The larger portion of it, however, is internal to the umbo and is solidly compact, with a firm insertion in a shallow pit. A conspicuous winged ear stands out on either side of the umbo.

Pecten irradians Lamarck COLOR PLATE XIV, 4. The Common Scallop. This is the edible scallop of our markets and is the most common scallop along our coast, where tons are dredged every year by the scallop fishermen. Only the large, tender adductor muscle is eaten, the rest of the mollusk being discarded. This is a large species, about 2 or 3 inches in diameter, with seventeen to twenty radiating ribs, rounded like furbelows, with somewhat narrower rounded grooves between, the shell being evenly scalloped around the margin. The wings are large and about equal in size. The color varies from gray to white, to yellowish brown or reddish, and usually shading into purple near the hinge. Sometimes various contrasting colors in bars are seen on the same shell. There are thirty to forty bril-liant blue eyes on the mantle margin.

This species is abundant from Cape Cod to Cape Hatteras, but especially so in the northern part of its range. It is also found locally farther north.

Pecten islandicus (Müller) PLATE 180 (1); COLOR PLATE XIV, 4. Iceland Scallop. This species is so called because it was first found near Iceland, though it is one of our well-known species. The valves are approximately equal in size, the left valve, as usual, being somewhat more arched than the right one. There are more than fifty fine radiating ribs of more or less scaly texture. The valves are handsomely colored, being banded concentrically in dark and light bars passing over purple, red, orange, and pink in different specimens, some of these colors even shading into each other on the same specimen. The wings on either side of the umbo are strikingly unequal in size, the anterior being the larger of the two. The diameter is about 3 inches. It ranges from Cape Cod to Greenland in about 10 to more than 100 fathoms.

Pecten dislocatus Say PLATE 180 (2). This is the southern counterpart of our common scallop, being abundant from North Carolina southward to Florida. It has arching valves with many close-set ribs, gaily decorated over a white ground with zigzag crossbars or mottlings of red or yellow, or variegated with an unusual assortment of colors and patterns. It is about 1 to 2 inches in diameter and is found in shallow water, especially in muddy regions.

Pecten ornatus Lamarck PLATE 180 (3). The Ornate Scallop. This is another southern form, spotted or blotched with red or purple, a few ribs being left free from the color pattern. Small bracketlike cups occur on some of the ribs. The posterior ear is practically lacking. This species measures 1 inch or less in diameter. It ranges doubtfully north into the Carolina region but commonly from Florida to the West Indies.

Pecten magellanicus (Gmelin) [= **Pecten grandis** (Solander)] PLATE 180 (4); COLOR PLATE XIV, 6. Giant Scallop. Deep Sea Scallop. This is the largest American scallop, measuring 5 to 6 inches across the firm, even shell. The upper valve is somewhat convex, the lower one practically flat. The valves gape anteriorly. The ears are practically symmetrical on either side of the small pointed umbo. Numerous fine, radiating ribs and grooves are crossed by concentric lines of growth, often in the form of delicate, upturned scales. The lower valve is practically white. The inside of the valves is polished white, also with fine radiating lines.

This mollusk is northern in range, which extends from New Jersey to Labrador. It is especially abundant off the coast of Maine in 10 to 100 fathoms.

Pecten nodosus Linnaeus PLATE 180 (5). The Knobbed Scallop. There are about ten strong ribs each with a series of raised knobs. These show as hollows on the inner side of the shell. Both valves are flattened and nearly equal in size. The color is dark orange or red. This is a very striking mollusk, about 4½ inches in height. It ranges from North Carolina, around the coast of Florida to the Gulf of Mexico.

Family Mytilidae
(The Mussels)

This family contains the commonest and most abundant of bivalves. Their elongate, narrowed shells are found on the shores of all continents. They hang in masses on wharf timbers. They cover mud flats with a continuous carpet, and all stationary or floating objects near the low-tide mark and for some distance between the tides, on rocky cliffs. They invade barnacle and oyster beds, and, in the latter respect, are a problem to fishermen. In European countries, they are an important source of food and so form the basis of a profitable industry. This would, doubtless, also be true in our own country were not oysters much more profitable and desirable here.

The shells of mussels are equivalved with the umbo at or close to the anterior end. As a rule the hinge is without teeth. The ligament is internal and long. The foot is cylindrical and spins a strong, coarse, hairy byssus, which has great clinging power. There is often a thick and coarse periostracum. There are two siphons connected at the base. Otherwise, the mantle is open. There are two leaflike gills on each side of the visceral mass, attached at their dorsal edges. There are two adductor muscles, the posterior being the larger. The shell is dark colored, dark brown, blue, or almost black. The interior often has a pearly, iridescent lining.

Mytilus edulis Linnaeus PLATE 180 (6); COLOR PLATE XIII, 2. The Common Edible Mussel. The anterior margin varies, being straight, convex, or concave, probably depending upon conditions of pressure in the crowded colony. The

---

Key to PLATE 180

1. *Pecten islandicus;* 2. *Pecten dislocatus;* 3. *Pecten ornatus;* 4. *Pecten magellanicus;* 5. *Pecten nodosus;* 6. *Mytilus edulis;* 7. *Mytilus exustus;* 8. *Mytilus recurvus* (*Mytilus hamatus*); 9. *Modiolus modiolus;* 10. *Modiolus demissus plicatulus;* 11. *Modiolus tulipa;* 12. *Modiolaria* (*Musculus*) *substriata,* 13, 14. *Modiolaria* (*Musculus*) *nigra;* 15. *Modiolaria* (*Musculus*) *corrugata;* 16. *Crenella glandula;* 17. *Modiolaria* (*Crenella*) *lateralis.*

PLATE 180

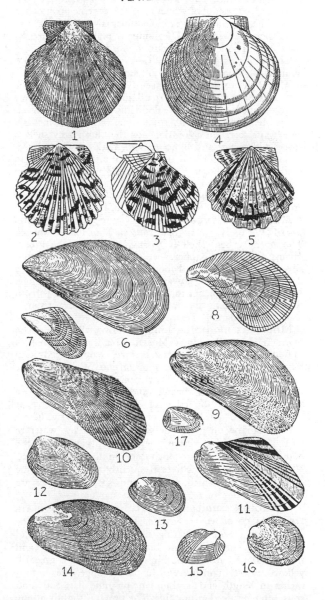

byssus is provided with a special opening. There are four teeth under the umbo, which is at the extreme apex of the shell. The general color is violet-blue, covered by a bluish black horny epidermis. The lining is pearly, margined by dark blue. The length is about 2½ inches.

The range is from North Carolina to the Arctic and abundantly along the European shore.

Mytilus exustus Linnaeus PLATE 180 (7). The Scorched Mussel. This is a small southern mussel. It may be recognized at once by the decidedly fan-shaped extension of its shell anteriorly, its small size (about 1½ inches), and by its scorched coloration, for the bluish gray shell is rayed with ocher and blotched with dark brown and red, both on the exterior and interior of the shell. It occurs in shallow water, clinging to other shells with its byssus in tangled masses.

The distribution is from North Carolina southward and around Florida to the Gulf of Mexico.

Mytilus recurvus Rafinesque (= **Mytilus hamatus** Say) PLATE 180 (8). The Bent Mussel. The Hooked Mussel. The strongly bent shell is twisted just below the umbo, giving the hooked appearance. The numerous radiating ribs often branch toward the posterior end. The color is a dark purplish, varying toward brown with a greenish tinge. It is from 1 to 2 inches in length. The distribution is from Rhode Island along the entire North Atlantic Coast southward to Florida and Texas.

Modiolus modiolus Linnaeus PLATE 180 (9); COLOR PLATE XIII, 3. The Horse Mussel. This is a large shell, 4 to 6 inches in length, of coarse texture, wedge-shaped, with the umbo at one side of the anterior end, but near it. The shell is more swollen in this region than elsewhere. The periostracum is dark brown and often produced in a ragged fringe at the edge of the shell. The animal is orange or red. The interior of the shell is pearly. These mussels burrow in gravel or sand from shallow water to 80 fathoms or more. Often, they prefer places on a rocky bottom to obtain secure anchorage in the rock crevices. This species and its relatives frequently spin a nest of the byssal fibers, in which pebbles and shell fragments are matted, as a den of refuge on the sea-bottom.

Modiolus demissus plicatulus (Lamarck) PLATE 180 (10); COLOR PLATE XIII, 4. The Ribbed Mussel. The shell has numerous radiating ribs, coarser posteriorly and much finer anteriorly. The brittle shell is delicately and finely scalloped around its thin edge. The color is greenish yellow, iridescent inside with a purple tinge. It is 2 to 3 inches in length and is abundant on mud flats and sand spits, often exposed at low tide. The umbo is slightly at one side of the apex, as in the previous species. This is not an edible species. It ranges from Prince Edward Island to South Carolina and Georgia.

Modiolus tulipa Linnaeus PLATE 180 (11). The Tulip Mussel. This is a small, but strikingly colored mussel. It is about 2 inches in length, yellowish brown, posteriorly striped with darker brown, while the inside of the shell is dark purple. The umbo is at one side of the apex. It ranges from North Carolina to the West Indies.

Modiolaria (Musculus) substriata (Gray) PLATE 180 (12). The approximately oval shell is widest at about its middle, with a prominent umbo near the anterior end. The valves are moderately arched and with coarse lines of growth. They are divided into three clearly distinguishable areas, the first located anteriorly, in front of the umbo, having about eight radiating ribs, with flat spaces between. The second is practically smooth, while the third or posterior area is separated from the second by a clearly elevated ridge running from the summit of the umbo straight to the outer margin of the shell, just where it turns upward for its posterior marginal sweep, and with an abrupt disjunction at the edge. This posterior area has numerous fine radiating ribs. The color of the shell is olive-green, shaded with chestnut. The interior shines like brilliant silver. The edges of the anterior and posterior areas are finely wrinkled. The shell is about 1 inch in length. It is northern in range, occurring from New York to Greenland, in 5 to 100 fathoms. It is also circumpolar and European.

Modiolaria (Musculus) nigra (Gray) PLATE 180 (13, 14). As this shell becomes older it changes from its original rusty brown or purple color to black. The shell is thin and the umbo is more distant from the anterior end than in previous species. The fine, concentric growth lines are crossed by numerous fine radiating ribs, producing the effect of a network. The inside of the shell has a silvery sheen, with the radiating lines visible. It averages ¾ inch to 1 inch in length, and ranges from Greenland to North Carolina, and from 1 to 60 fathoms of depth.

Modiolaria (Musculus) corrugata (Stimpson) PLATE 180 (15). This is a small species, being only ½ inch in length. The oval valves are considerably arched giving a heart-shaped effect to the shell when viewed from its anterior aspect. There are the three areas usual for this genus, with about sixteen ribs in the anterior area; ribs of minute fineness in the middle area; and fairly crowded, but distinct, ribs in the posterior area. Microscopic crosswrinkles are visible under a microscope. The color is yellowish green. The interior has a silvery luster. The range is from Greenland to North Carolina, in depths from 2 to 100 fathoms. It is also circumpolar and doubt-less European.

Modiolaria (Crenella) lateralis Say PLATE 180 (17). This little shell exhibits a series of finely beaded ribs on the anterior and posterior areas. The minute concentric growth lines are distinct. The inner margin is toothed except medially. The shell is conspicuously a deep chestnut color, becoming darker toward the umbones. It has the habit of spinning a fibrous nest. In length, it varies from ¼ to 1 inch.

The distribution is from Delaware Bay to Florida and the West Indies.

Crenella glandula Totten PLATE 180 (16). These are tiny mussels that are especially characterized by their habit of nest-building or of hiding among corals or alga hold-fasts. They have a thick epidermis, brown or yellow in this species, and pearly inside. The inner edge of the margin is toothed. The shell, as a whole, is oval, highly arched, somewhat truncate anteriorly, and rounded posteriorly. The umbones are not prominent. Numerous radiating lines are crossed by minute lines of growth giving a beaded effect. The length is about ¼ inch. It is a handsome, minute species, abundant on muddy bottoms. It ranges from Labrador to North Carolina, in depths of from 3 to 60 fathoms.

Family Anomiidae
(Jingle Shells)

The shell, in this family, is thin, almost translucent, and rounded. The two valves are unequal, the upper, or left valve, being the larger and dome-shaped; the under, or right valve, being smaller, concave, and perforated with a large hole through which the calcified byssus is exserted to fasten the mollusk firmly to a rock or another shell. The posterior adductor muscle is the larger of the two. There are no siphons and the mantle is open to the hinge. The foot is cylindrical but much reduced because of the permanently fixed habit of life.

Anomia aculeata Müller PLATE 181 (1, 2, 3). The Spiny or Thorny Jingle Shell. This shell is distinguished

Key to PLATE 181

1, 2, 3. *Anomia aculeata*; 4, 5. *Anomia simplex*; 6. *Periploma fragilis*; 7. *Periploma leanum*; 8. *Thracia conradi*; 9. *Thracia truncata (Thracia septentrionalis)*; 10. *Thracia myopsis*; 11. *Pandora gouldiana*; 12. *Lyonsia hyalina*; 13. *Lyonsia arenosa*; 14, 15. *Ostrea equestris*; 16. *Plicatula gibbosa*; 17. *Avicula atlantica (Pteria colymbus)*; 18. *Pinna (Atrina) serrata (Pinna seminuda)*; 19. *Lima scabra*; 20. *Lima squamosa*.

PLATE 181

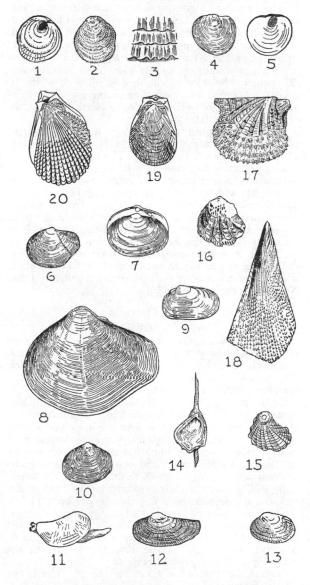

by the prickly scales that cover the upper valve (Figure 1). The lower valve (Figure 2) is very thin with an almost circular perforation. It is usually found along with the next species, and for the most part, attached to stones. The detail on the plate (Figure 3; after Gould) shows how the concentric edges formed by the lines of growth are thrown into folds to produce the prickly scales along the radiating rib vestiges. The color of this shell is yellowish white. It is smaller than the next species, measuring only ½ inch in diameter. It ranges from Labrador to North Carolina, at depths of 1 to 80 fathoms.

Anomia simplex d'Orbigny (= **Anomia ephippium** of various authors) PLATE 181 (4, 5); COLOR PLATE XIV, 1. The Smooth Jingle Shell. The Plain Jingle Shell. The upper valve is rounded, with an irregular margin, sometimes oval and occasionally jagged edges. The lower valve is flat with an ovate perforation (See Figures 4 and 5 on the plate). The shell is pale golden-yellow or with a silvery sheen, with a greenish pearly iridescence. It is usually 1 inch in diameter, but may be much larger. It is the upper valve of this species that is often thrown up on the beach. It is often fastened on oysters and stones. On scallops, its surface molds itself to conform to the surface sculpture of the scallop shell. It occurs abundantly from Nova Scotia to the West Indies.

Family Ostreidae
(The Oysters)

In this family there is but one genus, *Ostrea,* and about fifty species, among them the important oysters of commerce. There are but two species within our range, *Ostrea virginica* and *Ostrea equestris.* In describing them, we are describing the family as well.

Genus **Ostrea** Linnaeus. The shell is irregular, with unequal valves, the left being the larger. This is cemented to some fixed support and is immovable by the animal throughout its life. The rough and heavy shell is lead-gray in color. The interior is white like porcelain with a deep muscle scar, violet in color, and nearly central in position. There is a thick hinge with no teeth, on which the upper right shell is articulated. It is located just internal to the umbo at the anterior end. The shell is kept open by the elastic ligament or pad, against which the powerful single adductor muscle works. This is actually the posterior adductor muscle, the anterior one not existing in this genus. The shell is extremely variable throughout its growth, occasionally attaining a considerable size.

Ostrea equestris Say PLATE 181 (14, 15). The Horse Oyster. This is a small oyster, of variable size, not considered edible. Six to twelve teeth of the larger valve fit into corresponding hollows of the smaller valve, which is convex and attached to some stationary object. The larger valve is rather flat and not greatly folded. The narrow, irregularly pointed hinge is curved. This species ranges from North Carolina to Florida, entirely overlapping the range of *Ostrea frons* Linnaeus (the Mangrove or Coon Oyster) which often grows in clumps on the aerial roots and stems of the mangrove in Florida and the West Indies, but does not occur far enough north to come within our range.

Ostrea equestris ranges from Cape Hatteras to Florida.

Ostrea virginica Gmelin COLOR PLATE XIV, 3. The Virginia Oyster. The American Oyster. This species is considered to be the most valuable invertebrate animal from a commercial standpoint. It is extremely abundant from Massachusetts to the Gulf of Mexico, and is locally abundant along the coast of Maine and Canada to the Gulf of St. Lawrence. It has been transplanted to the Pacific Coast. It is the counterpart, in European waters, of *Ostrea edulis* Linnaeus, which, however, is smaller and not of as great commercial value.

The American Oyster, when of commercial size, varies from 3 to 4 inches in length. Six-inch specimens are not uncommon, though not so highly esteemed, and oysters measuring 12 inches have been found in northern waters.

The early part of the summer is the natural breeding season for the oyster, when the mantle cavity is loaded with milky fluid containing the eggs or sperm, depending on the sex of the individual; for, in oysters, the sexes are separate. This fluid is emptied out into the open sea and fertilization takes place, resulting in the hatching of multitudes of tiny top-shaped larvae, the *trochophores*. These metamorphose, in a day or two, into *veliger larvae,* which secrete the beginnings of a shell and settle down on some hard and rough object, perhaps, by good fortune, the dead shells of the clutch, where they are anchored immovably for the rest of their life. There, they feed and grow, also taking advantage of the lime-impregnated water to add to their shells. By this means, they endeavor to protect themselves from their enemies, for their mortality is very great.

It is estimated that a single large female oyster lays as many as 60,000,000 eggs at a time. Averaging oysters of all sizes, a conservative figure would be about 25,000,000. Many of these are caught in currents and drift out to sea. Many are consumed for food by copepods and other small crustaceans, while bottom-fishes and crabs devour great quantities, or even crush the shells of the young, developing oysters before they become too hard. The survivors are not secure, even after they have built up the stony shells; for starfishes, whelks, and sand-collar snails are able to force open or drill through the heavy shells. The oyster-drills and starfishes apparently do the most damage. The former bore tiny pinholes through the shell with the rasping teeth on their radulae and suck out the soft parts. The starfishes either envelop the smaller oysters with their five arms until they are smothered, or may even pry them apart by the opposing pull of their multitudinous tube-feet, until the oyster-valves open, and the starfish, everting its saclike stomach through its mouth-opening, inserts it like a swab between the oyster-valves, pours out digestive ferments, and digests the soft body *in situ*. It is remarkable that, in spite of the many enemies, so great an abundance of oysters can remain to form the most remunerative invertebrate fishery of our coasts.

Family Spondylidae
(Spiny Oysters, Thorny Oysters)

These mollusks have irregular shells and are attached to solid objects by the right valve. They have heavy radiating ribs, often with leaflike growths of spines. The hinge is formed of two interlocking, curved teeth in each valve. Many species are found in warm seas and are brightly colored.

Spondylus americanus Lamarck (= **Spondylus echinatus** Martyn). The Thorny Oyster. The Chrysanthemum Shell. This is a typically tropical species, but just verges into the southern limits of our territory at Cape Hatteras, and so will be briefly mentioned here. The shell is colored red, white, or purple with a border of the same color around the inner margin. The radiating ribs are ornamented by spines which vary from needlelike to broad and flat, or to irregular foliaceous expansions. Six of the ribs are more prominent than those between. The interlocking hinges are so closely fitted that they must be broken to separate them. The shell measures from 2 to 6 inches across. They range from North Carolina to the West Indies and the Gulf of Mexico, where the largest specimens occur.

Plicatula gibbosa Lamarck (= **Plicatula ramosa** Lamarck) PLATE 181 (16). The Plaited Shell. The Cat's Paw. The shell of this species is small, about 1 inch in length. It is irregular and clumsy in shape, and quite solidly built. It has six or seven radiating, rough folds making a fanlike pattern, and extending out from the margin with a saw-toothed effect. The color is white, variegated with yellow on the folds, and with red or gray markings. The range is from North Carolina to the West Indies.

Family Pinnidae
(The Pen Shells)

These remarkable fragile shells are triangular or wedge-shaped with the approximately equal valves gaping at the posterior expansion. There are no hinge teeth present on the laterally located hinge region. The ligament is in a long groove. The foot is proportionately long and is noted for its power of spinning a powerful byssus. Large muscles fasten the two valves together.

Pinna (Atrina) serrata Sowerby (= **Pinna seminuda** Lamarck) PLATE 181 (18). This species has delicate scales that are erected on the radiating ribs and are largest on the posterior part of the shell and are projections of the lines of growth. They become smaller and fewer anteriorly and toward the umbones. On this part, they become so insignificant that here the shell is practically bare, thus accounting for the scientific species name, *seminuda*, indicated above, as applied by Lamarck. The shell is brownish, semitransparent, and iridescent within. It is 6 to 10 inches in length. The muscles of this species are sold in the markets as large scallops and are in demand for that purpose.

It ranges from North Carolina to the West Indies in moderately deep water.

Pinna (Atrina) rigida Dillwyn (= **Pinna muricata** Linnaeus) COLOR PLATE XIV, 2. The Prickly Pen Shell. This is a larger and thicker shell with the hinge line nearly straight, sometimes curving inward. The strong ribs are beset with triangular scales or, at times, tubular. The color is dark brown. The ventral part of the shell tends to have prickles instead of scales. The length is 6 to 9 inches as a rule, though shells a foot in length are known, especially when growing under favorable conditions on a clean, sandy bottom.

One of the striking features for which the Pen Shells are famous is the remarkable byssus which they manufacture. In many shells of other species, the byssus is black and often coarse. In the case of the Pen Shells, it is exuded from the foot as a glutinous substance and passed through many fine holes. The delicate strands resulting from this process harden as golden threads, as fine as, if not finer than, silk. From ancient times, this soft-textured substance derived from the Mediterranean species of this genus (*Pinna nobilis* Linnaeus) has been woven into a fine cloth known commercially as "tarentine." It is also known as cloth of gold. Articles made of this marine silk can be folded into a remarkably small space, a pair of gloves fitting into a walnut shell. Black pearls of considerable value are also taken from *Pinna* shells.

Family Pteriidae
(Pearl Oysters, Wing Shells)

The valves of the shells in this family are very unequal, the smaller, or right valve, always being underneath. The shell is oblique with radiating lines or bands extending from the umbones to the margin. The hinge line is greatly elongated and straight. An ear extends out from either side of the umbo, the posterior one being prolonged and more or less pointed to form a wing. Beneath the wing of the right or undervalve is a notch for the byssus. There is a small foot and the mantle margins are free. This family is almost entirely confined to warm and tropic seas, where the species yielding pearls and mother-of-pearl abound.

Avicula atlantica Lamarck (= **Pteria colymbus** Roeding) PLATE 181 (17). The Atlantic Wing Shell. The shell is somewhat arched. Radiating bands of white from the umbones to the shell margin diversify the brown color of the shell, the bands being marked with brown arrowheadlike spots. It is 3½ to 4 inches in length. On this coast, it ranges from North Carolina to the West Indies.

Family Limidae
(The File Shells)

In this family, the shells are obliquely oval and equal in size. There are small, earlike projections of the valve on either side of a triangular ligamentary pit, beneath the umbo. The mantle is baglike and open, bordered with minute eyes. The anterior end is straight with the axis of the shell, while the posterior border is evenly rounded. The valves are yellowish or white, with the surface thrown into close-set radiating ridges made up of overlapping, pointed scales, suggesting a rasping function, hence the name, file shells.

Lima scabra Born PLATE 181 (19). The Rough File Shell. Small, pointed, overlapping scales make up the ridges. The yellow shell is oval and thick. The marginal ends of the ridge project to give a scalloped effect to the edges of the shell. The hinge area is triangular. The length is from 2 to 5 inches. The distribution is from North Carolina to the West Indies.

Lima squamosa Lamarck PLATE 181 (20). The Scaly File Shell. The shell, in this species, is set obliquely to the shell axis. Twenty to twenty-four ribs, crowded close together, radiate to the shell-margin, expanding in width as they do so, like a fan. They are covered with overlapping oval scales. The delicate shell is white and from 1 to 1½ inches in length. This shell is widely distributed in tropical waters, ranging from Florida through the West Indies. It does not come into the northern fauna, but is included here as a typical representative of the group of which *Lima scabra* is a northern example.

The File Shells swim actively about like the Pectens, by opening and closing their valves.

Order ANOMALODESMACEA

The families of this Order are mostly burrowing forms and represent a number of specialized groups, some of which appear to be survivals of ancient types. The mantle lobes are mostly united except for two apertures for the siphons, an opening for the foot, and occasionally a fourth opening. There are two adductor muscles and well-developed siphons. The shell valves are usually unequal. The hinge-region is poorly developed without a hinge-plate. They are also hermaphroditic.

Family Periplomatidae
(Spoon Shells)

These shells are so-called because they have a spoon-shaped tooth in the hinge of each valve for the insertion of the ligamentary cartilage. There is also a small ossicle-like process in front of the teeth and an internal rib from the hinge to the posterior margin.

Periploma fragilis (Totten) PLATE 181 (6). The Fragile Spoon Shell. This species has a very fragile and delicate shell, whitish and pearlaceous in color. The right shell is arched more highly than the left. The umbo is prominent and the lines of growth show clearly. The shell is extended posteriorly. This is a small shell, being only ⅜ inch in length. It is found from Labrador to New Jersey in depths of 4 to 30 fathoms.

Periploma leanum (Conrad) PLATE 181 (7). The Lantern Shell. This mollusk is larger than the preceding, being a little more than 1 inch in length. It is a pearlaceous white with a yellowish tinge. The right valve is convex and the left valve flat. The umbo is prominent and central, the oval shell being symmetrically rounded at both ends, but slightly angular posteriorly, a diagonal ridge to the posterior margin being barely indicated. This species ranges from the Gulf of St. Lawrence to North Carolina below low-tide mark on sandy bottoms.

Family Thraciidae
(The Duck-bill Shells)

These are shells with nearly equal valves, oblong, not greatly arched, extended posteriorly and gaping over the separate siphons. The shell is thin. The umbones are prominent, one being perforated.

Thracia conradi Couthouy PLATE 181 (8). The Giant Thracia. This is the largest species of the genus, being as large as the Soft Clam (*Mya arenaria* [COLOR PLATE XIII, 9]). The prominent, somewhat pointed umbones slope to the rounded anterior end, which sweeps around to an undulating ventral margin. The posterior end is expanded and truncate over the siphons. The ridge from the umbo to the posterior angle of the margin is quite clear. The point of the left umbo fits into a perforation in the right. The shell is an ashy white, with pearlaceous texture showing through. It is thin and fragile. The species ranges from Labrador to North Carolina, being especially abundant off the New England coast in 3 to 16 fathoms.

Thracia truncata Mighels & Adams (= **Thracia septentrionalis** Jeffreys) PLATE 181 (9). The Truncated Duck-bill Shell. This shell is short and rounded anteriorly. Posteriorly, it is extended and abruptly truncated, the umbones being thrown to the right. The shell is small, rather solid, and white, with a pale yellow epidermis. A ridge runs from the umbones to the posterior marginal angle. The ligament is rather large and the callosity is not spoon-shaped. The length is ¾ inch. It ranges from Greenland to Block Island.

Thracia myopsis Müller PLATE 181 (10). This little shell is solid, deep oval, with the umbones prominent and nearly centrally located, from which the shell slopes to the rounded anterior margin. It is short and truncated posteriorly, where it gapes for the siphons. The concentric lines of growth are conspicuous. The hinge callus is thick posteriorly and not clearly spoon-shaped. It is 1 inch long and ⁷⁄₁₀ inch high. The mantle is closed, the foot large and tongue-shaped, and the siphons separate and well developed. It ranges from Greenland to Massachusetts in 10 to 50 fathoms.

Family Pandoridae
(The Pandora Shells)

The shell, in this family, is small, with unequal valves, which are very thin and flat, with umbones inconspicuous. The color is white and the shells iridescent within. The right valve is flat and the left one slightly convex. The hinge has three teeth set at an angle to each other, fitting into grooves in the opposite shell.

Pandora gouldiana Dall PLATE 181 (11). This delicate and beautiful little shell is pearly-white and oval in shape. The hinge-line is usually concave and slopes upward anteriorly to the obtusely angled umbo, from which it rounds in a semicircular sweep on the anterior end to the gently curving ventral margin. Thence, it rises abruptly to the opening for the siphons at the upper posterior angle. The upper edge has two wrinkled diverging lines from the umbones. The shell is iridescent within. The mantle is closed except for an anterior marginal opening for the long, fingerlike foot, and the small upper posterior opening for the two short diverging siphons. These are purplish in color and fringed with filamentary projections. The length of this shell is 1 inch. Its range is from Prince Edward Island to North Carolina.

Family Lyonsiidae

These are small shells with unequal valves, somewhat triangular in shape and of pearly luster. There is a narrow ledge inside the shell for the attachment of the ligament. There is also an ossicle. The siphons are quite short and almost united, and fringed with filaments. The foot is slender, with a groove for the byssus.

Lyonsia hyalina (Conrad) PLATE 181 (12). The Transparent Lyonsia. The Glassy Lyonsia. The shell is very translucent, fragile, and of pearly luster. The umbones are prominent. The shell is rounded anteriorly and quite prolonged posteriorly. The umbones bend anteriorly. The valves have many radiating lines crossed by concentric wrinkles. Minute surface fringes cover the shell and catch sand-grains which often coat the valves. This species is found on sandy bottoms in shallow water from the Gulf of St. Lawrence to Texas. It is about ¾ inch in length.

Lyonsia arenosa (Müller) PLATE 181 (13). The Sandy Lyonsia. The Fingernail Shell. This shell is about the size of a fingernail, being about ½ inch in length. It is briefly rounded anteriorly and expanded and truncate posteriorly. The valves are strongly arched. It is gray-white in color, and has many radiating ridges which entangle sand. It occurs from Greenland to Cape Ann, Massachusetts, in from 13 to 60 fathoms.

Order TELEODESMACEA

This large Order includes the rest of the two-shelled mollusks. They are characterized by the possession of reticulate gills; that is, gills having a fine meshwork of gill filaments instead of simple parallel filaments, as in the Prionodesmacea. The edges of the mantle lobes are largely connected on the ventral and posterior margins.

Family Pleurophoridae
(The Black Clams)

These are large clams with a heavy, oval shell, closing tightly at the even margin. The valves are equal in size. There is a conspicuous ligament, showing outside, posterior to the umbones.

Cyprina islandica (Linnaeus) PLATE 182 (1). The large, conspicuous umbones point obliquely forward and also are directed inward so decidedly that they almost meet. There is a heavily developed periostracum in living specimens, forming a shaggy, shining, black covering. The length is from 3 to 4 inches. It is especially abundant in the northern part of its range, which extends from the Arctic Ocean to Cape Hatteras. It occurs in 6 to 90 fathoms, but is often tossed up on the beach after storms. In its general aspect, it resembles the Venus or Hard Clam (*Venus mercenaria*), but is without the purple border within the shell.

Family Astartidae

These are small brown bivalves, somewhat triangular in shape, with thick shells, and conspicuous concentric grooves and lines of growth. Two or three cardinal teeth are well-developed in the hinge, the laterals being weaker. The umbones are prominent and practically central.

Astarte castanea (Say) PLATE 182 (2). The Chestnut Astarte. The shell in this species is rich, reddish chestnut. The animal's body is bright red. The lining of the shell is clear white. It is about 1 inch in length. The range is from Nova Scotia to Cape Hatteras.

Astarte undata Gould PLATE 182 (3). The Wavy Astarte. The shell is dark brown, and distinctly marked with about ten to twenty-five concentric wavy ridges. The central umbones curve inward until they meet above the hinge. The interior of the shell is shining white. It is about 1½ inches in length. The distribution is from Labrador to Chesapeake Bay, in depths of from 5 to 104 fathoms, the greater depths of occurrence being the more southerly.

Astarte borealis Schumacher PLATE 182 (4). The Northern Astarte. This shell is of deep oval outline. The shell is irregularly grooved with concentric ridges, tending to disappear toward the margin. The outer surface is white with a yellowish brown periostracum. An abundant

---

Key to Plate 182

1. *Cyprina islandica;* 2. *Astarte castanea;* 3. *Astarte undata;* 4. *Astarte borealis;* 5. *Venericardia borealis;* 6. *Lucina tigrina* (*Conakia orbicularis*); 7. *Loripinus chrysostoma* (*Lucina edentula*); 8. *Lucina filosa;* 9. *Divaricella quadrisulcata;* 10. *Kellia* (*Chironia*) *suborbicularis;* 11. *Lepton lepidum;* 12. *Kellia* (*Rochfortia*) *planulata;* 13. *Turtonia minuta;* 14. *Aligena elevata* (*Montacuta bidentata*); 15. *Cardium pinnatulum;* 16. *Cardium magnum* (*Cardium robustum*); 17. *Cardium ciliatum* (*Cardium islandicum*).

PLATE 182

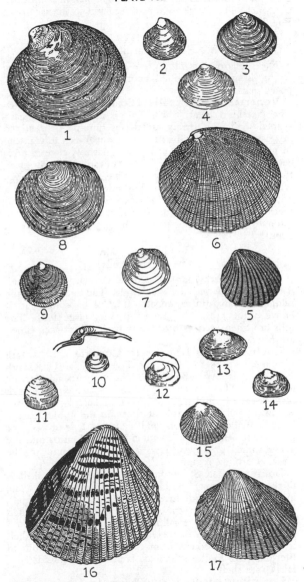

food for walruses in the far north. The length is upwards of 1 inch. The range is from Greenland to Massachusetts Bay, in 15 to 100 fathoms.

Family Carditidae

The shells of this family are characterized by the two strong hinge-teeth and an additional stout, erect tooth, posteriorly.

Venericardia borealis (Conrad) PLATE 182. (5). The Northern Heart Shell. This is a rounded to heart-shaped shell with strong radial ribs running in a curved fan from the apex to the margin, about fifteen to eighteen in number and rounded above with narrow, close grooves between. The umbones are curved inward to nearly meet, thus making a heart-shaped outline when viewed side-wise. The lining of the shell is shining white, contrasting with the dark brown periostracum of the exterior. This species is 1 inch in length. The distribution is from Labrador to Cape Hatteras, ranging from 3 to 250 fathoms of depth.

Family Lucinidae
(The White Shells)

The shell, in this family, is quite circular, with a small flattened umbo and a clear lunule. The shell is usually white. The margin is smooth. It folds back upon itself between the gills. The hinge has very large teeth. The gills are often used as brood-chambers and, at such times, are filled with eggs.

Lucina tigrina Linnaeus (= **Conakia orbicularis** Linnaeus) PLATE 182 (6). The Tiger Lucina. This handsome shell is large and heavy. The umbones are narrow and sharp. The surface is sculptured with a fine network of close-set ribs and lines of growth. The color is whitish yellow tinged with purple at times on the border. Abundant in shallow water on sandy bottoms. It is upwards of 3 inches in length. It is common through Florida and the West Indies to Texas. It is occasionally found in the North Carolina region.

Lucina filosa Stimpson PLATE 182 (8). The shell is thick and irregular with heavy lines of growth. The hinge-margin is straight. The umbones, though small, lean anteriorly over the smooth, narrow, and pointed lunule. There is one cardinal tooth in the left valve, and two diverging teeth in the right. The length of this shell is 1½ inches. It occurs from Casco Bay, Maine, south to Florida, in 16 to more than 500 fathoms. It is considered a fairly rare shell.

Loripinus chrysostoma Philippi (= **Lucina edentula** Linnaeus) PLATE 182 (7). The Apricot Shell. The

Buttercup Shell. This shell has large cup-shaped valves, bright yellow within and white outside. The outline is circular and the valves inflated. The teeth are rudimentary, and the area on which they are situated is a flat extension of the shell on either side of the umbo. The ligament of the living animal is bright red. The shell measures 1½ to 2 inches in diameter. It occurs on tidal flats and in shallow water as well as in moderate depths. The most northerly limit of its range is North Carolina and it is very abundant along the Florida coast and in the West Indies. In Florida, it is often used for making shell novelties.

Divaricella quadrisulcata (d'Orbigny) PLATE 182 (9). This is a white-shelled species, with a glossy surface that, starting with the posterior ridge, is decorated with close-set prominent grooves that run diagonally downward to the margin in both directions, on either side of the ridge. The diameter of the shell is 1 inch. This shell has a remarkably wide range, being found in 10 to 15 fathoms from Massachusetts to Brazil.

Family Leptonidae

In this family, the shell is minute, being 1/6 inch or less. The valves are equal in size. The hinge is variable. There is no pallial sinus. The mantle is united below, leaving three openings: a posterior anal opening; a median opening for the foot; and an anterior opening to supply the gills.

Kellia (Chironia) suborbicularis (Thomson) PLATE 182 (10). The shell is variable in form, but mostly round or quadrangular with rounded angles. It is thin and white in color, with a very thin epidermis. The umbones are nearly in the middle, small, pointed, and inclined inward toward each other. There is no lunule. The inside is white and polished. There are two teeth in one of the valves. The length is about ⅓ inch. The range is from Salem, Massachusetts, to Long Island Sound.

Kellia (Rochfortia) planulata (Stimpson) PLATE 182 (12). The shell, in this minute species, is nearly oval, white, and with a thin, purplish epidermis. The umbones are prominent and in contact with each other. A deeply excavated lunule is anterior to them. There are two muscular impressions with the pallial line between them without a pallial sinus. The hinge, in the right valve, consists of a single erect tooth. In the left valve there are two teeth, with a triangular space between to receive the tooth of the right valve. The length of the shell is ⅙ inch. This shell is found from the low-tide mark to about 48 fathoms and ranges from Nova Scotia to Texas.

Turtonia minuta (Fabricius) PLATE 182 (13). The length of this tiny mollusk is 1/12 inch. The shell is oval. The color is yellowish both within and without, but shades to purple at the umbones. It is usually attached by a byssus to stones and seaweed, commonly near the low-water mark. It is a northern species, extending from Massachusetts to Greenland, where it becomes circumboreal.

Aligena elevata Stimpson (= **Montacuta bidentata** Gould) PLATE 182 (14). This species, also minute, has a fragile, shining white, oval, or subtriangular shell, at times, with a thin straw-colored epidermis. Within, it is so polished that no pallial or muscular impressions are to be found. The hinge consists of two diverging teeth, one of which is excavated to receive the ligament. They are so arranged that they fit into the spaces between the teeth of the opposite valve. The length of the shell is less than ⅛ inch. The range is from Massachusetts to North Carolina.

Lepton lepidum Say PLATE 182 (11). This minute shell is quite symmetrical, the small but distinct umbo being exactly in the middle of the hinge area, with the anterior and posterior border of the shell arching in exactly similar and symmetrical curves to the rounded ends of the ventral margin. Numerous very fine ribs, separated by as fine intervals, pass from the umbo to the ventral border on each valve. They are crossed by about seven lines of growth, set at comparatively wide intervals. The valves are inflated.

Family Cardiidae
(Cockle Shells)

In this family, the valves are of equal size, and heart-shaped when viewed sidewise. The umbones are prominent and nearly centrally placed. The valves have saw-toothed margins. They often gape in the posterior region. The hinge-teeth are set in an arched pattern. The hinge has one or two cardinal teeth and two lateral teeth on each valve. The ligament is outside and posterior to the umbones. The pallial line is wavy posteriorly. The mantle is open anteriorly with ocelli on the border. There are two pairs of gills, connected posteriorly. The foot is large and compressed, without a byssus. The cockles are free and unattached mollusks.

Cardium pinnatulum Conrad PLATE 182 (15). This cockle has a small and fragile shell, quite thin and obliquely orb-shaped. The ribs are rounded with a creamy white general coloration, diversified by irregular brown markings. This is an abundant food for fishes, as is evidenced by the fact that the shells are often taken from their stomachs. It is a very active species, as it can travel about at a surprising speed by means of its long and powerful foot. The diameter of the shell is approximately ½ inch. It is found abundantly along the Atlantic Coast from Labrador to North Carolina.

Cardium magnum Born (= **Cardium robustum** Solander) PLATE 182 (16). The Great Cockle. The Strong Cockle. This cockle is one of the largest and finest cockles known. About twenty-seven to thirty deep and flat ribs are close set on its valves regularly radiating from the high, rounded umbo. The shell sweeps widely to its margin from the angle high up on its anterior side. The color is yellowish brown with spots and streaks of dark, purplish brown scattered over it. It is about 4 to 5 inches in length and is the handsomest as well as the largest cockle on the Atlantic seaboard. It ranges from Virginia to Brazil.

Cardium ciliatum Fabricius (= **Cardium islandicum** Lamarck) PLATE 182 (17); COLOR PLATE XIII, 8. The Iceland Cockle. It is an obliquely but transversely oval shell, with the anterior end shortest. The prominent rounded umbones are turned inward and nearly meet. There are about thirty-six spiny and angled ribs, flat at first on top and becoming rounded as they approach the margin. A gray-green to yellowish brown epidermis covers the whitish shell. The inside of the shell is light yellow. The reverse of the exterior sculpture shows within. The margins are distinctly notched. This shell is 2 inches long and 1 inch broad. It is abundant off the New England coast and ranges from the Arctic to Cape Hatteras.

Cardium muricatum Linnaeus PLATE 183 (1). The Southern Spiny Cockle. This is practically a circular-shelled cockle, the dorsal part of the outline rising on either side in a straight line to the pointed umbo. There are thirty-six ribs, all with the sharp cusps or scales. The spines of the middle ten to twelve ribs are pointed at a different angle from the rest. The yellowish valves are variegated by bands or streaks of purple or brown. The shell measures 1½ to 2 inches in diameter. This species ranges from North Carolina to the West Indies. It is quite common on the Florida west coast, in shallow water.

Cardium (Laevicardium) mortoni Conrad PLATE 183 (2). Morton's Cockle. This is a very smooth little shell. It is marked by a purple spot on the posterior margin and the bright yellow interior. It is not more than 1 inch in height. The figure shows the animal extended. It is abundant about Martha's Vineyard and Long Island Sound in 1 to 5 fathoms of depth. It is very brilliantly colored in Florida. Its distribution is from Nova Scotia to Brazil.

Laevicardium serratum Linnaeus PLATE 183 (3). Saw-toothed Cockle. This cockle has a fairly smooth shell, with a shining surface shading from white through light yellow to rose. It is 1 to 2 inches in length. It has a well-developed and powerful foot. Its range extends from North Carolina to the West Indies.

Serripes groenlandicus Bruguiere PLATE 183 (4). This shell is more compressed than the other species of this family described here. The small, centrally located umbones are slightly turned toward each other. The hinge lacks the cardinal teeth, although small lateral teeth are present. Radiating ribs are obvious on the anterior and posterior parts of the shell, especially on the latter, but are obsolete in the center. The lines of growth are coarse at intervals, between which finer ones occur. The shell is round anteriorly but is truncate and gapes posteriorly. The epidermis is olive-drab in color, and the shell outwardly somewhat resembles the Surf Clam, *Mactra* (see PLATE 185), but the hinge does not possess the spoon-shaped member characteristic of that genus. The edge of the foot is serrated, accounting for the generic name. This species is found at all depths from 2 to 260 fathoms, from Greenland to Cape Cod, Massachusetts.

Family Veneridae
(The Venus Clams)

This family is considered the group in which pelecypod shells have attained their best adjusted anatomical and physiological balance. In other words, these represent the highest attainment of bivalve evolution, including beauty of form and color as well as streamlined efficiency. The shell is thick and regular in shape, being evenly round or ovate. The hinge forms an efficient interlocking system with three cardinal teeth in each valve (INDEX DIAGRAM 178), the laterals being present in some species, while in others they are absent. There is a distinct and clean-cut lunule in front of the umbones and a prominent ligament behind them. The siphons are short, unequal in length, and more or less united with each other. The mantle margins are fringed. Both anterior and posterior adduc-

---

Key to PLATE 183

1. *Cardium muricatum;* 2. *Cardium (Laevicardium) mortoni* 3. *Laevicardium serratum;* 4. *Serripes groenlandicus;* 5. *Callocardia (Pitar) morrhuana;* 6. *Venus mercenaria;* 7. *Venus mercenaria notata;* 8. *Venus mortoni (Venus campechiensis);* 9. *Chione cingenda;* 10. *Liocyma (Tapes) fluctuosa;* 11. *Gemma gemma;* 12. *Callista gigantea (Macrocallista nimbosa);* 13. *Callista (Macrocallista) maculata.*

PLATE 183

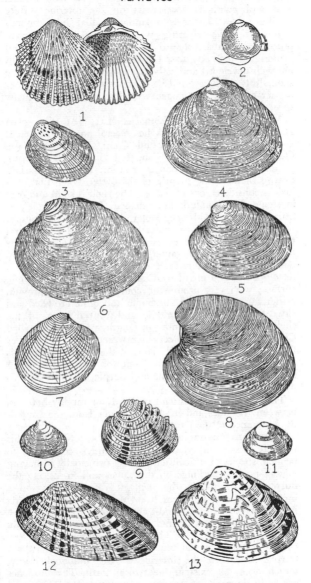

1

2

3

4

6

5

7

8

10

9

11

12

13

tor muscles are present and of equal size, with distinct oval and polished muscle-scars on the interior surface of the valves. There is a sinuate pallial line connecting them. The tapering well-developed foot is compressed and hatchet-shaped, being pointed anteriorly, and prolonging the body-mass ventrally. The two pairs of gills are well developed and rather quadrangular in shape. The shell shuts closely around its entire margin, with the inner border crenulated, or edged with fine markings, in many species.

Venus mercenaria Linnaeus PLATE 183 (6); COLOR PLATE XIII, 6. This mollusk has several popular names. It is variously called the Round Clam, Hard-shell Clam, Quahog, and Little Neck Clam. It is one of the most important of sea-food products, coming into the markets during the breeding months of the oyster, when that mollusk is considered out of season. The shell is solid and oval in shape. The lunule is heart-shaped. The inside is a porcellanous white, with deep violet blotches near the muscle-scars, and a purple or violet border around the ventral margin. There are three cardinal teeth present and the laterals are absent. The anterior end is short, the umbones being placed obliquely far forward, while the posterior is developed into a broad oval sweep. It has a dingy white surface, with very prominent, concentric lines of growth, rather far apart near the umbones and quite crowded and close together on the middle and ventral parts of the shell. It is 3 inches or more in length, while the so-called Cherry Stone Clams, as served in restaurants, are smaller than that, being immature clams of the same species. This is the shell that the Indians used for wampum, cutting small pierced beads of white and purple to string for this purpose.

These clams are abundant on sandy or muddy bottoms, between the tides and in shallow water from the Gulf of St. Lawrence to the Gulf of Mexico.

Venus mercenaria notata Say PLATE 183 (7). This form is closely related to the above and is considered to be a subspecies of it. It differs from it principally in having zigzag purple markings on the valves and in lacking the purple border within the shell. It varies from 3 to 4 inches in length. It ranges from Massachusetts to Florida in shallow water, but is most abundant in the South.

Venus mortoni Conrad (= **Venus campechiensis** Gmelin) PLATE 183 (8). This is also a closely related species. It has a large and much thicker shell and there is a purple blotch in the interior of the umbonal cavity, which does not exist in the typical form. The umbones are quite large in proportion. It occurs from Virginia to Texas and seems to take the place of *Venus mercenaria* in southern waters. It reaches a diameter of 6 inches, and its flesh is much coarser and of a stronger flavor than the northern species. It is eaten, nevertheless, by people in the Southern States, where it is often used for chowder.

Dosinia discus Reeve COLOR PLATE XIII, 7. This handsome shell is flat and circular in shape. It has a small, but prominent umbo, and the surface of the shell is sculptured by numerous fine and close-set concentric grooves. It has a thin, yellowish epidermis. When this is removed, the snowy-white shell beneath is disclosed. It is about 2½ inches in diameter. It is a relatively rare shell, ranging from Cape May, New Jersey to Vera Cruz, Mexico.

Callocardia (Pitar) morrhuana (Linsley) PLATE 183 (5). This mollusk somewhat resembles the Hard Shell, but is smaller and has thinner and more chalky valves, sometimes rusty in appearance. The shell is round and with arched valves. It has deeply incised concentric lines of growth. It is 2 inches in diameter. The distribution is from Prince Edward Island to Cape Hatteras.

Chione cingenda Dillwyn PLATE 183 (9). The shell is obliquely somewhat heart-shaped, with fine radiating grooves curving from the apex to the border of the shell. These are very close set on the anterior area. They are crossed by elevated flattened and thin-edged bands, indicating previous *varices* (former shell edges). These bands are more separated toward the apex of the shell and closer together toward the border. The shell is white with blotches or expanding stripes of red, purple, or bluish gray. The length of the shell is slightly less than 1 inch, the height ⅘ inch. It ranges from North Carolina southward.

Liocyma (Tapes) fluctuosa (Gould) PLATE 183 (10). The Wavy Carpet Shell. The shell, in this species, is thin, transversely ovate and one sided, the umbones leaning anteriorly. The hinge has three cardinal hingeteeth. The valves are white with a straw-colored epidermis. The siphons are separate beyond the middle, the incurrent tube with a branching tentacular fringe. The foot is equipped to spin a byssus. The shell has a series of concentric, wavelike lines of growth, forming compressed, thin ridges, inclined toward the umbones. The length varies from ⅘ inch to 1½ inches. This is a northern species ranging from Greenland to Nova Scotia.

Gemma gemma (Totten) PLATE 183 (11). The Amethystine Gem Shell. This shell is really a beautiful little gem. It is about the size of a pea, nearly orbicular, with the shining surface closely crowded with concentric furrows. The anterior part of the shell, toward the margin, is white or rose-color. The posterior and dorsal area is reddish purple. It is shining white inside, purple posteriorly, like the outside. It is very abundant in shallow waters of sandy coves, especially along the shore of New England, where it attracted the attention of the early settlers. It has a continuous distribution from Labrador to Cape Hatteras.

Callista gigantea Gmelin (= **Macrocallista nimbosa** Solander) PLATE 183 (12). The Giant Callista. This is a large and showy species, having an elongate porcelainlike shell with a smooth surface and even edges. The hinge and umbones are situated anteriorly, while the posterior part of the shell is long with a rounded point. The ground color is pale pink with radiating, diverging bands of lilac, crossing concentric bars of brown and blue to form a plaidlike pattern. The interior is white or, in some specimens, salmon-pink. It is typically a southern species, 4 inches in length, abounding in Florida sandy shallows, especially on the west coast. It overlaps into our area on the shore of North Carolina.

Callista (Macrocallista) maculata (Linnaeus) PLATE 183 (13). The Calico Shell. This is a very handsome species, popular with collectors, because of its gay plaid pattern of bright colors. It is oval, slightly triangular in shape, with a polished porcelainlike surface, having radiating bands of violet-brown broken into squarish spots on a yellowish buff background. There is a pattern of chevronlike markings, sometimes broken, between the bands. The length is from 2½ to 3 inches. It ranges from Cape Hatteras around the Florida Coast to the Gulf of Mexico and south to Brazil. It is more abundant on the Florida west coast than on the eastern shore.

Family Petricolidae
(The Rock Dwellers)

These are bivalve mollusks with greatly elongated shells, rounded shortly at the anterior end, and prolonged posteriorly to a narrowed curving termination. The hinge is practically toothless. The pallial sinus is deeply embayed. The thickened mantle at the margin is continued over the edge of the shell. It is closed anteriorly except for a small opening for the narrow, pointed foot. These animals bore into clay or soft rocks.

Petricola pholadiformis Lamarck PLATE 184 (1). The Rock Borers. The shell of the Rock Borer is an elongated, narrow oval. The umbones are far forward near the anterior end, which is very short and sharply rounded. The somewhat cylindrical shell is prolonged to a moderately gaping posterior termination for the outlet through which the long, narrow, divergent siphons may be extended. There are several strong, radiating ribs at the anterior end, but they are numerous, crowded, and fine throughout the rest of the shell, with the concentric growth lines emphasized at intervals. The length of this species reaches 2 to 2½ inches. It is found boring into clay and soft rocks, around the low-tide mark. The range is from Prince Edward Island to the West Indies and Texas.

Family Tellinidae
(Tellin Shells, Sunset Shells)

The shell, in this family, has equal valves, and is somewhat compressed, with the edges closing evenly. The valves are rounded anteriorly, but are angular and somewhat folded posteriorly. The hinge has two cardinal teeth. The umbones are usually posterior from center. The ligament is external and well developed. The fringed mantle is open in front to permit the extension of the long, flat foot. There is no byssus. The tentacles are remarkably long, separate, and very extensible. The gills are small and unequal. This is a large family, extending throughout the world, with about five hundred species known, of which only a few typical ones can be mentioned here. The shining, translucent surface of the shell, almost like porcelain, the graceful form, and variety and beauty of color place these mollusks with the Venus Shells as noteworthy for their attractive perfection.

Tellina tenera Say PLATE 184 (4). The Delicate Tellin. The shell is flat and fragile, a translucent white or rose in color and somewhat iridescent, with very fine concentric growth lines. The anterior end is rounded and the posterior end slopes somewhat more shortly and rounds to a point. There are two cardinal teeth in each valve, one being grooved. This species lives on sandy bottoms just below the water line. It is ½ to ⅔ inch in length. It occurs from Prince Edward Island to the Gulf of Mexico.

Tellina iris Say PLATE 184 (3). This is a thin, iridescent shell with faint yellow or rose-colored rays and circular patterns of rosy tint. The valves are cross-ridged and wrinkled on their upper surface. It is about ½ inch in length and ranges from North Carolina to the Florida Keys.

Tellina sayi Dall (= **Tellina polita** Say) PLATE 184 (2). Say's Tellin. This is a little, smooth, polished, white shell. The umbones are centrally located. It is rounded anteriorly and pointed posteriorly. It is ¾ inch in length. It is distributed from North Carolina to the Gulf of Mexico.

Tellina alternata Say PLATE 184 (5). This is a much larger species, being 2 inches or more in length, with a solid shell and broad, flat valves of shining white, light yellow, or rose color, and with widely spaced, concentric ridges. The umbones are somewhat posterior to the center of the shell, which has an angle and fold at the posterior end, but is broadly and bluntly rounded anteriorly.

Tellina similis Sowerby (= **Tellina decora** Say) PLATE 184 (6). The Pink-rayed Sunset Shell. This is a handsome shell, not quite 1 inch in length, with a convex shell with rosy pink rays expanding, fanlike, from the umbones to the elongated anterior margin of the shell with many fine sculptured rays between and beneath them. It has widely spaced concentric lines. The ventral edge of the shell is quite straight, and the short, posterior end is truncate and folded, with close-set rays posterior to the angle of the fold. This is one of the most beautiful of the Tellinas. It extends from Florida to the West Indies, and may possibly be found as far north as North Carolina, though this is doubtful.

Tellidora cristata Récluz (= **Tellidora lunulata** Holmes) PLATE 184 (7). This mollusk is largely represented by Pliocene and Pleistocene fossils from North Carolina to Florida and the Gulf States. It still survives, however, over the same area, especially in West Florida and south to Trinidad. It has a somewhat symmetrical triangular shell with slightly posterior umbones. The valves slope in a straight or slightly concave line anteriorly to the shell margin, and with a posterior ridge and fold to the hinder margin. The shell has heavy, fairly wide-spaced concentric lines of growth, intersecting the numerous finely sculptured rays radiating from the apex to the margin. It is about 1 inch in length. It occurs in shallow water below the low-tide mark.

Macoma balthica (Linnaeus) PLATE 184 (8). The Little Macoma. This is a small shell, less than 1 inch in length, deeply lenticular or slightly triangular in shape. It is thin, pure white, pinkish, or yellowish, when found on sandy bottoms; but in muddy regions, the shell is thick and bluish or dusky red. The interior is usually rose-colored. The valves are round anteriorly, but converging to a rounded point posteriorly. The range is from Arctic

---

Key to PLATE 184

1. *Petricola pholadiformis;* 2. *Tellina sayi (Tellina polita);* 3. *Tellina iris;* 4. *Tellina tenera;* 5. *Tellina alternata;* 6. *Tellina similis (Tellina decora);* 7. *Tellidora cristata (Tellidora lunulata);* 8. *Macoma balthica;* 9. *Macoma calcarea;* 10. *Macoma subrosea;* 11. *Macoma tenta;* 12. *Strigilla carnaria;* 13. *Strigilla flexuosa;* 14. *Psammobia lusoria;* 15. *Tagelus gibbus;* 16. *Tagelus divisus;* 17. *Donax fossor;* 18. *Donax variabilis;* 19. *Semele orbiculata (Semele proficua);* 20. *Semele radiata;* 21. *Cumingia tellinoides;* 22, 23. *Abra aequalis.*

PLATE 184

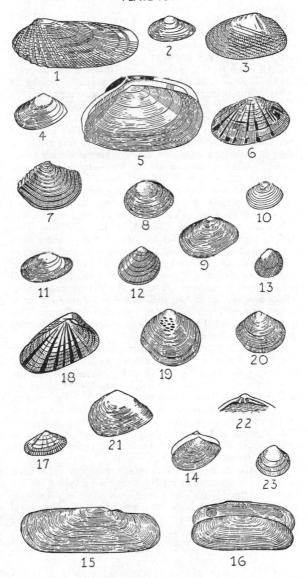

Seas to Georgia, in sheltered bays. It is also circumboreal in distribution.

Macoma calcarea Gmelin PLATE 184 (9). This is a thin, white shell of limy appearance with a greenish or somewhat olive epidermis. The rather insignificant umbones are situated somewhat posteriorly. There are two cardinal teeth in each valve and no laterals. The anterior end is broadly rounded, while the posterior border is rather abruptly narrowed to a bluntly curving angle. It is 1¼ inches in length and ranges from Greenland to Long Island Sound in 5 to 40 fathoms.

Macoma tenta (Say) PLATE 184 (11). This little oval shell has a shining white outer surface with fine radiating lines, the white interior also being white, but with a yellowish suffusion, and showing an indented radiating sculpture. The fragile hinge has two cardinal teeth on the right valve and one on the left valve. The posterior end gapes widely. It is ⅘ inch long. It ranges from Maine to Florida in sheltered harbors, floored with mud.

Macoma subrosea Conrad PLATE 184 (10). This shell is subtriangular, with the anterior and posterior sides sloping symmetrically from the centrally located umbones to rounded anterior and narrowed posterior ends. The shells are arched and very thin in substance. Minute, concentric lines of growth are quite distinct on each valve. The glossy surface of the shell is colored a rosy hue or is simply white. There is a pale brownish epidermis. This species occurs off the coast of New Jersey, in both Raritan and Delaware Bays.

Strigilla carnaria (Linnaeus) PLATE 184 (12). This is a small shell, less than 1 inch in length, deep rose in color near the apex, becoming paler toward the margin. The inside of the shell is also rich rose. The umbones are well developed. The surface of the shell is quite smooth, except for the numerous fine oblique lines which sculpture its valves and turn downward at a right angle posteriorly. This mollusk is very abundant from North Carolina to Brazil, especially just below the water line, in sandy shallows, in protected places.

Strigilla flexuosa (Say) PLATE 184 (13). This little orb-shaped shell is much smaller than the preceding species, being less than ½ inch in length. It is white in color with fine parallel striae which rise obliquely from the ventral margin and turn downward at a right angle over the posterior part of the shell. This species ranges from North Carolina to the West Indies.

Family Sanguinolariidae

The shells in this family are mostly convex and somewhat transparent. They are somewhat like the Tellinidae, to which they are closely related. They tend to have the sides of their shells more parallel and have very long siphons.

Tagelus gibbus (Spengler) PLATE 184 (15). The Stubby Razor Clam. The shell is quite elongated, having a length of about 4 inches, with equal valves, practically parallel sided, and only 1⅓ inches in height. It is rounded at each end. The umbones are somewhat posterior to central, in position, with two cardinals in each valve and no laterals. The foot remains exposed, extending from the shell anteriorly, as it is too large to be withdrawn into the shell. The extremely long siphons are separate and diverging for about three quarters of their length. The ligament is quite near the posterior end. The color varies from white to light yellow, with a yellowish brown epidermis. This mollusk is a mud-burrower, living in muddy bottoms in shallow water, below the low-water mark, where it digs in with its powerful foot, leaving only its long siphons exposed. Its range extends from Cape Cod, Massachusetts, to Florida and Texas.

Tagelus divisus (Spengler) PLATE 184 (16). This species is smaller than the preceding, the delicate, narrow elliptical shell being only 1½ inches in length. It has rounded ends, with the posterior narrower than the anterior. The umbo is nearly central. The surface of the shell is smooth, and yellowish gray in color, with a purplish tinge, and a band of purple or reddish passing posteriorly from the umbones across the shell. Inside the shell, it is also purple. This small species lives on shallow, sandy bottoms, usually in colonies of a number of individuals, from near the water line to somewhat deep water. The range is from Massachusetts to Florida, but it is more abundant in the south.

Psammobia lusoria Say PLATE 184 (14). This small species has an oblong, suboval shell with tiny concentric wrinkles. The anterior end is full and round, while the posterior end is narrowed and tapers to the rounded extremity. It is bluish white in color. The length is 1 inch and the height ⅗ inch. The range is from New Jersey to Florida.

Family Donacidae
(The Wedge Shells)

As the name implies, these shells are wedge-shaped. The posterior end is much elongated. Anteriorly, the shell is greatly shortened and truncate, the umbo being in a considerably forward position. The edge of the valves is usually crenulated. The ligament is external.

Donax fossor Say PLATE 184 (17). The Digger Wedge Shell. This species has a shell that is rounded posteriorly and somewhat prolonged in that direction. The radiating sculpture is overlaid with a thin layer so that it is smooth to the touch. The coloration is olive with bluish rays. The crenulations on the margin are fine but distinct. The length is about ½ inch. It is the most plentiful shell on the New Jersey coast, according to Maxwell Smith. It is abundant on the south shore of Long Island and ranges south to the Florida Keys, occurring in shallow water.

Donax variabilis Say PLATE 184 (18). The Variable Wedge Shell. The Pompano Shell. The Butterfly Shell. The Coquina Shell. This is one of the handsomest and daintiest of shells. The anterior end is truncate, just beyond the umbo, so that it is practically at a right angle to the rest of the shell. The posterior part is prolonged, taking up the greatest part of the shell, with a somewhat narrowed oval termination. The color is extraordinarily variable. Rays of color bands diverge fanlike from the umbones and are crossed by concentric bands in varying and contrasting hues, making every possible color combination, involving pink, rose, pale blue, green, yellow, white, lavender, fawn, and purple. Reddish brown bands frequently occur. The glossy inside of the valve also is suffused with color and is denticulated at the margin, so as to fit neatly and closely into the edge of the opposing valve. The shells are about 1 inch or less in length and range from North Carolina to Florida and Texas. They are very abundant on the Florida coast, between the tides and below the water line on sandy beaches, where they are gathered for making the delicious Coquina soup. The dead shells often spread out in pairs, looking like butterflies. They are frequently used for ornamental purposes.

Family Semelidae

The shells of this family are rounded to deep oval with an indefinite fold posteriorly. The umbones are practically central. There are two cardinal teeth and two laterals, the latter prolonged and tapering. These mollusks are mud- and sand-dwellers, digging with a powerful pointed foot.

Semele orbiculata (Say) (= **Semele proficua** Pulteney) PLATE 184 (19). The Orb-shaped Semele. As the name implies, the shell is orb-shaped. It is somewhat compressed. There is a small ligament. The umbones are nearly central with a lunule in front. There are strong, concentric lines of growth, sometimes expressed as wrinkles. The hinge has two cardinals on each side and long narrow laterals. The color is white to purplish. The length is about 1¼ inches. Its range extends from Virginia to the Gulf of Mexico and the West Indies.

Semele radiata (Say) PLATE 184 (20). The Rayed Semele. This related species also has orb-shaped shells, flat and slightly concave, posteriorly. The shell is white, sometimes with rays of rose color and lined with yellow. It is upwards of 1 inch in length. It occurs from Georgia southward.

Cumingia tellinoides (Conrad) PLATE 184 (21). The color of the valves is white in this species, except a yellow tinge near the apex. There are two cardinal teeth with a cup-shaped depression between them, and two very long laterals. The shell is broadly rounded anteriorly, but pointed and gaping posteriorly. The lines of growth are prominent. The length is ⅗ inch. The distribution is from Cape Cod to Florida. It also occurs as far north as Prince Edward Island.

Abra aequalis (Say) PLATE 184 (22, 23). The shell is orb-shaped with arched valves, which are rather thin and a polished white. The lines of growth show as very minute concentric wrinkles near the margin, which disappear dorsally and on the umbo. There are no lateral teeth, but there are two cardinals in the left valve and one in the right. The length is ⅖ inch. This species is found in fairly deep water from Connecticut to Florida and Texas.

Family Solenidae
(The Razor-shell Clams)

These are the true Razor-shells. They have greatly elongated shells, gaping at both ends and cylindrical in shape. There is a powerful cylindrical foot, capable of rapid digging. The siphons may be short and united, but in some species they are longer and divided at the ends. The gills are narrow and extend into the branchial siphons. These mollusks are usually found standing vertically, buried or partly buried, in the sand.

Solen viridis Say PLATE 185 (1). The Green Razor-shell. This mollusk is only about 2 inches in length. It is oblong and compressed. The hinge is nearly straight, but the ventral side is curved. The anterior margin is round, while the posterior end is obliquely truncated. The valves are open both anteriorly and posteriorly. The shell is smooth, with faint lines of growth, and is pale green in color. It burrows in shallow sand bottoms and is common from Rhode Island to Florida, but especially so in the southern part of its range.

Ensis directus (Conrad) PLATE 185 (2); COLOR PLATE XIII, 10. The Common Razor-shell Clam. The Sword-razor Shell. This is the common razor-shell of the Atlantic Coast of North America. It is the largest species of the family, being 6 to 7 inches in length. The shell is curved, truncately rounded, and has a long triangular area, due to the concentric lines of growth, which become parallel with the dorsal and ventral margins. The color is olive-green, with the triangular space a lavender-purple. This species lives on sandy bottoms at about the low-water mark, standing upright in the sand, the posterior end projecting up into the water with the siphons extended. If disturbed, it disappears as though by magic, shooting down out of sight in its burrow, drawn by the powerful action of its foot. Quick work with a shovel and bucket is necessary to dig the razor-shells out. Even when captured they are likely to spring out of one's grasp, propelled by the strong steel-spring-like action of the foot, which will send them yards away, when by a succession of jumps they will reach the water to disappear in a few seconds. The mollusk is larger than its shell, the foot projecting like a curved knife blade. The razor-shell is distributed abundantly from Labrador to the Florida Keys. It is quite edible, being sweet and of a fine flavor. Some people prefer it to any other kind of clam, though it is not extensively used in the markets.

Siliqua costata (Say) PLATE 185 (3). The Ribbed Pod Shell. This shell is elliptical, thin, and fragile. It is much compressed and the umbones are very minute. A rib reinforces the shell within the valve, extending from the upper edge, just posterior to the umbo, vertically downward, broadening somewhat to brace itself against the inside of the shell at about the middle point. The color of the valves is pale violet, blending into olive or light yellow-green. The length is 2 inches. This is quite a handsome and attractive shell, because of its coloration and smooth, glossy surface. It lives in sandy bottoms near the low-water mark, with a continuous distribution from the Gulf of St. Lawrence to North Carolina.

Siliqua squama (Blainville) PLATE 185 (4). The Scaly Pod Shell. This shell is thicker and more substantial than that of the preceding species. It is oblong-ovate, and with small umbones. The epidermis is very shining, yellowish green in color, and wrinkled. There is a prominent rib inside, bracing each valve, extending about halfway across the shell from the umbones. It is a larger mollusk than *Siliqua costata*, being about 3 inches in length. It is distributed over the fishing banks of Nova Scotia and along the New England coast.

Family Mactridae
(The Surf Clams)

In this family the shell-valves are equal in size, triangular, and often heavy. They close tightly or, at the most, are slightly gaping. The ligament is external or internal and, if the latter, it is contained in a deep, spoon-shaped pit. The hinge has two diverging cardinal teeth, with laterals usually present. The siphons are united, the openings being fringed. The gills are not prolonged into the branchial siphon.

Spisula (Mactra) solidissima (Dillwyn) PLATE 185 (5); COLOR PLATE XIII, 5. The Surf Clam. The Hen Clam. The shell of this species is large, solid, and somewhat triangular. It is the largest bivalve on the Atlantic seaboard, measuring up to 7 inches in length. The shell is thick and heavy. The umbones are nearly central, being at the apex of the shell. The hinge is very strong. The cardinal tooth is small and V-shaped. The lateral teeth are long, thin, and transversely striated. There is a large spoon-shaped receptacle for the internal cartilaginous ligament on the inside, just below the umbones. The surface of the valves is smooth or slightly roughened by the concentric growth lines and a thin, olive-brown epidermis is present. This clam lives in the surf just under the sand of the beach. It is not as tender as the Hard Clam, but nevertheless is eaten and is especially sought after for clambakes. It ranges from Labrador to Cape Hatteras in considerable abundance.

Spisula (Mactra) polynyma (Stimpson) PLATE 185 (6). The height of this shell is greater in proportion to its length than in the preceding species. It can also be distinguished by the fact that the laterals are smooth, instead of being transversely striated, as in the Surf Clam. The impressions of the anterior and posterior adductor muscles are very large. The pallial sinus is deep. The epidermis is tough and yellowish brown, while the shell lining is bluish white. This is also a smaller shell, having a length of only 3½ inches, about half that of the Surf Clam. This shell has a wide northern distribution, ranging from Hudson Bay to Cape Ann, Massachusetts, and Georges Bank.

Mactra fragilis Gmelin PLATE 185 (7). The Fragile Surf Clam. This clam is a still smaller shell, being 3 inches in length. It is white or cream in color. The epidermis is yellowish, darker posteriorly where there is a series of distinct, radiating ridges. There are also present numerous fine concentric growth lines, very close together. The umbones are centrally located. The anterior end is rounded, while the posterior area has a ridge or fold with an obliquely truncate margin, gaping somewhat as an opening for the siphons. This species, though fragile, is at home in the surf. It is very widely spread, ranging from North Carolina to the Gulf of Mexico and Brazil.

Mulinia lateralis (Say) PLATE 185 (8). The Little Surf Clam. This is a small species, quite triangular in shape, with arched valves, which are smooth, except for the close-set, very fine concentric wrinkles. It is a favorite source of food for fishes. It ranges from New Brunswick to Texas and the West Indies.

Anatina (Raeta) canaliculata (Say) PLATE 185 (9). Hat Shell. Channeled Duck Shell. The shell of this species is white to yellowish white in color. The shape is oval to orb-shaped and it is very thin and fragile. It is handsomely marked with distinct, fairly wide-spaced, concentric ribs, leaving the spaces between them as evenly rounded grooves or channels. It is clear, shining white within, with a spoon-shaped receptacle for the internal ligament as a part of the hinge structure. This beautiful and delicate little shell is 2½ inches in length, and is commonly washed ashore on beaches from New Jersey to Brazil.

Anatina (Raeta) lineata (Say) PLATE 185 (10). The Lined Duck Shell. This shell is more prolonged and flaring anteriorly than that of the previous species. The posterior end is shorter, gaping, and more abruptly sloping, and has a radiating ridge. The color is white to yellowish. It is 2½ to 3 inches in length and occurs in rather deep water from New Jersey to Brazil and Texas.

Mesodesma deauratum (Turton) PLATE 185 (11). This is a northern species about 1¾ inches in length, with an ovate triangular shell and a thick and massive surface with lines of growth emphasized at intervals and covered with a brown epidermis. Within, the shell is glossy-white. There is a deep, spoon-shaped cavity for the internal cartilaginous ligament, with a widely diverging V-shaped tooth. On either side is a very strong lateral tooth with a cavity above it for the tooth of the opposite side to fit into. It occurs from the Gulf of St. Lawrence to Georges Bank.

Family Myacidae
(The Soft-shell Clams)

These mollusks have a hinge equipped with a spoon-shaped tooth in one valve and a corresponding pit in the

---

Key to PLATE 185

1. *Solen viridis*; 2. *Ensis directus*; 3. *Siliqua costata*; 4. *Siliqua squama*; 5. *Spisula (Mactra) solidissima*; 6. *Spisula (Mactra) polynyma*; 7. *Mactra fragilis*; 8. *Mulinia lateralis*; 9. *Anatina (Raeta) canaliculata*; 10. *Anatina (Raeta) lineata*; 11. *Mesodesma deauratum*.

PLATE 185

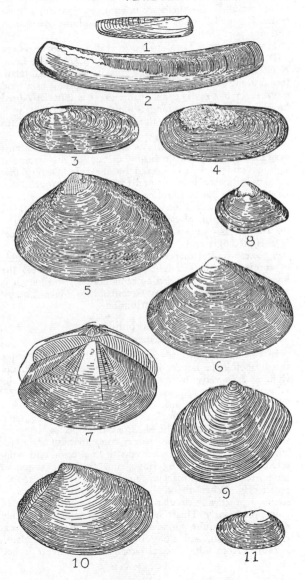

other valve for the reception of the cartilage holding the valves together. The shells are unequal and gaping at both ends. The pallial sinus is large. The siphons are united and are partly or entirely retractile.

Mya arenaria Linnaeus PLATE 186 (1); COLOR PLATE XIII, 9. The Long Clam. The Soft-shell Clam. The Long Neck Clam. The Sand Clam. This is the familiar clam found along all our shores and is very important as a food mollusk in our markets and fisheries. It is especially used for chowders and steaming, though, commercially, it is not so highly esteemed as the Hard or Little Neck Clam (*Venus mercenaria*).

The animal buries itself in shallow, muddy bottoms between the tides with just the tips of its extended siphons exposed when covered by the tide. During low tide, twice a day, it is exposed to the air. It ranges from Arctic seas to North Carolina.

Mya truncata Linnaeus PLATE 186 (2). The Short Clam. The shell is oblong, almost rectangular. Anteriorly, the margin is rounded. Posteriorly, it is truncated almost at a right angle and becomes flaring and widely gaping, the postero-ventral margin turning again at a right angle to continue as the straight ventral margin to meet the lower edge of the rounded anterior border. The length is 2¾ inches. It ranges from Greenland to Massachusetts. It also has a circumpolar distribution.

Family Corbulidae
(The Basket Shells)

In this family, the valves are unequal, the right valve usually being the larger. There is a single large tooth upright in each valve, fitting into a corresponding pit in the other valve. The siphons are short, united, and fringed. There is no pallial sunus.

Corbula contracta Say PLATE 186 (3). The Contracted Basket Clam. The shell, in this species, is white with regular, smooth, raised lines concentrically arranged. The anterior end is rounded and the posterior end truncated. A straight sloping ridge runs from the umbo to the posterior ventral margin, thus forming an angular fold posteriorly. When the shell is viewed from the end, it shows a practically circular outline, coming to a truncated point, posteriorly. This clam is found in sandy or muddy shallows. It is quite abundant in the Woods Hole, Massachusetts, region, and along the shores of Rhode Island. It ranges from Cape Cod to Jamaica, British West Indies.

Family Saxicavidae
(The Rock Borers)

The shells, in this family, are elongated and irregular. They have unequal valves and gape slightly at each end. The hinge is toothless or in some species there may be one or two cardinals. The mantle margins are closed, a small opening being left for the foot. The siphons are united, elongate, and well developed. They are borers in sand, mud, and soft rock.

Saxicava arctica Linnaeus PLATE 186 (4). The Arctic Rock Borer. This elongate shell has a rough, irregular surface, and is extremely variable. The umbones are prominent and placed near the anterior end. The posterior portion is more than twice the length of the anterior and is traversed by two diagonal roughened ridges from the umbones to the posterior end, one running near the posterior dorsal margin, the other diagonally to the lower angle. These ridges may have angular toothlike projections of the lines of growth, or they may be so worn that they are practically obsolete. The valves are generally gaping. The length is 1 to 1½ inches. The animal is symmetrical, with the mantle lobes united. The siphons are large and united almost to their openings, which are fringed. The opening for the foot is just large enough for that small fingerlike organ to be thrust out. It is equipped with a groove and secretes an effective byssus. The shell-surface is chalky-white, with an olive to yellowish epidermis.

This is a boring mollusk, excavating a home for itself in sand, mud, clay, or limestone or other soft rock. It excavates a hole about 6 inches deep, to the wall of which it attaches itself by spinning a strong byssus and settles down for life. It does much damage to cement or concrete sea walls and breakwaters by boring into them repeatedly, for the next generation often enlarges the parental burrows until the whole structure is weakened. It ranges from the low-water line to 100 fathoms, and from Greenland to the West Indies, but is especially common north of Cape Cod.

Cyrtodaria siliqua (Spengler) PLATE 186 (5). This is an elongate, heavy shell, with a black, shining epidermis. It is obliquely wrinkled especially at the posterior end. The umbones are not prominent. The animal is much larger than the shell. The mantle is entirely closed except for an opening for the small, conical foot and one for the siphons. The latter are long, united to the end, their muscular covering continuous with that of the mantle. The hinge has no teeth and the ligament is external. The length is 3½ inches and the height, 1½ inches. It is a northern species, ranging from the Arctic Ocean to Georges Bank.

Panomya arctica (Lamarck) PLATE 186 (6). The shell is thick and strong, the posterior part being about twice the length of the anterior. It is rounded anteriorly, slightly receding to a rounded angle ventrally. The posterior end is gaping, obliquely truncate and expanded, so that it is wider than the anterior end, giving a rhomboidal shape to the shell. The umbones are prominent and directed slightly anteriorly, with two wavelike ridges, one to the lower posterior angle, the other just back of the rounded lower anterior angle of the shell. The length of the shell is about 2½ inches. It is abundant on the Banks of Newfoundland, from which it ranges north to the Arctic Ocean.

Panope bitruncata Conrad PLATE 186 (7). The Oblong Panope. This shell is obliquely truncate anteriorly. It is short and rhomboidal in shape, with the ventral margin considerably convex. The posterior margin is oblique. The umbo is prominent. The length is 5¼ inches. This shell is variable in shape, largely through distortion caused by the environment, depending on whether they are buried in soft sand or mud, or in compact and firm gravel. It ranges from North Carolina around Florida to Mobile, Mississippi. It is also abundant as a Pliocene fossil.

Family Pholadidae
(Wing Shells, Angel Wings, and Piddocks)

These are boring clams capable of penetrating, not only wood and soft rocks, but quite hard rocks, as well. The shells are brittle, white, and gaping at both ends. They are usually elongate, narrowed, and often prolonged toward the posterior end. The anterior end is short and armed with abrading teeth or sharp, rough ridges. Some species have additional valves, reinforcing the hinge or the margin of the shell.

Pholas (Barnea) costata (Linnaeus) PLATE 186 (8). The Angel Wings. These mollusks are so called because of the snowy-white winglike valves. When found empty on the beach, attached by their anterior ligament, they have very much the appearance of white, outspread wings. The valves may be 6 to 8 inches in length, and are sculptured with about thirty radiating ribs, with toothlike elevations produced by the finer, concentric growth lines. The terminal ends of the anterior ribs are extended into strong

---

Key to PLATE 186

1. *Mya arenaria*; 2. *Mya truncata*; 3. *Corbula contracta*; 4. *Saxicava arctica*; 5. *Cyrtodaria siliqua*; 6. *Panomya arctica*; 7. *Panope bitruncata*; 8. *Pholas (Barnea) costata*; 9. *Barnea truncata*; 10. *Zirfaea crispata*; 11. *Pholas (Dactylina) campechiensis*; 12. *Martesia cuneiformis*.

PLATE 186

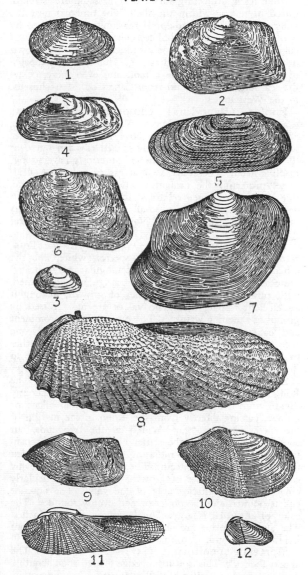

sawlike teeth, projecting forward. This sculpture is reproduced in reverse within the shell. The umbo is near the anterior end. The antero-dorsal margins are reinforced by two accessory horny shell-plates. The animal is yellow in color, the ends of the siphons sprinkled with reddish brown dots. The foot is large and strong. This species is capable of burrowing 10 inches to a foot, and even more, below the sea bottom. It is found from Cape Cod, Massachusetts, to the West Indies.

Pholas (Dactylina) campechiensis (Gmelin) PLATE 186 (11). The Campeche Wing. This is a smaller and slenderer species than the above, and with much finer sculpture. The radiating, widely spaced ribs fan out over the entire valves, but those situated anteriorly have strong, rasplike teeth. There are two accessory valves or shell-plates protecting the umbones. The color is pure white, like that of its larger relatives. It measures 3 inches in length and is grouped in small colonies throughout its range, which extends from North Carolina to Central America.

Barnea truncata (Say) PLATE 186 (9). The Truncated Borer. This very delicate species, white, like the others previously described, has a rectangular and truncated posterior end. The latter is short, triangular, and pointed, with ruffled and emphasized lines of growth, making it an efficient rasping tool. The valves are also crossed by groups of radiating wrinkles. The umbo is quite prominent and leans posteriorly. The hinge is reinforced by only one accessory valve. The shell gapes widely. It is about 3 inches in length. The species occurs abundantly from Maine to the Gulf of Mexico.

Zirfaea crispata (Linnaeus) PLATE 186 (10). The Rough Piddock. The valves of this shell are conspicuously divided into two areas by a nearly central radial sulcus, or groove, passing directly from the umbo to the margin of the shell. They also gape widely at the two ends, but converge and touch at the center of the margin. The anterior area is thrown into radiating foldlike wrinkles which terminate in rasplike teeth. These rays are crossed by coarse, concentric lines of growth, which are particularly obvious in the posterior area of the valve. The anterior end is pointed and the posterior end evenly rounded. The color of the shell is gray. The length is about 2 inches. The accessory plates are absent. This species ranges from Labrador to South Carolina.

Martesia cuneiformis (Say) PLATE 186 (12). The Wood Piddock. This is a little wedge-shaped shell about ¾ inch in length, remarkably well adapted for carrying on its habit of life, which is that of a wood borer. It has a shortened and rounded anterior end and is elongated, depressed, and tapering posteriorly. There is a transverse oblique groove or canal that passes in a staright line from the umbo to the shell margin and, as in the preceding species, divides the shell sharply into two areas. In the anterior area, the shell resembles a rasp, being covered with tiny rough scales, which edge the fine, close-set lines of growth and completely cover the area. This anterior part of the shell is rounded and inflated, the two similar valves having the effect of a burrlike buffer. The tapering posterior area is made up of concentric, coarsely spaced lines of growth. This end gapes for the protrusion of the siphons. The closely joined umbones, together with three marginal, accessory shell-plates, reinforce and strengthen this compact little shell, the whole thus being an efficient boring tool. This mollusk is widely distributed, occurring from Connecticut to the West Indies, and probably farther, because of its habit of boring into floating timber.

Family Teredinidae
(Ship Worms)

The Ship Worms are long, wormlike bivalve mollusks that bore into timbers of wharves and the hulls of wooden ships, causing great destruction. Their shells are reduced to two vestigial bilobed valves which are shaped like a double rasping organ, and only touch each other at two points. They are only about ½ inch long. By far the greater part of the soft-bodied animal is outside the shell for it may be 6 to 12 inches in length, when full grown, or even as much as two feet, and occupies the tunnel it has excavated in the timber, lining it with a shelly substance. When the Ship Worm hatches in the spring, from one of millions of eggs produced by one female, it is a minute free-swimming larva. After a week or two, when it is about the size of a pinhead, it settles on the surface of a submerged timber and bores a tiny hole just large enough to admit its body. Thereafter, it continues to bore, enlarging the hole as its body grows in length and diameter, keeping in communication with the outside only through its delicate, threadlike siphons, one of which pumps in the sea water to supply it with microscopic food and oxygen, while the other pumps out the waste products from its system. As the *Teredo* never enlarges the original entrance, it has to remain in its burrow for life, and continues to tunnel along the grain of the wood, turning aside only to avoid a knot or the tube of a neighboring *Teredo*. Eventually the timber becomes so weakened it falls apart. The best protection against these boring mollusks is to impregnate the timber of a wharf or of a vessel with creosote, or sheathe it with noncorrosive metal.

The shell of the mollusk, in this family, is reduced to two little bilobed valves at the anterior end of the creature and to two tiny leaflike or paddle-shaped *pallets* which can control the flow of fluids through the siphon openings or protect them from damage. Apparently the *Teredo* does not digest the wood cuttings, but ejects them unchanged in composition.

Teredo navalis Linnaeus PLATE 189 (1, 2). The Ship Worm. This species has been sufficiently described above in connection with the family. It ranges throughout the North Atlantic to Florida.

Xylotrya fimbriata (Jeffreys) PLATE 189 (3). This differs from the preceding species mainly in the pallets, which are here in the form of feather-shaped blades, the pinnate side pieces articulating obliquely from the main stalk. Each pallet is ½ inch in length. The tubes are a foot or more in length. This species is of common occurrence from Massachusetts to Texas.

CLASS SCAPHOPODA
(The Tooth Shells, the Tusk Shells)
INDEX PLATE 187

These are peculiar mollusks, so different from any others that they are put in a Class by themselves. Superficially, they resemble elephants' tusks or small curved trumpets. They vary in size from small species, like slender, curved needles 1 inch in length, to rather clumsy and heavy forms measuring 5 inches. Not many species (about two hundred) are known, but the individual shells exist in enormous numbers. They are exclusively marine and are found in all seas and in all depths, from shallow water to 2,600 fathoms or more. For the most part, they inhabit clear, sandy bottoms, but are also found in mud. The shell is open at both ends, the foot projecting from the larger opening. It is cylindrical in shape and is used for digging in sand or mud. There is no clearly defined head, but the mouth opens above the foot, at the end of a short snout, and is surrounded by a series of long, threadlike tentacles, each terminating in a small, beadlike enlargement, used in feeling for and capturing the Foraminifera, and other very small or microscopic organisms, which form its food. It has no eyes, but stands obliquely with its head buried in the sand, with the tentacles spread in all directions. The mouth opens into a U-shaped intestine which curves back upon itself to discharge into the mantle-cavity at the base of the foot. Just inside the mouth is a typical molluscan jaw and radula. A simple pulsating heart is present and a well-developed, characteristic molluscan nervous system, as well as a pair

PLATE 187

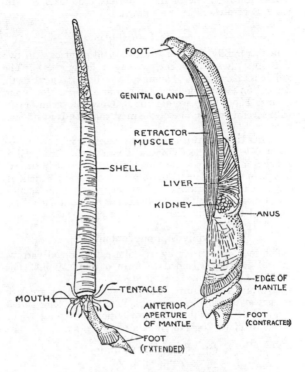

FOOT

GENITAL GLAND

RETRACTOR MUSCLE

SHELL

LIVER

KIDNEY

ANUS

TENTACLES

MOUTH

ANTERIOR APERTURE OF MANTLE

EDGE OF MANTLE

FOOT (CONTRACTED)

FOOT (EXTENDED)

ANIMAL WITH SHELL

ANIMAL REMOVED FROM SHELL

A TYPICAL SCAPHOPOD (DENTALIUM)

of nephridia discharging waste products into the mantle-cavity through two pores near the anus. The gonad is situated posteriorly, but the eggs and sperm reach the outside through one of the nephridia. The sexes are separate. Several families are known.

Family Dentaliidae

In this family, the foot is conical and pointed, with two side-lobes, and partly enclosed by a fleshy sheath. The radula is characteristic, having a large, broad, central tooth, flanked on either side by an arched and cusped lateral and a large bandlike marginal tooth. Only one genus exists with several species; one of the most common is mentioned here.

Dentalium entale Linnaeus PLATE 189 (4); COLOR PLATE XV (3). The Common Tooth Shell. This shell is 2 inches long, ivory-white in color, and moderately curved. It is vaguely annulated, but with no longitudinal striations, except a few indications of such markings at the smaller end. It occurs from Cape Hatteras northward to New England and the Arctic; also on the European coast.

Family Siphonodentaliidae

The foot, in this family, is quite extensile and narrow. Its end can be expanded to form a terminal disc. The smaller shell-opening is notched.

Siphonodentalium lobatum Sars. There are two notches at the smaller openings. It is ⅖ inch long and is thin and shining white. The distribution is from the Arctic Ocean to New England. It is also European.

CLASS GASTROPODA
(The Snails)

These are mollusks that usually have a twisted, one-sided anatomy, a spiral shell, and a broad, flat foot. If it were not for the twist, the shell would be essentially a cone, the apex of which is the middle of the back. The foot is theoretically shortened by this peculiarity, the anterior and posterior portions being brought together, nevertheless extending out forward and backward from underneath the shell. The head projects from under the rim of the mantle and its shell, anteriorly, and the anus opens under the posterior rim of the cone (INDEX PLATE 188).

In order to visualize what has taken place, during the evolution of the animal, to produce the twisted anatomy of the adult, it is necessary to imagine that the front border of the cone, together with the animal and its internal organs, has grown forward with a twist of 180 degrees to the right, until the opening of the anus is brought to the anterior edge of the shell near the mouth, the shell making a half turn in the process. If the shell-opening should continually grow around toward the right, more spirals would be added to the shell, each whorl representing a period in the growth and age of the mollusk, the number of twists being reflected in spirals added to the visceral mass of the animal within the shell. Meanwhile, the organs on the outside of the spiral have grown forward unimpeded, while those on the inside near the spire of the twisting shell are compressed and retarded. The paired structures, such as the ctenidia or gills, the kidneys, and the auricles of the heart are affected by this spiral growth with the result that the inner or right-hand member of each pair degenerates and finally disappears leaving only the left-hand members fully developed. At the same time, the right side of the ladderlike nervous system is twisted upon itself so that, while the cerebral commissure and its right and left ganglia remain in their original position, the lateral right visceral commissure with its ganglion becomes located dorsally to the intestine, and the corresponding left commissure and its ganglion are brought around under the intestine toward the left side. This twisting tendency of the animal is not the mechanical result of the coiling of the shell, but of the twist of both the animal and shell originated in the free-swimming veliger larva, and is even foreshadowed in the segmentation of the egg. In the larva, the original mantle and shell are cap-shaped and postero-dorsal in position, while the intestine is straight, the mouth being anterior and the anus posterior with the developing lobe of the foot between them. The twisting takes place during growth. This is substantially the process by which the coiled shell of the gastropod mollusk originates, and is especially characteristic of the so-called prosobranch or streptoneuran mollusks. In another group, containing opisthobranch or euthyneuran mollusks, the anatomy becomes secondarily untwisted, as will be shown later in this section.

The Class Gastropoda is divided into the Subclasses (1) *Prosobranchia,* and (2) *Opisthobranchia.*

SUBCLASS PROSOBRANCHIA (STREPTONEURA)

These are mostly marine snails, having a ctenidium (the characteristic gastropod gill) located anteriorly in the mantle cavity in front of the heart and pericardium. Except in the more primitive species, which retain a pair of ctenidia, only a single ctenidium is present. In two terrestrial families, the Helicinidae and Cyclostomatidae, the ctenidia do not exist, being replaced by lungs, but as these are not marine forms, they are not included here. They all have the typical twisted condition of the internal anatomy, the ladderlike nervous system being crossed over, so as to have the form of a figure 8. The head has a single pair of tentacles. Teeth in the radular ribbon are of several different kinds in each row, and are of great use in classifying the various subgroups and species in this Subclass. On the inner side of the mantle, in the branchial cavity, is situated the *hypobranchial gland,* a pallial mucous gland, the use of which is not known. In the genera *Murex* and *Thais,* the so-called Purple Snails, it secretes a purple fluid, formerly often used as a dye. In almost all species, a large, univalve, coiled shell is present, which may be of large size and weight, often characteristically and handsomely sculptured and colored, varying in different species, and often extensively within the same species. These shells are much sought after by private collectors and are often featured extensively in museum collections.

There is almost always an *operculum* present. This is a horny or calcareous plate secreted on the posterior upper surface of the foot, and so located that, when the heavy muscular foot is withdrawn into the shell, the operculum just fits the shell-opening and acts as a protective door. It may be circular and spirally formed, with a nucleus in the center; the spiral may be leaf-shaped, with the nucleus on one side; it may be irregular in outline to fit closely into the hollow spinelike projections bordering the aperture of the shell; or it may have the form of a polished knob or button (INDEX PLATE 188).

The prosobranchiate *head* projects forward from under the mantle, equipped with a pair of nonretractile *tentacles* bearing eyes, either at their base, on their sides, or terminally. There is a *proboscis* in many species, at the end of which is the mouth, opening into the buccal cavity with its radula and opposing jaws (the latter present only in non-carnivorous species). In many species, the shell-opening is prolonged to form an *anterior siphonal canal,* through which a *siphon* (a spoutlike prolongation of the upper border of the mantle) may be thrust out for inhaling sea water to bathe the gill.

The Subclass Prosobranchia is divided into three Orders: (1) *Archaeogastropoda*; (2) *Mesogastropoda;* and (3) *Stenoglossa.*

Order ARCHAEOGASTROPODA (ASPIDOBRANCHIA)

This Order includes the most primitive living gastropods, certain species having a pair of ctenidia, others a *bipectinate* (double-branched) gill. It consists of two Suborders: (1) *Docoglossa,* and (2) *Rhipidoglossa.*

PLATE 188

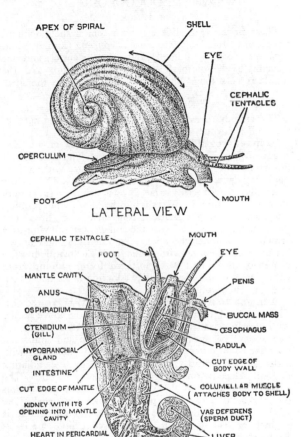

APEX OF SPIRAL

SHELL

EYE

CEPHALIC TENTACLES

OPERCULUM

FOOT

MOUTH

LATERAL VIEW

CEPHALIC TENTACLE

MOUTH

FOOT

EYE

MANTLE CAVITY

PENIS

ANUS

OSPHRADIUM

BUCCAL MASS

CTENIDIUM (GILL)

ŒSOPHAGUS

RADULA

HYPOBRANCHIAL GLAND

CUT EDGE OF BODY WALL

INTESTINE

CUT EDGE OF MANTLE

COLUMELLAR MUSCLE (ATTACHES BODY TO SHELL)

KIDNEY WITH ITS OPENING INTO MANTLE CAVITY

VAS DEFERENS (SPERM DUCT)

HEART IN PERICARDIAL CAVITY

LIVER

TESTIS

BLOOD VESSEL

STOMACH

DORSAL VIEW WITH SHELL REMOVED AND MANTLE CAVITY CUT AND THROWN OVER TO LEFT SIDE

Suborder DOCOGLOSSA
(The Limpets)

These primitive mollusks have a conical shell, without a twist or spiral. There are paired *nephridia* (kidneys) and *osphradia* (organs of smell), but only one auricle and one bipectinate ctenidium. There is no operculum and the radula is very long. There is no slit or hole in the shell.

Family Acmaeidae

The ctenidium extends from left to right. The apex of the shell is turned anteriorly.

Acmaea testudinalis (Linnaeus) COLOR PLATES XV, 4, 4a; XVI, 6. The Tortoise-shell Limpet. The shell of this limpet is tent shaped and rather elongate, with a low, unpierced apex. It is about 1½ inches in length. The surface is sculptured with cross-striae. Brown stripes or spots radiate from the summit, diversifying the bluish white ground color, and crossing a series of concentric, black lines. The inner surface is white, with the muscle-scar showing as a brown patch under the apex. A mottled gray and brown border edges the inner rim of the shell. The mantle margin is not fringed. This is a northern form, ranging from Labrador to Connecticut, closely adhering to rocks between tides and in shallow water.

Acmaea testudinalis alvea (Conrad) PLATE 189 (9). This is a small, thin, and fragile variety of the above species with nearly parallel sides about equally rounded at the two ends. The apex of the shell is sharp and somewhat hooklike. The outer surface is beautifully checkered with a delicately sculptured pattern produced by fine radiating lines and close-set lines of growth crossing each other. The color is a reddish brown with oval spots and round dots of light yellow, regularly patterned like a network. The shell is so thin that it is practically translucent. It is ½ inch or less in length. This attractive little species is found abundantly on eelgrass exactly matching the blades in width. It ranges from the Arctic Ocean southward to Cape Cod, Massachusetts.

Suborder RHIPIDOGLOSSA

The shell, in this Suborder, is usually spiral, but, in such cases, the spiral is low and with only a slight coil. In non-spiral species, a slit, or closed slot, is present in the shell. These mollusks have a paired jaw, not being carnivorous, and a long radula with many teeth.

Family Fissurellidae
(Keyhole Limpets)

At first glance, the shell, in this family, resembles that of the limpets already described, but this similarity is only superficial. Like the Acmaeidae (page 614), the shell is low, with a tentlike spire, and is apparently uncoiled. It differs, however, from that family in having a slot, or keyholelike aperture, penetrating the shell at the apex, or it may be on the side, or even represented by a notch in the shell-margin.

The life history of these keyhole limpets betrays their true relationship. The young limpet begins life with a spiral shell, having an elongate slit rising from the margin. During its growth, the marginal opening of the slot is closed and the slot, itself, gradually travels up the slope of the shell, becoming proportionately narrower and shorter until it reaches the apex. At the same time, the apical spiral becomes smaller and smaller until it is reduced to a diminutive curved knob, or is lost altogether.

Fissurella (Diadora) alternata Say PLATE 189 (11). The Eastern Keyhole Limpet. This is the common keyhole limpet occurring within our region. It is upwards of 1 inch in length. The cone-shaped shell is pierced by a keyhole-shaped slot at the summit of quite an elevated peak, which curves distinctly forward. The radiating ribs, crossed by concentric striae, give the surface a latticed effect. The color, varying from gray to yellow with about eight radiating black or brown bands, makes this quite a handsome shell. The range of this species is from southern New Jersey to the West Indies and Mexico.

Puncturella princeps Mighels & Adams PLATE 189 (10). The Little Chink. This shell forms a steep cone with curving, corrugated sides sculptured with about twenty-two strong radiating ribs, with smaller ribs between. The color is a bluish white. There is a diamond-shaped slit on the anterior side of the apex, which rolls backward at the tip and represents the last remnant of the spiral coil of the younger shell. The opening communicates with the interior through a circular hole. This is quite a small shell, being only ⅛ inch in length. It is found at depths ranging from 25 to 310 fathoms, from Labrador to North Carolina.

Family Trochidae
(The Top Shells)

The shells in this family are noted for their pearly lining. They have a top-shaped conical spire, with a smooth and even-edged aperture. The periostracum is often highly colored but thin. When this is removed, the nacreous pearly substance is immediately exposed, as it comprises practically the entire thickness of the shell. The operculum is thin, horny, and usually circular, with central nucleus and spiral pattern. The spiral, as is always the case in an operculum, is opposite to that of the spire of the shell, that is, counterclockwise. The snout is short and broad. The tentacles are long, with simple eyes on the outer side of their base. There is one ctenidium, or gill, being, of course, the left-hand one.

This is a large family, usually of tropical seas, but a few species are within our range.

Margarites olivacea (Brown) (= **Margarites argentata** Gould) PLATE 189 (13). This is a tiny shell, about ¼ inch in diameter, globose in outline, and olive-brown in color. It is thin and delicate, with four or five whorls and a circular aperture. The interior is pearly and highly iridescent. It is a northern species, ranging from Labrador to Massachusetts Bay in 7 to 80 fathoms.

Margarites helicina (Fabricius) COLOR PLATE XV, 6. This is also a small, but beautiful shell, thin, iridescent, and shining with pinkish brown luster, varying to yellow or olive. Fine spiral lines are present on the lower part of the shell. It is very convex in shape, with four to five whorls. It is often found on the fronds of the brown kelp (*Laminaria*) cast up on the beach. The range is from Greenland to Massachusetts Bay, in depths of 2 to 100 fathoms.

Margarites groenlandica (Gmelin) PLATE 189 (14). The Wavy Top Shell. Dark reddish brown to flesh-color, the Wavy Top Shell is another of the beautiful little pearly shells of our coast. It is about ⅓ inch in diameter, but a number of these mollusks, in a rock crevice at low tide,

---

Key to PLATE 189

1, 2. *Teredo navalis;* 3. *Xylotrya fimbriata;* 4. *Dentalium entale;* 5. *Chaetopleura apiculata;* 6. *Lepidochiton (Tonicella) marmorea;* 7. *Lepidochiton (Trachydermon) ruber;* 8. *Amicula vestita;* 9. *Acmaea testudinalis alvea;* 10. *Puncturella princeps;* 11. *Fissurella (Diadora) alternata;* 12. *Mölleria (Margarites) costulata;* 13. *Margarites olivacea (Margarites argentata);* 14. *Margarites groenlandica;* 15. *Margarites cinerea;* 16. *Calliostoma occidentale;* 17. *Turbo castaneus;* 18. *Melanella oleacea;* 19. *Pyramidella producta;* 20. *Pyramidella fusca;* 21. *Odostomia seminuda;* 22. *Odostomia impressa;* 23. *Odostomia bisuturalis;* 24. *Odostomia gibbosa;* 25. *Odostomia dealbata;* 26. *Couthouyella striatula;* 27. *Obeliscus (Pyramidella) crenulatus;* 28. *Epitonium (Scalaria) multistriatum;* 29. *Epitonium (Scalaria) humphreysi (Scalaria sayana);* 30. *Epitonium (Scalaria) groenlandicum.*

PLATE 189

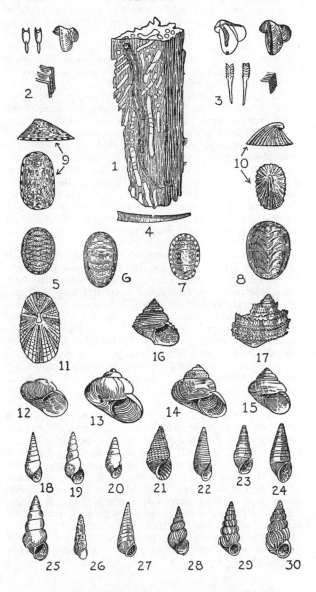

make a shining display of iridescence. They are found living near the lower tidal mark but range chiefly from 7 to 50 fathoms. The spire is marked by regular revolving lines on its four to five whorls, which have a wavy junction at the suture. The umbilicus is broad and funnel-shaped. There is a thin and horny operculum. Though it is handsome enough to be a tropical shell, its occurrence is from Labrador to Massachusetts Bay.

Margarites cinerea (Couthouy) PLATE 189 (15). The Ridged Top Shell. This is an ashy-gray shell tinted with greenish tones, somewhat more than ⅓ inch in height, pyramidal in shape, with five to seven strongly sculptured revolving whorls, crossed by fine lines of growth. The umbilicus is quite open and deep. It ranges from Greenland to Massachusetts Bay in depths from 5 to 200 fathoms.

Margarites (Solariella) obscura Couthouy COLOR PLATE XV, 5. The Little Sun Shell. This shell has shorter but broader proportions than those described above, being ⅖ inch high and ½ inch in diameter. The revolving ribs are coarser, there being only two or three to each of the whorls. The lines of growth also are somewhat coarse. There is a brownish periostracum, but when removed, it discloses a pearly iridescence. The umbilicus is broad and deep. This species ranges from Labrador to Marthas Vineyard, Massachusetts. It is found in from 6 to 35 fathoms.

Calliostoma occidentale (Mighels & Adams) PLATE 189 (16). The Pearly Top Shell. This is quite a beautiful and attractive shell, ½ inch in length, pearly-white in color, almost translucent, and with rounded whorls, with raised spiral ridges which terminate at the shell aperture to produce a crenulated margin. It ranges from Nova Scotia to southern New England, being found in depths of from 25 to 980 fathoms.

Mölleria (Margarites) costulata (Möller) PLATE 189 (12). The shell of this species is only ⅒ inch in diameter. It is white in color and rather thick near the minute apex. The body-whorl is thin and delicate, and very convex, rounded, and sculptured with prominent, crowded ribs. On the outer surface of the whorl, each rib is divided into two, thus taking up the increased space. They join to form one rib again as the space is crowded with them on the concave side at the deep umbilicus, and disappear before crossing the five separated, spiral striae on the umbilical side of the whorl. The shell-aperture is rounded, with a complete peristome. This shell is found in 4 to 30 fathoms, ranging from Greenland to New England.

Family Turbinidae
(The Turban Shells)

The shell is large, spiral, and turban-shaped with a circular or oval aperture. The operculum is calcareous, rounded, almost hemispherical on the outer side, with a flat, horny layer of spiral pattern on the inside. There is a large body-whorl. The periostracum is often brilliantly colored with the pearly substance directly beneath and forming the entire thickness of the shell. The tropical species are of considerable value for making mother-of-pearl ornaments. A few species come into the southern part of our range.

Turbo castaneus Gmelin PLATE 189 (17). The Knobby Top Shell. The Chestnut Top. The shell is colored orange, variegated with brown, often with white spots. The five or six whorls are decorated with many spiral lines made up of a succession of beadlike tubercles, the largest being on the shoulders of the whorls. The aperture is large and round. There is a heavy callus on the columella. The length is about 1½ inches. It is found from shallow water down to 25 fathoms, from North Carolina to the West Indies and the Gulf of Mexico.

Order MESOGASTROPODA
(PECTINIBRANCHIA)

The mollusks in this Order have the typical coiled shell structure. There is but one of the ancestrally paired organs surviving in each set, with the result that only one auricle survives of the original pair, as well as one kidney, one osphradium, and one ctenidium, with rare exceptions. The proboscis and siphon are uniformly present, also an anterior canal and a penis. The sexes are separate. The reproductive organ empties by its own duct and not through the kidney. This is a large group comprising more than half of the known species of the Phylum Mollusca.

Suborder PTENOGLOSSA

The chief characteristics of the families in this Suborder are the short and broad radula, without a central tooth, but with a large and indefinite number of hooklike lateral teeth; the conical or discoid shell; and the small, simple circular or oval aperture, usually with a complete lip encircling it.

Family Janthinidae
(The Violet Snails)

This very interesting family has a thin, translucent, violet-colored shell, a prominent snout, and an operculum transformed into a long raft of gelatinous material filled with bubblelike vesicles, to the underside of which the egg-capsules are attached. This contrivance enables the mollusk to float on the surface of the sea, so that it is entirely pelagic. It occurs in schools or fleets, often far from land in both the Atlantic and Pacific Oceans. It has no eyes, but possesses a featherlike ctenidium or gill. The sexes are separate. There is but one genus and three species.

Janthina fragilis Lamarck (= **Janthina janthina** Linnaeus) color plate XV, 7. The Fragile Purple Shell. The graceful, delicately colored shell has three or four sloping whorls, the outer one with a sharp ridge encircling it. This is the largest species of the Janthinidae on the North Atlantic Coast, the shell being 1½ inches in diameter. It is carnivorous, feeding chiefly on jellyfish, which it catches by shooting out its prehensile proboscis. Its chief enemies are sea gulls, but the violet color of the shell camouflages it, rendering it inconspicuous in the sea. Besides, when disturbed, it discharges a purple liquid, causing it to disappear in a violet cloud in the water.

Family Epitoniidae (Scalidae)
(Wentletraps, Staircase Shells)

This family is characterized by the white, turreted shell, each whorl having longitudinal ribs in the form of outstanding, conspicuous plates. The whorls are very convex with a polished surface. The animal has a retractile proboscis, with a short siphon. Like the previous family, these mollusks discharge a purple fluid, but, unlike it, they have no float, being creeping animals. There are quite a number of species, widely distributed and of carnivorous habits. The conspicuous ribs are the successive lips of the mollusk, representing resting stages when the forward growth stops and the lip of the aperture becomes thickened. They are also known as *varices* (plural of *varix*). The present lip surrounding the aperture will become a varix as the shell resumes its growth.

Epitonium (Scalaria) groenlandicum (Chemnitz) plate 189 (30). The Ladder Shell. This species has an elongated shell, with eight to ten whorls, close together and slightly flattened, each with about ten stout oblique ribs. The fairly wide spaces between the ribs are barred with close-set revolving ridges that show an underlying continuity from the apex to the lip of the aperture. The general color of the spire is bluish brown, while the ribs are white. The animal is yellowish gray, marked with dull, whitish spots. The shell is 1 inch in length. It is found from Greenland to Block Island, in 10 to 109 fathoms.

Epitonium (Scalaria) multistriatum (Say) plate 189 (28). The Crowded Wentletrap. The word wentletrap is a Dutch word meaning "spiral staircase" and is quite appropriately applied to these shells, with their ascending, winding spire of flat, steplike ribs. This species is distinguished by the many closely crowded ribs decorating the eight whorls, from the round aperture, up to the very tip of the spire, crowned by the tiny clear *protoconch*, or embryonic shell. This species ranges from Vineyard Sound, Massachusetts, to the Florida Keys, in depths of 10 to 109 fathoms. It measures 1 inch in length.

Epitonium (Scalaria) humphreysi (Kiener) (= Scalaria sayana Dall) PLATE 189 (29). This is a much smaller shell, being about ½ inch in length. It is glossy white in color. It occurs in deep water from Massachusetts to Texas.

Suborder GYMNOGLOSSA

This group contains species with the radula and jaw absent. The shell is turret-shaped and the aperture is round. There are three families, two of which are included here.

Family Melanellidae

These are small shells, elongated and slender, smooth, polished, and white in color. The spire is many whorled and often curved to one side. There is no jaw or radula. The proboscis is very long and is used for sucking. They are often parasitic on sea urchins and other echinoderms, living on the juices of their host. There are many species.

Melanella oleacea (Kurtz & Stimpson) PLATE 189 (18). This is a many-whorled species with a slender, sharply tapering, smooth and polished shell. It is white in color, marked with pale brown, transverse bands. The twelve whorls are quite compact, with close sutures. The aperture is small and ovate. The length is only ¼ inch. It is found in Vineyard Sound, where it is parasitic on the Sea Cucumber, *Thyone briareus,* in 4 to 10 fathoms, and ranges south to deeper waters off Georgia, where it is recorded at 440 fathoms.

Family Pyramidellidae
(The Pyramid Shells)

The shell is turreted and pyramidal or conical, with many whorls. The aperture is ovate. The lips are not continuous posteriorly. The columella is thrown into folds (*plicate*). The surface is white and polished. The tentacles are ear-shaped and joined at the base. The operculum is horny, fits the semicircular aperture, as well as being notched to fit the plications of the columella.

Pyramidella producta (C. B. Adams) PLATE 189 (19). This species has a small, very slender, light yellowish brown shell. It is composed of eight rounded, but rather flattened whorls. The aperture is about one fourth the length of the shell. There is no umbilicus and the operculum is very thin. The body-whorl is slender. The length is about ¼ inch. It occurs from Massachusetts Bay to New Jersey.

Pyramidella fusca (C. B. Adams) PLATE 189 (20). This is very similar to the previous species but has a somewhat stouter body-whorl. The aperture is large and ear-shaped. It is of the same size as *Pyramidella producta,* being ¼ inch in length. It ranges from Prince Edward Island to Florida.

Odostomia seminuda (C. B. Adams) PLATE 189 (21). This shell is sharply conical, glossy-white and translucent. There are six or seven slightly convex whorls, with numerous cross-ridges and revolving lines giving a granulated appearance to the sculpture. The cross-ridges terminate abruptly about the middle of the body-whorl, while the revolving lines continue to the aperture, four more being added at the base. The very thin outer lip is cut into and scalloped by the revolving lines. The shell is about ⅐ inch in length and ranges from Prince Edward Island to the Gulf of Mexico.

Odostomia impressa (Say) PLATE 189 (22). This is a species of slightly larger size with an acute apex and six whorls, sculptured with four clearly impressed revolving lines and without cross-lines. The columella is very stout. The base is sculptured with seven spiral grooves. The outer lip is thin, showing the undulations of the interrupted revolving lines at the edge. This species often occurs on oyster beds. The range is from Massachusetts Bay to the Gulf of Mexico.

Odostomia bisuturalis (Say) PLATE 189 (23). This shell is distinguished by a single revolving line parallel to the suture, thus giving the impression of a double suture. It is light green in color with a brownish epidermis. It has a more northern but overlapping range, as compared to the previous species, extending from the Gulf of St. Lawrence to Delaware Bay. The size is very small, being only about ⅒ inch in length.

Odostomia gibbosa Bush (= **Odostomia modesta** Stimpson) PLATE 189 (24). The shell, in this species, is yellowish white and with a shining surface. The body-whorl is well developed with faint growth and revolving lines. It is about ⅛ inch in length and ranges from Maine to Woods Hole, Massachusetts.

Odostomia dealbata Stimpson PLATE 189 (25). This is a white, smooth, and shining shell, with six convex whorls and clearly indented sutures. The ovate aperture has an inconspicuous fold. It is about ⅙ inch in length.

This species occurs from Boston Harbor to Long Island Sound.

Couthouyella striatula (Couthouy) PLATE 189 (26). This is a larger shell, about ⅜ inch in length. It has a slender spire, bluish white in color, with seven to nine rather flattened whorls and many fine revolving lines. The lines of growth are quite distinct and farther apart than the revolving lines. The aperture is ovate with an angle above. It is a fairly rare shell, being found sparsely from Halifax, Nova Scotia to Cape Ann, Massachusetts.

Obeliscus (Pyramidella) crenulatus Holmes PLATE 189 (27). The spire of this shell is turretlike, being slender and pointed. The fourteen to sixteen whorls are compact with angular troughlike sutures. The columella has three folds, the uppermost being the largest. The lower whorls are somewhat crenulated. This species occurs off North and South Carolina. It is less than ⅜ inch in length.

Suborder TAENIOGLOSSA

The radula is present in this Suborder. It is long and narrow and characterized by having a central tooth, one pair of laterals, and two pairs of marginals in each row. The shell is variable in shape and may or may not have a posterior prolongation for a siphonal canal.

This is the largest Suborder of the Mollusca, having about fifty families, including by far the greater number of the Subclass Prosobranchia.

The Suborder Taenioglossa is divided into two Divisions: (1) *Platypoda,* including the families of the Suborder having a creeping foot with a broad sole; (2) *Heteropoda,* including pelagic, swimming mollusks with a fin-shaped foot.

Division PLATYPODA

The shell, in this group, is well developed, from the aperture of which the mollusk extrudes a broad, flat foot, upon which the creature creeps about. There are about forty-eight families, including marine, fresh-water, and terrestrial species. As only the marine species come within the scope of this field book, our attention will be confined to the families containing them.

Family Naticidae
(Moon Shells, Sand-Collar Snails)

The shell is globose, usually with a flattened spire. The lip of the aperture is sharp-edged. These are sometimes very large species and noteworthy, because of the enormous foot, which, in some species, cannot be entirely withdrawn into the shell.

Natica clausa Broderlip & Sowerby PLATE 190 (1). The Little Moon Shell. The color of this shell is pale brown. It is quite globular in shape, with four to five whorls and a scarcely elevated spire. The body-whorl is very large and expanded, nearly submerging the rest of the spire. The sharp outer edge of the aperture is strongly arched around the oval opening. It becomes thicker and rounded on its margin as it joins the umbilicus, which it closes with a polished white callus.

There is a calcareous operculum. This species measures from less than 1 inch to 1½ inches in length. It ranges from Labrador to North Carolina and is found in depths of 16 to 1537 fathoms.

Natica pusilla Say PLATE 190 (2). This tiny shell measures only ¼ inch in length. It is suboval, sometimes faintly banded, and with the callus almost closing the umbilicus. It ranges from 2 to 15 fathoms occurring abundantly from Casco Bay, Maine, to the Gulf of Mexico.

Polinices heros (Say) COLOR PLATE XV, 8. The Moon Shell. This is the well-known Moon Shell of our Atlantic Coast. It is a thick, globose shell, having about five rotundly convex whorls, grayish brown in color, with a thin, brown periostracum. The body-whorl is broadly and posteriorly expanded, overlapping the greater part of the spire, so that the apical whorls project but little above its upper suture. It is a large shell, 3 or 4 inches in height. The aperture is oval and pointed above. The umbilicus is open, exposing the inner sides of the whorls nearly to the apex. The horny operculum distinguishes these shells from those of *Natica* which has a calcareous one.

This species, like the others of the family, burrows in the sand, using its huge and powerful foot, which is so large that it seems impossible for the animal to pack it completely within its shell. It is abundant from the Gulf of St. Lawrence to North Carolina.

Polinices (Neverita) duplicata (Say) COLOR PLATE XV, 9. The Sand-Collar Snail. This popular name is really applicable to all the members of this family. The eggs of these species are laid on the underside of a glutinous collar that is exuded from under the frontal reflected flap, or apron, of the foot, and is molded on the outside of the shell, being pushed around the entire rear portion of the body-whorl and finally shed onto the sandy bottom, where a layer of sand adheres to its sticky surface. It has very much the appearance of a capelike collar of pure sand. When cast ashore and dried, it is very fragile, so that, when picked up, it crumbles easily in the fingers.

This species differs from the preceding in having a thick, brown callus that covers the opening of the umbilicus entirely or partially, in having a lower, more compressed spire, so that it has a flatter appearance, and in having a darker chestnut-brown coloration with a bluish tinge. The burrows of these larger species of the Naticidae are readily recognized on the sandy sea bottom and on the wet sand of the beach between tides as small elevated circular mounds rising above the surface. Both these species of *Polinices* are carnivorous, boring neat round holes, ⅛ inch or more in diameter, in the shells of the Surf Clam and of the Ark Shells, and sucking out their soft parts.

Polinices duplicata ranges from Massachusetts Bay to the Gulf of Mexico.

Polinices triseriata (Say) PLATE 190 (4). This little Moon Shell is only about ¾ inch in height. It is quite attractively colored, being yellowish white with three rows or bands of rhomboidal, brown spots on the body whorl, and a single spiral band of the same pattern visible on the upper whorls. It has an ivory-white callus on the inner lip. It is found on sand flats at low tide, from the Gulf of St. Lawrence to North Carolina.

Polinices immaculata (Totten) PLATE 190 (5). The shell of this very small species is immaculately white (hence its name), especially when the very thin, greenish yellow epidermis is peeled off. There are about five whorls. The spire is pointed, very short, and continues the outline of the shell smoothly to the apex. There is an ivory-white callus on the margin of the inner lip, not interfering with the umbilicus, which is open. The operculum is horny. The length is ⅓ inch. It ranges from the Gulf of St. Lawrence to North Carolina, in 5 to 110 fathoms.

Polinices groenlandica (Möller) PLATE 190 (6). The shell in this species is oval, almost globular, and grayish in color, with a glossy surface. There are four convex whorls, each with a deep suture. The umbilicus is partly covered with a white callus. The operculum is horny. It is found from 70 to 80 fathoms from Greenland to North Carolina. It is about ¾ inch in length.

Sinum (Sigaretus) perspectivum (Say) PLATE 190 (3). The Ear Shell. The body-whorl of this shell is so tremendously expanded and flaring that, when viewed from the aperture, the name, Ear Shell, is quite appropriate. The spire is somewhat flattened, the shell being 1½ inches in diameter and less than ½ inch in height. There are three or four whorls. The surface of the whorls has many impressed, wavy, transverse lines crossed by revolving striae which are more distinct on the upper side of the whorls than below. The color is white with a yellowish epidermis. Within, it is smooth and shining, with a slight iridescence. The mantle is greatly developed and reflected on to the shell. It cannot be withdrawn entirely into the shell. It is found on the beaches from New Jersey to the West Indies.

Amauropsis islandica (Gmelin) (= **Natica helicoides** Johnston) PLATE 190 (7). The shell of this species is whitish with a dark yellow epidermis. There are four whorls. The umbilicus is very small. The suture is channeled. There is a horny operculum. The shell is about 1 inch in length. It occurs from Labrador to Georges Bank in 27 to 80 fathoms.

Bulbus (Acrybia) smithii (Brown) PLATE 190 (8). This shell is inflated and globular. It is very light and thin with a golden epidermis. There are four rounded whorls. The aperture is a broad oval, occupying fully one half of the front area of the body-whorl. The outer margin of the aperture is very sharp. The umbilical opening is within the inner margin of the left side of the aperture. The length of the shell is about 1 inch. The shell is found in about 50 fathoms, from the Gulf of St. Lawrence to Georges Bank.

Family Lamellaridae

The aperture in this family is very large, due to the combined expansion of the last two whorls. The species are small with a very thin shell. There is no operculum. These mollusks have carnivorous habits.

Velutina laevigata (Linnaeus) PLATE 190 (9). The Velvet Shell. This is a thin, transparent shell, the large, round aperture and pink color give it an earlike appearance. The texture is calcareous and fragile, while the surface, due to the texture of the epidermis, has a velvety appearance, especially along the minute revolving striae. There is no operculum. The foot is large and elongate.

Key to PLATE 190

PLATE 190

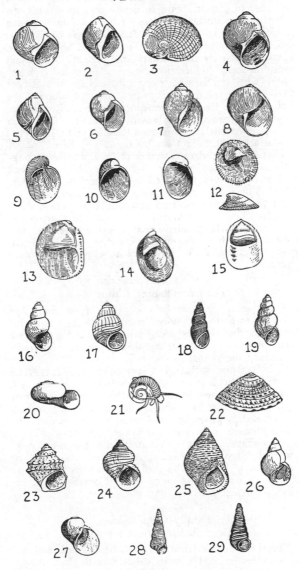

This shell is about ½ inch in length and ranges from Labrador to Massachusetts, in depths of 3 to 50 fathoms.

Velutina undata Brown (= **Velutina zonata** Gould) PLATE 190 (10). The Striped Velvet Shell. This shell is thin and translucent when stripped of epidermis. There are scarcely three whorls, the first two very small and practically hidden by the greatly expanded body-whorl with its flaring, trumpet-shaped aperture, larger than the body of the shell. Instead of an epidermis, the shell is covered by a calcareous incrustation, white or flesh-colored and zoned with brown stripes. It is less than ½ inch in length. It occurs from the Gulf of St. Lawrence to Massachusetts, in 20 to 30 fathoms.

Marsenina glabra (Couthouy) (= **Lamellaria per-spicua** (Stimpson)) PLATE 190 (11). This little shell consists of but two whorls, the apical whorl and the body-whorl. The former is very minute and is merely an adjunct to the latter, which is practically the whole shell, with its elongate oval aperture and thin and sharp-edged lip. It is ½ inch in length and ⅔ inch in breadth. The color is a translucent white. It is found in 15 to 34 fathoms from the Gulf of St. Lawrence to Cape Cod, Massachusetts.

Family Calyptraeidae
(Cup-and-Saucer Limpets)

These are limpetlike mollusks living a stationary life adhering to shells and stones by means of their powerful foot. The shell is subconical, the apex inclining to one side. There is an internal cup-shaped process which aids in keeping the animal in the shell.

Crucibulum striatum (Say) PLATE 190 (12). The Cup-and-Saucer Limpet. This is a small, circular shell, fairly solid in structure, and white, varying to pinkish or yellowish in color. Sometimes, it is marked with brownish streaks and is generally lined with polished white. The summit inclines posteriorly and toward the left side. There is a cup-shaped process inside attached to the anterior inner wall. Numerous radiating, raised lines cross the shell from apex to border. The shell is ½ inch in height and ⅘ inch in diameter. It ranges from Nova Scotia to the Florida Keys in 3 to 189 fathoms.

Family Crepidulidae
(Boat Shells, Slipper Limpets)

The shell, in this family, is oval, boat-shaped, and has an imperfect spire. The inner cavity is partly divided by a horizontal shelf or internal plate, situated posteriorly.

Crepidula fornicata (Linnaeus) PLATE 190 (13). The Boat Shell. The Slipper Limpet. The Quarter Deck.

These shells are about 1½ inches in length. They are often found closely pressed together in groups, one shell mounted on top of another, and piled on the outer or inner side of the shell of another species. This is the largest species of the genus, and the arched, whitish shells are conspicuous objects on the beach. The limy internal diaphragm takes up about one half of the concave interior, so that it has much the appearance of the quarter deck of a vessel. This habit of clinging together makes the boat shells useful to oyster fishermen, who buy them by the boatload to spread them over the sea bottom as a clutch, on which to plant seed-oysters. This species ranges from Prince Edward Island to Texas and the West Indies.

Crepidula glauca Say (= **Crepidula convexa** Say) PLATE 190 (14). The Gray Slipper Shell. This species is related to the previous one, but is smaller, being ⅜ inch in length. It is grayish green in color, sprinkled with specks of darker and lighter color. The interior is mottled with dark brown, while the horizontal diaphragm is white, with a yellowish edge. They are not so common as the previous species, but are found on shells of other mollusks and on seaweed, from Nova Scotia to Florida and Texas.

Crepidula plana Say PLATE 190 (15). The Flat Slipper Shell. This is a thin, translucent, and pure white shell, with a minute apex, turned somewhat off center, and with a highly polished and iridescent lining. The interior shield is less than half the length of the shell. The general shape is adaptable to the character of the surface of the shell to which it adheres. It is often attached and flattened on the interior of the shells borne by hermit crabs, that formerly belonged to a whelk or a moon shell. They are often carried about on the shells of horseshoe crabs, as well. This species is of common occurrence from Prince Edward Island to Texas.

Family Rissoidae
(The Spire Shells)

These are small, often minute, snails with a spiral turret and usually with an umbilicus. The operculum is horny, and the sculpture is variable. They are cosmopolitan and more than two hundred species are known.

Hydrobia (Rissoa) minuta (Totten) PLATE 190 (16). This is a minute, smooth snail with a blunt apex. It has a shining surface of a yellowish color. There are five whorls, with a translucent surface, finely striate with growth lines. The length is about ⅐ inch. The species is found in salt-marsh ponds from Labrador to New Jersey.

Alvania (Cingula) carinata (Mighels & Adams) PLATE 190 (17). This shell is quite minute, being about

⅒ inch in length. It is comparatively stout, its approximately five whorls being quite convex, especially the body-whorl. The shell is conical, very thin, and brown in color. The upper whorls have vertical striae, while the body-whorl shows a series of revolving lines. It is a northern form, ranging from the Gulf of St. Lawrence to Casco Bay, Maine. It is found in 96 to 200 fathoms.

Rissoa (Cingula) multilineata Stimpson PLATE 190 (18). This is also a minute species, being about ⅒ inch in length. It has a slender turret, with a blunt apex, and is white in color. There are five convex whorls with about twenty minute revolving lines. The aperture is ovate, somewhat pointed at both ends. It occurs from the Gulf of St. Lawrence to Casco Bay, Maine, in 96 to 200 fathoms.

Onoba (Rissoa) aculeus (Gould) PLATE 190 (19). The shell is minute, with six convex whorls, separated by deep sutures, the body-whorl being more than half the length of the shell, and the aperture, one third the length. The surface of the whorls is finely sculptured with minute revolving lines. The color is light yellow and the operculum is horny. The length is slightly more than ⅐ inch. It is found from the Bay of Fundy to Long Island Sound, around the low-water mark, on stones and decaying timbers.

Family Skeneidae
(The Orb Shells)

The shells of the species included in this family have a worldwide distribution. They are very minute and flattened with the whorls practically in one plane, coiled around a central, slightly elevated apex. The aperture is small and rounded.

Skenea planorbis (Fabricius) PLATE 190 (20, 21). The Orb Shell. The Trumpet Shell. This very minute shell is about ⅒ inch in diameter. It is flat and with only four whorls, surrounding a slightly raised spire. The sutures are distinct and the umbilicus is circular. These mollusks are found under stones and the holdfasts of algae, as well as on oyster shells and those of other mollusks. In the southern part of their range they are found creeping over sponges and corals and any other marine growths. On the Atlantic Coast they range from Greenland to Florida. They are also European in habitat.

Family Architectonicidae (Solariidae)
(The Sundial Shells)

These shells are characterized by their flattened cone shape, the sharp-edged aperture with acute outer angle, and the wide umbilicus, with the inner edges of the whorls visible, and margined by a beaded to knobbed keel. The operculum is horny and spiral. The mollusk has a large, oval foot, indented anteriorly.

Architectonica (Solarium) granulata (Lamarck) PLATE 190 (22). The Granulated Sundial Shell. This essentially tropical shell invades the southern part of our region off the North Carolina coast. The flattened toplike spire has a practically continuous outline, due to the close-set sutures over the sharp edges of the flattened whorls. The crossing of the radiating ridges with the equally raised spiral lines produces a conspicuous granulated sculpture of brown and purple tubercles standing out against the generally white or gray background color of the shell. The somewhat contracted, but open, umbilicus discloses a beautiful perspective of beaded spiral inner whorl-margins gradually and regularly narrowing toward the apex. The aperture is sharp-edged and rounded, except for the acute outer angle. This species inhabits moderately shallow water from North Carolina to the Gulf of Mexico and the West Indies.

Family Littorinidae
(The Periwinkles)

This is a widespread family of common, well-known mollusks, worldwide in range, occurring abundantly, often in crowded groups on rocks, not only between the tide limits, but often up to the ultimate zone reached by the highest tides. They can survive long stretches of drought, and in many respects seem transitional to the condition of air-breathing land shells. The shell is a conical spire of a few whorls, with a round aperture and without an umbilicus. It is not pearly. The columella is thick and relatively flat. The animal has a short, broad snout and long tentacles, furnished with eyes on the outer side of their bases. There is a broad, squarish foot, divided into two parts longitudinally, each side being pushed forward alternately as the animal progresses. The radula is long and narrow, each row of rasplike teeth consisting of a large, variable central tooth of several cusps, a single cusped lateral on either side, flanked by two hooked marginal teeth. Several hundred species of periwinkles are known throughout the world. They are vegetarian in habit, feeding on algae.

Littorina litorea Linnaeus COLOR PLATE XV, 10. The Shore Periwinkle. The Edible Periwinkle. The Common Periwinkle. The shell is a thick cone, rather squat, with seven or eight whorls, having spiral ribs and a sharp spire, often worn somewhat on exposed, rocky coasts. The color is olive, varying to brownish yellow or gray, often banded with brown or dark red; the whole shell may be practically black. The columella is broad and white, almost flattened. The outer lip is thick sometimes beveling to a sharp edge, and lined with black.

This species was originally European, but has spread around the North Atlantic to the coast of North America, gradually working southward along the coast of Canada, Maine, and Massachusetts. For a time, Cape Cod acted as a barrier but, during the past century, it surmounted that barrier, and now ranges along the Long Island Shore, even to the pilings on the sandy shores of New Jersey. It is a common article of food in England and on the Continent, tons of winkles being sold in the European markets, or roasted and hawked about the streets of London during the year. This periwinkle measures about ¾ inch both in height and in diameter. The sexes are separate, the female being larger than the male.

Littorina irrorata (Say) PLATE 190 (25). The Lined Periwinkle. The Southern Periwinkle. The shell is about 1 inch in height, and is quite heavy and well developed. It is yellowish white with numerous chestnut-brown dots on the whorls in spiral rows. The columella is brown to orange in hue. The apex is sharply pointed and there are about five whorls. The travels of this species have been in the opposite direction to those of *Littorina litorea*. Just as that species invaded New England from the north, so *Littorina irrorata* has spread from the Gulf of Mexico and Florida, northward, finally reaching Massachusetts, and overlapping the territory of the former species, so it is now intermingled with it. Nevertheless, this southern *Littorina* seems to prefer quiet locations in salt marshes, away from wave action.

Littorina rudis (Donovan) (= **Littorina saxatilis** Olivi) PLATE 190 (24); COLOR PLATE XVI, 2. The Rough Periwinkle. The shell of this species is very solid and thick, with four or five strong and convex whorls, sculptured with raised revolving lines crossing fairly elevated lines of growth, giving the shell a rough appearance. The color is gray and banded with inconspicuous hues varying from yellow to brown and black. It can withstand exposure to the air for a week or more, so that its habitat extends to the upper limits of the tidal zone like that of *Littorina litorea*. It is generally a smaller shell than the two previous species, varying from ⅙ to ½ inch in height. It ranges from Labrador to New Jersey.

Littorina palliata (Say) (= **Littorina obtusata** Linnaeus) COLOR PLATES XV, 11; XVI, 3. The Pale Periwinkle. The Obtuse Periwinkle. This shell is small with a low spire and comparatively large body-whorl. It is of substantial texture and fairly thick. The surface is smooth and shining. The color varies considerably. It is often yellow, brown, or red, and is often banded with a contrasting spiral stripe, such as bright red on a dark brown background, or a brown spiral on yellow. The length of the shell varies from about ½ to ⅞ inch. It is abundant, clinging to rock-weeds and in tide-pools, as well as on the rocks themselves, where it feeds on algae. It is very common from New Jersey to the Arctic Ocean.

Littorina dilatata D'Orbigny PLATE 190 (23). The Knobbed Littorina. The shell is a broad cone, rather thick, and bluish gray in color. The four to five whorls are encircled spirally with rows of conspicuous, white nodules, giving them an angular appearance. The columella is considerably excavated and is purplish brown in color. This is a southern species, ranging from North Carolina to the West Indies.

Family Lacunidae
(The Chink Shells)

These are conical, thin-shelled mollusks, with an expanded half-moon-shaped aperture, having a long groove, or chink, on the columella leading to an umbilicus. The lip is sharp. There is a thin membranous operculum, spiral in character.

Lacuna vincta (Montagu) PLATE 190 (26). The Atlantic Chink Shell. This species superficially resembles a thin, elongate *Littorina*. The shell is yellowish in color, sometimes, with two spiral bands of brown on the spiral whorl and four on the body-whorl. This color scheme varies, some shells having brown bands on a purplish ground, others with purple bands on a whitish ground. There are about five rather convex whorls, with rather deep sutures. There are very fine lines of growth and a half-moon-shaped aperture. The columella has a thin groove, terminating in a very small umbilicus. This shell is about ⅓ inch in height. It is often found entangled in the holdfasts of kelp and other algae. It occurs abundantly from 1 to 120 fathoms, and ranges from Labrador to New Jersey.

Lacuna pallidula neritoidea Gould PLATE 190 (27). The Pale Chink. This little shell has 3½ whorls, the body-whorl being very large. The epidermis is greenish yellow in color and quite rough. There is a large, expanded aperture, the outer lip being very sharp and the rounded inner lip leading to the deep umbilicus. The length is ⅕ inch. Like the previous species, this mollusk is often found on floating seaweed. The distribution is from Greenland to Connecticut.

Family Turritellidae
(The Screw Shells, the Tower Shells)

These are shells with long, slender spires, having many whorls sculptured with numerous revolving ridges. There is no umbilicus. The aperture is oval and with a thin lip. The operculum is spiral. While this is a large family, most of the species belong to the Pacific fauna, only a few being found in the Atlantic Ocean.

Turritella (Tachyrhynchus) erosa Couthouy PLATE 190 (28). This is an elongate, slender high-turreted shell of about ten whorls, each grooved with three to five blunt furrows. The aperture is practically circular. This shell is about 1 inch in length. It is difficult to get perfect specimens because of the fragile, slender tip. The species ranges from Labrador to Massachusetts Bay, in 7 to 60 fathoms.

Turritella (Turritellopsis) acicula Stimpson PLATE 190 (29). The Needle Shell. This is a very slender white or brownish shell with ten very convex whorls with strong, spiral ribs, three of which are especially strong. There are also very weak and fine vertical striations. The aperture is almost a perfect circle with a thin edge. This shell is less than ¼ inch in length. It ranges from Labrador to Massachusetts Bay and Georges Bank, in 1 to 50 fathoms.

Family Vermetidae
(Worm Shells)

The shell is tubular. At the apex it forms a somewhat irregular, turreted spiral which is tightly coiled. This upper portion was the young shell and, during that stage, resembled the adult shell of a *Turritella*. After a number of such coils, the shell apparently became free of restraint and grew aberrantly in a loose, irregular, wormlike course, so that the shells of the mollusks of this family have been popularly, but erroneously, called "worm shells." They are, at times, found in tangled masses, or attached to shells of other mollusks, and in tropical regions are frequently entwined in sponges and corals. Only a few species come into our range.

Vermicularia (Vermetus) spirata (Philippi) PLATE 191 (1). The Worm Shell. This is a yellowish to violet-brown, or white shell, with tight coils near the apex, the remainder being loosely and irregularly winding. The tubelike portion is longitudinally keeled and striated, and also has transverse lines of growth. The length is 6 to 9 inches. The open end of the tube may be closed by a membranous operculum having a central nucleus and concentric growth lines.

Family Caecidae
(The Tube Shells)

This family contains a single genus of minute, tubular shells, spiral at first, and then forming a straight, slightly curved portion. Soon, the spiral part is lost, leaving only the straight tube, closed at the top by a septum. After a time, a new septum forms a short distance below the previous one and a second section drops off. The remainder of the tube, closed at the top, by the second septum, then becomes the shell of the animal during the remainder of its life.

Caecum pulchellum Stimpson PLATE 191 (2). The Northern Blind Shell. The Beauty Blind Shell. This shell is so called because, in the adult, it ends blindly at the truncated and sealed summit. The adult, curving, cylindrical shell has about twenty-five regular encircling rings, each formed by a raised rib and the equal space between it and the next rib. The sealed septum covering the apex has the form of a slightly convex, rounded cap. It has a concave operculum of about eight concentric spirals. Because of its minute size and peculiar shape, it is often overlooked by collectors. The distribution of this species is wide, extending from New Hampshire to the Florida Keys.

Family Trichotropidae
(The Hairy Keeled Snails)

These are thin top-shaped, elongate shells with a hairy periostracum, the prolongations of which stand out from the angles of the whorls. The sutures are deeply channeled and there are a number of spiral ribs.

Trichotropis borealis (Broderlip & Sowerby) PLATE 191 (3). The Northern Hairy Keel. This species has a yellowish periostracum. There are about four whorls, of which the last is quite large and sculptured by two prominent revolving ribs, from which prolongations of the periostracum stand out like spines. The rounded aperture tapers almost to a point below. There is an umbilicus. This shell is about ¾ inch in length and ranges from Labrador to Massachusetts Bay, in 7 to 60 fathoms.

Family Triphoridae

These are minute shells with an elongated spire and many reversed or sinistral (left-handed) whorls. The aperture is small and with a short anterior canal.

Triphora perversa nigrocincta (Adams) PLATE 191 (4). The Perverse Triple-lined Shell. This pale brown, elongate, spiral shell has about fifteen whorls which are sinistral, or left handed, and sculptured with three rows of prominent tubercles, separated by two revolving grooves on each whorl, except on the first four or five apical whorls which are smooth, and except the body whorl, which has four rows. Some shells are blackish red and a blackish revolving ridge follows the suture in most whorls. The length of the shell is about ⅓ inch. This variety ranges from Massachusetts to Florida, in depths of 1 to 30 fathoms.

Family Cerithiopsidae

The shells, in this family, are small and, as in the previous family, are many whorled and with a small aperture with a nearly straight anterior canal forming a notch at its lower termination. The whorls are ornamented by a spiral sculpture.

Cerithiopsis greenii (Adams) PLATE 191 (5). The shell of this species is small, slender, and turreted with ten to twelve whorls. The body-whorl has twenty to twenty-five ridges, crossed by three revolving, impressed lines, thus producing three series of granules, the lower being the largest. The small aperture is about one eighth of the shell length, terminating anteriorly in a very short but deep anterior canal over which the lips curve to a degree. This species occurs in shallow water, just below the low-tide mark on marine algae. It ranges from Massachusetts Bay to the West Indies.

Cerithiopsis subulata (Montagu) PLATE 191 (6). This is a pale brown shell, darker at the sutures. The whorls are flat, making an even and slender spire. There are about fifteen whorls with deep sutures, sculptured by three rows of granules produced by the crossing of indented spirals with the cross-lines of growth. The length is ½ inch. The distribution is from Massachusetts to the West Indies, in 2 to 15 fathoms.

Seila adamsii (Lea) (= **Cerithiopsis terebralis** Adams) PLATE 191 (7). This is a small, turreted sea snail ⅖ inch in height, with ten to twelve quite flat whorls, each with three or four sharp, elevated, spiral ridges. The aperture is small and the body-whorl is short. There is a short canal. These are quite common throughout their range, which extends from Massachusetts to Florida.

Family Cerithiidae
(Horn Shells)

The shells in this family are elongated and many-whorled, each whorl often convex in outline. The aperture is set at an oblique angle. There is an inconspicuous, short anterior canal.

Cerithium ferrugineum Say (= **Cerithium variabile** Adams) PLATE 191 (8). This shell is about ½ to

⅔ inch in length, with seven rather rotund whorls, each spirally ribbed with about three rounded ridges, with seven ridges on the body-whorl. The color is dark with a reddish tinge. The lining of the aperture is also dark. It ranges from the Carolinas to the Florida Keys and the Gulf of Mexico.

Bittium alternatum (Say) (= **Bittium nigrum** Totten) PLATE 191 (9). This is a brown, conical shell, about ⅕ inch in length. There are six to eight whorls covered by a network of spirals and cross-ridges, with spirals alone on the body-whorl. The aperture is oblique and rounded, and the anterior canal is reduced to a small notch. The operculum is membranous with four to five spirals. This shell is common on eelgrass and algae in shallow water, or on stones. They are abundant from Prince Edward Island to North Carolina.

Family Aporrhaidae
(The Pelican's Foot Shells)

These are small but solid shells, with a long spire and numerous tuberculated whorls. The aperture is long and narrow, with a greatly expanded and thickened outer lip, in some species, especially those in European seas, having toelike projections, hence the name Pelican's Foot.

Aporrhais occidentalis Beck COLOR PLATE XV, 12. The Duck's Foot Shell. The whorls of the spire are eight or nine, convex in outline, with numerous wavelike folds of ribs, more conspicuous than the close-set revolving lines. The aperture is vertical and long and narrow. The outer lip is greatly expanded and triangular with a blunt process at its upper angle. There is a nearly obsolete anterior canal. This expanded lip makes the species easy to identify. There are several varieties of this species, but the typical form inhabits relatively deep waters from the Gulf of St. Lawrence to North Carolina, in 50 to 350 fathoms. It is from 2 to 2⅖ inches in length.

Family Strombidae

These are large, heavy shells with a thickened and expanded lip in adults, notched near the canal. The body-whorl is greatly enlarged, with a long and narrow aperture. The operculum is horny, clawlike, and pointed. It does not close the aperture and is not well adapted for creeping. The animals progress by a series of leaps, turning the shell from side to side. They are carrion-eaters and very active. Their large eyes are mounted on thick pedicels, are more perfect than those of most other gastropods. They also have a pair of slender, sensitive tentacles.

Strombus pugilis alatus (Gmelin) PLATE 191 (10).

The Winged Strombus. This is a variety of the Fighting Conch, (*Strombus pugilis pugilis* Linnaeus), common on the Florida coast. It is about 3 or 4 inches in height, yellowish brown in color, buff below blending into suffusions or stripes of orange and purple. The fairly solid shell has about seven whorls, the upper ones with revolving ribs. The typical form has blunt spines on the shoulders of the lower whorls, but this variety is said to be spineless, though some individuals have them. The variety, *alatus,* also has a mottled color pattern, while the typical form is not variegated. These carrion-eaters are noted for their pugnacity. This variety ranges from North Carolina to Florida and to the Gulf of Mexico.

Family Cassididae
(The Helmet Shells)

The shells of the mollusks in this family are very heavy, thick, and either globular or triangular. The aperture is long and narrow, ending in a recurved anterior channel. The columella is thick and often folded. The spire is partly immersed by the extensively developed body-whorl. The outer lip is broad and thickened at the edge. It is ribbed within. These are active mollusks, carnivorous and predatory. They live in warm seas, on sandy bottoms, where they prey upon bivalves.

Cassis cameo Stimpson PLATE 191 (11). The Cameo Shell. The Queen Conch. These are large shells, 10 inches, or even more, in length. The color is yellowish white, tinged with brown. The lip and columella are extremely broad. The lip is light coffee-brown in color with a number of spaced outer teeth, while the inner and columellar teeth are more numerous. These teeth and ridges are light in color, with the spaces between them a deep, chocolate-brown.

The shell of this species and that of the large King Conch (*Strombus gigas* Linnaeus), have always been much sought after for making cameos, great numbers being exported to Italy and Great Britain, especially for that purpose. *Strombus gigas* does not come as far north as our range, but *Cassis cameo* is found in North Carolina waters.

Cassis granulosa Bruguiere PLATE 191 (12). The Granular Helmet Shell. The shell of this species is thinner than that of the previous one. It is ovate and more or less globular in shape, with the body-whorl considerably inflated, especially around the thickened and reflected outer lip of the aperture. The spire is sharp. The rounded whorls are smooth with vestigial indications of transverse grooves. The columella has smooth plications and has a conspicuous granulose surface. The inner margin of the outer lip has fine toothlike indentations. The general coloration is bluish white, encircled by five bands of quadrangular, irregularly spaced reddish brown spots. The length of the shell is 4 inches and the diameter, 2¾ inches. It is found on sandy bottoms from North Carolina to the West Indies.

Family Tonnidae (Doliidae)
(The Tun Shells)

The shell, in this family, is large, thin, and practically globular. There is a short, stout spire and a greatly expanded body-whorl with numerous revolving ridges. There is no operculum. The head of the animal is large, with eyes on the sides of the tentacles. The head is massive and the proboscis, also, is large and very long. There is a horizontal groove in the anterior margin of the wide, lobed foot. These are essentially tropical shells, but some of them impinge on the extreme southern portion of our territory, as limited for this field book.

The large size, capacity, and shape of these shells have made them useful as utensils, in the regions where they are abundant. For that reason, they are often popularly known as Cask Shells and Wine Jars.

Tonna (Dolium) galea (Linnaeus) PLATE 191 (13). The Helmet Tun Shell. This shell is light and very thin. There are seven whorls. The spire is quite small and sunken within the curve of the enormous, thin-walled basin of the body-whorl, which makes up the greater part of the shell. The sutures are sunken. The surface is sculptured with many spiral ribs, parallel to each other, deeply cut, and crossed by many fine lines of growth. The body color is a clear, smooth fawn, diversified by touches of darker brown on the spire, lip, and columella. The columella is considerably twisted. The shell is 6 to 10 inches in height, and the animal is much larger than the shell. It is found in shallow water from Cape Hatteras, North Carolina, to Texas and the West Indies.

Tonna (Dolium) perdix (Linnaeus) PLATE 191 (14). The Partridge Tun Shell. The Partridge Cask Shell. This shell is marked with spirals of elongated, crescent-shaped blocks, outlined by curving white lines, suggesting the plumage of a partridge. The spire is much more elevated than in the preceding species. The aperture is considerably expanded. The height of the shell varies from 4 to 9 inches. It is largely found in and about the Florida Keys and the West Indies, but as it seems to have much wider distribution, it may some day be recorded from the North Carolina neighborhood. At any rate, it is a good species for comparison.

Ficus (Pyrula) papyracea (Say) PLATE 192 (10). The Paper Fig Shell. This shell is pear shaped, inflated, very thin, and light. The name, Paper Fig Shell, is very appropriate. The spire is not elevated and the body-whorl is without shoulders. The sutures are thin. The color is yellowish with small reddish spots. The whorls are marked by numerous revolving striae, about thirty in number, that tend to be alternately heavy and light. They are crossed by smaller striae. The interior is shining orange-brown. There is no operculum. This species is quite common along the entire Florida coast, and extends as far north as North Carolina.

Family Cypraeidae
(The Cowries)

This is a remarkable family of brightly colored shells, brilliantly polished by the activity of the mantle, a fold of which is reflected from either side to cover completely one half of the shell, meeting the fold of the outer side at the mid-line of the upper surface. The young animal has a spiral shell, the successive whorls, during growth, being laid on horizontally, with the body-whorl so wide that it nearly conceals the spire. The aperture is narrow, but elongate, reaching nearly the entire length of the shell on one side. At first, the outer lip is thin, but soon thickens and becomes toothed, corresponding teeth also developing on the columella. The laterally reflected folds of the mantle lay down successive thin layers of enamel, alternately colored and white, covering more and more of the spire, until, in the adult shell, it is completely buried, when the final coat of shining, colored enamel is applied. The adult shell is ovate, narrowed at both ends, the toothed aperture extending the entire length of the shell, notched

---

Key to PLATE 191

1. *Vermicularis* (*Vermetus*) *spirata*; 2. *Caecum pulchellum*; 3. *Trichotropis borealis*; 4. *Triphora perversa nigrocincta*; 5. *Cerithiopsis greenii*; 6. *Cerithiopsis subulata*; 7. *Seila adamsii* (*Cerithiopsis terebralis*); 8. *Cerithium ferrugineum* (*Cerithium variabile*); 9. *Bittium alternum* (*Bittium nigrum*); 10. *Strombus pugilis alatus*; 11. *Cassis cameo*; 12. *Cassis granulosa*; 13. *Tonna* (*Dolium*) *galea*; 14. *Tonna* (*Dolium*) *perdix*; 15. *Atlanta peronii*; 16. *Cypraea exanthema*; 17. *Trivia quadripunctata*; 18. *Simnia* (*Ovula*) *uniplicata*; 19. *Murex fulvescens* (*Murex spinicostata*); 20. *Eupleura caudata*; 21. *Trophon clathratus*; 22. *Trophon truncatus*; 23. *Urosalpinx cinerea*; 24. *Thais floridana*; 25. *Columbella* (*Anachis*) *avara*; 26. *Columbella* (*Mitrella*) *lunata*; 27. *Columbella* (*Pyrene*) *mercatoria*; 28. *Columbella* (*Anachis*) *translirata*; 29. *Columbella* (*Mitrella*) *rosacea*.

PLATE 191

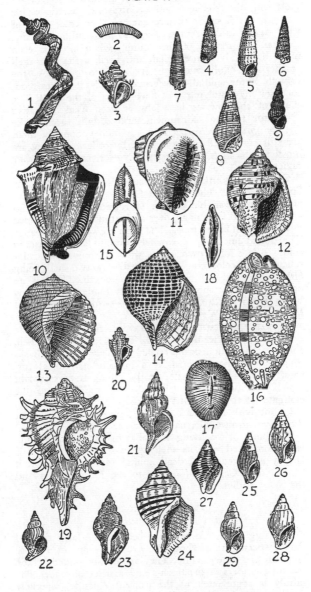

at both extremities. The final color pattern shows bright spots on the surface with contrasting bands visible through the layer of surface enamel. The color patterns vary greatly in different species, and also within the same species. The mantle of the animal, when alive, is even more brilliantly colored than the shell. After the shell reaches the adult condition, it ceases to grow. As the growth of the animal, however, continues, it makes room for itself by dissolving the inner layers of the shell. The shells of the cowries have always been used by native tribes for personal adornment, and certain species, like *Cypraea moneta,* have been used as money. Some of them are still considered of great value by collectors. They are mostly tropical. A few species, however, extend into our region.

Cypraea exanthema Linnaeus PLATE 191 (16). The Spotted Cowrie. The Measled Cowrie. This shell shows an extremely variable pattern of round white spots and rings scattered irregularly over a chestnut ground blended with gray and bluish tones. The teeth are very dark brown. The dorsal line is approximately straight and whitish in color. Bands of brown often show through this color scheme. This coloration is very variable, no two shells being alike. The size is 3 to 4 inches in length. There is no operculum. This species is found in moderately shallow water, from North Carolina to the Florida Keys, Gulf of Mexico, and the West Indies.

Trivia quadripunctata Gray PLATE 191 (17). The Four-spotted Coffee-bean Shell. This is an ovoid shell, about ⅓ inch in length, related to *Cypraea* but always smaller and characterized by a longitudinal dorsal furrow, from which radiate nearly equal transverse ribs which continue around the edge of the shell to the elongate, slotlike aperture. The color is light to purplish rose, but with four dark red dots, two on either side of the dorsal groove, alternating with each other.

The body of the living animal is bright red, and quite large compared with its shell, when fully extruded. It is largely a scavenger of dead animal matter. Its range is from North Carolina (Tryon) to the Florida Keys and the West Indies.

Family Ovulidae
(The Egg Shells)

The Egg Shells are so called because the large tropical Pacific species are of about the size and shape of a goose egg and are snowy white. They are highly valued by the Pacific Islanders as ornaments and articles of trade. The family is represented in the tropical Atlantic, especially Florida and the West Indies, and as far north as North

Carolina, by a few much smaller and slenderer species found on sea fans and other gorgonians. They are related to the Cypraeidae.

Simnia (Ovula) uniplicata (Sowerby) PLATE 191 (18). The Slender Egg Shell. The shell of this species is long and slender, similar in construction to that of *Cypraea*, notched at each end to form anterior and posterior canals, and rolled in upon itself at the narrow, slitlike aperture, which is smooth on the columellar side and faintly toothed within the outer lip. This species is distinguished by having a single distinct fold on the posterior end of the columella. The outside of the shell is smooth and polished. This species ranges from North Carolina to the West Indies. It is practically always attached to the stems of sea fans and other gorgonians. The color of the shell harmonizes with the color of the gorgonian, being purple if the latter is purple, or yellow if the stem is yellow. The length of the shell is about ¾ inch.

Division HETEROPODA
(Pelagic Sea Snails)

These are pelagic, free-swimming Gastropoda, having the foot developed into a swimming-organ, instead of a creeping sole, as is the case in the Division Platypoda. This swimming structure is made up of two parts, a flattened fin, projecting ventrally, often with a sucker, and a posterior tail, in some cases, with an operculum. The visceral sac, which normally occupies the spire of the streptoneuran mollusk, is here reduced to a small posterior hump, the nucleus, usually covered by a transparent coiled shell. The head is large, with a pair of short tentacles, having stalked eyes at their base. The entire body is transparent, so that the internal organs can be clearly seen. The nucleus is usually brightly colored.

Family Carinariidae

These Heteropods have an elongate, transparent body, with the foot divided into two parts, one of which acts as a fin. There is a diminutive transparent, conical shell situated posteriorly, which contains the visceral hump (nucleus) alone, with the ctenidium or gill projecting forward from beneath it.

Carinaria mediterranea Peron & Lesueur. The elongate gelatinous body of this species is about 2 inches in length, with a well-defined head bearing a violet-colored proboscis. The ventral, fin-shaped anterior, or foot-lobe, is red in color and bears a sucker with which the animal attaches itself, when not moving about. It feeds on various small pelagic animals, seizing them with the powerful snout. This creature swims in the open ocean and occurs from New Jersey to Florida, the West Indies, and in the Mediterranean Sea.

Family Atlantidae

In this family, the shell is coiled and much more completely developed than in the previous family. It is transparent and fragile, with the whorls equipped with a distinct keel, or carina.

Atlanta peronii Lesueur PLATE 191 (15). The shell is coiled and sufficiently large to contain the entire body, when retracted. It is discoid in section, as shown in the figure. The aperture is narrow with a deep notch at the beginning of the keel, which is at first in the form of a depressed groove and then becomes elevated. The operculum is ovate. The shell and body are completely transparent. The diameter of the shell is about ½ inch.

Order STENOGLOSSA

This order comprises gastropods with a well-developed shell, usually having a thick spiral, an elongated aperture, and a distinct siphonal canal, often long, and sometimes a short but distinct notch. There is a retractile proboscis, an unpaired oesophageal gland (at times, a poison gland), and a siphon originating from a fold in the mantle to form a closed tube, for inhaling water and excreting wastes from the mantle cavity. A penis is always present in the male. The osphradium, or organ of smell, is well developed and is *bipectinate* (branched like a feather on both sides of the main stem). This is usually the case with carnivorous gastropods. The radula is narrow, and either has a single lateral on either side of the median, or *rachidian,* tooth, or there is a lateral on each side with the median tooth lacking.

The order Stenoglossa is divided into two Suborders: (1) *Rachiglossa,* and (2) *Toxiglossa.* Only the Rachiglossa occurs within our territory.

Suborder RACHIGLOSSA

The Suborder Rachiglossa includes Stenoglossa with a highly developed proboscis, a pallial siphon, and vestigial jaws. Each row of teeth on the radular ribbon consists of a strongly cusped median or rachidian tooth and one lateral on either side, or the laterals may be lacking. The shell is usually entirely external and well developed.

Family Muricidae
(The Rock Shells)

In this family, the shell has a moderately long spire and straight posterior siphonal canal, usually ornamented with ribs, which often bear spines. The foot of the animal is broad and truncated anteriorly.

Murex fulvescens Sowerby (= **Murex spinicostata** Valenciennes) PLATE 191 (19). The Spine-ribbed Murex. This is a fine large shell, about 6 inches in length. The color of the shell is grayish white with a brownish epidermis and a series of many prominent spines connected with the raised horizontal ribs. The siphonal canal is long, narrow, and nearly closed. There are about seven or eight whorls. The aperture is large and rounded, with a white interior. There are three or more varices, vestiges of the outer lips of previous successive apertures, thickened during resting stages in the past history of the shell. The present outer lip and the siphonal canal are also adorned with spines. This handsome shell is distributed from North Carolina to Florida and around the Gulf of Mexico to Texas.

The species belonging to the Family Muricidae are all carnivorous and are highly organized mollusks capable of creeping and swimming. They prey especially on bivalves. Where their range extends to clam- and oyster-beds, they commit extensive depredations, boring holes through one valve of their victim and sucking out the flesh. The ancient Tyrians made the famous Tyrian purple dye from a fluid secreted by the anal glands of the Banded Murex (*Murex trunculus*) of the Mediterranean. As they did not know how to extract the brownish fluid, which, on exposure to the air, became the glorious royal purple for the robes of Roman emperors, the Tyrian fishermen crushed the shell in hollows of the rocks along the coast and filtered out the fluid, which they purified to produce the dye. About 1,000 species of *Murex* are known.

Eupleura caudata (Say) PLATE 191 (20). The Borer. The radula of this small species shows that it belongs in the Family Muricidae. The shell is 1 inch, more or less, in height. The color of the outside of the shell varies from reddish to whitish gray, while the outer lip is often bluish. There are about five whorls, with flattened shoulders, around a relatively steep spire. There are from nine to eleven strong, vertical ribs, with opposite varices. Many close revolving lines descend the spire, crossing the ribs. Beadlike granules border the outer lip. The siphonal canal is short, straight, and almost closed. The foot of the animal is yellow. This species is common from Massachusetts to Florida in 1 to 8 fathoms.

Trophon clathratus Linnaeus PLATE 191 (21). This is a small, light brown shell, with six rounded whorls, having the suture well defined. During its growth the repeated expansion of the lip produces a series of fifteen to twenty raised folds, which are actually varices transformed into ribs rounded gradually as they become older. The small aperture has an evenly rounded outer lip terminating in a curved canal that bends to the left. The aperture is brown. The length is ½ inch. This American *Trophon* ranges from the Arctic Ocean, south to Georges Bank and Massachusetts. It is often found in the stomachs of haddocks.

Trophon truncatus (Ström) PLATE 191 (22). The Common Trophon. This shell is also about ½ inch in height and brownish gray in color. There are six whorls. The varices are similar to those of the preceding species, but they are much more numerous and, therefore, more closely set together. Also, the canal is shorter and more curved, and is abruptly truncate. This is the most common North Atlantic *Trophon*. It ranges from Greenland to Georges Bank, but it is usually found in the stomachs of fishes. It is recorded from 10 to 50 fathoms.

Urosalpinx cinerea (Say) PLATE 191 (23). The Oyster Drill. The Oyster Borer. This little fusiform shell has about six convex whorls, crossed by numerous, vertical, rounded ribs or folds. A number of revolving, raised lines cross these folds, about twenty being on the body-whorl, while on the spire, the lines cease, leaving only the vertical ribs. The shell color is light brown or yellowish, with the aperture lined with dark brown or purple. The oval aperture has a sharp outer lip, and there is a short, rather open canal, and a horny operculum. Next to the starfish, this species is the worst enemy of the oyster-beds. Scores of these oyster drills mount on a clump of oysters and bore neat little round pinholes through the shells. They then destroy the oysters by sucking out their juices. In this way, thousands of dollars in damages are done in a single season. This is one of the commonest sea snails of the North Atlantic Coast, and ranges from Prince Edward Island to Florida.

Family Thaisidae
(The Purple Snails, the Dog Whelks)

This family contains shells of great interest because of their variability, their adaptive resourcefulness, and because of their former usefulness in producing dye. Their striated, nodular, and thick-walled shells have a short spire, a large body-whorl, and a large, elongate, and thick-lipped aperture, which is pointed at the top and has a short, open canal below. In some specimens, on the other hand, the lip may be comparatively thin at the edge, though stouter away from it. The color also is very variable, running through a large number of hues and combinations of them. They are carnivorous, devouring bivalve mollusks and especially mussels, and even invading the rock barnacle zone to feed upon its inhabitants. They are able to withstand exposure to the air at the summit of the tidal zone because of their capacity for breathing air when it is passed over the water imprisoned in their mantle cavity. Their anal glands secrete a crimson or purple dye which was made use of not only by American Indian tribes, but also by the ancient Phoenicians, who combined its secretions with that derived from the Phoenician *Murex* to produce certain varieties of the famous Tyrian purple.

Thais lapillus Linnaeus COLOR PLATE XVI, 1. The remarkable color variation of this species is shown in the color plate, as well as its habit of gathering in large colonies in rock crevices between the tides to feed upon the crowded mussel and barnacle colonies. The eggs of this snail are deposited in vaselike capsules, in clusters, each capsule being mounted on a slender stalk (COLOR PLATE XVI, 1a).

Thais floridana Conrad PLATE 191 (24). The Florida Dye Shell. This species has a strong, rugged shell, with about five whorls with sutures not clearly visible and sloping shoulders. The body-whorl is large, sculptured with two rows of tubercles. The surface, generally, has strong revolving ridges. The outer lip is thick and heavy, crenulated within. The canal is short. The general coloration is grayish white, clouded, and streaked with brown. This is a southern species, occurring on rocks between the tides, from North Carolina to Florida, Texas, and the West Indies.

Family Columbellidae (Pyrenidae)
(The Dove Shells)

These are small shells with a long and narrow aperture. The outer lip is thickened in the middle and toothed. The inner lip is wrinkled. These shells are found in warm seas. Their coloration is striking and they have a polished surface.

Columbella (Mitrella) lunata (Say) PLATE 191 (26). The Lunar Columbella. This species is distinguished by the crescent-shaped markings of chestnut-color on the whitish ground of its surface. The shell is fusiform and quite smooth in texture. It has a small oval aperture, with the lip indistinctly toothed. The animal is light-colored, with black eyes. It is very small, measuring about ⅛ inch in length. This species occurs abundantly in shallow water on sandy bottoms or crawling over stones and algae. It ranges from Prince Edward Island to the Gulf of Mexico. It is very common along the shore of southern New England.

Columbella (Mitrella) rosacea Gould PLATE 191 (29). The Rosy Columbella. This little shell has an acutely tapering spire, and is white tinged with rose-color.

It has six whorls, completely covered with minute revolving lines. The lip is sharp-edged, and without teeth. It measures only ⅕ inch in length. It is a northern species occurring from Labrador to New Jersey.

Columbella (Anachis) avara Say PLATE 191 (25). The Greedy Columbella. This shell has an elongate, somewhat ovate spire, of a light straw-color, with a fine network of reddish brown. The lower half of the body-whorl is marked with about fifteen smooth ribs running lengthwise on the shell, interrupting a series of fine revolving lines. Above the ends of the ribs and on the rest of the spire to the apex, the shell is covered by the revolving lines alone and without interruption. The small aperture is narrow and oval, both lips being provided with teeth inside the margin. The length is about ⅗ inch. This shell is of common occurrence from Massachusetts to the Florida Keys.

Columbella (Pyrene) mercatoria Linnaeus PLATE 191 (27). The Trader Columbella. The Common Columbella. The Mottled Dove Shell. This shell is about ½ inch in height. The spire of this species is short, cone-shaped, and with an acutely formed apex. There are six whorls, all spirally grooved. The body-whorl is expanded above and contracted narrowly below. The aperture is long, narrow, and of sinuous outline. It is quite thick, especially in the middle where the outer lip has several calluslike denticles. The coloration is light gray, mottled and blotched longitudinally with brown, but quite variable in different individuals. This species is very abundant on the beaches from North Carolina to Florida and the West Indies.

Columbella (Anachis) translirata Ravenel PLATE 191 (28). This is the commonest of all the Columbellas. It is very brightly colored, varying from straw-yellow to dark brown. It ranges abundantly from North Carolina to the Florida Keys and the Gulf of Mexico.

Family Nassidae (Nassariidae)
(The Dog Whelks, the Mud Snails)

This is an exceedingly widespread family, being found throughout the shallow waters of the entire world, and includes the commonest marine snails found along our Atlantic Coast. They are predaceous mollusks, feeding not only on living animals but also on dead and decaying animal matter, which they consume voraciously. They are, therefore, of great importance in the economy of protected mud flats, where they act as scavengers and keep such waters sweet and clean by disposing of all kinds of dead and decaying organisms within an exceedingly short space of time.

The shell is small with a tapering spire and rotund body-whorl, thus having a generally ovate outline. The aperture is oval, being usually covered with a layer of enamel over the lower part of the columella and extended to form a callus closing the umbilical region. There is a terminal notch forming a short anterior canal. The body of the animal is well developed, being lobed anteriorly and terminating in a forked tail. There is a pair of long appendages, each with an eye on the outer side of its base. A long tubular siphon extends forward and waves back and forth as the snail crawls actively over the mud.

Nassa (Alectrion) obsoleta (Say) PLATE 192 (2). The Mud Snail. The Eroded Basket Shell. This is the most abundant species of our Atlantic seaboard. The shell has about six whorls, completely covered with fine revolving lines crossed by equally fine lines of growth, thus giving it the appearance of a finely woven basket, except for the fact that the naturally tapering spire is badly eroded to a rounded apex, obliterating the markings completely in that region. Older shells also become covered with mold or loose material caught by the cross-markings. The color varies from olive to dark brown or purplish. In fact, the shell is so nearly the color of the mud in which the mollusk crawls that it would be difficult to detect it when not moving, if it were not for the groovelike trail which it always leaves behind it. These trails crisscross in all directions, for the animals have a remarkably keen sense of smell which causes them to move actively about as the odor of their prospective food attracts them. Sometimes, there are so many of these mollusks congregated on the mud flats, crowding so closely that they practically crawl over each other in their eagerness to get at their prey. They will often devour living bivalves, by boring through their shells with their narrow but rapidly moving, rasplike lingual ribbons, the central and lateral teeth of which, in each row, are equipped with powerful and sharp cusps. They will even attack each other, often boring through the shell of their nearest neighbor.

These snails lay their minute, spiny egg-capsules, crowded close together on short stalks on dead shells, the collars deposited by the *Polinices* snail (page 624), and other objects on the sea bottom.

The Mud Snail measures up to 1 inch in length and ranges along the coast from Nova Scotia to Florida.

Nassa (Alectrion) bivittata (Say) PLATE 192 (3). The Dog Whelk. The Triple Banded Basket Shell. This mollusk often overlaps the habitat of the preceding species, but prefers a protected sand-flat rather than a muddy one. It is smaller than the Mud Snail and is white to greenish white in color, with a sharp spire, about six or seven clean-cut whorls covered with a fine, but clear, network of revolving lines and vertical ridges, giving it a woven, or dotted appearance. There are about three rows of these dots on the body-whorl. The color of the animal is white with purple dots. It ranges, like the preceding species, from Nova Scotia to Florida.

Nassa (Alectrion) vibex (Say) PLATE 192 (1). The Mottled Dog Whelk. The spire is pointed and there are about six whorls with wavelike folds and revolving lines, giving the surface a checkered appearance. The body-whorl is enlarged and has about twelve conspicuous, undulating corrugations and about ten revolving lines. A reddish brown band continues from the spire to the body-whorl on the upper portion of each whorl. There are three such bands alternating with white ones on the body-whorl, so that the shell has a strikingly colorful appearance. The outer lip is thick, with four to five teeth just inside the margin. The columella is excavated, the smooth lining of the shell forming an enameled surface over the inner lip, being expanded to form a callus over the umbilical region. The anterior canal is very short and clearly distinct from the main aperture. This is the handsomest of the Nassas, with its alternating brown and white bands and the rows of conspicuous nodules formed at the crossings of the spirals with the vertical wavy ridges. The length of the shell is ¾ inch. The species is more abundant in the South, but ranges from Vineyard Sound, Massachusetts, to the Gulf of Mexico.

Nassa (Alectrion) unicincta (Say) PLATE 192 (4). This shell is ovate with a sharply pointed spire. There are eight whorls with ten to twelve revolving lines crossed at intervals by transverse undulations. The outer lip is

---

Key to PLATE 192

1. *Nassa (Alectrion) vibex;* 2. *Nassa (Alectrion) obsoleta;* 3. *Nassa (Alectrion) bivittata;* 4. *Nassa (Alectrion) unicincta;* 5. *Nassa (Alectrion) acuta;* 6. *Neptunea despecta tornata;* 7. *Colus (Sipho) stimpsoni;* 8. *Colus (Sipho) ventricosus;* 9. *Colus (Sipho) pygmaeus;* 10. *Ficus (Pyrula) papyracea;* 11. *Busycon (Fulgur) perversum;* 12. *Busycon (Fulgur) pyrum;* 13. *Oliva literata (Oliva sayana);* 14. *Olivella mutica;* 15, 16. *Marginella guttata;* 17. *Marginella roscida (Marginella limatula);* 18. *Voluta (Maculopeplum) junonia;* 19. *Mitra nodulosa (Mitra granulosa);* 20. *Fasciolaria gigantea;* 21. *Fasciolaria tulipa;* 22. *Fasciolaria distans;* 23. *Admete viridula;* 24. *Cancellaria reticulata;* 25. *Terebra dislocata.*

PLATE 192

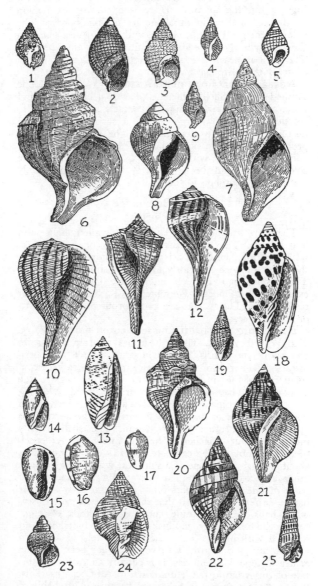

dentate on its margin and there are ten revolving markings within the aperture. There is a curving excavation of the columellar lip at about its middle border. The color of the shell is light yellow, with a brownish band on the body-whorl. There is a rosy tint within the aperture. The shell is nearly 1 inch in length. It occurs along the coast of the Carolinas.

Nassa (Alectrion) acuta (Say) PLATE 192 (5). The Pointed Basket Shell. This shell has a slender spire and acute apex. The surface appears coarsely granular, due to six deeply cut spiral grooves and a series of still more deeply indented transverse grooves. The spire is longer in proportion than the body-whorl. The lips are thickened and the outer lip with a scalloped outer margin. The color is white and the length is ½ inch. It occurs rarely from North Carolina to the Gulf of Mexico.

Family Buccinidae
(The Whelks)

These are mollusks with large, thick-walled shells with few whorls. They are usually fusiform or pear-shaped, with a pointed spire and a large body-whorl and aperture, the latter notched anteriorly to form a short, wide canal. The periostracum is thick and horny. The columella is expanded and smooth. The outer lip is thin and without teeth inside. The whelks are carnivorous and inhabitants of northern seas.

Buccinum undatum Linnaeus COLOR PLATE XV, 13. The Waved Whelk. This whelk has a prominent spire and about six whorls, grayish in color with a thin periostracum. There are about twelve rounded ridges, conspicuous on the upper whorls but fading away on the body-whorl. These are crossed by many raised revolving lines, the combination presenting a wavy effect, from which the name of the species is derived. The aperture is oval in shape, often yellow within. The shell usually measures about 3 inches in height, though larger specimens are known. The eggs are laid in yellowish capsules about the size and shape of a split pea, which overlap each other and are attached in a mass about the size of the palm of one's hand. Sailors often use them to wash their hands, instead of soap, so that they are often called "sea-wash balls." Each capsule contains hundreds of eggs.

The body of this mollusk is white, blotched and streaked with black. This is the edible whelk of northern Europe and the British Isles, where it has been a staple article of food for centuries. It is equally abundant on this side of the Atlantic, but is unknown in American markets. It is a great nuisance to fishermen because of its habit of stealing bait in lobster pots and cod lines.

Family Neptuneidae
(The Neptune Shells)

This is a very widespread family existing in all seas from polar, through temperate, to those of the tropics. The shells vary from small to large size. They are all carnivorous.

Neptunea (Chrysodomus) decemcostata (Say) COLOR PLATE XV, 14. The Ten-Ridged Neptune. This is the large whelk characteristic of the northern New England coast, well known and conspicuous because of the ten winding ridges on its large body-whorl, the upper three being continued on up the spire. The shell has six or seven whorls and is large and strong, measuring 3 to 4 inches in height. The general color is grayish white, but the upper edges of the raised revolving bands are striking because of their reddish brown hue. Their habits are similar to those of *Buccinum undatum*. They are often found among the rocks below the low-water line and range into deep water from Cape Cod to Nova Scotia and Georges Bank.

Neptunea despecta tornata (Gould) PLATE 192 (6). This large species is 4 inches in height. It has a high, steeplelike spire of about eight whorls, each quite convex in outline. There are high revolving ridges as in the previous species but they are fewer in number, the body-whorl having five high ridges, colored dark yellow, contrasting with the light yellow of the general shell surface. Between these high, colored ridges there are three lower ridges without distinctive color. The whorls of the spire have three colored ridges on each. The aperture is yellow inside. This species is more abundant in deep water, occurring in from 10 to 471 fathoms from the Gulf of St. Lawrence to Marthas Vineyard, Massachusetts.

Colus (Sipho) stimpsoni (Mörch) PLATE 192 (7); COLOR PLATE XV, 17. Stimpson's Distaff Shell. This graceful, spindle-shaped shell varies from 3 to 5 inches in height. The spire is elongate and tapering to a very small apex. The body-whorl is about two thirds the length of the shell, which has about eight whorls in all. The removal of the periostracum shows that distinct revolving lines mark the bluish white shell. The oval aperture is white within, and has a somewhat elongated canal, which bends backward from the axis of the shell. The animal is white, speckled with black, and with a pair of black eyes. While occasionally found on the beaches, this is a distinctly deep-water mollusk, but is often brought by fishermen. It ranges from 1 to 471 fathoms, and is found from Labrador to North Carolina.

Colus (Sipho) ventricosus Gray PLATE 192 (8). This is a smaller shell, rather stout and about 2 inches in height. The somewhat inflated body-whorl occupies more than half the shell, which has about five whorls. There is a brownish periostracum. The wide aperture terminates in a short but distinct, obliquely inclined canal. The smooth inner lip is covered by a polished enamel-like layer. This shell ranges from Nova Scotia to Georges Bank, in relatively deep water.

Colus (Sipho) pygmaeus (Gould) PLATE 192 (9). The Pygmy Distaff Shell. This little shell is about 1 inch in height. There are six to eight whorls with a sharply pointed apex. It is gray in color with a greenish periostracum. The oval aperture terminates in a short siphon which bends backward. It ranges from the Gulf of St. Lawrence to North Carolina, in depths of from 1 to 640 fathoms.

Busycon (Fulgur) caricum (Gmelin) COLOR PLATE XV, 15. The Giant Whelk. The Knobbed Whelk. This is the largest mollusk north of Cape Hatteras, though some specimens of the next species are a close second. It is a great pear-shaped snail, each whorl formed by a convolution around the preceding whorl, so that it is completely enclosed, resulting in a low spire. There are six whorls, the body-whorl being marked by large, blunt tubercles on the shoulder, there being one for each stage of growth. The general color is gray, while the lining of the aperture is brick-red. The expanded body-whorl forms an elongate, oval aperture, with a long and open canal. The outer lip has a thin, sharp edge, while the inner lip is rolled into a twisted arch. The operculum is horny. The eggs of this species are laid in double-edged, parchmentlike and disc-shaped capsules attached together on one edge by a cord of the same substance. The string may have as many as one hundred capsules and be a yard in length. These egg-strings are often cast ashore and picked up on the beach.

The Giant Whelk has a large fleshy body with a broad foot upon which it crawls, bearing the shell with the canal extended upward and forward containing the siphon, with its incurrent and excurrent tubes. The head projects from beneath the siphon, equipped with a pair of stout, tapering tentacles each with an eye at its lower outer edge. A long proboscis extends forward beneath the head, terminating in a mouth with its rasping, filelike lingual ribbon with which it bores a neat, round hole through the shells of other mollusks to suck out their soft contents. It is one of the important enemies of oysters and clams, though the smaller snails, like the Oyster Drill (page 646).

and the starfish (pages 727-8) are probably much more destructive because of their greater numbers.

Busycon (Fulgur) canaliculatum (Linnaeus) COLOR PLATE XV, 16. The Channeled Whelk. This mollusk is nearly as large as the Knobbed Whelk, described above. It reaches a length of 6 to 9 inches and is distinguished by having a deep channel-like groove following each whorl at the suture. The spire is turreted with five to six whorls. The color is yellowish gray and the interior is lined with yellow. The body-whorl is much swollen, taking up fully two thirds of the shell-height, and is prolonged below into a narrow, nearly straight, tubular canal. There is a brownish periostracum and the shell is marked by numerous revolving lines. The shoulders of the whorls are quite square. The egg-string in this species is similar to that of *Busycon caricum* except that the capsules have a single sharp edge to each disc, instead of a double one as in that species. This is a very common shell, occurring abundantly in a sandy environment in shallow water, from southern New England to northern Florida.

Busycon (Fulgur) perversum (Linnaeus) PLATE 192 (11). The Left-handed Whelk. The Lightning Shell. This whelk is peculiar in having a spiral that winds to the left instead of to the right. The coloration is quite striking, consisting of lightninglike, rich brown markings radiating from the apex, on a light fawn background. Otherwise it much resembles *Busycon caricum,* having shoulders adorned with knoblike projections. It is also a somewhat more slender shell and cleaner cut. It practically replaces the northern species along the southern coasts, ranging from North Carolina to Florida and Texas.

Busycon (Fulgur) pyrum Dillwyn PLATE 192 (12). The Pear Conch. The Fig Shell. This whelk is similar to the Channeled Whelk, but is somewhat smaller, slenderer, and more graceful, varying from 3 to 5 inches in length. The suture has a deep, but narrow channel and the spire is quite low, the body-whorl taking up most of the shell height. The shell is flesh-color, somewhat streaked and banded with brown. The canal is long and quite open. This shell is found in shallow water, for the most part in a sandy environment, from North Carolina to Florida and Texas.

Family Marginellidae

These are small shells of porcellanous texture, being highly polished by the reflected mantle of the mollusk. They are somewhat pear-shaped, with a very short, or even completely hidden spire. The aperture is long and narrow, with the outer lip thickened, often as long as the shell.

Marginella guttata (Dillwyn) PLATE 192 (15, 16). The Spotted Marginella. This is a small, polished shell, about ¾ inch in length, with an elongate aperture, extending the length of the shell, and notched at the base. It is flesh-colored, mottled with brown, and speckled with white spots. The thickened outer lip is white with some brown spots. The columella has a number of narrow folds. It measures up to 1 inch in length. The distribution is from North Carolina to Florida and the West Indies.

Marginella roscida Redfield (= **Marginella limatula** Conrad) PLATE 192 (17). This little, polished shell is somewhat more than ½ inch in height with a moderate spire showing about four whorls. The columella has four narrow folds or plaits. The thickened lip is white with three brown spots on the outside and slightly toothed within. The porcellanous surface of the shell is grayish brown in color, sprinkled with minute white spots blending into fine lines toward the spire. This species occurs off the North Carolina coast in 25 to 100 fathoms.

Family Mitridae
(The Mitre Shells)

This is a large family, which really belongs to the Pacific and Indian Oceans, where many large and beautiful species are abundant. Only a few small and relatively insignificant species occur on our coasts. They are elongate, spindle-shaped shells often brightly colored, with an acutely pointed, steeplelike spire, and a small, narrow aperture.

Mitra nodulosa Gmelin (= **Mitra granulosa** Lamarck) PLATE 192 (19). The Knobbed Mitre Shell. This is a small shell, about 2 inches in height. There are about ten whorls converging to a sharp apex. The surface is distinctly granular, due to the crossing of transverse ribs by revolving lines. The aperture is short and notched. The columella has four folds or plaits. The species ranges from Cape Hatteras to the West Indies.

Family Volutidae
(The Volutes)

This is another large family characteristic of the tropical waters, of which a few species enter the southern limits of our territory. Included in the family are many beautiful species, much sought after by collectors. They are mostly vase-shaped, with a gracefully tapering spire, usually capped by a nodule, or more or less hemispherical protoconch, which is the shell of the animal at birth. One species will be described here.

Voluta (Maculopeplum) junonia Hwass PLATE 192 (18). The Junonia Volute. This beautiful species is spindle-shaped with a relatively pointed spire. It is about 3 inches in height and is marked by conspicuous rhomboidal spots of orange-red or chocolate-brown rising in a spiral from base to apex, contrasting with the rosy-white surface tint of the shell background. There are about five whorls, including the body-whorl, which is very large, taking up, by far, the greater part of the shell, leaving room only for the short but acute spire. The aperture is elongate and relatively narrow. The outer lip is thin and arched below. The columella has four plaits. There is only a short canal and no operculum. This has always been considered a rare shell by collectors in the past, but it is found, from time to time, around the Florida coast. The range, as now known, extends from Cape Lookout, North Carolina, to the Florida Keys and the Gulf of Mexico.

Family Fasciolariidae
(The Band Shells)

This is a family of large, strong, thick-walled shells. They are spindle-shaped and rise in a sharp spire, from a much expanded body-whorl with a large oval aperture which terminates in an open, usually straight canal, twisted, however, in some species. The whorls are marked with wide spiral bands. The large operculum is claw-shaped. This is a family widespread throughout the shallow waters of warm seas.

Fasciolaria gigantea Kiener PLATE 192 (20). The Giant Band Shell. The Horse Conch. This magnificent shell is one of the largest known snail shells in the world and the largest known to American waters. It is very heavy and massive, growing to 2 feet in length. There are about ten whorls tapering to form an elongate spire, yellowish in color, with a brown epidermis. The aperture is lined with orange red. The whorls bear a succession of heavy nodules, while heavy, dark, revolving ridges cross strong growth lines. The widely oval aperture narrows to form a tubular open canal. The animal is bright red in color and an excellent fighter because of its great strength. It inhabits fairly shallow waters from North Carolina to Brazil.

Fasciolaria tulipa Linnaeus PLATE 192 (21). The Tulip Shell. The Pepper Conch. This is a smaller but extremely handsome Band Shell, gracefully tapering with smooth, convex whorls to a well-formed, symmetrical spire. It averages 5 to 6 inches in length, but shells measuring 8 inches are occasionally found. The color is a warm gray, marked by spiral lines of brown, often interrupted by quadrangular blotches of brown, banded by broad, light-colored spirals. The color pattern, however, varies greatly in different individuals. The columella has three plaits. The lining of the aperture is a flesh tint. This species ranges, in shallow water, from North Carolina to Florida and Texas.

Fasciolaria distans Lamarck PLATE 192 (22). The Banded Tulip Shell. This species is distinguished by its small size and the fact that its revolving dark lines are farther apart than in the preceding species. It is a much smoother and more delicate shell and the designs are more finely drawn. The ground color is bluish gray, while the pattern is in deep brown with whitish areas. The graceful spindle-shaped spire has seven to eight whorls. This species, closely related to the previous one, is also distributed throughout the same area, extending from North Carolina to Florida and Texas.

Family Olividae
(The Olive Shells)

These shells are characterized by the fact that the oval, polished body-whorl is so extensive that it hides all or the greater part of the spire within its volution. There is no epidermis, the shell being kept polished by the two folds of the mantle which completely cover it when the animal is expanded. The outer lip is smooth and the aperture is very long and narrow, and has a notch at the lower end. The operculum is usually wanting or insignificant. The foot is large, rounded in front, and pointed behind. This is a large tropical family, remarkable for the lustrous shell and the infinite variety of bright color patterns.

Oliva litterata Lamarck (= **Oliva Sayana** Ravenel) PLATE 192 (13). The Lettered Olive. This is a slender olive shell, more or less pointed at both ends. It is not large, seldom being more than 2 or 3 inches in length. The color is bluish gray, especially evident on the spire. Various shades of chestnut-brown and pink cover the shell with many fine markings reminding one of hieroglyphics. Hence the name, "Lettered Olive." There is a quite short spire as each new body-whorl, when it is laid on, nearly covers most of the underlying ones. The long, narrow aperture has an oblique notch at the lower end. The outer lip is quite thick. The individuals of this species group together in colonial fashion in shallow water. When they are moving about, the expanded mantle and the foot exhibit the same color markings as the shell.

Olivella mutica Say PLATE 192 (14). The Little Olive. This common little mollusk is very abundant throughout its range, extending from North Carolina to Texas and the West Indies. It is ½ inch or less, forming a slender narrow oval, tapering at both ends. The pollshed shell is extremely variable in color, the general background usually being a light yellow or cream, with bands of purplish brown or even chocolate. There are about five whorls, with more of the pointed spire showing than in the previous genus. The outer lip is thin and delicate. There is also a thin operculum, which is lacking in the Genus *Oliva*. Also, the aperture does not extend as far toward the spire as in that genus. This animal and its relatives often swim through the water by flapping the mantle lobes.

Family Cancellariidae
(The Cross-barred Shells)

These spiral shells are remarkable for the strongly developed cross-ribs upon the shells. There is an oblong aperture drawn out into a short canal anteriorly. There is no operculum and no radula, as these mollusks are vegetable-eaters.

Cancellaria reticulata (Linnaeus) PLATE 192 (24). The Netted Cross-bar. The close cross-ridges, produced by the spirals and the lines of growth, are so deeply cut as to become a noteworthy feature of the shell, giving the effect of coarse granulations. The color is white with patches and bands of brownish color. The height of the shell varies from 1 and 1½ to 2½ inches. These little mollusks are found abundantly from Cape Hatteras to Florida.

Admete viridula (Fabricius) PLATE 192 (23). The Greenish Admete. The shell of this mollusk is about ½ inch in height with five to six whorls. The apex of the spire is quite sharp. The surface of the whorls is sculptured with coarse spiral lines crossed by vertical ribs which are especially prominent near the shoulder. There are three folds on the columella. The *Admete* is frequently eaten by fishes, as well as by hermit crabs, which dig it out of the shell and occupy the latter as a home. It occurs in depths of 10 to 60 fathoms from Labrador to Massachusetts Bay.

Family Terebridae
(The Auger Shells)

As the name implies, these shells are almost augerlike, having a long, slender, coiled spire with a sharp apex, and many whorls. The aperture is small and located just at the base with an anterior notch.

Terebra dislocata Say PLATE 192 (25). The Little Auger Shell. This small and slender species is grayish or brownish in color marked with yellowish brown. The very elongate spire tapers to a fine point. The shell has about fifteen whorls, sculptured with both spiral grooves and vertical ribs. The aperture is proportionately quite small. These are common mollusks on shallow sand bars from Virginia to Texas.

Family Turridae (Turritidae)

This is a large family, composed mostly of small mollusks with spindle-shaped shells, the outer lip of the aperture often having a slit or notch at the upper angle near the suture for purposes of excretion and with the lower portion narrowed for a more or less elongated canal. They are found in relatively deep water in seas of all climatic zones.

Lora (Bela) scalaris (Möller) PLATE 193 (1). This is a white or yellowish snail with seven or eight shouldered whorls narrowing to an acute apex. It measures about ¾ inch in height. The surface is sculptured with twelve to fourteen vertical, narrowly compressed ribs, crossed by many slightly raised spiral lines. The vertical ribs vanish on the lower part of the body-whorl. The outer lip is thin and sharp, and the terminal canal is open and short. It ranges from the Arctic Circle to Massachusetts in relatively deep water.

Lora (Bela) cancellata (Mighels & Adams) PLATE 193 (2). The shell of this species is about ⅜ inch long, with a slender turret of about seven convex whorls. About twenty longitudinal ribs, crossed by many raised revolving lines, break up the surface into distinct squared cancellations. The aperture is small and compressed, the outer lip serrated by the revolving striations. The color is white, slightly suffused with purple. This species occurs from Labrador to Massachusetts in 7 to 312 fathoms.

Lora (Bela) harpularia (Couthouy) PLATE 193 (3). This is an ovate, tapering shell, rather stout in outline, and about ½ inch in height. There are six to eight round-shouldered (not angular) whorls, having about eighteen rounded ribs crossing numerous threadlike revolving lines, the ribs disappearing on the lower part of the body-whorl. The general coloration is a tan flesh-color. The aperture is oval, narrowing to the vestige of a canal, with an arching, sharp outer lip.

Lora (Bela) pleurotomaria (Couthouy) PLATE 193 (4). This is a very graceful little shell, about ¾ inch in length, rather elongated and tapering with rounded, slightly shouldered whorls to an acute apex. It is of a reddish fawn color. There are eight whorls, ornamented with obliquely undulating ribs, standing out sharply with equal spaces between. These ribs are most prominent on the spire and fade out at about the middle of the body-whorl. This species ranges from Labrador to Marthas Vineyard, Massachusetts, occurring at depths of from 5 to 255 fathoms.

Lora (Bela) bicarinata (Couthouy) PLATE 193 (5). This beautiful little shell is only ⅕ to ⅖ inch in height. It is grayish white or slate-color, and is distinguished particularly by a pair of keel-like revolving ribs, with an excavated groove between them, that ornament the middle of the body-whorl and continue as a spiral along the whorl and up the spire to the apex. This species is distributed from Labrador to New York, in 6 to 100 fathoms.

Mangelia filiformis Holmes PLATE 193 (6). This shell is about ¼ inch in length. It is stout and spindle-shaped, with the five or six whorls thrown into waves or vertical nodules. It occurs off the Carolina coast.

SUBCLASS OPISTHOBRANCHIA
(EUTHYNEURA)

The chief characteristics of the Opisthobranchia, or Marine Euthyneura, are as follows:

(1) The twisted condition of the ladderlike nervous system, peculiar to the Subclass Prosobranchia (Streptoneura), becomes untwisted secondarily, in adult Opisthobranchia, with all its elements concentrated around the oesophagus.

(2) The head usually bears two pairs of tentacles.

(3) The radula is composed of a large number of uniform teeth on either side of the central tooth in each row. The jaw is usually composed of two pieces.

(4) The animals are hermaphroditic.

(5) The branchiae, for the most part, are located posteriorly, instead of anteriorly.

(6) The mantle and shell are, for the most part, entirely absent. If present, they are frequently small, the shell being usually spiral in form.

(7) The body is unsymmetrical, the kidney, genital pores, and anus usually being located on the right side.

(8) In the Naked Mollusks (Order Nudibranchia), there are no ctenidia (gills) and no osphradia (organs of smell), respiration being effected by branched projections from the dorsal body-wall or by the general body-surface.

(9) The lateral divisions of the foot (epipodia) become greatly enlarged and specialized for various functions, such as swimming and shell production.

(10) The Opisthobranchia are largely shallow-water animals, hiding among the seaweed, in rock crevices, or under stones; except the Pteropoda, which are pelagic.

The Subclass Opisthobranchia is divided into three Orders, as follows: (1) *Tectibranchia;* (2) *Pteropoda;* (3) *Nudibranchia.*

Order TECTIBRANCHIA
(The Shell-bearing Sea Slugs)

This is a transitional order. The shell is usually present, though in a progressively reduced condition. The right gill or branchia (ctenidium) is present and functions for respiration. It is contained within a mantle cavity.

There are twenty-five families in this Order, from which five have been selected for inclusion here.

Family Acteonidae

The mollusks in this family still retain a spiral shell which completely covers the body. There is a well-developed spire and a horny operculum. The visceral loop of the nervous system still has a twist. The foot has no epipodial lobes. The radula has many rows of numerous, very small, rasplike teeth.

Acteon punctostriatus (Adams) PLATE 193 (7). This minute species retains a solid, ovate shell with a conical spire and an elongate, narrow aperture. The inner lip has a long twisted plication or fold. The large body-whorl takes up more than half the shell and is marked, on the lower half, with numerous revolving lines composed of punctate dots. The color of the shell is white. It is about ¼ inch in length. This species is widely distributed, from Vineyard Sound, Massachusetts, to Florida and the Gulf of Mexico, in 2 to 63 fathoms.

Family Tornatinidae (Acteocinidae)
(The Lathe Shells)

The shell of the mollusks in this family is nearly cylindrical with the body-whorl so large that it nearly hides the flat or slightly raised conical spire. It has the appearance of having been turned on a lathe, hence the name, Lathe Shell. The spiral suture is channeled forming a continu-

---

Key to PLATE 193

1. *Lora (Bela) scalaris;* 2. *Lora (Bela) cancellata;* 3. *Lora (Bela) harpularia;* 4. *Lora (Bela) pleurotomaria;* 5. *Lora (Bela) bicarinata;* 6. *Mangelia filiformis;* 7. *Acteon punctostriatus;* 8. *Tornatina (Acteocina) canaliculata;* 9. *Retusa pertenuis;* 10. *Scaphander punctostriatus;* 11. *Diaphana debilis;* 12. *Cylichna alba;* 13. *Cylichna oryza;* 14. *Haminea solitaria;* 15. *Philine sinuata;* 16, 16a. *Limacina retroversa;* 17. *Corolla calceola;* 18. *Creseis conica;* 19. *Cavolina trispinosa;* 20. *Cavolina tridentata;* 21. *Cavolina unicinata;* 22. *Hyalocylis striata;* 23. *Clione limacina;* 24. *Creseis alicalis;* 25. *Cuvierina columella;* 26, 27. *Alexia myosotis;* 28. *Melampus lineatus (Melampus bidentatus).*

PLATE 193

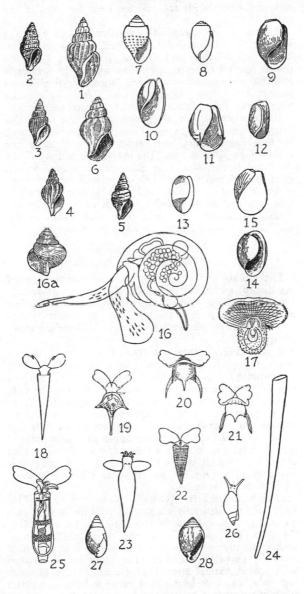

ous groove. The head is divided and the foot is split into epipodial lobes which are reflected over the sides of the shell.

Tornatina (Acteocina) canaliculata (Say) PLATE 193 (8). The Channeled Lathe Shell. The nearly cylindrical shell is white and shining, and shows a slightly projecting, but flattened spire. The top of the whorls is grooved with a narrow channel. There are five whorls present. The length varies from ⅛ to ¼ inch. This species ranges from Prince Edward Island to Florida and Texas.

Retusa pertenuis (Mighels) PLATE 193 (9). The Fragile Blunt Shell. The raised margin of the body-whorl, in this species, completely enfolds and conceals the sunken spire with its apex. The aperture is as long as the shell and is narrowed to a thin crevice above, though quite broad below. The shell is smooth, without any sculpture, white in color, and with a shining surface. This is a tiny mollusk, only ⅒ inch in length. Its unusually wide range extends from Greenland to the northern border of Florida in 10 to 294 fathoms.

Family Scaphandridae
(The Canoe Shells)

The mollusks in this family have an external, nearly egg-shaped, sometimes thin shell, with the aperture narrowed, but open above, and widely open below. The outer lip is sharp-edged and the inner lip is spirally convoluted. The epipodia are well developed. There is a short, square head.

Scaphander punctostriatus (Mighels & Adams) PLATE 193 (10). The Striated Canoe Shell. The white, somewhat solid, finely shaped, but punctate shell, with its egglike form, characterizes this beautiful species. The spire is completely concealed. The very large aperture has an outer lip with an evenly arched and sharp edge that extends upward above the apex. The body-whorl rolls into the cavity of the aperture in the upper part, narrowing it considerably, and forming a thin inner lip that also rises above the apex. It is less than ⅖ inch in length. It is found in 46 to 1467 fathoms from the Gulf of St. Lawrence to the West Indies.

Diaphana debilis (Gould) PLATE 193 (11). This tiny, thin, and delicately transparent shell has four whorls all rising to almost exactly the same height, concealing the apex. The aperture is as long as the shell, open at both ends, narrowed above, and widened below, with a generally pear-shaped outline. The inner lip is surfaced with a thin enamel layer. It is greenish white in color and only ⅙ inch in length. The range is from Greenland to Connecticut in 6 to 16 fathoms.

Cylichna alba (Brown) PLATE 193 (12). The White Cup Shell. This little glossy white shell somewhat resembles a grain of rice. The outer whorl rises so that the apex is at the bottom of a narrow, circular pit. The outer lip is the higher of the two, arching upward and then curving in a semicircle at the top to follow a downward course parallel to the left border of the shell. The inner lip forms a broad curve, the two together producing a long, very narrow aperture, widening suddenly at the base. The length is less than ¼ inch. It ranges from Greenland to Block Island, in 10 to 1091 fathoms. It is also circumboreal in distribution.

Cylichna oryza (Totten) PLATE 193 (13). The Rice Cup Shell. This is a similar but broader shell, a trifle shorter than the above, measuring about ⅛ inch in length. It also closely resembles a grain of rice. The aperture is broader at the bottom where it is scored by microscopically fine revolving lines. The columella is twisted and has a blunt tooth at its base. There is no umbilicus. It frequents moderately shallow water, from 2 to 4 fathoms, and ranges from Maine to Connecticut.

Family Akeridae

In this family, the shell is still external but reduced and usually concealed by the large epipodia which are reflected around it on either side. It is ovate to cylindrical, and very fragile. The body-whorl, which is the largest and envelops all the others, is covered with numerous almost microscopic, revolving lines. The large aperture has a sharp-edged outer lip.

Haminea solitaria (Say) PLATE 193 (14). This is a very fragile, egg-shaped shell, bluish white in color, the body-whorl completely enclosing all the others, with the spire depressed and hidden, though sometimes a very small opening is above it. The aperture is narrow above and broadened below, with a very sharp outer lip rising in a regular curve above the top of the shell. There is a slight fold at the umbilical region, which is covered over, together with the inner margin, by a thin layer of enamel. The surface of the shell has a lustrous texture, with incised spiral grooves. The shell is ⅖ inch in height.

The animal is much too large for the shell, which is thus in a very rudimentary condition.

Family Philinidae

The shell, in this family, is apparently in the last stages of reduction. It is internal, and hidden completely in the mantle of the mollusk. It is oval, translucent, and delicately thin. The spire is vestigial. Sometimes, the shell is entirely absent.

Philine sinuata Stimpson PLATE 193 (15). The animal is sluglike, as its rudimentary shell is entirely concealed and internal, being enclosed by the mantle. It is quite minute, being less than ½2 inch in length. It is oval in shape, white in color, and practically transparent. The spire is obvious and the aperture is dilated below. The color is yellowish, rather dark above, variegated with white patches and dots. These animals have no eyes and burrow in slimy mud for their food, consisting of still more minute bivalves, which they swallow whole, breaking the shells in their muscular oesophagus. They have a universal distribution, but are particularly recorded along our coast from Maine to Massachusetts, in 4 to 7 fathoms.

Order PTEROPODA
(The Sea Butterflies)

The Pteropoda are pelagic, free-swimming gastropods with the sides of the foot in the form of expansions (*epipodia*) which have become modified into fins, innervated by the pedal ganglia. The asymmetrical internal organs show that they are derived from the Gastropoda. Because they are hermaphroditic, and because their nervous system is secondarily untwisted, they have features in common with the Euthyneura (Opisthobranchia). This is confirmed by similarities in their circulatory and reproductive systems.

The Order Pteropoda is divided into two Suborders: (1) *Thecosomata,* the Pteropoda with shells, and (2) *Gymnosomata,* the Pteropoda without shells.

Suborder THECOSOMATA

The Pteropoda in this Suborder always have a shell, from which the finlike lobes project on either side. The ctenidia are absent, being replaced by secondarily developed branchiae. There is no definite head and no eyes are present and but one pair of tentacles. These animals are vegetable-eaters. The lingual ribbon has but three teeth in each row, a central tooth and a lateral on each side.

Family Limacinidae

These creatures have a left-handed spiral shell. The anal and generative openings are on the right side within a mantle cavity. They are pelagic animals, usually in northern seas.

Limacina retroversa Fleming PLATE 193 (16, 16a). This species has a snail-like, transparent, sinistrally coiled shell, with a low spire, the two fin-lobes projecting from the opening and spreading out on either side. These butterflylike creatures flit about at the water surface, especially at night, in vast schools. They are very abundant in Arctic seas, where they form an important food for whales.

Family Cymbuliidae

The shell in this family is a transparent test of a cartilaginouslike substance which is really a thickening of the mantle, and is somewhat slipper-shaped. This is a secondary structure, peculiar to the adult animal, the embryo being provided with a coiled calcareous shell, having an operculum.

Corolla calceola (Verrill) PLATE 193 (17). The expanded wings, or epipodia, of this species are united in front, forming a continuous swimming appendage, like a thin, simple, tegumentary disc. It was discovered by Verrill, swimming in the open sea, one mile off Gay Head, Massachusetts, and described by him. The shell is a transparent, membranous, slipperlike pouch, covered by a thin layer of the mantle, of which it is apparently a thickening, and not a true shell. It contains the internal organs and hangs down from the disc in the swimming position, in which the animal is inverted, with the swimming disc uppermost. The embryo has a true calcareous molluscan shell, which is discarded after hatching.

Family Cavoliniidae

In this family, the mantle secretes a shell, which is not spiral, but is a symmetrically straight or curved covering for the internal organs. There is no operculum. Two large, symmetrically paired fin-lobes extend from the shell opening.

Cavolina trispinosa (Lesueur) PLATE 193 (19). The shell is transparent and globular with three posterior spines, the middle spine being three times longer than the other two, with the shorter ones symmetrically disposed on either side. They are about ⅖ inch in length, and swim in large schools in the open sea from Greenland to the latitude of New Jersey.

Cavolina tridentata Forskäl (= **Cavolina telemus** Linnaeus) PLATE 193 (20). The animal of this species is short and globular, equipped with thin, transparent, lateral epipodia, broadened at their outer extremities, which are scalloped terminally. They have the appearance of balancing organs and doubtless so function. The shell, also, is globular, thin, and often brightly colored. The shell has a fissure on each side, closed anteriorly. The dorsal surface is convex and prolonged forward over the opening. There is a pair of shelflike prolongations laterally, with two curved, saberlike spines extending backward on either side of a short, stubby median spine. This species is pelagic in the open sea off Marthas Vineyard Island, Massachusetts.

Cavolina unicinata (Rang) PLATE 193 (21). This species is similar to the previous one, except that the fins expand from a narrow median junction quite rapidly to form symmetrical, fanlike expansions, trilobed at their outer margins, and much shorter than in the previous species. The shell is also more quadrangular in shape. It is pelagic off the coast of southern New England and New Jersey.

Creseis conica Eschscholtz PLATE 193 (18). This species has a long, slender, straight shell. It is evenly tapering and sharply pointed at the end. The epipodia are oval, with a thumblike notch on their inner border. The length is about ½ inch. They are pelagic from southern New England to the tropics.

Creseis alicalis Rang PLATE 193 (24). This is a closely related species to the preceding, and with about the same distribution. Only the shell is figured here to show the slight curvature of its outline as compared with the straight shell of *Creseis conica,* above.

Hyalocylis striata (Rang) PLATE 193 (22). This species has a conical shell, stouter and comparatively shorter than in *Creseis,* with a slightly flattened or ovoid cross-section. The aperture is ovoid, but not oblique. The apex is pointed. The surface of the shell is transversely grooved throughout. The fins are narrowed at their median junction with the minute anterior extremity of the foot, but broaden to a wide, bilobed border at their truncate ends. The larval period of this species is very short, the embryonic shell disappearing soon after hatching. This species ranges widely in the open Atlantic, being found from the latitude of New Jersey to that of Argentina, also in the Gulf of Mexico.

Cuvierina columella (Rang) PLATE 193 (25). The swimming organs have practically parallel sides and are bilobed at their external border. The straight shell is shaped like a nearly cylindrical vial or vase. Its apex is acute in young shells, then becomes rounded and finally truncate in the fully grown, adult shell. The opening is simple, oval, and slightly compressed. It is cosmopolitan in distribution, occurring in all seas. Off our coast, it ranges from the open sea off New Jersey to Argentina.

Suborder GYMNOSOMATA

These are Pteropoda entirely without shells except in the embryo.

Family Clionidae

This family is noteworthy because, in general, the species included are entirely without a branchia, mantle cavity, and shell. Respiration takes place through the integument or through projections from the dorsal surface, known as *cerata*. It is thus considered by many to be transitional to the nudibranchs. There is a distinct head, which is rather elevated, with earlike tentacles bearing eyes. The anterior part of the somewhat depressed body is expanded into two large, leaflike wings or fins, which stand out at right angles to the body and enclose branches of the liver.

Clione limacina (Phipps) PLATE 193 (23). This species, as is indicated by the family definition above, has no shell, branchia, or mantle cavity. However, a coiled shell is present in the embryo. The body is spindle-shaped, tapering to a point posteriorly. The head, clearly separated from the body by a necklike constriction, bears two pairs of tentacles, with eyes on the posterior pair. The animal is 1½ inches in length, with leaf-shaped fins standing out on either side of the body, just back of the neck. It is pale blue in color and transparent. These creatures swim in great schools near the ocean surface, ranging from the Arctic Ocean to New York, sometimes coloring the water for miles. They are a great source of food for the Greenland Whale which devours them in immense quantities.

Order NUDIBRANCHIA
(The Sea Slugs)

In this Order, the shell is entirely absent in the adult, though a coiled shell occurs in the embryo, but is discarded soon after birth. There is no ctenidium or branchia proper, respiration taking place either through the general integument, through posterior adaptive gills, or through branched, or club-shaped, symmetrically arranged projections of the dorsal or dorso-lateral surface, known as cerata. The nervous system is concentrated, and the kidney is branched or ramified throughout the body. Jaws and radula are present. There are two pairs of tentacles.

Family Aeolididae

The sea slugs in this family have simple unbranched cerata arranged in transverse ranks on either side of the median line, into which projections from the liver extend. The head has a pair of tentacles and a second pair, especially adapted for smell perception, known as *rhinophores,* which perform the function of the osphradia in the Proso-branchia. Sting cells (nematocysts) often occur in the cerata. These sting-cells have been swallowed alive by the nudibranchs, along with the coelenterates to which they belong, and are then incorporated into the cell-structure of the nudibranchs themselves, where they function as in the coelenterates that produced them originally.

Aeolis (Aeolidia) papillosa (Linnaeus) COLOR PLATE XVII, 6. The Plumed Sea Slug. The back of this slug is covered with elongated, tapering papillae, or cerata, which tend to part in the middle and fall away on either side. The body is broad and flattened and tapers posteri-orly. The general color is orange-color or gray, spotted with white, or green and purple. It also takes on the color of the anemones, hydroids, or algae it feeds on, for particles of their substance permeate the fluids of the body and are drawn up into the cerata, altering their color. Nematocysts from their coelenterate prey are also taken, preserved, and their properties put to work for the mollusk's own use. When fully grown, this species may be 4 inches in length, though smaller ones are often found. It occurs in tide-pools and among algae and hydroids between the tidal limits. Its vertical range, however, ex-tends down to 200 fathoms or more. It is distributed abundantly from Greenland to Watch Hill, Rhode Island. It is also European.

Family Flabellinidae

In this family are contained sea slugs with cerata ar-ranged as in the preceding family, but not so abundantly. The two pairs of tentacles are unequal in length and the front angles of the foot are prolonged.

Coryphella salmonacea (Couthouy) COLOR PLATE XVII, 7. The elongate body tapers back to an acute point. The head is large with a V-shaped mouth. The tentacles are large and blunt. The body color is yellowish white. The cerata are rather long and tapering, and deep salmon-colored within. In full-grown specimens there are about one hundred on each side in regular transverse series, perforated at the tip. The anterior angles of the broad foot are prolonged into attenuated appendages. It is about 1¾ inches in length. It ranges from Greenland to Boston Harbor.

Coryphella rufibranchialis (Johnston) COLOR PLATE XVII, 8. This nudibranch has a slender, tapering body of an almost translucent white, with a median opaque white line running lengthwise along the back. The second (dor-sal) pair of tentacles is long and wrinkled transversely, and variegated with brownish tints, with a pale white line running down the posterior side. The oral tentacles extend to about the same length, but are very contractile. The cerata are slenderer than in the preceding species and are arranged in six or seven clusters, each consisting of two to six rows of four cerata in every row. The interior of each ceras is bright vermilion, the tip encircled with an opaque-white ring. The anterior angles of the foot are prolonged into narrow lobes which are often folded transversely. The length of this species is about 1 inch. It is a northern species. The author has frequently found it at Bar Harbor, Maine, and it is recorded from Massachusetts. It also seems to be European.

Family Dendronotidae
(The Bushy-backed Slugs)

The sluglike body is rather flattened in shape, elongate, and tapering posteriorly. There are two rows of branching, treelike cerata rising from the somewhat raised and tuberculated dorsal surface. The frontal margin has arborescent and fringed papillae, instead of tentacles. The rhinophores are also fringed.

Dendronotus frondosus (Ascanius) (= **Dendronotus arborescens** O. F. Müller) COLOR PLATE XVII, 1. The color of this species is brown to reddish, mottled with yellowish to whitish spots. The branching, treelike cerata are translucent. There are about seven pairs in all. The surface of the body is elevated and somewhat tuberculous or warty. The blunt head has about six branching appendages extending forward. There are small eyes present on the lateral base of the tentacular sheath. This species is often found crawling over rocks and seaweeds and in tide-pools. It occurs from Labrador to Watch Hill, Rhode Island, from the tidal zone to 60 fathoms.

Family Onchidoridae

In this family, the mantle is large, completely covering the head. There are no marginal appendages. The rhinophores (second pair of antennae) are ringed with lamellae and are retractile. The first pair of tentacles is replaced by a veil. The branchiae form a circle of pinnate structures united at the base, surrounding the anus, which is posteromedian and dorsal in position. They are almost always retractile into a cavity.

Onchidorus aspersa (Alder & Hancock) COLOR PLATE XVII, 2. The body of this species is elongate, with nearly parallel sides, the two ends being about equally rounded. The general coloration is pale cream, with a central dusky spot. The back is stellate with tubercles of a lighter color. They are smaller and more numerous toward the margin.

The tentacles are encircled by about ten oblique laminae. Eight branchial plumes surround the anus, all retractile into separate sheaths. They are pinnate in form. The length of this species is about ½ inch. It ranges from Eastport, Maine, to Newport, Rhode Island.

Lamellidoris bilamellata (Linnaeus) COLOR PLATE XVII, 3. The body shape of this species is like that of the above, the outline, elliptical, with nearly parallel sides and evenly rounded ends. The color is a clouded or marbled suffusion of reddish brown and flesh-color, sometimes slaty-blue. The surface is covered with short club-shaped papillae, standing out conspicuously and of various sizes, the larger ones being light yellow at the tips. The tentacles are short, rather oval in section, with the upper three fourths obliquely ridged, except posteriorly, and with yellow-brown tips. The branchial plumes are long and slender, with simple side-branches of lamellate, leaflike form. The plumes are arranged in an oval series of about twenty-two across the back, with a gap posteriorly. A number of scattered tubercles are enclosed within the oval. The broadly crescentic head is as broad as the foot and overhung around the margin by the mantle. The tail is pointed and is on the middle of the foot. The length of the body is about 1 inch. This species is common along the northern New England coast.

Lamellidoris diademata (Agassiz) COLOR PLATE XVII, 4. The body, in this species, is elongate-oval in outline, a little broader anteriorly, both ends being rounded. It is maroon to brown in color, lighter around the edges and in the center, the color produced by many crowded brown dots. The tentacles have a series of symmetrically oblique folds close together on the terminal half. A cylindrical, sleevelike sheath encloses the base of the tentacles, into which they may be retracted. It is somewhat toothed at the margin. The branchial star is composed of nine simple pinnate plumes partly folded and lighter at their edges. The length of this animal is about 1½ inches. The breadth is a little less than 1 inch. It is found in fairly deep water along the New England coast.

Lamellidoris grisea (Stimpson) COLOR PLATE XVII, 5. The oval body is relatively short in proportion to its width and is broadly rounded at both ends. The back is covered with bluntly rounded papillae crowned with star-shaped clusters of spicules, rather roseate in appearance, due to the reddish brown tips of the papillae, while the bases are dotted with a golden yellow. The six branchial plumes are arranged like a radiating star. They are yellow in color and surround a brown area from which protrudes a central, dark-colored bristle. This is quite an actively moving nudibranch. It is about 1 inch in length, the width approximating ⅓ inch. It occurs along the northern New England coast as far south as Boston Harbor.

Family Iduliidae (Dotonidae)

In this interesting family, the slender, elongated body is surmounted by a single series of clublike tuberculated cerata, on each side. The tentacles are retractible into a sheath. The lingual ribbon is narrow, with a single series of similar teeth in each row.

Doto coronata (Gmelin) COLOR PLATE XVII, 9. The color of this nudibranch is pale rose or yellow marked thickly with brown dots. The tentacles are filamentary, extending from obliquely truncated, trumpetlike sheaths. The club-shaped cerata are narrowed at the summit and adorned with two or three tubercular rings, each tubercle tipped with a dark red dot. These tubercles are capable of extension and contraction. They are also dark red within. The cerata form two single parallel lines along the back, varying from five to eight on a side in different individuals. This is one of the most attractive of the nudibranchs, both in color, which is widely variable, and in its graceful and unusual form. It ranges from Labrador to New Jersey, occurring on hydroids and Bryozoa in shallow water.

Family Euphuridae (Polyceratidae)

In this family, the body is sluglike and elongate, with a marginal ridge on each side with prolongations either tubercular or fingerlike. The rhinophores and cerata are not retractile. The latter have lateral projections and usually surround the anus.

Palio (Polycera) lessonii (D'Orbigny) COLOR PLATE XVII, 12. This animal is yellowish green in color. The longitudinal marginal ridges on either side give it a four-sided appearance. There are six tubercles on each ridge, and another row on the median line, with a scattering of similar projections on the sides and tail. All the tubercles are sulphur-yellow in color. There is a semicircular head, with six projections on each side and a pair of tentacles having about a dozen close-set laminae on each. There are three pairs of branchial plumes posteriorly, in the region of the anus, flanked by two smaller pairs. They are not retractile and are yellow at the base. The foot is light-colored and has a square anterior margin. The length of this species is about ¾ inch and the breadth, ¼ inch. It is quite common from Labrador to Long Island Sound, in 3 to 20 fathoms.

Family Elysiidae

This family consists of slender, creeping species with distinct head and tapering tail. There are no cerata, but the ciliated body carries on respiration through the general surface of the integument. The sides of the body are expanded into winglike expansions folded over the back when the animals are creeping, but expanded into undulating fins when swimming. The lingual ribbon is narrow, with the rasplike teeth in a single series in each row. The tentacles are finger-shaped or linear, with eyes near their bases.

Elysia chlorotica (Agassiz) COLOR PLATE XVII, 10. The lateral ridges of the body are expanded in the form of winglike flaps used as undulating fins, when swimming, and folded over the back of the body so as to overlap when crawling. There are no cerata, but the body surface and the wings are permeated by ramifying veinlike canals. There is a clearly distinct head, with a necklike connection with the body. Extending forward from the front of the head are two delicate, fingerlike tentacles, folded to form a groove beneath. The paired eyes are set just behind the tentacles. The head is rounded and somewhat bilobed on its anterior margin. The color of the animal is emerald-green marked by opaque white spots with red dots scattered between them. The species ranges from Boston Harbor to New Jersey, abundantly found in shallow salt and brackish water.

Elysia catula (Agassiz) COLOR PLATE XVII, 11. This animal is sea-green in color, shading into brownish, especially forward. A whitish longitudinal mark is on the median line between the short, blunt, earlike tentacles, and two lateral, oblique, whitish marks just behind them. A round, whitish spot is also present near the middle margin of the wings. These wings, or fins, extend for about two thirds of the body-length and do not quite meet when folded over the back. The large, rounded head, with earlike tentacles, gives a very kittenlike appearance and accounts for the specific name. The back is marked by fine, parallel folds running lengthwise, doubtless increasing the area for respiration, which takes place through the integument, generally. This species is found in shallow water from Boston, Massachusetts, along the southern New England coast, to New Jersey.

SUBCLASS PULMONATA
(Fresh-water and Land Snails)

In these snails, there are no ctenidia but air-breathing is carried on by means of a *lung,* which is the vascular wall of the mantle cavity. This cavity is entirely enclosed except for a small opening on the right side of the body, which can be closed at will, by the animal, to keep out water in the case of aquatic species and to prevent drying out, in terrestrial forms. Even the fresh-water snails must come to the surface to fill their mantle-cavity with air for breathing purposes.

The majority of the pulmonates, living on land or in fresh water, are thus outside the range to which this book is devoted. A few species, nevertheless, are marine and two of these will be mentioned here, as typical of such forms.

The Subclass Pulmonata is divided into two Orders: (1) *Stylommatophora;* and (2) *Basommatophora.*

Order STYLOMMATOPHORA

These are land pulmonates. They have eyes on the tips of their two pairs of tentacles. Their mantle-cavity has been transformed into a lung-cavity with vascular lining for air-breathing. Therefore, none of them are marine.

Order BASOMMATOPHORA

This Order includes mostly fresh-water pulmonates, with a few found in brackish and salt water. There is but one pair of solid and flattened tentacles with a pair of eyes located at their base. Most of them have a spiral shell. About twelve families are recognized, one of which includes the brackish and salt-water species.

Family Ellobiidae (Auriculidae)

While the breathing organ is a pulmonary sac or true lung, nevertheless, these species cannot endure fresh water, but a few are terrestrial. It seems to be a transitional family.

Alexia myosotis (Draparnaud) PLATE 193 (26, 27). This little shell is ovoid with a conical spire and is only about ⅓ inch in length. It has a shining surface, yellowish brown in color, often verging into reddish or violet, with very faint lines of growth. The spire has seven or eight whorls, with clearly defined sutures. The body-whorl takes up about two thirds of the shell. The animal is light drab with darker head and tentacles. The tentacles are finger-like and diverging from the angles of the quadrangular head. The eyes are situated just inside the base of the tentacles. It is found near high-water mark along the shores especially in the crevices of decaying wooden wharves. It is distributed abundantly from Nova Scotia to the West Indies.

Melampus lineatus (Say) (= **Melampus bidentatus** Say) PLATE 193 (28). This shell is broadest at about the upper third, thus producing a short conical spire. It is of a translucent brownish horn-color with a shining surface. There are five or six whorls, the body-whorl being three fourths the length of the shell. It has a narrow aperture, quite long and rounded at the bottom. The inner lip is covered with enamel with two teeth or plications. The bottom of the aperture rounds upward, including the lower fold in its course. The shell is upwards of ½ inch in height. It is found in abundance from Prince Edward Island to the Gulf of Mexico, in salt marshes not far from the high-tide mark, usually climbing to keep out of the tidal reach.

CLASS CEPHALOPODA
(Squids and Octopuses)

In the Cephalopoda, the key to the anatomy is indicated by the name of the Class, which is derived from two Greek words, *cephalos,* meaning "head," and *pous,* genitive *podos,* meaning "foot." In other words, it is the "head-footed animal." This term emphasizes the fact that the foot of the mollusk has come to be situated around the mouth and divided to form the arms of the octopuses, squids, nautiluses, and argonauts included in this group, though a part of the foot also has developed into the *siphon,* situated within the mantle-cavity. In the Gastropoda, we found that, in the Subclass Prosobranchia, the front of the foot is extended to the neighborhood of the mouth. This has been carried further in the Cephalopoda, so that the foot surrounds the head. The anterior and posterior regions of these animals, thus, have come to be located close together. Just as, in the Prosobranchia, the apex of the twisted spire represents the middle of the dorsal part of the body and the contained digestive system forms a loop bringing the mouth and anus near together; so, in the Cephalopoda, the anatomy of the digestive system forms a loop, also bringing the anus and the branchial cavity, into which it empties, forward to the neighborhood of the mouth, while the body, with its visceral organs, forms a pointed or pouchlike extension behind the combined head and foot region, and the mid-dorsal part of the anatomy is at the hindermost part of this extension, or visceral trunk. In the case of many of the squids, this visceral trunk is pointed or cigar-shaped (PLATE 195, [1, 3]; COLOR PLATE XVIII; INDEX PLATE 194). In others, it is rounded and oblong (PLATE 195 [4, 5, 6]). Finally, in the octopuses, it is like a bulbous sac (PLATE 195 [7]). The chief features of the internal anatomy of the squids are indicated in the INDEX PLATE 194.

In the nautilus of the South Pacific and East Indies, there is a coiled external shell. The female argonaut, of worldwide distribution in the open seas, has a parchment-like external shell secreted by expansions of its dorsal

PLATE 194

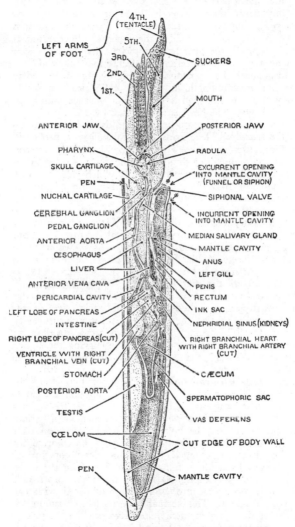

4TH. (TENTACLE)
5TH.
3RD.
2ND.
1ST.

LEFT ARMS OF FOOT

SUCKERS

MOUTH

ANTERIOR JAW

POSTERIOR JAW

PHARYNX

RADULA

SKULL CARTILAGE

EXCURRENT OPENING INTO MANTLE CAVITY (FUNNEL OR SIPHON)

PEN

SIPHONAL VALVE

NUCHAL CARTILAGE

CEREBRAL GANGLION

INCURRENT OPENING INTO MANTLE CAVITY

PEDAL GANGLION

MEDIAN SALIVARY GLAND

ANTERIOR AORTA

MANTLE CAVITY

ŒSOPHAGUS

ANUS

LIVER

LEFT GILL

ANTERIOR VENA CAVA

PENIS

PERICARDIAL CAVITY

RECTUM

LEFT LOBE OF PANCREAS

INK SAC

INTESTINE

NEPHRIDIAL SINUS (KIDNEYS)

RIGHT LOBE OF PANCREAS (CUT)

RIGHT BRANCHIAL HEART WITH RIGHT BRANCHIAL ARTERY (CUT)

VENTRICLE WITH RIGHT BRANCHIAL VEIN (CUT)

CÆCUM

STOMACH

POSTERIOR AORTA

SPERMATOPHORIC SAC

TESTIS

VAS DEFERENS

CŒLOM

CUT EDGE OF BODY WALL

PEN

MANTLE CAVITY

LEFT HALF OF COMMON SQUID SHOWING INTERNAL ANATOMY

arms for a brood-chamber. *Spirula peronii,* one of the squids, has a partially external spiral shell (PLATE 195 [2]) at the termination of its body. The rest of the squids have internal, elongate shells, either calcareous or chitinous, buried in the anterior wall of the visceral body covering. In the octopuses, the shell has completely disappeared except for a pair of vestigial remnants of chitinous material.

In general, the cephalopods are highly organized, swiftly moving marine mollusks with a cylindrical or saclike body and a head-region having a pair of large, highly developed eyes. The head is surrounded by a circle of eight or ten arms in the octopuses and squids, and about ninety in the nautilus. These arms are furnished with prehensile sucking discs or hooks. The body consists of the internal organs, contained in a thin membrane, but protected by the thick, muscular wall of the mantle, which closely invests the visceral mass on all sides, being fastened on the antero-dorsal wall of the body and enclosing a mantle-cavity on the postero-ventral side (INDEX PLATE 194). The mantle-cavity contains the gills and the anus and the openings of the excretory and genital organs. The anterior opening is crescent-shaped and allows water to be admitted freely. At the lower part of the opening is the siphon, a funnel-shaped tube with its smaller end protruding from the mantle-opening. When the powerful muscular walls of the mantle are contracted, the inner edge of the siphon is locked against the inner side of the mantle wall, so that the only exit is through its cavity, and a forcible stream of water is ejected, driving the animal backward by jet propulsion. By curving the siphon opening backward, the cephalopod is driven forward. An ink-sac is present in the visceral mass, from which a jet-black or dark brown fluid may be ejected to cloud the water, as if with a smoke-screen, enabling the animal to escape, when molested. The outer surface of the mollusk is patterned by *chromatophores,* pigmented spots of various colors, which may be enlarged by the contraction of a retinalike structure around them, so that the color of the surface may be changed rapidly, or floods of various colors may be made to follow each other along the body. The mouth is circular and is armed with a protrusible parrotlike beak of chitin, sometimes reinforced with calcareous material. This acts as a formidable weapon for attack against prey or enemy, and is worked by the powerful muscular pharynx just behind it. Also in the pharynx is the lingual ribbon with its radula. This leads into the long, narrow oesophagus and the stomach and a large caecum or blind sac, which acts as a receptacle for the secretion of the liver. The intestine passes forward from the stomach to complete the loop and connect with the anal opening into the mantle-cavity. The pair of gills (ctenidia) are in the mantle-cavity, each with an auricle to receive the purified blood from the gills and pass it on to a single median ventricle for distribution through the body by the aorta and the arterial system, whence it is returned by means of veins to the branchial hearts for passing it on to the gills again; thus, these animals have three hearts. A pair of excretory organs connect with the mantle-cavity and also with the pericardium. Typical molluscan ganglia are massed around the anterior end of the oesophagus. The eyes have a lens, except in the nautilus, together with retina and often a cornea, and are quite similar to the vertebrate eye from a superficial standpoint. There are also olfactory organs. The sexes are separate, the gonads emptying their products into the mantle-cavity through a genital pore.

All the species of the Cephalopods are carnivorous and quite a pest for fishermen.

The Cephalopods include the largest invertebrates known. The Giant Squid (*Architeuthis princeps*) may reach a length of sixty feet and has been known to do battle with the Sperm Whale.

Squid and octopuses are used for food by man in many parts of the world, and the former for bait for fishermen. The Mediterranean squid (*Sepia officinalis*) is the source of the India ink utilized by artists.

The Class Cephalopoda is divided into two Subclasses: (1) *Tetrabranchia;* and (2) *Dibranchia.*

SUBCLASS TETRABRANCHIA

This Subclass includes the nautiluses, of which the Chambered or Pearly Nautilus (*Nautilus pompilius*) is the best known. It has an external, coiled, chambered shell, four ctenidia, four auricles, and four nephridia, but no ink-sac, and about ninety tentacular arms. This group is found in the Pacific and Indian Oceans and does not come within our territory, and so need not be further mentioned here.

SUBCLASS DIBRANCHIA

In this Subclass, but one pair of gills, one pair of auricles and one pair of nephridia are present. The shell is internal (except in the genus *Spirula*) where it exists. In many species it is absent. An ink-sac is present, and there are eight or ten tentacular arms. The eyes have a crystalline lens.

Order DECAPODA
(The Squids)

The body is oblong or cigar-shaped. There are ten arms, eight of which are of equal length, surrounding the mouth-opening, and equipped with suckers for their entire length; and two, longer than the others, with the suckers only on terminal enlargements and usually mounted on peduncles and reinforced by a chitinous ring. These two are more or less retractile. The shell is present, but internal, except in one species.

Suborder PHRAGMOPHORA

This Suborder is characterized by the presence of a calcareous spiral shell with a siphuncle.

Family Spirulidae

The characters of this family are the *shell,* which is partly external and partly internal; the fact that it consists of two or three loose, *spiral coils;* and the *siphuncle,* which is a spiral, calcareous tube, housing a continuous canal, passing through the entire series of coils. There is but one living species, the survivor of a group which contained the fossil *Belemnites* of the Mesozoic Age.

Spirula peronii Lamarck (= **Spirula spirula** Linnaeus) PLATE 195 (2). This spiral shell is occasionally thrown up on beaches from Cape Cod to the Gulf of Mexico. The animal that secretes it lives in deep water. It is a white, pearly shell of two or three loose coils which do not touch each other. The shell is constricted at intervals, corresponding to internal partitions dividing the shell into chambers. A siphuncle of calcareous material is at the inner side of the coil. It is about 1 inch in diameter. The animal is but seldom seen. It is red in color with brown spots and has a terminal sucker. There are eight short sessile arms tapering to a point and equal in size, with numerous, very small suckers with short pedicels, and two long, retractile tentacular arms. The body is nearly cylindrical with a rounded end. The eyes are large. The length of the animal is about 3 inches.

Suborder SEPIOPHORA

In this Suborder, the internal shell is calcareous and straight, not coiled, and contains a series of air-chambers, but no siphuncle.

Family Sepiidae

The body is flat and oval, with narrow fins bordering the sides and end of the body. The suckers are in four rows.

Sepia officinalis Linnaeus. This is the Common Sepia or Cuttlefish. It is Mediterranean and European, so does not enter our territory. The color is brownish with light yellow or whitish stripes and bluish fins. It is mentioned here as the representative of its Suborder, and because of general interest in its shell (the cuttle bone), and the sepia ink which the animal secretes.

Suborder CHRONDROPHORA
(The Squids)

The squids, which are included in this Suborder, have a short and rounded, or elongate, tapering, or spindle-shaped body, with a pair of rounded or triangular fins, usually at the hinder end. The shell is internal. It is a straight, chitinous structure, often suggesting a quill pen, in shape. In some species, it is slender, like a sword blade. Therefore, it is usually spoken of as the *pen* or *gladius*.

Family Sepiolidae

In this family, the body is short and thimble-shaped or globose, while the fins are rounded and on the sides of the body toward the middle. The two long, tentacular arms are retractile. The eyes are well developed, possessing both lens and cornea.

Rossia hyatti Verrill PLATE 195 (5). The body is short and thimble-shaped. The postero-dorsal surface is covered with small, conical, whitish papillae, including the upper part of the head. The fins are large in proportion, oval or semicircular in shape, with the front rounded margin free. The siphon is long, conical, and with a small opening. The head is large and rounded, with large eyes with a prominent lower eyelid. The short, sessile arms are joined by a moderate web at their bases. The arms have numerous suckers, fairly large, in two series near the base of the arms, and in four rows on the rest of these structures. The two tentacular arms are about twice as long as the sessile arms. The terminal enlargements have about eight to ten rows of small globular suckers. The color of this species is pinkish, spotted with purplish brown, with the anterior edge of the mantle and the inside surface of the arms paler. The length from the bases of the arms to the end of the body is about 1⅜ inches, the tentacular arms also having the same length. This species occurs from Newfoundland to Massachusetts, in 7 to 217 fathoms.

Rossia sublevis Verrill PLATE 195 (6). The body in this species is a little shorter than that of the preceding one, but with the tentacular arms adding another inch. There are two rows of suckers throughout the entire length of the arms. The fins are farther forward than in

Rossia hyatti. The head is large and broader than the body, with very large eyes. The sessile arms are slender and unequal in size. The color is about like that of the preceding species. The pen is short and thin, not as long as the mantle, with a narrow shaft and a blade wider and shorter than the shaft. This species ranges from Newfoundland to Charleston, South Carolina, in 45 to 460 fathoms.

Family Loliginidae

The squid in this family have an elongate, cylindrical body, tapering to a point at its extremity. The triangular fins are terminal, tapering toward the apex. The internal shell (pen) is as long as the mantle and is chitinous. It begins at a point on the antero-dorsal margin of the mantle at the center, buried within the mantle, where it is comparatively slender, like a pen point. Then it broadens out like the feather of a quill pen, but symmetrical in outline, with a flange on either side to taper to a point at the hinder apex of the body. The mantle is attached to the animal at the nape of the neck and along the mid-antero-dorsal line. It is otherwise open on the sides and antero-ventral sides of the neck to give a free, slotlike entrance to the mantle-cavity from the center of which the smaller opening of the siphon protrudes. The eight sessile arms have two rows of suckers, and the long, tentacular arms, which are partially retractile, have four rows of suckers on the terminal clubs. The arms are large, three upper pairs successively longer, the lowest pair a little shorter than the third pair. The fourth arm on the left side is *hectocotylized* at the tip; that is, the suckers become transformed into swollen papillae during breeding, and are charged with sperm-carrying capsules (*spermato-phores*), which are transferred to the female, and attached to a horseshoe-shaped sucker, on her inner buccal membrane, below the beak, for fertilizing her ova.

Loligo pealii Lesueur PLATE 195 (3); COLOR PLATE XVIII. The Common Squid. The paired triangular fins are united at their tips meeting at the hinder end of the pointed body. They are more than half the length of the trunk. The pen has been described above. It is longer and narrower in the male than in the female, which also has a stouter body than the male. The average length of the mantle in grown specimens is 4 to 5 inches, with a total length of about 8 inches. The color is steel-gray with red to purplish spots, in the form of dilatable chromatophores. The eggs are deposited in many spindle-shaped gelatinous capsules which are attached by one end in clusters to seaweeds or other submerged objects. The capsules are about 2 or 3 inches in length, combined into clusters about 6 or 8 inches in diameter. The eggs within each capsule vary from about twenty to more than two hundred and are closely crowded. The embryos, distorted dwarfs of the adult, may be seen swimming around inside the eggs before hatching. This species ranges along the Atlantic Coast from Massachusetts Bay to South Carolina. It is common from Cape Cod to Cape Hatteras. It is taken in great quantities from fish pounds and seines, and used by fishermen for bait. It occurs in all depths from the low-water mark to 50 fathoms. It is an important source of food for most of our valuable food fishes.

Loligo brevis Blainville PLATE 195 (4). This is a short-bodied, small species, having short, rounded, terminal fins practically united into an oval disc at the terminal end of the body. The two upper pairs of sessile arms are very short, much shorter than the two lower pairs, with the dorsal pair the shortest of all. The tentacular arms are about as long as the body, when extended, the terminal clubs having four rows of suckers. The suckers of the sessile arms, in two rows, are very deep and obliquely cup-shaped. The pen is short with a broad, pointed blade and a short, narrow stem. The body surface is covered with purplish chromatophores, closely crowded above the eyes forming dark blotches. The length of the mantle, in this species, is less than 3 inches. Occasionally much larger specimens are found, especially in southern waters. This species is found from Delaware Bay to southern Florida and the Gulf of Mexico.

Family Ommastrephidae
(The Sea Arrows)

The body of the squid in this family is streamlined for speed. It is cylindrical, slender, and elongate. The fins are terminal, united at their point of meeting at the terminus of the body, where their outer edges join at a right angle, and their forward margins, if produced across the body, would form a practically perfect quadrant. The arms are usually short and can be held together in a streamlined group. The number of suckers varies in different species. The eyes have no cornea. The siphon is bound by bands to a concavity on the underside of the head, into which it fits closely. The tentacular arms are not retractile.

Ommastrephes illecebrosa (Lesueur) PLATE 195 (1). The Sea Arrows. The Flying Squid. This species has the characters of a well-balanced organization for swift motion through the water. It swims in schools, shooting backward, with the sharp end of the body and the balancing plane of its fins in advance, the tentacles and mouth, armed with parrotlike beak, trailing behind, but ready to strike right and left as the school overtakes and plunges through shoals of fish. These squid travel with such speed that they often hurl themselves out of water, planing through the air and even shooting on the deck of vessels at sea.

The head is large and cylindrical, continuing the line of the body. A lateral transverse ridge on either side, back of the eyes, separates the head from the neck. From these ridges three folds of skin extend backward on either side, finally joining to lead toward the mantle-opening, apparently directing a flow of water over the sensitive olfactory and hearing organs in the mantle-cavity. The tentacular arms are long and adapted to act in conjunction with the sessile arms in quickly seizing prey. They make their kill by seizing fishes in a school, striking right and left, grasping them with their arms, adhering with the pneumatic discs of their suckers, and biting them in the back of the neck, even killing many that they do not eat. During this process, apparently they are under great excitement, changing color rapidly. Their distribution is worldwide in the open sea.

Architeuthis princeps Verrill. The Giant Squid. This huge creature is the largest invertebrate known, even far exceeding the great octopus of the Pacific coast (*Octopus apollyon*) in size and strength. This species and *Architeuthis harveyi* were discovered and named by the eminent naturalist, A. E. Verrill, who recorded and described more than a score of instances in which they were seen in the neighborhood of the Banks of Newfoundland, while similar observations have been published by other well-known naturalists. Among the Giant Squid described by Verrill was one that measured 10 feet from tip of tail to mouth, while the tentacular arms were 42 feet in length, a total of 52 feet for this enormous creature. Apparently the Giant Squid are inhabitants of deeper waters and have come to the surface through accident. They have been reported from widely separated parts of the world, so that they are apparently of cosmopolitan distribution.

Battles between this monster and the Sperm Whale have been recorded and these are corroborated by frequent finds of fragments of these creatures in the stomachs of such whales.

Key to PLATE 195

1. *Ommastrephes illecebrosa;* 2. *Spirula peronii* (*Spirula spirula*); 3. *Loligo pealii;* 4. *Loligo brevis;* 5. *Rossia hyatti;* 6. *Rossia sublevis;* 7. *Octopus bairdii;* 8. *Octopus rugosus.*

PLATE 195

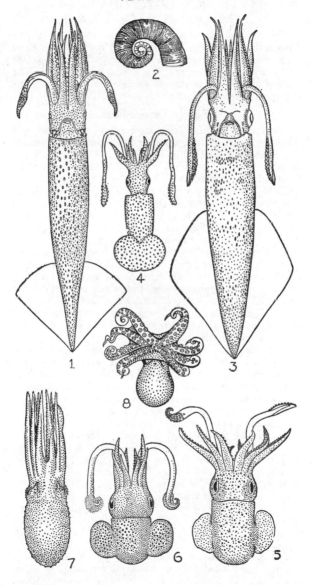

Order OCTOPODA
(The Octopuses, the Devil Fishes)

The mollusks in this Order have a round or saclike body, usually without fins. The head is large with eight arms, no tentacular arms being present. The suckers are fleshy and usually sessile. The oviducts are paired. The shell is absent, or consists of vestigial bars, except in the argonaut.

Family Octopodidae

The species in this family have a very large head, and similar, elongated arms, more or less webbed. The suckers are sessile and usually in two rows. The mantle is fastened to the head by fleshy bands. The third arm on the right side is hectocotylized.

Octopus bairdii Verrill PLATE 195 (7). The body, in this species, is short and thick, somewhat flattened and rounded behind. The head is nearly as broad as the body, enlarged around the eyes and concave between them. There are numerous rough and irregular tubercles, somewhat conical, around the eyes. There is a pair of conical, erectile cirri above and inward from each eye, both papillose on their surface. The entire upper side of the body is covered with minute, irregularly scattered papillae, which, in the larger males, may have the form of warts. The siphon is large, long, and tapering. It can be bent in any direction, movement in any opposite direction being correlated with that factor.

The arms are connected for about one third of their extent by a web, which is continued along their edges toward the termination. The suckers are in two rows. The right arm of the third pair in males of this species is modified into a large spoon-shaped organ for reproductive purposes. This organ has a series of ten to thirteen transverse folds and other features to adapt it for such functions. The body of this octopus is about 2 inches in length, exclusive of the arms, which are about ¾ inch long. Larger examples have been found. One, recorded by Verrill, measured 6½ inches from the end of the dorsal arms to the end of the body.

The general coloration is a translucent bluish white, closely dotted with light orange-brown and dark purplish brown, changing in hue to a certain degree. This species ranges from the Bay of Fundy to South Carolina, in 75 to 524 fathoms.

Octopus rugosus Bosc PLATE 195 (8). This is a larger rough-backed octopus found as far north as Beaufort, North Carolina, but it is typically a West Indian species.

Family Argonautidae
(The Paper Nautiluses, the Argonaut)

This family is remarkable for the thin, paperlike shell secreted by the expanded ends of the two upper arms of the female. It has no internal septa and is used as a depository for eggs. The animal can leave and return to it at will. The male has no shell.

Argonauta argo Linnaeus. The shell is fragile, whitish, and ribbed, showing an external spiral character. There are two rows of sharp tubercular prominences around the periphery of the shell, which may be 8 inches or more across. The female also may measure 8 inches in length. The male is much smaller, being 1 inch in length. The color of the female is very changeable. It may be light yellow with red dots, or floods of rose and purple may pass through its body in succession. This species is pelagic in the Atlantic and Pacific Oceans. It has been recorded from south of Marthas Vineyard and Newport, Rhode Island, in 64 to 365 fathoms, and also at various times off the coast of New Jersey. It also ranges to the Florida coast.

12
Phylum Chaetognatha

(ARROW WORMS)

THIS small but important group has a structure so distinct from that of any other group in the animal kingdom that it must be placed as a Phylum by itself. It is especially significant because a number of its characteristics seem to show that it is near the point of departure which leads toward that circle of transitional forms from which emerges the line leading toward the origin of the vertebrate stem. These incipient indications will be touched upon in summarizing the fundamental structure of the animals composing the group.

They are pelagic animals of small size, which swarm in the open sea and suddenly appear in vastly increased swimming masses, at certain times of the year, and even at certain hours of the day (see PLATE 196). They vary in length from ⅖ inch to about 2 inches and are slender, transparent animals, with lateral and tail-fins resembling the wings of an arrow. These fins are flattened horizontally and act as balancing organs, for the animal progresses by the movements of its body. They are called *Chaetognatha* because of the *chaetae,* or spines, and circlets of sickle-shaped hooks borne on their blunt heads, the latter being used as seizing jaws. These hooks are tipped with small, movable points. The body, viewed externally, is clearly divided into head, trunk, and tail, which corresponds to an internal structure divided in like manner. The blunt, rather triangular or domelike head-region has a vertical slitlike mouth, situated either terminally or ventrally, and is surrounded, in some species, by a thin, transparent fold of skin to form the *hood* or *collarette*. Within this, on the summit of the head, there are one or two rows of small teeth, or spinules, flanked on either side by a paired row of long, sickle-shaped, prehensile hooks, the ends of which can be drawn together over the mouth, or stiffly spread apart when the animal is disturbed.

The body-cavity is divided into three chambers by two transverse partitions. The head-compartment is nearly filled with the powerful muscles that move the grasping hooks and the small spines. The other cavities contain the digestive and reproductive organs and are more crowded in certain species than in others, and especially when they are filled with ova and sperm. The digestive system consists of a straight tube passing directly from the mouth to the anus, the latter situated at the junction of the trunk

PLATE 196

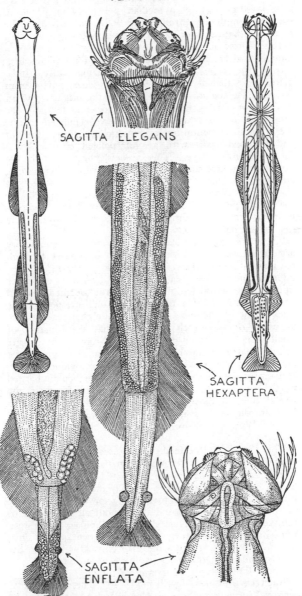

SAGITTA ELEGANS

SAGITTA HEXAPTERA

SAGITTA ENFLATA

with the tail, usually on the ventral surface. The digestive tube is suspended by a median mesentery or partition, running lengthwise through the body, thus dividing the three compartments of the body-cavity into right and left halves. These six compartments are lined with a peritoneum and are filled with a peritoneal fluid. Thus, they form a true *coelom,* apparently of the same nature, fundamentally, as that of vertebrates. During development from the egg, the coelom is formed from the original gut, or *archenteron* (the primal cavity of coelenterates), by the growth of paired pouches, which become inflated to line the original segmentation cavity which is between the gut and the body-wall, with an interpolated cellular layer, the *mesodermal layer.* This process, together with the division into three compartments filled with coelomic fluid, and the subsequent division of each of these lengthwise by the mesentery, is exactly the process by which the coelom, or peritoneal cavity, is formed in the various protochordate groups leading to the vertebrates, as well as by the vertebrates themselves.

There are no special excretory, respiratory, or circulatory organs present, respiration doubtless taking place through the general body-surface. There is a dorsal "brain" or ganglion situated in the head, connected by nerves on either side, with a ventral ganglion in the trunk-segment. Paired optic nerves lead from the brain to small eyespots in the integument of the head. There is also, here, a median, unpaired organ, which apparently has the function of smell. The Chaetognatha are hermaphroditic, the ovaries being situated in the trunk and the male organs in the tail. The sperm are introduced into the oviduct where, apparently, the eggs are fertilized. They are then discharged to the outside through openings just in front of the lateral fins. In most cases, the extruded fertilized eggs float in the open sea, where they develop into young Arrow Worms that exactly resemble the adults, except in size.

The Arrow Worms feed on microscopic diatoms, protozoans, and small larvae of other animals, as well as copepod crustaceans and even larval fishes. They are also cannibalistic, attacking each other. As they exist in unbelievable numbers, they are an important factor in the economy of the seas. They are found throughout all the oceans of the world, where their vast horizontal and vertical migrations have been the study of many oceanographers. They occur from the surface to the greatest depths known. Six genera and about thirty species have been described.

The following will be mentioned here:

Sagitta elegans Verrill PLATE 196. These are slender Arrow Worms with two pairs of lateral fins, separated by

PLATE 197

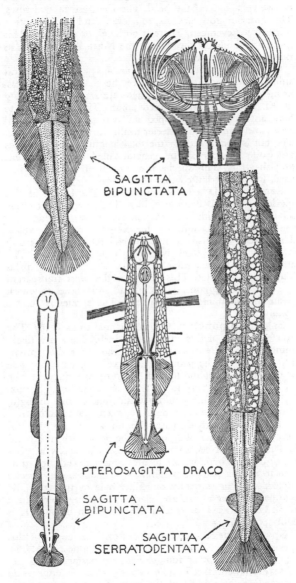

SAGITTA
BIPUNCTATA

PTEROSAGITTA DRACO

SAGITTA
BIPUNCTATA

SAGITTA
SERRATODENTATA

a distinct interval, as well as the caudal fin. There are nine to twelve hooks on the head. The teeth are in two rows. The anterior row has six to eleven, and the posterior, thirteen to seventeen. There is no hood, or collarette. This species is abundant throughout the North Atlantic, but its range is cosmopolitan.

Sagitta hexaptera D'Orbigny PLATE 196. The adult animals are among the largest of the chaetognaths, measuring 2⅘ inches in length. There are six to nine seizing hooks, smooth with uncurved points. There are three to four anterior teeth, grouped on two triangular skeletal areas, and two to five posterior teeth. There is no collarette. The tail is about ¼ or ⅕ the total length. The lateral fins are quite separated. The general color is a translucent grayish white. This species is abundant off Marthas Vineyard, but is distributed through all seas.

Sagitta enflata Grassi PLATE 196. The length of this species is from about ½ to ⅘ inch. There are eight to nine seizing hooks, with the ends not bent. The anterior teeth are five to eight in number; the posterior, eight to twelve. The head is quite small, with no collarette, and the trunk is proportionately thick but with a thin epidermis. The anterior fin is triangular in shape. The posterior fin is longer and broader. This species is the most transparent of all the chaetognaths, with the head and ovaries yellowish cream in color and more opaque. The species is cosmopolitan.

Sagitta bipunctata Quoy & Gaimard PLATE 197. The greatest length of this species is ¾ inch. There is a thickening of the epidermis behind the head and a short collarette is present. The paired seminal vesicles, on either side of the peduncle of the tail fin, protrude prominently. The olfactory organ is very long. There are seven to eight seizing hooks, while the anterior teeth number five to eight, and the posterior ones, nine to fourteen. Cosmopolitan.

Sagitta serratodentata Krohn PLATE 197. In this very slender species, the point of the hooks is bent around and the edge of the shaft is toothed. The hooks number six to eight. There are six to nine anterior teeth and thirteen to nineteen in the posterior row. The seminal vesicles project very prominently on either side of the tail. The two pairs of lateral fins are relatively close together. There is no collarette. This species is ⅖ to ¾ inch long. It is cosmopolitan.

Spadella draco Krohn PLATE 197. The length of this species is nearly ⅓ inch. There are about nine hooks. The anterior teeth number four to five; the posterior teeth six to seven. There is a bundle of long setae on either side forward of the middle of the body. There is a large collarette, or expansion of the epidermis, behind the head, having very large cells. There is but one pair of lateral fins at the forward part of the tail. The body is broad, because of the thickening of the epidermis along the sides from behind the head. The tail and the trunk are about the same length. This species is cosmopolitan.

13

Phylum Echinoderma

(SEA-STARS, BRITTLE-STARS, SEA-URCHINS, SEA-LILIES, AND SEA-CUCUMBERS)

THE word *Echinoderma* is derived from two Greek words, *echinos,* a hedgehog, and *derma,* meaning skin. Literally, therefore, they are the "spiny-skinned" animals. This refers to the fact that their skeleton consists of calcareous plates with projecting spines imbedded in the skin. These plates, in certain groups (those containing the sea-stars, brittle-stars, and sea-lilies) articulate with each other so as to form a multitude of movable joints. In such cases, the animals are quite flexible and can change the position of various parts of the body in any direction. In other groups (the sea-urchins, cake-urchins, and sand-dollars), the plates are closely locked together to form an immovable protective shell, with the soft parts of the animal inside. Finally, the group containing the sea-cucumbers has its skeletal calcareous plates scattered loosely within the skin, so that these creatures have a flexible, leathery body.

Another distinctive characteristic is the possession of a radial symmetry or starlike pattern, instead of the bilateral or elongate symmetry of all other animals above the Coelentera. This radial arrangement of parts in the Echinoderma is acquired secondarily, however, for the larvae, when hatched from the egg, are distinctly bilateral, free-swimming animals, which, by a remarkable metamorphosis, become transformed into the radiate, creeping adult, although even in this state, in certain features, a disguised bilateral symmetry still persists. There is no definite circulatory system, no special nephridium or other organ of excretion, and a diffuse nervous complex, in close association with the integument, with no concentrated ganglia but with a nerve-tract or cord running along the underside of each arm just above the ambulateral groove. In these respects, we are reminded of the Coelentera; but that the Echinoderma have traveled a long road from that group is obvious from the rest of their anatomy, most of which is peculiarly correlated with their radiate condition. Even the diffuse nerve-net, with its radiating cords is, doubtless, due to this factor. In all bilateral animals, the end which comes in contact with the environment first has become specialized as the head, with the nervous system and all organs of special sensation, as well as active prehension and food intake concentrated in and around it.

There the cephalic ganglia (directive brain) have become highly evolved. The radiate echinoderm, however, is likely to travel in any direction, so that all parts of its periphery have become equally sensitive, but with emphasis on projecting features such as, for example, the tips of the arms of the sea-star, where there are eyespots terminating the radial nerve cords. A good idea of the arrangement of echinoderm anatomical features may be obtained by studying INDEX PLATE 198, where the internal organization of the sea-star (asteroid), viewed dorsally, is graphically indicated, the integument being shown as partly removed to expose the internal organs, some of the latter, in turn, being lifted to show those situated underneath.

The diagram represents a five-rayed sea-star (*Asterias*). The *stomach,* with its five radiating pouches, is seen in the center, surmounted by the five-branched *pylorus,* the function of which is to receive the digestive secretions from the five radiating, paired *hepatic caeca.* It will be noted that each of these paired and bipinnately lobulated glands lies in one of the five arms of the sea-star. These arms are said to lie along the *radii* of the typical echinoderm ground plan. Midway between the radii are situated the *interradii,* along which certain other parts of the anatomy may be located. From the dorsal center of the pylorus rises the *rectum* to terminate in the *anus,* which empties to the outside at the mid-dorsal point. Two small pouches, the *rectal caeca,* are connected with the rectum. The central mouth enters directly into the stomach beneath it, and is located at the midventral center on the underside of the animal.

One of the most remarkable systems characteristic of echinoderms is the *water-vascular system.* If one examines the underside of the arms of the common sea-star, multitudes of *tube-feet* become visible, extending and contracting in four crowded rows in a central groove (the *ambulacral groove*) running lengthwise along the arm. These tube-feet, shown in the upper figure in the INDEX DIAGRAM, are extensions from a tube running along within each of the five arms, known as a *radial canal.* Small bulblike *ampullae,* one for every tube-foot, extend inward from the radial canal, within the arm, in crowded series. The radial canals arise from a *ring-canal* at the center of the animal, which completely surrounds the mouth beneath the lobes of the stomach. A canal, known as the *stone-canal,* branches off from the ring-canal at one of the interradii between two of the radial canals. It terminates at the dorsal surface by means of a disc-shaped sieve-plate, known as the *madreporite* (shown in the diagram with the slender tube of the stone-canal just above it). The interior of the stone-canal and of the ring- and radial-canals is lined with fine, but powerful, hairlike cilia that continually beat inward, thus drawing in a strong current of sea water keeping the entire ambulacral system full and turgid with fluid, especially including the ampullae. When these little bulblike appendages are squeezed by surrounding muscles, the fluid with which they are filled is forced, in each case, into the adjoining tube-foot, thus extending it. When the muscle tension is decreased, the water returns to the ampullae and the corresponding tube-feet are shortened. This motion seems to be under perfect control, due to the fact that each tube-foot, at its terminus, appears to be a sense organ. At the end of each tube-foot, in most species, there is a pneumatic disc, which will adhere strongly to any surface. It acts in this way: when the tube is extended, the disc is flattened against the surface it touches. Muscles in the tube at the top of the disc are retracted, raising the center and creating a vacuum, the surrounding water pressure causing it to adhere. Hundreds of these discs acting together enable the sea-star, by further contracting the muscles, to draw itself slowly forward. This is the method by which the sea-star moves from place to place, and is also the source of the steady pull by means of which the sea-star overcomes the resistance of bivalves, like the oyster and mussel, in order to force them to open their shells so that it may devour them.

This water-vascular system is also noteworthy as being a part of the coelom, with which the body-cavity of the echinoderm is lined, and from which the gonads are developed. The presence of this coelom groups the echinoderms with the series of Phyla from which, eventually, the protochordates and, thus, the vertebrates, sprang, in the course of evolution. The gonads are quite simple. A pair is located in each arm of the sea-star and opens directly to the outside. The sexes are usually separate in echinoderms. Fertilization takes place in the open sea. The fertilized eggs hatch into free-swimming larvae, mentioned above. These differ in the five main classes into which the Echinoderma are divided. For the most part, they are quite minute. Except for the larvae of the crinoidea (sea-lilies), they are of four main types: *Auricularia,* the larva of the Holothuroidea (sea-cucumbers); *Bipinnaria,* for the Asteroidea (sea-stars); *Ophiopluteus,* for the Ophiuroidea (brittle-stars); and *Echinopluteus,* for the Echinoidea (sea-urchins). These larvae are propelled through the water by means of moving microscopic cilia, arranged in *ciliated bands.* When the larvae are first hatched, this band merely surrounds the mouth, but, as it develops, it is extended into a series of folds or fingerlike

PLATE 198

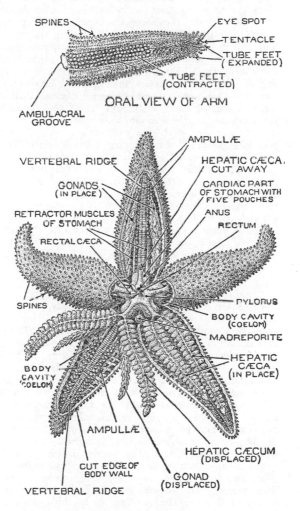

SPINES — EYE SPOT

TENTACLE

TUBE FEET (EXPANDED)

TUBE FEET (CONTRACTED)

ORAL VIEW OF ARM

AMBULACRAL GROOVE

AMPULLÆ

VERTEBRAL RIDGE — HEPATIC CÆCA, CUT AWAY

CARDIAC PART OF STOMACH WITH FIVE POUCHES

GONADS (IN PLACE)

ANUS

RETRACTOR MUSCLES OF STOMACH

RECTUM

RECTAL CÆCA

PYLORUS

BODY CAVITY (COELOM)

SPINES

MADREPORITE

HEPATIC CÆCA (IN PLACE)

BODY CAVITY (COELOM)

AMPULLÆ

HEPATIC CÆCUM (DISPLACED)

CUT EDGE OF BODY WALL

GONAD (DISPLACED)

VERTEBRAL RIDGE

INTERNAL ANATOMY OF A TYPICAL ASTEROIDEAN
(BODY WALL REMOVED FROM ABORAL SURFACE OF DISC AND THREE ARMS)

outgrowths, which are definite in form for each type. They are very abundant in the sea, but are so different from the adult that they were considered to be independent species of organisms, until their life history was known. The *Auricularia* is characterized by a continuous ciliated band thrown into a series of symmetrical folds. In the *Bipinnaria*, these have become narrowed into a series of flexible, fingerlike processes and separated into two unconnected sets, one of which, much shorter than the other, is located above the mouth. The *Ophiopluteus* has the processes lengthened into very narrow fingers, each of which is supported by a stiff, skeletal rod, all of the processes pointing upward, diagonally or vertically, in symmetrical pairs. The *Ophioglypha* is similar to the *Ophiopluteus*, also with skeletal rods, but two of the processes project out horizontally, one on each side, and a single median process projects vertically downward. The larva of the Crinoidea (sea-lilies) is barrel-shaped, with parallel, ciliated bands at intervals.

The Phylum Echinoderma is most conveniently divided into five Classes, as follows: (1) *Asteroidea;* (2) *Ophiuroidea;* (3) *Echinoidea;* (4) *Crinoidea;* (5) *Holothuroidea.*

CLASS ASTEROIDEA
(The Sea-stars)

These are echinoderms having a flat body, usually the shape of a five-pointed star, or pentagonal, with five arms. In some species there are more than five. There is also mutation within the species, so that there may be more or less than the normal number of arms. The tube-feet occur in an open groove on the underside of the arms. The main features of a typical asteroid have already been described above. In addition, it may be stated that the epithelium is ciliated and that the calcareous plates embedded in the integument are diversified by spines and tubercles, which push up the integument to form an irregular, or more or less patterned, surface. Some of the spines are movable, especially on the margins. Modified spines form special organs, called *pedicellariae,* and *paxillae.* The former are pincerlike, with various modifications, and are used for cleaning the body-surface or as a means of defense. The paxillae are brushlike and often form mosaic patterns when they cover the surface. Through holes between the spines, delicate fingerlike papillae (*papulae*) project, probably to act as gills.

The Class Asteroidea is divided into three Orders: (1) *Phanerozonia;* (2) *Spinulosa:* (3) *Forcipulata.*

Order PHANEROZONIA

In this order, the marginal plates are well developed and show distinctly in one or two rows, being set close together so as to make a definite border. The arms have two rows of tube-feet. Papulae are found on the upper side, for the most part, which may be covered with paxillae, or it may have scattered spines, or be entirely naked.

Family Porcellanasteridae

These are somewhat pentagonal sea-stars, with the dorsal side covered with paxillae and often with a central projection. The anus is lacking. On the lower side, the interradial areas are covered with elongate, parallel, scalelike plates. *Cribriform organs* (vertical grooves bordered by folds of membrane), are situated in the interradial angles.

Ctenodiscus crispatus (Retzius) PLATE 199; COLOR PLATE XIX, 1. The Mud-star. In this species, the form of the body varies from almost pentagonal, through intermediate stages, to nearly star shape. There are five arms. The marginal plates and those on the oral (lower) side are covered with a thin, soft skin. The plates bordering the wide ambulacral grooves (adambulacral plates) have three to four short spines. The color is yellowish. The diameter is 3 to 4 inches. This is a circumboreal species, ranging, on our coast, from the Arctic southward to Panama and South America. It is quite common off Cape Cod and the New England coast generally. It is found from shallow water to 1000 fathoms.

Family Astropectinidae

These are sea-stars that have no anus. The upper surface is covered with paxillae, forming a close, mosaiclike layer. There are no cribriform organs and no aboral protuberance. The border of marginal plates is thick and laid flat. They are covered with spinules. The tube-feet are without suckers.

Leptychaster arcticus (M. Sars) PLATE 199. This small species has a relatively large disc, with arms broad at the base and flattened, but with rounded edges. It measures about 1¼ inches in diameter. The marginal plates are without large spines; the upper series has smaller plates than those on the lower edge. There are no pedicellariae. The plates bordering the ambulacral grooves each have three to four long, slender spines. This sea-star is orange to reddish in color. It is circumboreal, ranging from Greenland to Delaware Bay on the Atlantic Coast, and to the Scandinavian peninsula and the British Isles on the European side of the Atlantic. It also occurs in the North Pacific Ocean.

Plutonaster rigidus Sladen PLATE 199. In this species the disc is proportionately large with the arms long and tapering to a sharp point, separated interradially by a broad, sweeping curve. The paxillae on the aboral (upper) side are small and very numerous, being set close together, and consisting of columnar plates with diverging spinules. They are without definite arrangement. The marginal plates, for the most part, are small and form a distinct, narrow border. Each has one or two sharp spines. The interradial plates on the under (oral) side are scalelike, forming diverging rows toward the center. Those forming the border of the ambulacral groove have eight to ten spines. There are often a few pedicellariae of simple structure near the mouth region. Four-rayed and six-rayed individuals are found occasionally. This is a relatively deep-water species, occurring most commonly from 300 to 1700 fathoms from the latitude of New York to Cape Hatteras.

Psilaster andromeda (Müller & Troschel) (= **Archaster florae** Verrill) PLATES 199; 202. This sea-star has a comparatively small disc, with tapering, acutely pointed arms diverging at the disc by a somewhat sharp angle. The arms are thick, with almost vertical sides and high and narrow marginal plates, making a narrow, but distinct border. The plates of the lower series each have a single spine, which lies flat. There are three to four series of small plates on the large interradial oral areas. The madreporite is distinct. There are no pedicellariae. The paxillae on the upper side are close set, and fall into fairly regular rows toward the base of the arms. This species, when adult, measures about 4 inches in diameter. The color is pale pink to nearly white, with a gelatinous, somewhat slimy secretion covering the body. It feeds on small bivalves, small sea-urchins, and foraminifera, which it finds on the muddy bottoms it frequents. It occurs most commonly from about 380 to 450 fathoms, though at times it is taken in waters as shallow as 10 fathoms. It is circumboreal, ranging from Davis Strait to Delaware Bay on the American side of the Atlantic, and from the British Isles to the Azores on the European side.

Astropecten articulatus (Say) PLATE 200. Fairly large sea-stars. There are two relatively broad rows of marginal plates; the upper row is fringed with spines and granules, and the lower row is very thickly edged with spines. Near the tip of the arm the upper marginal plates each have a small, wartlike tubercle. There are no pedicellariae. The diameter of these sea-stars is 8 to 10 inches. This species occurs from New Jersey southward to the Gulf of Mexico. This is a very variable species. It is more often orange, but it may be purplish on the upper side.

PLATE 199

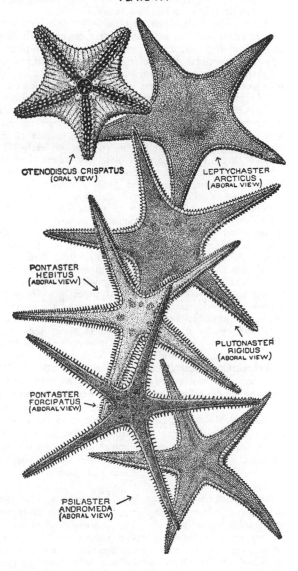

OTENODISCUS CRISPATUS
(ORAL VIEW)

LEPTYCHASTER
ARCTICUS
(ABORAL VIEW)

PONTASTER
HEBITUS
(ABORAL VIEW)

PLUTONASTER
RIGIDUS
(ABORAL VIEW)

PONTASTER
FORCIPATUS
(ABORAL VIEW)

PSILASTER
ANDROMEDA
(ABORAL VIEW)

bordered by orange-red on the marginal plates, edged with purple spines, and yellow beneath.

Astropecten duplicatus Gray PLATE 200. The arms radiate from the disc at equal abrupt angles, with their bases close together, and taper symmetrically to narrow tips. The marginal plates of the lower series project beyond the upper ones, the two together forming the borders of a vertical groove on the sides of the arms, which is felted with fine spines. The upper marginal plates form a thick border, elevated above the central part of the disc. There is a stout spine on the first seven plates on each arm, the first two being the largest. The surface of the plates is granular. From the outer edge of each plate project three to four broad, flattened spines, beneath which, on the oral side, there are three or four flattened, bladelike, tapering spines, the general surface between them being thickly sown with bristling spinules. The ambulacral groove is edged with plates, each bearing a three-tined fork of spines, pointing inward, and each group joined at its base with two outwardly directed flat spines of quite unequal size. The paxillae on the upper side of the disc thickly cover the surface with their cylindrical stems, from the top of which radiate spinules to form a starlike cluster, interlocking with those of neighboring paxillae when extended. At times they are withdrawn and folded up in a bundle, exposing the pores of the integument between. The madreporic plate is usually overhung by the paxillae, so that it is nearly concealed. This species is 3 to 4 inches in diameter. It ranges from North Carolina to Florida and the West Indies.

Astropecten cingulatus Sladen PLATE 200. This is an unusually short-rayed species, bordered with broad marginal plates. They are broadest at about the center of the ray, so that there the plate border is wider than the median paxilla-covered surface. Each plate on the margin of the undersurface has two projecting marginal spines, and a sparse series of smaller spines projecting from the spinule-covered surface. There are three series of spines on the plates bordering the ambulacral groove. This is a species from deep water.

Astropecten comptus Verrill PLATE 200. This species has somewhat stout, tapering, elongate arms, diverging at an acute angle from the disc. The marginal plates on the upper side are transversely oblong, with rounded corners, close-set to each other, forming a conspicuous, embossed border. Their surface is spineless, but covered with closely crowded granules which gradually become short spinules toward the margin. The paxillae of the upper surface are closely crowded together, each crowned

PLATE 200

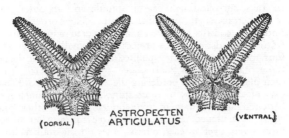

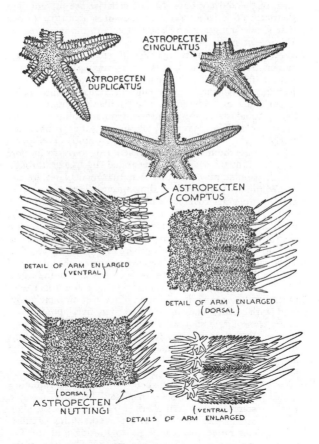

ASTROPECTEN
ARTICULATUS

(DORSAL)　　　(VENTRAL)

ASTROPECTEN
CINGULATUS

ASTROPECTEN
DUPLICATUS

ASTROPECTEN
COMPTUS

DETAIL OF ARM ENLARGED
(VENTRAL)

DETAIL OF ARM ENLARGED
(DORSAL)

(DORSAL)
ASTROPECTEN
NUTTINGI

(VENTRAL)
DETAILS OF ARM ENLARGED

by a flowerlike rosette, consisting of a circlet of five or six rays, surrounding a central spinule and an outer ring of numerous, small, petal-like spinules. The border on the underside consists of similar plates covered with granules, from the midst of which project many small spinules and four to six small, sharply pointed spines, while two large, acute, tapering marginal spines project outward from each plate. The series bordering the ambulacral groove consists of small groups of three spines each, the outer ones flattened, and the median spine longer than the others and vertically flattened. Two rows of three still smaller spines successively overlap each others' bases on the stalk behind each of the above groups. No pedicellariae are present. The diameter of a large specimen measures about 10 inches. The species ranges from Cape Hatteras to the west coast of Florida in 11 to 26 fathoms.

Astropecten nuttingi Verrill PLATE 200. This is a rather flat and thin species. It is regularly star-shaped with a flat disc, which often has a central bosslike projection. It is smaller than the previous species, being about 4 inches in diameter. The paxillae are small and of about equal size, forming nearly regular, obliquely transverse rows. The stems or columns of the paxillae are fairly long and slender, with convex, round, or elliptical caps. Along the median line of each arm they are in close contact, but otherwise are separated by pores through which papulae may protrude. The marginal plates are not so prominent as in the preceding species. They are smaller and completely covered with short and regularly arranged spinules of about the same size as those on the paxillae, so that at first glance they seem to blend with them. They are convex on the upper side and at the approximate center of each plate there is a short, stubby, but acute spine, larger on the basal margin of the arm and gradually decreasing in size as one approaches the apex. The lower marginal plates correspond with the upper ones in size and position but are flatter. They are completely covered with small spines of irregular size, overlapping each other transversely so that they point outward. Two long spines point outward at the edge of each upper plate and two or three of intermediate size are beneath them at the margin of the lower plate. Bundles of three or four finger-like spines project over the margin of the ambulacral groove from each plate, with about two clusters of radiating spines just behind these on each plate. These are movable and act somewhat as pedicellariae. The madreporic plate is small and obscure because of the overhanging paxillae. This species ranges from Georgia to Florida and the Bahamas, and probably also occurs off the Carolina coast. The known depth range is from 90 to 116 fathoms.

Family Luididae

The sea-stars in this family have long and narrow arms and a small flat disc. There is no border of marginal plates on the upper side, these structures being replaced by the continuation over the edge of the covering of paxillae. The single border of ambulacral plates is on the underside of the arms. Pedicellariae are usually present. There are no cribriform organs. No intestine, no intestinal caeca, or anus are present in this family, waste material being regurgitated through the mouth.

Luidia clathrata (Say) PLATE 201. This species has five long, narrow arms. The upper surface is covered with quadrangular paxillae closely fitted together in ten to twelve fairly regular rows, the central paxillae being smaller and more irregularly placed. The lateral rows are composed of larger, almost rectangular paxillae, with a remarkably regular arrangement. All are ornamented with coarse, tuberclelike spinules. The underside has a series of marginal plates close to the ambulacral groove, filling out the sharp interradial angles which widen, V-like, to the junction of the bases of adjacent arms. Each of these plates bears two spines of unequal length. These sea-stars bury themselves just below the surface of sandy bottoms, but as they draw water through their bodies by ciliary action from underneath and exhale it through the pores between the paxillae on the upper sides, their location is marked by star-shaped grooves in the sand caused by the expelled water currents just above their bodies. These patterns move about following the rapid creeping movements of the sea-stars, as they are propelled from place to place by the oarlike action of their powerful flattened tube-feet. They also swim through the water by the same means. They are about 4 inches in diameter, and are salmon to rose-salmon or gray in color. These are shallow-water sea-stars, found most commonly in less than 20 fathoms of water, but range down to 48 fathoms or more. They occur abundantly from North Carolina to Florida, the West Indies, and Brazil. They have also been recorded off the southern New Jersey coast.

Luidia elegans Perrier PLATE 201. This is a large sea-star, measuring, when adult, up to 14 inches in diameter. The upper surface is rich orange in color. It is lighter underneath. The paxillae, on the upper side, are of about uniform size, star-shaped, and not quadrangular as in the previous species. They form a rosette with one to three spinules in the center, surrounded by a circle of very slender spinules. There are no upper marginal plates. The lower series are short and nearly vertical, with three long, acute spines, the largest being uppermost. Two-valved pedicellariae are present. This species is very abundant from New Jersey to south of Cape Hatteras. It also occurs in the West Indies. It is found most often from 53 to 146 fathoms and has been dredged from 200 fathoms. When handled, this sea-star frequently amputates its arms, so that it is difficult to collect complete specimens.

Family Benthopectinidae

In this family, the upper side of the sea-star is covered with paxillae or spines. The upper and lower marginal plates alternate, promoting greater flexibility as compared with the previous family, in which the two sets are opposite to each other. They are covered with spines. The pedicellariae are simple or comblike (pectinate). The tube-feet have a small pneumatic disc. The upper side of each arm has a pair of strong muscles, enabling the sea-star to utilize the flexibility of the arms, due to the alternating upper and lower marginal plates. The *papulae* (fingerlike gills) are in a specialized group, extending through the skeletal openings in areas at the base of each arm and neighboring regions. Such an area is called a *papularium*. An intestine, anus, and intestinal caeca are present.

Pontaster hebitus Sladen [= **Pontaster tenuispinus** (Düben & Koren)] PLATES 199; 201. In this species the disc is comparatively small and the arms are long, slender, and tapering to an acute tip. The narrow border of marginal plates, each with its single large spine, stands out conspicuously. There is no odd marginal plate at the interradial junction of the arms, as in *Benthopecten armatus* (see below).

On the underside, the plates bordering the ambulacral groove have a comblike series of small, even spines standing out from the plate into the groove, and one to three larger spines standing up from the surface of the plate itself. The paxillae of the upper side of the sea-star are small, often with a central spine standing up, surrounded by the radiating spinules. The arms in this species often vary in length. The color is bright red, varying to pink or orange, and light underneath. This is usually a deep-water species but may be brought to the surface by fishermen. The vertical range is from 10 to about 1100 fathoms. It is a circumboreal species, occurring from the Arctic to Southern New England and around to Scandinavia and the British Isles.

Pontaster forcipatus Sladen PLATE 199. This species is closely related to the preceding. The marginal plates on the upper side are smaller, thus producing a narrower border. They are covered with fine spinules, and a large spine stands out conspicuously from about every third

PLATE 201

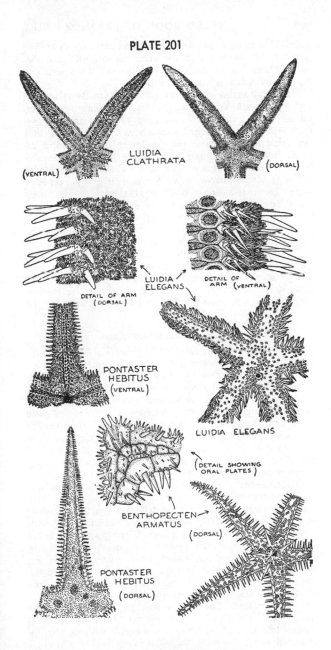

LUIDIA
CLATHRATA

(VENTRAL) (DORSAL)

DETAIL OF ARM
(DORSAL)

LUIDIA
ELEGANS

DETAIL OF
ARM (VENTRAL)

PONTASTER
HEBITUS
(VENTRAL)

LUIDIA ELEGANS

(DETAIL SHOWING
ORAL PLATES)

BENTHOPECTEN
ARMATUS
(DORSAL)

PONTASTER
HEBITUS
(DORSAL)

plate. The paxillae are very small and close set. The five papularia at the bases of the arms are compact and distinct. There is a central elevation around the anus. The madreporic plate is also quite distinct.

Benthopecten armatus (Sladen) (= **Benthopecten spinosus** Verrill) PLATE 201. The marginal plates, on both the upper and lower sides, are long and narrow, each with a single, large, conspicuous spine, tapering to a very sharp point, those on the lower margin being directly beneath the upper ones. Those bordering the ambulacral groove have a row of small cylindrical spines over the edge of the furrow, as well as one large spine on each plate. There is a single odd marginal plate at the interradial angle, between the bases of the arms (see the small figure on PLATE 201). Five large, spikelike spines radiate from an interradial position at the upper angles at the bases of the arms. There is an anal elevation, located centrally. The madreporic plate may be clearly seen. This species is circumboreal, though the European and American forms may have local differences. It ranges from the latitude of New York to the Gulf of Mexico, on the Atlantic Coast, and from the British Isles to Portugal on the European shores.

Family Odontasteridae

The sea-stars in this family are either star-shaped, with a broad disc with short arms, or pentagonal. The marginal plates are widely developed and quite large. There is an odd interradial marginal plate between the bases of the arms, on both the upper and undersides. The upper side of the disc and arms is flattened. On the upper sides there are short, flat spines arranged in radiating groups like paxillae. The pedicellariae are either in close-set pairs to form a valve, closing sidewise (*valvate*), or formed of two short beaklike parts, like half cones, set so as to snap together on an oval depression as a base (*alveolate*).

Odontaster robustus Verrill PLATE 202. In this species, the form is that of a star having a broad center with concave margins and short, acutely tapering arms ending in a rounded apex. The margins are quite thick and with large and heavy marginal plates. The upper and lower series are opposite each other and match in size and shape. There are about twenty-seven plates in each set, which overlap the disc to a marked degree. They are oblong in shape, with the longer sides joining. At the ends of the arms about four pairs are practically in contact on the middle line. The plates covering the disc on the upper side are circular and separate from each other. They rise as vertical columns, topped with a slightly rounded head, those on the arms being higher. On their

PLATE 202

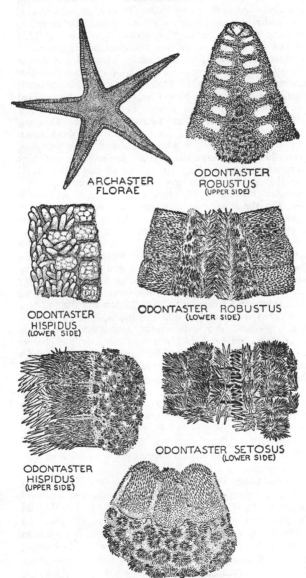

ARCHASTER FLORAE

ODONTASTER ROBUSTUS (UPPER SIDE)

ODONTASTER HISPIDUS (LOWER SIDE)

ODONTASTER ROBUSTUS (LOWER SIDE)

ODONTASTER HISPIDUS (UPPER SIDE)

ODONTASTER SETOSUS (LOWER SIDE)

ODONTASTER SETOSUS (UPPER SIDE)

tops, they have a spreading cluster of slender, pointed spinules. The conspicuous pores for the papulae are in five radial groups besides a central pore. The plates on the underside are rectangular, arranged in rows on either side of the ambulacral groove, and each is surmounted by a cluster of long, slender spinules. Around the mouth there is a series of five recurved, flat spines, conspicuously translucent and bladelike with sharp tips. This species is found off the southern New England coast in depths from 300 to 400 fathoms. It is about 3 inches in diameter.

Odontaster hispidus Verrill PLATE 202. This sea-star also has a flat, broad disc. The arms are short, tapering regularly, and are acutely pointed. The marginal plates have an average size and are not so large and thick as those of the preceding species, nor do they encroach on the disc to a marked degree. They are convex and quadrangular, rounded at the corners on the upper side of the disc. On the lower side they are quite square, somewhat separated, and higher than long. The odd, interradial plate is practically triangular and smaller than its neighbors. All the marginal plates, in both sets, are thickly covered with spinules. On the upper side they are slender and sharp. On the lower side, they are longer and stouter. The pores for papulae are large and well distributed, especially over the surface of the arms. The numerous, spinous plates on the underside are convex and well separated, their surface sculptured with low, knoblike elevations. They form about five rows on either side of the ambulacral groove, to which they are parallel. Those bordering on the grooves are transversely quadrangular and narrow, with a knobbed surface, like the rest. The disc-plates on the upper side are thickly covered with groups of radiating spinules, closely adjacent to each other, the papulae and their pores showing distinctly between them. These sea-stars are 4 to 5 inches in diameter. The small marginal plates are distinctive. Mutations having four or six arms are occasionally found. The range is from Marthas Vineyard Island to Florida, in depths varying from 43 to more than 480 fathoms.

Odontaster setosus Verrill PLATE 202. This species, in its general aspect, resembles the preceding, but is readily identified by the higher marginal plates, encroaching on the disc to a considerable degree on both the upper and under sides, and the abundant covering of fine spinules on the latter. The outline is star-shaped with five concave sides. The marginal plates are transversely longer than broad, with rounded ends, and covered with sharp spinules pointing uniformly outward toward the margin in a feltlike pattern. The plates are well separated from each other by deep grooves. The upper and lower series almost exactly correspond in the position of their plates, so that the grooves separating the plates are continuous around the edge of the disc. Toward the tips of the arms several of the plates on either side are in contact with those of the opposite side. The plates covering the upper surface of the arms are quite separated and resemble paxillae, having a rounded top covered with a radiating cluster of small, slender, acute spinules. The papular pores are numerous and conspicuous, being scattered singly between the plates. The plates on the underside are more or less square. Three or four rows are on either side of the ambulacral grooves arranged parallel to them. Each one has a thick cluster of diverging spinules. The plates bordering the ambulacral groove are narrower than the others and have three or four slender, almost parallel spinules extending over the groove, nearly interlocking with those of the opposite side. A cluster of more numerous spinules, longer and more slender than the others, stands out from the surface, pointing in various directions. The five dentary plates surrounding the mouth have short, prismatic spines at their apices flanked by two or three shorter, curved spines of larger size. There are also five recurved spines radiating from the mouth, bladelike in character, and translucent at their extremely sharp tips. This species is about 3½ inches in diameter. It ranges from off Marthas Vineyard Island to the Carolina coasts in 56 to upwards of 400 fathoms.

Family Goniasteridae

In this family the marginal plates are large and thick on both the upper- and underside of the disc, which is somewhat broad, flat, or slightly convex. It is quite rigid, sometimes pentagonal, with large discs and short arms, often star-shaped, with concave sides and somewhat prolonged arms. The nearly equal upper and lower marginal series together form a thick, practically vertical margin, with the two series closely sutured at the point where they join at the periphery. The plates on the upper surface of the disc are joined to form a mosaic. They are usually polygonal or rounded and sometimes lobed. They are either joined directly or with the aid of smaller intervening plates. Their surface may be granulate or they may approximate paxillalike structures. The tube-feet are in two rows and have pneumatic suckers. Pedicellariae are usually present. This is a very large family with many genera. Only a few of the most typical species will be mentioned here, especially those occurring in comparatively shallow waters, or that are likely to be dredged by fishermen.

Pseudarchaster intermedius Sladen PLATE 203. In this species the arms are fairly long, and the disc moderate in size. The dorsal side is covered with paxillae, which continue to the end of the arms. The size of the marginal plates is gradually reduced as they approach the tips of the arms so that the paxillae are not blocked off. The marginal plates are largest in the region of the interradii. The plates on the arms are in radial rows. They are in the form of paxillae. Their columns are surmounted by round or oval tops, with a star-shaped basal-region having six radiating lobes. The marginal plates are moderately large and paired on the upper and lower sides, with their junctions forming a groove on the edge of the star. The plates on the upper disc are separated from each other in the central part of the disc and the arms and upper surface are covered with small granules. The lower plates are numerous, arranged in chevronlike rows parallel to the ambulacral groove and are completely covered with granules. The plates adjoining the groove are large and regularly arranged, somewhat overlapping the groove with their rounded inner margins. The spines adjacent to the groove are in more or less radiating clusters but are not real paxillae, though superficially resembling them. This is the most common species of this genus off our coast. It is often brought in by Gloucester fishermen. It is about 6 inches in diameter. It is red or reddish brown in color. The range is from the latitude of Nova Scotia to that of New Jersey. It is also circumboreal, extending around through the Arctic to the British Isles.

Pseudarchaster fallax (Perrier) PLATE 203. This species is quite closely related to the above. It can be recognized by the larger and much thicker marginal plates, which are closely appressed and much broader than long. They overlap the upper surface of the disc to a much greater degree and nearly cover the entire surface of the arms, leaving very little space for the disc-plates. On the underside, the granules are much more crowded and the groove-bordering spines are much shorter. The range is about the same on the Atlantic Coast.

Goniaster americanus Verrill PLATE 203. This is a broadly pentagonal sea-star with concave sides and short arms. The disc-plates on the upper side are large and polygonal or more or less circular. The marginal plates are usually large and convex. They are quadrangular with rounded inner sides, shaped somewhat like an axhead, and quite thick. They are not numerous, there being from six to nine on each side of an arm, depending on the age of the individual. There are many conical spines on the radial and disc-plates, but not on the marginal plates, which are bare of all spines. The radial plates extend up

PLATE 203

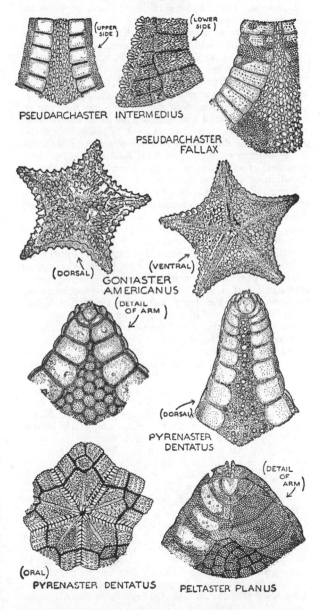

PSEUDARCHASTER INTERMEDIUS
(UPPER SIDE)
(LOWER SIDE)

PSEUDARCHASTER FALLAX

GONIASTER AMERICANUS
(DORSAL)
(VENTRAL)

(DETAIL OF ARM)

PYRENASTER DENTATUS
(DORSAL)

PYRENASTER DENTATUS
(ORAL)

PELTASTER PLANUS
(DETAIL OF ARM)

into the arms, but are excluded from the apex by one or two pairs of marginal plates, the inner edges of which are in contact, as shown in the detail on the plate. There are many pedicellariae of a type that has two spoon-shaped blades, which lie with their stem-ends in contact and their spatulate spoons away from each other, in little hollowed-out concavities just fitting them. When the surface of the animal is touched or irritated the spoons spring together, their bowls forming a pair of nippers, which grip and cling to whatever they touch until they are relaxed. Pedicellariae of this kind are on many of the plates between the arms as well as on some of the marginal and disc-plates. On the underside, there are also pedicellariae of the same type, but larger. This species measures about 5 inches in diameter. It ranges from the Carolinas to Brazil from 21 to 129 fathoms.

Pyrenaster dentatus (Perrier) PLATE 203. The form of this species varies from more or less pentagonal to star shape with a broad disc. The arms are narrower and more tapered than in the previous species. The upper marginal plates are fairly large, similar to, and nearly paired with the lower series. The upper marginals are often separated somewhat from each other by a row of small disc-plates. All marginal plates in both series have a granulated surface. The plates on the underside bordering the grooves are also large and somewhat quadrangular, while the others which fill the interradial angles are rounded and convex. They are of two sizes, the smaller surrounding the larger plates This is one of the distinguishing characters of this species. This species occurs from the Carolinas to the West Indies in 41 to 1639 fathoms.

Peltaster planus. Verrill PLATE 203. This is a pentag onal species with the arms very short and broadly rounded at the apex. The marginal plates are quite large in proportion. Those median to the sides are nearly square, while toward the tips of the arms they are much appressed, so that they are much broader than long. The lower series on the underside practically corresponds to the upper. The three large terminal-paired plates are in contact with each other. The apical plate is small and shield-shaped. The general surface covering of the upper side consists of a small, quadrangular or hexagonal plates fitted together to form a tesselated pavement. They are closely sculptured with coarse granules, slightly separated and of uniform size. The plates bordering the groove on the underside are similar to the other plates on that side but are larger and longer. The pores for the papulae are abundantly distributed among the plates, but there are apparently no pedicellariae. This species is about 4 inches in diameter. It occurs off southern New England in 156 fathoms.

Pentagonaster (Tosia) granularis (O. F. Müller) PLATE 204. This is a pentagonal species with a very broad disc and very slightly projecting arms. The sides of the pentagon are almost straight until the vicinity of the ray is reached, when the arm rises as a short triangle to the apex. Practically the entire upper surface is closely tessellated with small hexagonal to rhomboidal plates of small size. They are more clearly hexagonal in the neighborhood of the arms. All are covered with very fine granules. The madreporic plate is small and fairly near the center. The marginal series, above and below, is closely covered with granules and is quite narrow. On the underside, the surface is also closely crowded with small polygonal plates like those of the upper side, especially in the wide interradial areas. They become smaller toward the marginal plates. The inner spinules bordering the groove form a simple row with three or four spines on each plate. Beyond this series there are about seven to eleven on each plate on this side, so that it is only the proportionate abundance of spines to a plate that characterizes and distinguishes the various areas on the lower side of the surface in this species inside the marginal border, rather than variation in the form of the spinules and spines. This species has been recorded along the entire New England coast, as well as on the Banks off Nova Scotia, in depths between 50 and 150 fathoms. It also occurs off the Scandinavian peninsula and the British Isles.

Hippasteria phrygiana (Parelius) PLATE 204; COLOR PLATE XIX, 2. This sea-star has a large disc with short arms. The upper surface is covered with thick spines, each one of which is encircled by a series of smaller granules. There are many bivalve pedicellaria. These are pedicellaria composed of two small, elongate, narrow plates, lying close together lengthwise, hinged on their outer margin, so that the crevice between can open and close, catching whatever may come in contact with it, thus differing from the various forcipate or pincer types hitherto mentioned. The plates on the upper side are of various kinds and sizes. Scattered thickly over the surface are larger plates, each with a thick, stumpy spine, or a bivalvate pedicellaria in the middle with a series of granules around the edge. Irregularly disposed between them are smaller ones, also bearing granules or pedicellariae. The marginal plates each have one to three thick spines rising from their center and are granulated around their edges. The interradial areas on the underside form large triangles completely filled with large pedicellariae surrounded by an oval ring of granules. A large series of these plates borders each side of the ambulacral grooves in an even line, the pedicellariae directed obliquely to the groove. Two or three spines project over the groove from each plate, while a single spine is on the outer surface in each case. This seastar grows to a large size, full-grown specimens measuring 16 inches in diameter. The general coloration in life is a beautiful coral-red, with a golden-yellow border. It is omnivorous, devouring mussels, worms, and other echinoderms indiscriminately. It ranges from the Arctic down both sides of the Atlantic; from Greenland to New York, on the American Coast, and from Scandinavia to the British Isles, on the European side, in depths varying from 11 to 437 fathoms.

Family Oreasteridae

These are large, swollen, and massive sea-stars, with a high somewhat angular disc and with regular, pointed arms which are stout and rigid-looking. The upper surface is supported by a reticulate skeleton of barlike plates surrounding triangular areas, partly covered by a leathery or parchmentlike dermis, giving a good opportunity for many papular openings. The marginal plates are small and covered with granules. They are inconspicuous, partly because of their relative size and partly because of being largely covered by dermis. The marginal plates, however, tend to be more quadrangular than the disc-plates, and are characterized by large conical spines. On the underside, the interactinal regions are covered by thick plates laid down like a mosaic pavement, equipped with small bivalve pedicellariae, a few strong, central spines, and with granulated surfaces.

Oreaster reticulatus (Linnaeus) PLATE 204. The reticulate sea-star. This is the largest sea-star on our Atlantic Coast. It is typically West Indian or subtropical and is especially abundant and common in the shallow waters, on sandy bottoms, of Florida and the Bahamas. It is recorded, however, as far north as South Carolina, and is included here in the hope that it may be found also in the North Carolinian region. The upper surface, with its triangular and quadrangular reticulations made by the bar-shaped plates, is striking in its color pattern. The nodes where the plates join are each marked by a short, stout, cone-shaped spine. These and the plates are bright yellow in color, and frame in the dermal meshes which, in some specimens, are deep red or rose, in others a rich maroon, or in still others, varying from yellow, orange, or brown to a deep purple, blue, or greenish, or various shades of each of these. These great, richly colored sea-stars, scattered over the white sandy bottom of a sheltered lagoon, showing clearly through its quiet, transparent waters, are

PLATE 204

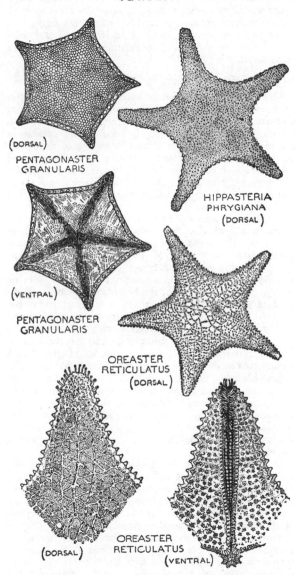

(DORSAL)
PENTAGONASTER
GRANULARIS

HIPPASTERIA
PHRYGIANA
(DORSAL)

(VENTRAL)
PENTAGONASTER
GRANULARIS

OREASTER
RETICULATUS
(DORSAL)

(DORSAL)
OREASTER
RETICULATUS
(VENTRAL)

a remarkable sight. The arrangement of the plates on the upper and lower sides, including those along the sides of the ambulacral grooves, is readily seen in the figures on PLATE 204. Specimens 12 to 16 inches in diameter are common. They are also found measuring 20 inches or more from tip to tip.

Family Poraniidae (Asteropidae)

This family also contains sea-stars with wide discs and relatively short arms. It is distinguished by the thick skin, or dermis, which covers the convex upper side. In various species, this may have short isolated spines, conical in shape; or there may be a close-set covering of fine, practically microscopic spinules; or it may be entirely bare of spines of any kind. There are no pedicellariae, but papulae are present, scattered indiscriminately over the upper surface. Genital organs are interradial in position, but confined to the disc.

Porania grandis Verrill PLATE 205. This sea-star has a broad, convex disc. The upperside is entirely without spines and is covered with a thick skin. The lower marginal plates have three to five rather coarse, distinct spines forming a definite fringe around the edge. The lower side has a series of symmetrical, scalelike plates on each arm on either side of the ambulacral groove and extending to the tip of the arm in a series of transverse, parallel plates, curving interradially at the base of the arm to meet the plates of the adjoining arm in mutually symmetrical curves. The ambulacral grooves are narrow. They are bordered with a narrow series of plates, each having two or three spines extending over the groove. The upper side has a double band of papulae extending to the tip of each arm, curving outward slightly at the center, and stopping short near the center of the disc, to leave bare a circular area immediately surrounding the anus. This species is found along our coast at depths ranging from 66 to 673 fathoms. The specimen illustrated was about 6 inches in diameter.

Porania insignis Verrill PLATE 205. This is a similar species, but shown here by two figures of a young specimen. The upper side is covered by skin which hides the skeletal structure. Two indefinite bands of papulae extend out toward the tips of the arms from near the center of the disc. Fine marginal spines form a delicate fringe around the upper border, showing interradially but disappearing toward the arm tips. Indications of the marginal plates show indefinitely through the dermis. The marginal ends of the lower series extend out beyond this fringe and show conspicuously from above. Each plate of this lower series ends in two or three irregularly serrate

PLATE 205

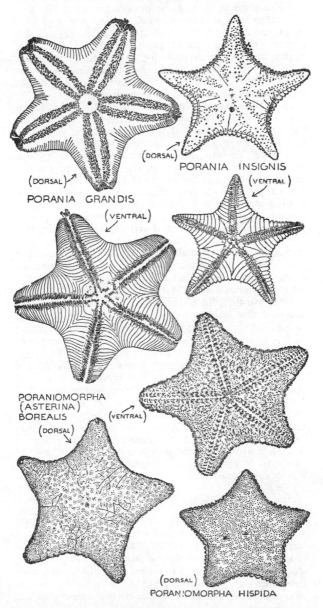

(DORSAL)

PORANIA INSIGNIS

(VENTRAL)

(DORSAL)

PORANIA GRANDIS

(VENTRAL)

PORANIOMORPHA
(ASTERINA)
BOREALIS

(VENTRAL)

(DORSAL)

(DORSAL)

PORANIOMORPHA HISPIDA

projections. The lower side has a similar arrangement of scalelike plates to that of the preceding species. The ambulacral grooves are narrow, with a narrow row of grooveplates, each projecting a single spine over the edge of the groove. The five central jaw-plates are approximately square, but set cornerwise to the mouth-opening with two teeth projecting inward from the inner corner of each. The diameter of this young specimen is about 2 inches. It has the same range as the previous species.

Poraniomorpha (Asterina) borealis Verrill PLATE 205. The disc, in this species, is large and convex, with short arms. The upper side is covered with a close coating of fine spines or granules, scarcely, if at all, visible to the naked eye. The groups of papulae are numerous but distinctly separated from each other. They are in circular groups of ten or less, but are more evenly distributed near the margin, both on the interradii and on the sides of the arms. The underside is quite spinose, the spines being arranged in more or less crescentic or overlapping groups pointing outward. The ambulacral grooves are quite narrow, bordered by groove-plates each having about five spines, all directed radially. This is a small species, being only about 1 inch in diameter. It is a deep-water species, being found in 192 to 225 fathoms. Its occurrence is rare. Its range extends from New England northward.

Poraniomorpha hispida (M. Sars) PLATE 205. The shape of this sea-star is similar to that of the preceding species. The upper side is entirely covered with a coating of fine spines. The numerous papulae are distributed over the entire surface in groups of twenty or more. The marginal plates form a distinct, narrow, but more or less vertical edge. The lower marginal border has a delicate fringe of short spines showing around the periphery. The lower interradial areas have fine spines scattered over them irregularly. The groove-plates have two spines turned inward over the groove and three or four spines turned directly outward. The color varies from yellow to reddish brown. The adult measures 2½ inches or more in diameter. It ranges from Greenland to Virginia, and is also circumboreal.

Order SPINULOSA

In this order the disc has inconspicuous marginal plates which do not form a vertical edge to the disc. Both the upper and lower sides are covered with spines. For the most part, these are arranged in groups mounted on small elevations rising from the plates, themselves, but sometimes they occur singly. Papulae occur on both the upper and underside. The tube-feet are in two series, with one

COLOR PLATES
XVII-XXIV

PLATE XVII

TYPICAL NUDIBRANCHS

1. Bushy-backed Sea Slug *Dendronotus arborescens* O. F. Müller.

2. Tuberculated Nudibranch *Onchidorus aspersa* (Alder & Hancock).

3. Leaf-plumed Sea Slug *Lamellidoris bilamellata* (Linnaeus).

4. Diadem Nudibranch *Lamellidoris diademata* (Agassiz).

5. Star-clustered Sea Slug *Lamellidoris grisea* (Stimpson).

6. Plumed Sea Slug *Aeolis* (*Aeolidia*) *papillosa* (Linnaeus).

7. Salmon-gilled Nudibranch *Coryphella salmonacea* (Couthouy).

8. Vermilion-gilled Nudibranch *Coryphella rufibranchialis* (Johnston).

9. Crowned Sea Slug *Doto coronata* (Gmelin).

10. Green Elysia *Elysia chlorotica* (Agassiz).

11. Sea Cat Nudibranch *Elysia catula* (Agassiz).

12. Ridged Sea Slug *Palio* (*Polycera*) *lessonii* (D'Orbigny).

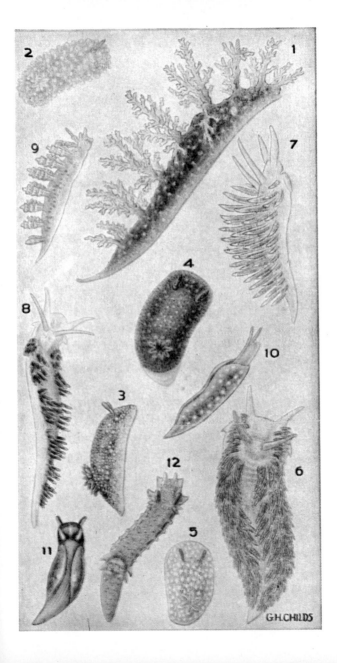

G.H.CHILDS

PLATE XVIII—THE COMMON SQUID

Loligo pealii Lesueur

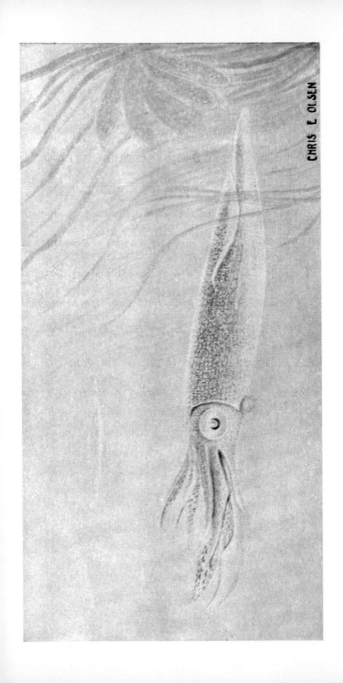

CHRIS E OLSEN

PLATE XIX

TYPICAL SEA STARS

1. Mud Star *Ctenodiscus crispatus* (Retzius). See also PLATE 199.

2. Red Gold-bordered Sea Star *Hippasteria phrygiana* (Parelius). See also PLATE 204.

3. Blood Sea Star *Henricia (Cribrella) sanguinolenta* (O. F. Müller). See also PLATE 206.

4. Purple Sun Star *Solastar endeca* (Linnaeus). See also PLATE 206.

5. Common Sun Star *Crossaster (Solaster) papposus* (Linnaeus).

6. Common Starfish *Asterias forbesi* (Desor). See also PLATE 207.

7. Purple Starfish *Asterias vulgaris* Verrill. See also INDEX PLATE 198.

8. Slender-armed Sea Star *Asterias (Leptasterias) tenera* Stimpson.

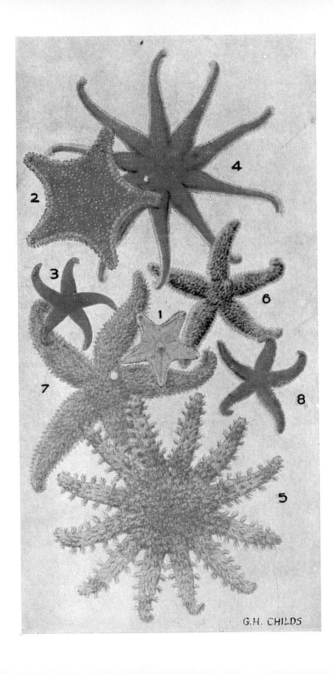

G.H. CHILDS

PLATE XX

BRITTLE-STARS, SEA-URCHINS, AND SEA-CUCUMBERS

1. Daisy Brittle-star *Ophiopholis aculeata* (Linnaeus). See also PLATE 212.

2. Long Armed Snake-star *Amphipholis squamata* (Delle Chiaje). See also PLATE 212.

3. Purple Sea Urchin *Arbacia punctulata* (Lamarck). See also PLATE 220.

4. Green Sea Urchin *Strongylocentrotus droehbachiensis* (O. F. Müller). See also PLATE 220.

5. Sand Dollar *Echinarachnius parma* (Lamarck). See also PLATE 222.

6. Keyhole Urchin *Mellita testudinata* Klein = *Mellita quiesquiesperforata* (Leske) See also PLATE 222.

7. Large Northern Sea-cucumber *Cucumaria frondosa* (Gunnerus).

8. Common *Thyone briareus* (Lesueur). See also INDEX PLATE 228.

9. Common Synapta *Synapta (Leptosynapta) inhaerens* (O. F. Müller). See also PLATE 232.

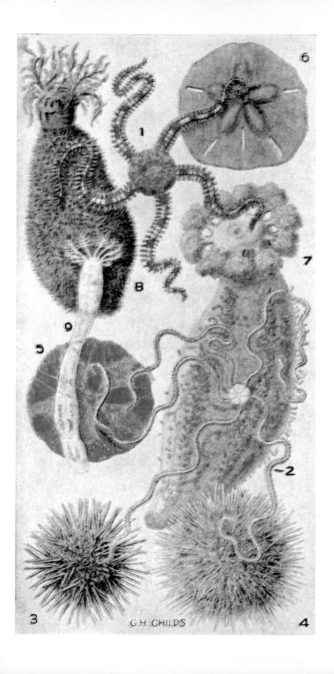

G.H. CHILDS

PLATE XXI

SYNAPTIDAE AND PSOLIDAE

1. Tufted Synapta *Chirodota laevis* (Fabricius). Entire animal. 1a. Mouth with tentacle-circlet.

2. Brown Psolus *Psolus phantapus* (Strussenfeldt). Side view. 2a. Ventral view. 2b. Detail of tentacle.

3. Scarlet Psolus *Psolus fabricii* (Düben & Koren). Side view. 3a. Ventral view. 3b. Mouth region with tentacle-circlet. 3c. Detail of tentacle.

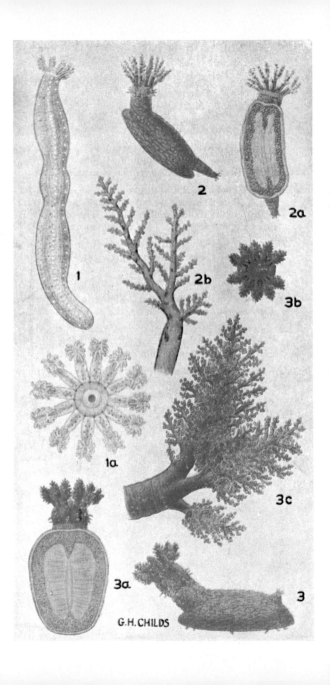

G.H. CHILDS

PLATE XXII

TYPICAL BRYOZOA

1. Creeping Bryozoan *Aetea anguina* (Linnaeus).

2. Turreted Bryozoan, Spiral-tufted Bryozoan *Bugula turrita* (Desor). Entire colony, one-half natural size. 2a. Branchlet of tuft, enlarged. 2b. Tip of branchlet greatly enlarged to show individual animal expanded.

3. White Oval-windowed Bryozoan *Membranipora pilosa* (Linnaeus). Moderately enlarged. 3a. More highly magnified. See also PLATE 235.

4. Brick-red Bryozoan *Schizoporella unicornis* (Johnston). Part of colony magnified. 4a. Young individuals. 4b. Two nearly adult individuals. See also PLATE 236.

5. Disc-encrusting Bryozoan *Lepralia pallasiana* (Moll). Colony, life-size. 5a. Colony enlarged twice. 5b. Portion of colony greatly enlarged. See also PLATE 236.

6. Vase-clustered Bryozoan *Bowerbankia gracilis* Leidy. Part of colony enlarged.

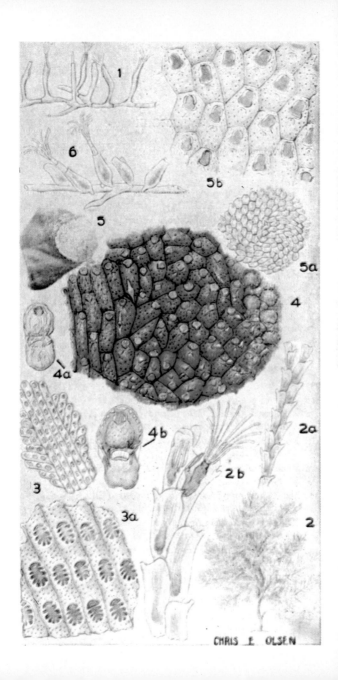

CHRIS E OLSEN

PLATE XXIII

SEA-ANIMALS OF THE WHARF-PILES

ASCIDIANS

1. Sea Grapes *Molgula manhattensis* De Kay. See also COLOR PLATE XXIV, 1; PLATE 249.

2. Pink Sea Pork *Amaroucium pellucidum* Leidy. See also COLOR PLATE XXIV, 9, 9a.

3. Sea Vase *Ciona intestinalis* (Linnaeus). See also COLOR PLATE XXIV, 6; PLATE 247.

4. Solitary Ascidian *Styela* (*Cynthia*) *partita* (Stimpson). See also COLOR PLATE XXIV, 2; PLATE 248.

4a. Red Solitary Ascidian *Dendrodoa carnea* (Agassiz). See also COLOR PLATE XXIV, 3; PLATE 248.

5. Green Beads *Perophora viridis* Verrill. See also COLOR PLATE XXIV, 7, 7a; PLATE 248; INDEX PLATE 245.

6. White Crust *Didemnum albidum* (Verrill). See also COLOR PLATE XXIV, 10, 10a; PLATE 247.

VARIOUS INVERTEBRATES

7. Redbeard Sponge *Microciona prolifera* (Ellis & Solander). See also COLOR PLATE II, 4.

8. Rock Barnacle *Balanus crenatus* Brugière. See also PLATE 136.

9. Eyed Sponge *Chalina oculata* Pallas. See also COLOR PLATE II, 2.

10. Sea Anemone *Metridium dianthus* (Ellis). See also COLOR PLATE I (Frontispiece); PLATE 73.

11. Brick-red Bryozoan *Schizoporella unicornis* (Johnston). See also COLOR PLATE XXII, 4; PLATE 236.

12. Purple Starfish *Asterias vulgaris* Verrill. See also COLOR PLATE XIX, 7.

13. Carnation Warm *Hydroides dianthus* Verrill encrusting wharf-pile with calcareous worm-tubes, these in turn being encrusted with *Schizoporella unicornis*.

14. Edible Mussel *Mytilus edulis* Linnaeus. See also COLOR PLATE XIII. 2; PLATE 180 (6).

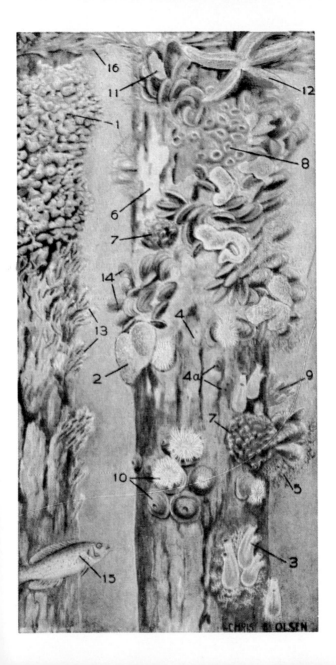

PLATE XXIV

TYPICAL ASCIDIANS

1. Sea Grapes *Molgula manhattensis* De Kay. See also COLOR PLATE XXIII, 1; PLATE 249.

2. Solitary Ascidian *Styela (Cynthia) partita* (Stimpson). See also COLOR PLATE XXIII, 4; PLATE 248.

3. Red Solitary Ascidian *Dendrodoa carnea* (Agassiz). See also COLOR PLATE XXIII, 4a; PLATE 248.

4. Sea Peach *Halocynthia pyriformis* Rathke. PLATE 249; INDEX PLATE 244.

5. Stalked Ascidian *Boltenia ovifera* (Linnaeus).

6. Sea Vase *Ciona intestinalis* (Linnaeus). See also COLOR PLATE XXIII, 3; PLATE 247.

7. Green Beads *Perophora viridia* Verrill. Natural Size. 7a. Enlarged. See also COLOR PLATE XXIII, 5; PLATE 248; INDEX PLATE 245.

8. Colonial Ascidian *Botryllus schlosseri* (Pallas). Life size. 8a. Colony enlarged. 8b. Free-swimming larva of *Botryllus*.

9. Pink Sea Pork *Amaroucium pellucidum* Leidy. 9a. Enlarged. See also COLOR PLATE XXIII, 2.

10. White Crust *Didemnum albidum* Verrill, natural size. 10a. Enlarged.

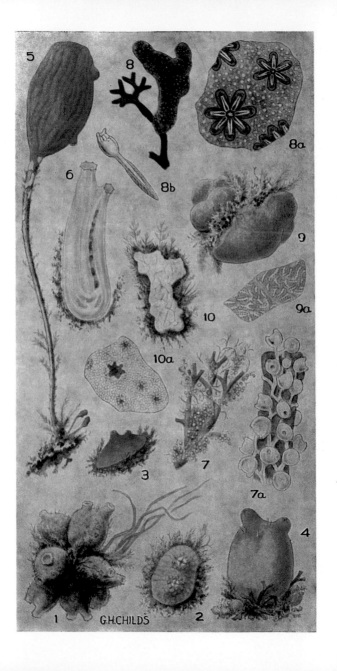

G.H.CHILDS

exception. They are always equipped with suction discs. The number of rays is five or more.

Family Echinasteridae

In this family, the sea-stars have a very small disc and five very long, slender arms, cylindrical in cross section, with no important differentiation between upper and underside. The skeleton is a fine network. The spines may be grouped or may occur singly, but not as paxillae. There are no pedicellariae. The tube-feet are in two series.

Henricia (Cribrella) sanguinolenta (O. F. Müller) PLATE 206; COLOR PLATE XIX, 3. The Blood Sea-star. This beautiful little sea-star has slender, gracefully pointed arms and a small disc, the radius of which is about one fifth the radius measured from the center of the disc to the tip of an arm of the sea-star. The arms are cylindrical, the sides curving around evenly to the narrow ambulacral groove on the underside. The general color is quite variable. It is most commonly a rich red, but orange, purple, rose, or cream-colored individuals are often found, some even with red and purple mottlings on the same specimen. The body and arms are covered evenly with small spinules on a network of very fine skeletal meshes, and the ambulacral groove has only two rows of tube-feet, instead of four as in the common sea-star depicted in INDEX DIAGRAM 198. Another peculiarity is the fact that the young are not born directly as free-swimming larvae, but the eggs are deposited around the mouth, the underside of the disc and the bases of the arms being drawn together to form a brood-pouch in which the eggs lie freely, being retained there until they develop into minute sea-stars and are able to fend for themselves. There is no metamorphosis, the bipinnaria stage being lacking. This species is very abundant on rocky coasts, especially in and around tide-pools and in rock crevices in the intertidal area. Though the entire extent of its range on our shores is from Greenland to Cape Hatteras, it is especially common from Woods Hole, along the north shore of Massachusetts, the coast of Maine, and in the Bay of Fundy. It is also circumboreal, extending down the European shores from northern Scandinavia and the British Isles to the Bay of Biscay and the Azores, from the tidal zone to a depth of about 547 fathoms. It seldom exceeds 2½ to 4 inches in diameter.

Echinaster sentus Verrill PLATE 206. This species has two marginal rows of plates with stout, almost wart-like spines, mounted on a rounded base with a wide area around the edge of the arms, between the two marginal rows. This area is without spines, or with a short series of plates having one spine each. On the upper surface there are five irregular rows of spines along the arms between the marginal series and they are also scattered irregularly over the disc. The madreporic plate is raised but flat and covered with rough projections. It is about halfway between the center of the disc and the interradial junction of two of the arms. On the underside, the ambulacral grooves have two rows of quite extensible tube-feet, shown in the figure on the plate. A detail is also pictured of a portion of the arm magnified in and around the groove showing the shape and arrangement of the groove-plates with their spines. The groove-plates are much smaller than the adjacent spines of the undersurface. The inner plates are the smallest. They are oval in shape and each has a spine pointing in toward the groove. The next row has larger plates, with several spines on each, pointing outwardly. They are united by the dermis, which partly covers their bases, thus forming a continuous border of two rows of plates on either side of the groove. The rest of the lower side is covered with spines much like those of the upper surface. The diameter of the adult star is upwards of 4¼ inches. There are about six irregular rows of papulae interspersed between the spines on the upper side of the arms. This species is found in shallow water from North Carolina southward to the Florida reefs and to Yucatan, as well as the West Indies generally.

Family Solasteridae
(The Sun-stars)

The species in this family, with one exception, have more than five arms, usually from seven to seventeen. The disc is large, yet the rounded arms are fairly long. The skeleton of the upper side forms a close and fine network (*reticulate*) with paxillae. Around the edge is a single or double series of marginal papillae, representing the marginal plates. The underside has interradial plates. The groove-spines are of two series at right angles to each other. There are two rows of tube-feet and no pedicellariae. They are animals of temperate and shallow seas.

Solaster endeca (Linnaeus) (= **Solaster intermedius** Sluiter) PLATE 206; COLOR PLATE XIX, 4. The Purple Sun-star. The Eleven Armed Sun-star. The arms may be eleven in number, but they vary from seven to thirteen, and most frequently they are nine to ten. There are two rows of small inconspicuous marginal paxillae in two series, the upper much smaller than the lower. The entire upper side is covered with small, close-set paxillae with short columns and with circlets of quite short spines. In large specimens the lower marginal paxillae are more conspicuous, being broad and comb-shaped. The groove-spines number two to four on a plate and are nearly hidden in the groove, with an outer series of six to eight short spines pointing transversely.

The general color of this striking sun-star is red-violet with golden-yellow marginal paxillae and a conspicuous light yellow madreporic plate at one side of the disc. This species grows to a large size, measuring upwards of 16 inches in diameter. It ranges in shallow water from Cape Cod northward and from Scandinavia to the British Isles on the European side of the Atlantic. There is no free-swimming larval stage as the development from the egg is direct.

Crossaster (Solaster) papposus (Linnaeus) COLOR PLATE XIX, 5. The Common Sun-star. The Spiny Sun-star. This is the most magnificent of the sun-stars. Its large disc and many spreading arms, varying from eight to fourteen, but usually ten to twelve, in number, display a coloration, often brilliant scarlet in the center of the disc, surrounded by a band of crimson spreading around the bases of the arms, which are also broadly banded by pink or white in the middle, and tipped with crimson. It is more nearly a sunburst of color than any other of the echinoderms. This color scheme is also variable, being more purple in some individuals. It adds to its conspicuousness by growing to 14 inches or more in diameter. The skeleton on the upper-side is made up of narrow bars forming an irregular net-work, enclosing spaces covered with membrane, each penetrated by several papulae. The underside is whitish. The paxillae are large, crowned with cylindrical clusters of spines, giving them the appearance of circular bristling brushes. The marginal paxillae form a single series and stand out stiffly around the arms. This animal feeds greedily on all kinds of bottom-creatures, especially other echinoderms no matter what their size, also on mollusks, especially bivalves, including oysters, and also on sea-anemones. Like the previous species, it has no free-swimming larval stage, the development being direct from the egg. The distribution of this species is circumboreal. On the American side of the Atlantic, it ranges from the Arctic to New Jersey, and on the European side from Scandinavia to the English Channel. In the Pacific Ocean it extends as far south as Vancouver. Its vertical distribution is from the tidal region to a depth of about 550 fathoms.

Lophaster furcifer (Duben & Koren) PLATE 208. Although this species has only five arms, nevertheless, it is a member of the Family Solasteridae, for it has typical papillae covering the upper side, with a tendency to arrangement in series. The groove-spines are in successive groups of three or four, united by a thin membrane. The groove-plates also have a transverse series of four to five spines united in the same way. It is primarily an Arctic species, growing to a diameter of less than 7 inches. The color of this sea-star is dull red, with the lower side whitish. It is circumboreal, being found from Greenland to New Jersey on the American side of the Atlantic, and from Scandinavia to Britain on the European side, in depths ranging from about 16 to 734 fathoms.

Family Pterasteridae

The remarkable sea-stars included in this family have a finlike membrane around the edge of the body instead of marginal plates reinforced by spines standing out at regular intervals. The upper side has a membranous roof covering its entire surface, supported by circlets of long, slender spines arising from the columns of the paxillae like the ribs of an umbrella, somewhat like tent poles holding up the roof of a huge tent. The cavity thus formed is utilized by the sea-star as a brood-pouch, the eggs being detained here until they are developed into young resembling miniatures of the parent, without the interposition of a free-swimming larval stage. This enclosed space is also respiratory in function, water being drawn in through pores on the underside and expelled through the large cloacal opening in the center of the upper side. The ambulacral grooves on the underside have two or four rows of tube-feet.

Pteraster militaris (O. F. Müller) PLATE 206. In this species, the membrane covering the upper (aboral) side has many small calcareous concretions embedded in it. The disc is quite large, and the arms short and bluntly rounded at their tips. The upper, tentlike covering has the characteristics mentioned in the family diagnosis. On the underside, the spines bordering the ambulacral grooves are united by a thin membrane so as to form a successive series of transverse combs supported by a fanlike series of spines, with long, lateral spines extending out horizontally to support the lateral membrane at the edge of the disc. The paxillae have from two to five spines. The five jaws surrounding the mouth have a pair of strong spines on the outer surface. The general coloration of this species is yellowish or yellowish red. The adults have a diameter of about 6 inches. The range extends from Greenland to New Jersey, in about 2 to 600 fathoms. It is also circumboreal occurring on the Scandinavian and British coasts.

Diploptereaster multipes (Sars) PLATE 206. This species is distinguished from the preceding by having a practically pentagonal shape, with the five arms projecting to only a slight degree. The tube-feet are in four rows instead of two, with the groove-spines quite long and projecting beyond the edges of the membrane connecting

PLATE 206

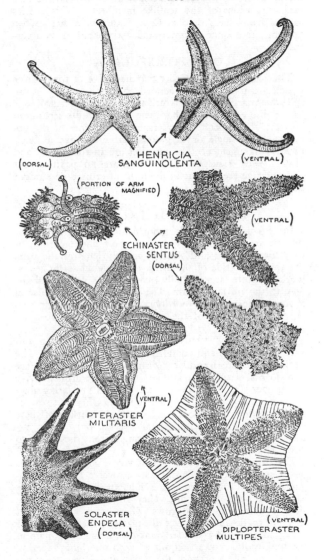

(DORSAL)

HENRICIA
SANGUINOLENTA

(VENTRAL)

(PORTION OF ARM
MAGNIFIED)

(VENTRAL)

ECHINASTER
SENTUS
(DORSAL)

(VENTRAL)

PTERASTER
MILITARIS

SOLASTER
ENDECA
(DORSAL)

(VENTRAL)

DIPLOPTERASTER
MULTIPES

them. There is a great development of the aboral and oral expansions of the tentlike membrane. This species ranges from the Arctic to Cape Hatteras in 124 to 640 fathoms. It is quite common and widespread in its occurrence.

Order FORCIPULATA

The sea-stars in this Order may have five or many arms which are more or less rounded and with usually inconspicuous marginal plates which never form a vertical edge to the disc and arms so that there is no definite separation between the upper and undersides. The spines of the upper side are single or in groups that may have a longitudinal arrangement. The tube-feet are in four series and always with a suction disc. There are no paxillae, but pedicellariae are present in the form of crossed or straight forciculate structures.

Family Pedicellasteridae

In this family, five or more arms, sometimes ten or twelve, are present. They may be short and tapering, or they may be long and slender, not restricted at the base. On the upper side of the arms, the skeleton forms a network of quite large, usually quadrangular meshes all the way to the tip of the arm. The marginal and ambulacral groove-spines are not very long. The tube-feet are in two series. Pedicellariae of the crossed and straight types are present.

Pedicellaster typicus M. Sars PLATE 207. In this species the lateral and aboral spines are not elongated. The pedicellariae are irregularly distributed over the surface and do not occur in wreathlike groups. The arms are five in number. On the underside the grooves are larger than those on the upper surface of the body. Only one row of spines borders the grooves. A second row outside of these is lacking. This is quite a small species, only about 2½ inches in diameter. This species ranges from the Arctic to New York.

Coronaster briareus Verrill PLATE 207. This species has a small disc, with about ten or twelve slender, elongated arms radiating from it, each about five times as long as the diameter of the disc. They are covered with long, slender spines in radial rows. There is a weak aboral skeleton made up of rows of disc-plates connected with the upper marginals by slender transverse bars. Each plate in the longitudinal rows is equipped with one long, tapering spine. The plates of both the upper and lower marginal rows are furnished with spines. There are large pedicellariae, shaped like a pair of cats' paws clasped with interlocking claws (*felipedal pedicellariae*), scattered over both

PLATE 207

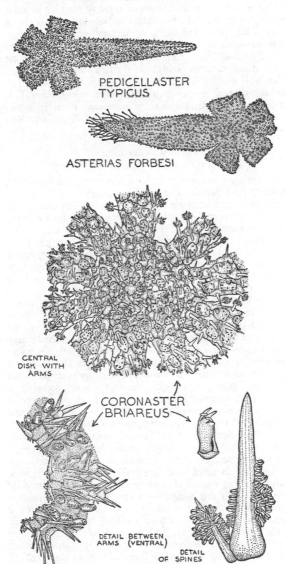

PEDICELLASTER
TYPICUS

ASTERIAS FORBESI

CENTRAL
DISK WITH
ARMS

CORONASTER
BRIAREUS

DETAIL BETWEEN
ARMS (VENTRAL)

DETAIL
OF SPINES

the upper and lower surfaces. In the spaces formed by the
skeletal network are membranous areas pierced by papular
openings, through which clusters of papulae extend themselves. The spines are quite similar to each other. They
often have dense clusters of small pedicellariae draped
around them. The lower right-hand figure on the plate
shows these together with the clusters of small pedicellariae, and one of the larger "cats' claw" type just above.
The ambulacral groove-plates each bear two spines. This
handsome, many-armed sea-star measures about 6 inches
in diameter. It ranges from the latitude of Virginia to Key
West, Florida, in 31 to 373 fathoms.

Family Asteriidae
(The Common Sea-stars or Starfishes)

The sea-stars in this family have five to eight arms in the
species found within our range, though certain Pacific
species may have as many as forty-five arms. There are four
rows of tube-feet. The spines are single, usually in somewhat longitudinal series. The skeleton of the upper disc
forms an irregular, open network. There are generally
both crossed (scissorslike) and straight (pincerslike) pedicellariae. This family has many species throughout its
cosmopolitan range, mostly in temperate and northern
seas.

Asterias forbesi (Desor) PLATE 207; COLOR PLATE
XIX, 6. The Common Starfish. The normal number of the
arms is five, but specimens are found with four, six, or
even seven from time to time. Adults of this species range
from 6 to 11 inches in diameter. The arms are stout and
somewhat cylindrical and blunt at their tips. The disc is of
moderate size, often domelike. The upper surface has
numerous, closely interlocked, strong plates, forming a
firm mosaic, without a regular pattern. Each plate bears a
single prominent spine, usually blunt and rough at the
tip, encircled by a few smaller spines. Clusters or festoons
of small pedicellariae encircle each spine about halfway
to the tip. Additional, larger pedicellariae are scattered
over the surface. On the underside, the groove-plates have
one or two flattened and truncate, long, slender spines,
many of them encircled with pedicellariae. The papular
areas vary, but are unusually large and with about five
papulae in each. The madreporic plate is usually of a
bright orange-red color. There are four rows of tube-feet,
closely crowded together. The color of this species is very
variable, ranging through brown, purple, bronze, green,
and orange. It is distributed from Maine to the Gulf of
Mexico, but is rare north of Massachusetts, where it overlaps the more abundant range of the next species in that
area. It is found from the low-water mark to 27 fathoms.

This and the next species are very important economically, because of the destruction they cause to oyster beds.

Asterias vulgaris Verrill. COLOR PLATE XIX, 7. The Northern Starfish. The Purple Star. In this species, the arms are flattened, as compared with the previous species, and more pointed. The disc is fairly large and often rises to an arched dome. The upper side is made up of a network of narrow, barlike plates, with large meshes, making a much weaker skeleton than in *Asterias forbesi,* and much flabbier to the touch. Usually there is a clearly perceptible median series of plates on each arm much closer longitudinally than the rest, set off by the large papular areas formed by the meshes on either side. The plates all have one or more blunt spines one or two millimeters high, with rough or prickly tips, festooned with wreaths of very blunt pedicellariae. The side of the arms is bordered by a series of lateral spines above a spine-free zone, but with many large and acute pedicellariae rising directly from the surface. This is also true of the pedicellariae along the edge of the upper surface. On the undersurface is another much more conspicuous series of spines, often reaching three or four millimeters in length, very blunt and squarely truncate at the tips. Each of the plates bordering the ambulacral groove has one or two rather long and usually flattened, bladelike spines. The madreporic plate is about the size of that in the preceding species and light yellowish in color, as compared with the bright orange-red of the plate of *Asterias forbesi,* aiding greatly in quickly distinguishing between the two species. The general color of this species is very variable and usually brighter or lighter than that of *Asterias forbesi*. Sometimes it is variegated with yellow and brown or purple. The range of color in different individuals includes blue, pink, rose, or even bright red. The spines are usually lighter than the body-surface. There is a wide variation in size, usually between 6 and 12 inches in diameter, the more northerly individuals from Passamaquoddy Bay, the Bay of Fundy and Nova Scotia reaching 17 inches. The species ranges widely from Labrador to Cape Hatteras; but south of Cape Cod it is not so often seen, as from then on it verges off into deep water. It is the dominant shallow-water species from Cape Cod northward, gradually replacing *Asterias forbesi*.

The method used by these two species in opening and feeding on oysters is of considerable interest. The starfish simply mounts on the oyster, humping up the central part of its body and spreading its five arms so that they surround the two valves of the mollusk, applying hundreds of tube-feet, some on one valve and some on the other, and bracing the tips of its arms on the surrounding objects. It then contracts the muscles of the middle part of its arms, exerting a steady pull on the two shells of the oyster in opposite directions. The single muscle by which the oyster keeps its shells together gives way sooner or later, yielding to the steady, tireless pull of the multitudinous tube-feet, and the oyster-valves begin to part. The mouth of the starfish is located centrally on the underside of its body and through its round opening, the starfish immediately protrudes its stomach, turning it inside out as it does so, thrusting it between the oyster shells and pouring out its digestive fluids as it envelopes the soft parts of the oyster. It actually digests the oyster within its own shell, assimilating the digested products through the walls of its stomach, until the inside of the shell is completely cleared of its former inhabitant.

Asterias (Leptasterias) tenera Stimpson COLOR PLATE XIX, 8. The Slender-armed Sea-star. The arms of this starfish are nearly cylindrical and slender, tapering to a small, slightly blunt apex. The disc and arms are rough with conspicuous, slender spines rising from a skeleton having a somewhat open network, with no clearly defined median row on the arms. This is a rather pale species, light purple or pink in color. It is about 2½ to 4 inches in diameter, but usually not more than 3 inches. The female carries her eggs and newly hatched young in an extemporized brood-sac made by partly everting the borders of the mouth. There are red eyespots at the tips of the arms. This species ranges from Nova Scotia to New Jersey in 10 to 85 fathoms of depth.

Asterias tanneri Verrill PLATE 208. Tanner's Sea-star. This species is closely related to the foregoing. It occurs abundantly in somewhat deeper water from New Jersey to Cape Hatteras, ranging vertically from 48 to 194 fathoms. The plate figures show clearly the details of the shape and distribution of the blunt spines with their circlets of pedicellariae.

Leptasterias groenlandica (Lütken) PLATE 208. The Greenland Starfish. This is a northern, circumboreal species with five slender, robust arms. It is especially characterized by the irregular, transverse series of skeletal bars, with single or grouped spinules, crossing the arm to connect the longitudinal, central plates with the marginal plates. This species measures about 4½ inches in diameter. It is extremely variable, several forms being recognized, the typical one extending from Bering Strait to Greenland and down the east coast of North America to Labrador, Nova Scotia, the Bay of Fundy, and the Grand Banks, in depths ranging from 5 to about 60 fathoms.

Leptasterias polaris Müller & Troschel PLATE 208. The Polar Starfish. This is another and related Arctic

PLATE 208

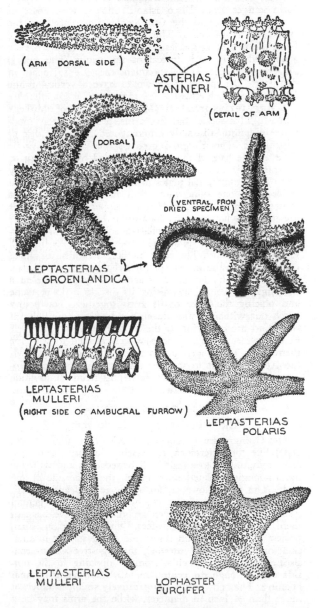

(ARM DORSAL SIDE)

ASTERIAS
TANNERI

(DETAIL OF ARM)

(DORSAL)

(VENTRAL, FROM
DRIED SPECIMEN)

LEPTASTERIAS
GROENLANDICA

LEPTASTERIAS
MULLERI

(RIGHT SIDE OF AMBUCRAL FURROW)

LEPTASTERIAS
POLARIS

LEPTASTERIAS
MULLERI

LOPHASTER
FURCIFER

species, with a number of circumboreal forms. The typical form ranges from Disco Island, on the west coast of Greenland, south to the Gulf of St. Lawrence and the Banks off Nova Scotia. The most conspicuous difference from the preceding species is that it almost always has six arms. Otherwise it is typical of the genus. The size is also very variable. Large specimens measure 12 inches in diameter. The species is known to have a vertical range from 1 to 200 fathoms.

Leptasterias mülleri (M. Sars) PLATE 208. Müller's Starfish. This species has five arms, proportionately moderate in length, distinctly differentiated from the disc at their bases. The marginal groove-spines are in a single series at the base of the arms, succeeded by two rows or by spines directed alternately toward the groove or away from it. The marginal plates in both the upper and lower series have one spine each, thus making two rows of spines outlining the arms. On the upper side, the spines are in somewhat irregular longitudinal rows, and tend to be knob-shaped. The pedicellariae are mainly in the intervals between the spines. The species measures up to 8 inches in diameter. The color, in life, is reddish or violet on the disc and arms, except toward the tips, where they are white. A brood-chamber is arranged by the female for the eggs and young, by raising its disc to a dome shape and placing the bases of its arms together. The young hatch out without going through a free-swimming larval stage and are cared for by the mother starfish until their first tube-feet appear, when they are released to fend for themselves. This is a circumboreal species, extending down the Atlantic Coast to southern Maine and, on the European side to the British Isles, in depths from the low-tide mark to about 430 fathoms.

CLASS OPHIUROIDEA
(The Brittle-stars, the Snake-stars)

The Ophiuroidea (COLOR PLATE XX, 1, 2; INDEX PLATE 209), like the Asteroidea, are starlike in form, with five arms radiating from a central, flattened disc, and with the mouth-opening located centrally on the underside of the body. The arms, however, are many jointed and contain no extensions of the stomach, or usually, of the genital system, and there is no open ambulacral groove beneath them. Two series of tube-feet, without suction discs, project through pores on either side of the jointed internal skeleton. There is no intestine, the digestive system consisting of a simple, saclike stomach opening to the outside only through the central mouth, there being no anal opening. The body-disc is comparatively small, usually not more than ¾ inch in diameter, while the arms may be 3

PLATE 209

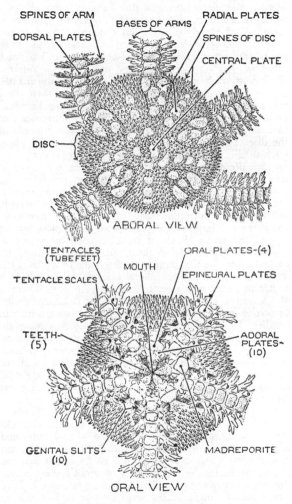

SPINES OF ARM
DORSAL PLATES
BASES OF ARMS
RADIAL PLATES
SPINES OF DISC
CENTRAL PLATE
DISC

ABORAL VIEW

TENTACLES (TUBE FEET)
MOUTH
ORAL PLATES-(4)
EPINEURAL PLATES
TENTACLE SCALES
TEETH-(5)
ADORAL PLATES-(10)
GENITAL SLITS-(10)
MADREPORITE

ORAL VIEW

EXTERNAL ANATOMY OF A
TYPICAL OPHIURAN

inches long. *Gorgonocephalus,* the Basket Star, is a note-worthy exception, having a disc varying from 2½ to 4 inches in diameter, with branching arms 9 to 14 inches in length. With the above exception, the arms are simple and have an internal skeleton made up of a series of calcareous pieces somewhat resembling vertebrae, fitting into each other in such fashion that they only allow a sidewise movement, with no possibility of rolling in toward the disc, except in the case of the Basket Stars and their allies, which have hourglass-shaped vertebrae. These vertebrae permit a vertical as well as a horizontal movement, so that the arms may roll in toward the oral or underside of the disc. There is also an external skeleton of flat plates on both disc and arms, arranged in regular fashion, vary-ing in different species, thus being of value for classifica-tion (see INDEX PLATE 209). The madreporite is on the oral side instead of the aboral, as in the asteroids, occupy-ing one of the five oral plates, surrounding the mouth, interradially. The circular mouth is armed with five teeth, consisting of sharp-pointed plates with their apices inward toward the center. Each of these is based on a pair of *adoral plates* just behind them, and these, in turn, are backed up by the five large *oral plates,* one of which is the madreporic plate. On the aboral side of the disc, there is a pair of *radial plates* at the base of each arm. There is also a central plate in the middle of the disc, surrounded by one or two sets of five plates each, alternating with one another. The arms are typically covered by four plates on each joint, one *dorsal,* one *ventral,* and two *lateral* plates. Each of the latter bears a series of spines varying in num-ber in the different species. In some cases, they stand out from the sides of the arms. In other cases, they are held closely appressed to them. The openings for the tube-feet are in the intervals on either side of the ventral plates, partly protected by small, scalelike pieces, the *tentacle-scales.* These details are shown in INDEX PLATE 209. On the oral side, on either side of the base of each arm, and parallel to it, is a long, narrow radial slit, one of the ten *genital slits.* These each open into an expanded sac, the *genital bursa,* into which a series of small *gonads* empty the reproductive elements. The bursae are also said to have a reproductive function. The sexes are separate and usually the genital products are discharged into the open sea, where they are fertilized, and hatch out in the form of a free-swimming larva, with a series of long, slender, paired projections in the form of ciliated rods, one pair of which is often much longer than the rest. This is known as the *Ophiopluteus* larva. After a time, it metamorphoses into a small brittle-star resembling the adult. It usually takes two or three years to grow to the full adult size. In some species there is no metamorphosis, the newly hatched young being held in a broad chamber near the mother's mouth, made by everting the edges of the stomach or by clustering together the spines surrounding the mouth. The larvae assume the form of minute brittle-stars, having arms of a few segments before they are released. The brittle-stars move about rapidly by means of the flexible arms, in a series of jumps. They also utilize the arms to secure the mollusks, worms, and other small sea-animals which form their food, and to carry them to the mouth. They, in turn, are preyed upon by fishes and other larger sea-creatures.

The Class Ophiuroidea is divided into two Orders, as follows: (1) *Euryalae;* (2) *Ophiurae.*

Order EURYALAE
(The Basket Stars)

This Order is characterized by the hourglass-shaped surfaces of the joints or vertebrae of its arms, which permit them to be moved vertically, though horizontal motion is possible as well. There is no distinct armature of plates or scales, but both the disc and arms are invested with a soft skin or with granules. Only rarely are there distinct scales. The spines on the arms are usually directed downward, often in the form of hooks. The arms, due to their vertical movement, roll in toward the mouth or in the opposite direction, or coil about various undersea growths. The genital slits are located vertically on the disc, on either side of the base of the arms. They are short, with comparatively wide openings.

Family Gorgonocephalidae

In this family the arms branch from the base, forming repeated V-shaped divisions. The disc is large, covered by naked skin, granules, or short spines. There are ring-like groups of minute hooks, especially on the finer divisions of the branches. The tentacle-scales are spinelike and small. There is a single interradial madreporite.

Gorgonocephalus arcticus Leach (= **Astrophyton agassizii** Stimpson) PLATE 210. The Basket Star. This remarkable ophiuroid, when its branching, tentaclelike arms are rolled up, has a very basketlike appearance; hence its popular name. The arms are branched from the base. The arm-spines (tentacle-scales) begin and continue serially with the second pair of tube-feet. The disc, as already stated, may be from 2½ to 4 inches in diameter, with arms from 9 to 14 inches long, though smaller specimens with a disc of 1½ inches are often found in this region. The animal may walk about on its branch tips, or may coil about the stems of gorgonians and other submarine growths. Individuals of this species are often found grouped together, sometimes in entangled masses, when they form a mutual network in which all kinds of marine organisms may be caught and worked by their coiling arms within reach of the five sharp jaws, to be torn apart for food. This animal makes a remarkable item for an invertebrate collection. If taken alive and submerged in fresh water, it dies in a spread-out relaxed condition, and then may be preserved in a 4- or 5-per cent formalin solution. This species ranges from Nantucket northward to the Arctic from below the lowest water mark to about 800 fathoms. Its coloration, in life, varies from chocolate-brown to yellow or cream-color, the darker color being in the depressed areas.

Family Asteronychidae

In this family the disc, as in the preceding species, is covered with skin, with the large radial plates showing indistinctly through. The arms are branched, the segments each bearing three or more arm-spines. There is a single madreporic plate on the oral side. The disc is moderately large, averaging about 1½ inches in diameter in adult specimens. The five arms are unequal, but the longer ones may be ten times the diameter of the disc. The genital slits are small, in diverging pairs, just outside the oral plates.

Asteronyx loveni Müller & Troschel PLATE 211. The disc is naked, and covered with skin, the large, narrow, riblike radial plates showing through, and giving the disc a pentagonal shape. As above stated, the five arms are quite unequal in length, some being considerably longer and thicker than the others. The arm-spines are long and club-shaped, with spiny tips, there being three or more to a segment. As the arms taper toward the tips, the spines are replaced by hooks in segmental groups of eight or nine. All the spines are hook-shaped on the shorter and thinner arms. The tentacle pores are without scales, and there are no spines at the first pair of pores. The coloration is reddish. This species often occurs with its long, snakelike arms entwined around the stems of gorgonians or sea-pens (pennatulids), stretching out one or two of its arms into the water to capture small free swimming or other crustaceans for food. It has a cosmopolitan distribution and, on the Atlantic Coast, it ranges from the Arctic to the West Indies, at depths of 55 to 1,000 fathoms.

PLATE 210

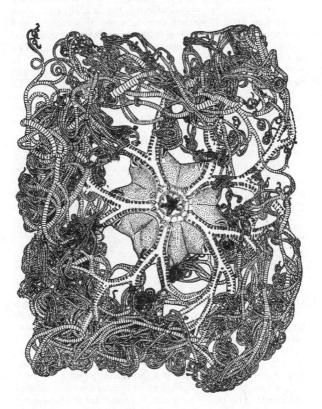

GORGONOCEPHALUS ARCTICUS

Order OPHIURAE
(The True Brittle-stars)

This Order contains most of the Ophiuroidea. The disc and arms are covered with scalelike plates, sometimes covered by skin, spines, or granules, and often exposed. The arm-plates are well developed, the lateral plates often extending around so that they meet on the midoral and midaboral line, alternating with the dorsal and epineural plates. The arm-spines are not directed downward. The arms are never branched and move, for the most part, in a horizontal plane, their motion being limited by the series of pits and knobs of the articulating surfaces. The genital slits are always horizontal in position, and are narrow and elongate, located on either side of the arm bases. There is a single madreporite, occupying one of the five oral positions.

Family Ophiomyxidae

In this family, both the disc and the arms are covered by a thick skin, the scales and plates being hidden beneath. The radial plates are not well developed, while the scales covering the disc are very small, polished, and elliptical in shape. The dorsal plates on the arms are vestigial, while the ventral plates are normally developed. The arm-spines are covered with skin and stand erect.

Ophioscolex glacialis Müller & Troschel PLATE 211. In this species, the skin of the disc is entirely bare of spines. The dorsal plates of the arms are in an exceedingly vestigial condition and difficult to make out. The outline of the interlocking vertebrae shows through the skin. They are obvious in dried specimens, superficially appearing to be plates. The ventral plates are normally developed with convex outer margin, and slightly overlapping. There are three fairly acute arm-spines on each segment, continuing as such to the arm tips, without being replaced by hooks. The triangular interradial jaw has three papillae on each side, and a cluster of papillae at its apex, in well-developed specimens. The oral plate is small, triangular with rounded angles. The elongated adoral plates each have an acute spine. The disc reaches about 1 inch in diameter, while the length of the arms is about 5 inches. The coloration, when alive, varies from yellow to red or violet. The arms are luminescent in the dark. This species ranges from Greenland to Virginia, in from 27 to about 1,000 fathoms, on muddy bottoms.

Ophioscolex purpureus Düben & Koren PLATE 211. Small spines are distributed over the disc, in this species, and the dorsal arm-plates are sufficiently well developed as transverse, rectangular plates, usually two to a seg-

PLATE 211

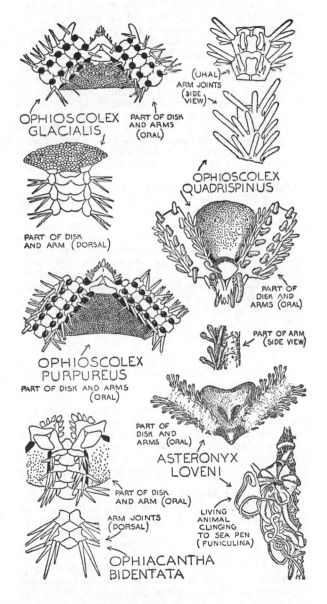

OPHIOSCOLEX
GLACIALIS

PART OF DISK
AND ARMS
(ORAL)

(ORAL)
ARM JOINTS
(SIDE VIEW)

PART OF DISK
AND ARM (DORSAL)

OPHIOSCOLEX
QUADRISPINUS

PART OF
DISK AND
ARMS (ORAL)

PART OF ARM
(SIDE VIEW)

OPHIOSCOLEX
PURPUREUS
PART OF DISK AND ARMS
(ORAL)

PART OF
DISK AND
ARMS (ORAL)

ASTERONYX
LOVENI

PART OF DISK
AND ARM (ORAL)

ARM JOINTS
(DORSAL)

LIVING
ANIMAL
CLINGING
TO SEA PEN
(FUNICULINA)

OPHIACANTHA
BIDENTATA

ment, so that they completely cover the upper surface, except that near the disc they are somewhat irregular. The ventral plates resemble those of the preceding species. The oral plates are transversely elongate, rounded at the ends, and with a slight but distinctly projecting median apex. The adoral plates are similar to those of *Ophioscolex glacialis,* but without a spine. There are six to ten papillae projecting on either side of each jaw. There are three fairly robust arm-spines to a segment, but toward the arm tips, the two upper ones become hooks. There is a small, spinelike tentacle-scale projecting forward over each ambulacral pore. This species is slightly smaller than the preceding, but resembles it in color. It is circumboreal and occurs from the Arctic southward on the American east coast, in depths of about 40 to 760 fathoms, on muddy bottoms.

Ophioscolex quadrispinus Verrill PLATE 211. The disc and base of the arms are covered with soft skin, wrinkled, and with small, wartlike papillae on the upper side, becoming smoother beneath and covering the vestigial arm-plates completely. There are about four pairs of blunt arm-spines on each segment, and a very small acute tentacle-scale. There are about six or eight acute teeth on each side of each jaw, besides several mouth papillae. The disc measures up to ¾ inch in diameter, while the arms are nearly 3 inches long. This species is relatively rare, but has been found from about the 100-fathom line to a depth of 234 fathoms, off Nova Scotia and the Gulf of Maine.

Family Ophiacanthidae

In this family the disc is largely covered with granules or small spines, which tend to conceal the scales. There is a practically continuous series of papillae bordering the jaws and mouth-region, for the most part pointed and some even spinelike. The spines stand erect and are usually quite long and evenly tapering to a nearly acute point. The arms often appear to be knotted, the segments having their proximal waists narrowed, but expanding distally. This is one of the largest brittle-star families, mostly deep sea in habitat.

Ophiacantha bidentata (Retzius) PLATE 211. The disc is thickly covered with short stumps or tubercles, on the aboral, and, to a certain degree, on the oral side, as well. The dorsal arm-plates are diamond-shaped and separated by the laterals, which meet on the median line between them, bearing long arm-spines on their distal facet, and continuing around to the oral side of the arm, where they also meet on the median line, well separating the convex scale-shaped ventral plates. Six to eight long, tapering arm-spines are borne on each segment, graduated in length to the dorsal aspect, where they are longest. There is a moderately large tentacle-scale present. Three or four mouth-papillae are on either side of the jaw. The oral-plates are roughly diamond-shaped, with the transverse axis the longer. The color of this species is dark brown. The disc is about ½ inch in diameter, with the arms 1½ to 2½ inches in length. This is a circumboreal species, extending, on the American coast, from the Arctic to South Carolina, from 5½ to 2,460 fathoms. It is a luminescent species.

Family Amphiuridae

The disc, in this family, is furnished with clearly distinct scales or plates, and frequently with spines. There is a pair of *infradental papillae* on the inner angle of each jaw, with which the papillae immediately on either side may or may not be adjoined. There is a single series of square teeth and no tooth-papillae. The arm-spines are small, solid, and stand out from the sides of the arms.

Ophiopholis aculeata (Linnaeus) PLATE 212; COLOR PLATE XX, 1. The Daisy Brittle-star. The disc is covered with small spines which conceal the scales, but do not conceal the radial and central plates which stand out distinctly, oval in shape, usually forming a starlike figure of ten rays. The transversely oval dorsal plates of the arms are surrounded by a single series of small plates. The ventral arm-plates are squarish, separated from each other by a pitlike area. There are five or six somewhat flattened, tapering arm-spines on either side of each segment, standing out fanlike in a vertical series, the uppermost spine being quite minute; the three succeeding spines, long and similar to each other; and the lowest spine hook-shaped, with a small tooth below the hook. There is a fairly well-developed tentacle-scale with each of the ambulacral pores on the proximal joints of the arms. The color of this brittle-star is very variable. It is often reddish on the disc, with deeper red plates, and the arms banded alternately red and white; or the center may be a blue star, bordered with brown and the arms green and brown; or countless other combinations, so that the bottom of a tide-pool frequented by these brittle-stars presents a colorful sight.

The disc of this species measures up to ⅘ inch in diameter, having arms 3½ inches in length. It is very abundant from the Arctic to Long Island Sound, from the low-water mark to 900 fathoms or more.

Amphipholis squamata (Delle Chiaje) PLATE 212; COLOR PLATE XX, 2. The Long Armed Snake-star. This species is extremely delicate and fragile. The disc is about ⅛ inch in diameter, while the threadlike arms may be nearly 1½ inches in length. The disc is covered with small scales, both on the upper and lower sides, to such an extent that it is difficult to see the primary plates. The radial shield-plates, however, above the bases of the arms are clearly visible, each pair being in contact throughout its entire length. The dorsal arm-plates are triangular with rounded corners, somewhat broader than long, their apices and bases being in contact successively. The outer border of the triangular ventral plates is slightly concave, and similarly adjoining, tip to base, being also in close contact on their oblique sides with the flanking lateral plates. Each segment has a pair of arm-spine clusters of four spines each, except as the arm narrows farther out, there are three spines. The color of this species is grayish white with a pale bluish tinge. It is viviparous and hermaphroditic. This is a cosmopolitan species, occurring on our coast from the Arctic to Long Island Sound. On the European side it is very abundant around the British Isles. It ranges, vertically, from the low-tide mark to 60 fathoms.

Amphiura denticulata Koehler PLATE 213. The aboral side of the disc, in this species, is covered with scales, concealing the primary plates, but the oral side is entirely devoid of them. The radial shields at the base of the arms on the aboral side are wedged apart by a few elongate, narrow scales. The dorsal plates of the arms are rounded, while the ventral plates are polygonal and somewhat concave, laterally. The arm-spines vary from five to seven, the upper and lower being smooth and tapered, with the intervening spines flattened, and the outer edge finely saw-toothed. There are no tentacle-scales. The disc is about ⅕ inch in diameter, with the arms about 2 inches long. This is a northern, circumboreal species, known, on the American North Atlantic Coast from Greenland south to Newfoundland, in depths from about 58 to 600 fathoms.

Hemipholis elongata (Say) PLATE 213. The disc, on the upper side, is covered with rounded scales with large radial shields, so shaped that each pair has a heart-shaped outline, having the points directed inward toward the center of the disc, and slightly split apart by narrow wedge-shaped scales, pushing in from the apex in a radial direction. Each shield measures about one fifth the diameter of the disc. There are no tooth-papillae but there are two mouth-papillae for each angle of the mouth. Lyman describes and figures three arm-spines for each segment (the middle figures on the plate), but Boone shows and describes seven (see the three lower left-hand figures) from the specimen collected off the coast of Florida by the "Ara" expedition of 1923.

The shape of the dorsal and ventral arm-plates are

PLATE 212

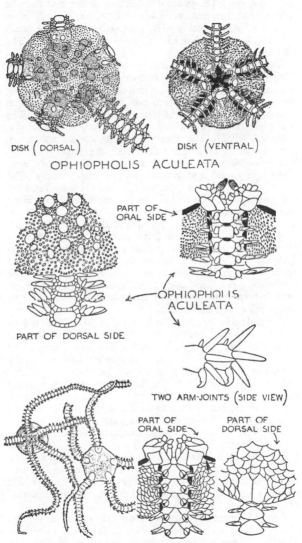

DISK (DORSAL) DISK (VENTRAL)

OPHIOPHOLIS ACULEATA

PART OF ORAL SIDE

OPHIOPHOLIS ACULEATA

PART OF DORSAL SIDE

TWO ARM-JOINTS (SIDE VIEW)

PART OF ORAL SIDE PART OF DORSAL SIDE

AMPHIPHOLIS SQUAMATA

shown in the figure. This is another variable species in color patterns. The general coloration of the disc may be indigo blue, greenish, yellow-brown, yellow, or flesh-color, with the radial shields of a contrasting color; the arms are usually banded and different from the disc. The tentacles are red.

Ophiophragmus wurdemani (Lyman) PLATE 213. This species was formerly known only from Florida, but it is now known to occur off the coast of North Carolina, and therefore impinges into our zone at that point. The disc-scales are smooth, but not regularly arranged. The oral plates are long and narrow. The diameter of the disc is about ⅖ inch. The arms are flat and wide, and about 4 to 5 inches in length. The teeth are broad and flat. The oral plates are long and narrow. The upper arm-plates are broad and narrow and overlap distally. The scales of the disc are very small and about evenly of the same size. The radial shields are broad and blunt and in each pair are separated throughout their length. The two plates of a pair together make a roughly heart-shaped figure. There are three pairs of arm-spines to a segment. They are short and stout, as well as somewhat flattened and rounded terminally. There are two short and broad tentacle-scales to each tentacle-pore. The color is variable, the disc being either cream-color, grayish, or dark brown, with the arms irregularly cross marked by cream-color and dusky gray.

Amphiodia erecta Koehler PLATE 214. This species was described by Koehler from "Albatross" dredgings off Cape Hatteras in 52 fathoms. As it is not likely to be found by the users of this book, unless brought in by fishermen, only a brief mention will be made.

The disc is roughly oval and measures between 6 and 7 millimeters (a little over ¼ inch) in diameter. The arms are about 1⅖ inches in length. The upper side is covered with fairly thick plates, but the primary plates are not visible. The radial shields are small and adjoin for most of their length. The genital slits are narrow. The oral plates are diamond-shaped and longer than wide. The adoral plates are long and narrow triangles with somewhat concave sides. The dorsal arm-plates are large and wider than long. The characteristics of the undersurface are clear from the figure.

Amphilimna olivacea (Lyman) PLATE 214. The disc of this species is covered with spinules and is swollen aborally. There is a notch over the base of each arm. The radial shields are parallel and are in contact for the most part. On the underside, the oral-papillae are four or five in a series. The tooth-papillae are two to four. There are usually two spinelike tentacle-scales located on either side

PLATE 213

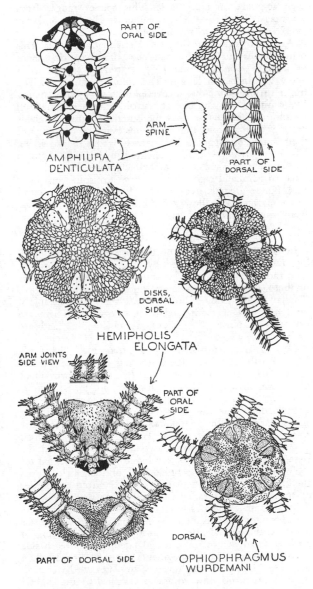

PART OF
ORAL SIDE

ARM
SPINE

AMPHIURA
DENTICULATA

PART OF
DORSAL SIDE

DISKS,
DORSAL
SIDE

HEMIPHOLIS
ELONGATA

ARM JOINTS
SIDE VIEW

PART OF
ORAL
SIDE

PART OF DORSAL SIDE

DORSAL

OPHIOPHRAGMUS
WURDEMANI

of each tentacle-pore. There are nine to ten arm-spines to each segment on either side. This species ranges from Marthas Vineyard to Cape Hatteras, Florida, and the West Indies, in 40 to 192 fathoms.

Amphioplus macilentus Verrill PLATE 214. This brittle-star is small, with a five-lobed disc measuring about ⅛ inch in diameter with long, extremely slender arms about 2½ inches in length. The color is light gray. The upper surface of the disc is covered with scales, overlapping like rounded shingles, entirely devoid of spines, sometimes forming a distinct rosette at the center. The radial shields are long and narrow, the outer ends being in contact, and their inner ends separated by narrow wedge-shaped scales. There are five oral-papillae, unequal in size, and rounded at their ends. There are two tentacle-scales for each ambulacral pore, and each joint has three arm-spines on either side. These animals live in the soft mud and are found in comparatively shallow water in this region. They occur from southern New England to Cape Hatteras.

Family Ophiotrichidae

In this family, the scales on the disc are well developed, but they may be concealed by small spines or bristles. The radial shields are large and distinct. The arm-plates on both the upper and lower sides are well developed. The jaws have a row of broad, strong teeth on their apices, with a group of tooth-papillae outside them. There are no mouth-papillae. The spines are outstanding and are usually thorny.

Ophiothrix angulata Ayres PLATE 214. The Little Spiny Brittle-star. This little brittle-star has a disc measuring up to ½ inch in diameter and five slender arms about 2½ inches in length. It is remarkable both for its spinose condition and for the range of its color variation. The upper side of the disc is densely covered with bristling spines except for the five paired radial shields, which are comparatively without spines. Together, each pair forms a shield-shaped area, with the point inward toward the center of the disc and their combined suture conjoined for their entire length. The broad end of the shield covers the base of the arm articulating below it, from the border of the mouth. The radial shields confine the aboral disc bristles to an elevated star-shaped area of which the rays are interradial in position. The arms of the brittle star bristle with long, slender, blunt-tipped spines, varying in number from two to six, directed laterally from each side of the segments. The arm-segments are much broader than they are long, with the upper arm-plates wedge-shaped, their points turned inward and overlapped by the slightly convex broad end of the previous plate. The lateral plates

PLATE 214

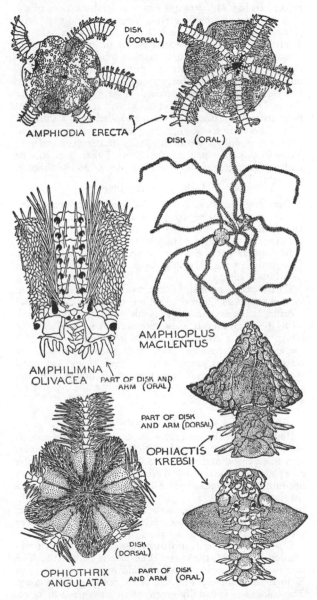

AMPHIODIA ERECTA

DISK (DORSAL)

DISK (ORAL)

AMPHIOPLUS
MACILENTUS

AMPHILIMNA
OLIVACEA

PART OF DISK AND
ARM (ORAL)

PART OF DISK
AND ARM (DORSAL)

OPHIACTIS
KREBSII

OPHIOTHRIX
ANGULATA

DISK
(DORSAL)

PART OF DISK
AND ARM (ORAL)

are covered with skin and bear the spines on a median ridge, curving with straight edges around the sides of the arm to form a junction with the squarish lower arm-plates. The basal arm-spines have thorny sides and tip. There is a thorn-tipped tentacle-scale on each segment of the arm from base to tip. Agassiz recorded color varia-tions of this species with the disc ranging through ver-milion, pink, purple, blue, green, brown, and yellow, in various shades, the radial shields always of a contrasting shade. The general coloration of the arm is always different from that of the disc, and always banded with a different color. There are about eighteen tooth-papillae to each jaw.

This is mainly a southern species, but is very common from Chesapeake Bay to the West Indies and Rio de Janiero, from very shallow water to depths of 200 fathoms.

Family Ophioactidae

The disc, in this family, has well-developed scales, usually not concealed by the spines or granules which are often present on its surface. The mouth-papillae are not contiguous with the infradental papillae. There are no tooth-papillae but there is a single series of square teeth. The genital organs are in a large, concentrated group in each bursal slit.

Ophiactis krebsii Lütken PLATE 214. This is also a southern species, found through the West Indies and Florida. It is recorded as far north as South Carolina and, with the idea that it may sometimes be found off the North Carolina coast, it is briefly mentioned here. This species usually has six arms and often reproduces by direct fission. It is green in color, marked and patterned with white or gray. It is a very small species, the disc measuring only about ⅛ inch in diameter, the arms being about ¾ inch in length.

Family Ophiodermatidae

Both the aboral and oral sides of the disc are covered with a close investment of granules, concealing the scala-tion completely, and even invading the jaws, though the oral-plates, or mouth-shields, are left clearly exposed. There are numerous mouth-papillae in a continuous row around the jaws. There is a single series of teeth, while tooth-papillae are absent. There are two pairs of genital slits located along the arm-bases interradially. The arm-spines are held closely against the sides of the arms.

Ophioderma brevispinum (Say) (= **Ophiura vi-olacea** Lyman) PLATE 215. The Green Brittle-star. The disc in this species is pentagonal and measures about ⅖ to ⅗ inch in diameter, with the arms nearly 3 inches long. The coloration is usually green, often olive-green or olive-

PLATE 215

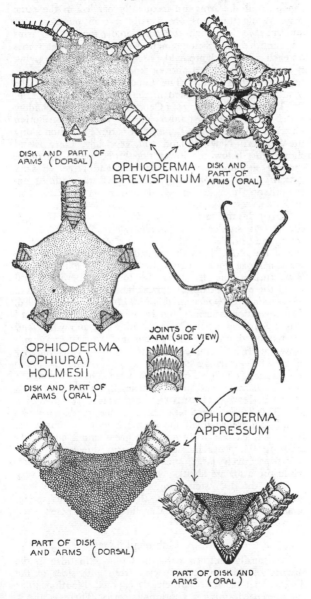

DISK AND PART OF
ARMS (DORSAL)

OPHIODERMA
BREVISPINUM

DISK AND
PART OF
ARMS (ORAL)

OPHIODERMA
(OPHIURA)
HOLMESII

DISK AND PART OF
ARMS (ORAL)

JOINTS OF
ARM (SIDE VIEW)

OPHIODERMA
APPRESSUM

PART OF DISK
AND ARMS (DORSAL)

PART OF DISK AND
ARMS (ORAL)

brown, varying on the disc to darker or lighter
shades, and the arms are frequently banded in the same
way. While the arms are usually five in number, four
and six-rayed specimens are occasionally found. The arms
are rounded and each segment has seven or eight spines
on each side, which are held closely against the arm, giving
it somewhat the appearance of smoothness, a characteristic
feature of this family. The important characters of the
mouth-parts are mentioned in the description of the family. The species ranges from Cape Cod to Brazil in shallow
water along the coast, also with a vertical distribution
down to more than 100 fathoms. It is quite common along
the southern New England and, especially, Long Island
shores, just below the lower tide limit, usually in quiet,
shallow situations such as tide-pools and protected sand
flats, its color harmonizing almost perfectly with its environment. It feeds on small worms, crustaceans, and
mollusks.

Ophioderma appressum (Say) PLATE 215. This species is very similar to the previous one. It is one of the
commonest brittle-stars along the southern coast, as well as
one of the most widely distributed. Its range extends from
the Carolinas southward to Brazil and the Bahamas and
West Indies generally. It is also found at Bermuda and
along the coast of tropical Africa. It therefore overlaps and
supplements *Ophioderma brevispinum* to the southward.
The coloration is similar, but is more strikingly green and
white. Some specimens have a white disc and white and
green-banded arms. Some specimens are also gray and
brown with all kinds of intergrades. While the majority
of the individuals are of about the same size as the previous species, a number are much larger, having a disc 1
inch in diameter and arms 5 inches in length.

Ophioderma (Ophiura) holmesii Lyman PLATE
215. This is another South Carolina species that may be
found to impinge upon the southern limits of our zone.
It has a thick disc with very fine granulations completely
covering the plates including the arm shields. The disc
is comparatively large, measuring ⅘ inch in diameter,
while the arms are about 3 inches long. The color is very
variable, the disc often being nearly white and the arms
green, banded with yellow or lighter green. This species
occurs off the coast of South Carolina and may be expected
to extend farther north.

Family Ophiolepididae

This family contrasts with the Ophiodermatidae in the
absence of skin, in most species, from both sides of the
disc, so that the scales are clearly exposed. Mouth-papillae
are present, forming a continuous series. There is also a

PLATE 216

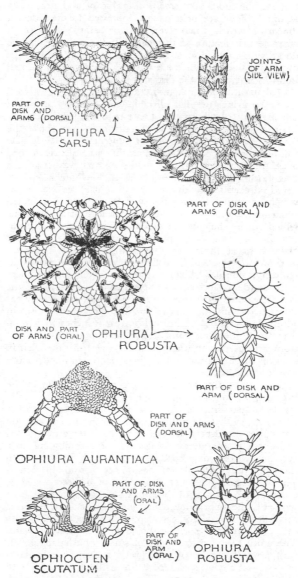

PART OF
DISK AND
ARMS (DORSAL)

JOINTS
OF ARM
(SIDE VIEW)

OPHIURA
SARSI

PART OF DISK AND
ARMS (ORAL)

DISK AND PART
OF ARMS (ORAL)

OPHIURA
ROBUSTA

PART OF DISK AND
ARM (DORSAL)

PART OF
DISK AND ARMS
(DORSAL)

OPHIURA AURANTIACA

PART OF DISK
AND ARMS
(ORAL)

PART OF
DISK AND
ARM (ORAL)

OPHIOCTEN
SCUTATUM

OPHIURA
ROBUSTA

single series of teeth but no tooth-papillae. The arm-spines are, for the most part, small, insignificant and practically vestigial. They are held closely appressed to the sides of the arms which, themselves, are comparatively short. A characteristic feature of this family is the presence on the dorsal side of the disc, at the base of each arm, of a fringe of small spines, called the *arm-comb*. It is usually located in an indentation of the disc at this point.

Ophiura sarsi Lütken PLATE 216. The numerous small scales covering the flat disc, in this species, surround the primary plates, so that they are often inconspicuous. There is a distinct notch in the disc-edge just above the base of the arms, which appear superficially to originate from the aboral side though, if the specimen is turned over, they are seen to issue in the normal way from the neighborhood of the mouth-corners. This notch is bordered on each side with a comb of papillae, the *arm-comb*, which continues around the arm laterally, like a frilled collar, to the oral side, to the neighborhood of the papillae, which border the edges of the bursal slits. The radial arm-shields are ovoid and separated, in each pair, by smaller plates or scales, those following having two pairs. There are three arm-spines, which, in this species, are diagonally outstanding. The oral shields are comparatively short. There are four to six tapered mouth-papillae on either side of the jaw. The color of this species is red to dark red, somewhat variegated with mottlings. The diameter of the disc, in adults, is about 1½ inches, with arms 6 inches in length. The distribution is circumboreal, extending down our coast from the Arctic to Cape Hatteras, and to the British Isles on the European side of the Atlantic, in depths from 5½ to 1,640 fathoms.

Ophiura robusta Ayres PLATE 216. As shown in the third figure on the right side of the plate, the scales of the upper side of the disc are of uniformly rather large size, so that the primaries, such as the arm-shields, do not stand out clearly. In this case, the latter are rounded and entirely separated by scales. The arm-combs are present, but weakly developed, and the notch is also small, showing only two dorsal arm-plates within its limits. The dorsal arm-plates are arched and with the outer edges quite convex, and with three pairs of arm-spines on each segment, the upper one being the longest. There is one small tentacle-scale for each pore. The mouth-shields are shorter than broad, with a broad apex pointing inward. There are three or four pairs of small mouth-papillae for each jaw. The color of this species is gray-blue to dark-brown, sometimes sprinkled with white spots and with light-colored radial shields. The arms are usually banded. The disc is ⅖ inch in diameter, the arms being 1⅓ inches in length. The American distribution is from Greenland to Cape Cod. On the European side, it ranges from the Arctic to the northern part of the British Isles, in depths from 3¼ to as much as 547 fathoms.

Ophiura (Ophiopleura) aurantiaca (Verrill) PLATE 216. The disc is covered with very small, imbricated scales, almost like a coat of armor, and nearly concealing the primary plates. The radial shields, however, show clearly. They are oval and widely separated by the scales, set diagonally, with their outer ends tilted toward each other. The notch above the arms shows only very slightly. The dorsal arm-plates are quadrangular, with their outer corners expanded and rounded. They are smaller and narrower near the base of the arms. The ventral plates are fan-shaped with a convex outer edge. The mouth-shields are triangular with a small, rounded lobe on either side. The mouth-papillae are very small and closely adjoin each other. The genital slits are long and narrow, extending from the mouth-shields to the edge of the disc. The color of this species is bright orange. The diameter of the disc is about ¾ inch, but at least one specimen has been found with a disc 1⅜ inches in diameter. The arms vary in proportion from 2¼ to more than 6 inches in length. This brittle-star occurs along the New England coast and is circumboreal.

Ophiocten scutatum Koehler PLATE 216. In this species, the disc is covered with very small scales, leaving the small primary plates clearly visible. It has a sharp edge with a clear boundary for the upper and lower sides of the disc. A circle of small scales surrounds each primary plate. The dorsal arm-plates are very broad and keeled. The ventral arm-plates, as exposed, are fan-shaped, the convex outer border touching the pointed inner border of the next plate in the basal segments, but becoming separated in the rest of the arm by the lateral plates, which join each other on the median line. A large oval tentacle-scale covers the pore completely on either side of each segment. The five mouth-shields are very conspicuous, being much longer than broad, and reaching almost to the border of the disc. There are three to four mouth-papillae on either side of each jaw, the outer one very broad and flat on its summit. There are two pairs of arm-spines with blunt, rounded tips to each segment. The disc measures up to ⅓ inch in diameter, with the arms about 1 inch in length. This species occurs off Newfoundland in about 85 fathoms, also in British seas and in the Bay of Biscay.

Ophiolepis elegans Lutken PLATE 217. The aboral side of the disc shows clearly all its primary plates, which, together with the well-developed scales, completely cover its surface. Each plate and scale is completely surrounded by a close-set belt or border of small ones. There is a small notch over the base of each arm. The primary plates are all very flat and regularly arranged in a symmetrical pattern. There is a flowerlike rosette in the center of the disc composed of five petal-like plates surrounding the circular center plate. A row of three plates borders each interradial space and one small primary plate is radially located in front of each notch. The radial plates are pear-shaped and, in each case, are separated by scales. There are nine to eleven mouth-papillae set in an even row around each jaw, the central one, being the longest, forming the apex. There are four teeth on each side, the three lowest with flat tops and the one at the apex being longer, narrower, and pointed at the tip. Two genital slits follow closely along the sides of each arm. The dorsal arm-plates are broader than long, each end formed by two angular sides. Toward the arm tips, they become hexagonal, with about equal sides. The ventral arm-plates are broader than long, with slightly convex outer edges. There are two tentacle-scales to each pore, each pair with one flat side in contact, and together forming a lens-shaped outline. The color of this species is variable from greenish gray to brown. A color plate by Agassiz shows a reddish brown disc, a light yellow central rosette, and five interradially located oval, light-yellow plates, the arms being banded alternately brown and bluish gray. This species ranges from the Carolinas to the West Indies in 2 to 20 fathoms. The disc measures ¾ inch in diameter, the length of the arms being nearly 2 inches.

CLASS ECHINOIDEA
(The Sea-urchins, Cake-urchins, and Sand-dollars)

The Echinoidea are echinoderms having their body enclosed in a hard shell, or *test,* made up of immovable plates joined together in a regular pattern. The test may be somewhat globular in shape, or it may be ovoid or flattened to form a thin, circular disc. The outside of the test (INDEX DIAGRAM 218) is covered with stiff spines articulating in any direction on tubercles or bosses, in ball-and-socket fashion. The tube-feet, in ten equally spaced bands, radiate from the upper center of the test, or *apical pole,* passing, like the meridians around the globe, to converge again, on the underside, at the margin of the typically central oral-opening of the test. The test is divided into ten regular areas, of which five alternating areas are perforated with a double series of openings for the tube-feet, and therefore correspond, anatomically, to the five arms of a sea-star. Each one of these is known as a radius or ambulacral zone, while the areas between are the inter-

PLATE 217

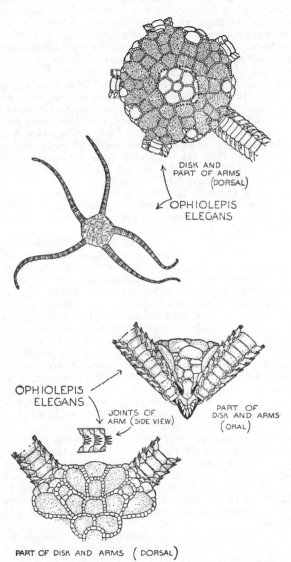

DISK AND
PART OF ARMS
(DORSAL)

OPHIOLEPIS
ELEGANS

OPHIOLEPIS
ELEGANS

JOINTS OF
ARM (SIDE VIEW)

PART OF
DISK AND ARMS
(ORAL)

PART OF DISK AND ARMS (DORSAL)

radii or interambulacral zones and are devoid of openings. Each zone is composed of two rows of plates, each rectangular in shape, except that the ends where the two rows meet are pointed and interdigitate with each other to form a zigzag line of junction. The ambulacral plates are narrower than the interambulacral plates, with an ambulacral pore near each end. Tubercles for the spines are present on the plates of both areas. The mouth-opening is typically situated in the center of the underside, though in certain ovoid forms it may be considerably off center. It usually includes a membranous area (the *peristome*) with the central circular mouth, from which project five calcareous, sharply pointed teeth, their tips converging at the center. Their bases articulate from a complex apparatus constructed of a symmetrical framework of narrow ossicles and muscular bands, known as *Aristotle's lantern,* because it was originally observed by him. The peristome, in some species, is quite without plates, but, most frequently, a number of small plates may be found partially covering it.

At the apical pole of the test, in the "regular" echinoids, is a starlike series of characteristic plates, known as the *apical system.* There are ten plates in this series surrounding a central enclosure containing a number of small movable plates, known as the *periproct,* because the anal opening is included in it, usually somewhat to one side of the center. The plates composing this apical system are five interradially situated *genital plates* and five radial *ocular plates.* Each of the former has a *genital pore* opening through it, and one of the five, a little larger than the others, is also a *madreporite* and opens directly into the *madreporic duct,* which connects with the water-vascular system.

In some species, the plates of the ambulacral zones are coalesced to form compound plates of three to five original plates, but each containing the original number of paired ambulacral openings for the tube-feet included in the plates from which they were combined. This coalescence permits the enlargement of the tubercles and spines arising from them. The spines may be short, as in *Echinus;* they may be long, cylindrical, and needlelike, even a foot in length in certain tropical species; or they may be very thick, flattened, or oval in section, and short and club-shaped.

Pedicellariae of various characteristic types exist on the surface in scattered abundance. They are usually mounted on long, flexible stalks, with threefold pincerlike parts at their summit, sometimes globular in form, when closed, and sometimes elongate. When opened, these jaws are tripartite, to close suddenly when touched, grasping any-

PLATE 218

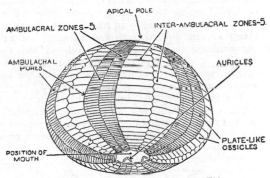

APICAL POLE

AMBULACRAL ZONES-5.

INTER-AMBULACRAL ZONES-5.

AMBULACRAL PORES

AURICLES

PLATE-LIKE OSSICLES

POSITION OF MOUTH

LATERAL VIEW OF SHELL WITH SPINES OMITTED

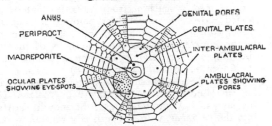

ANUS

GENITAL PORES

PERIPROCT

GENITAL PLATES.

MADREPORITE

INTER-AMBULACRAL PLATES

OCULAR PLATES SHOWING EYE-SPOTS

AMBULACRAL PLATES SHOWING PORES

APICAL VIEW WITH SPINES OMITTED

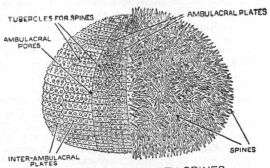

TUBERCLES FOR SPINES

AMBULACRAL PLATES

AMBULACRAL PORES

INTER-AMBULACRAL PLATES

SPINES

LATERAL VIEW WITH SPINES REMOVED FROM LEFT HALF

thing within their reach. Thus they act as weapons of defense, clinging to any moving object that touches them, and discharging an irritating poison from triple poison glands, found especially in those with globular heads. They are also utilized to remove sediment and other foreign substances from the outer side of the test, thus keeping it clean. When such material is loosened, the spines, successively moving, also carry it to the periphery of the body, to be dropped behind.

The tube-feet in the "regular" echinoids end in a pneumatic sucking-disc, while in the oval, "irregular" forms, such as the spatangoids, they may be leaf-shaped or of other various types. They contain a complex skeleton of supporting calcareous rods and spicules. Each tube-foot, except certain simple types, requires two ambulacral pores for its functioning in extension.

Around the mouth, on the peristome, ten branching gills are located, while projecting from the mouth-opening are the five teeth articulating from Aristotle's lantern, as mentioned above. The muscles for holding this apparatus in place, and for extending and retracting it, are attached to the *auricles,* five internal projections of the test surrounding and just inside of the mouth-opening (shown in the upper figure of INDEX PLATE 218).

Within the test, the internal organs (INDEX PLATE 219) are surrounded by the body-cavity or *coelom.* Through the jaws and Aristotle's lantern, the mouth leads directly into the *oesophagus,* from which is given off, at one side, a thin, tubular *siphon,* or *accessory gut* that joins the oesophagus again just before it connects with the *stomach.* This part of the digestive tract completely encircles the body-cavity and then turns back and encircles it again in the opposite direction becoming the *intestine,* which finally empties into the *anus* at the *periproct,* through the *rectum.* Just above the mouth apparatus is the pentagonal ring-canal, with five blind sacs, the interradial *polian vesicles,* radiating from it. From one side rises the *madreporic duct,* a slender vessel, which expands into an *ampulla,* just below its junction with the madreporite in the apical system. The five radial canals with their ampullae also branch from the radial angles of the ring-canal, each ampulla corresponding to a tube-foot. The latter is distended by the water forced into it through the contraction of the ampulla so that the tube-foot elongates and attaches itself by its pneumatic disc to whatever it contacts in its environment. The reproductive organs or *gonads* lie interradially between the branches of the radial canals, and discharge their products through the genital pores located in the appropriate genital plates in the apical system. In the "irregular" ovoid echinoids, such as the spatangoids

PLATE 219

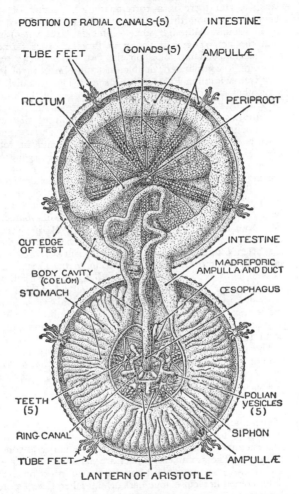

POSITION OF RADIAL CANALS-(5)   INTESTINE

TUBE FEET   GONADS-(5)   AMPULLÆ

RECTUM   PERIPROCT

CUT EDGE
OF TEST   INTESTINE

BODY CAVITY
(COELOM)   MADREPORIC
AMPULLA AND DUCT

STOMACH   ŒSOPHAGUS

TEETH
(5)   POLIAN
VESICLES
(5)

RING CANAL   SIPHON

TUBE FEET   AMPULLÆ

LANTERN OF ARISTOTLE

INTERNAL ANATOMY OF A
TYPICAL ECHINOID
(TEST BISECTED HORIZONTALLY AND
OPENED OUT TO SHOW INTERNAL
ORGANS)

(to be treated later), one or two of the gonads may be lacking, and there is a corresponding reduction of the genital pores and their plates to four, or even three in some groups. Although some echinoids (*Hemiaster*) retain the newly hatched young in brood-pouches formed by certain petal-like areas on the test, most species pass through a complicated double metamorphosis involving two free-swimming *Echinopluteus* stages. The cake-urchins and other ovoid forms burrow 7 or 8 inches in the sandy or gravelly bottom, hiding from their enemies and feeding on mussels, snails, and other small animals of that environment. The round sea-urchins crawl about more openly, and are often found in tide-pools and in rock crevices feeding upon algae and small animal organisms. They have considerable powers of regeneration, easily repairing injuries to the test and quickly replacing spines and other external parts when lost or injured. Some sea-urchins are of economic value, their reproductive organs being utilized as food by the inhabitants of southern European countries and certain other parts of the world, especially in the tropics. Because of their hard parts, they are often found as fossils, being abundantly represented in all formations from the Ordovician to the Cretaceous, as well as in Tertiary times, the fossil species contributing largely to our knowledge of their interrelationships. Pratt estimates that about 600 living species and 2,000 fossil species are known. Our present space will allow the description of only a few outstanding and common forms occurring within the limits of our zone.

The Class Echinoidea is divided into five Orders, containing the existing species as follows: (1) *Cidaroidea;* (2) *Diadematoidea;* (3) *Clypeastroidea;* (4) *Cassiduloidea;* and (5) *Spatangoidea.*

Order CIDAROIDEA

These are regularly round sea-urchins with the anal opening in the central part of the apical system. The ambulacral zones are narrow, while the interambulacral zones are broad. The ambulacral plates are narrow and simple; that is, there are only two pores for the tube-feet on each plate, sometimes close together, or, in other cases, more distant and connected by a groove or furrow. In the interambulacral zone, the plates are regular but much wider and with only one single, large, primary spine articulating from each plate on a large hemispherical tubercle, surrounded by a deep, circular groove (the *areole*), and pierced in the center by a pit. The tubercle may be smooth, or the pit may be at the summit of a nipplelike dome, surrounded by a ring of toothlike crenulations. The primary spine is cylindrical and blunt at the tip. It is clothed with a hairy coat, the *ostracum*, having a smooth, uncoated base, the *collar*. Surrounding the primary spine is a series of small, flattened, secondary spines. The ambulacral and interambulacral plates invade the peristome, completely covering it with a continuation of their regular zonal plates. Gills are absent and the teeth have no keel. Globe-shaped and triple-toothed pedicellariae are present and have poison glands. Toward the apex, the primary spines are smaller and lack the outer coat.

Family Cidaridae

This is the only family of this Order, and therefore has the characters outlined in its definition.

Cidaris (Eucidaris) tribuloides (Lamarck) PLATE 220. This sea-urchin is of moderate size, measuring up to 2¼ inches in diameter. The stout spines are about equal in length to the diameter of the test, but some individuals with shorter or longer spines are known, the latter, especially, from deeper water. The color is light brown shaded with a darker brown and sometimes mottled with white; some specimens vary toward olive-green, while others are red. In some cases, the spines are banded with purplish red and yellow. At times, they are covered with bryozoa and crusts of other marine growths, modifying their apparent coloration. This species is common in the West Indies in shallow water, often occurring in colonies in great abundance. It occurs at Bermuda, throughout the Bahamas, along the Florida coast, the Lesser Antilles, and the northern coast of South America to Brazil, and even ranges to the eastern Atlantic. It is found along the Atlantic Coast of the southern United States as far north as the Carolinas. It is, therefore, preeminently a southern and tropical species.

Order DIADEMATOIDEA (CENTRECHINOIDEA)

In this Order the general shape of the test and the position and arrangement of the apical system are similar to those of the preceding Order. The test is regular, round, and either spherical or flattened. The anal opening is in the center of the apical pole, and surrounded by the ocular and genital plates, fundamentally as in the Cidaroidea. But the peristome is different. Here, the zone of interambulacral plates is not continued over the peristome, though the radial or ambulacral series may be represented by one or a few plates in this area. Gills and gill-indentations are usually present at the margin of the test. On the surface of the test, the ambulacral plates themselves are usually fused into compound groups, as represented by the number of ambulacral pores in each, and the vestiges of their united edges. Both ambulacral and interambulacral plates have large primary tubercles and spines, while the secondaries often are as large as the primaries and tend to be arranged in regular series like them. The spines usually have no outer coat. The teeth are with or without a keel. Four kinds of pedicellariae are present. This Order includes all the "regular" echinoids, except those in the Order Cidaroidea, embracing hundreds of species; but only a few of the most typical, representing our region, can be included here, due to the limits of space.

Family Arbaciidae

These sea-urchins usually have short, stout, and smooth spines articulated on smooth tubercles without crenulations, one or more spines being on each interambulacral plate. The secondary spines, appressed, are not outstanding. The ambulacral plates are fused from, usually, three primary plates, with the pores in three series. The periproct is usually covered by four triangular valves, rarely five, to protect the anus. The tube-feet on the aboral surface are without suckers.

Arbacia punctulata (Lamarck) PLATE 220; COLOR PLATE XX, 3. The Purple Sea-urchin. The living animal has a test almost hidden by the multitude of long, stiff spines, which vary in shape and length in the different regions of the body. The apical pole is practically without spines, the apical plates and periproct being clearly exposed. All the spines are cylindrical on the general surface of the test, and fluted or grooved longitudinally. Those situated apically are acutely pointed, while the rest are blunt at the tip. On the under or oral side, the long spines have flattened but rounded tips, while short, spatulate spines immediately surround the peristome. On the oral side, and immediately surrounding the peristome, and extending out toward the oral periphery are ten groups of fine ambulacral perforations in the test, marking the position of ten clusters of very slender tube-feet, which can be extended to great length, as shown in the lower left-hand figure on PLATE 220. This species is widely distributed from Cape Cod to the Gulf of Mexico, in shallow water. It is the most common species of sea-urchin on the southern New England shores, and is particularly abundant from Woods Hole, Massachusetts, to New Haven, Connecticut. However, for some unexplained reason, its occurrence varies greatly from year to year, intervals of scarcity recurring from time to time. It is usually found on rocky or shelly bottoms, and large numbers hide in rock crevices, between the tides, or are seen on the bottoms of tide-pools, among the seaweed. The test of this species usually measures 1 to 2 inches in di-

PLATE 220

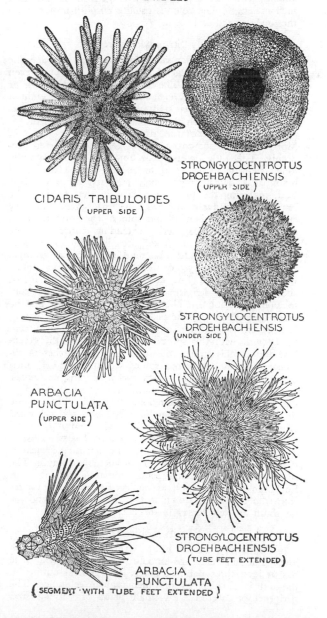

CIDARIS TRIBULOIDES
(UPPER SIDE)

STRONGYLOCENTROTUS
DROEHBACHIENSIS
(UPPER SIDE)

STRONGYLOCENTROTUS
DROEHBACHIENSIS
(UNDER SIDE)

ARBACIA
PUNCTULATA
(UPPER SIDE)

STRONGYLOCENTROTUS
DROEHBACHIENSIS
(TUBE FEET EXTENDED)

ARBACIA
PUNCTULATA
(SEGMENT WITH TUBE FEET EXTENDED)

ameter, while the larger spines average from ½ inch to 1 inch in length. The color is usually purplish brown, with the tube-feet red or brown.

Family Strongylocentrotidae

These are also regular sea-urchins, circular in shape, the fused groups of ambulacral plates having four to eleven pairs of pores in each. The test is without depressions or pits. The pedicellariae are of the globiferous type without lateral teeth, having a stalk with an extensible and re-tractile neck to which the globelike head is attached.

Strongylocentrotus droehbachiensis (O. F. Müller) PLATE 220; COLOR PLATE XX, 4. The Green Sea-urchin. This little green sea-urchin, with the remarkably long scientific name (said to be the longest zoological binomial known), is extremely common north of Cape Cod, replacing the previous species in that region. The test is comparatively low, with a broad arch, and very closely set with tubercles and spines. The former are in quite distinct vertical series extending entirely to the periproct, which has no naked area like that in *Arbacia*. The secondary tubercles also tend to a vertical arrange-ment. Usually, only two of the ocular plates are in contact with the periproct. The crowded spines are usually of about the same length, the primaries not being con-spicuously distinguishable. There are no spines on the oral-plates. The tridentate pedicellariae usually have broad, leaf-shaped valves. The color of the test is usually green-ish brown, with the spines almost always bright green. The test of this species measures 2 to 3½ inches in di-ameter, but the numerous spines seldom exceed ½ inch in length. This species prefers rocky bottoms, tide-pools, and rock crevices. It is very abundant between the tides on the rocky coast of northern New England with its wide tidal limits, hiding among the festoons of rock-weed (*Fucus* and *Ascophyllum*), and crawling around on the pool bottoms. This species, like *Arbacia,* has ten clusters of very extensible oral tube-feet, with pneumatic suckers, that can be stretched out for a considerable distance. The species is circumboreal, being found abundantly on European shores as well as on Pacific Coasts. It ranges from the tidal zone down to 650 fathoms. It extends as far south as New Jersey in the deeper waters.

Family Echinidae

In this family, the test has no depressions or pitlike hol-lows. The tubercles are smooth. Each ambulacral plate has at least three pairs of pores. The general outline of the test is circular, as in other regular echinoids. The periproct is covered with small plates of varying size.

There are peristomial gills, situated in shallow indentations of the peristome. The pedicellariae are globe-shaped with one or two teeth on either side of the valves. The attachment to the stalk is direct, without a neck.

Echinus norvegicus Düben & Koren PLATE 221. In this species, which may be a variety of *Echinus acutus* Lamarck, the general shape of the shell is somewhat more acute than globose in outline, but smaller and more depressed than the typical *Echinus acutus*. The spines are few and scattered on the upper side. The species is very variable in color, but is usually whitish, with a red-brown stripe along each vertical series of plates, which vary in width. Alternating, parallel brown and white lines often occur on the plate-margins. The lower part of the spines is usually reddish, the tips being white. *Echinus norvegicus*, either as a species or variety, is distinguished by five red-brown spots in a ring around the apical system. This form is very abundant on Georges and Browns Banks and off Cape Sable, Nova Scotia, in deep water varying from 888 to 1,497 fathoms, while, with its variants of the *Echinus acutus* series, it ranges from about 100 to 500 fathoms.

Echinometra subangularis (Leske) PLATE 221. The Rock-boring Sea-urchin. While this species is clearly a member of the Family Echinidae, yet it is elliptical in shape, sometimes with the suggestion of angularity in its outline, and the long axis of the body is oblique to the axis passing through the mouth and the madreporite. The primary spines are long and pointed, and about ⅘ inch in length. There are usually many small spines around the anus. The test, itself, measures 2 inches or less in length, and varies considerably in shape and proportions, as well as in color. The latter ranges usually from reddish brown to nearly black or violet. The spines vary from light green or pink, tipped with violet, to light or dark reddish brown. Often, more than half the spine is violet. This is generally known as the "rock-boring sea-urchin" due to its practice of living in rock crevices in shallow water. This is distinctly a littoral species. It ranges from the Carolinas southward to Florida and the West Indies and Brazil. It also occurs at Bermuda.

Family Toxopneustidae

The test, in this family, is approximately as wide as long. The surface is without depressions or pits. The ambulacral plates are fused, so that there are three or more pairs of pores to each. There are peristomial gills present, located in acute peristomial indentations. The heads of the pedicellariae are globe-shaped, but without lateral teeth, attaching directly to the stalk, without a neck.

Toxopneustes variegatus (Lamarck) PLATE 221.
The spines, in this species, are all short and slender, with
the tubercles tending to be of approximately the same size
and closely set in quite distinct rows. The peristome is
comparatively large. The diameter of the test, which is
approximately circular, is about ½ to ¾ inch. The color
varies greatly, ranging from deep violet or purple through
rose to bright green or white, or having combinations of
these hues. The spines are often tipped with reddish or
may be entirely rose-pink. This is the common sea-urchin
of our tropical waters, ranging from North Carolina to
the West Indies and Brazil. It is also found in Bermuda.
It occurs from low-water mark to 30 fathoms. It frequents sandy bottoms, often covering itself with bits of
seaweed and fragments of other material it may chance to
pick up.

Order CLYPEASTROIDEA

This Order includes echinoids with an elongate or
round, depressed, or flattened test. The mouth is centrally situated on the underside. The anal opening, for the
most part, is located on the underside, or at the posterior
margin of the disc, or exceptionally, on the upper side a
short distance from the hinder margin. There are no
peristomial gills or indentations. The upper and underside
of the test are usually braced interiorly by an elaborate
set of pillars and partitions, sometimes forming a network
surrounding the internal organs. In some cases this is
vestigial or wanting. The ambulacral plates are simple
(i.e., not fused). On the upper side, each pair of ambulacral openings is connected by a groove, and so grouped
that the system forms a flowerlike (petaloid) pattern. The
jaw apparatus (Aristotle's lantern) is strikingly developed.
The spines are very small, forming a close-set covering almost like a velvety coat, each spine mounted on a per-
forate tubercle. There are many tube-feet, many to each
plate, sometimes even invading the interambulacral system. The pedicellariae are present, but small and not
readily seen, and this is especially true of the sphaeridia,
which are located in grooves and are almost invisible. In
this Order and the succeeding one, the initial almost
radial symmetry of the echinoderms has been transformed
into a secondarily evolved bilateral symmetry.

Family Clypeastridae
(The Cake-urchins)

In this family, while the test is depressed, it is not discoidal. The mouth is centrally located on the underside.
The madreporite is in the center of the upper surface with

PLATE 221

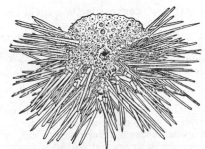

ECHINOMETRA SUBANGULARIS

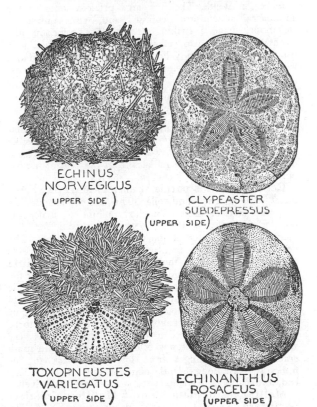

ECHINUS
NORVEGICUS
(UPPER SIDE)

CLYPEASTER
SUBDEPRESSUS
(UPPER SIDE)

TOXOPNEUSTES
VARIEGATUS
(UPPER SIDE)

ECHINANTHUS
ROSACEUS
(UPPER SIDE)

the five ambulacral areas radiating from it in petaloid fashion.

Clypeaster subdepressus Gray PLATE 221. The test is more or less five-sided but with sweeping rounded angles. It is quite flat, but usually raised in the center. There are five genital grooves. The color is yellowish, reddish, or deep brown. Adult specimens measure 6 to 7 inches in length, by 5 to 5⅝ inches wide. They occur from the tidal area to 40 fathoms and range from North Carolina to Brazil.

Echinanthus rosaceus (Linnaeus) PLATE 221. This large species is well known throughout the West Indies, being of quite common occurrence. It ranges from the Carolinas to the Bahamas and Barbados. It also occurs in the Greater Antilles. It is 4 to 6 inches in length and over 5 inches in width. The five large petaloid lobes of the ambulacral system are depressed and, with contrasting elevations, make a striking pattern. The color, in life, varies from reddish to yellowish or greenish brown. It is usually found on sandy bottoms below low-water mark, though, at times, it prefers open beaches where it is exposed to the surf.

Family Scutellidae
(The Sand-dollars)

The species in this family have a very flat, thin, circular test covered with a coating of very fine spines, with a silky or hairy feeling. The five-armed petal-like ambulacral figure on the upper side radiates from the central madreporite.

Echinarachnius parma (Lamarck) PLATE 222; COLOR PLATE XX, 5. The Sand-dollar. The circular shape, thin test, and size of these echinoids combine to make the popular name, sand-dollar, very appropriate for this species. The diameter of the test is about 3 inches. The petal-like rays of the ambulacral figure on the upper side of the disc are open at their outer ends. The mouth is in the center of the underside and the anal opening is at the edge of the test. The ambulacral areas on the underside are marked by the narrow, branching grooves which radiate from the central mouth. The hairy covering is purplish brown while the animal is in the water, but turns green when it is exposed to the air. This species is very abundant on sandy bottoms, often covering them in moderate depths. It ranges from low-water mark to 800 fathoms, from Long Island Sound northward. Flounders, cod, and haddock feed upon the sand-dollars extensively.

Mellita testudinata Klein [= **Mellita quinquiesperforata** (Leske)] PLATE 222; COLOR PLATE XX, 6. The Keyhole-urchin. The disc of this species is rounded, but

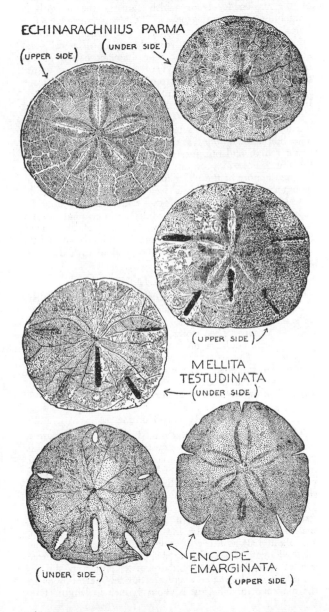

PLATE 222

ECHINARACHNIUS PARMA

(UPPER SIDE)

(UNDER SIDE)

(UPPER SIDE)

MELLITA
TESTUDINATA
(UNDER SIDE)

(UNDER SIDE)

ENCOPE
EMARGINATA
(UPPER SIDE)

flattened on the rear margin. The mouth is in the center of the underside, from which radiates the irregularly branching ambulacral grooves. The test is pierced by five holes. As seen on the upper side, one is interradial, the other four each being between the tip of a lateral petal and the margin of the disc. The diameter of the disc is from 2⅓ to 4⅖ inches in diameter. This species occurs sparingly in shallow water from Vineyard Sound to Cape Hatteras, but abundantly from that Cape to the West Indies.

Encope emarginata (Leske) PLATE 222. This species has a solid, stony disc, which is very variable in outline. The holes, or *lunules,* are typically six in number, five being radial, and one interradial, in the posterior part of the test. These may be entirely enclosed within the disc or one or more of the plates may be open to the margin at its outer end, thus making a deep indentation in its periphery. In some specimens all the radial lunules may be reduced to marginal notches, while the interradial lunules may remain or may be entirely sealed (see two lower figures in PLATE 222). The size may be 5 inches in length, with the breadth slightly less. The petaloid rays are open at their ends.

Order CASSIDULOIDEA

This is an aberrant Order. The test is round, somewhat elongate, and not flattened or disc-shaped. No peristomial gills are present. There is no internal supporting skeleton, and no lantern of Aristotle or other complex jaw apparatus. The ambulacra on the upper side may be simple or petaloid. The spines are quite small. The series of five groups on the lowermost ambulacral plates are usually larger, flattened, and bent over to protect the mouth. There is only one family in our region.

Family Cassidulidae

The ambulacra are not arranged in a petaloid pattern on the upper side of the test, but an imperfect one is present around the peristome on the underside. The mouth is somewhat anterior of the center. The anus opens posteriorly at the edge of the test in the middle of a small, depressed area marked by an encircling ridge.

Neolampas rostellata A. Agassiz PLATE 223. The test is rather flattened but arched on the upper side, shallowly concave on the lower side around the mouth, and about half as thick as wide, thus tending to a somewhat elongate, thick, saucer shape. There are only three genital pores around the madreporite, larger in the female than in the male. There are but few perforations in the madreporite. The test is about ⅖ inch in length. This species is commonly distributed throughout the West Indies in about 80 to 680 fathoms. It may sometime be found to occur off the Carolina coast.

Order SPATANGOIDEA
(The Heart-urchins)

The Order Spatangoidea includes echinoids with elongate tests that are rounded and not flattened. They are bilateral in symmetry, this feature obviously being secondary, due to the elongation or displacement of originally radial parts. The mouth is located anteriorly on the underside, and the anus posteriorly, instead of being centrally located as in the regular echinoids. The areas between the petaloid ambulacral regions (*interambulacra*) are of importance for classification, the posterior interambulacrum on the oral side being especially modified, its first plate often being specialized to form a lower lip, or *labrum,* which is prominently elevated as the posterior border of the mouth. The following plates are usually specially developed as a *sternum* or *plastron,* having a special function. Often, narrow bands of very small, close-set spines, covered with cilia, surround parts of or all of the petaloid patterns of ambulacral areas. These are known as *fascioles* and are of importance in moving water currents over certain areas, to keep them free from detritus. Pedicellariae of five types are conspicuously present, as well as sphaeridia.

Family Spatangidae

In this family the ambulacral region on the upper surface of the test has a petaloid pattern, with the arms more or less sunk below the level of the surface to form wider grooves, the anterior arm being hollowed more deeply than the rest. On the oral side, the labrum, formed by the first plate of the plastron, is quite prominent, partially overhanging the transverse, slitlike mouth, with its elongate peristome. A continuous fasciole closes the subanal region, apparently functioning to drive excreted material away from the body by its water currents.

Echinocardium cordatum (Pennant) PLATE 223. This is a little heart-shaped urchin about 3½ to 4 inches in length, covered with long, light yellow spines, except in the ambulacral areas, and with a deeply hollowed-out anterior ambulacral petal. This animal burrows in the sand to a depth of 8 to 10 inches, keeping a channel open to the surface by gluing the lining sand-grains together by means of a slime secreted by it, which also lines the cavity in which it rests. The frontal ambulacral groove is provided with unusually long and extensible tube-feet which have little fingerlike divisions at their tips instead of sucking-discs. These tube-feet reach out through the tube-opening, one at a time, and capture small animals and food particles dragging them down to the buccal tube-feet, which transmit them to the mouth for consumption. Besides the subanal fasciole, there is also present in this species an inner fasciole surrounding the frontal ambulacrum and the apical system of plates, apparently to keep these regions free of detritus by the motion of its cilia. The paired interambulacral regions have both long and short spines. The mouth is surrounded with an area bearing peculiar buccal tube-feet. They are short, thick, and pointed, with many club-shaped processes. Most of the tube-feet in the petaloid areas have broad, flat bases, but no pneumatic disc, being respiratory in function. The pedicellariae are tridentate, having three leaflike valves with serrate edges; or they are globe-shaped, mounted on stalks with spicules imbedded in them. The plastron has an abundance of long, peculiarly curved spines with flattened tips which are the chief organs of locomotion, the tube-feet not being adapted for this purpose. This species occurs from the tidal zone to a depth of about 121 fathoms on European and British coasts. It is said to be cosmopolitan, but its occurrence on North American shores needs verification.

Echinocardium flavescens (Müller) PLATE 223. In this species the frontal ambulacral petal is not sunk below the surface of the test, and there is only a very slight depression or indication of a notch at the anterior end of the test. The tube-feet here are fairly sparse but in regular series. The labrum is prolonged backward. Otherwise it is quite similar to the preceding species, though it is somewhat smaller. The color, in life, is yellowish rose. The vertical distribution and range are similar to *Echinocardium cordatum,* with the same need for verification of its extent.

Family Hemiasteridae

The test, in this family, is more or less heart-shaped. The frontal ambulacral area is quite widened and somewhat sunk below the general surface. The first plate of the posterior ambulacral region, on the underside, forms a prominent labrum overhanging the transverse mouth and peristome. The plastron below the periproct is not especially developed.

Schizaster (Briaster) fragilis (Düben & Koren) PLATE 224. The test of this species is more or less flattened but is somewhat higher posteriorly. The anterior margin is deeply notched. The frontal petal of the ambulacral area is considerably deepened below the level of the others. The anterior paired petals are much longer than the posterior pair, which are quite short and

PLATE 223

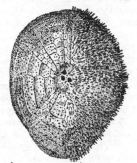

(UNDER SIDE) (UPPER SIDE)

NEOLAMPAS ROSTELLATA

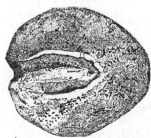
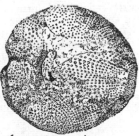

(UPPER SIDE) (UNDER SIDE)

ECHINOCARDIUM CORDATUM

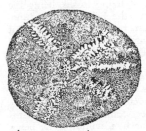
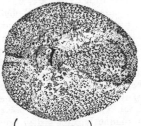

(UPPER SIDE) (UNDER SIDE)

ECHINOCARDIUM FLAVESCENS

stumpy. There is a distinct median keel in the posterior interambulacral region. The apical plates and the whole ambulacral system have their center posterior to the middle point of the test. There are only three genital pores, with none in the madreporite. The heads of the conspicuous pedicellariae are globular with a tooth at the end of each valve, the poison gland opening at its base. The color is dark brown. The test is upwards of 3½ inches in length. This is a circumboreal species, ranging on our shores from the Arctic to Florida, in depths from 36 to 711 fathoms, on muddy bottoms.

Moira atropos (Lamarck) PLATE 224. This species is egg-shaped, high-bodied, and with a depth about equal to its width. The apical area is back of the middle. All the ambulacral grooves are very deep slits. On the underside, the mouth and peristome are near the anterior margin, with a conspicuous labrum overhanging the mouth. Hubert Lyman Clark * states that this species spends its life buried in soft mud, and that the extraordinarily deep and narrow ambulacral furrows probably enable it to maintain a current of water from which the sediment has been strained, flowing over the tube-feet of the petaloid areas, which apparently are adapted for respiratory and excretory functions. He considers it, in many respects, one of the most highly specialized of the echinoids. The size of the body is approximately 1½ inches long, 1 inch wide, and 1 inch high. It ranges from North Carolina southward to the West Indies. It is common in shallow water.

CLASS CRINOIDEA
(The Sea-lilies, the Feather-stars)

The Class Crinoidea is regarded as one of the five Classes of the Phylum Echinoderma as it exists at the present time. They are, in reality, living fossils, being the remnants of a great Subphylum, the Pelmatozoa, echinoderms attached to the sea-bottom by a base or stem, that existed in great abundance and diversification in the Mississippian and even in the Devonian Periods.

About two thousand fossil species of crinoids are known and about eight hundred living species. Although they are fastened to a stem at some time during their life, many of them later become detached and swim freely about. Certain species, however, remain on their stems permanently, unless they become free-swimming by being broken off accidentally.

* "A handbook of the littoral echinoderms of Porto Rico and the other West Indian Islands, N. Y. Academy of Sciences." *Sci. Survey of Porto Rico and the Virgin Islands*, 16(1):80, 90. 1933.

PLATE 224

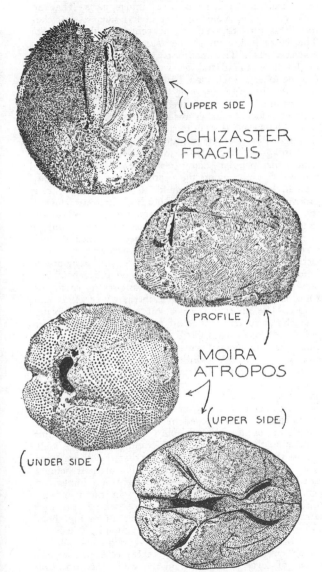

(UPPER SIDE)

SCHIZASTER
FRAGILIS

(PROFILE)

MOIRA
ATROPOS

(UPPER SIDE)

(UNDER SIDE)

Like other members of the Phylum, they are built on a radiating pattern of five similar parts. They are attached by the center of their aboral side, so that their mouth is upward, and in the center of the oral disc. The latter is known as the *theca,* or *calyx* (see INDEX DIAGRAM 225). The mouth is pentagonal and from its angles, five ambulacral grooves extend radially toward the periphery, each one branching like a "Y" before reaching the edge. Each of the ten grooves, so formed, is continued on one of the ten branched radial arms, each of which branches twice, successively, in the same way. The branchlets, in turn, give rise, on either side, to a series of close-set, but alternating, smaller branchlets or *pinnules,* giving each arm a featherlike appearance, hence the popular name sea-feather. The ambulacral grooves continue along the ventral (upper) side of each branch, branchlet, and pinnule, to the very tip. These grooves are lined with cilia, beating vigorously toward the mouth, so that any small organism or food-particle caught in the net of the spread feathery arms will be swept into it. Ambulacral appendages extended through a row of pores on either side of the groove are sensitive tactile organs and are also respiratory and excretory in function. Cilia are lacking, however, on the general surface of the body, and the crinoid possesses no special organs of sight or hearing. The theca, or calyx, is cup-shaped. The upper surface is soft without visible plates. The aboral center is attached to the stem by five interradial polygonal plates, fitted neatly together (PLATE 226). These are the *basals,* which are closely welded to five *radials,* which interlock with them above. Around the edge of the disc, located interradially, are five pairs of unbranched spines, the *oral pinnules.* The anus is mounted on the summit of the anal papilla, near the edge of the disc, between two of the oral pinnules. The outer plates of the theca are continued on to the branched arms in the form of disc-shaped joints (*brachials*), becoming smaller on the branchlets, and becoming very small joints out to the tip of each pinnule, so that the entire structure is extremely flexible. The stalk, also, is jointed, and bears circlets of five to ten pointed and jointed appendages (*cirri*) at regular intervals. In the free-swimming species a circlet of a number of jointed cirri, each terminated by a curving claw, is attached to the aboral end of the theca (PLATE 227). The mouth, which has no jaws, opens internally into a short oesophagus, which empties into a wide stomach, equipped with a series of oval extensions in its wall, the *stomachic pouches,* and with a pair of branched *hepatic diverticula.* The stomach extends halfway around the internal periph-

PLATE 225

ANATOMY OF TYPICAL CRINOIDS

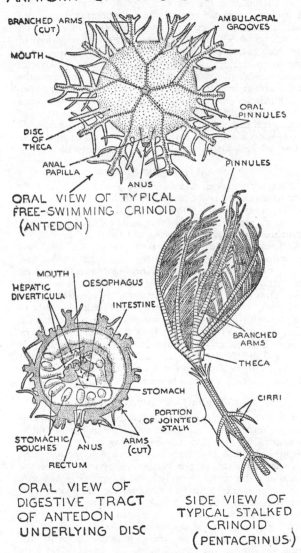

BRANCHED ARMS (CUT)

AMBULACRAL GROOVES

MOUTH

ORAL PINNULES

DISC OF THECA

ANAL PAPILLA

ANUS

PINNULES

ORAL VIEW OF TYPICAL FREE-SWIMMING CRINOID (ANTEDON)

MOUTH

HEPATIC DIVERTICULA

OESOPHAGUS

INTESTINE

BRANCHED ARMS

THECA

STOMACH

CIRRI

STOMACHIC POUCHES

ANUS

ARMS (CUT)

PORTION OF JOINTED STALK

RECTUM

ORAL VIEW OF DIGESTIVE TRACT OF ANTEDON UNDERLYING DISC

SIDE VIEW OF TYPICAL STALKED CRINOID (PENTACRINUS)

ery of the theca, then narrows somewhat to continue the rest of the way around as the intestine, through the *rectum,* in the anal-opening on the upper surface of the disc. Surrounding the digestive system is the body-cavity, or coelom, as in the rest of the echinoderms. It is filled with a network of connective tissue fibers in the theca, as well as blood mixed with sea water. Prolongations of the body-cavity penetrate the arms as well as all the branchlets and pinnules. A ring-canal around the mouth, together with five radial canals branching throughout the entire arm-system, form the ambulacral system. The tube-feet bordering the ambulacral groove have no ampullae or terminal sucking discs. The sexes are separate. The ovaries or testes also branch and subbranch through all the arm-divisions, releasing ova or sperm through minute pores, in the body, or breaks in the pinnule walls.

Family Bourgueticrinidae

These are stalked crinoids with a slender, gracefully formed theca and branching arms, with five basal and five radial plates, usually closely compacted together, with few or no cirri on the long stalk, and with rootlike, many-branched appendages extending out from it.

Rhizocrinus lofotensis Sars PLATE 226. The basals are fused together without sutures to form a solid cup. There may be four to seven branching arms. The slender stalk may be nearly 3 inches in length with about sixty-five joints and no cirri, rooted to the bottom by its anchoring appendages. The arms are about ½ inch in length, with a half-dozen pinnules branching, fernlike from each side. The color, in life, is a handsome shade of yellow, though grayish in some species. This species is widely distributed in the North Atlantic. On our coast it occurs from the Arctic to the latitude of Florida, in depths ranging from 77 to 1,640 fathoms.

Family Antedonidae

These crinoids pass through a stalked stage (*Pentacrinus* stage) but become detached and free-living as adults (*Comatulids*). In this free-swimming stage, the only vestiges of a stalk that remains are the pentagonal welded *centrodorsal plate,* at the bottom or aboral side of the theca, and the circlet of curved and jointed *cirri* that arise from it, usually with a terminal spine. These cirri articulate from the centrodorsal plate by means of sockets into which their first joint is set. In some families this socket is bordered by a horseshoe-shaped rim. In the Family Antedonidae this rim is absent. There are ten arms, dividing at the second joint. The centrodorsal plate may be hemispherical, conical, or discoidal in shape.

PLATE 226

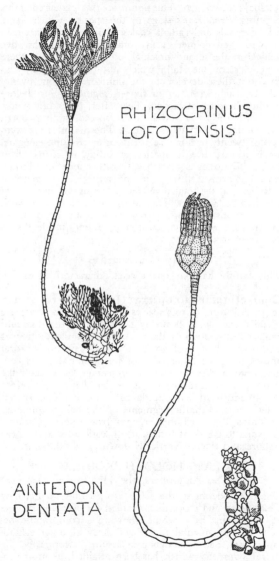

RHIZOCRINUS
LOFOTENSIS

ANTEDON
DENTATA

Antedon dentata (Say) (= **Hathrometra tenella** [Retzius]) PLATE 226. The figure on this plate represents the young *Pentacrinus* stage of the species, which has a theca of basals and radials coalesced into a compact cup, and with ten jointed arms branching from the five brachials at the second brachial joint. In this stage, there are no cirri on the stalk, which has thirty to forty segments, but these develop to the number of about twenty to thirty, each with ten to sixteen segments, just before the adult becomes detached. Thereafter, the adult swims about with the arms and pinnules spread, settling down on its circlet of cirri when at rest. The pinnules are composed of twenty to thirty segments and are quite elongate. This is a very fragile species, shedding its arms when handled. The color is grayish with rather indefinite brown bands. The arms of this species measure 3½ to 4 inches in length, so that the total diameter of the swimming animal is about 7 to 8 inches. This species is circumboreal with local variations, ranging, on our coast, from the Arctic to Massachusetts and New York. It is found in depths of about 15 to 975 fathoms.

Family Comasteridae

This family has but one species, characterized as follows:

Comactinia echinoptera (J. Müller) PLATE 227. The general form of this species is shown on the plate. As to details, the mouth is not in the center of the disc, and is replaced in position by the anus. The ambulacral grooves are also off center and are of unequal length. The oral pinnules have the outer edge of the terminal joints continued into a thin, triangular projection, as a comblike structure. The centrodorsal plate is disc-shaped. There are about twenty cirri without dorsal processes. This species has ten arms, with the segments of the genital pinnules very short. Its distribution ranges from North Carolina southward to the West Indies. It is occasionally found near the shore and extends vertically down to 280 fathoms.

CLASS HOLOTHUROIDEA
(The Sea-cucumbers, the Holothurians)

The echinoderms in this Class are peculiar in that they are elongated and wormlike, adapted for creeping on one side, the group, as a whole, showing a compromise between the fundamental radial symmetry of other echinoderm classes, and a tendency to assume, secondarily, the bilateral symmetry which has been attained, as most progressive and effective, by most of the higher groups in the Animal Kingdom.

Retention of a radial symmetry in holothurians is

PLATE 227

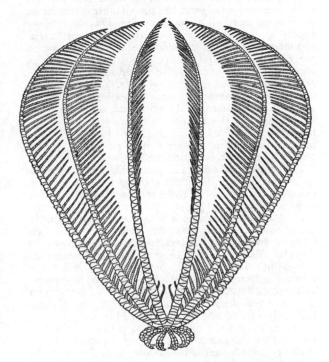

COMACTINIA ECHINOPTERA

CIRRUS (DORSAL
AND LATERAL VIEWS)

CENTRODORSAL
(VENTRAL VIEW)

RADIAL PENTAGON
(DORSAL VIEW)

shown by viewing them from the head end in an antero-posterior direction, when it will be noted also that the radial arrangement of parts, like that of other echinoderms, tends to be based on multiples of five. For example, see Figure 7, in COLOR PLATE XX, which represents a sea-cucumber (*Cucumaria frondosa*) with ten tentacles arranged around the central circular mouth. In this species, also, the tube-feet occur in five bands at equal distances around the practically cylindrical body. Thus, it follows, at least to this extent, the same principle of five-starred arrangement exhibited by the brittle-star, sea-urchins, and sand-dollars also shown on the same plate. A similar tendency is exhibited in certain internal structures, like the five longitudinal muscle bands, spaced at approximately equal distances around the inside of the body-wall. There are, as in all echinoderms, variations as to a greater or less number of such parts, but the general pentamerous pattern is obvious as well as the tendency for such parts to form a radiating pattern around the central body-axis. Throughout the echinoderms, however, the conflicting bilateral tendency has remained as a vestigial trait from the bilateral ancestors of the echinoderms, as indicated by their larval stages. As will be seen, it is very strongly developed in various groups, in certain features, in both the external and internal anatomy. A dissection of the internal structure of a typical holothurian is shown in INDEX PLATE 228, in which the excellent diagram of Wesley Coe has been redrawn and adapted for this field book.

The elongate bodies of holothurians have a mouth at one end surrounded by a peristome equipped with a circle of usually ten arborescently branched tentacles, rising from a calcareous ring surrounding the oesophagus, and connected with the base of the tentacles by a thin-walled neck-region. The elongate tube, or sac-shaped body, terminates posteriorly in the *cloacal aperture,* or *anus,* the opening of which is strengthened by five radially arranged calcareous plates, each armed with an *anal tooth.* In many holothurians, as already mentioned, there are five tracts of tube-feet or ambulacra extending longitudinally along the outside of the body from the "neck" to the anal region. Since the animal habitually creeps on the same side (which, therefore, in this group, may be known as the ventral side), the three most ventral tracts differ from the two dorsal sets in having tube-feet with pneumatic suckers at their pits, adapted for creeping, while the latter usually have no suckers and are fingerlike and sensitive, adapted for respiration and sensation.

Many species, including *Thyone briareus* (INDEX PLATE 228; COLOR PLATE XX, 8), have tube-feet scattered thickly

PLATE 228

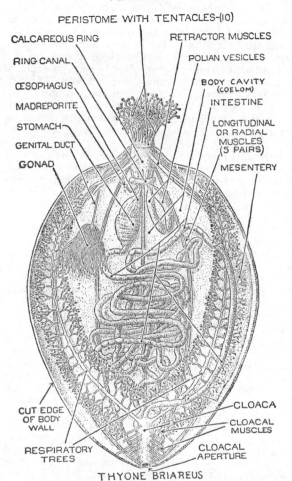

PERISTOME WITH TENTACLES—(10)

CALCAREOUS RING

RING CANAL

ŒSOPHAGUS

MADREPORITE

STOMACH

GENITAL DUCT

GONAD

RETRACTOR MUSCLES

POLIAN VESICLES

BODY CAVITY (COELOM)

INTESTINE

LONGITUDINAL OR RADIAL MUSCLES (5 PAIRS)

MESENTERY

CUT EDGE OF BODY WALL

RESPIRATORY TREES

CLOACA

CLOACAL MUSCLES

CLOACAL APERTURE

THYONE BRIAREUS

INTERNAL ANATOMY OF A TYPICAL HOLOTHURIAN

(BODY OPENED BY MEDIAN INCISION DOWN RIGHT VENTRAL INTERRADIUS AND BODY WALL REFLECTED TO EACH SIDE) and indiscriminately over the entire body; while others like *Psolus* (COLOR PLATE XXI, 2, 2a; 3, 3a) have a distinct sole bordered with tube-feet. The ten oral tentacles, likewise, are ambulacral in character, actuated by the ambulacral system. In *Synapta* (PLATE 232) there are no tube-feet whatever, the oral tentacles alone representing the external appendages of the ambulacral system. The skin, in certain species, is thick, leathery, and muscular (*Thyone*). In others (*Synapta*), it is thin, delicate, and transparent. The muscular body-wall of *Thyone* is capable of vigorous contractions and is one of the chief means of propulsion and digging, while the tube-feet function for creeping over the surface.

Internally, below the calcareous ring, the lower part of the delicate, thin-walled oesophagus expands and leads into the thick-walled, muscular stomach, which narrows to be succeeded by the exceedingly long, thin-walled intestine. Its many coils, involving a length several times that of the body, with S-shaped loops, pass down to the vicinity of the anus, being held in place by a mesentery attached to a neighboring radial muscle. Then it passes anteriorly again, still coiling and supported by another radial mesentery, back to the region of the stomach. Finally, it turns again on the right side, and, attached to the right radial mesentery, returns to the mid-posterior region to empty into the upper end of the muscular cloaca, which opens by the cloacal aperture, or anus, to the outside.

From the upper angles of the cloaca rise the two respiratory trees. These are long, tapering, thin-walled tubes, extending one on each side, nearly to the anterior end of the body-cavity, giving off treelike branches from either side. When oxygen-bearing sea water is pumped into them by the expansions and contractions of the muscular cloaca, it fills the branches to their delicate tips until they are turgid, and forces the water through into the surrounding coelomic fluid of the body cavity, producing pressure against the body-wall, thus enabling the animal to keep its shape at the same time that the blood is aerated. The walls of the cloaca are equipped with strong circular muscles and also with radiating muscles extending from its walls on all sides, and inserted in the neighboring body-wall. By the contraction of these muscles, the interior of the cloaca is expanded, drawing in sea water. Then the circular muscles squeeze the cloaca, forcing the water through the respiratory trees. A repetition of the action also draws the refuse from the rectum and discharges it to the outside, so that this rhythmic action gets rid of detritus at the same time that it purifies and aerates the system, keeping the body turgid, meanwhile. Five paired longitudinal muscles run the whole length of the body, along the walls of the body-cavity, while the body-wall, itself, is lined with powerful transverse muscle-bands. The contraction of the latter squeezes water out of the cloacal opening, at the same time lengthening the body, while the longitudinal muscles act in the contrary direction, shortening the body, the pressure in the body-cavity being restored by the water pumped in through the respiratory trees. A series of five powerful muscle-bands (the *retractor muscles*) is attached to the calcareous ring, extending back diagonally and inserting on the longitudinal muscles near the middle of the body-wall. The contraction of these pulls into the body-cavity the entire anterior portion of the body including the tentacles. These muscle-bands are sometimes split into two bands for a part of their length, before inserting on the double longitudinal muscles.

Another part of the ambulacral or water-vascular system, is the *ring-canal* which surrounds the outer side of the calcareous ring investing the oesophagus. This ring has a series of ten bulblike ampullae connected with the bases of the oral tentacles, and two or three elongate Polian vesicles. When they contract, they force the water they contain into the interior of the hollow tentacles, thus enabling the latter to distend and lengthen. The water is renewed and kept tense by the small "stone-canal" and the madreporite, with which it is connected. We have seen that the madreporite of the sea-star opens directly to the outside. In the holothurian, however, it opens into the body-cavity, and, by the uniform motion of the cilia on its surface, it draws fluid into the ring-canal, thus effectuating the action of the oral tentacles. These latter organs may extend out for considerable distances into the surrounding mud or sand, capturing small organisms or collecting sandy or muddy particles with organic remains in them. The tentacles then contract and transfer this food material to the mouth, which rejects the indigestible material and passes the remainder into the alimentary tract to be assimilated.

The ring-canal also opens into five ambulacral tubes which run the full length of the body and are situated between the paired retractor muscle bands and connect with the ampullae of the outer surface of the body. The reproductive system consists of a single gonad, having the form of a brushlike cluster of filaments. This discharges the sexual products through a genital duct to the outside by means of a pore situated on the mid-dorsal side of the head between the bases of the two dorsal tentacles. The sexes are separate in the holothuroids, except in the genus *Mesothuria* and in the Family Synaptidae, where the gonads develop both ova and sperm, but at different times. The egg hatches out as a free-swimming *Auricula* larva, which swims about for a time by means of its convoluted tracts of cilia. Later on, these tracts break up into parallel bands surrounding the now barrel-shaped larva. After a few weeks, this larval stage metamorphoses into a small sea-cucumber.

The previous classes of echinoderms have a skeleton of closely interlocking calcareous plates. The holothurians, however, have no continuous skeleton; but, imbedded in the thick, leathery skin of most species, there are many small, sometimes microscopical, calcareous plates, not connected together, but sometimes so numerous as to add considerable stiffness to the integument; at other times, the plates are scattered or even lacking. In one family, the Psolidae, they overlap each other like scales. These plates are often of beautifully symmetrical designs, resembling wheels, anchors, or round tables with a central standard. Each species has a characteristic series of plates, so they are useful in classification. To utilize them for this purpose, a piece of the outer skin must be cleared in Canada balsam or Javelle water and examined with a microscope in watch glasses or on a microscope slide.

Except for the Synaptidae, the sea-cucumbers bury themselves in the sea-bottom by lying out flat upon it and removing the particles of sand or mud by pushing them continually from beneath them by means of their ventral tube-feet, so that their bodies gradually sink below the surface, completely hidden except for the head with its tentacles and the anal aperture. These usually project, unless disturbed, the tentacles continually searching for food, and the anus, by the forcible contractions and expansions of the cloaca, drawing in and ejecting streams of water. Surrounding the cloacal opening are extremely sensitive papillae. Even if a shadow falls across them, their sensitive perception of light and shade causes the cloaca to contract violently, throwing a jet of water for some distance. When violently disturbed, the holothurian will contract its body so powerfully that it will eject the greater part of its internal organs through its thin neck wall. In some cases, the animal dies thereafter. In others, it regenerates the lost organs and goes on living. If holothurians are cut apart, the section with the head-region will regenerate all the rest of the anatomy. The sections having no head, however, may live for a time, but with no power of regeneration, and soon die.

The Class Holothuridea is divided into five Orders, as follows: (1) *Elasipoda*; (2) *Aspidochirota*; (3) *Dendrochirota*; (4) *Molpadonia*; (5) *Apoda*.

PLATE 229

MESOTHURIA INTESTINALIS
(SIDE VIEW)

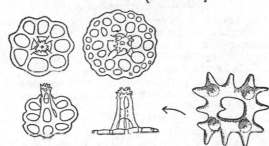

MESOTHURIA INTESTINALIS
(CALCAREOUS)
DEPOSITS

(CALCAREOUS)
DEPOSITS

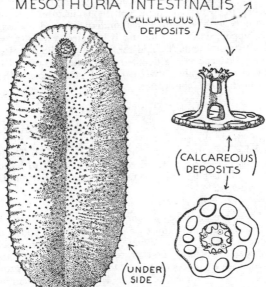

(UNDER)
SIDE

BENTHODYTES GIGANTEA

Order ELASIPODA

In this Order, the tentacles have shield-shaped ends, and tube-feet are usually present. There are no retractor muscles and no internal respiratory trees. Many of the calcareous bodies are in the form of pointed rods. They are deep-sea forms, occasionally brought to the surface by fishermen.

Family Psychropotidae

This family is characterized by the elongate, bisymmetrical, depressed or arched body with a thick, gelatinous integument. There is a border of appendages around the ventral surface. There is a circlet of large tentacles with a broad disclike top. Tube-feet are present along the midline on the ventral side. The calcareous bodies are sparse, but usually are spinous rods, either simple or cross-shaped with a central projection.

Benthodytes gigantea Verrill PLATE 229. This holothurian was originally brought up in a dredge off the New England coast and described by Verrill. It is a huge species, measuring up to 18 inches in length and 5 to 6 inches in width, of firm, gelatinous texture, and quite translucent. The body is flat underneath and arched on the upper side. The mouth is situated ventrally, with about twenty tentacles, and the anus is on the dorsal side. The tube-feet are in a double row on the mid-ventral line. It occurs in depths between 938 and about 2,000 fathoms in considerable abundance.

Order ASPIDOCHIROTA

These holothurians, like those of the previous order, have shield-shaped tentacles, tube-feet, and no retractor muscles. Respiratory trees, however, are present. The calcareous bodies are pointed rods, tables, and also buttons. The body is bilaterally symmetrical and either cylindrical or flattened.

Family Synallactidae

These are also deep-sea forms of fairly large size. The tube-feet are much reduced and the calcareous bodies also reduced or lacking. When present, they are tables, C-shaped structures, and at times, buttons. The stone-canal, instead of opening into the body-cavity, is usually in contact with the body-wall. These species often have foreign bodies adhering to their skin, such as pteropod shells, sponge spicules, etc.

Mesothuria intestinalis (Ascanius) PLATE 229. The mouth is terminal but slightly ventral in this species, while the anus is posterior. The body, for the most part, is cylindrical, narrowing toward both ends, without a marginal fringe. There are twelve to twenty tentacles. The skin is thin, with calcareous bodies in the form of tables. There are no C-shaped spicules. The general coloration, in life, is grayish white, slightly tinted with violet or pink. This species is hermaphroditic, but the sexual products ripen and are discharged at different times. It grows to 12 inches in length and lives on muddy bottoms, covering itself with various kinds of foreign material, including shell fragments. It occurs in depths of from 10 to more than 1,000 fathoms.

Order DENDROCHIROTA

The most outstanding characters peculiar to this order are the arborescent tentacles, the presence of retractor muscles capable of withdrawing the tentacles and anterior part of the body into the body-cavity, the presence of well-developed respiratory trees, the stone-canal with its madreporite hanging freely within the body-cavity, the gonads located on both sides of the dorsal mesentery, and the calcareous plates which are irregular and fenestrated with openings. The tentacles are very extensible and utilized for capturing food.

Family Cucumariidae

The body of the holothurians in this family is spindle-shaped and cylindrical. There is no ventral flattened surface or any indication of a distinct sole.

Cucumaria frondosa (Gunnerus) COLOR PLATE XX, 7. This species has a thick-walled cylindrical body narrowing toward the rounded anal end, and somewhat toward the base of the oral tentacles. There are ten branching, treelike tentacles and the tube-feet are arranged in five longitudinal radial tracts, with a few scattered sparsely over the interradial regions. They can be retracted completely or may be extended as much as 1 inch in anchoring and manipulating the body. This sea-cucumber well deserves the name because of its shape and size, which varies from 6 to 12 inches in length and 3 to 4 inches in thickness. The color is reddish brown, lighter underneath. It is the largest species on our shores and is found from Nantucket northward, being especially abundant on the rocky coast of northern Massachusetts and Maine. It is also circumboreal, occurring in large numbers on the British and European Coasts. It abounds along the lower tide limits, hiding under kelp, in rock crevices, and in tide-pools, its expanded bushy tentacles presenting a magnificent appearance. It ranges from the tidal zone to a depth of 200 fathoms.

Cucumaria pulcherrima (Ayres) PLATE 230. This is a much smaller species varying from 1½ to 2 inches in length. There are ten much-branched tentacles, the two ventral being shorter than the rest, like those in *Thyone briareus*. The five ambulacral tracts, each having two double rows of tube-feet, are very distinct, with none on the interradii. It ranges from Vineyard Haven to South Carolina, but is seldom seen living in shallow water in the northern part of its territory. Nevertheless, it is frequently cast ashore after storms, especially entangled with seaweed. It is more of a shallow-water animal in the sheltered muddy coves of North Carolina where it is often found on eelgrass. Its ovate body narrows at both ends. The color is white or pale yellow.

Thyone briareus (Lesueur) COLOR PLATE XX, 8; INDEX PLATE 228. The Common Thyone. The body is elongate, changing to ovate, depending on degree of inflation. There are ten treelike tentacles. The tube-feet are scattered thickly over the surface. The length is 4 to 5 inches and the color, dull brown or olive to black. The internal anatomy is fully described in INDEX PLATE 228 and the neighboring text, where its habits also are dealt with briefly. The species is found from Vineyard Sound southward. It is quite common in shallow, muddy water.

Thyone scabra Verrill PLATE 230. The Rough-skinned Thyone. This is a related but much smaller species, seldom exceeding 2 inches in length. The most striking peculiarity is the multiplicity of the calcareous plates in its integument. They are so numerous and so closely situated that the entire body-surface is extremely rough. The calcareous plates are irregular plates pierced by a dozen or more holes, with a small upright or handle in the middle. The species ranges from Georges Bank and the Bay of Fundy to Vineyard Sound and possibly Delaware Bay, from shallow water to more than 600 fathoms.

Thyone unisemita (Stimpson) PLATE 230. The Single-striped Thyone. The body of this sea-cucumber is curved so that the ends give it the appearance of a shallow U. It is fairly stout in the middle and tapered toward both extremities. The tube-feet are uniformly distributed over the dorsal and lateral surfaces, but on the ventral side there is only one double row along the median line with a bare area on either side, giving it the appearance of a single stripe; hence its name. The coloration of the body is white, flesh-colored, or yellowish white, with the tentacles orange-yellow. There are ten tentacles, the two ventral tentacles being shorter than the others, which are long and slender, sparsely branching above the stalk. The calcareous plates are flat with many holes on the irregular units, but with four holes on the more regular ones. The species ranges from the Banks of Newfoundland to southern New England and Long Island Sound, but

PLATE 230

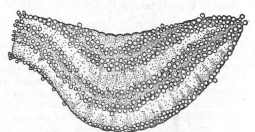

CUCUMARIA PULCHERRIMA
(AMBULACRAL AREAS AND ARRANGEMENT OF
TUBE FEET)

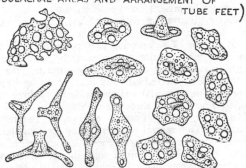

CUCUMARIA PULCHERRIMA
(CALCAREOUS PLATES.
UPPER LEFT-HAND
PLATE FROM TENTACLE,
THREE LOWER LEFT-
HAND PLATES FROM
TUBE-FEET, ALL OTHERS
FROM BODY WALL)

THYONE
SCABRA

THYONE
UNISEMITA

sparsely rather than abundantly. It occurs on sandy bottoms from 17 to 22 fathoms.

Family Psolidae

The species in this family have a more or less flattened body with a sharply defined ventral sole. The dorsal and lateral sides are covered with large plates, overlapping like imbricated scales. The ventral side is flattened with a sharp, limiting border to form an oval or elongate sole, with a tract of tube-feet, two to three rows wide, completely encircling the central bare space of the sole, itself, with a triangle of tube-feet projecting inward along the median line anteriorly and posteriorly. There are ten to fifteen much-branched tentacles. Scattered tube-feet may or may not be present on the dorsal side.

Psolus phantapus (Strussenfeldt) COLOR PLATE XXI, 2, 2a, 2b. The dorsal side has an evenly convex, dome-shaped outline. The anterior and posterior ends of the body are turned prominently upward, the former with the mouth and crown of ten branching tentacles; the latter, tapering like an erected tail, and bearing the anal opening at the tip. The tentacular stalk is divided into three slender, tapering branches, of three sizes: a long, a middle-sized, and a short, stubby branch, each with serrated side-branchlets. The ventral sole is almost rectangular. The color is yellowish brown with the scales outlined in darker brown; the peristome, pink; and the tentacles mottled with darker brown. This holothurian is fed upon by the Cod, the large Sun-stars (*Solaster*), and other species of sea-star. The length of this species is about 6 inches when fully grown. It ranges from the Arctic to Cape Cod, and is circumboreal, being also found from Spitzbergen to Britain. Vertically, it occurs from the low-water mark to 150 fathoms.

Psolus fabricii (Düben & Koren) COLOR PLATE XXI, 3, 3a, 3b, 3c. The Scarlet Psolus. This remarkably brilliant *Psolus* was collected by the author in Frenchmens Bay, Mount Desert Island, in 1928, in about 10 fathoms, and was identified by him as *Psolus fabricii* (Düben & Koren). The dorsal and lateral sides are covered by imbricated scales. The peristome is longer than in the preceding species and the ten tentacles have closely arborescent branches, each arising from a stalk that divides into three trunks of three graduated lengths, the anterior being the longest, and the posterior much the shortest. The anal projection is relatively short as compared with the previous species. The sole is clearly defined, broader in proportion to the length as compared with *Psolus phantapus*. The tube-feet form a similar encircling border around the margin with a triangular projection from the ambulacral

PLATE 231

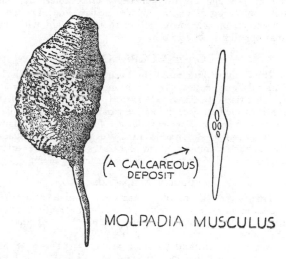

(A CALCAREOUS) DEPOSIT

MOLPADIA MUSCULUS

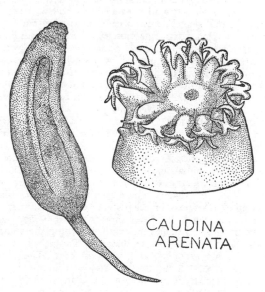

CAUDINA ARENATA

border pointing inward, anteriorly and posteriorly, but not continuing along the whole median line. The anal projection, or tail, forms only a short elevation with the anal opening at its summit.

Order MOLPADONIA

The body is thick and cylindrical, constricted anteriorly and enlarging posteriorly to a rounded termination, from which arises an elongated, narrow, tapering tail. There are no tube-feet, except for five small clusters of papillae around the anus. The tentacles are finger-shaped, usually with ampullae. Respiratory trees are present and usually the retractor muscles. The calcareous plates are often anchor-shaped. Fifteen tentacles are usually present.

Family Molpadiidae

This is the only family of the Order and therefore has the same characters. In most species, there are fifteen cylindrical tentacles, usually slightly branched or divided at their tips.

Molpadia musculus Risso PLATE 231. There are fifteen fingerlike tentacles and no tube-feet. The body is constricted anteriorly and expanded posteriorly, especially on the ventral side. There is a slender, tapering tail. There are well-developed retractor muscles. The calcareous bodies are narrowly spindle-shaped, with the median portion slightly expanded and pierced by four holes. These are present throughout the body. The species is cosmopolitan, at least in the Northern Hemisphere, and is present along our North Atlantic seaboard, the vertical range being roughly from 55 to 618 fathoms.

Caudina arenata Gould PLATE 231. This interesting species has a cylindrical body, without tube-feet, tapering abruptly posteriorly to a long, narrow tail about one third the length of the body proper. The anterior part of the animal narrows to the circlet of tentacles surrounding the mouth. These are fifteen in number, cylindrical in shape, and each with four short, fingerlike divisions or digits at the tip. Internally, each is actuated by an ampulla. The body, itself, varies from 4 to 7 inches in length, including the tail, and from about ½ to ⅞ inch in diameter. The skin is smooth or with fine granules, and is translucent. The cloacal opening is at the end of the tail, surrounded by five sensitive papillae. The color of the living animal varies from flesh-color to pink, reddish, or even purple. The range is from the Gulf of St. Lawrence to Rhode Island, from the low-water mark to about 18 fathoms, often quite common. It is usually buried in the sandy mud, with the tip of its tail extending up into the water.

Order APODA
(The Synaptas)

These are holothurians with elongate, usually translucent bodies, without tube-feet, with ten to twenty-five
branched tentacles, their canals connected with the ring-
canal and effectuated by Polian vesicles, which in various
species may number from 1 to 50. There are no respiratory trees or radial canals, and, of course, the ampullae
are also wanting. There are no *Cuvier's organs* (simple
tubes, occurring in certain echinoderms, attached to the
cloaca). These forms are mostly hermaphroditic. There is
but one family.

Family Synaptidae

The single family has the characters of the Order, as
above outlined. Other features in common are that the
calcareous ring often has more than the five interradial
segments usually found in echinoderms, and these are
either perforated or notched. Series of small, ciliated fun-
nels are present in the body-cavity. The calcareous bodies
are characteristic and peculiar, being mostly anchors associated with anchor-plates, wheels, or sigmoid bodies.

Synapta (Leptosynapta) inhaerens (O. F. Müller) PLATE 232; COLOR PLATE XX, 9. The Common Synapta.
The flexible, wormlike body of this beautiful little holothurian is long, slender, and so translucent that certain
internal organs and the five white longitudinal muscle-
bands can be clearly seen through the body-wall. The
general color is whitish, tinged sometimes with yellowish
or pale red. The body-length varies from 4 to 6 inches,
the diameter ranging from ¼ to ⅜ inch. The twelve
tentacles each have five to seven tapering, tubular branches
besides the long and slender terminal branch. The side-
branches gradually increase in length from the stalk outward. There is a group of specialized sense organs at the
base of each branch. There is usually one Polian vesicle
and one stone-canal. The calcareous ring, beneath the
tentacles, consists of twelve pieces or segments, which are
broad and without side-projections. Those located radially
are centrally perforated for the radial nerves to pass
through. The spiral intestine is large and passes through
the interior of the body-cavity to the terminal cloaca. The
gonads are composed of very slender filaments, the single
genital duct opening to the outside through a pore at the
tip of the tentacle located at the right of the mid-dorsal
line.

The remarkable calcareous bodies are peculiarly characteristic of this species. They are minute structures, about
³⁄₅₀₀ inch in length, shaped like an anchor, having a

slender shank with parallel sides and a knob at the end. The flukes of the anchor curve evenly and symmetrically from the bottom of the shank, bending slightly forward, and have minute spines on their outer sides. These *anchors* are always found in combination with an oval *anchor-plate,* with the upper margin of which they articulate by means of the knoblike handle, though they are not actually attached to each other. Multitudes of these almost microscopic, coupled bodies are imbedded in a horizontal position, just under the surface of the delicate skin of the *Synapta,* the points of the anchors pushing out the skin without penetrating it; but if any foreign body scrapes across the outer surface of the *Synapta,* the points are dragged out, penetrate the skin, and cling to the passing substance. Thousands of these anchor tips, acting in this way, cling so firmly that they are separated only with difficulty. They also serve as a locomotory apparatus, and possibly as a means of defense.

The *Synapta* lies buried in sand or even clear mud, particles of which it grasps with its tentacles and passes into its mouth. The stomach is thus usually loaded with foreign granules from which nutritive material is extracted and the residue passed out through the cloaca. The burrows of the *Synapta* can be spotted on the sea-bottom by small mounds of fine sand with a central hole about ¼ inch in diameter. They may also be found in black mud or even gravel. They are often exposed between the tides, where the sand is still wet. The habitat of the species extends down to the 100-fathom line, from Maine to South Carolina. It is also found on British and European shores.

Synapta roseola (Verrill) PLATE 232. The Rosy Synapta. This holothurian closely resembles the preceding species, but the fact that its coloration is usually a deep rosy-red identifies it at once. Particles of red pigment occur, thickly distributed through its integument, and cause the color which gives rise to its specific name. Like the previous species, it has twelve tentacles, but with fewer branches, there being only two or three pairs besides the terminal branch. Its maximum length appears to be 4 inches, and it is often less, so that, in general, it is somewhat smaller than the related species. The calcareous bodies are more irregular than those of *Synapta inhaerens* and the anchors somewhat slenderer, but they work on the same principle. *Sigmas* are also abundant. These C-shaped bodies, sometimes doughnut-shaped, and certain other irregularly branched plates are also frequently found. The plates of the calcareous ring are similar to those of the previous species, but the radial plates are notched instead of being perforated for the passage of the radial

PLATE 232

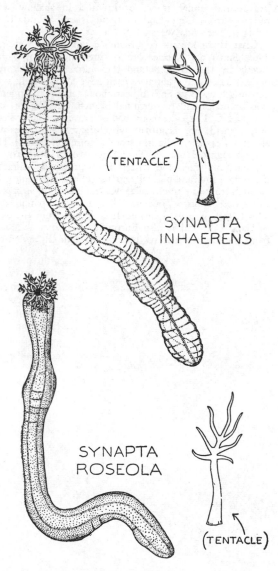

(TENTACLE)

SYNAPTA
INHAERENS

SYNAPTA
ROSEOLA

(TENTACLE)

nerves. This species is also less common, but is found in gravel and under stones or in sand in shallow water, ranging from Cape Cod to Long Island Sound. It also exists in Bermuda waters.

Chiridota laevis (Fabricius) COLOR PLATE XXI, 1, 1a. This genus and species are distinguished from *Synapta* chiefly by the tentacles and the characteristic calcareous bodies. The twelve tentacles each have a short stalk which expands toward its end to bear about ten short, fingerlike, side branches and no terminal branch (see Figure 1a on the plate). The calcareous bodies are not anchor-shaped but, instead, are beautiful wheel-shaped structures with about six spokes radiating from a common center. There are no sigmoid bodies. There are two to three rows of papillae, in which the wheels are segregated, in each of the dorsal interambulacral regions. There are one to three of such rows in the similar ventral areas. The color of this species is often pink, but varies to a transparent white. The length is 4 to 6 inches. It is found from the Arctic to Cape Cod and is also European. It occurs abundantly from the low-water mark to about 45 fathoms and deeper.

14
Phylum Prosopygia
(MOSS ANIMALS AND LAMP SHELLS)

THIS Phylum, as here treated, includes two important groups of the Animal Kingdom; namely, the BRYOZOA (Moss Animals) and the BRACHIOPODA (Lamp shells). These divisions were formerly retained as separate Phyla because of their apparent lack of affinities with other groups, and their separate treatment is still regarded by many zoologists as more convenient, because of their striking external differences. It is generally acknowledged, however, that certain fundamental structures and features of their life history indicate that they have a nearer approach to each other than to other Phyla. They are here designated, therefore, as two Subphyla of the *Phylum Prosopygia*.

Following this conception, the Phylum Prosopygia is regarded as including those animals that have tentacular arms supported by a lophophore, or ridge, which may be circular, oval, horseshoe-shaped, or in the form of a double spiral. These tentacles are ciliated, and surmount the anterior end of the body, either surrounding the mouth, or in immediate association with it. The mouth opens into an alimentary tract consisting of an oesophagus, stomach, and intestine, which tends to bend upon itself in U-shaped form, though, in certain cases, like the Lamp shells, it may end blindly without an anus. The coelom is present in both Subphyla and the development, in both cases, passes through a free-swimming "trochophore" larval stage.

SUBPHYLUM BRYOZOA (POLYZOA)
(The Moss animals)

These are minute animals which form colonies on rocks, water plants, mollusk shells and other objects in the sea and in fresh water, though they are, preeminently, marine animals, about three thousand marine species being known as compared with thirty-five fresh-water species. If a stone, shell, or bit of seaweed is picked up in the shallow ocean margin, below the tidal area, various patches of hard crust, white, yellowish, or brick-red in color, may be seen upon their surface. If these are examined with a hand lens or placed in a dish of sea water under a dissecting microscope (a binocular, if possible), the crusts (if bryozoan in nature) will resolve themselves into close-set colonies of shells of beautiful form and sculpture. After watching them for a while, gradually various trapdoors will open, one on each shell, and brush-like clusters of tiny filaments will emerge, to expand into flowerlike circlets of tentacles, often golden-yellow in color (see COLOR PLATE XXII). The shells (*zooecia*) built by these animals (*polypides*), usually start from one individual, which settles down and undergoes a metamorphosis from the free-swimming larval trochophore stage, and builds the first zooecium, the next generation budding out from it by asexual gemmation, and building a new zooecium just in advance of that occupied by the parent (see Figures 4a and 4b on the PLATE). This process keeps on until an extensive colony grows up. Certain species, like *Bugula turrita* (COLOR PLATE XXII, 2, 2a, 2b), instead of forming crusts, grow up as fluffy treelike colonies, composed of spiral branchlets, the final twigs of which are filamentary, and comprise a double, alternate row of transparent zooecia, with the animals (polypides) and their anatomy plainly showing through their walls. Still others, like *Aetea anguina,* and *Bowerbankia gracilis* (Figures 1 and 6, on the same PLATE) stand erect in separate zooecia, mounted on a horizontal stolon, visible to the naked eye as white, threadlike networks of seaweeds like *Laminaria* (Kelp), *Fucus* (Rockweed), and *Rhodymenia* (Dulse).

The Subphylum Bryozoa, therefore, consists of minute prosopygians, usually colony-forming, reproducing both sexually and asexually, with the latter feature developed to a high degree through budding. A retractile lophophore is present bearing a corona of ciliated tentacles. The digestive system, consisting of oesophagus, stomach, and intestine, is U-shaped. There is a coelom or true body-cavity. The nervous system is essentially a simple nerve-ganglion, and there is no definite circulatory system (INDEX PLATE 233).

This Subphylum is divided into two Classes as follows: (1) *Entoprocta;* (2) *Ectoprocta;* the former, consisting of Bryozoa having the anus situated inside the circle of tentacles near the mouth, and the latter, with the anus just outside the circle of tentacles.

CLASS ENTOPROCTA

In this Class, the anus is situated within the circular lophophore which bears the single row of tentacles. There is a cuplike hollow within the lophophore, known as the *vestibule,* into which the tentacles are rolled, in contraction, and partly covered by a fold of membrane, but they are never retracted into the body-cavity. The tentacular crown, with vestibule, mouth, and anus, constitutes the *head* of the animal. The rest, or *body,* is contained within the zooecium and includes the U-shaped digestive system

PLATE 233

CLASS ECTOPROCTA

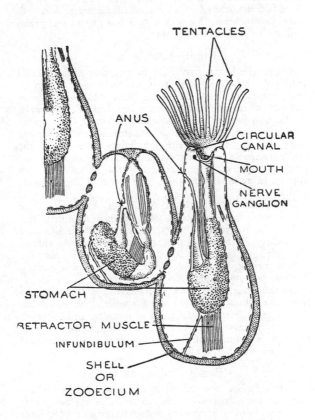

TENTACLES

ANUS

CIRCULAR
CANAL

MOUTH

NERVE
GANGLION

STOMACH

RETRACTOR MUSCLE

INFUNDIBULUM

SHELL
OR
ZOOECIUM

ANATOMY OF A TYPICAL
MARINE BRYOZOAN

and the genital organs which open into the vestibule. The body-cavity is reduced to a more or less gelatinous matrix. In some species the sexes are separate, while others are hermaphroditic, but with the sexual products maturing at different times. Primitive kidneys with flame-cells are present. The nerve fibers radiate from a central ganglion. The body is supported on a contractile stalk. There are three families, one of which inhabits fresh water and so is not included here. There are only a few genera comprised within the two marine families.

Family Loxosomidae

The species in this family are an exception to the general rule in Bryozoa and are not colonial in habit, the asexual buds separating from the parent after maturing and attaching themselves by means of a pedal gland, separately, to the substratum. Thereafter, the individual leads a solitary life. The lophophore is situated obliquely on the body, which, together with the habit of detaching the buds, is regarded as indicating that this is perhaps the most primitive family of the existing Bryozoa, in spite of what appears to be a secondary breaking down of the coelomic cavity.

Loxosoma davenporti Nickerson PLATE 234. The lophophore, in this species, has eighteen to thirty tentacles. The foot is only slightly enlarged. There is a pair of flask-shaped organs depending from the ventral side of the body, just below the stomach. The animal is about $\frac{1}{12}$ inch in height. It has been found attached to worm-tubes, in shallow water in the Woods Hole region.

Loxosoma minuta Osburn PLATE 234. The body is more oval than in the preceding species. The somewhat stouter tentacles are about eight in number, and the stalk is comparatively short. The height is not more than $\frac{1}{50}$ inch. It is found attached to the outside of sipunculid worms on the New England coast.

Family Pedicellinidae

In this family, the animal has a cup-shaped zooecium mounted on a stalk which is contractile at certain points and rises from a horizontal stolon forming a branching network. The body is separated from the stalk by a horizontal diaphragm and can be cast off, being replaced by regeneration from the stump. The lophophore encircles the top of the body and is placed horizontally.

Pedicellina cernua (Pallas) PLATE 234. The stalk is stout and simple, having the same diameter for the entire length. The stolon, from which it rises, is rather transparent and slender, with a branching habit. The cup-shaped body is somewhat swollen on one side. There are fourteen to twenty-four tentacles. Spines may be present on the stalk and body. It often occurs on wharf-piles and similar situations with other sessile and encrusting organisms. The species ranges from the Gulf of St. Lawrence, along the Atlantic Coast to Beaufort, North Carolina, and even to Florida. It is quite abundant on the southern New England coast, especially in the Woods Hole region, from near the surface down to 18 fathoms.

Barentsia discreta (Busk) PLATE 234. The individuals of this species rise from a very slender delicate stolon, which is jointed at intervals, with the pedicels or stalks rising from the joint, where also the branches take their origin. There is an annulated cylindrical enlargement, muscular in nature, at the base of the stalk, enabling the animal to swing from side to side. The stalk, itself, is extremely slender where it leaves the cylinder, but gradually expands to a slight degree as it joins with the globular body. The inner layer of the stalk is perforated with tiny funnel-shaped pores, visible through the outer layer, which they do not penetrate. The polypide body and cylinder are of whitish color, while the stalk and stolon are yellowish brown. This species ranges along our coast from Vineyard Sound to Tortugas, Florida, in shallow water or deeper.

Barentsia major Hincks PLATE 234. The stalk of this species is without the funnel-shaped perforations of the above species. The stolon is comparatively stout and is jointed. The stalks, or pedicels, are of considerable length, slender below and gradually enlarging somewhat as they approach the polypide. The muscular, cylindrical base terminates in a cone-shaped summit, from which the stalk takes origin. The body of the polypide is quite large, white in color, and swollen on one side. The tentacles are numerous. A fleshy peduncle connects the body with the stalk. The species, though not common, is found throughout the Woods Hole region, individual colonies being found on wharf-piles, as well as on shells and stones, to a depth of 13 fathoms.

CLASS ECTOPROCTA

The important characteristics of this Class are that the anal opening is situated outside the lophophore; the coelom or body-cavity is well developed; and that, in contraction, the entire lophophore is drawn down into the zooecium. Practically all the species form large colonies, encrusting stones, shells, wharf-piles, seaweed and other submerged objects. The body-cavity is large and spacious and is lined with a cellular peritoneum. The alimentary tract is U-shaped, the stomach at the bottom with a retractor muscle to hold it in position and a connective tissue strand or funiculus connecting its base with the body-wall (INDEX PLATE 233). There is a circular canal around the mouth and a nerve ganglion is situated just below it on one side. The animals are hermaphroditic, with the gonads in the peritoneum, the testes usually on the funiculus, and the ovary on the wall of the cavity. The fertilized eggs develop in the body-cavity and the embryo may be released after the death of the parent. In some species, the embryos develop in *ovicells,* which are globular prolongations of the wall of a zooecium.

Order PHYLACTOLAEMATA

These are fresh-water Ectoprocta, having a horseshoe-shaped or oval lophophore. Since they are not marine, they are not included here. The group contains comparatively few species.

Order GYMNOLAEMATA

The Ectoprocta in this Order have a circular lophophore. They include all the living marine species.

Suborder CYCLOSTOMATA

The tubular zooecia have a wide opening, usually round, and without an operculum. They are fully calcified, with no appendages, no brood-pouch, and with a zooecium transformed into an *ooecium,* for the development of eggs.

Family Crisiidae

In this family, the colony (*zoarium*) of each species is jointed and has an erect habit of growth of bushlike form, attached to the substratum by tubular fibers. The ooecium is an overgrown zooecium, swollen to a balloonlike shape.

Crisia eburnea (Linnaeus) PLATE 234. The erect, branching colony, from ½ to ¾ inch in height, has cylindrical zooecia curving outward, with calcareous walls and horny joints. The zooecia are arranged nearly alternately in two rows. They are white in color. This is a cosmopolitan species, ranging from Long Island Sound to the Arctic Ocean, from the low-water mark to 80 fathoms. It is also circumboreal occurring in European seas and along the California coast. It is commonly found on any submarine object that will give it a foothold.

Crisia denticulata (Lamarck) PLATE 234. These colonies are similar to the preceding, but are larger and more loosely branching. They are about 1 inch in height, and of a generally sinuous outline. The zooecia are alternating, as a rule. The internodes, between branches, average about eleven zooecia. The ovicell is large and usually near the end of a branch. The basal fibers have black joints. The range is from the Gulf of St. Lawrence to Florida.

PLATE 234

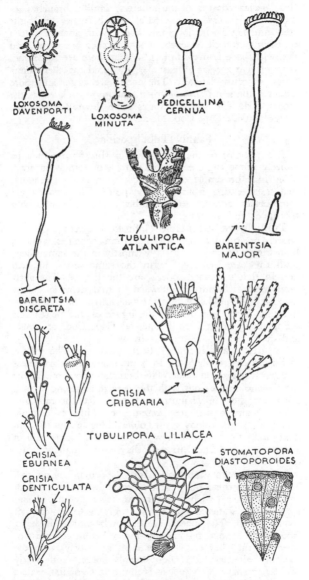

LOXOSOMA
DAVENPORTI

LOXOSOMA
MINUTA

PEDICELLINA
CERNUA

TUBULIPORA
ATLANTICA

BARENTSIA
MAJOR

BARENTSIA
DISCRETA

CRISIA
CRIBRARIA

CRISIA
EBURNEA

TUBULIPORA LILIACEA

STOMATOPORA
DIASTOPOROIDES

CRISIA
DENTICULATA

Crisia cribraria (Lamarck) PLATE 234. The colony of this species consists of quite erect, fanlike branches attached by a very narrow base. The branches are quite stout and rigid with long internodes, with about eighteen or twenty zooecia to each. The branches are broad and flat, with zooecia overlapping, so that there are sometimes parts of five zooecia abreast, largely fused together, sometimes projecting laterally. The ooecia are larger and more elongate than in *Crisia eburnea,* and more inflated at the larger end. The species ranges from Labrador to Crab Ledge, outside Cape Cod, Massachusetts.

Family Tubuliporidae

The colonies of the bryozoans in this family may be entirely prone and creeping in growth or somewhat erect. They may be simple or branched, or may be spreading, that is, radiating from a single point. The zooecia are more or less attached to each other along their sides with the upper ends separate.

Tubulipora atlantica (Johnston) PLATE 234. The zooecia are tubular, in more or less fan-shaped expansions, branching two and two serially, mostly in the same plane, until they are four or five in the same series, in such fashion that the inner zooecia are the longest. The apertures tend to be turned outward so that there is a clear space in the middle, where the ooecium is located in an irregular form, as shown in the figure on the plate. This species is found at Crab Ledge, off Cape Cod, on stones and shells in about 14 to 18 fathoms.

Tubulipora liliacea (Pallas) PLATE 234. The colony, in this species, is about ⅛ inch in height. It is white, or frequently purple in color. The branches are about in the same plane fanning out with the zooecia adhering to each other for their full length, with the effect of radiating ridges. Many ooecia are present, becoming even more numerous as the colony grows older. This species is abundant along the southern New England coast, especially in Vineyard Sound and Buzzards Bay, from shallow water to 15 fathoms.

Stomatopora diastoporoides (Norman) PLATE 234. The colony forms a thin, crustlike growth, the entire patch having a wavy or lobed outline, transversely striped and with evenly scattered punctures. It grows to a width of about ¾ inch. The zooecia are narrowly conical in shape, tapering to a point posteriorly, and adherent for most of their length. They are slightly erect anteriorly, with the openings alternate and about evenly spaced and nearly circular in shape. This species is found in Canadian waters as well as at Crab Ledge, and may, therefore, be considered to have a New England coastal distribution.

Suborder CHILOSTOMATA

The colony (zoarium) may be either erect or flat in this suborder, with calcareous zooecia, the orifice of which is closed by a movable *operculum* or lid. Appendages in the form of *avicularia* and *vibracula* are usually present. The former are like the head of an eagle or hawk in shape, resembling a rounded bird's head, with a mandible and hooked upper beak, capable of grasping and seizing, and with a jointed necklike attachment to the outside of the zooecia. This beak opens and shuts vigorously, by means of powerful muscles, and seizes any worm or other organism that may come within its grasp. The *vibracula* are long, whiplike organs which lash through the water and aid in attaching the colony to the substratum on which it is growing. In this Suborder, also, there are usually external brood-pouches or fertile zooecia for harboring the developing embryos. This Suborder includes most of the Bryozoa.

Family Aeteidae

These bryozoans have tubular, erect zooecia rising from a creeping stolon, enlarged at intervals at the points where the upright extensions of the stolon form the zooecia of which the expanded portions of the stolon are a part. The aperture is at the summit, closed by a movable operculum. A membranous area extends laterally down from the aperture on one side for a short distance.

Aetea anguina (Linnacus) COLOR PLATE XXII, 1. The erect part of the zooecium is about ⅒₅ inch in height. It is white and shining, more or less curved and, at times, nearly straight. It is slightly expanded at the summit, with the membranous area flat, but spoon-shaped in outline. The stem is closely annulated. This species is very common but inconspicuous. It occurs on stems of hydroids, shells, stones, and seaweeds. It is distributed all along the New England coast.

Family Eucrateidae

The colony is erect and branching. The zooecia are trumpet-shaped, often widest at the summit. They are arranged in a single series or in double series with the zooecia back to back. The aperture is obliquely subterminal, but without an operculum. There are no avicularia or vibracula.

Eucratea chelata (Linnaeus) PLATE 235. There is a creeping stolon from which arise upright branching stems, composed of single lines of zooecia, each somewhat trumpetlike in shape and slightly bent forward, mounted by its tapering lower end on the upper edge of the oval aperture of the preceding zooecium. The branches arise on the lower edge of the aperture. The fertile individuals are dwarfed and rise from the upper edge of the orifice of normal individuals. This species is locally abundant off the southern New England coast on algae, hydroids, and other bryozoa. It also ranges northward from Vineyard Sound in shallow water and in the tidal zone.

Gemellaria loricata (Linnaeus) PLATE 235. The colony of this species is erect and branching, with the zooecia in two series, closely adherent, back to back, in very regular succession. It grows to a height of 6 to 10 inches, often assuming a bushy aspect. The aperture is oval in shape, very oblique, and quite large. There is a very thin rim or collar around the aperture. There are no ovicells or appendages. It ranges from the Arctic to Vineyard Sound and is circumboreal occurring both around Alaska and along the European coast.

Scruparia clavata Hincks PLATE 235. The filamentary colony has few branches and tends to be trailing and straggling. The zooecia are in a single series or in a double series, when they are back to back. Each zooecium is elongate, somewhat club-shaped, and slightly constricted around the suboblique, rounded aperture, and tapering to a slightly bent termination below, which stands like a foot on the bent shoulder of the preceding zooecium. Sparsely perforated ooecia are situated on the summit of small zooecia mounted back to back with the lower part of the larger zooecia. This species seems to be only sparingly found off the southern New England coast, in from 8 to 18 fathoms, but may be most abundant elsewhere in our region.

Family Cellulariidae

In this family, the colonies are erect and branched dichotomously. The zooecia are always in the same plane in two or more rows. Avicularia and vibracula usually are present, also an operculum. The aperture is not terminal, often with spines at its margin.

Caberia ellisii (Fleming) PLATE 235. The colony, in this species, is in one plane, somewhat fan-shaped, with stout branches wider at the top, and about 1 inch in height. The zooecia are close-set in two to four rows, quadrangular in shape, with large, elliptical apertures, which take up nearly the whole face of the zooecia. The marginal zooecia have two toothlike spines on the outer side and one on the inner side. The others all have one spine on each side. Avicularia and vibracula are present, the latter, very long and saw-toothed, especially at the tip. The ooecia are flattened and miter-shaped. This species is common in shallow to deep waters off the coast of New

PLATE 235

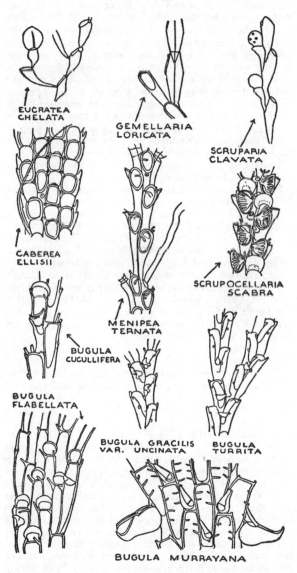

EUCRATEA
CHELATA

GEMELLARIA
LORICATA

SCRUPARIA
CLAVATA

CABEREA
ELLISII

MENIPEA
TERNATA

SCRUPOCELLARIA
SCABRA

BUGULA
CUCULLIFERA

BUGULA
FLABELLATA

BUGULA GRACILIS
VAR. UNCINATA

BUGULA
TURRITA

BUGULA MURRAYANA

England from Vineyard Sound to the Arctic Ocean, as well as on European and Alaskan shores.

Menipea ternata (Solander) PLATE 235. The colony forms delicate, bushy, treelike tufts, white in color, with dichotomous branches. The internodes consist of three, sometimes five, or even seven zooecia. They are long, slender, and tapering below, with considerable variation in length. At the top of the zooecium, there are two spines and another at the outer edge of the oval opening. There are avicularia of two kinds, one, prominently located at the upper, outer margin of the opening, and the other just below the aperture. An operculum is present. Long tendril-like structures are also present, extending out from the sides of the zooecia near the lateral avicularia. Abundant in the Woods Hole region in the neighboring outer waters from 8 to 25 fathoms.

Scrupocellaria scabra (Van Beneden) PLATE 235. This is a rather rare species, but has been found from time to time in the Woods Hole, Massachusetts, region, especially in the outer waters off Cape Cod. The colony is erect with dichotomous branches, having five to twelve zooecia in the internodes. There is an oval aperture occupying about half the front of the short, spreading zooecia. There are one or two stout spines on the outer margin and another smaller one on the inner margin of the aperture. There is an oval shield surmounted by an antler-like figure covering the aperture. There are wedge-shaped vibracular cells situated crosswise on the back of the zooecia, each with a short vibraculum.

Family Bicellariidae

The colony is erect, forming flexible, branching treelike growths. The zooecia are typically quadrate and arranged in two or more rows, the apertures facing in the same direction. The avicularia are stalked and are definitely shaped like birds' heads.

Bugula turrita (Desor) PLATE 235; COLOR PLATE XXII, 2, 2a, 2b. This beautiful and graceful colony grows up to 12 inches in height, when fully developed. It is composed of many branches, each one of which is a symmetrical spiral tuft of flat fanlike branches, succeeding each other around a spiral axis, gradually decreasing in size until the final small spiral at the summit is reached. Each fanlike branch divides into branchlets, composed of two rows of zooecia, each zooecium with a spine at the upper, outer angle and with an aperture occupying about two thirds of the front, turned somewhat inward. The avicularium, shaped very much like a bird's head, with a curved beak with smooth margin, and a narrow, flexible neck, is situated on the outer margin of the aperture about halfway down its edge. The ooecium is somewhat globular and is situated at the upper margin of its zooecium set at an angle with it. The color is pale yellow, often varying to a brown or bright orange, with the tentacles of a golden-yellow. This species is our largest and most common *Bugula* and is distributed abundantly from Casco Bay to North Carolina, from shallow water to all depths. It is very luxuriant on wharf-piles and sea-walls.

Bugula cucullifera Osburn PLATE 235. This is a similar species with four spines at the upper end of the zooecium. The ooecium is set in line with the axis of the zooecium and is short, wide, almost hemispherical, with the front edge turned upward. The beak of the avicularium has a saw-toothed margin, while the head is compressed and the beak is much elongated. The zooecia are in two rows and in alternating positions. They are quite long and narrow with the aperture taking up most of the front, and tapering narrowly at the bottom. It ranges from Maine to Cape Cod and has been found in depths from 14 to 75 fathoms.

Bugula gracilis var. **uncinata** Hincks PLATE 235. This species is a small one, the colony growing to only about 1 or 2 inches in height, forming a small bushy tuft of somewhat spiral branches, light yellow in color, with three spines at the summit of the zooecium. The avicularium is quite small and placed as in *Bugula turrita*. Anchorlike processes replace the rootlike tubes at the base of the colony. This species has been repeatedly brought up in the dredge in the Woods Hole region, and there is a record for Lynn, Massachusetts, by Hincks.

Bugula flabellata (Thompson) PLATE 235. This colony seldom exceeds 1 inch in height, and is branched in whorls of broad fanlike pattern, with the larger branches near the base because of the very short main stem. The species is unlike those mentioned hitherto, because the zooecia are arranged in three to six series instead of two, and have marginal spines only at the top. The avicularia and ovicells are small, the latter being hemispherical and hoodlike. This species grows abundantly on wharf-piles and occurs in Vineyard Sound at depths of 6 to 8 fathoms. Its distribution continues northward in shallow water, along the entire New England coast. Elsewhere it is cosmopolitan.

Bugula murrayana (Johnston) PLATE 235. The colony in this species is a bushy tuft with broad, lobate, or flattened branches, about 2 inches in height, with zooecia multiseriate, in three to twelve rows, the colony dividing dichotomously into broad ribbonlike strips. The zooecia are elongate, oblong, and squarely truncate at the top. The aperture reaches almost to the bottom, with a series of marginal spines on either side bending inward over the aperture. There are avicularia of two kinds, large and small. The small ones are situated in front of the zooecia near the bottom of the aperture, and the exceedingly large ones are attached only on the outer margin of the lateral zooecia. In both cases, they are turned with the jaw upward, and both kinds have strongly hooked beaks. The color is light yellow or brown and the height of their colonies is from ½ to 1½ inches. They resemble small frills standing up from the stones or shells to which they are anchored. This species is circumpolar in distribution, and on our Atlantic shore ranges southward from the Arctic to Vineyard Sound in fairly deep water. In the Woods Hole region it is found in depths of 8 to 25 fathoms.

Family Membraniporidae

This family contains strongly calcified encrusting Bryozoa, mostly with the aperture of the zooecium widely open, exposing a membranous area, usually surrounded by the raised margin of the aperture and often with a calcareous extension in front, which may or may not be perforated. The membranous area may take up the greater part of the zooecium, the calcareous rim being equipped with spines, avicularia being present or wanting.

Membranipora lacroixii (Audouin) PLATE 236. The encrusting colony of this species occurs on shells, stones, and other material, in patches of most delicate network. The zooecia are quite small, having the large membranous areas with calcareous margins not raised above the general level and finely granulated around the edge.

Membranipora (Electra) monostachys Busk PLATE 236. This species forms irregular or radiating colonies on shells, stones, algae, the carapaces of crabs and other crustacea, from shallow water to depths of 2 to 19 fathoms and deeper along the southern New England coast. It ranges from the Arctic Ocean to New Jersey, and, in fact, is cosmopolitan. The zooecia are rather small with oval membranous areas and with well-calcified basal portions, often impressed with fine dots, and raised borders which, frequently, are armed with eight to ten sharp spines arching over the membranous areas, including a single median basal spine larger than the others. In some cases, this is the only spine to be found, and so accounts for the specific name, *monostachys*. There are no avicularia or ovicells.

Membranipora (Electra) pilosa (Linnaeus) PLATE 235; COLOR PLATE XXII, 3, 3a. This very common encrusting bryozoan is often found in large, white patches irregular in outline, on stones and shells, or in long, regular

ranks of zooecia on the fronds of algae, and especially on
eelgrass. The large oval membranous areas are located on
the upper part of the zooecia, the basal portion calcified
and perforated with distinct rounded holes. The oval
areas are framed by high, smooth borders from which
seven to nine stout and rather flat, curved spines project
over the membranous portion of the zooecium in pairs,
the odd projection being the basal spine, which varies
greatly in position and length. In some colonies it is similar
to the other spines, bending in the same way and parallel
to the membranous area (see COLOR PLATE XXII, 3, 3a).
In others, especially when the colony is located on rounded
surfaces, like stems, it may be much longer than the
zooecium and project with an undulating outline for a
considerable distance, and, in combination with the
others in the colony, it gives the patch a pilose effect (see
the figure in the upper right corner of PLATE 236), hence
the specific name. Many intermediate variations of this
spine are readily found. This is also a cosmopolitan species.
On our coast it ranges from the Arctic Ocean to Long
Island Sound, from low-tide mark to 17 fathoms and
deeper.

Membranipora lineata (Linnaeus) PLATE 236. This
species forms its colonies in more or less circular crusts,
the zooecia being of moderate size with fairly elongate
oval apertures limited by a narrow, calcareous rim from
which eight to twelve spines project inward at a curving
oblique angle in pairs, except for the first two, which are
inclined anteriorly. An avicularium is sometimes present,
attached to the base of the zooecium. Above each aperture, a large, globular ovicell is located with a rib crossing
it transversely. This species occurs rather sparsely in southern New England waters, on stones, shells, and wharf-
piles from near the surface to 15 fathoms.

Membranipora (Tegella) unicornis (Fleming)
PLATE 236. This bryozoan forms round, whitish colonies on
shells. It has a large ovoid aperture, somewhat narrower
at the top, with a broad rim finely scalloped on its inner
edge. There are usually two pairs of spines anteriorly. The
first pair is small and vertical, if existent. The second pair
is longer but unequal in length and position, the longer
one often inclined over the membranous portion. The
ovicell is large, turban-shaped, and with a transverse line.
The texture of the hard parts is shining and translucent.
The species ranges from Canada to Woods Hole, Massachusetts, where it is found in 8 fathoms.

Membranipora (Callopora) aurita Hincks PLATE
236. The colonies encrust shells or algae. When on shells,
the colonies are circular, the zooecia forming a regular
pattern. On the stems of seaweed they are usually irregu-

lar and crowded. The zooecia are large and broad. Their apertures have a high, broad margin and are narrowed anteriorly, their S-shaped lateral margins giving them a flask-shaped outline. The rounded ovicells are somewhat buried in the zooecium, directly above the aperture, with a broad, chevron-shaped rib enclosing a triangular area. There is a curious circumstance regarding the avicularia. There are always two avicularia pointing forward and outward, when the zooecium just posterior to them has an ovicell, but if there is no ovicell, there is never more than one avicularium, and in that case it invariably points backward. This species is common all through the Buzzards Bay and Vineyard Sound region in 3 to 18 fathoms. Its further American distribution is not known but it is likely that it will be found much farther north. It is probably circumboreal, since it also occurs in the waters around England and Denmark.

Membranipora tehuelcha (d'Orbigny) PLATE 236. This species is only known in this region because it encrusts Gulfweed (*Sargassum bacciferum*), which drifts into Vineyard Sound and the Nantucket-Marthas Vineyard neighborhood from the Gulf Stream. Its colonies form patches of beautiful white network on the brown fronds of the weed. The apertures are elongate and narrowly oval, producing an alternating pattern of remarkable regularity. The aperture is often covered on the base and sides by a calcified layer. The walls of the margin are high rimmed and the anterior angles of the zooecium are produced into two blunt, diverging horns. They are convex on the posterior side and concave anteriorly.

Since this species is on Sargassum Weed, it is of worldwide distribution.

Family Cribulinidae

These are encrusting colonies of zooecia, arranged like a mosaic. The front of the zooecia is considered to have originated from the fusing of spines, because of the arrangement of the pores and the manner of their development, resulting finally in a fissured surface.

Cribrilina punctata (Hassall) PLATE 236. In this species, the zooecia are small and more or less cylindrical. Their front is perforated quite irregularly by various openings or pores of irregular shape, resembling lacunae. The aperture is more or less semicircular with a small toothlike point rising from the middle of the lower lip, which is sometimes doubled. There are two pairs of marginal spines on the margin of the aperture, of which the longer, second pair is visible in the figure, somewhat inclined over the aperture. The shorter, first pair is fused with the mouth of the hoodlike ovicell which surmounts each zooecium as shown in the illustration. The ovicell is smooth and shining, perforated by small, pinholelike openings. There are two small avicularia, one on each postero-lateral angle of the aperture, inclined forward and outward. This species is quite abundant in the outer waters off the New England coast, on shells and pebbles, from beyond the low-tide mark to moderate depths. It is less common in sheltered areas. It also occurs along the European coast.

Cribulina annulata (Fabricius) PLATE 236. This species forms small, round crusts of a reddish to brown color on stones and kelp. The zooecia are more or less oval, but of irregular shape, coarser in appearance, and standing out in distinct relief. The apertures are oval to almost round in the younger specimens but become considerably flattened horizontally in the older individuals, especially when ovicells appear. There is also a low median tooth on the lower border of the aperture in young zooecia. This becomes irregular or overgrown in later stages. The upper margin of the aperture has two pairs of spines, the upper being the shorter and turned outward. Later on, with the development of the ovicell, a thick, secondary lip overgrows the first, largely formed on the upper side by a hypertrophy and median junction of the second pair of spines, the first pair then becoming completely obscured and submerged. The ovicells are small, hemispherical, and pierced by a few small perforations, often overgrown by the secondary lip. The front of the zooecium tends to be marked by about six or seven annular cross ridges between which, in each groove, there is a transverse row of distinct perforations. The upper rows are fairly straight, but posteriorly they become chevron-shaped, with the angle pointing upward. In many cases a longitudinal median ridge is present. There are no avicularia.

This species ranges from the Bay of Fundy to the outer waters of Massachusetts. It is circumboreal, occurring also in Europe.

Family Porinidae

The chief family characteristics are the tubular character of the zooecia, with a circular aperture at the summit, and the presence of a small, median pore on a raised mound.

Porina tubulosa (Norman) PLATE 236. Many stones and shells show on their surface small, white, rounded patches formed by the colonies of this species. The zooecia are in close ranks, being uniformly alternate in position, with prostrate, perforated, flasklike bodies, narrowing to semierect tubular necks terminating in a round aperture with an irregular, somewhat flattened rim. At the base of the tubular portion on the median line is a ringlike eminence with a round pore at the summit. The ovicells are small and flattened and more or less concealed by the tubes which rise around them. There are no avicularia. This species ranges from the Arctic to Nantucket Shoals, where it occurs in depths of 7 to 20 fathoms.

Family Microporellidae

Like the preceding family, the Microporellidae possess a median pore below the aperture. The zooecium, however, has no tubular necklike extension so that the pore is close to the lower rim of the aperture where it may be partly concealed by an umbo and the calcifications of the aperture-margin. The latter is approximately semicircular in form, with a straight posterior border.

Microporella ciliata (Pallas) PLATE 236. The colonies formed by this species are silvery or frosty discs, sometimes irregular, about 1 inch or less in diameter, on stones, shells, or seaweed. The zooecia are oval in shape, hexagonal when crowded, and punctured on their rough surface, but with the punctures obscured as the calcifications thicken. The aperture is semicircular, and with a slightly raised border having two diverging pairs of curving spines. The median pore is just in front of the aperture, usually somewhat crescent-shaped, having thin teeth or spinules projecting into it, giving a somewhat starlike appearance to the opening. A projecting mound, or umbo, is often just in front of it tending to obscure it to the view. The ovicell is rounded and frequently has radiating ridges and scattered punctures. There is usually a small avicularium situated on the right side, somewhat below the aperture, with its beak pointing forward and outward. This is a cosmopolitan species, occurring along our coast from the Arctic to Nantucket Shoals and the outer waters generally, from the lower-tide mark to 300 fathoms.

Family Hippothoidae

The Family Hippothoidae contains species with thin walls of shining, translucent texture. The zooecia are somewhat cylindrical in form, with a rounded notch, or *sinus,* in the middle of the posterior border of the aperture. The wall is not perforated but has irregular, transverse ridges. There are no spines or avicularia.

Hippothoa divaricata Lamouroux PLATE 236. The zooecia, in this species, are pear-shaped but slender and produced into a long, slender stem at the posterior end. They grow in a loose, branching network, with the zooecia often nearly at a right angle to each other. The surface of the zooecia may be smooth or with fine horizontal striae. There is often a vertical keel down through

PLATE 236

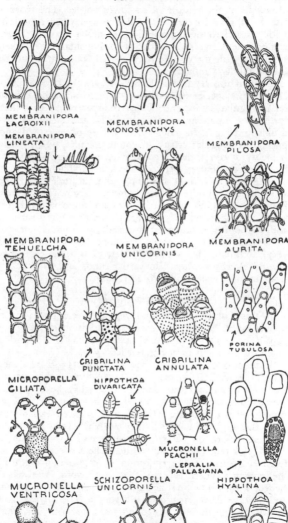

MEMBRANIPORA
LACROIXII

MEMBRANIPORA
MONOSTACHYS

MEMBRANIPORA
PILOSA

MEMBRANIPORA
LINEATA

MEMBRANIPORA
TEHUELCHA

MEMBRANIPORA
UNICORNIS

MEMBRANIPORA
AURITA

CRIBRILINA
PUNCTATA

CRIBRILINA
ANNULATA

PORINA
TUBULOSA

MICROPORELLA
CILIATA

HIPPOTHOA
DIVARICATA

MUCRONELLA
PEACHII

LEPRALIA
PALLASIANA

MUCRONELLA
VENTRICOSA

SCHIZOPORELLA
UNICORNIS

HIPPOTHOA
HYALINA

the middle. The aperture has a small, semicircular sinus, or notch, in the middle of its lower border. The ovicells rise from dwarfed zooecia and are somewhat spherical, with a small rounded projection, or umbo, on top. There are no avicularia. This species is cosmopolitan. It is taken sparingly with the dredge in Vineyard Sound and outside Cape Cod at 18 fathoms.

Hippothoa hyalina (Linnaeus) PLATE 236. The zooecia of this species are elongate, cylindrical, often closely set in regular series, and almost transparent, so that they form glossy patches on stones, shells, and stems of hydroids and algae. In older colonies, they often crowd and pile up in irregular crusts. In young colonies, where there is plenty of room, they are often separated here and there by enclosed openings between the zooecia. The aperture is rounded or arched at the top, with an indentation or sinus in the middle of the bottom margin. The latter, however, is usually hidden by a broad umbo which overhangs it. The ovicell is globular, with a punctured surface, and surmounts a somewhat dwarfed zooecium. There are no avicularia. This is also a cosmopolitan species and is very abundant in southern New England, especially around Buzzards Bay, Vineyard Sound, and Nantucket, from the low-water mark to 20 fathoms.

Family Schizoporellidae

In this family, the frontal region is composed of a double layer, having perforations in addition to marginal gaps (*areoles*). The aperture is circular with a rounded notch, or sinus, in its lower border.

Schizoporella unicornis (Johnston) PLATE 236; COLOR PLATE XXII, 4, 4a, 4b. The colonies of this species are wide-spreading and dominant on the shells, stones, worm-tubes, and wharf-piles that they encrust. Sometimes they rise into free, vertical, and irregular expansions from the surface on which they are anchored. The most frequent coloration varies from an orange to a bright or dark brick-red, sometimes white. The zooecia vary in form according to the condition of crowded growth in the colony. When isolated they are ovoid, but when crowded they may be hexagonal, rectangular, elongate, and narrow, or short, broad, and square. The surface may be smooth, but usually it is rough and beset with tubercles. The outer layer is punctured with many round holes irregularly disposed over the surface. Larger irregular openings, or areoles, are found around the margin. An umbo of varying length is situated, as a rule, just beneath the aperture (hence the name, *unicornis*). The aperture may be circular or semicircular, with the posterior border somewhat widened for the accommodation of the rounded sinus. The individuals may be separated by a groove or by a raised wall. The ovicell is nearly spherical, with a punctured surface, often with radiating grooves, rough in texture, and with a rounded umbo in the middle. There may be one or two avicularia at either side a little below the aperture, usually pointing forward and outward, but in certain variations they point backward and outward. This is one of the most abundant species in southern New England. It ranges from Massachusetts Bay to South Carolina, from the low-tide mark to 19 fathoms and deeper. It is also found in Europe.

Family Escharidae

In this family there is no special pore in front, and no distinct sinus, or notch, in the lower margin of the aperture, though there may be denticles developed there instead and also on either side of it. There is a varied development of secondary characters. Avicularia may or may not be present.

Mucronella peachii (Johnston) PLATE 236. This species forms crusts with regularly arranged zooecia, which are rhomboid or hexagonal in shape, not separated by deep grooves or walls, and with a more or less flat surface. In the young zooecium, areoles appear around the margin in a regular row. As the calcification increases with age, these become obliterated, since radiating ridges grow between them, with the pores at the intervening grooves, so that, as the ridges become more calcified, the pores are overgrown and often disappear. The aperture is rounded with a tooth, or denticle, usually double-pointed, growing up on the midline. Lateral teeth are also present. The margin of the aperture is raised and gives rise to six oral spines in the position indicated by the dots in the figure. The ovicells are globe-shaped and smooth, without perforations. There are no avicularia in this species. This species is abundant in outside waters in 6 to 20 fathoms, but less common in sheltered situations in southern New England.

Mucronella ventricosa (Hassall) PLATE 236. The colonies of this encrusting species form white or silvery patches with the zooecia usually arranged in regular radiating lines. They are individually large and of swollen configuration, and with deep grooves between them. There is a single row of round areoles around the margin. The surface of the zooecium is smooth in young individuals, but granular in the adult, with radiating rows of small, round tubercles which begin at a double ring of tubercles surrounding the aperture and fan out to terminate near the areoles at the margin. The aperture is rounded anteriorly and with a straight posterior rim, a large double-pointed denticle occupying the greater part of it. The margin of the peristome is quite high and thin, at times almost spout-shaped. The ovicells are globular in form and smooth, without perforations, but they are more or less granular when calcification is complete. There are no avicularia. The species ranges in depth from 14 to 20 fathoms or more, at Crab Ledge, Massachusetts, and also occurs at various points along the New England coast.

Lepralia pallasiana (Moll) PLATE 236; COLOR PLATE XXII, 5, 5a, 5b. The encrusting colonies of this interesting species are circular in shape, whenever the substance on which they are built up will allow them to expand, and the zooecia are arranged in an approximate spiral (see Figures 5, 5a on the COLOR PLATE). The zooecia are large, elongate, often somewhat hexagonal. They are depressed posteriorly but raised anteriorly, with the surface perforated with large pores, having thick tubercles and ridges between in heavily calcified specimens. The aperture is quite large, longer than wide, arched anteriorly, with sides at first parallel, then expanding about the middle, the greatest width being at the posterior end. The rim of the peristome is thin and raised, especially around the anterior half of the opening. There are no ovicells and no avicularia. There is a small, rounded umbo below the aperture on the median line. The range is from the Arctic Ocean to New Jersey. The specimens pictured on COLOR PLATE XXII, 5, 5a, 5b, were collected by the author near Mount Desert Island, in 1929. The distribution, vertically, is from the tidal zone to 8 fathoms and deeper.

Rhamphostomella ovata (Smitt) PLATE 237. The zooecia of this species have large punctures scattered over the surface in front and a series of areoles along the margin. In the younger cells, these are numerous and there are strong ribs extending a short distance to the center. In the older stages, such as that pictured, these are partially overgrown and covered over. The aperture is large and ovate in outline with the smaller end pointing downward. There is a low peristomial rim and a small, oval avicularium is present, a little to one side of the terminus, mounted on a rounded, smooth elevation (the *rostrum*). There is no median tooth, a part of the rostrum occupying its position. The ovicells, when present, are globular and smooth. This is a northern species ranging from the Arctic to Nantucket and Vineyard Sound, but rare in the southern part of this range. It is found to a depth of 20 fathoms.

Smittia porifera (Smitt) PLATE 237. This bryozoan forms a more or less irregular, flat, and smooth crust. The zooecia are large, elongate, and practically urn-shaped.

In young stages, the surface is smooth and polished, but roughens up with the calcifications of age. The aperture is round, with a small median tooth, which may have one or two points. In some cases it is entirely lacking. An oval avicularium is present immediately behind the tooth, having a rounded mandible, which points forward and is seated on the peristome, which is widened here, though quite thin around the rest of the aperture. This species occurs off the southern New England coast in 8 to 20 fathoms.

Porella concinna (Busk) PLATE 237. This is an encrusting species, or it may form low, erect frills. The zooecia are flat with punctures in the adult state or they may be apparently lacking due to overgrowth by calcification. There is a single row of marginal pores around the edge. The primary aperture is rounded anteriorly and straight on its posterior edge, which has a broad tooth forming a shelflike projection or rostrum, bearing a round avicularium. This species ranges from the Gulf of St. Lawrence to Woods Hole, Massachusetts, where it is fairly common.

Porella acutirostris Smitt PLATE 237. This species forms whitish or yellowish encrustations which, when young, are thin and quite smooth, but become roughened with age. The zooecia are usually in radiating lines. There is a row of areoles along the margin of the zooecia, which are compressed and elongate in the colony. The ooecium is large and globular. This species ranges along the entire New England coast from the Gulf of St. Lawrence to the Woods Hole region. It is very common at Crab Ledge in 14 to 20 fathoms.

Suborder CTENOSTOMATA

The chief characteristics of this Suborder are, as follows: the complete lack of calcification of any kind; the integument is chitinous or soft, without strengthening support, or they may be strengthened by introducing earthy material or other foreign matter into their walls; the absence of appendicular organs, such as avicularia, vibracula, and ooecia; and the colony may be encrusting or stolonate, or may have branched, plantlike supports, or fleshy lobes.

Family Flustrellidae

In this curious family, the zooecia are embedded in a gelatinous layer or crust on stones or seaweed, from the surface of which are extended long, tapering, pointed spines. The aperture has two lips, one of which is movable and acts like an operculum.

Flustrella hispida (Fabricius) PLATE 237. The colony forms a brownish encrustation from which bristle many pointed spines of a reddish color. The zooecia are ovate, or, when pressed against their neighbors, more or less hexagonal. Their surface is smooth and flat and bordered with more of the spines, while still others are around the raised double-lipped opening.

Family Alcyonidiidae

The gelatinous crust, in the Family Alcyonidiidae, has no spines, but sometimes absorbs a certain amount of earthy material. Occasionally the colony rises as upright or, at least, free cylindrical or leaflike growths. The zooecia are fairly closely united and usually somewhat submerged in the jellylike crust. The aperture is without the double lips, and the orifice is closed by simply retracting the tentacle sheath.

Alcyonidium mytili Dalyell PLATE 237. This is an encrusting colony on stones, shells, and seaweed, of rather substantial consistency, and of varying color tints, ranging through whitish, gray, yellow, bright red, and light to dark brown. Sometimes the colony is quite transparent and colorless. The zooecia are usually hexagonal, varying at times to five- or four-sided cells. There are no ovicells but the eggs are developed in any of the regular zooecia. The colony expands by asexual budding. The range of this species extends from Nova Scotia to Long Island.

Alcyonidium verrilli Osburn PLATE 237. This species forms erect, branching colonies consisting of firm and solid gelatinous matter, with the zooecia in very close contact. The colonies branch luxuriantly and grow to a height of 10 to 12 inches. They are dichotomous, but irregularly so; the branches often flattened toward the tips. The surface is smooth and glassy, and the zooecia of small size with about fifteen to seventeen tentacles. The color is grayish brown to rusty brown.

Family Cylindroecidae

These bryozoans have a creeping stolon from which the zooecia arise singly and directly continuous with the stolon or in somewhat flat and palmate branches, the vertical branches bearing the zooecia which are continuous with each other. The outer integument is opaque being impregnated with foreign, earthy material.

Anguinella palmata Van Beneden PLATE 237. This species has erect branches with cylindrical zooecia, not constricted at the base but freely continuous with the branches themselves. They are rounded at their tips, irregularly distributed over the branches, and each has about ten tentacles. The integument is opaque because of the presence of foreign earthy material. The colonies grow about 1 inch in height. This species is abundant along the

PLATE 237

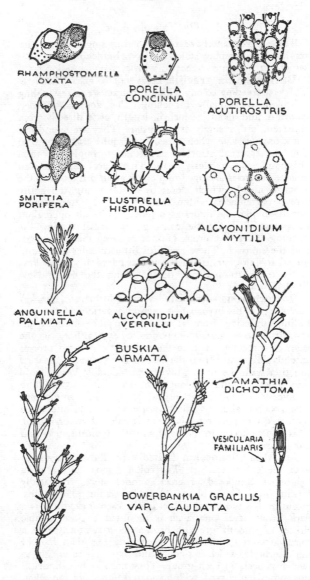

RHAMPHOSTOMELLA OVATA

PORELLA CONCINNA

PORELLA ACUTIROSTRIS

SMITTIA PORIFERA

FLUSTRELLA HISPIDA

ALCYONIDIUM MYTILI

ANGUINELLA PALMATA

ALCYONIDIUM VERRILLI

BUSKIA ARMATA

AMATHIA DICHOTOMA

VESICULARIA FAMILIARIS

BOWERBANKIA GRACILIS VAR CAUDATA

Atlantic coast from New England to Beaufort, North Carolina.

Family Vesiculariidae

These bryozoans have zooecia rising singly or in clusters from a creeping stolon or from branching structures which, in turn, are connected with a creeping stolon.

Bowerbankia gracilis Leidy COLOR PLATE XXII, 6. This is a creeping colony with a prostrate stem, resembling a stolon, occasionally branching. The zooecia, slender, colorless, and about ⅓₆ inch in length, arise directly from this stem, either singly or in clusters. They are cylindrical (or elongate-ovate when closed) and quite transparent, so that the internal structure is visible through the thin, chitinous, almost glassy wall. There are eight to ten ciliated tentacles arranged in a circle around the top of the tentacle sheath, which closes by withdrawing the entire crown of tentacles within the sheath, the latter turning outside-in like the finger of a glove, while an operculum of spines, set in a circle, converges behind it to close the opening. There is a strong gizzard between the oesophagus and the stomach. These beautiful little colonies are found on wharf-piles, stones, shells, and seaweed from the low-water mark to moderate depths along the entire New England coast.

Bowerbankia gracilis var. **caudata** (Hincks) PLATE 237. This bryozoan is merely a variety of the preceding, differing from it, mainly, in the biserially arranged zooecia, usually opposite to each other, on the stem of the colony, and in the fact that a pointed process extends downward from the base of the zooecium, near its junction with the stem. There is considerable variation in this short, tail-like prolongation, since it may have a double or a triple point instead of the usual single one. The zooecia, also, may be truncate at the top, and often with a square opening. The color is pale yellow or brown. This variety occurs in company with the typical species and has the same range.

Amathia dichotoma (Verrill) (= **Amathia vidovici** Heller) PLATE 237. The colony, about 2 inches in height, is composed of erect, slender stems, repeatedly forking in different planes, like a branching plant, translucent and white in color. Just below each fork, there is a dark brown area on which is mounted a close, double cluster of smooth, greenish brown zooecia, attached in a spiral around the stem, and occupying less than half of the internode, which is smooth and bare. There are six to twelve zooecia in each group. They are nearly cylindrical and somewhat curved, with a squared upper portion when closed, and an operculum of clustered spines which open out to allow the eight long and slender, ciliated tentacles to emerge and spread out into a circlet. The range is from northern waters south to New Jersey, usually common on wharf-piles and rocks, in shallow water.

Vesicularia familiaris (Gros) PLATE 237. This is a doubtful species, said to have a tall, slender, flexible stem with a spindle-shaped zooecium at the summit, "occurring repeatedly over the surface of small algae, standing out in all directions" (Verrill), with a distribution from Casco Bay to Long Island Sound.

Family Buskiidae

The colony, in this family, grows from a stolon. The zooecia converge at the base to a sessile attachment by a joint to the stolon. Each zooecium has a flat, membranous area on one side.

Buskia armata (Verrill) PLATE 237. In this species, the zooecia are attached in pairs by a movable joint to the stolon, which is creeping, for the most part, but with occasional erect shoots. It is found in shallow water on other bryozoans, and on hydroids and algae, from New England to the Carolinas.

SUBPHYLUM BRACHIOPODA
(The Lamp-shells)

The Brachiopoda are marine animals that, like the Subphylum Bryozoa, have a pair of ciliated tentacular arms, borne by a lophophore, or ridge, originating on either side of the mouth, which, in this case, like that of some of the Bryozoa, is two-lobed and horseshoelike, but has gone further as an elaboration of that plan. The alimentary tract consists of oesophagus, stomach, and intestine, typically bent into a U-shaped pattern. There is a coelom, or true body-cavity, present and the free-swimming larva is a trochophore.

This simple bryozoanlike organization, in the Brachiopoda, is enclosed in a bivalve calcareous shell, with a superficial resemblance to the shell of bivalve mollusks, so that zoologists originally related the brachiopods to that group, under the name of Molluscoida. As we have seen, however, the animal contained in the shell is far from being a mollusk or any animal related to that group, but has strong resemblance to the fundamental bryozoan plan, instead.

The brachiopod shell consists of an upper and lower, or dorsal and ventral valve; the ventral valve being the larger, and extending beyond the dorsal valve posteriorly to accommodate a circular opening from which projects a muscular stalk, the *peduncle* (see INDEX PLATE 238, the lower figure). This is an extension of the posterior end of the brachiopod body by means of which the animal attaches itself to a rock or some other object on the sea-bottom. The body proper is situated between the posterior portions of the two valves, enclosed within an integument consisting of a dorsal and a ventral expanded fold. The mantles extend forward and enclose the body above and below, their outer sides secreting the shell. Two other prolongations forward form the double ridge known as the *lophophore,* which is supported by a calcareous framework or skeleton that grows out from the dorsal valve. The lophophore extends forward on either side. The two parts are also known as the *tentacular arms.* They are hollow extensions of the body-cavity or coelom and have on their surface a ciliated groove that runs along their coils to the tip. On one side of the groove is a fringe of ciliated tentacles. These are both sensory and respiratory, as well as the chief means by which the animal obtains its food, for it is by the vibratile motion inward of the cilia covering the outside of this apparatus that food particles and small organisms are sent in a continuous stream back into the mouth-opening between the bases of these two arms. There are no jaws or other appendages, the mouth leading directly into the oesophagus, which, in turn, opens into the enlarged stomach, into which a pair of saclike digestive glands, or livers, pour their secretions. The stomach, in turn, leads into the intestine, which in the majority of the brachiopods hangs in the body-cavity as a blind sac, there being no anus, the excreta apparently being broken up to pass through the nephridia from the body-cavity to be cast out between the shells.

The *nervous system* consists of two pairs of ganglia, one pair dorsal and the other ventral to the oesophagus, connected by commissures, and various branching nerves. There is a heart connected with an anterior vein and posterior arteries. The *nephridia* open into the body-cavity at their inner end and into the cavity between the mantles at the other. They are not only excretory but act as genital ducts as well. The sexes are separate, except in the Ecardines, the gonads in each case being situated in the body-cavity. As stated above, there is a trochophore larva. There is a pair of adductor muscles to close the shells, a pair of muscles attached to the umbo of the hinge to open the shells, and a retractor muscle attached to the stalk.

Brachiopods are one of the most ancient groups of animals, and in the course of ages have come down relatively unchanged, especially the genus *Lingula,* which is the oldest genus of animals, being unchanged since the Cambrian, and still existing plentifully in the depths of the sea. That remote age and the others of the Paleozoic Era were the heyday of brachiopods, and they have had representatives

PLATE 238

TYPICAL BRACHIOPODA
(LAMP SHELLS)

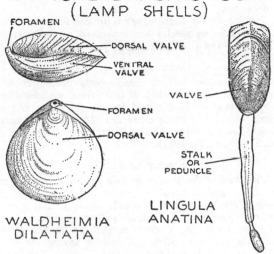

FORAMEN

DORSAL VALVE

VENTRAL VALVE

VALVE

FORAMEN

DORSAL VALVE

STALK OR PEDUNCLE

LINGULA ANATINA

WALDHEIMIA DILATATA

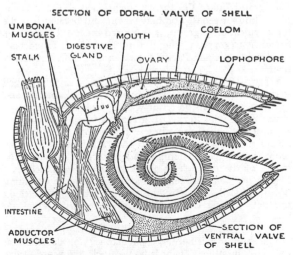

SECTION OF DORSAL VALVE OF SHELL

UMBONAL MUSCLES

MOUTH

COELOM

DIGESTIVE GLAND

STALK

OVARY

LOPHOPHORE

INTESTINE

ADDUCTOR MUSCLES

SECTION OF VENTRAL VALVE OF SHELL

SECTION SHOWING TYPICAL BRACHIOPOD ANATOMY

in all ages down to the present. The fossilized remains of about 2,500 species are known to us and only about 120 living species now exist in our seas, though numerous in individuals.

The Subphylum *Brachiopoda* is divided into two Orders, so far as living species are concerned, as follows: (1) *Ecardines;* and (2) *Testicardines.*

Order ECARDINES

The *Ecardines* include Brachiopoda having either a hornlike or calcareous shell of two valves, not joined by a hinge. They are kept closed by muscles alone and are more primitive in many characters. They are most nearly related to the oldest fossils, some being generically related to them. They include three families.

Family Lingulidae

The shell of this species is oblong, almost quadrilateral in shape, and of hornlike texture instead of being calcareous. The valves are practically equal in size, tapering more or less behind. The fleshy stalk or peduncle is quite long and contractile. There is no skeleton but the tentacular arms are spiral, with stiff bristles around the edges. There are two genera, *Lingula* and *Glottidia*. The former is not found in the Atlantic Ocean but is common in the Pacific and Indian Oceans. As mentioned above, it is the oldest known genus. For that reason and because it is the most typical of its group, it is figured on INDEX PLATE 239, for comparison with other forms. *Glottidia* is found both on the Atlantic and Pacific Coasts of the American Continent.

Glottidia audebarti (Broderip) PLATE 239. The shell is elongate, truncate anteriorly with rounded corners, and tapering to a point posteriorly. The color of the valves is cream-white with transverse green markings, especially on the anterior half. The peduncle is very long and secretes a mucus to which grains of sand adhere. The shell is a little more than 1 inch in length and ⅖ inch in breadth. The length of the peduncle is about ¾ inch. This brachiopod lives in the sand between the tides, the peduncle extending down vertically and with the shell openings just reaching the surface of the sand, when it is covered with water.

Family Craniidae

The shell, in this family, is circular varying to somewhat quadrate in outline. There is no peduncle, the ventral valve being closely adherent to the rocky bottom.

Crania anomala (O. F. Müller) PLATE 239. The dorsal valve of this species is conical, flattened anteriorly from the apex to the margin. The apex may be hooked or

PLATE 239

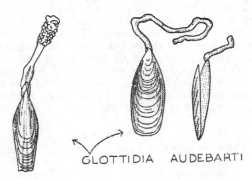

GLOTTIDIA AUDEBARTI

CRANIA
ANOMALA
(SHOWING SETAE)

EXTERIOR OF SHELLS
CRANIA
ANOMALA

ATTACHED VALVE
(INTERIOR)

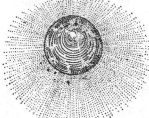

PELAGODISCUS ATLANTICUS
UPPER VALVE WITH SETAE   LOWER VALVE

pointed. Concentric lines of growth on the valve are conspicuous. The color is a reddish chocolate-brown. The attached lower valve molds its surface to the stones or shells to which it is attached. The animal is white in color, tinged with yellow and brown. The mantle is very thin, closely adhering to the shell, and extending to the edges of the valve. The marginal cirri are long, stiffly outstanding, and numerous. The range is from Greenland along the Atlantic seaboard to Florida Keys and the West Indies from 20 to 100 fathoms.

Family Discinidae

These are Ecardines with circular valves, the upper being convex, and the lower, convex or flattened. The lower valve has a small somewhat triangular, longitudinal septum or prominence at its center of growth, with a small opening beneath it.

Pelagodiscus (Discinisca) atlanticus (King) PLATE 239. The shell is small, in this species, slightly oval longitudinally, broadest at its anterior margin, sometimes practically circular. It is horny, very thin, and semitransparent. The color is a light yellowish brown. The margin of the mantle has very long, slender setae of stiff, hairlike cilia, which radiate in all directions around the shell to a distance fully as great as the diameter of the shell, itself. This, while a very abundant species, occurs only at great depths.

Order TESTICARDINES

The brachiopods included in the Order are the most abundant and most typical of the present-day representatives of the Subphylum. The typical anatomy has been described already, at the beginning of this section, and is figured in INDEX PLATE 238. The Order includes the brachiopods having the valves of the shell joined by a hinge. The shell is calcareous, with the ventral valve larger than the dorsal one and prolonged to a beak posteriorly. There is a circular opening through this beak for the muscular peduncle to pass through. Inside the shell, the tentacular arms (lophophore), are supported by calcareous arms or loops of a skeleton extending forward from the dorsal valve. The intestine ends blindly without an anus.

Family Terebratulidae

The shape of the shell, in this family, is round or oval, with a prominent beak with a relatively large circular foramen. There are two curved hinge-teeth. The dorsal valve has a hinge-process and a slender calcareous loop which may be long or short.

PLATE 240

TEREBRATULINA
SEPTENTRIONALIS

INTERIOR OF
DORSAL VALVE
SHOWING
LOOP

TEREBRATULINA
SEPTENTRIONALIS

TEREBRATULINA
SEPTENTRIONALIS
DORSAL VALVE
SHOWING LABIAL
APPENDAGES

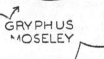

GRYPHUS
MOSELEY

INTERIOR OF DORSAL VALVE
SHOWING LOOP

Terebratulina septentrionalis (Couthouy) PLATE 240. The shell, in this species, is rather thin, ovate, narrowed posteriorly, so that it approximates a pear shape. Within the shell, the loop of the skeleton is short and simple. The oral procesess are united, transforming the loop into two rings. The tentacular arms are united by a membrane. The shell is about ½ inch long and ⅓ inch broad. This is a common species ranging along the entire New England coast. It is found in 20 fathoms off Cape Cod, and in shallow water, at about the low-water mark in the northern part of its range.

Gryphus (Liothyris) moseleyi (Davidson) PLATE 240. This species has a broadly ovate shell, slightly longer than wide, broadest anteriorly. Both valves are quite convex, with a straight margin, viewed anteriorly, having an almost continuous oval line from one valve to the other. The beak is moderately produced with an almost circular foramen, separated from the hinge by a small triangular area. The shell is perforated by many small canals. The loop within the valve is short and simple, with the oral processes not meeting. The color is white. This species occurs in northern waters at a depth of 240 fathoms.

Macandrevia (Waldheimia) cranium (Müller) PLATE 241. The dorsal and ventral valves, in this species, are evenly convex, being quite symmetrically arched. They are about evenly rounded, being widest in the middle. The beak is curved inward to a slight degree, having an incomplete circular foramen. The surface of the shell is smooth, marked by the lines of growth only. The loop of the skeleton is long, extending to about four fifths of the length of the valve before being reflected. It is very delicate and fragile. This is an abundant shell in northern Atlantic waters, being dredged off the coast of Greenland. It is not known as to how far south it extends. It is a good typical example of the reflected loop. The known depth varies from 5 to 650 fathoms.

Terebratella spitzbergensis (Davidson) PLATE 241. The shell of this species is light or whitish yellow, oval, and longer than wide. The beak is conspicuously incurved with an incomplete, longitudinal, oval foramen, two small lateral triangular plates forming its lateral margins, while the umbo of the dorsal plate bounds it anteriorly. The loop in the dorsal valve is doubly attached and extends two thirds of the valve length before becoming reflected. It is first attached to the hinge-plate and then again on the upper edge of the elevated median septum which rises from the middle line of the valve itself. The outside of the shell is about ⅜ inch. Its distribution is circumpolar, ranging south on the eastern American seaboard to the Gulf of St. Lawrence in depths of 40 to 400 fathoms.

PLATE 241

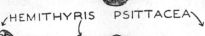

HEMITHYRIS PSITTACEA

INTERIOR OF
VENTRAL VALVE

INTERIOR OF
DORSAL VALVE

PROFILE VIEW OF
VENTRAL VALVE

SECTION OF
INTERIOR
SHOWING
MESIAL
SEPTUM

ATRETIA GNOMON

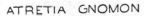

INTERIOR OF
DORSAL VALVE

TEREBRATELLA SPITZBERGENSIS

INTERIOR OF ADULT
WITH FULLY
DEVELOPED LOOP

MACANDREVIA CRANIUM

Family Rhynchonellidae

In this family the shell is fibrous. It is triangular and the beak is very sharp, hooklike, and resembles the beak of a parrot, when viewed sidewise. The internal median septum is only insignificantly developed. The foramen is widely open at the anterior end, forming a slot flanked by two slender, triangular lamellae with curved margins. This brachiopod has two elongated and turreted spiral lamellae directed inward toward the concave interior of the dorsal valve.

Hemithyris (Rhynchonella) psittacea (Chemnitz) PLATE 241. This brachiopod has a shell slightly over 1 inch in length, and about 1 inch in width. It is rather triangular in shape and globose. The dorsal valve is inflated, especially toward the umbo. The dorsal valve is about equally divided into three areas, the middle one depressed, hollowed out, and shortened; the two lateral divisions convex and extended down on the flanks, resembling ear-lappets from the front view. The ventral valve fits into this outline. The central division has a hollowed-out upward median extension fitting into the depression of the upper valve, and a depressed convex surface on either side but with the lateral margins cut out to fit the lateral expansions of the dorsal valve. The figure on the plate makes this clear. The color is bluish or very dark brown. The species is circumpolar, ranging around the north of the American continent from the Gulf of St. Lawrence to Alaska.

Atretia gnomon (Gwyn Jeffreys) PLATE 241. The shell is very small, being only about ⅕ inch in length. The shape is a triangular pear shape, with a very sharp parrotlike beak. The shell is much flatter, smoother, and more regular than in the case of the previous species. On the inside of the dorsal valve there is a large, vertical bladelike plate extending downward from the median line, like the keel of a yacht. This species occurs in Davis Strait and near the southern tip of Greenland as well as farther south in the North Atlantic. It has not yet been determined how far south in Atlantic waters its range extends.

15
Phylum Chordata

(THE PROTOCHORDATES AND VERTEBRATES)

THIS Phylum includes both the vertebrates, or back-boned animals, and the transitional groups that tend to bridge the gap between them and the invertebrate groups of backboneless animals to which this volume has been devoted hitherto. The vertebrates comprise the cyclostomes, fishes, amphibians, reptiles, birds, and mammals, and are dealt with in other volumes of this field book series. This chapter will exclude these, but will briefly review the protochordates, comprising those primitive groups that exhibit structures, either in their larval or adult anatomy, or both, obscurely in some, but more clearly in others, that foreshadow a number of features characteristic of vertebrates. These features are: the notochord; dorsal nerve-cord with a neural canal; and a series of paired gill-slits. Finally, in *Amphioxus,* we even find a ventral mouth and anus; a segmented muscular layer; and a portal system; that is, a provision for the blood from the alimentary tract to pass through the liver, before being distributed to the general circulation. Not all the transitional groups show this entire list of incipient vertebrate features, but in the most primitive forms some are indicated, while the more complex types cover them more completely.

The Phylum Chordata, for our purposes, is divided into four Subphyla, as follows: (1) *Hemichorda;* (2) *Urochorda;* (3) *Cephalochorda;* and (4) *Vertebrata.*

SUBPHYLUM HEMICHORDA

This Subphylum includes a series of marine burrowing animals that, either in their larval or adult organization, or both, show a primitive division into three coelomic and corresponding external segments, and various other structures that appear to be vestigial beginnings of the notochord and gill-slits. True chordate, metameric segmentation is not yet clearly present or with few, if any, indications of it.

This Subphylum is divided into three Classes, as follows: (1) *Phoronidea;* (2) *Pterobranchia;* and (3) *Enteropneusta.*

CLASS PHORONIDEA

This Class consists of the single genus *Phoronis,* an elongate, burrowing, wormlike animal, having, in the adult condition, a U-shaped digestive system; a double, fundamentally horseshoe-shaped lophophore bearing numerous ciliated tentacles, suggesting those of the Phylum Prospygia; and a free-swimming Actinotroch larva of peculiar interest. About six species of *Phoronis* are known from various parts of the world, only one of which lives within our habitat.

Phoronis architecta Andrews PLATE 242. This is a long, slender, burrowing animal with a straight body about 5 inches in length, and about ⅟₂₅ inch in width. It is flesh-colored anteriorly, shading into a reddish or yellowish hue in the posterior region. At the upper or dorsal end, a partition, the *epistome,* separates the mouth and anus and extends as a fold of the body-wall (enclosing a small portion of the coelom) between the two rows of tentacles forming the *lophophore.* This latter structure, in *Phoronis,* is a double horseshoe-shaped ridge coiling into a spiral at both ends of each of the two parallel edges, bearing a single row of ciliated tentacles.

The body-cavity, or coelom, is divided into three segments, the upper or prostomial segment being lost during metamorphosis from the larval stage, when the preoral hood containing it is discarded. The second, or collar segment, is marked externally by the lophophore region and is, therefore, still present in the adult, as is the third or trunk-segment.

Phoronis is hermaphroditic. The ovaries and testes form two white masses on the outside of the stomach, which discharge their products into the body-cavity ultimately to reach the outside through the kidney ducts. The development takes place through metamorphosis from a free-swimming larva, as above mentioned, known as the Actinotroch larva (PLATE 242). This is a peculiar form quite unlike the parent. The mouth is anterior, opening into a straight digestive tube, expanded to form a capacious stomach, then narrowed to a short intestine to discharge through the anus at the end opposite to the mouth. An expanded structure, the *preoral hood,* overhangs the mouth. A single circlet of larval tentacles surrounds the body. After a time, a fingerlike tubular opening grows into the body on the ventral surface just below the circlet of tentacles. The larva settles to the bottom and a strange metamorphosis takes place. The tubelike opening suddenly turns inside out to form a conspicuous projection on the ventral surface. The intestine bends up and enters this tube, closing the old anal opening and forming a new one at the end of the new tube, so that the digestive tract is now U-shaped. At the same time, the expanded preoral hood and, in company with it, the ganglia and eyespots, enter into the mouth to be swallowed and digested. Next, the larva devours the larval tentacles, which are replaced by a new set forming the adult lophophore. In this way, the

PLATE 242

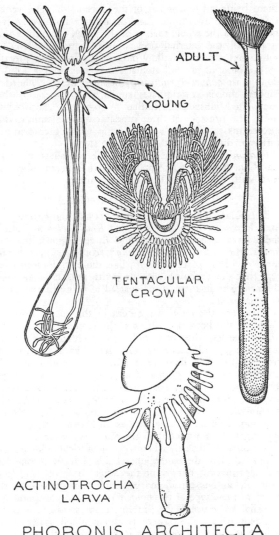

YOUNG

ADULT

TENTACULAR
CROWN

ACTINOTROCHA
LARVA

PHORONIS ARCHITECTA

U-shaped adult organization is attained, so that the mouth and anus are close together, the short distance between them being all that is left of the dorsal side. The ventral side, in the meantime, has expanded enormously, and now forms the whole surface of the body, containing practically all the internal organs. It is now considered by some that a pair of hollow outgrowths from the junction of the oesophagus and stomach may represent a kind of double *notochordal rudiment,* because the notochord of higher chordates originates similarly and because their vacuolated substance is similar to so-called "chordoid tissue." The presence of three fundamental coelomic cavities also seems to point to a relationship with other primitive forms leading toward the vertebrate stem.

Phoronis architecta is found in the sand-flats of North Carolina, near the low-water mark, in isolated tubes covered with sand-grains. It is quite common.

CLASS PTEROBRANCHIA

This Class is based on the discovery of the curious animals known as *Cephalodiscus* and *Rhabdopleura.* Both of these have a body divided into three regions, the *proboscis,* the *collar,* and the *trunk,* corresponding to the three divisions of the *coelom,* like those in *Phoronis,* except that the proboscis with its cavity persists as an adult characteristic in these forms, instead of being merely larval as in *Phoronis.*

These are the only two genera in this Class. Both are found at the bottom of the sea, the former having about fifteen species; the latter, only one. Neither of them occurs strictly within our territory, but they are mentioned here simply as a link between the Phoronidea and the Enteropneusta. In *Cephalodiscus,* the body is divided into proboscis, collar, and trunk, each with a corresponding division of the body-cavity or coelom. The trunk-cavity is subdivided into two lateral cavities by a longitudinal partition. The alimentary tract is U-shaped with the anal opening near the mouth. There is a dorsally located nerve concentration, beneath which is a cylindrical cellular cord connected with the epithelium of the pharynx at one end and terminating blindly at the other. It is of solid construction, and is considered by many zoologists to be the incipient prototype of the notochord, and to correspond to a similar structure in the Enteropneusta. Behind the collar is a pair of gill-slits. There is also a blood system with heart and closed blood vessels resembling those of the Enteropneusta.

Rhabdopleura also has a small proboscis, collar, and trunk-region, with corresponding segments of the body-cavity, arranged similarly to those in *Cephalodiscus.* There is also a dorsally concentrated nerve-tract and beneath it a rodlike cellular structure, almost exactly corresponding to that of *Cephalodiscus*. There are, however, no gill-slits.

These genera, therefore, have structures which seem to foreshadow the dorsal nerve-cord, notochord, and, in the case of *Cephalodiscus,* the gill-slits of vertebrates, in their fundamental structure, their relative position, and in their origin and method of development. It may be added that their larval stages, also, while not free-swimming, nevertheless show strong points of similarity with those of the Echinoderma, on the one hand, and with that of the Enteropneusta, on the other. Therefore, even if they do not represent actual stages in the evolution of the higher types, they must have affinities to the general stock from which the higher chordates sprang.

CLASS ENTEROPNEUSTA
(The "Acorn-worms")

These are elongate, wormlike Hemichorda, which are quite common in sand- and mud-flats. The body is divided into proboscis, collar, and trunk-region (PLATE 243). The proboscis is fairly short in some species, and elongate in others. It is somewhat cylindrical and tapering to a blunt, rounded point at the apex, enlarged and rounded at the base, and connected with the collar by a narrow, flexible neck. In the species with the shorter proboscis, it is somewhat acorn-shaped, so that these animals are often called "Acorn-worms." Although about ten genera are known, they are often familiarly called *"Balanoglossus,"* the name applied to one of the two first-described genera and now restricted, from the zoological standpoint, to only one.

The three regions of the body, as we have seen in the Pterobranchia, correspond to similar divisions of the coelom, there being a single cavity in the proboscis; a paired cavity in the collar; and also in the trunk, the cavity is divided into two by a longitudinal partition that encloses the digestive tract and subsidiary glands between its double walls and thus acts as a supporting mesentery. The alimentary tract extends as a straight tube from the mouth (located ventrally below the neck, between the proboscis and the collar), to the anus, which terminates the trunk at its posterior tip. At the anterior end of the digestive tube, just back of the mouth, is the pharynx, from which on the dorsal side there extends forward a narrow tubular prolongation, with closely appressed, stiffened cellular walls, into the cavity of the proboscis. This is considered by Bateson and many other comparative anatomists to be homologous to the *notochord* of vertebrates, which is derived in the same way as a corresponding structure in the embryo of vertebrates from which the notochord is actually developed. As previously mentioned, it corresponds in origin and anatomy with the smaller similar structure in the Pterobranchia.

The lateral walls of the digestive tract, in its entire anterior portion, are pierced with a series of *gill-slits* on either side, and, with certain exceptions, a series of paired liver sacs is posterior to these. On the dorsal side of the collar there is a tubular concentration of nerve tissue forming a *neural canal* that extends backward in a similar way to that in the central nervous system in vertebrates. There is a smaller, but similar nerve concentration beginning on the ventral median line of the trunk, connected by a nerve ring with the dorsal nerve-tube. There are also a dorsal and a ventral blood vessel above and below the intestine throughout its entire length. The dorsal vessel passes anteriorly above the notochordal prolongation and connects with a blood sinus in the proboscis and collar, which acts as a heart. A kidney is located in this region and connects with the outside by means of a pore. The sexes are separate. The gonads form a paired series, each opening to the outside by a reproductive pore, extending for a considerable distance on either side of the trunk. The eggs hatch out as a free-swimming, top-shaped larva known as a *tornaria* (PLATE 243, lower figures). In a number of respects it resembles certain echinoderm larvae.

Dolichoglossus kowalevskii Spengel PLATE 243. This is a slender, wormlike species characterized by an elongate, tapering proboscis, which it uses as a burrowing organ. The proboscis has a single pore at its tip, as compared with two pores in other genera of the group. The length is about 6 inches. The proboscis is pink, or salmon-colored; the collar, bright orange, sometimes orange-red; and the body an orange-yellow, sometimes mottled in various shades. The species is found burrowing in sand and sandy mud quite abundantly, and ranges from Massachusetts Bay to Beaufort, North Carolina. This creature burrows quite actively by elongating its proboscis and inflating it with water to stiffen it. Then, by clinging with its tip, it draws the body forward and repeats the process. The free-swimming Tornaria larva is illustrated in the plate. A half-grown larva is also represented with the notochord showing through the transparent wall of the proboscis.

SUBPHYLUM UROCHORDA (TUNICATA)

This is a small, exclusively marine group of degenerate Chordata which will be best understood from the description given below of its principal Class, containing the Ascidians. The other Classes of the Subphylum are peculiar

PLATE 243

HEMICHORDA

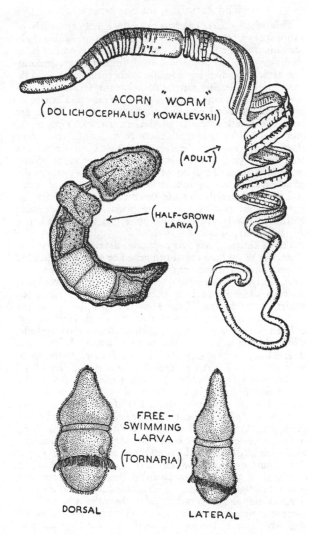

ACORN "WORM"
(DOLICHOCEPHALUS KOWALEVSKII)

(ADULT)

(HALF-GROWN LARVA)

FREE-
SWIMMING
LARVA
(TORNARIA)

DORSAL

LATERAL

pelagic forms especially modified for a free-swimming existence.

CLASS ASCIDIACEA
(The Ascidians, the Sea Squirts)

This small Class, comprising only a few hundreds of valid species, probably contains nine tenths of the Sub-phylum. It affords one of the most striking examples of evolution that has gone backward, instead of progressing.

A typical ascidian has a saclike body enclosed in a tough, more or less flexible outer tunic, known as the *test,* and lives either permanently attached to some solid object or buried in the sand or mud of the sea-bottom. There are only two small openings in the test (INDEX PLATE 244); one, the oral or branchial aperture or mouth (*incurrent siphon*), serving for the intake of water for respiration and for carrying in the minute organisms or organic matter which form the food of the ascidian; the other, the *atrial* or excurrent siphon, serving for the escape of water and waste material, and for the discharge of the eggs or larvae. These two apertures are often raised on papillae which may be lengthened into projecting tubes. and hence are called *siphons.*

The ascidians have very poorly developed organs of sense, but when the animal is touched or otherwise alarmed by any sudden movement of the water, its muscles contract, and the water contained in the body is forced out through these apertures in small jets, hence the name sea squirts. If we cut one of these animals open, as represented in the INDEX PLATE, we find that the tough external test is lined with a layer containing muscles and blood vessels, while the remainder of the body is largely hollow, the internal organs being of small bulk compared to the space in which they lie. An exception to this is the very large, membranous sac (*pharynx*) lying rather loosely in the cavity of the body, but so attached to the inner side of the body-wall, at its front end, that the *branchial aperture* (*incurrent siphon*) opens directly into it. Its walls are pierced with such vast numbers of minute clefts that it is, in fact, a net or sieve. It serves not only for respiration (its walls being full of blood vessels), but also for straining out the minute organisms which form the food supply of the ascidian. As the water taken in at the branchial aperture passes through the minute clefts, called *stigmata,* into the outer cavity, and then out through the *atrial aperture* (*excurrent siphon*), it leaves the food within the branchial sac, which opens at its rear end into the stomach and intestine.

The oesophagus, stomach, and other parts of the digestive tract, as well as the heart, reproductive, and excretory

PLATE 244

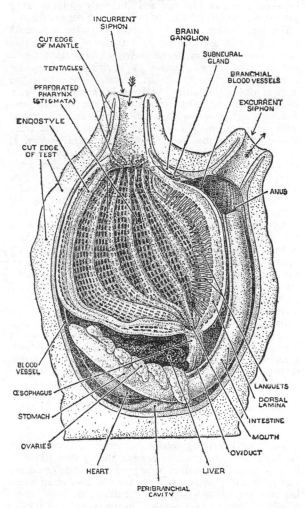

INCURRENT
SIPHON

BRAIN
GANGLION

CUT EDGE
OF MANTLE

SUBNEURAL
GLAND

TENTACLES

BRANCHIAL
BLOOD VESSELS

PERFORATED
PHARYNX
(STIGMATA)

EXCURRENT
SIPHON

ENDOSTYLE

CUT EDGE
OF TEST

ANUS

BLOOD
VESSEL

ŒSOPHAGUS

LANGUETS

STOMACH

DORSAL
LAMINA

OVARIES

INTESTINE

MOUTH

OVIDUCT

HEART

LIVER

PERIBRANCHIAL
CAVITY

MEDIAN SECTION OF
A TYPICAL ASCIDIAN

organs, lie either in the *peribranchial cavity* (the space between the branchial sac and the body-wall) or in a posterior extension of the body. The other organs that require mention are: a circle of *tentacles* (often branched) inside the oral aperture at the entrance to the branchial sac; a *brain ganglion* in the body-wall, between the two siphons; the *dorsal lamina,* a membrane projecting freely into the cavity of the branchial sac along the median dorsal line (often replaced by a row of tongue-like processes, or *languets*); and on the median ventral line, the *endostyle,* a wide, densely ciliated furrow with raised edges. The *heart* is an elongate tube lying at the bottom of the body in the peribranchial cavity. It possesses the peculiarity of reversing its pulsations at frequent intervals, so that the vessels leading to and from it serve, at times, as veins and, at other times, as arteries. This remarkable characteristic can be easily observed under the microscope in small, transparent ascidians, such as *Perophora* (INDEX PLATE 245).

Ascidians are mostly hermaphroditic. In some species, the eggs pass out of the atrial aperture and develop into larvae outside (oviparous species), or do so in the parent's body (viviparous species). Many ascidians possess, besides the power of sexual reproduction, the faculty of reproducing asexually by budding or gemmation (INDEX PLATE 245). This is usually confined to species in which the individuals are very small (⅖ to ⅘ inch in length). The individuals, so formed, remain connected with their parents, producing a more or less compact colony. Such forms are distinguished as "compound ascidians" but do not form a natural division of the class, as some families include certain species that have the budding habit, as well as others that do not.

The Larvae of Ascidians and Their Relation to the Vertebrates

The most interesting feature of the ascidians remains to be dealt with. As the above description shows, there is little in the adult ascidian to suggest a relationship to the vertebrates. If, however, we examine the larva of an ascidian, we see, at once, striking resemblances, both superficially and in its organization, to the tadpole of a frog, except that the larval ascidian is very much smaller (only a few millimeters long). A study of the figures on INDEX PLATE 246 will give the reader an understanding of these points of resemblance more clearly than a long description would do. It was these larval characters, which the ascidian loses after a brief period as a free-swimming animal, that led the great naturalist Kowalevsky to the

PLATE 245

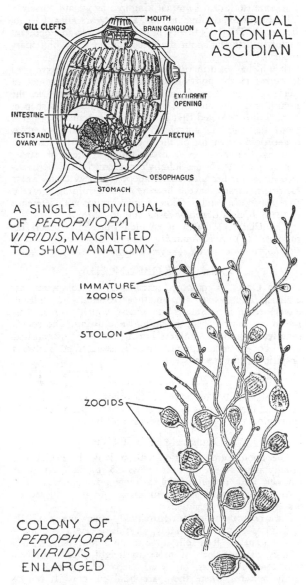

A TYPICAL
COLONIAL
ASCIDIAN

GILL CLEFTS

MOUTH
BRAIN GANGLION

EXCURRENT
OPENING

INTESTINE

TESTIS AND
OVARY

RECTUM

OESOPHAGUS

STOMACH

A SINGLE INDIVIDUAL
OF *PEROPIIORA
VIRIDIS*, MAGNIFIED
TO SHOW ANATOMY

IMMATURE
ZOOIDS

STOLON

ZOOIDS

COLONY OF
*PEROPHORA
VIRIDIS*
ENLARGED

conclusion that the ascidians are a degenerate branch of the same stock of the animal kingdom as we are ourselves. This discovery, coming in 1866, a few years after the publication of Darwin's theory of evolution, was an important factor in bringing about the acceptance of the evolutionary theory.

It will be noted in INDEX PLATE 246 that the nerve cord is dorsal to the notochord; that the brain, or center of nerve concentration, is on the dorsal side between the mouth and anus; and that the digestive system is U-shaped. It may also be stated that in the development of the larva from the egg the notochord is originally developed as a chordoid extension of the integument of the pharynx, and that the dorsal nerve cord is tubular. These, of course, are all features of the Subphylum Hemichorda, here carried to a further and more adaptive elaboration. These factors, naturally, have a bearing in determining the relative relationship and position of these groups with reference to the Subphyla *Cephalochorda* and *Vertebrata*.

The Class Ascidiacea is divided into four Orders, as follows: (1) *Krikobranchia;* (2) *Diktyobranchia;* (3) *Ptychobranchia;* and (4) *Pyrosomida.*

Order KRIKOBRANCHIA

This Order is composed exclusively of compound ascidians. The zooids are small and usually completely enveloped in a common mass of test, which may be massive or variously lobed, or flat and encrusting. The zooids may have the body transversely constructed or demarcated into two or three regions. The digestive tract is always posterior to the branchial sac.

Family Synoicidae

In this family, the body of the mature zooids is composed of three regions, the most posterior (post-abdomen), containing the reproductive organs and heart.

Genus AMAROUCIUM

The zooids are elongate, with a long, branchial sac, usually with twelve or more rows of stigmata, an atrial languet, and (when adult) a long post-abdomen. The wall of the stomach is longitudinally plicated and red or orange, in living specimens.

Amaroucium pellucidum Leidy COLOR PLATE XXIII, 2; XXIV, 9, 9a. The colony, in this species, is densely sand encrusted. It is split up into numerous narrow, tall lobules, often 1 inch or more in height, closely packed into rounded masses, but easily separable. It occurs on sandy bottoms where there are tidal currents. It ranges from Cape Cod to Long Island Sound.

PLATE 246

UROCHORDA
METAMORPHOSIS OF AN
ASCIDIAN LARVA

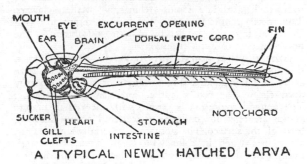

MOUTH

EYE

EAR

BRAIN

EXCURRENT OPENING

DORSAL NERVE CORD

FIN

SUCKER

HEART

GILL CLEFTS

INTESTINE

STOMACH

NOTOCHORD

A TYPICAL NEWLY HATCHED LARVA

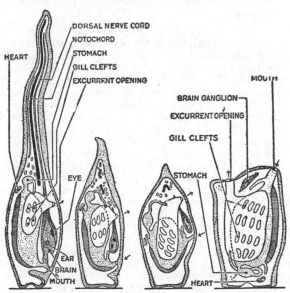

HEART

DORSAL NERVE CORD

NOTOCHORD

STOMACH

GILL CLEFTS

EXCURRENT OPENING

MOUTH

BRAIN GANGLION

EXCURRENT OPENING

GILL CLEFTS

STOMACH

EYE

EAR

BRAIN

MOUTH

HEART

SUCCESSIVE STAGES IN THE
METAMORPHOSIS TO THE ADULT

Amaroucium stellatum Verrill PLATE 247. Sea Pork (this popular name is also applied to the various allied species). This species has a tough, translucent test, suggesting raw salt pork in color and consistency. The colonies are in the form of large, elongate, erect plates, often ⅜ to ⅘ inch thick, and sometimes 8 inches or more in length. The zooids are in small, stellate clusters. This species ranges from the Woods Hole region to North Carolina. It occurs in depths of 2 to 3 fathoms in the northern part of its distribution.

Amaroucium constellatum Verrill. The colonies in this species are massive, sometimes 1 to 2 inches or more across, usually divided into turbinate or capitate lobes by deep clefts. The test is rather soft, fleshy, semiopaque. The general coloration is cream, with the red or orange zooids arranged in confluent or scattered groups showing through the surface. The stomach is especially conspicuous, being bright red in color with about twenty-five longitudinal fine folds visible on its surface. The distribution is from Massachusetts southward and is common on wharf-piles.

Family Didemnidae

The colonies included in this family are usually flat and encrusting, with the test often so densely packed with minute spherical or stellate calcareous spicules as to make it opaque, white, and rather hard and brittle. The zooids are minute, with only three or four rows of stigmata. These forms have no post-abdomen. The method of budding is unique, taking place from the middle, constricted region of the body, and often temporarily forming double zooids suggesting Siamese twins.

Didemnum albidum Verrill PLATE 247; COLOR PLATES XXIII, 6; XXIV, 10, 10a. This species forms chalky-white, yellowish, or flesh-colored encrustations, about ½ inch to 3 inches across, on stones, wharf-piles, and other undersea objects. Spherical spicules are present, studded with round knobs. This species is chiefly found north of Cape Cod, but is also quite common on the wharf-piles at Martha's Vineyard.

Didemnum lutarium Van Name PLATE 247. This species is similar to the previous one, but has stellate spicules with conical points. It is common on wharf-piles, rocks, and other objects, chiefly from Cape Cod southward. It is probably a variety of *Didemnum candidum* widely distributed in the tropics.

Family Polycitoridae

In this family, the body of the zooids is constricted into two divisions by a long, narrow neck. The zooids are much larger than in the Didemnidae. Their buds develop on vascular stolons from the posterior end of the abdomen. Spicules are usually not present.

Polycitor (Endostoma) convexus (Van Name) PLATE 247. Both apertures are situated on tubes, their margins usually cleft into about six lobes. There are no spicules. The longitudinal muscles of the thorax are composed of strong, thick bands. The reproductive organs are located beside the alimentary tract in the abdomen. The larvae develop in the peribranchial cavity. The colonies are gelatinous and translucent. They are sessile, rounded, or elliptical masses from ⅗ inch to 4 inches or more in diameter. They are yellowish to brownish violet in color. The zooids have only three rows of stigmata. This species ranges from North Carolina southward, from low-water to 10 fathoms or more.

Order DIKTYOBRANCHIA

These are mostly simple ascidians with a transparent or translucent test and a branchial sac without folds. Usually there is a system of internal longitudinal vessels raised on short papillae on its inner surface. The tentacles are not branched. The oral aperture (incurrent) is usually eight lobed, the excurrent six lobed, and the ovaries and testes are branched, ramifying on the digestive tract.

Family Ascidiidae

The species in this family include rather large, simple ascidians having the digestive tract along the left side of the branchial sac.

Ascidia callosa Stimpson PLATE 247. The body in this species is elliptical, obliquely compressed, and usually obliquely attached by a large part of the left side. The apertures usually are not prominent. The test is translucent, grayish, greenish, or yellowish, and rather firm and fairly smooth except in old specimens. The diameter varies from about 1½ to 2½ inches. It is found in shallow water along the coast of Maine and northward, and in deeper water as far south as Cape Cod.

Ascidia hygomiana (Traustedt) PLATE 247. The normal shape, in this species, is rather elongate, tapering anteriorly to the terminal oral aperture. The atrial (excurrent) aperture is situated far back at about the middle of the test, but the shape is very variable because of its habit of growing in crowded clusters on the substratum. The test is usually yellowish and the surface rather rough and opaque. The length varies from 1⅗ to 2½ inches or more. The distribution is from North Carolina southward.

Ciona intestinalis (Linnaeus) PLATE 247; COLOR PLATES XXIII, 3; XXIV, 6. This species is readily distinguished from *Ascidia* by the strong longitudinal muscle bands, which are often visible through the translucent test, and the more posterior location of the digestive tract. The body is elongate, attached at the rear end, and tapering anteriorly. The oral aperture is terminal, with the atrial aperture close beside it, both on very short tubes. The test is transparent, of a light golden yellow. It measures from about 1½ to 2½ inches in length. It ranges all along the New England coast on piles, submerged timbers and rocks.

Family Perophoridae

These are small ascidians resembling the Ascidiidae, except that they produce stolons on which buds develop, forming colonies of usually loosely connected individuals.

Perophora viridis Verrill PLATE 248; INDEX PLATE 245; COLOR PLATES XXIII, 5; XXIV, 7, 7a. The little zooids in this species are only 1/10 to 1/7 inch in diameter. They are ovoid in shape, colorless, or greenish yellow, and borne on the branches of a slender stolon that grows like a vine over piles, rocks, and algae. The individuals are very transparent, allowing the internal structures, and even the reversible beating of the heart to be easily observed. The species ranges from Cape Cod southward, in shallow water.

Order PTYCHOBRANCHIA

This is the most highly organized Order of the ascidians. It is characterized by usually having an opaque, coriaceous test; a branchial sac with internal longitudinal vessels and with large longitudinal folds or pleats to increase its surface, the tentacles often branched; a digestive tract beside the branchial sac; and reproductive organs borne on the inner surface of the body-wall. The Order contains both compound and simple species.

Family Botryllidae

The ascidians in this family form soft, fleshy colonies in which the zooids are arranged in systems or groups discharging by common cloacal apertures. The zooids are small, and the branchial sacs without folds. The test is penetrated by branching vessels ending in bulbs. The colors are often brilliant and varied during life, but fade quickly after death. Budding takes place from the lateral regions of the body.

Botryllus schlosseri (Pallas) PLATE 248; COLOR PLATE XXIV, 8, 8a, 8b. This colonial species forms smooth, fleshy encrustations of varying thickness, often 4 inches across, on wharf-piles, bottoms of boats, floats, eelgrass, and similar places. The zooids embedded in these are arranged in small, round, or oval groups. The colors are

PLATE 247

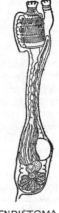

DIDEMNUM
ALBIDUM

DIDEMNUM ALBIDUM
(COLONY)

ENDISTOMA
CONVEXA

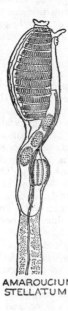

AMAROUCIUM
STELLATUM

DIDEMNUM LUTARIUM
(SPICULES)

CIONA
INTESTINALIS
(PART OF
BRANCHIAL SAC)

CIONA
INTESTINALIS

ASCIDIA
CALLOSA
(PART OF
BRANCHIAL SAC)

ASCIDIA
CALLOSA

(PART OF
BRANCHIAL
SAC)

ASCIDIA
HYGOMIANA

very variable and often handsome during life, varying from olive-green to yellowish olive, with brown or purple zooids, conspicuously marked with white and bright yellow. The species is very common in shallow water from Massachusetts southward.

Family Styelidae

Although both simple and compound species occur in this family at large, only simple forms are found in the region covered by this book. The test is opaque, usually very tough, and is often colored red or reddish, especially about the apertures, which are either four lobed or square. The branchial sac has up to four large folds or pleats on each side. The tentacles are simple. The digestive organs are situated on the left side of the interior cavity. The stomach-wall has plications and there is no liver or kidney. Two genera are represented here: *Styela,* with one or more elongate gonads on each side of the body, and *Dendrodoa,* with one gonad on the right side and none on the left.

Styela partita (Stimpson) PLATE 248; COLOR PLATES XXIII, 4; XXIV, 2. The body, in this species, is irregularly oval. In some cases it is attached by the whole ventral surface; in others, the body is more or less upright and attached only near the rear end. The usual length is ¾ to ⅘ inch. The test is brown or yellowish in color, and is opaque, leathery, and wrinkled, with minute rounded tuberculations near the apertures, which are often purplish with radiating white stripes. There are two elongate, sinuate gonads on each side of the body. This species is common on stones, shells, and similar objects, in shallow water, from Massachusetts Bay southward.

Styela plicata (Lesueur) PLATE 248. This is a larger species, often 1½ inches to 2½ inches in length. The body is oval or tapering toward the rear end, by which it is attached. The test, where not discolored, is dull whitish, usually with wide rounded ridges which break up into rounded elevations about the apertures. There are two elongate gonads on the left side of the body and usually four or more on the right. The distribution is similar to that of the above.

Dendrodoa carnea (Agassiz) PLATE 248; COLOR PLATES XXIII, 4a; XXIV, 3. The body, in this species, is depressed, conical, or dome-shaped, and attached by the whole lower surface, the test spreading beyond its margin. The surface is usually smooth and pink or red in color. The apertures are on low papillae. The gonads are not branched. This species is usually not more than ½ inch in diameter. The distribution is from Long Island northward, on stones, shells, and wharf-piles.

PLATE 248

BOTRYLLUS SCHLOSSERI

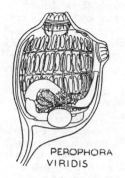

PEROPHORA
VIRIDIS

(LEFT
SIDE)   (RIGHT
SIDE)

STYELA PLICATA

DENDRODOA CARNEA

CNEMIDOCARPA MOLLIS

BOLTENIA
ECHINATA   STYELA PARTITA

BOLTENIA
ECHINATA   SPINOUS
                 PROCESSES OF
                 BODY   BOLTENIA
                             ECHINATA

Cnemidocarpa mollis (Stimpson) PLATE 248. The body is elliptical or nearly spherical. It is slightly less than ½ inch in diameter and evenly coated with sand-grains. The apertures are near together, usually only slightly raised. There are several elongate gonads on each side of the body. It is found from Long Island Sound northward, living on stones, shells, wharf-piles, and the like.

Family Pyuridae

The ascidians, in this family, are simple in habit and often large. They are most easily distinguished from the Styelidae by the branching tentacles, more numerous folds in the branchial sac, usually six or more on each side, and the elongate, narrow stomach, which bears a liver of minute branching tubules. Both the apertures are four lobed or square. There is no kidney.

Boltenia ovifera (Linnaeus) COLOR PLATE XXIV, 5. In this peculiar species, the body is about the size of a hen's egg or larger. It is borne on the summit of a slender stalk, 1 to 4 inches in length. The body-surface is variable, being smooth or wrinkled, and sometimes spiny. The color is yellowish orange, or partly or entirely red. This species is chiefly found along the coast of Maine and farther north, in shallow water. It also occurs southward to Cape Cod in deeper water.

Boltenia echinata (Linnaeus) PLATE 248. The body of this *Boltenia* is not stalked like that of the previous species. It is slightly attached to rocks and similar situations. It is covered with large tubercles, each bearing a group of rather stiff, radiating spines, rather suggesting those of a cactus. The color is salmon-pink to red. The diameter is usually not more than ⅗ to ⅘ inch in our region. The range is chiefly north of Cape Cod.

Halocynthia pyriformis Rathke PLATE 249; COLOR PLATE XXIV, 4. The Sea-peach. The body of this handsome species is ovate or barrel-shaped and attached by one end. The apertures are mounted on large papillae. The body-surface is generally even, but rough to the touch, like sand-paper. The size, shape, and color, which is yellow or orange, more or less tinged with pink or red, suggest the popular name, Sea-peach. The distribution is chiefly along the coast of Maine and northward, in shallow water.

Pyura vittata (Stimpson) PLATE 249. This is a large species of very variable external appearance. It measures up to 2 inches in diameter. It is best distinguished by the gonads, usually one on each side, each consisting of a slender, tubular oviduct with many small sacs arranged along it. There are six branchial folds on each side. It ranges from North Carolina southward.

PLATE 249

HALOCYNTHIA PYRIFORMIS

PYURA
VITTATA

MOLGULA ARENATA

PYURA
VITTATA

MOLGULA MANHATTENSIS (PART
OF
BRANCHIAL
SAC)

MOLGULA RETORTIFORMIS

MOLGULA
OCCIDENTALIS

BOSTRICHOBRANCHUS
PILULARIS

MOLGULA
OCCIDENTALIS

Family Molgulidae

These are simple ascidians with a usually rounded or ellipsoidal body, often unattached, and living buried in sand or mud. The oral aperture is usually six lobed and the atrial aperture, four lobed or square. The tentacles are branched. The stigmata are often arranged in more or less perfect spirals, especially on the folds of the branchial sac. A kidney in the form of a large, closed sac is present, attached to the inside of the body-wall, on the right side.

Molgula manhattensis DeKay PLATE 249; COLOR PLATES XXIII, 1; XXIV, 1. Sea Grapes. The body of this ascidian is rounded and is about 1 inch in diameter. The apertures are on more or less prominent papillae or diverging tubes. The test is tough, slightly translucent, and rough. The stigmata are curved or spiral. There are six branchial folds on each side. There is a hermaphroditic gonad on each side. That on the right side is dorsal to the kidney. This interesting species grows, often in dense clusters, on piles, rocks, eelgrass, and floating timbers, in shallow water. The tests are often the basis of attachment for colonies of *Botryllus*. This is the commonest simple ascidian from Massachusetts southward.

Molgula arenata Stimpson PLATE 249. This is a small species living buried in sandy bottoms. It is usually found in a contracted state, when it is much flattened laterally, like a thick disc with rounded edges, the tubes being retracted. The diameter is ½ inch or more. It is usually densely and evenly encrusted with coarse sand. It ranges from Cape Cod to New Jersey.

Molgula retortiformis Verrill PLATE 249. This is a large species, 1¼ to 1⅗ inches in diameter, with a somewhat translucent test, often covered with debris, and with long tubes, usually found retracted in preserved specimens. There are seven branchial folds on each side. The stigmata are mostly straight. The range is from Maine northward on rocky bottoms.

Molgula occidentalis Traustedt PLATE 249. This is a larger species than *Molgula manhattensis,* with shorter, nonretractile tubes. The test is often covered with sand or debris. The stigmata are small, short, and mostly straight. The right gonad is long and curved around the kidney. The distribution is from North Carolina southward, attached to piles, mangrove-roots, and other submerged material.

Bostrichobranchus pilularis (Verrill) PLATE 249. The body, in this species, is globular and from ½ inch to 1¼ inches in diameter. The tubes are retractile and placed quite near together. There are no branchial folds and the stigmata form very perfect spirals. The body-surface is so fibrous that mud or fine sand adhere to it. There is an oval, definitely circumscribed area about the bases of both tubes, free from adhering material. The latter is quite a distinguishing character. This species ranges from Canada to Florida. It is quite common, but is usually buried out of sight.

Order PYROSOMIDA
(The Pyrosomas)

This is a very small Order of pelagic, compound ascidians, having a tubular colony closed at one end. The zooids are arranged around this tube with their branchial apertures on the outside and their atrial openings on the interior surface. The test is transparent, luminous at night. the zooids having luminous organs.

CLASS THALIACEA

This is a very small Class of pelagic tunicates, often large in size, approximating 4 inches or more in length, which drift or swim slowly in the open sea. They have a more or less spindle-shaped, or cylindrical, body. It is almost transparent, with the incurrent (branchial) aperture and the excurrent (atrial) aperture at or near their opposite ends. They are provided with luminous organs, so that they are a brilliant sight at night. The body is largely hollow, the principal viscera usually forming a small, compact mass, or nucleus. There are conspicuous, transverse muscle-bands in the walls of the body. The contraction of these bands, forcing the water out posteriorly, enables the animal to swim by jet propulsion.

Order HEMIMYARIA
(The Salpas)

The body is more or less spindle-shaped or cylindrical, sometimes prismatic in cross section. The muscle-bands are usually interrupted ventrally. Alternating generations of sexually produced *solitary individuals* and asexually produced *aggregated individuals* occur, the latter brought about by budding and by remaining for a time connected with each other in chains. The individuals of the solitary generation differ from those of the aggregate generation in form, in arrangement of muscles, in the presence of the stolon with its chain of buds, and in other ways.

Family Salpidae

This is the principal family of the Order Hemimyaria and has the same characters.

Salpa democratica Forskal PLATE 250. This is a very small species, at times extremely abundant off southern

New England in summer. As above stated, the muscle-band arrangement on the PLATE should be utilized for purposes of identification.

Salpa fusiformis Cuvier PLATE 250. This is a species of medium size, measuring 1⅝ inches in length, sometimes smooth, externally, and sometimes rough with minute points. It is found drifting north in the Gulf Stream.

Salpa (Iasis) zonaria (Pallas) PLATE 250. This species is easily recognized by the broad, closely spaced muscle-bands, especially on the solitary form, which is elongate. It is of frequent occurrence off our coast.

Salpa (Thetys) vagina Tilesius PLATE 250. This is a very large species, being sometimes more than 6 or 7 inches long. It is more common in warmer regions than off our coast.

Salpa (Pegia) confederata Forskal PLATE 250. This species is fairly large, ranging from 3 to 6 inches in length. It can be easily recognized by its scanty musculature. The aggregate form is quite common and is reddish in color. The solitary form is quite rare and probably inhabits deep water only.

Cyclosalpa affinis (Chamisso) PLATE 250. This is a cylindrical salp with narrow, nearly complete muscle-bands. The aggregate form has two characteristic, ventral projections (see PLATE). It is commoner in southern regions.

Order CYCLOMYARIA

In this Order, the transparent body is barrel-shaped, with terminal apertures, and a diagonal platelike partition within, pierced by stigmata, and the muscle-bands usually completely encircling it. The life history is complex and requires too detailed an explanation for inclusion here. The manner in which the small, detached buds, produced by the sexual generation on a ventrally placed stolon, migrate to a dorsal process of the parent's back, by amoeboid movements, and attach themselves to it in three perfectly regular rows, is one of the most astonishing mysteries that zoology affords.

Family Doliolidae

This is the only family and has the characters of the Order.

Doliolum denticulatum Quoy & Gaimard. The oblique respiratory partition has about forty stigmata on each side. A member of the genus *Doliolum,* possibly this species, has been reported as occurring off Gay Head, Massachusetts.

PLATE 250

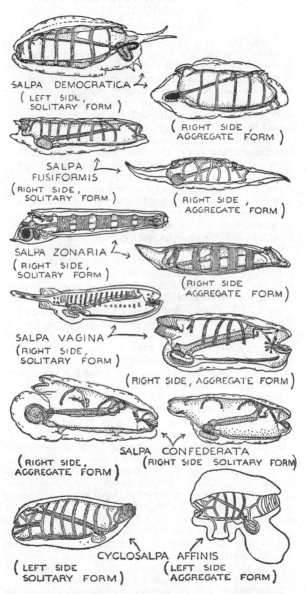

SALPA DEMOCRATICA
(LEFT SIDE,
SOLITARY FORM)

(RIGHT SIDE,
AGGREGATE FORM)

SALPA
FUSIFORMIS
(RIGHT SIDE,
SOLITARY FORM)

(RIGHT SIDE
AGGREGATE FORM)

SALPA ZONARIA
(RIGHT SIDE,
SOLITARY FORM)

(RIGHT SIDE
AGGREGATE FORM)

SALPA VAGINA
(RIGHT SIDE,
SOLITARY FORM)

(RIGHT SIDE, AGGREGATE FORM)

(RIGHT SIDE,
AGGREGATE FORM)

SALPA CONFEDERATA
(RIGHT SIDE SOLITARY FORM)

CYCLOSALPA AFFINIS

(LEFT SIDE
SOLITARY FORM)

(LEFT SIDE
AGGREGATE FORM)

SUBPHYLUM CEPHALOCHORDA
(AMPHIOXUS)
(The Lancelets)

At the beginning of this chapter it was stated that the Phylum Chordata is divided into four Subphyla, namely: *Hemichorda; Urochorda; Cephalochorda;* and *Vertebrata.* It was also indicated that certain features in the anatomy of the Hemichorda seemed to show beginnings and early steps toward fundamental structures which differentiate vertebrates from invertebrates. These structures, which are found in all vertebrates and do not occur in invertebrates, except to a degree in transitional forms, are (1) a backbone, appearing in the vertebrate embryos as a cartilaginous rod or notochord, becoming jointed in the adult, and developing into cartilaginous or bony vertebrae; (2) a dorsal nerve-cord, enclosing a hollow canal, or neurocoele, situated above the notochord, afterward developing into a spinal nerve and becoming enlarged at its anterior end to form a brain; (3) a series of paired gill-slits as perforations through the pharynx wall, present in all vertebrates either temporarily in their embryonic condition, or permanently in adults; and (4) the development of a special portal circulatory system.

In the Hemichorda, there are indications of a possibly rudimentary notochord, doubtful in the larva of *Phoronis,* apparently in *Cephalodiscus* and *Rhabdopleura,* and more clearly in *Enteropneusta.* In the Urochorda, a well-developed notochord is evident in the ascidián larva, but not in the adult. A nerve concentration is dorsal to the notochord rudiment in *Cephalodiscus* and *Rhabdopleura,* in a very primitive condition, and without a neurocoele. In the Enteropneusta, there are both ventral and dorsal nerve-tracts, but with a neurocoele in only the anterior portion of the dorsal tract. The dorsal nerve-cord, with neurocoele, is present in the ascidian larva but there is only a solid ganglion in the adult. There is a pair of gill-slits in *Cephalodiscus,* but none in *Rhabdopleura,* while they are conspicuous in both Enteropneusta and ascidians. In a word, some or all of these structures or their apparent rudiments are present in the Hemichorda and Urochorda, either in the larval or adult stages, in varying assortments, but in the Subphylum Cephalochorda, for the first time, we find the full assortment, though in a stage more primitive in the adult than in any groups of the Subphylum Vertebrata. The Subphylum Cephalochorda, therefore, has reached the highest stage of progress toward the vertebrate structure from invertebrates exhibited by any animal group now known to zoologists.

This group centers around the animals known as

Branchiostoma or, more generally, as *Amphioxus* or the Lancelets.

Amphioxus is a little fishlike chordate, about 2 inches in length, which has a well-developed unsegmented, but undoubted, notochord extending the entire length of the body. In the vertebrates proper, the notochord extends only as far as the mid-brain stopping just posterior to the pituitary body. In *Amphioxus* (that is, the Cephalo-chorda) it extends to the anterior end of the head and to the tip of the tapered tail, thus forming the axis of the entire body. The fact that it extends through the entire head gives rise to the name *Cephalochorda* (head-chord). The general shape of the body is seen on PLATE 251. It is tapered in fishlike fashion at both ends and is laterally compressed. The body-surface is divided into V-shaped muscle-segments, or *myotomes*, with the point of the "V" directed forward. A *dorsal fin* extends along the crest of the entire animal from the anterior tip to near the end of the tail, where it expands to form the *caudal fin*, shaped like an arrowhead. Thence, it extends forward ventrally, as the *ventral fin*, terminating at the *atriopore*, or posterior opening of the *atrium* (branchial cavity). This is not the *anus*, which is situated ventrally on the left side of the caudal fin. *Amphioxus* has no head, but just ventral to the anterior extremity and extending posteriorly and obliquely downward is the *oral hood* surrounding a cup-like cavity, the *vestibule*, at the bottom of which is the *mouth*. Around the frill-like oral hood is a fringe of numerous tentacles or *cirri*. The anterior two thirds of the ventral side is flattened and bounded by a longi-tudinal fold on either side, known as the *metapleural folds*. The small, circular mouth opens into the greatly en-larged *pharynx*, which is a high, narrow chamber oc-cupying the anterior half of the body. More than one hundred oblique *gill-slits* or *branchial apertures* pierce its walls, which open into the *atrium*. This occupies the greater part of the space between the pharynx and the body-wall and surrounds the ventral and lateral sides of that organ. It ends blindly forward, but posteriorly opens to the outside through the atriopore, already mentioned. The pharynx opens posteriorly into the *intestine*, into which the median ventrally located *liver* or *hepatic caecum* empties its secretion. The intestine narrows to the posterior anus on the left side of the caudal fin. On the floor of the pharynx is the median groove, known as the *endostyle*, homologous with the similar organ in the pharynx of ascidians, and on the dorsal median line is an *epipharyn-geal groove*. These aid in digestion, the former secreting a cord of mucus which entangles and compacts the food particles and carries them on to the intestine to be digested. There is a complex circulatory system, forming loops around the gill-clefts on either side of the pharynx, and connecting below with the median central aorta, which is contractile, acting like a heart and driving the blood forward. From it, on either side, are given off contractile branches to the gills, which force the blood through those organs to be purified and discharged into the paired dorsal aortae above. Anteriorly they supply the anterior tip of the body, and posteriorly they unite to supply the intestine, dividing into capillaries from which blood is collected and poured into a hepatic portal vein to be carried to the liver, whence it passes forward again through the ventral aorta. This is a typical *vertebrate portal system* in principle, and is the most primitive such system known.

The nervous system consists of a *dorsal nerve-cord,* running lengthwise along the upper side of the notochord and completely filling a longitudinal *neural canal,* the wall of which is secreted by the notochordal sheath and is composed of connective tissue. The nerve-cord continues forward to terminate some distance posterior to the anterior end of the notochord and extends posteriorly to taper to a filament at about the posterior end of the notochord. It contains a neurocoele for its full length and, anteriorly, becomes enlarged to form a *cerebral ventricle.* The neurocoele connects on the median line with the dorsal connective tissue region on the mid-line, by means of a longitudinal cleft, the *dorsal fissure.* This expands anteriorly to a trough, just behind the cerebral ventricle, covered over by a connective tissue roof. These two dilated cavities at the anterior end of the nerve-cord are considered to be a primitive brain. Hence, it is obvious that *Amphioxus* has all the essential organs of a vertebrate but in a very primitive and elementary stage. It has (1) a notochord; (2) a dorsal nerve-cord with true neurocoele; (3) paired gill-slits in the pharyngeal wall, by which the blood is purified; and (4) a closed circulatory system that includes a true portal system. In addition it shows, for the first time, a true metameric muscular segmentation of the vertebrate type. At the same time, it carries certain features which relate it to the Urochorda, of which the endostyle in the ventral median line of the pharynx is an outstanding example. The structure of the pharynx is also quite similar to the urochord pharynx and, together with the incurrent oral hood, the atrium, and the atripore, is reminiscent of the incurrent and excurrent system of the ascidian. Finally, the notochord and dorsal nerve-cord and neurocoele of the ascidian larva are clear foreshadowings or at least affinities of the similar structures in *Amphioxus.*

PLATE 251

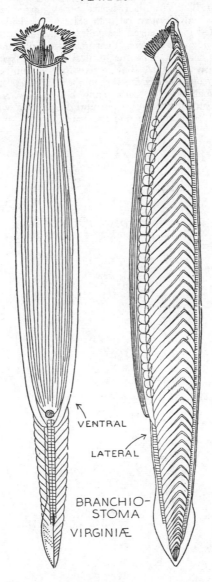

VENTRAL

LATERAL

BRANCHIO-
STOMA

VIRGINIÆ

Branchiostoma (Amphioxus) virginiae Hubbs
PLATE 251. The Virginia Lancelet. Serial gonads represent
the reproductive system on both sides of the body. They
are situated in the paired coelomic cavities on either side
of the body, discharging their products into the peribranchial chamber. The metapleural folds are symmetrical. The myotomes are sixty to sixty-four in number. The
range is from Chesapeake Bay to Florida. These animals
live in shallow bays with sandy bottoms, where they
partially bury themselves in an upright position with the
oral hood projecting up into the water.

Selected References

GENERAL

ARNOLD, A. F. The sea-beach at ebb-tide. New York, 1901.
BUCHSBAUM, R. Animals without backbones. Chicago, 1938.
CAMBRIDGE NATURAL HISTORY. (10 Volumes.) London and New York.
CROWDER, W. Between the tides. New York, 1931.
FLATTELY, F. W. and C. L. WALTON. The biology of the sea-shore. New York, 1922.
GALTSOFF, P. S. and others. Culture methods for invertebrate animals. Ithaca, N.Y., 1937.
HYMAN, L. H. The Invertebrates: Protozoa through Ctenophora. New York and London, 1940.
LANKESTER, E. R. A treatise on Zoology. (Several volumes.) London.
MINER, R. W. Sea Creatures of our Atlantic Shores. Nat. Geog. Mag. 70(2):209-231. 1936.
MINER, R. W. Denizens of our Atlantic Waters. Nat. Geog. Mag. 71(2):198-219. 1937.
PARKER, T. J. and W. A. HASWELL. Textbook of Zoology. Fifth Edition. London, 1930-1938.
PRATT, H. S. A manual of the common invertebrate animals. Philadelphia, 1935.
VERRILL, A. E. and S. I. SMITH. Report upon the invertebrate animals of Vineyard Sound and adjacent waters. Washington, D.C., 1874.

1. PHYLUM PROTOZOA

CALKINS, G. N. Marine Protozoa from Woods Hole. Bull. U.S. Fish Comm. 21:412-468. 1901.
CALKINS, G. N. The biology of the Protozoa. New York, 1926.
CUSHMAN, J. A. Foraminifera: Their classification and economic use. Cushman Lab. Foramin. Res. Contrib. 3. Boston, 1928.
DELAGE, Y et E. HÉROUARD. Les Protozoaires. Traité de Zoologie concrète. 1. Paris, 1901.
KENT, W. S. A manual of Infusoria. (3 vols.) London, 1880-1882.
MINCHIN, E. A. Introduction to the study of the Protozoa. London, 1912.

2. PHYLUM PORIFERA

BOWERBANK, J. S. A monograph of the British Spongidae. (Ray Society.) 1-4. London, 1864-1882.
DELAGE, Y. et E. HÉROUARD. Les Spongiaires. Traité de Zoologie concrète. 2. (1). Paris, 1899.
DE LAUBENFELS, M. W. Sponge Fauna of the Dry Tortugas, with material for the revision of the families and orders of the Porifera. Carnegie Inst. Wash. 30. 1936.
GEORGE, W. C. and H. V. WILSON. Sponges of Beaufort, N.C., Harbor and vicinity. Bull. U.S. B. F. 36:129-180. 1919.
JOHNSTON, G. History of British sponges and lithophytes. Edinburgh, London, Dublin, 1942.
LAMBE, L. M. Sponges from the Atlantic Coast of Canada. Trans. Roy. Soc. Canada. 2(2):181-208. 1896.
LAMBE, L. M. Catalogue of the recent marine sponges of Canada and Alaska. Ottawa Naturalist. 14(9):153-172. 1900.
LAMBE, L. M. Sponges from the coasts of Northeastern Canada and Greenland. Trans. Roy. Soc. Canada. 6(2):19-50. 1900.
LUNDBECK, W. Porifera. Part I: Homorrhaphidae and Heterorrhaphidae. Danish Ingolf-Expedition. 6:1-108. 1902.
LUNDBECK, W. Porifera. Part II: Desmacidonidae (Pars). Danish Ingolf-Expedition. 6:1-219. 1905.
LUNDBECK, W. Porifera. Part III: Desmacidonidae (Pars). Danish Ingolf-Expedition. 6:1-124. 1910.
MINCHIN, E. A. Porifera. In Lankester's "A treatise on Zoology." Part II. London, 1900.

MINER, R. W. A Guide to the Sponge Alcove. Amer. Mus. Jour. 6(4):219-250. 1906.

MOORE, H. F. The commercial sponges and the sponge fisheries. Bull. U.S. Bur. Fish. 28:399-511. 1923.

RIDLEY, S. O. Report on the Monaxonida collected by H. M. S. "Challenger" during the years 1873-1876. "Challenger" Reports. 20(1):i-lxviii, 1-275. London, 1887.

SOLLAS, W. J. Report on the Tetractinellida collected by H. M. S. "Challenger" during the years 1873-1876. "Challenger" Reports. 25:i-clxvi, 1-458. London, 1888.

TOPSENT, E. Contribution à l'Étude des Spongiaires de l'Atlantique Nord. Resultats des Campagnes Scient. Albert I de Monaco. 2:1-165. 1892.

TOPSENT, E. Matériaux pour servoir à l'étude de la Faune des Spongiaires de France. Mém. Soc. Zool. France. 9:113-133. 1896.

TOPSENT, E. Éponges à l'étude monographique des Monaxonides de France. Classification des Hadromerina. Arch. Zool. Expér. 6:91-113. 1898.

TOPSENT, E. Étude Monographique des Spongiaires de France. III: Monaxonida (Hadromerina). Arch. Zool. Expér. 8:1-331. 1900.

TOPSENT, E. Spongiaires de l'Atlantique et de la Méditerranée. Résultats des Campagnes Scient. Albert I de Monaco. 74: 1-276. 1928.

3. PHYLUM COELENTERA

AGASSIZ, A. The Porpitidae and Velellidae. Mem. Mus. Comp. Zool. 8. 1883.

AGASSIZ, A. and A. G. MAYER. Dactylometra. Mus. Compar. Zool. Bull. 32. 1898.

AGASSIZ, L. Contributions to the Natural History of the U.S. 3; 4(1,3). 1862.

ALLMAN, G. J. Monograph of the Gymnoblastic or Tubularian hydroids. (Ray Society). London, 1872.

BIGELOW, H. B. Albatross Medusae. Mus. Compar. Zool. Mem. 37. 1909.

CLARK, H. J. Lucernariae and their allies. Smithson. Inst. Contrib. 23(242). 1878.

DELAGE, Y. et E. HÉROUARD. Les Coelenteres. Traité de Zoologie concrète. 2. 1901.

FEWKES, J. W. Anatomy and development of Agalma. Amer. Zool., Bull. 8. 1880.

FEWKES, J. W. Jellyfishes of Narragansett Bay. Mus. Compar. Zool. Bull. 8. 1881.

FRASER, C. M. Hydroids of the west coast of North America. Iowa State Univ., Lab. Nat. Hist. Bull. 6. 1911.

FRASER, C. M. Some Hydroids of Beaufort, N.C. U.S. Bur. Fish. Bull. 30:337. 1912.

FRASER, C. M. Development of Aequorea. Roy. Soc. Canada, Proc. Trans. 10. 1916.

HAECKEL, E. Das System der Medusen. 1879.

HAECKEL, E. Siphonophora. "Challenger" Reports. Zool. 28. 1889.

HARGITT, C. W. The Medusae of the Woods Hole Region. Bull. Bur. Fish. 24:21. 1904.

HARGITT, C. W. Behavior of sea-anemones. Biol. Bull. 12. 1907.

HARGITT, C. W. Anthozoa of the Woods Hole Region. U.S. Bur. Fish. Bull. 32. 1912.

HARVEY, E. N. Luminescence in the coelenterates. Biol. Bull. 41. 1921.

HEYMANS, C. and A. R. MOORE. Luminescence in Pelagia. Jour. Gen. Physiol. 6. 1924.

HINCKS, T. A history of the British hydroid zoophytes. London, 1868.

MAYER, A. G. Some medusae from the Tortugas. Mus. Compar. Zool. Bull. 37. 1900.

MAYER, A. G. Medusae of the World. (3 vols.) Carnegie Inst. Wash. 1910.

MCMURRICH, J. P. Structure of Cerianthus americanus. Jour. Morph. 4. 1890.

MCMURRICH, J. P. Development of Cyanea. Amer. Nat. 25. 1891.

MCMURRICH, J. P. Report of the Actinia. Proc. U.S. Nat. Mus. 16:119. 1893.

MCMURRICH, J. P. Ceriantharia. Siboga Exped. Monog. 15a. 1910.

MCMURRICH, J. P. Genus Arachnactis. Jour. Expt. Zool. 9. 1910.

MURBACH, L. Hydroids from Woods Hole. Quart. Jour. Micros. Sci. 42. 1899.

NUTTING, C. C. Hydroids of the Woods Hole Region. Bull. U.S. Fish. Comm. 19. 1899.

NUTTING, C. C. American Hydroids, Part I, The Plumularidae. U.S. Nat. Mus. Spec. Bull. 4. 1900.

NUTTING, C. C. American Hydroids, Part II, The Sertularidae. U.S. Nat. Mus. Spec. Bull. 4. 1904.

NUTTING, C. C. American Hydroids, Part III, Campanularidae and Bonneviellidae. Smithson. Inst. Spec. Bull. 1915.

PARKER, G. H. Synopsis of North American Invertebrates, The Actiniaria. Am. Nat. 34:747. 1900.

PARKER, G. H. Interrelations of zooids in soft corals. Nat. Acad. Sci. Wash., Proc. 11. 1925.

POTTS, E. On the Medusa of *Microhydra*. Quart. Jour. Mic. Sci. 50:623. 1906.

POTTS, E. *Microhydra* in 1907. Proc. Delaware Co. Inst. 3:89. 1908.

VERRILL, A. E. Radiata in the museum of Yale. Conn. Acad. Arts Sci. Trans. 1. 1869.

VERRILL, A. E. Invertebrate Animals of Vineyard Sound. Rep. U.S. Fish. Comm. 1871.

VERRILL, A. E. Anthozoa dredged by the Blake. Mus. Compar. Zool. Bull. 11. 1883.

VERRILL, A. E. New American actinians. Amer. Jour. Sci. 6(4). 1898-1899.

VERRILL, A. E. Descriptions of imperfectly known and new Actinians, with critical notes on other species, II-V. Brief contributions to Zoology from the Museum of Yale College, No3. 59-62. Amer. Jour. Sci. 7(4):41-50, 143-146, 205-218, 375-380. 1899.

WILSON, E. B. Development of *Renilla*. Roy. Soc. London, Phil. Trans. 174. 1883.

WILSON, E. B. Merogeny and regeneration in *Renilla*. Biol. Bull. 4. 1903.

4. PHYLUM CTENOPHORA

ABBOTT, J. F. Morphology of Coeloplana. Zool. Jahrb., Abt. Anat. Ontog. Tiere 24. 1907.

AGASSIZ, L. Ctenophorae. Contributions to the Natural History of the U.S. 3:155. 1860.

MAYER, A. G. Ctenophores of the Atlantic Coast of North America. Carnegie Inst. Wash. Pub. 162. (3 vols.) 1912.

WILLEY, A. Ctenoplana. Quart. Jour. Micros. Sci. 39.

5. PHYLUM PLATYHELMIA

VON GRAFF, L. Monographie d. Turbellarien, I. Rhabdocoelida. 1882.

VON GRAFF, L. Acoela, Rhabdocoela and Alloeocoela des Ostens der Vereinigten Staaten. Zeit. f. Wiss. Zool. 99132 1911.

HYMAN, L. H. Studies on the Morphology, Taxonomy, and Distribution of North American Triclad Turbellaria. I-V. Trans. Amer. Micr. Soc. 47:222; 48:406; 50:124, 316, 336. 1928, 1929, 1931.

VERRILL, A. E. Marine Planarians of the New England Coast. Trans. Conn. Acad. 8. 1893.

6. PHYLUM NEMERTEA

COE, W. R. On the Anatomy of a Species of Nemertean (*Cerebratulus lacteus* Verrill). Trans. Conn. Acad. 9:479. 1895.

COE, W. R. Synopsis of the Nemerteans. Part I. Am. Nat. 39: 425.

VERRILL, A. E. Marine Nemerteans of New England and adjacent waters. Trans. Conn. Acad. 8:382. 1892.

VERRILL, A. E. Additions to the Turbellaria, Nemertina, and Annelida of the Bermudas, with revisions of some New England Genera and species. Trans. Conn. Acad. 10(18):595-672. 1899-1900.

7. PHYLUM NEMATHELMIA

MONTGOMERY, T. H. Synopsis of the Gordiacea. Am. Nat. 33:647. 1899.

WARD, H. B. On *Nectonema agile* Verrill. Bull. Mus. Comp. Zool. 23:135. 1892.

8. PHYLUM TROCHELMIA

BEAUCHAMP, P. M. Recherches sur les Rotiferes; les Formations Tegumentaires et l'Appareil digestif. Arch. Zool. Exp. et Gen. (4)10:1-410. 1909.

BLAKE, C. H. Three new species of worms belonging to the Order Echinodera. Publ. Biol. Sur., Mount Desert Region. 3. 1930.

BRONN, H. G .Klassen und Ornungen des Tier-Reichs. Rotatorien, Gastrotrichen und Kinorhynchen by A. Remane. Leipzig, 1929.

HARRING, H. K. and F. J. MYERS. The Rotifer Fauna of Wisconsin, Parts I-IV. Trans. Wis. Acad. Sci., Arts, Letters. 20: 553-662; 21:415-550; 22:315-424; 23:667-680. 1923-1929.

HUDSON, C. T. and P. H. GOSSE. The Rotifera, or Wheel Anamalcules, Both British and Foreign. (2 vols.) London, 1886-1889.

MINER, R. W. A Drama of the Microscope. Nat. Hist. (Spec. Pub.) 1928.

MYERS, F. J. The Rotifer Fauna of Wisconsin, Part V, The Genera Euchlanis and Monommata. Trans. Wis. Acad. Sci., Art, Letters, 25. 1930.

ZELINKA, C. Die Gastrotrichen. Zeit. f. Wiss. Zool. 49:209. 1889.

ZELINKA, C. Monographie der Echinoderen. Leipzig, 1928.

9. PHYLUM ANNULATA

(a) POLYCHAETA

ANDREWS, E. A. The Annelida Chaetopoda of Beaufort, N.C. Proc. U.S. Nat. Mus. 14:277. 1891.

ARWIDSSON, I. Studien über die skandinavischen und arktischen Maldaniden. Zool. Jähr. 25(Syst.):1-301. Upsala, 1906.

EFLERS, E. Die Borstenwürmer (Annelida Chaetopoda). Leipzig, 1864-1868.

HARTMAN, OLGA. New England Annelida, Part 2, including the unpublished plates by Verrill with reconstructed captions. Bull. Am. Mus. Nat. Hist. 82 (7):327-344. 1944.

MCINTOSH, W. C. Monograph of the British Marine Annelids. (4 vols.) (Ray Society.) London, 1873-1923.

MINER, R. W. The Sea Worm Group. Amer. Mus. Jour. 12: 244-250. 1912.

SUMNER, F. B. and others. A biological survey of the waters of Woods Hole and vicinity. Bull. Bur. Fish. 31. 1913.

VERRILL, A. E. Invertebrate animals of Vineyard Sound. Rep. U.S. Bur. Fish. 1871-1872.

VERRILL, A. E. Dinophilidae of New England. Trans. Conn. Acad. 8:457.

VERRILL, A. E. New England Annelida. Pt. I. Historical sketch, with annotated list of the species hitherto recorded. Trans. Conn. Acad. Arts and Sci. 4(8):285-324. 1877-1882.

WEBSTER, H. E. Annelida Chaetopoda of New Jersey. 32nd Rep N.Y. State Mus. Nat. Hist. 1879.

WEBSTER, H. E. Annelida Chaetopoda of the Virginia Coast. Trans. Albany Inst. 9:202-269. 1879.

WEBSTER, H. E. and J. E. BENEDICT. The Annelida Chaetopoda from Provincetown and Wellfleet, Mass. Ann. Reprt. Comm. Fish & Fisheries. 1881.

(b) OLIGOCHAETA

MOORE, J. P. Some Marine Oligochaeta of New England. Proc. A.N.S. Philadelphia, 1905.

STEPHENSON, J. The Oligochaeta. 1930.

(c) ECHIURIDA

BALTZER, F. Echiurida. Kükenthal's Handbuch der Zoologie, Bd. 2. 1931.

CONN, H. W. *Thalassema mellita*. Stud. Biol. Lab., Johns Hopkins Univ. 3. 1884.

WILSON, C. B. North American Echiurida. Biol. Bull. 7:163. 1900.

(d) SIPUNCULIDA

ANDREWS, E. A. Notes in the anatomy of the *Sipunculus gouldii* Pourtales. Stud. Biol. Lab.. Johns Hopkins Univ. 4:389. 1890.

BALTZER, F. Sipunculida and Priapulida. Kükenthal's Handbuch der Zoologie, Bd. 2. 1931.
GEROULD, J. H. The Sipunculids of the Eastern Coast of North America. Proc. U.S. Nat. Mus. 44:373. 1913.

(e) HIRUDINEA

MOORE, J. P. Leeches of the U.S. Nat. Museum. Proc. U.S. Nat. Mus. 21:543. 1898.

10. PHYLUM ARTHROPODA

(a) ENTOMOSTRACA

SHARPE, R. W. Notes on the Marine Copepoda and Cladocera of Woods Hole. Proc. U.S. Nat. Mus. 38:405. 1911.
WILLIAMS, L. W. Marine Copepoda of Rhode Island. Amer. Nat. 40:639. 1906.
WILSON, C. B. North American Parasitic Copepods. Proc. U.S. Nat. Mus. 25:635; 28:479; 31:669; 33:323; 39; 47:565; 53:1; 60:1. 1903-1922.
WILSON, C. B. The Genus Lernaea. Bull. U.S. Bur. Fish. 35:165. 1917.
WILSON, C. B. Copepods of the Woods Hole Region. Bull. 156, U.S. Nat. Mus. 1932.
WHEELER, W. M. Copepoda of the Woods Hole Region. Bull. U.S. Bur. Fish. 19:157. 1900.

(b) OSTRACODA

CUSHMAN, J. A. Marine Ostracoda of Vineyard Sound and adjacent waters. Proc. Bost. Soc. Nat. 32. 1932

(c) CIRRIPEDIA

DARWIN, C. A monograph of the Subclass Cirripedia. 1851-1854.
PILSBRY, H. A. The Barnacles (Cirripedia) contained in the Collections of the United States Natural Museum. Bull. 60, U.S. Nat. Mus. 1907.
PILSBRY, H. A. The sessile Barnacles, etc. Bull. 93, U.S. Nat. Mus. 1916.

(d) MALACOSTRACA

BIGELOW, R. P. Report on the Crustacea of the Order Stomatopoda. Proc. U.S. Nat. Mus. 17:489. 1891.
BROOKS, W. K. and F. H. HERRICK. Embryology and Metamorphosis of the Macrura. Mem. Nat. Acad. Sci. 5. 1892.
CALMAN, W. T. The Crustacea of the Order Cumacea in the collection of the United States National Museum. Proc. U.S. Nat. Mus. 41:603. 1912.
HOLMES, S. J. Synopsis of the Amphipoda. Am. Nat. 37:267. 1903.
HOLMES, S. J. The Amphipods of Southern New England. Bull. U.S. Fish. Com. 24:457. 1904.
KINGSLEY, J. S. Synopsis of Astacoid and Thalassinoid Crustacea. Am. Nat. 33:819. 1899.
KUNKEL, B. W. The Arthrostraca of Connecticut. Bull. 26, State Geol. and Nat. Hist. Surv. 1918.
PAULMEIER, F. P. Higher Crustacea of New York City. Bull. 91, N.Y. St. Mus. 1905.
RATHBUN, MARY J. Synopsis of the Cyclometopous or Cancroid Crabs of North America. Am. Nat. 34. 1900.
RATHBUN, MARY J. Synopsis of the Oxyrhynchous and Oxystomatous Crabs of North America. Am. Nat. 34. 1900.
RATHBUN, MARY J. The Catometopous or Grapsoid Crabs of North America. Am. Nat. 34:583. 1900.
RATHBUN, MARY J. The Grapsoid Crabs of America. Bull. 97. U.S. Nat. Mus. 1917.
RATHBUN, MARY J. The Spider Crabs of America. Bull. 129. U.S. Nat. Mus. 1925.
RATHBUN, MARY J. The Cancroid Crabs of America. Bull. 152. U.S. Nat. Mus. 1931.
RICHARDSON, HARRIET. Synopsis of North American Isopoda. Am. Nat. 34:207, 295.

RICHARDSON, HARRIET. Monograph of the Isopods of North America. Bull. 54. U.S. Nat. Mus. 1905.

VAN NAME, W. G. American Land and Fresh-water Isopod Crustacea. Bull. Amer. Mus. Nat. Hist. 71. 1936.

(e) ARACHNOIDEA

KINGSLEY, J. S. The Embryology of Limulus. Jour. Morph. 7:35; 8:195. 1892-1893.

LANKESTER, E. R. Limulus an Achnid. Quart. Jour. Mic. Sci. 21. 1881.

11. PHYLUM MOLLUSCA

BARTSCH, P. Monograph of the North American Shipworms. U.S. Nat. Mus. Bull. 122. 1922.

DALL, W. H. Synopsis of the Family Cardiidae and of the North American Species. Proc. U.S. Nat. Mus. 23:381. 1900.

DALL, W. H. Synopsis of the Family Veneridae and of the North American Recent Species. Proc. U.S. Nat. Mus. 26:335. 1901.

GOULD, A. A. Report on the Invertebrata of Massachusetts, etc. 2nd ed., Edited by W. G. Binney. 1870.

JOHNSON, C. W. List of Marine Mollusca of the Atlantic Coast from Labrador to Texas. Proc. Bost. Soc. Nat. Hist. 40(1): 1-204. 1934.

MINER, R. W. Marauders of the Sea. Nat. Geog. Mag. 68(2):185-207. 1935.

MORRIS, P. A. A Field Guide to the Shells of our Atlantic Coast. New York, 1947.

PILSBRY, H. A. Manual of Conchology, Second Series. 1889.

SMITH, MAXWELL. East Coast Marine Shells. Ann Arbor, Mich., 1937.

VERRILL, A. E. The Colossal Cephalopods of the North Atlantic. Am. Nat. 9:21. 1875.

VERRILL, A. E. Report of the Cephalopods of the Northeastern Coast of America. Rep. U.S. Fish Comm. for 1879. 1882.

12. PHYLUM CHAETOGNATHA

CONANT, F. S. The known Chaetognatha of American Waters. Johns Hopk. Univ. Cir. 15:82. 1896.

MICHAEL, E. A. Classification, etc., of the Chaetognatha. Univ. of Cal. Pub. 8:21. 1911.

VON RITTER-ZAHONY, R. Chaetognathi. Das Tierreich. 1911.

13. PHYLUM ECHINODERMA

AGASSIZ, A. Revision of the Echini. 1872-1874.

AGASSIZ, A. and L. F. de POURTALES. Echini, Crinoids, and Corals. Illus. Cat. Mus. Comp. Zool. 8(1). 1874.

AGASSIZ, A. Echinoids of the "Challenger" Expedition. 1881.

CLARK, A. H. The Coamtulids. Bull. 82, U.S. Nat. Mus. (1-3). 1915-1931.

CLARK, H. L. Echinoderms of the Woods Hole Region. Bull. U.S. Fish. Com. 22:543. 1902.

COE, W. R. Echinoderms of Connecticut. Bull. 19, Geol. and Nat. Hist. Sur. 1912.

FISHER, W. K. Asteroidea of the North Pacific and adjacent waters. Bull. 76, U.S. Nat. Mus. (1-3). 1911-1930.

LYMAN, T. Ophiuridae and Astrophytidae. 1. Illus. Cat. Mus. Comp. Zool. Cambridge, Mass., 1865.

MACBRIDE, E. W. Echinodermata. In Cambridge Natural History. 1. 1906.

MORTENSEN, T. Handbook of the Echinoderms of the British Isles. London, 1927.

VERRILL, A. E. Invertebrate animals of Vineyard Sound. Rep. of U.S. Fish. Comm. 1871.

VERRILL, A. E. Distribution of the Echinoderms of Northeastern America. Am. Jour. Sci. 49:127. 1895.

VERRILL, A. E. Asteroidea. Am. Jour. Sci. 49. 1895.

VERRILL, A. E. Revision of Certain Genera and Species of Starfish. Trans. Conn. Acad. 10:145. 1899.

14. PHYLUM PROSOPYGIA

(a) BRYOZOA

OSBURN, R. C. The Bryozoa of the Woods Hole Region. Bull. U.S. Bur. Fish. 30. 1912.

VERRILL, A. E. Report upon the Invertebrate Animals of Vineyard Sound. Rep. U.S. Comm. Fish. 1871-1872.

(b) BRACHIOPODA

BEECHER, C. E. Revision of the Families of Loop-bearing Brachiopoda Trans. Conn. Acad. 9. 1893.
DALL, W. H. Annotated List of the Recent Brachiopoda in the U.S. Nat. Mus., Proc. U.S. Nat. Mus. 57. 1920.
DAVIDSON, T. A monograph of recent Brachiopoda. Trans. Linn. Soc. Lond. 4. 1886-1888.

15. PHYLUM CHORDATA

(a) PHORONIDEA

COWLES, R. P. Phoronis architecta. Mem. Nat. Acad. 10:76. 1905.

(b) HEMICHORDA

AGASSIZ, A. The History of Balanoglossus and Tornaria. Mem. Amer. Acad. 9:421. 1873.
BATESON, W. The Development of Balanoglossus. Quart. Jour. Mic. Sci. 24-26. 1884-1886.
DELAGE, Y. et E. HÉROUARD. Les Procordés. Traité de Zool. Concr. 8. 1898.
MORGAN, T. H. Growth and Development of Balanoglossus. Jour. Morph. 5:407. 1891.

(c) TUNICATA

BROOKS, W. K. and M. M. METCALF. The Genus Salpa. Mem. Johns Hopk. Univ. 2. 1893.
METCALF, M. M. The Salpidae: A Taxonomic Study. Bull. 100. 2(2), U.S. Nat. Mus. 1918.
MINER, R. W. Animals of the Wharf Piles. Amer. Mus. Jour. 13:86-92. 1913.
RITTER, W. E. and E. S. BYXBEE. The Pelagic Tunicata. Mem. Mus. Comp. Zool. 26. 1905.
VAN NAME, W. G. Compound Ascidians of the Coasts of New England, etc. Proc. Boston Soc. Nat. Hist. 34(11). 1910.
VAN NAME, W. G. Simple Ascidians of the Coasts of New England, etc. Ditto. 34(13). 1912.
VAN NAME, W. G. Ascidians of Porto Rico and the Virgin Islands. Sci. Survey Porto Rico and the Virgin Islands. 10(4). 1930.
VAN NAME, W. G. North and South American Ascidians. Bull. Amer. Mus. Nat. Hist. 84:1-476. 1945.

(d) CEPHALOCHORDA

WILLEY, A. Amphioxus and the Ancestry of Vertebrates. 1894.

Index

873